COMPUTERS IN SCIENCE AND MATHEMATICS

COMPUTERS IN SCIENCE AND MATHEMATICS

Editor

Boris Waxweiler

scitus academics

computers in changing the face of the sciences and mathematics. It is the only periodical devoted specifically to using information technology in the teaching of mathematics and science. It provides a medium of exchange for those engaged in fields where there exists a non-trivial interplay between mathematics and computers. This book shows scientists and engineers how Mathematics can be used to do scientific computations.

Table of Contents

CHAPTER 1

Random numbers for parallel computers: Requirements and methods, with emphasis on GPUs

Pierre L'Ecuyer[a,b], David Munger[a], Boris Oreshkin[a], Richard Simard[a]

[a]*DIRO, Pavillon Aisenstadt, Universit´e de Montr´eal, C.P.6128, Succ. Centre-Ville, Montr´eal (QC), Canada H3C 3J7*

[b]*Inria Rennes Bretagne Atlantique, Campus Universitaire de Beaulieu, 35042 Rennes Cedex, France*

ABSTRACT

We examine the requirements and the available methods and software to provide (or imitate) uniform random numbers in parallel computing environments. In this context, for the great majority of applications, independent streams of random numbers are required, each being computed on a single processing element at a time. Sometimes, thousands or even millions of such streams are needed. We explain how they can be produced and managed. We devote particular attention to multiple streams for GPU devices.

Keywords: Random number generators; Multiple streams; Parallel computing; Simulation; Monte Carlo

1. INTRODUCTION

Random number generators (RNGs) are fundamental ingredients for stochastic simulation and for the application of Monte Carlo methods in general. Conceptually, these RNGs are designed to produce sequences of real numbers that behave approximately as the realizations of independent random variables uniformly distributed over the interval (0,1), or i.i.d. $U(0,1)$ for short [23]; [24]; [26]; [34] ; [60]. These numbers are then transformed to simulate random variables from other distributions, stochastic processes, and other types of random objects [11] ; [19].

In this review paper, we examine the design and implementation of RNG facilities for parallel processing, with a special attention to discrete *graphical processing units* (GPU) devices. Such facilities are increasingly important, because computing power now improves by increasing the number of *processing elements* (PEs), that can operate in parallel in a computer, rather than by increasing clock speeds of the PEs [4] ; [56], mainly because faster clock speeds produce too much heat.

Parallel computers are generally organized in a hierarchic fashion, both in terms of PEs and memory. A single chip may contain several PEs (or cores) that execute instructions in parallel. In many cases, several PEs can execute different instructions in parallel, almost independently, with only sparse communication between them. In some cases, certain groups of PEs on the chip work in the *single instruction multiple data* (SIMD) mode, which means that they must all execute the same instructions at each time step, usually with different data. This happens in array processors and GPU devices, for example, which are used as accelerators to perform the same instructions in parallel on an array (or vector) of different data. The purpose of this restriction is to speed up the processing by reducing the work required for task scheduling. On the other hand, it puts important constraints on the design of algorithms that run on such hardware.

Most often, there is a mixture of these two cases. The largest supercomputers in 2015 have over a million PEs. The PEs execute *threads*, where a thread can be seen as a sequence of instructions that can execute on a single PE (although the notions of thread and PE can have various meanings that differ in the scientific and commercial literature). The memory has a matching hierarchical organization, in which each PE can have access to a small amount of very fast-access memory, then groups of PEs share a larger memory that is slower to access, and there can be many levels of that. There is a large variety of such hierarchic organizations. On some common chips, all the PEs have fast access to a large shared memory (with a single address space) of several Gbytes. On others, such as discrete GPU chips, each PE has a fast read–write access only to a small private memory for its data, fast read-only access to a larger shared memory, and much slower access to the shared read–write memory. The read and write access times depend on the type of memory and on how it is physically connected to the PEs or to the host (on the same chip, on the same board, in the same machine, in a different machine from a same cluster, etc.).

In recent years, there has been a strong interest and much published articles on RNGs for GPU devices. Those devices were originally designed for fast high-quality image rendering on computer screens and video-game consoles, but are now widely used as low-cost alternatives to accelerate computations in several other areas such as statistics, computational finance, and simulation in general, and have been extended to general-purpose GPUs (GPGPUs). This special interest for RNGs that run on GPU devices comes from the strong restrictions (mentioned earlier) that one faces when computing on those devices, and which are not present on other common types of processors such as ordinary CPUs (single-core or multi-core) and parallel processors typically found in the largest supercomputers. Our review gives special emphasis to GPUs for this reason. A traditional GPU board (named *discrete* GPU) contains specialized chips, each one containing multiple copies of a hardware unit with PEs that can execute a *warp* (or *wavefront*) of (typically 32 or 64) threads (also called *work items*) in parallel, in a SIMD fashion. The actual number of physical PEs is typically less than 32 (e.g., it can be 16, with one instruction per thread every two or four clock cycles). There are several variations in the architectural design, and explaining this is beyond the scope of the present article. The important aspects for our purposes are the SIMD restriction for groups of threads and the limited size of fast access private memory per thread, mentioned earlier.

To take advantage of new parallel-computing architectures, and account for their specificity and constraints, algorithms and software in general, and for RNGs in particular, must be adapted and sometimes radically redesigned. Feeding all the PEs with a single source of random numbers is generally unacceptable, first because it would create too much overhead and a large bottleneck. In highly-parallel systems, one may need thousands or even millions of virtual RNGs. They can be either different RNGs or copies of the same RNG starting from different states, that run in parallel without exchanging data between one another, and behave from the user's viewpoint just like independent RNGs. These virtual RNGs are often called *streams* of random numbers.

Another important requirement is *reproducibility of the results* : it is often required that simulations must be exactly replicable and produce exactly the same results on different computers and architectures, either parallel or purely sequential, and when running the program again on the same computer. The latter is important for debugging and in the (frequent) situation where we want to simulate a complex system with slightly different configurations or decision making rules (e.g., to optimize these rules), while making sure that exactly the same random numbers are used at exactly the same places in all configurations of the system, and repeat this n times independently. To reduce the variance in the comparisons, it is important to use well-synchronized *common random numbers* (CRNs) [24]; [32]; [33]; [36]; [45] ; [41]; that is, to ensure that the same random numbers are used for the same purpose across configurations. To achieve this, one would use a separate stream for each required source of random numbers in the system, and use one substream for each of the n independent runs [24]; [32]; [33]; [36] ; [41].

Reliable software facilities that provide RNGs with multiple "independent" streams and substreams have been available for some time for that purpose [33]; [37]; [45] ; [38]. Most were initially designed primarily for simulations over a single processor, for synchronizing CRNs, but they can be used as well to provide multiple streams for parallel processing. In particular, the RngStream package of [45] has been incorporated in the parallel package which supports parallel programming in R [70]. RngStream can also be used directly in OpenMP, which is the most standard interface for parallel programming in shared-memory environments, and in MPI, a popular parallel programming interface based on message passing. Examples are given in [22].

In these software tools, all the new streams are created and managed by a single central monitor. The streams are defined so they are all distinct, long enough to make sure they cannot overlap, and they behave as statistically independent. For reproducibility, the user must make sure that they are created in the same order and used for the same purpose in different configurations. This single-monitor design means that all streams must be passed or copied from the single location where they are created to all other places where they are to be used. For most parallel applications, this is acceptable and sufficient.

This setting can be extended to multiple monitors (or creators) that create the streams. Each creator will create exactly the same sequence of streams in exactly the same order, provided that the creators are created themselves in the same order. Once created, the creators no longer have to interact with each other and can be distributed in loosely connected groups of nodes.

The streams and substreams are most often constructed by partitioning the long period of a single base RNG into pieces of equal length, as in [33]; [45] ; [41]. Other approaches such as using counter-based RNGs with different initial values for the counter, or different hashing keys, or using different RNGs from the same family (with different parameters), are also used to define streams. We will return to this later on.

There are situations where using one or more central monitor(s) to create the streams is not acceptable, e.g., because new streams have to be created dynamically and randomly within threads as a simulation goes on, without resorting to external information, and with a guarantee that the results are exactly reproducible [14] ; [53].

In this setting, we want each stream to be able to create children streams by itself at any time, using a deterministic mechanism. The possibility of collisions or overlap between streams is hard to rule out in this case, but the probability that it occurs can be made extremely small, as we shall see.

Most good RNGs proposed over the past decades have been designed for single-processor environments with plenty of memory. Some popular ones have a very large state (e.g., [10]; [54] ; [63]), which makes them inappropriate for computations on a single PE having limited fast memory, such as the PEs on discrete GPUs, and adds overhead when storing and restoring stream states, which is required, e.g., to checkpoint programs and restart them from a saved checkpoint, an essential activity in highly-parallel computations.

In those types of setting, several PEs can be used simultaneously to advance the RNG state by one step, so these PEs all work on the same stream. But this often does not match the need of users, e.g., if one wishes to run one simulation thread per PE. RNG frameworks and implementations specifically adapted to GPUs, and other parallel processing environments such as programmable arrays, have also been proposed in recent years; see for example [5]; [18]; [49]; [58]; [65]; [64]; [73]; [74]; [75] ; [80]. Parallel processing accelerators can be exploited in different ways in a simulation. On a GPU, for example, one can either run a piece of simulation on each PE, using one or more random stream per PE, or one can just use the GPU to rapidly fill up a large buffer of random numbers to be used on the host computer or elsewhere.

The rest of this paper provides a (brief) survey of the main issues, requirements, and recent proposals, for RNGs on parallel computing environments. In Section 2, we provide some background on algorithmic RNGs and their (classical) quality criteria. Section 3 quickly summarizes the main classes of RNGs used for simulation. In Section 4, we outline a set of requirements and ideas to provide multiple streams for parallel computing, and discuss what we think application programming interfaces (APIs) should contain. In Section 5, we describe various efforts made to adapt existing RNGs to parallel settings, and to define new ones that can be more appropriate.

2. BACKGROUND

One way to generate (approximately) $U(0,1)$ random numbers is to generate random bits from physical devices and use these bits to construct real numbers represented in floating-point with finite precision. Those random bits can be obtained from thermal noise in semiconductors, photon counters, photon trajectory detectors, etc. With such devices, there is generally no mathematical proof or guarantee that the successive bits are statistically independent and that each bit is 0 or 1 with probability 1/2 each, but some of them appear reliable enough so we can make this assumption, based on empirical statistical tests that check for detectable bias or dependence. However, they are cumbersome to install and use (particularly on parallel processing elements) and, more importantly, they cannot reproduce exactly the same sequence twice. This reproducibility is a key requirement for simulation applications, e.g., for program verification and for comparing similar systems with common random numbers [24]; [32]; [33]; [41] ; [65].

Algorithmic generators, often called *pseudorandom* , are more appropriate and much more popular than physical devices for simulation and Monte Carlo methods. They are in fact deterministic finite automata that produce a periodic sequence of numbers which behave like typical i.i.d. $U(0,1)$ when viewed externally [26]. In the rest of this paper, the term RNG will always refer to an algorithmic generator. An RNG has a finite set of *states* S, a transition function $f\colon S\to S$, an output function $g\colon S\to(0,1)$, and an initial state (or *seed*) s_0. Sometimes, the seed s_0 is chosen randomly (via an external mechanism) from some probability distribution on S. The state evolves according to $s_i=f(s_{i-1})$ and the output value returned at step i is $u_i=g(s_i)\in(0,1)$, for $i\geq 0$.

Because S is a finite set, there are always finite integers $l\geq 0$ and $0<j\leq|S|$ such that $s_{l+j}=s_l$. Then, $s_{i+j}=s_i$ and $u_{i+j}=u_i$ for all $i\geq l$. The smallest $j>0$ for which this holds is the *period* ρ of the RNG. Note that $\rho\leq|S|\leq 2^k$, where k is the number of bits used to represent the state. Well-designed RNGs typically have $l=0$ and ρ near 2^k.

Basic requirements for good RNGs include high running speed, long period (e.g., 2^{200} or more), exact repeatability on various computing platforms, ease of implementation, preferably in a platform-independent way, and efficient ways of splitting the sequence into long disjoint streams and of jumping quickly between them. On top of these basic properties, we also want the successive output values to have an i.i.d. $U(0,1)$ behavior, which can be captured by the following: for any dimension $s>0$, if we select the seed s_0 at random uniformly over S, the vector $\mathbf{u}_{0,s}$ = $(u_0,\ldots u_{s-1})$ should have (approximately) the uniform distribution over the unit hypercube $(0,1)^s$.

This vector cannot have *exactly* the uniform distribution over $(0,1)^s$, because S is a finite set, but it has a uniform distribution over the set

$$\Psi_s=\{(u_0,\dots,u_{s-1})=(g(s_0),\dots,g(s_{s-1})):s_0\in S\}.$$

The best we can ask for is that Ψ_s covers the unit hypercube $(0,1)^s$ very evenly, in some sense, so that the uniform distribution over Ψ_s is a good approximation of that over $(0,1)^s$. Good RNGs must be constructed based on a mathematical analysis of this uniformity, which is measured by figures of merit that must be easily computable without generating the points explicitly. These measures generally depend on the structure of the RNG [16]; [23]; [34] ; [42]. With a larger Ψ_s (i.e., larger S), one can potentially cover $(0,1)^s$ more uniformly, and this is the main motivation for having a larger state (more than trying to increase the period). On the other hand, a larger state and longer period does not necessarily imply a better RNG.

A large state also has many drawbacks: it requires more memory to store the states, and more overhead to compute the seeds of the multiple streams and to store and restore the states when needed.

After selecting an RNG based on proper mathematical analysis, one submits it to empirical statistical tests, to try to detect observable non-uniformity or dependence [23] ; [43]. A test takes a stream of successive output values, computes the value t taken by a test statistic T, then computes the p-value of the test, defined as the probability p that $T\geq t$ under the hypothesis H_0 that the output values are independent $U(0,1)$ random variables. A p very close to 0 usually indicates strong departure from uniformity, whereas p very close to 1 indicates excessive uniformity, which also represents departure from randomness.

For poor RNGs, p-values smaller than 10^{-15} (and often much smaller) are often returned [43], and it is then very clear that the RNG fails the tests. Collections of statistical tests for RNGs can be found in [23]; [43] ; [52], for example. The most extensive collection and software is TestU01 [43]. Among other things, it includes predefined batteries of tests called SmallCrush, Crush, and BigCrush, which have become very popular. RNGs that pass all tests in those batteries are called *Crush-resistant* [74]. However, it is only possible to apply a finite (small) number of statistical tests in practice, and this can never prove that a RNG is flawless.

For this reason, theoretical tests that measure the uniformity by studying the mathematical structure are deemed more important and convincing than empirical tests, when they can be applied.

3. MAIN CLASSES OF RNGS FOR SIMULATION

The most popular classes of RNGs used for simulation are based on linear recurrences modulo m, either for $m=2$ (which amounts to doing linear operations in the finite field F_2) or for a large integer m. A large class of F_2-linear RNGs can be represented as:

$$x_i = Ax_{i-1} \bmod 2, \quad (1)$$

$$y_i = Bx_i \bmod 2, \quad (2)$$

$$u_i = \sum_{\ell=1}^{w} y_{i,\ell-1} 2^{-\ell} \quad (3)$$

where x_i is the k-bit *state vector* at step i, $y_i = (y_{i,0}, \ldots, y_{i,w-1})^T$ is the w-bit *output vector*, k and w are positive integers, **A** and **B** are binary matrices of appropriate sizes, and $u_i \in [0,1)$ is the *output* at step i. In practice, the output function is modified slightly to avoid returning 0. Several fast RNGs such as the linear feedback shift register (LFSR) generator, generalized feedback shift register (GFSR), twisted GFSR, Mersenne twister (MT), WELL, xorshift, shift registers in lookup tables (LUT-SR), and combinations of these, belong to this class [31]; [34]; [42]; [54]; [63] ; [77]. The maximal period for the state is 2^k-1 and is reached when the characteristic polynomial of **A** is primitive in F_2. The matrices **A** and **B** usually represent simple binary operations that are fast to execute on binary computers, such as or, exclusive-or, shift, and rotation, on blocks of bits. The matrices should also be selected in a way that the point sets Ψ_s have good uniformity, which can be assessed by exploiting the linear structure to compute measures of equidistribution of the points in dyadic rectangular boxes [31] ; [42]. Empirically, all these RNGs fail statistical tests designed to detect linearity in the bits, such as tests that compute the linear complexity of successive bits at a given position, $\{y_{i,j}, i \geq 0\}$, or the rank of "random" binary matrices constructed by the RNGs, so they are not Crush-resistant, but they are still appropriate for applications in which the bits of the u_i's are used nonlinearly. Some of the most popular ones use a very large k, which make them not so convenient for GPUs, because the state occupies too much memory. For example, the most popular MT instance, named MT19937, has $k=19937$, whereas the WELL uses the same k and even larger ones [63].

Linear recurrences modulo a large integer m are usually written as

$$x_i = (a_1 x_{i-1} + \cdots + a_k x_{i-k}) \bmod m, \quad (4)$$

for some coefficients $a_1,\ldots,a_k$ in $\{-m+1,\ldots,0,1,\ldots,m-1\}$, with $a_k \neq 0$, and k is the order of the recurrence. This can be written equivalently as (1) with 2 replaced by m, $\mathbf{x}_i = (x_i - k+1, \ldots, x_i)^{\mathrm{T}}$, and the appropriate $k \times k$ matrix . Typically, m is a prime number slightly smaller than 2^{31} or 2^{32} or 2^{63}, and the coefficients are selected so that the period is $m^k - 1$ and the sets Ψ_s have good uniformity, measured again by exploiting the linearity (via the spectral test, which measures the quality of the lattice structure) [23]; [30] ; [34]. The output can be defined as $u_i = x_i / m$, or by $u_i = (x_i + 1)/(m+1)$ or $u_i = (x_i + 1/2)/\mathrm{m}$ to avoid returning 0, for example. This is known as a *multiple recursive generator* (MRG). For $k=1$, it gives a *linear congruential generator* (LCG), now considered obsolete because its period is much too small and its lattice structure is much too coarse (the point sets Ψ_s are too small). Taking k too large, on the other hand, makes the state too large for convenient use on traditional GPUs.

The multipliers a_j are usually selected in a way that (4) is very fast to compute, which could mean taking many of them equal to 0, the other ones equal to ±1 or to the same constant a, etc. But doing this can lead to bad generators [29]; [34] ; [44]. For example, the lagged-Fibonacci RNGs, as well as the add-with-carry and subtract-with-borrow (which are slightly modified variants of the MRG) employ only two nonzero coefficients, say a_r and a_k, both equal to ±1, and all their output vectors of the form (u_i, u_{i-r}, u_{i-k}) lie in only two parallel planes in the unit cube $[0,1)^3$ [29]. These generators give wrong results in certain simulations and they fail several statistical tests [43].

For all these linear RNGs, one can jump ahead directly by ν steps for an arbitrarily large ν by computing $\mathrm{x}_{i+\nu} = (\mathrm{A}^{\nu} \bmod m)\mathrm{x}_i \bmod m$, where $\mathrm{A}^{\nu} \bmod m$ can be precomputed in advance [25]; [34] ; [45], provided that k is not too large. This is useful for computing the initial states for separate streams of random numbers whose starting points are very far apart.

Two or more small F_2-linear RNGs can be combined via a bitwise xor of their outputs and it gives another F_2-linear RNG with much larger period and better quality point sets Ψ_s than its components [42], and whose uniformity measures can still be computed. This can also be done for MRGs with different moduli, where the combination is via addition modulo 1, for example [27]. See [30]; [35]; [47] ; [43] for specific constructions of this type. They include MRG32k3a and MRG31k3p, which come with multiple streams and substreams [30]; [33]; [45] ; [41]. If we combine MRGs with F_2-linear RNGs, the structure becomes nonlinear and the uniformity becomes harder to measure other than by empirical statistical tests; but see [39] for some theoretical results.

Besides the linear ones, there are also various classes of RNGs for which either f or g is nonlinear. For example, the multiplicative lagged Fibonacci generators proposed by [51]replace the additions in (4) by multiplications and use only two nonzero coefficients a_j, both equal to 1. They perform well empirically in statistical tests [43].

As a general rule, there should be no easily detectable dependence between successive output values, and in particular for any given bits in those values. To achieve this, either for g or both must perform a sufficient amount of work to transform the bits of the state at each step. For the conventional RNGs discussed so far, almost all of this work is done by the transition function f, and g does very little. But it is also possible to do the opposite, or to balance the work in a different way.

In *counter-based RNGs* [17]; [43]; [74]; [78] ; [80], f simply increments a counter. The state at step i is just i, so $f(i)=i+1$, and all the hard work is performed by g, which can be taken as a bijective block cipher encryption algorithm such as MD5, the tiny encryption algorithm (TEA), the secure hash algorithm (SHA), the advanced encryption standard (AES), ChaCha, Threefish, etc. [7]; [43]; [59]; [69]; [74]; [78]; [80]. An important advantage is that the output value u_i at an arbitrary position (or step) i can be generated directly and quickly regardless of i.

These values can then be generated in any order, they are easy to replicate, and it is easy to split the entire sequence into long disjoint streams. Since g is a bijection, the period is 2^k where k is the number of bits used to represent the counter. This k will usually be a multiple of 32, say in the range from 128 to 1024.

Good encryption algorithms satisfy the *avalanche criterion*, which says that changing a single bit in the counter changes approximately half the bits in the output, on average. One drawback is that they are typically slower than popular RNGs when implemented in software. But they can be simplified and still remain good enough for many simulation applications. Salmon et al. [74] propose counter-based RNGs that use simplifications of the AES and Threefish algorithms, named ARS and Threefry, which trade security for speed, and a new counter-based method called Philox.

These new proposals are Crush-resistant and this was a prime criterion in their design. One important limitation of all these counter-based RNGs is that there is no theoretical analysis of uniformity for their point sets Ψ_s. For image rendering in computer graphics, Crush-resistant may be too strong a requirement; one would prefer a faster RNG as long as it produces acceptable visual effects.

A fast counter-based RNG for GPUs is proposed for that using MD5 in [78] and faster ones using TEA in [80]. Other ones that can fit in one thread in a traditional (discrete) GPU can be found in [7]; [49]; [59] ; [69].

4. HOW TO PRODUCE PARALLEL STREAMS AND SUBSTREAMS

There are various ways of providing random numbers for parallel processors. We discuss and compare the main ones. The effective methods use multiple streams of random numbers. Those streams can be obtained in many ways, for instance by using a different RNG (e.g., different parameters in the definition), or by a leap-frog technique with a single RNG, or by splitting the sequence into long disjoint blocks of equal length, or by splitting it using random starting points for the streams. Using a single stream for everything is not a solution, as we shall see.

The easiest and cleanest way to create the streams is via a central monitor, which creates the streams in a specific order and passes them to the threads or other software entities that need them. As an indirect but equivalent way of doing this, the monitor can provide only an ID number for each stream instead of creating it explicitly, and there can be a well-defined mechanism that allow any entity to reconstruct the stream (and its initial state) from its ID number. A totally different setting is if streams can be created in a distributed fashion, e.g., for example, if we want to allow each stream to have children streams.

A single source of random numbers (single stream). A naive setting would be to have all random numbers generated on demand by a single RNG, or produced in advance and stored in global memory or in a file. The generation could be done either on a host CPU or on a parallel device to speed up the production. The methods that return the random numbers to the threads must be thread-safe, so that things work properly when several threads invoke them simultaneously. This involves overhead, especially when the random numbers are consumed by a large number of PEs. Data exchange between the different memories would also involve overhead and create a bottleneck, which would be unsustainable on highly parallel systems. Finally, this scheme is unacceptable because the way the random numbers are consumed would vary between runs, depending on how the different parallel threads execute on the PEs, and therefore the results would not be reproducible [18] ; [64].

A different generator for each stream. This usually means using the same type of RNG, but with different parameters. For example, one can use LCGs or MRGs with the same modulus but different multipliers [12] ; [25]. Finding many different good parameter sets is usually feasible, but this approach is not very convenient to manage, because finding those good parameters on the fly or precomputing and storing them adds overhead either way, in time or space. Moreover, different parameters give different streams but it does not necessarily imply that the streams can be considered as independent [3] ; [7], so this independence must be tested in some way [16]; [45] ; [74]. Some have suggested to choose parameters at random among those that give a maximal period, but this is dangerous, because maximal period does not suffice, as we saw earlier; some parameters may still give point sets Ψ_s that are far from uniform.

As an example of this approach, the dynamic creator program [55] permits one to create dynamically new instances of good-quality MT generators. It is used in [73] to obtain parallel streams based on different parameterizations. SPRNG [13]; [48] ; [53] also uses a parameterization approach to create new streams during execution. With counter-based RNGs from block ciphers which require an encoding key in addition to the counter, a simple and elegant parameterization is just to select a different key for each stream, among the huge set of admissible keys [50]; [59]; [69]; [74]; [78] ; [80]. There is no need to search for good keys or precompute tables of keys. For example, to assign a different stream to each thread (or software entity), one can just take its ID number (or a bijective function of it) as the key [59]. If we assume that block ciphers are perfectly safe, this implies that the streams produced with different keys are statistically independent. However, this assumption is not formally proved.

Leap-frogging with a single RNG . Given p processors and a single RNG with transition function f, the leapfrog approach produces p streams as follows. For $j=0,\dots,p-1$, stream j outputs the subsequence $\{u_{ip}+j,\ i = 0, 1, 2, \dots\}$ from the original RNG. The values $u_{ip},\dots,u_{ip+p-1}$ can be computed in parallel at each time step i. This is how the vectorized implementations in [58] ; [73] operate. However, these implementations work only for specific values of p and the p streams do not evolve independently. The p values must be updated together for each i and must be shared by all processors, and each stream must consume one value at each time step, which is not always convenient. More generally, one could think of using the recurrence based on f^p for an arbitrary p and run it separately for each stream, e.g., in independent threads. But most RNGs are designed so that f (not f^p) can be computed quickly. In popular linear generators, jumping ahead by p values typically takes significantly more time than advancing by one step.

Splitting a single RNG into equally-spaced blocks (streams) . The most common approach to produce multiple streams from a single RNG is to split the sequence into long subsequences of equal length, by starting the streams at different seeds. To compute those seeds, spaced say ν steps apart for a very large ν, we must be able to compute quickly the ν-step transition function f^ν. For linear RNGs, this can be achieved as we saw earlier; see also [46] ; [45]. Although jumping ahead is generally slower than generating one value, it is normally used more sparingly and it is fast enough unless k is large [5] ; [33]. When k is large, e.g., for $\mathbb{F}_2$-linear RNGs such as MT19937 and the WELL RNGs [54] ; [63], the matrix **A** is huge and squaring it repeatedly to precompute $\mathbf{A}^\nu$ becomes impractical. By standard matrix multiplication, this requires $O(k^3 \log \nu)$ time. A more efficient method for that situation has been developed in [15], based on a polynomial representation. But this method is still slow when k is in the thousands, such as for MT19937 [5]. We think this is one of the good reasons for staying away from such large values of k. If one insists on a very large period (large k) and still wants fast jump ahead, a good way to achieve it is to use a combined generator, for which the jump ahead is done by jumping ahead for each (smaller) component separately. This is done in [33]; [41] for various combined RNGs. For a counter-based generator with a fixed key, jumping ahead is trivial: just add ν to the counter.

In most software with multiple streams, the length ν of the streams is fixed to a very large constant (e.g., $\nu = 2^{127}$ in the RngStream package of [45], based on MRG32k3a). If we want to allow the user to choose any ν,$\mathbf{A}^\nu$ mod m (for linear RNGs) cannot be precomputed in advance. But when streams are used for parallelization, some users may want to have the flexibility to decide on the exact length of the streams, i.e., the distance between their starting points. This is useful for example to ensure that in a parallel version of a program, the streams can be defined in a manner that the random numbers are used in exactly the same way (and the results are exactly the same) as in a sequential version of the same program with a single stream. To do this, one needs to know how many random numbers are used from each stream, and in what order they are used in both the parallel and the sequential versions. (Another (easier) way to obtain the same results on the sequential and parallel computers, is to run the program with the same streams and substreams on both computers, with standard spacings.)

To offer efficient jump-ahead facilities by an arbitrary ν with MRG32k3a, Bradley et al. [5]precompute and store $\mathbf{A}^p$ for all p of the form $p = ib^e$ for some base b, $i = 1, \ldots, b-1$, and $e = 0, \ldots, e_{max}$, and for $p = b^{e_{max}}$. They choose $b = 8$ and $e_{max} = 20$ in their code. Whenever one needs $\mathbf{A}^\nu \mathbf{x}$ for some $\nu < b^{20}$ and $\mathbf{x}$, one writes ν in base b, i.e., as a sum of terms of the form ib^e, which effectively writes $\mathbf{A}^\nu$ as a product of matrices that have been precomputed. The vector $\mathbf{x}$ is then multiplied by those matrices, in succession. This technique applies more generally to all generators based on a linear recurrence.

In [33]; [45] ; [41], each stream is also divided into substreams, and when comparing similar systems (using a single processor), each simulation run (or replication) uses a new substream. After each run, we advance all streams to their next substream. This is convenient in a single-processor setting.

In a situation where each simulation run uses multiple processors and requires an unknown number of independent streams, it may be more convenient to assign the streams to the runs, and the substreams to the different parallel threads or tasks that need them, because it may seem easier to provide the seeds of the successive substreams of a given stream than to provide a specific substream number for many streams when making a simulation run. But the latter is also possible: To get the seed of substream number j for successive streams of length v, start with the seed of substream number j for the first stream, and jump ahead repeatedly by v steps at a time.

One potential concern with splitting is the dependence between the different streams. For example, for LCGs for which both the modulus m and the spacing v are powers of 2, the streams are strongly dependent [9]; [12]; [25]. In general, one should measure or test the uniformity of vectors of the form $(u_i, \ldots, u_{i+d-1}, u_{i+v}, \ldots, u_{i+v+d-1}, u_{i+2v}, \ldots, u_{i+2v+d-1}, \ldots)$, for various choices of $d \geq 1$. This was done in [45] with the spectral test to select good values of v. It is advocated (and easy) to apply statistical tests to vectors of this form, using TestU01 [43]; [74]. This recommendation holds more generally, to test the dependence across streams regardless of how they are defined (e.g., by using different parameters for the different streams).

A single RNG with a "random" seed for each stream . When jumping ahead is too expensive and the RNG has a huge period, it can be reasonable to just select a (pseudo)random seed for each stream, using another RNG if we want reproducibility. There is a possibility of overlap, but the probability is often negligible. If the RNG has period ρ and we take s different streams of length ℓ, with random starting points in the sequence, the probability that none of those streams overlap anywhere is approximately $p=(1-s\ell/\rho)^{s-1}$; see [12]. This gives $\ln p=(s-1)\ln(1-x)$ where $x=s\ell/\rho$. When x is very small, we have $\ln p \approx -(s-1)x$ and then the probability that there is overlap somewhere is $1-p \approx -\ln p \approx (s-1)x \approx s^2\ell/\rho$. As an illustration, if $s=\ell=2^{20}$, then $1-p \approx 2^{60}/\rho$ is near 2^{-68} for $\rho=2^{128}$ and near 2^{-964} for $\rho=2^{1024}$. For counter-based RNGs parameterized by a random key, with s streams and ρ possible keys, the probability $1-p$ that the s random keys are not all distinct is $1-p \approx s^2/\rho$ (this corresponds to $\ell=1$ in the above formula). For example, if $s=2^{30}$ (about one billion) random 128-bit keys are selected, the probability that they are not all distinct is approximately $2^{60}/2^{128}=2^{-68}$, which is really negligible.

Another important situation where "random seeds" are useful is when the streams must split during execution, so that new streams are created dynamically. This evolution can be represented as a *random tree of streams*. Any given stream may have to split in two streams (or perhaps more) at any given step. This splitting is not fully predictable (it depends on the evolution of the simulation) and the new streams must behave independently after the split. This type of splitting occurs in nuclear particle simulations in high-energy physics, where a stream is assigned to each particle, and the particles can split when they collide [14]; [53]. It occurs in a similar way in computer graphics, where the particles are replaced by rays of light, which can split when they hit a surface (some light is absorbed, some is reflected, and some may be refracted) [80]. Relying on a central provider to manage the streams is not convenient or acceptable for these applications, at least if we insist on reproducibility, because the calls to the central manager are likely to change order across replications. The SPRNG software [13]; [53]was designed for this type of setting. Conceptually, it contains a binary tree of distinct streams, numbered according to their position in the tree. When a stream splits, its two children in the tree are uniquely determined, regardless of the time at which the split occurs. The number of levels in the tree depends on the number of bits used to number the nodes. In SPRNG, the different streams are defined by the parameterization method: to each node number corresponds a set of RNG parameters. With the RNGs and implementation proposed in [53], certain parameter choices may give rise to poorly behaved streams, and some of the proposed RNGs are poorly behaved (e.g., the additive lagged-Fibonacci and some simple LCGs). Splittable streams are also proposed in [7], using a hash function to determine the new streams when splitting occurs, and a 256-bit version of the Threefish block cipher to produce the random numbers in the streams.

How to assign streams. In parallel processing, to generate the random numbers locally on each PE, it suffices to have at least one stream on each PE. In some multithread programming models, a large number of threads run on a collection of physical PEs, any given thread can run sequentially on different PEs, and a physical PE executes various threads in succession, in a time-slice fashion. These threads can be created dynamically during execution, or a large pool of threads can be created at the beginning and used by the different programming subtasks, as is the case in Java JDK 7, for example. In this context, since each thread has its own private data (not each core), the threads can be seen as (logical) PEs [64]; [66], and it appears more relevant to have one stream per thread rather than one stream per physical PE. This is done for example in JAPARA [8], in which a synchronized method in a central monitor computes (sequentially) the seeds of the different streams and assigns them to the threads, using a splitting technique as in[45]; [46]. Once the thread gets its seed, it can evolve independently; there is no further need for the central monitor. The one-stream-per-thread strategy is also discussed and implemented in [50]; [64]; [67].

However, with one stream per PE or per thread (when the threads act as logical PEs), the simulation results may depend on how the hardware is organized and on how the computations are assigned to the PEs or the threads, which may vary from one execution to the next, even on the same hardware. To ensure reproducibility, one should assign streams at a higher level, in terms of computing tasks (or subtasks) that are executed on threads, and the specific usages of random numbers in the simulation model. For example, when simulating a large service system with waiting queues, one stream can be devoted to generate the arrivals of each specific type of customer, another stream for the service times of each type, etc., so the random numbers remain well synchronized when comparing similar systems with CRNs. These assignments and the simulation results should not depend on the hardware in any way, neither on how the tasks are assigned to threads.

Passerat-Palmbach [64] points that out and proposes a Java class named TaskLocalRandom [66], based on the RngStream package of [45], and designed for parallel simulation programming in Java. In this class, each task is created with a unique ID number and a stream number is assigned to each ID number. Precomputed tables in global memory permit one to quickly find the seed for any stream number. When performing multiple independent simulation runs, the different runs should use different streams (or substreams), but this can be easily achieved even with one stream per task (and no substreams) by defining different task numbers for the different runs.

This way of assigning one stream per task can achieve reproducibility, since each task always gets the same stream regardless of the hardware. However, in many cases this is not sufficient, because it does not permit one to have more than one stream per task, which is often required to facilitate CRN synchronization [24]; [32] ; [36], as we saw earlier. One should be able to assign multiple independent streams to any given task. The streams can be created by a central monitor and passed to the tasks in the same way as any other data or objects used by those tasks. For reproducibility and good synchronization, one must make sure that they are always created in the same order, regardless of how the tasks are executed. This is done in [41], for example. See also Section 5.1.

5. RNGS ADAPTED TO PARALLEL-PROCESSING HARDWARE

We distinguish here two main schemes (or models) for exploiting parallel computing for random number generation and simulation, and discuss specific methods and software that have been proposed for each. In the first scheme, several streams can evolve in parallel, each stream running on a single PE at a time. In this model, each stream evolves in the same way as on an ordinary sequential computer, even though it may switch its execution from one PE to another, sequentially. In the second scheme, the goal is to produce random numbers, from either a single stream or many streams at a time, at a faster rate than on a single PE, by running a vectorized implementation on a group of several PEs. We name them *vectorized RNGs*. Which scheme is more appropriate depends on the type of hardware and the intended application. In the first scheme, the random numbers are often consumed locally on the PE where they are generated, whereas in the second scheme they are usually copied to a global memory and consumed elsewhere or stored for later use. In many RNG libraries, the two schemes are offered and can be mixed.

5.1. Each stream running on a single PE at a time

Most of the best currently available RNGs have been designed for conventional CPUs with "standard" instruction sets and plenty of fast-access memory. To use them on a parallel computer whose PEs have these characteristics and can execute their instructions independently of each other at any given time step, it suffices to make multiple streams as explained earlier. There is no need to change their implementation. The PEs (cores) in recent multi-core CPUs and APUs share a large common fast-access memory in addition to their separate registers, so they can accommodate the same RNGs as in traditional CPUs. The hundreds of thousands of PEs in largest supercomputers today also behave much like traditional CPUs. In this type of setting, a standard multi-stream package such as RngStream can be used directly [22].

However, on certain types of widely-used parallel-compute devices, most notably discrete GPUs, but also others such as vectorized (array) processors, there are various types of limitations such as a very small fast-access private memory for each PE, limited instruction sets, and the SIMD constraint that groups of PEs or threads must execute the same instructions simultaneously, in parallel. The smaller fast-access (private) memory and also (more generally) the cost of communication between PEs, especially when there are many of them, should discourage the use of RNGs with a very large state, such as those in [43]; [44]; [54]; [63] for example. The type of hardware may also impact what functions f and g are appropriate by favoring or ruling out certain types of instructions, due to the different architectural design of the processors [75]. We discuss those issues in the rest of this section.

Different instruction sets and hardware constraints. On discrete GPUs, warps (or wavefronts) of 32 or 64 threads must execute the same instructions simultaneously, in parallel. At each step, some of the threads can be deactivated, so they do nothing at that step. But doing too much of this would waste clock cycles. Each PE has only a limited amount of fast-access memory, so if we decide to run a stream in a single PE (or thread) at a time, the RNG state must be small, say no more than about six to eight 32-bit words. Instruction sets on traditional GPUs are also limited and RNGs must be chosen in accordance with those constraints. For example, double precision floating point arithmetic was either slow or nonexistent until recently. Recent GPGPUs and APUs do not have these limitations, however.

RNGs with a small state. Examples of recommendable RNGs with a small state, that can run easily on a single PE in a discrete GPU and have been implemented for that, are LFSR113 [3]; [31]; [41], MRG31k3p [47]; [41], MRG32k3a [3]; [5]; [30]; [41], a hybrid Tausworthe-LCG [20] which combines the taus88 generator of [28] with an LCG, LFSR113 combined with an LCG [57], and a xorshift with a running sum modulo 1 as output (to break the linearity) [75, Section 7]. There are other good RNGs whose state is small enough so they can be implemented in a single thread; see [43] for example.

Counter-based RNGs. Recently, counter-based RNGs have been advocated as an easy and attractive solution to provide millions of streams, each one having a small state [7]; [50]; [69]; [74]. Some say that the state should fit in 128 bits, for example [50]; [69]. With such a small state, it is possible to have more than one stream in a thread. In computer graphics, it sometimes happens that the same stream (at specific positions) must be accessed by different threads running on different cores. Counter-based RNGs are very handy for this situation [80]. Neves and Araujo [59] propose the Tyche RNG, which uses the ChaCha encoding algorithm over 128 bits and can provide one stream per thread. Phillips [69] propose one stream per thread per kernel call, based on a hash function, which uses a global seed broadcast to all threads, the thread id, and a counter, and hashes all this information to get the output. Block cipher encoding with a different key for each stream is used in [59]; [74]. Note that both the key and the counter use memory; the state can be seen as their juxtaposition.

Some available libraries. We now briefly discuss a small selection of available RNG libraries that offer multiple streams for parallel simulation, with emphasis on those that support GPUs.

The CUDA programming language offered by NVIDIA for their GPUs comes with the CURAND library [61], which currently implements five types of RNGs: Xorwow (not recommended; see [72]), MRG32k3a from [30], MT19937 from [54], MTGP from [73], and PHILOX-4×32-10 from [74]. Multiple streams (they are called "generators") can be created from each type, but only a limited number of them can be created. The random numbers can be generated and consumed either on the host computer or on the GPU device.

For OpenCL, a more general C-like programming environment for parallel processing, but which targets primarily GPUs for general computations, the recently-proposed clRNG library [40]; [41] offers various types of RNGs, with arbitrary numbers of streams and substreams. The streams can be created in practically unlimited number. They are created on the host computer by a central monitor. They can generate and consume random numbers either on the host or on a device (such as a GPU). Each stream also has multiple substreams, and one can skip ahead to the next substream or rewind to the beginning of the current substream or the beginning of the stream, as in [45]. It currently implements four RNGs: MRG31k3p from [47], MRG32k3a from [30], LFSR113 from [31], and PHILOX-4 × 32-10 from [74].

Barash and Shchur [3] propose a library called PRAND, with selected RNGs implemented for both CPU and GPU usage, in Fortran, Cuda, and C with streaming SIMD extensions (SSE) for improved performance. It includes MGR32k3a [30], LFSR113 [31], MT19937 [54], and a series of RNGs named GL and GQ, based on linear recurrences in the two-dimensional unit torus, all with good statistical behavior. The GL and GQ are generally slower and also have shorter periods than the first three. The authors provide facilities for jumping ahead in the sequence, to obtain starting points for multiple streams, using essentially the same algorithms as in [45]; [33]. One can produce random numbers with one or more streams per PE. In their tests and comparisons, the authors are mainly interested in how fast one can fill a large array of random numbers on a GPU, using multiple threads and multiple streams. The array is divided into contiguous sections and each section is filled by a group of threads that run one stream.

Bradley et al. [5] implement MGR32k3a and MT19937 in a CUDA environment, with jump-ahead facilities to provide multiple streams, in a setting where the users can decide on the exact length of each stream. In other software, such as in [45]; [33]; [41], this length is usually fixed. To provide efficient facilities to jump ahead by an arbitrary number of steps, for MGR32k3a they pre-compute and store several matrices, as explained in Section 4. For MT19937, they have groups of 224 threads working on each stream in a similar way as in [73], and they use the method of [15] to jump ahead. For MRG32k3a, each stream can run in a single thread. In speed benchmark tests, to generate 2^{25}random numbers in multiple streams on GPUs with CUDA, the MRG32k3a turned out to be faster than MT19937, due to its faster jumping ahead. Their software is included in the NAG library.

5.2. Multiple PEs for a single stream and vectorized RNGs

Several authors propose and implement methods that exploit parallel processing to generate random numbers at a faster rate, mostly to speed up the generation for a single stream of random numbers. Note that methods that return an array of random numbers are useful even in a single-processor setting, to amortize the function call, which often takes more time than computing the next random number.

RNG libraries using vectorized instructions. In the Intel Math Kernel Library, the Vector Statistical Library (VSL) [21, Chapter 9] offers tools to generate vectors of random numbers via the vectorized functions found in C with streaming SIMD extensions (SSE), optimized to take advantage of SIMD instructions available in recent Intel processors. One can create and use multiple streams of random numbers, each one from a base RNG. Eight specific RNGs are available: MCG31m1, R250, MCG59, MRG32k3a, WH, MT2203, MT19937, and SFMT19937. The first three fail several tests and should not be used; see [43]. The last one is a version of MT19937 running on several PEs [73] in parallel. As a downside, the user must provide the seed explicitly for each stream, by providing either a single 32-bit integer or an array of 32-bit integers, used to construct the seed. This gives no guarantee of sufficient spacing between the streams. For 6 RNGs out of 8, a function is available to jump ahead by ν steps, where ν is a 32-bit integer specified by the user. That is, ν must be less than 2^{32}, which is quite small for the maximum length of a stream.

Barash and Shchur have proposed RNGSSELIB [2], which resembles their PRAND library and offers the same RNGs, also with multiple streams, but was targeted at vectorized operations and programming via SSE, whereas PRAND is also for GPU programming.

Vectorized RNGs for GPUs. The following methods and software have been developed for the setting in which a CPU host uses a block of threads on a discrete GPU to produce a large array of random numbers.

Saito and Matsumoto [71]; [73] have done that for MTs. In [71], they propose a fast implementation of MT19937 for a specific single-instruction multiple data (SIMD) architecture that offers fast operations on 128-bit integers. The tight connection with the specific hardware is an important limitation. In [73], they propose a class of MTs for graphic processors (MTGP) adapted to the architecture of GPUs. It exploits the fact that their MT recurrence can be written as

$$x_i = f_0(x_{i-k}, \ldots, x_{i-k+r})$$

where the RNG state at step i is written $\mathbf{x}_i = (x_{i-k+1}, \ldots, x_i)$ and each x_i is a block of 32 bits. The idea is to set up a circular buffer of length $\ell \geq 2k - r$ that will contain vectors of successive values $(x_{i-k+1}, \ldots, x_i, x_{i+1}, \ldots, x_{i+k-r})$. At any step, a portion of the vector contains $\mathbf{x}_i = (x_{i-k+1}, \ldots, x_i)$, and the next values $x_{i+1}, \ldots, x_{i+k-r}$, which depend only on $\mathbf{x}_i$, are computed in parallel with $k - r$ threads. The table is circular in the sense that the indices i are always computed modulo ℓ, so $\mathbf{x}_i$ can actually be at any k successive positions (modulo ℓ) in the table. This idea applies more generally to parallelize RNGs whose recurrence has the form (5); see [1]. One would usually choose ℓ as a power of 2 and $k-r$ no larger than the number of PEs that can share a fast-access memory in a chip. They propose specific MTs for $k=11213, 23209$, and 44497. They also include a dynamic creator tool that can create new ones at will, and encode their ID number in the recurrence. This is useful to produce multiple streams, with different ID numbers. However, several PEs are needed to run each stream. This RNG is intended to be called from a host CPU to obtain a large array of random numbers using a GPU device. It can also be invoked from a program running in the same block. It is available in CUDA in 32-bit and 64-bit versions.

Nandapalan et al. [58] propose parallel implementations of xorgen generators [6], which combine an F_2-linear xorshift generator [6]; [62] with an additive Weyl sequence to break the F_2-linearity, and obtain a Crush-resistant RNG. They use a circular buffer as in [73]. The speed on discrete GPUs is comparable to that of MTGP.

Other software, such as PRAND and clRNG for example, also offer facilities to fill up an array of random numbers using several PEs in parallel on a GPU device, with one or more streams.

Special RNGs for array processors. Massively parallel processor arrays (MPPAs) offer an architecture in which small cores (or PEs) are arranged in a two-dimensional rectangular grid, with communication between neighbors, and limited local memories. Instruction sets are limited (e.g., there can be no floating-point, no division, etc.). For example, [75] describe a device that allows shifts of bits by one position at a time, fast permutations of blocks of bits, but no multiplicator. They design an F_2-linear RNG that exploits these features to produce a block of 32 bits at each step. To break the linearity, they add the successive 32-bit blocks modulo 2^{32} and return as output the running sum divided by 2^{32}.

Field programmable gate arrays (FPGAs) are another class of parallel computing devices, more flexible than those previously discussed: instead of having a fixed instruction set as in conventional devices, they can be programmed at the circuit level, in terms of bitwise operations. They allow extremely fast implementations of F_2-linear RNGs with general matrices $\mathbf{A}$ in (1). Tian and Benkrid [79] propose an FPGA implementation of the MT19937 that runs 25 times faster than a multi-core CPU implementation and 9 times faster than a GPU implementation they had. It is also faster than previous RNGs available on FPGAs [68]. Thomas, Howes, and Luk [76]; [75]; [77]propose faster F_2-linear RNGs in which $\mathbf{A}$ is constructed so that the RNG has maximal period, good uniformity (measured in terms of equidistribution), and where very efficient FPGA implementations are constructed using lookup tables to implement shift registers, and other variations. Concrete constructions are given for k up to 19,937. These RNGs can produce over a thousand bits per clock cycle. For the situation where such devices are available, they seem to be the fastest generators. An FPGA implementation of the SPRNG library [53] is proposed in [48], for the Cray XD1 and for Xilinx XUP.

6. SUMMARY AND CONCLUSION

Parallel computers are used in at least two very different ways to provide random numbers, and appropriate software facilities are needed for each. In one scheme, a host computer invokes a function that uses several PEs to fill up a large array of random numbers that are returned or stored in a buffer for further usage. In the other scheme, several (up to millions or more) independent streams of random numbers are produced in parallel. One some type of hardware such as discrete GPUs, if we want each stream to run on a single PE at a time, its state must be small. Streams should be assigned preferably not to PEs or threads, but at a higher software level, e.g., to tasks and other software entities, and with the possibility of having multiple streams in a task or in a thread. There are also applications where one may want to create (and seed) the streams dynamically, because the need for new streams depends on events that occur in the simulation. In some of those applications, seeding the new streams by a central monitor is not acceptable because it would not meet the reproducibility requirement, and one needs a method that produces a tree of streams created dynamically as the simulation goes on, and where each stream can create its children by itself, without resorting to external information. Work remains to be done to construct efficient and reliable software that provides all these facilities.

ACKNOWLEDGMENTS

This work has been supported by an NSERC-Canada Discovery Grant Number 110050and a Canada Research Chair to the first author. It was written while the first author was at Inria-Rennes, France, under an Inria International Chair, and during invited visits to Université de Savoie, in Chambéry, France, and the University of New South Wales, in Sydney, Australia. We thank the following people for their comments and corrections: David Hill and Jonathan Passerat-Palmbach from Blaise Pascal University in Clermont-Ferrand; Natarajan Bragadeesh, Chip Freitag, Ken Knox, Timmy Liu, and Brian Sumner, from Advanced Micro Devices; AbdelAlim Farag and Nabil Kemerchou from Université de Montréal.

REFERENCES

1. S.L. Anderson Random number generators on vector supercomputers and other advanced architecture SIAM Rev., 32 (1990), pp. 221–251
2. L.Y. Barash, L.N. Shchur RNGSSELIB: Program library for random number generation: More generators, parallel streams of random numbers, and Fortran compatibility Comput. Phys. Comm., 184 (2013), pp. 2367–2369
3. L.Y. Barash, L.N. Shchur, PRAND: GPU accelerated parallel random number generation library: Using most reliable algorithms and applying parallelism of modern GPUs and CPUs, 2014.
4. B. Barney, Introduction to parallel computing, 2014. https://computing. llnl. gov/tutorials/parallel_comp/.
5. T. Bradley, J. du~Toit, R. Tong, M. Giles, P. Woodhams Parallelization techniques for random number generations GPU Computing Gems Emerald Edition, Morgan Kaufmann (2011), pp. 231–246 Chapter 16
6. R.P. Brent Some long-period random number generators using shifts and xors ANZIAM J., 48 (2007), pp. C188–C202
7. K. Claessen, M.H. Pałka Splittable pseudorandom number generators using cryptographic hashing Proceedings of the 2013 ACM SIGPLAN symposium on Haskell, Haskell'13, ACM (2013), pp. 47–58
8. P.D. Coddington, A.J. Newell Japara—a java parallel random number generator library for high-performance computing Proceedings of the 18th International Parallel and Distributed Processing Symposium, IPDPS'04, IEEE Computing Society (2004) Article 156
9. De Matteis, S. Pagnutti Parallelization of random number generators and long-range correlations Numer. Math., 53 (1988), pp. 595–608
10. L.Y. Deng, J.J.H. Shiau, H.H.S. Lu Large-order multiple recursive generators with modulus $2^{31}-1$ INFORMS J. Comput., 24 (2012), pp. 636–647
11. L. Devroye Non-Uniform Random Variate Generation Springer-Verlag, New York, NY (1986)
12. M.J. Durst Using linear congruential generators for parallel random number generation Proceedings of the 1989 Winter Simulation Conference, IEEE Press (1989), pp. 462–466
13. S. Gao, G.D. Peterson GASPRNG: GPU accelerated scalable parallel random number generator library Comput. Phys. Comm., 184 (2013), pp. 1241–1249
14. J.H. Halton Pseudo-random trees: Multiple independent sequence generators for parallel and branching computations J. Comput. Phys., 84 (1989), pp. 1–56
15. H. Haramoto, M. Matsumoto, T. Nishimura, F. Panneton, P. L'Ecuyer Efficient jump ahead for F_2-linear random number generators INFORMS J. Comput., 20 (2008), pp. 385–390
16. P. Hellekalek Good random number generators are (not so) easy to find Math. Comput. Simulation, 46 (1998), pp. 485–505
17. P. Hellekalek, S. Wegenkittl Empirical evidence concerning AES ACM Trans. Model. Comput. Simul., 13 (2003), pp. 322–333
18. D.R.C. Hill, C. Mazel, J. Passerat-Palmbach, M.K. Traore Distribution of random streams for simulation practitioners Concurrency Comput. Pract. Exp., 25 (2013), pp. 1427–1442
19. W. Hörmann, J. Leydold, G. Derflinger Automatic Nonuniform Random Variate Generation Springer-Verlag, Berlin (2004)
20. L. Howes, D. Thomas GP gems 3: Efficient Random Number Generation and Applications Using CUDA Addison-Wesley (2007) Chapter 37
21. Intel math kernel library reference manual, MKL 11.2, Intel Corporation, 2015. URL https://software.intel.com/en-us/mkl_11.2_ref_pdf, document Number 630813-065US.
22. A.T. Karl, R. Eubank, J. Milovanovic, M. Reiser, D. Young Using RngStreams for parallel random number generation in C++ and R Comput. Statist., 29 (2014), pp. 1301–1320
23. D.E. Knuth The Art of Computer Programming, Volume 2: Seminumerical Algorithms (third ed.)Addison-Wesley, Reading, MA (1998)
24. A.M. Law Simulation Modeling and Analysis (fifth ed.)McGraw-Hill, New York (2014)

25. P. L'Ecuyer Random numbers for simulation Commun. ACM, 33 (1990), pp. 85–97
26. P. L'Ecuyer Uniform random number generation Ann. Oper. Res., 53 (1994), pp. 77–120
27. P. L'Ecuyer Combined multiple recursive random number generators Oper. Res., 44 (1996), pp. 816–822
28. P. L'Ecuyer Maximally equidistributed combined Tausworthe generators Math. Comp., 65 (1996), pp. 203–213
29. P. L'Ecuyer Bad lattice structures for vectors of non-successive values produced by some linear recurrences INFORMS J. Comput., 9 (1997), pp. 57–60
30. P. L'Ecuyer Good parameters and implementations for combined multiple recursive random number generators Oper. Res., 47 (1999), pp. 159–164
31. P. L'Ecuyer Tables of maximally equidistributed combined LFSR generators Math. Comp., 68 (1999), pp. 261–269
32. P. L'Ecuyer, Variance reduction's greatest hits, in: Proceedings of the 2007 European Simulation and Modeling Conference, EUROSIS, Ghent, Belgium, pp. 5–12.
33. P. L'Ecuyer, SSJ: A Java Library for Stochastic Simulation, 2008. Software user's guide, available at http://www.iro.umontreal.ca/~lecuyer.
34. P. L'Ecuyer Random number generation J.E. Gentle, W. Haerdle, Y. Mori (Eds.), Handbook of Computational Statistics (second ed.), Springer-Verlag, Berlin (2012), pp. 35–71
35. P. L'Ecuyer, T.H. Andres A random number generator based on the combination of four LCGs Math. Comput. Simulation, 44 (1997), pp. 99–107
36. P. L'Ecuyer, E. Buist Variance reduction in the simulation of call centers Proceedings of the 2006 Winter Simulation Conference, IEEE Press (2006), pp. 604–613
37. P. L'Ecuyer, S. Côté Implementing a random number package with splitting facilities ACM Trans. Math. Software, 17 (1991), pp. 98–111
38. P. L'Ecuyer, N. Giroux, A process-oriented simulation package based on Modula-2, in: 1987 Winter Simulation Proceedings, pp. 165–174.
39. P. L'Ecuyer, J. Granger-Piché Combined generators with components from different families Math. Comput. Simulation, 62 (2003), pp. 395–404
40. P. L'Ecuyer, D. Munger, N. Kemerchou, clRNG: A library for uniform random number generation in OpenCL, 2015.
41. P. L'Ecuyer, D. Munger, N. Kemerchou, clRNG: A random number API with multiple streams for OpenCL, 2015. http://www.iro.umontreal.ca/~lecuyer/myftp/papers/clrng-api.pdf.
42. P. L'Ecuyer, F. Panneton F_2-linear random number generators C. Alexopoulos, D. Goldsman, J.R. Wilson (Eds.), Advancing the Frontiers of Simulation: A Festschrift in Honor of George Samuel Fishman, Springer-Verlag, New York (2009), pp. 169–193
43. P. L'Ecuyer, R. Simard TestU01: A C library for empirical testing of random number generators ACM Trans. Math. Software, 33 (2007) Article 22
44. P. L'Ecuyer, R. Simard On the lattice structure of a special class of multiple recursive random number generators INFORMS J. Comput., 26 (2014), pp. 449–460
45. P. L'Ecuyer, R. Simard, E.J. Chen, W.D. Kelton An object-oriented random-number package with many long streams and substreams Oper. Res., 50 (2002), pp. 1073–1075
46. P. L'Ecuyer, S. Tezuka Structural properties for two classes of combined random number generators Math. Comp., 57 (1991), pp. 735–746
47. P. L'Ecuyer, R. Touzin Fast combined multiple recursive generators with multipliers of the form $a = \pm 2^q \pm 2^r$ Proceedings of the 2000 Winter Simulation Conference, IEEE Press, Piscataway, NJ (2000), pp. 683–689
48. J. Lee, Y. Bi, G.D. Peterson, R.J. Hinde, R.J. Harrison HASPRNG: Hardware accelerated scalable parallel random number generators Comput. Phys. Comm., 180 (2009), pp. 2574–2581
49. C.E. Leiserson, T.B. Schardl, J. Sukha Deterministic parallel random-number generation for dynamic-multithreading platforms 17th ACM SIGPLAN symposium on Principles and Practice of Parallel Programming, PPoPP'12, ACM (2012), pp. 193–204
50. M. Manssen, M. Weigel, A.K. Hartmann Random number generators for massively parallel simulations on GPU Eur. Phys. J. Spec. Top., 210 (2012), pp. 53–71

51. G. Marsaglia A current view of random number generators L. Billard (Ed.), Computer Science and Statistics, Sixteenth Symposium on the Interface, Elsevier Science Publishers, North-Holland, Amsterdam (1985), pp. 3–10
52. G. Marsaglia, DIEHARD: A battery of tests of randomness, 1996. See http://www.stat.fsu.edu/pub/diehard.
53. M. Mascagni, A. Srinivasan Algorithm 806: SPRNG: A scalable library for pseudorandom number generation ACM Trans. Math. Software, 26 (2000), pp. 436–461
54. M. Matsumoto, T. Nishimura Mersenne twister: A 623-dimensionally equidistributed uniform pseudo-random number generator ACM Trans. Model. Comput. Simul., 8 (1998), pp. 3–30
55. M. Matsumoto, T. Nishimura Dynamic Creation of Pseudorandom Number Generators H. Niederreiter, J. Spanier (Eds.), Monte Carlo and Quasi-Monte Carlo Methods 1998, Springer, Berlin (2000), pp. 56–69
56. S. McIntosh-Smith, The GPU computing revolution: From multi-core CPUs to many-core graphics processors, 2011. URL http://www.lms.ac.uk/sites/ default/ files/ files/reports/GPU-KT-report-screen.pdf.
57. S. Mohanty, A.K. Mohanty, F. Carminati Efficient pseudo-random number generation for Monte-Carlo simulations using graphic processors J. Phys. Conf. Ser., 368 (2012), Article 012024
58. N. Nandapalan, R. Brent, L. Murray, A. Rendell High-performance pseudo-random number generation on graphics processing units Parallel Processing and Applied Mathematics, Lecture Notes in Computer Science, vol. 7203, , Springer, Berlin/Heidelberg (2012), pp. 609–618
59. S. Neves, F. Araujo Fast and small nonlinear pseudorandom number generators for computer simulation Parallel Processing and Applied Mathematics, Lecture Notes in Computer Science, vol. 7203, , Springer (2012), pp. 92–101
60. H. Niederreiter Random Number Generation and Quasi-Monte Carlo Methods, SIAM CBMS-NSF Regional Conference Series in Applied Mathematics, vol. 63, , SIAM, Philadelphia, PA (1992)
61. NVIDIA, CURAND Library: Programming Guide, Version 7.0, NVIDIA, 2015. URL http://docs.nvidia.com/cuda/curand.
62. F. Panneton, P. L'Ecuyer On the xorshift random number generators ACM Trans. Model. Comput. Simul., 15 (2005), pp. 346–361
63. F. Panneton, P. L'Ecuyer, M. Matsumoto Improved long-period generators based on linear recurrences modulo 2 ACM Trans. Math. Software, 32 (2006), pp. 1–16
64. J. Passerat-Palmbach Contributions to Parallel Stochastic Simulation: Applications of Good Software Engineering Practices to the Distribution of Pseudorandom Streams in Hybrid Monte Carlo Simulations (Ph.D. thesis) Graduate School of Enginerring Sciences, Blaise Pascal University, Clermont-Ferrand (2013) http://tel.archives-ouvertes.fr/tel-00858735
65. J. Passerat-Palmbach, C. Mazel, D.R.C. Hill Pseudo-random streams for distributed and parallel stochastic simulations on GP-GPU J. Simul., 6 (2012), pp. 141–151
66. J. Passerat-Palmbach, C. Mazel, D.R.C. Hill TaskLocalRandom: A statistically sound substitute to pseudorandom number generation in parallel Java tasks frameworks Concurrency Comput. Pract. Exp., 27 (13) (2015), pp. 3383–3398 http://dx.doi.org/10.1002/cpe.3214
67. J. Passerat-Palmbach, C. Mazel, D.R.C. Hill, ThreadLocalMRG32k3a: A statistically sound substitute to pseudorandom number generation in parallel Java applications, in: International Conference on High Performance Computing and Simulation, pp. 543–550.
68. D. Pellerin, E. Trexel, M. Xu, FPGA-based hardware acceleration of C/C++ based applications, 2007. URL http://www.pldesignline.com/howto/201800344.
69. C.L. Phillips, J.A. Anderson, S.C. Glotzer Pseudo-random number generation for brownian dynamics and dissipative particle dynamics simulations on GPU devices J. Comput. Phys., 230 (2011), pp. 7191–7201

70. R: A Language and Environment for Statistical Computing, Reference Index R Core Team R Foundation for Statistical Computing, Vienna, Austria (2015) URL http://cran.r-project.org/doc/manuals/r-release/fullrefman.pdf
71. M. Saito, M. Matsumoto SIMD-oriented fast Mersenne twister: A 128-bit pseudorandom number generator A. Keller, S. Heinrich, H. Niederreiter (Eds.), Monte Carlo and Quasi-Monte Carlo Methods 2006, Springer-Verlag, Berlin (2008), pp. 607–622
72. M. Saito, M. Matsumoto, A deviation of CURAND: Standard pseudorandom number generator in CUDA for GPGPU, 2012. http://www.mcqmc2012.unsw. edu.au/slides/MCQMC2012_Matsumoto.pdf, Presented at MCQMC'2012.
73. M. Saito, M. Matsumoto Variants of Mersenne twister suitable for graphic processors ACM Trans. Math. Software, 39 (2013), pp. 12:1–12:20
74. J.K. Salmon, M.A. Moraes, R.O. Dror, D.E. Shaw Parallel random numbers: As easy as 1, 2, 3 Proceedings of the 2011 International Conference for High Performance Computing, Networking, Storage and Analysis, ACM, New York (2011), pp. 16:1–16:12
75. D.B. Thomas, L. Howes, W. Luk A comparison of CPUs, GPUs, FPGAs, and massively parallel processor arrays for random number generation Proceedings of the ACM/SIGDA International Symposium on Field Programmable Gate Arrays, ACM, New York (2009), pp. 63–72
76. D.B. Thomas, W. Luk High quality uniform random number generation using LUT optimised state-transition matrices J. VLSI Signal Process. Syst., 47 (2007), pp. 77–92
77. D.B. Thomas, W. Luk The LUT-SR family of uniform random number generators for FPGA architectures IEEE Trans. Very Large Scale Integr. (VLSI) Syst., 21 (2013), pp. 761–770
78. S. Tzeng, L.Y. Wei, Parallel white noise generation on a GPU via cryptographic hash, in: Proceedings of the 2008 symposium on Interactive 3D graphics and games, pp. 79–87.
79. T. Xiang, K. Benkrid, Mersenne twister random number generation on FPGA, CPU and GPU, in: NASA/ESA Conference on Adaptive Hardware and Systems, AHS 2009, pp. 460–464.
80. F. Zafar, M. Olano, A. Curtis, GPU random numbers via the tiny encryption algorithm, in: Proceedings of the Conference on High Performance Graphics, HPG'10, pp. 133–141.

CHAPTER 2

Non-prismatic Timoshenko-like beam model: Numerical solution via isogeometric collocation

Giuseppe Balduzzi[a], Simone Morganti[b], Ferdinando Auricchio[c,e], Alessandro Reali[c,d,e,*]

[a]*Institute for Mechanics of Materials and Structures (IMWS), Vienna University of Technology, Vienna, Austria*

[b]*Department of Electrical, Computer, and Biomedical Engineering, University of Pavia, Pavia, Italy*

[c]*Department of Civil Engineering and Architecture (DICAr), University of Pavia, Pavia, Italy*

[d]*Institute for Advanced Study (IAS), Technical University of Munich, Garching, Germany*

[e]*Institute for Applied Mathematics and Information Technology (IMATI), National Research Council (CNR), Pavia, Italy*

ABSTRACT

The present paper combines an effective beam theory with a simple and accurate numerical technique opening the door to the prediction of the structural behavior of planar beams characterized by a continuous variation of the cross-section geometry, that in general deeply influences the stress distribution and, therefore, leads to non-trivial constitutive relations. Accounting for these peculiar aspects, the beam theory is described by a mixed formulation of the problem represented by six linear Ordinary Differential Equations (ODEs) with non-constant coefficients depending on both the cross-section displacements and the internal forces. Due to the ODEs' complexity, the solution can be typically computed only numerically also for relatively simple geometries, loads, and boundary conditions; however, the use of classical numerical tools for this problem, like a (six-field) mixed finite element approach, might entail several issues (e.g., shear locking, ill-conditioned matrices, etc.). Conversely, the recently proposed isogeometric collocation method, consisting of the direct discretization of the ODEs in strong form and using the higher-continuity properties typical of spline shape functions, allows an equal order approximation of all unknown fields, without affecting the stability of the solution. This makes such an approach simple, robust, efficient, and particularly suitable for solving the system of ODEs governing the non-prismatic beam problem. Several numerical experiments confirm that the proposed mixed isogeometric collocation method is actually cost-effective and able to attain high accuracy.

Keywords: Non-prismatic beams; Tapered beams; Isogeometric analysis; Mixed collocation methods; B-splines

1. INTRODUCTION

Non-prismatic structural elements are widely used in several engineering fields, e.g., large span structures, mechanical components, aeronautical applications [1] ; [2]. Unfortunately, their modeling is a non trivial task since the variable geometrical properties of the cross-section lead to scarcely manageable solutions, also when considering simple geometries (i.e., linearly tapered homogeneous beams), loads, and Boundary Conditions (BCs) [3] ; [4]. As a consequence, it is necessary to take advantage of numerical tools (mainly, Finite Element (FE) analysis), which researchers continuously aim at improving in terms of efficiency and effectiveness [5]; [6]; [7]; [8] ; [9]. Furthermore, recent papers have highlighted that smooth changes of the cross-section geometry lead to non trivial stress distributions that deeply influence the whole beam behavior [10]; [11] ; [12]. In this context, the use of prismatic beam Ordinary Differential Equations (ODEs) simply assuming that the cross-section area and inertia are variable parameters results in a non-effective approach, as noticed since the '60s of the past century [13].

A significant contribution overcoming the problems so far discussed was recently proposed by Balduzzi et al. [14] that derive a novel and effective non-prismatic beam theory based on a simple and consistent definition of kinematics, equilibrium, and constitutive relations. Specifically, all variables are represented with respect to a global Cartesian coordinate system, avoiding possible complications arising from the definition of local coordinate systems. Furthermore, the three cross-section displacements usually adopted in prismatic Timoshenko beam (i.e., cross-section rotation ϕ, horizontal u and vertical v displacements) and the three internal forces (i.e., bending moment M, horizontal H and vertical V internal forces) are used as unknowns and the resulting beam theory is naturally expressed as a system of six first order ODEs. The numerical results discussed in [14] and the application of the proposed model to several engineering problems [1] ; [4] have already been shown the highly improved performances of the adopted beam theory in terms of ability in predicting stress, strain, displacements, and stiffness.

However, even if it is a 1D theory (hence representing a simplification of the 2D problem), the above mentioned beam model is still represented by a system of ODEs which requires a numerical treatment to obtain solutions in non-trivial cases. Standard numerical approaches such as a displacement-based or mixed FE approach have been already considered in the literature [10], but their use leads to non trivial numerical schemes, for which a high computational cost has to be paid in order to accurately capture the complexity of the solution.

Accordingly, in the present paper, we resort to IsoGeometric Analysis (IGA) (see, e.g., [15] and references therein), and in particular to the family of methods referred to as isogeometric collocation. Initially introduced in [16], aiming at optimizing the computational cost still taking advantage of geometrical flexibility and accuracy typical of IGA, the fundamental idea of isogeometric collocation consists of the direct discretization of the (system of) equations of interest in strong form, adopting the isoparametric paradigm and making use of the higher-continuity properties typical of the spline-based shape functions used in IGA (see, e.g., [17] and references therein).

Isogeometric collocation has been particularly successful in the context of structural elements. In particular, Bernoulli–Euler beam and Kirchhoff plate elements have been proposed by [18], and shear-deformable structural elements have been considered in a number of papers. Mixed formulations both for Timoshenko initially-straight planar beams [19] and for curved spatial rods [20] have been proposed and studied, and then successfully extended to the geometrically nonlinear case [21]. Isogeometric collocation has been moreover successfully applied to the solution of Reissner–Mindlin plate problems in [22], and a new single-parameter formulation for shear-deformable beams, recently introduced by Kiendl et al. [23], has been solved also via IGA collocation.

In the case of the beam theory considered in the present paper, isogeometric collocation seems to be an ideal solution strategy, allowing the creation of a unique combination of a simple and effective analysis tool with a simple and effective structural theory. Therefore, also supported by a number of convincing numerical experiments, we believe that the approach herein proposed may have a significant impact on non-prismatic structural elements modeling.

The paper is structured as follows: In Section 2, we summarize the differential equations governing the beam model under investigation and provide some highlights on the beam model properties. In Section 3, we introduce B-splines and describe the isogeometric collocation method adopted for the numerical solution. In Section 4, we provide several numerical results showing the good behavior of the proposed approach. Finally, in Section 5, we draw our conclusions and discuss possible future developments.

2. SYNOPSIS OF THE NON-PRISMATIC TIMOSHENKO-LIKE BEAM

This section recaps the Timoshenko-like beam model ODEs derived in [14]. Readers may refer to the so far mentioned paper for further details on the derivation procedure. The beam behaves under the hypothesis of small displacements and plane stress state and is made of a homogeneous and linear-elastic material. Being l the *beam length*, we introduce the beam *longitudinal axis*

$$L := \{x \in [0, l]\} \tag{1}$$

that coincides with the domain of the functions we are going to introduce. Thereafter, we introduce the *beam center line* $c: L \rightarrow \mathrm{R}$ and the *cross-section height* $h: L \rightarrow \mathrm{R}^+$(where R^+ indicates strictly positive real values). We assume that both the center line and the cross-section height are sufficiently smooth function, as specified in the following. The *beam lower and upper boundaries* $b_l, b_u: L \rightarrow \mathrm{R}$ are defined as

$$b_l(x) := c(x) - \frac{1}{2}h(x); \qquad b_u(x) := c(x) + \frac{1}{2}h(x) \tag{2}$$

and, the 2D region occupied by the beam body Ω is defined as

$$\Omega := \{(x, y) | \forall x \in L \rightarrow y \in [b_l(x), b_u(x)]\} \tag{3}$$

Fig. 1 represents the beam longitudinal axis L, the 2D region occupied by the beam body Ω, the Cartesian coordinate system Oxy, the lower and upper boundaries $y=b_l(x)$ and $y=b_u(x)$, and the center line $y=c(x)$.

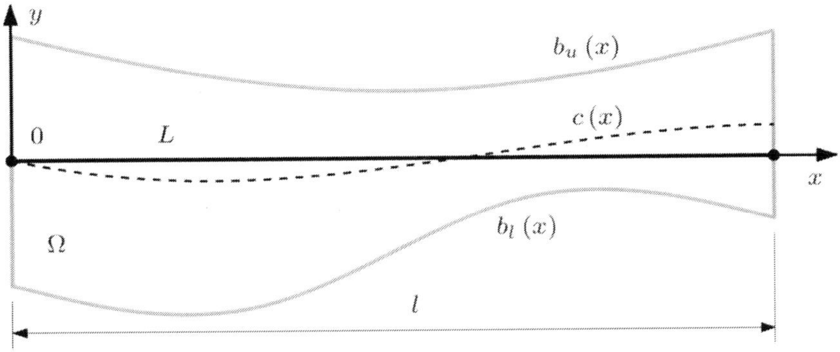

Figure. 1. Beam model domain, 2D beam geometry, coordinate system, dimensions and adopted notations.

Assuming that the lower and upper boundaries $b_l(x)$ and $b_u(x)$ are unloaded, being $\sigma : \Omega \to \mathbb{R}_s^{2\times 2}$ the 2D symmetric stress tensor and $\boldsymbol{n} = [n_x, n_y]^T : b_l \cup b_u \to \mathbb{R}^2$ the outward unit vector defined as

$$\boldsymbol{n} = \begin{Bmatrix} n_x \\ n_y \end{Bmatrix} = \pm \frac{1}{\sqrt{1+b'^2(x)}} \begin{Bmatrix} b'(x) \\ -1 \end{Bmatrix} \tag{4}$$

where the notation $(\cdot)'$ indicates the first derivative with respect to the independent variable x and $b(x)$ represents either $b_l(x)$ or $b_u(x)$, depending on the point where the boundary equilibrium is evaluated. The equilibrium on lower and upper boundaries $(\sigma \cdot \boldsymbol{n})|_{b_l \cup b_u} = \boldsymbol{0}$ allows to express the shear stress τ as a function of the axial stress σ_x

$$\tau = -\frac{n_x}{n_y}\sigma_x = b'\sigma_x \tag{5}$$

Remark 2.1. Eq. (5) highlights that the shear at the boundary is defined only if the slopes of the lower and upper boundaries are limited, i.e., $b_l'(x)$ and $b_u'(x) < \infty$. Furthermore, discontinuities in $b_l'(x)$ and $b_u'(x)$ lead to meaningless discontinuous shear. As a consequence, requiring $\{c(x), h(x)\} \in C^1(L)$ is a reasonable hypothesis to ensure that the ODEs are a well-posed problem and the solution has a meaningful physical meaning.

The displacement field $\mathbf{s} : \Omega \to \mathbb{R}^2$ is approximated as in prismatic Timoshenko beam i.e., assuming that the cross-section behaves as a rigid body

$$\mathbf{s}(x,y) = \begin{Bmatrix} s_x(x,y) \\ s_y(x,y) \end{Bmatrix} \approx \begin{Bmatrix} u(x) + (c(x) - y)\,\phi(x) \\ v(x) \end{Bmatrix} \tag{6}$$

where $u:L\rightarrow R$ is the *centerline horizontal displacement* , $\phi:L\rightarrow R$ is the *cross-section rotation* , and $v:L\rightarrow R$ is the *centerline vertical displacement.*

The **beam compatibility** is expressed through the following ODEs

$$\boxed{\begin{aligned} &\varepsilon_0(x) = u'(x) + c'(x)\,\phi(x) \\ &\chi(x) = \phi'(x) \\ &\gamma(x) = v'(x) - \phi(x) \end{aligned}} \tag{7}$$

where the *horizontal deformation* $\varepsilon_0:L\rightarrow R$, the *curvature* $\chi:L\rightarrow R$, and the *shear deformation* $\gamma:L\rightarrow R$ represent the *generalized deformations.*

According to a consolidated approach in structural mechanics [24, Section 1.4], we introduce the *internal forces,* i.e., the *horizontal internal force* $H:L\rightarrow R$, the *resulting bending moment* $M:L\rightarrow R$, and the *vertical internal force* $V:L\rightarrow R$, respectively defined as follows

$$H(x) = \int_{b_l(x)}^{b_u(x)} \sigma_x(x,y)\,dy; \quad V(x) = \int_{b_l(x)}^{b_u(x)} \tau(x,y)\,dy; \quad M(x) = \int_{b_l(x)}^{b_u(x)} \sigma_x(x,y)\,(c(x) - y)\,dy \tag{8}$$

Being $q, m, p:L\rightarrow R$ the *horizontal, bending,* and *vertical loads,* respectively, the **beam equilibrium** reads

$$\boxed{\begin{aligned} H'(x) &= -q(x) \\ M'(x) - H(x)\cdot c'(x) + V(x) &= -m(x) \\ V'(x) &= -p(x)\,. \end{aligned}} \tag{9}$$

As usual in elementary beam models and taking into account the changes of geometry, we assume that the horizontal stress has a linear distribution within the cross-section and the shear stress has a quadratic distribution (with non-vanishing values at boundaries). In more detail, the distribution of the horizontal stress turns out to be consistent with the cross-section kinematics (see Eq. (6)), whereas the distribution of the shear stress was constructed according to the Jourawsky formula, opportunely modified in order to take into account the boundary equilibrium (5) [25, Section 3.4]. Therefore, the stresses distribution within the 2D region occupied by the body Ω can be expressed as

$$\sigma_x(x,y)=\sigma_H(x,y)H(x)+\sigma_M(x,y)M(x) \tag{10a}$$

$$\tau(x,y)=\tau_H(x,y)H(x)+\tau_M(x,y)M(x)+\tau_V(x,y)V(x) \tag{10b}$$

where

$$\begin{aligned}
\sigma_H(x,y) &= \frac{1}{h(x)}\\
\sigma_M(x,y) &= \frac{12(c(x)-y)}{h^3(x)}\\
\tau_H(x,y) &= -\frac{h'(x)(c(x)-y)}{h^2(x)}+\frac{c'(x)}{h(x)}\left(-\frac{1}{2}+\frac{3}{2}\left(\frac{2(c(x)-y)}{h(x)}\right)^2\right)\\
\tau_M(x,y) &= \frac{12c'(x)(c(x)-y)}{h^3(x)}-\frac{3h'(x)}{h^2(x)}\left(-\frac{1}{2}+\frac{3}{2}\left(\frac{2(c(x)-y)}{h(x)}\right)^2\right)\\
\tau_V(x,y) &= \frac{3}{2h(x)}\left(1-\left(\frac{2(c(x)-y)}{h(x)}\right)^2\right).
\end{aligned} \tag{11}$$

Remark 2.2. The recovery relation (10b) leads to a non-trivial distribution of the shear stress within the cross-section and introduces non-trivial dependencies of the shear stress on horizontal internal force and bending moment [14] ; [25]. This issue is well known since the first half of the 20th century. In particular, referring to the analytical solution of the 2D equilibrium equation for an infinite long wedge, stress distribution can be expressed as the combination of some trigonometric functions [26]; [27] ; [28]. Furthermore, Timoshenko and Goodier [28] state that a parabolic shear distribution is a reasonably accurate approximation in the case of small boundary slope (i.e., $b_l'(x)$ and $b_u'(x)$ should be smaller than $\tan(15°)\approx 0.25$). Later on, Krahula [29] extends the so far mentioned results to tapered beams, recovering equations substantially identical to (10). Similar results were obtained also by Bleich [30] through an accurate generalization of the Jourawsky theory.

We consider the following simplified expression of stress potential:

$$\Psi^* = \frac{1}{2}\left(\frac{\sigma_x^2(x,y)}{E} + \frac{\tau^2(x,y)}{G}\right) \tag{12}$$

where E and G denote Young's and shear modulus, respectively. Substituting the stress recovery relations (10) into Eq. (12) and considering the integral with respect to y of the partial derivatives

$$\varepsilon_0(x) = \int_{b_l(x)}^{b_u(x)} \frac{\partial \Psi^*}{\partial N(x)} dy; \quad \chi(x) = \int_{b_l(x)}^{b_u(x)} \frac{\partial \Psi^*}{\partial M(x)} dy; \quad \gamma(x) = \int_{b_l(x)}^{b_u(x)} \frac{\partial \Psi^*}{\partial V(x)} dy. \tag{13}$$

we finally obtain the **beam constitutive relations** consistent with the so far introduced kinematics and internal forces:

$$\boxed{\begin{Bmatrix} \varepsilon_0(x) \\ \chi(x) \\ \gamma(x) \end{Bmatrix} = \begin{bmatrix} \varepsilon_H(x) & \varepsilon_M(x) & \varepsilon_V(x) \\ \chi_H(x) & \chi_M(x) & \chi_V(x) \\ \gamma_H(x) & \gamma_M(x) & \gamma_V(x) \end{bmatrix} \begin{Bmatrix} H(x) \\ M(x) \\ V(x) \end{Bmatrix}} \tag{14}$$

where

$$\begin{aligned} &\varepsilon_H(x) = \left(\frac{c'^2(x)}{5Gh(x)} + \frac{h'^2(x)}{12Gh(x)} + \frac{1}{Eh(x)}\right); \quad \varepsilon_M(x) = \chi_H(x) = -\frac{8c'(x)h'(x)}{5Gh^2(x)}; \\ &\varepsilon_V(x) = \gamma_H(x) = -\frac{c'(x)}{5Gh(x)}; \quad \chi_M(x) = \left(\frac{9h'^2(x)}{5Gh^3(x)} + \frac{12c'^2(x)}{Gh^3(x)} + \frac{12}{Eh^3(x)}\right); \\ &\chi_V(x) = \gamma_M(x) = \frac{3h'(x)}{5Gh^2(x)}; \quad \gamma_V(x) = \frac{6}{5Gh(x)}. \end{aligned} \tag{15}$$

Remark 2.3. Differently from prismatic beams in which each generalized deformation depends only on the corresponding internal force, constitutive relations (14) highlight that all the generalized deformations depend on all internal forces. In authors' knowledge, the only papers that notice the non-trivial dependence of generalized deformations on all internal forces are [31]; [10]; [11] ; [32]. Specifically, deriving a model for a tapered beam, Rubin [32] and Aminbaghai and Binder [31] consider the fact that the bending moment produces also shear deformation and the shear force produces a curvature. Nevertheless both papers do not consider the effect of a non-horizontal centerline and use different coefficients with respect to the ones that naturally result in Eqs. (14). Conversely, Auricchio et al. [10] and Beltempo et al. [11] consider implicitly these aspects through enhanced model derivations.

Substituting the constitutive relations (14) into the compatibility Eqs. (7) we obtain the beam model ODEs in the following mixed form:

$$\begin{Bmatrix} H'(x) \\ V'(x) \\ M'(x) \\ \phi'(x) \\ v'(x) \\ u'(x) \end{Bmatrix} = \left[\begin{array}{ccc|ccc} 0 & 0 & 0 & & & \\ 0 & 0 & 0 & & \mathbf{0} & \\ c'(x) & -1 & 0 & & & \\ \hline \chi_H & \chi_V & \chi_M & 0 & 0 & 0 \\ \gamma_H & \gamma_V & \gamma_M & 1 & 0 & 0 \\ \varepsilon_H & \varepsilon_V & \varepsilon_M & -c'(x) & 0 & 0 \end{array}\right] \begin{Bmatrix} H(x) \\ V(x) \\ M(x) \\ \phi(x) \\ v(x) \\ u(x) \end{Bmatrix} - \begin{Bmatrix} q(x) \\ p(x) \\ m(x) \\ 0 \\ 0 \\ 0 \end{Bmatrix}. \tag{16}$$

Obviously, the six first order ODEs (16) must be equipped with six suitable BCs (three per each beam end) in order to ensure the uniqueness of the solution. In Section 4, BCs for every considered numerical example are specified.

Remark 2.4. Within the herein discussed beam model all variables are referred to the global Cartesian coordinate system Oxy and the domain of the independent variable functions is L, a subset of the x axis defined in Eq. (1) and highlighted with a bold line in Fig. 1.

This modeling strategy is substantially different from the one usually adopted for curved beams that are formulated with respect to a curvilinear coordinate running along the beam centerline [33] ; [34], but has the following main advantages: (i) it avoids complications coming from the handling of a curvilinear coordinate (e.g., curve parameterization, mapping, total derivatives); (ii) it allows to obtain linear and simple ODEs (see Remark 2.5); and (iii) in numerical discretization, it reduces the mapping between real and reference elements to a trivial scaling function.

Remark 2.5. In Eq. (16), the matrix that collects equations' coefficients has a lower triangular form with vanishing diagonal terms.

As a consequence, from a theoretical point of view the ODEs' solution can be easily obtained through an iterative procedure of row by row integration, starting from $H(x)$ and arriving at $u(x)$. Several other beam models have this peculiar property, among others we would like to mention the famous Timoshenko beam model and the 3D beam model proposed by Gimena et al. [35].

Remark 2.6. As usually done by standard beam theories and according to the adopted kinematics and stress representation, the introduced beam model cannot tackle boundary effects like stress concentrations occurring nearby the constrains [36].

Furthermore, according to Remark 2.2, the formulas for the recovery of stress distributions (10) and consequently the whole beam model provide meaningful solutions only for values of $b_l'(x)$ and $b_u'(x)$smaller than $\tan(15°) \approx 0.25$.

3. NUMERICAL SOLUTION VIA ISOGEOMETRIC COLLOCATION METHODS

The aim of this section is to present a short description of B-splines and of their use in isogeometric analysis, followed by an introduction on isogeometric collocation in 1D.

We finally present here the application of isogeometric collocation in mixed form for the solution of the system of ODEs describing the beam model introduced in the previous section. The good behavior of the proposed method is then confirmed by the numerical experiments reported in the following section.

3.1. Basics on B-splines and their use in isogeometric analysis

We limit the description in the following to the basic concepts on B-splines and isogeometric analysis essential for the proposed method. For more details, the interested reader is referred to [15] and to the references therein.

A knot vector is a set of non-decreasing real numbers representing coordinates in the parametric space which we assume here to be $[0,1]$:

$$\Xi=\{\xi_1=0,\dots,\xi_{n+p+1}=1\}, \tag{17}$$

where p is the degree of the B-spline and n is the number of basis functions necessary to describe it. A knot vector is said to be *uniform* if its knots are uniformly-spaced and *non-uniform* otherwise; it is moreover said to be *open* if its first and last knots have multiplicity $p+1$.

In what follows, only open knot vectors are considered. Basis functions formed from open knot vectors are interpolatory at the ends of the parametric interval $[0,1]$ but are not, in general, interpolatory at interior knots.

Given a knot vector, univariate B-spline basis functions are defined recursively starting with $p=0$ as follows:

$$N_{i,0}(\xi)=\begin{cases}1 & \text{if } \xi_i \le \xi < \xi_{i+1}\\ 0 & \text{otherwise.}\end{cases} \tag{18}$$

For $p>1$:

$$N_{i,p}(\xi)=\begin{cases}\dfrac{\xi-\xi_i}{\xi_{i+p}-\xi_i}N_{i,p-1}(\xi)+\dfrac{\xi_{i+p+1}-\xi}{\xi_{i+p+1}-\xi_{i+1}}N_{i+1,p-1}(\xi) & \text{if } \xi_i\le\xi<\xi_{i+p+1}\\ 0 & \text{otherwise,}\end{cases} \quad (19)$$

where, in (19), we adopt the convention $0/0=0$.

As an example, in Fig. 2 we report the $n=12$ quartic basis functions generated from the open knot vector $\Xi=\{0,0,0,0,0,1/8,1/4,3/8,1/2,5/8,3/4,7/8,1,1,1,1,1\}$.

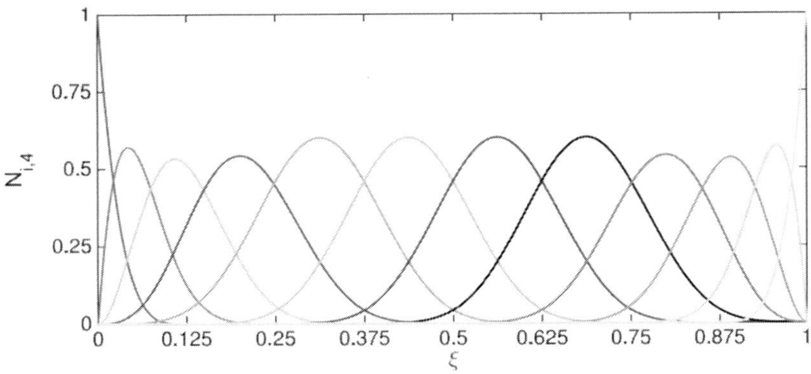

Figure. 2. Quartic basis functions formed from the open knot vector $\Xi=\{0,0,0,0,0,1/8,1/4,3/8,1/2,5/8,3/4,7/8,1,1,1,1,1\}$.

If internal knots are not repeated, B-spline basis functions are C^{p-1}-continuous (as in the case of Fig. 2). If a knot has multiplicity k, the basis is C^{p-k}-continuous at that knot. In particular, when a knot has multiplicity p, the basis is C^0 and interpolates the control point at that location. We define

$$\mathcal{S}_n=\text{span}\{N_{i,p}(\xi),\ i=1,\ldots,n\} \quad (20)$$

the spline space spanned by the basis functions $N_{i,p}(\xi)$. Following the isogeometric approach [15], the space of B-spline functions defined on a generic interval $[a,b]$ is given by:

$$\mathcal{V}_n=\text{span}\{N_{i,p}\circ F^{-1},\ i=1,\ldots,n\}, \quad (21)$$

where $x=F(\xi)=a+(b-a)\xi$ is the linear parameterization mapping $[0,1]$ onto $[a,b]$. The images of the knots through the function F naturally define a partition of the interval (a,b), which is referred to as "mesh" and is defined by a mesh-size h (being h the largest size of the elements in the mesh).

3.2. The adopted mixed isogeometric collocation method

As anticipated in Section 1, isogeometric collocation methods have been introduced in [16] for the numerical solution of ordinary and partial differential equations in strong form by means of an isoparametric approach based on spline functions. They have been shown to be an interesting and efficient alternative to isogeometric Galerkin methods, attracting in particular a lot of attention in the context of structural elements and mixed methods, where equal order approximations seem to be stable and accurate. Such a unique feature can be analytically proven in the univariate context and has been exploited to develop effective Timoshenko-like beam formulations in [20] ; [19].

Following these works, we herein propose to discretize the system of ODEs of Eq. (16)using a mixed isogeometric collocation approach where splines of the same degree are adopted for the discretization of each unknown field. Furthermore, the simple assumptions behind the beam model do not require special treatment of the problem's data (see Remark 2.4). As a consequence, due to the relative simplicity of the numerical examples we are going to discuss, we decide to handle the center line $c(x)$, the cross-section height $h(x)$, and the distributed loads $q(x)$, $p(x)$, and $m(x)$ as analytical functions. Nevertheless, according to Remark 2.1, splines represent the most natural and effective choice for the approximation of both the geometry and the loads in more complex situations. We therefore substitute in Eq. (16) the approximated fields:

$$\psi(x) = \sum_{j=1}^{n} N_{j,p}(x)\hat{\psi}_j \tag{22}$$

where $\psi(x)$ indicates one of the six generic unknown functions (i.e., $H(x)$, $V(x)$, $M(x)$, $\phi(x)$, $v(x)$, $u(x)$) and $\hat{\psi}_j$ $(j=1,\dots,n)$ the n corresponding control variables (i.e., the unknown coefficients), while $N_{j,p}(x)$ $(j=1,\dots,n)$ are the n basis functions of degree p generated by the knot vector $\Xi=\{\xi_1=0,\dots,\xi_{n+p+1}=1\}$. The obtained strong-form equations are then collocated at the images $\hat{x}_i = F(\hat{\xi}_i)$ of the Greville abscissae of the first-derivative spline space $\hat{\xi}_i$ $(i=1,\dots,n-1)$, which can be easily computed as:

$$\hat{\xi}_i = \frac{\xi_{i+2} + \xi_{i+3} + \cdots + \xi_{i+p}}{p-1}, \quad i = 1, \ldots, n-1 \tag{23}$$

The resulting algebraic system of equations, consisting of $6(n-1)$ equations in the 6 n control variables (i.e., n control variables for each of the six unknown functions), has to be finally completed by six suitable BCs to be imposed strongly as additional equations.

Remark 3.1. The possibility of using the same approximation space for all unknown fields, without affecting the stability of the solution, makes the proposed approach particularly simple and effective, and its implementation straightforward. On the other hand, building an equivalent Galerkin approach, dealing with the possible locking effects typical of mixed FEs, may be cumbersome.

4. NUMERICAL RESULTS

The proposed mixed isogeometric collocation method for the solution of non prismatic Timoshenko-like beams is tested on three different examples: (i) a shear-loaded tapered cantilever beam, (ii) an axially-loaded arch-shaped cantilever beam, and (iii) an arch-shaped beam clamped at both the extremities and subjected to self-weight load. Examples (i) and (ii) are taken from [10] ; [14], respectively, which provide also the analytical solution for the ODEs reported in Eq. (16). For Example (iii) we refer to Beltempo et al. [11], where only a numerical estimation of the solution is given due to the high problem complexity, which does not allow to obtain an explicit form of the analytical solution. All investigated examples highlight the non-trivial behavior of a non-prismatic beam body.

For Examples (i) and (ii), the results obtained with the proposed mixed collocation method are reported in terms of convergence analysis. In particular, considering the numerical approximation of a generic solution variable $\psi_{num}(x)$ and its analytical counterpart $\psi_{an}(x)$, we introduce the following error definition

$$err_{\psi}^{L2} = \left(\frac{\sum_{i=1}^{a \cdot n} \left(\psi_{num}(x_i) - \psi_{an}(x_i)\right)^2}{\sum_{i=1}^{a \cdot n} \left(\psi_{an}(x_i)\right)^2} \right)^{\frac{1}{2}} \tag{24}$$

where the points x_i are uniformly distributed within L and a⍰n is the number of points used for the error evaluation (the results that follow are obtained setting a equal to 10). It is worth noting that Eq. (24) is an estimation of the error evaluated in L^2 norm.

For Example (iii), being the analytical solution not available, the obtained isogeometric collocation results are compared with an overkill solution computed with 2D FE analysis.

4.1. Example (i): tapered cantilever

We consider the symmetric tapered beam illustrated in Fig. 3 with the following dimensions: $l = 10\ \mathrm{mm}, h(0) = 1\ \mathrm{mm},$ and $h(l) = 0.5\ \mathrm{mm}$. We assume $E = 10^5\ \mathrm{MPa}$and $G = 4 \cdot 10^4\ \mathrm{MPa}$ as material parameters. The beam section at $x = 0$ is clamped and a vertical load $P = -1\ \mathrm{N}$ acts on the section at $x = l$ (as illustrated in Fig. 3), x being the axis coordinate.

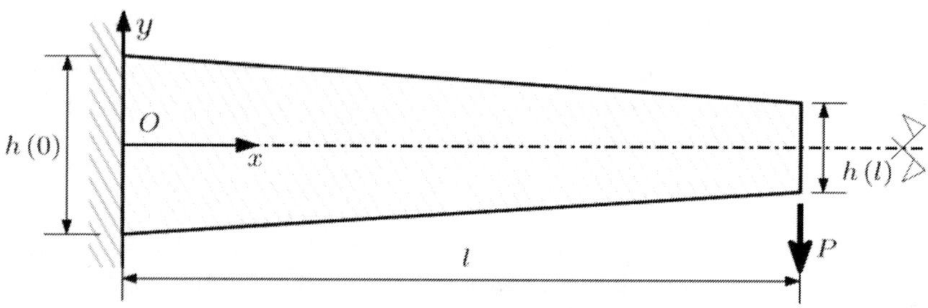

Figure. 3. Example (i): Symmetric tapered cantilever beam.

In the present example, $c(x) = 0$, therefore, following Eqs. (15), $\gamma_H(x) = \chi_H(x) = \varepsilon_M(x) = \varepsilon_V(x) = 0$. As a consequence, the axial and shear-bending equations become independent. In particular, the ODEs governing the problem read

$$\begin{cases} H'(x) = 0 & (\text{BC } H(l) = 0) \\ u'(x) = \varepsilon_H(x) H(x) & (\text{BC } u(0) = 0) \end{cases} \tag{25a}$$

$$\begin{cases} V'(x) = 0 & (\text{BC } V(l) = 1) \\ M'(x) = V(x) & (\text{BC } M(l) = 0) \\ \phi'(x) = \chi_V(x) V(x) + \chi_M(x) M(x) & (\text{BC } \phi(0) = 0) \\ v'(x) = \gamma_V(x) V(x) + \gamma_M(x) M(x) + \phi(x) & (\text{BC } v(0) = 0) \end{cases} \tag{25b}$$

ODEs (25a) have a trivial solution $H(x)=u(x)=0$ that the proposed isogeometric collocation method is able to compute exactly (i.e., $H_{num}(x) = u_{num}(x) = 0$). As a consequence, the error estimations for the horizontal internal force H and for the centerline horizontal displacement u (i.e., err_H^{L2} and err_u^{L2}, respectively) are meaningless and, in the following, we do not consider them.

The analytical solution (also reported in [14]) consists in a constant vertical internal force $V(x)=1$ and a linear bending moment $M(x)=x-10$. Since both the distributions can be exactly represented by any non-trivial (at least linear) approximating B-spline, with the developed collocation method they can be computed up to machine precision, independently from the number of used collocation points n. As a consequence, their convergence is trivial and it is not reported in the following.

Fig. 4 reports the variation of the error estimations err_v^{L2} and err_ϕ^{L2} for different number of collocation points n, chosen always equal for each field. All polynomial orders are chosen equal to $p=2,4,$ and 6, respectively, for the shape functions of each of the six independent fields. The obtained results show that the convergence rates of the collocation method agree with the expected ones [19].

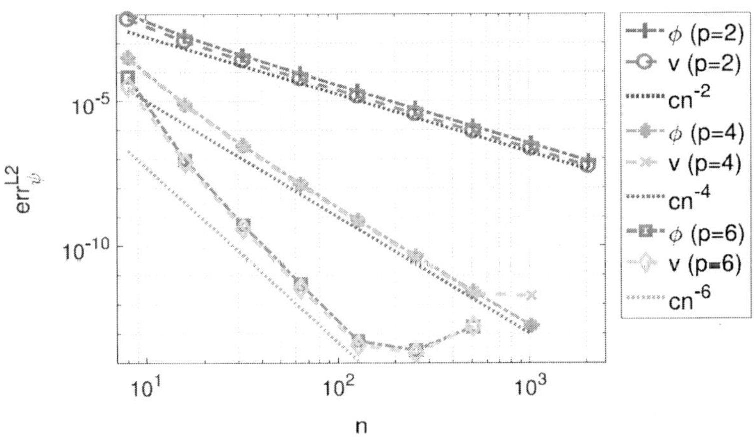

Figure. 4. Symmetric tapered cantilever: convergence of the L^2-norm of the displacement error estimations err_v^{L2} and err_ϕ^{L2}.

4.2. Example (ii): Arch-shaped cantilever beam

We consider the arch-shaped beam depicted in Fig. 5 with the following dimensions: $l = 10\ \text{mm}, \Delta = 0.5\ \text{mm}, h(l) = h(0) = 0.6\ \text{mm}, q = 1\ \text{N/mm}$. We assume $E = 10^5\ \text{MPa}$ and $G = 4 \cdot 10^4\ \text{MPa}$ as material parameters. For this example, the beam centerline and the section height are defined as

$$c(x) := -\frac{1}{100}x^2 + \frac{1}{10}x; \qquad h(x) := \frac{1}{50}x^2 - \frac{1}{5}x + \frac{3}{5} \tag{26}$$

respectively. The beam section at $x=0$ is clamped and a horizontal load $Q = 0.6\ \text{N}$ acts on the centroid of the section at $x=l$ (as illustrated in Fig. 5). Consequently, the BCs for the ODEs (16) read

$$H(l) = 0.6; \quad V(l) = 0; \quad M(l) = 0; \quad \phi(0) = 0; \quad v(0) = 0; \quad u(0) = 0 \tag{27}$$

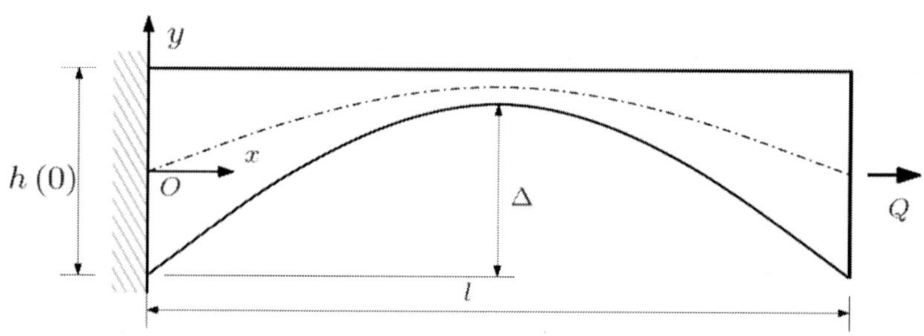

Figure. 5. Arch-shaped cantilever:
$l = 10\ \text{mm}, \Delta = 0.5\ \text{mm}, h(l) = h(0) = 0.6\ \text{mm}, Q = 0.6\ \text{N}, E = 10^5\ \text{MPa}$ and $G = 4 \cdot 10^4\ \text{MPa}$.

The analytical solution is provided in [14] and consists in a constant horizontal internal force $H(x)=0.6$, in a quadratic distribution of the bending moment $M(x)=0.6 \cdot c(x)$, while the vertical internal force vanishes (i.e., $V(x)=0$).

Since, also in this case, the distributions of the internal forces can be exactly represented by any (at least quadratic) approximating B-spline, with the proposed isogeometric collocation method they can be computed up to machine precision, independently from the number of adopted collocation points n. Consequently, in the following we do not report convergence results of internal forces solution.

We rather represent in Fig. 6 the error estimations err_v^{L2}, err_u^{L2}, and err_ϕ^{L2} for each cross-section displacement evaluated using different number of collocation points n. Also in this case, we keep equal the number of collocation points for each field, as well as the polynomial orders (i.e., p=2,4, and 6, respectively) of the shape functions of the six fields. Expected convergence rates, in agreement with Beirao da Veiga et al. [19], are obtained.

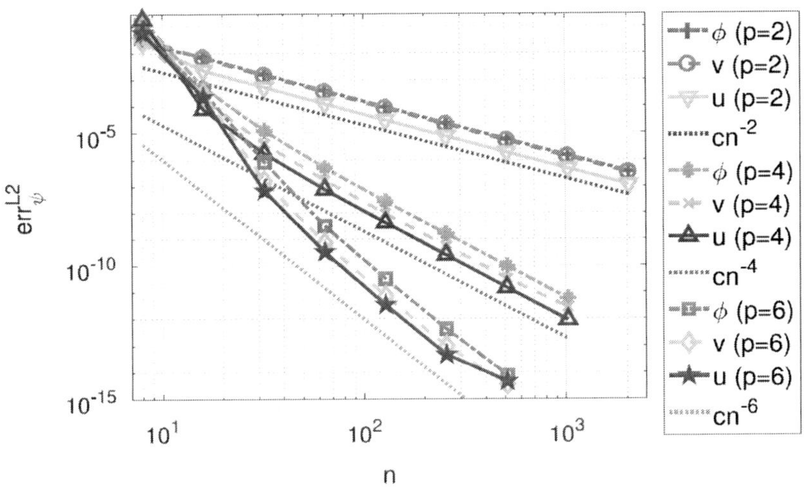

Figure. 6. Arch-shaped cantilever beam: convergence of the displacement error estimations according to L^2 norm.

4.3. Example (iii): statically indeterminate arch-shaped beam

We consider the statically undetermined arch-shaped beam depicted in Fig. 7 with the following dimensions: $l = 10$ m, $\Delta = 0.5$ m, $h(l) = h(0) = 1$ m. We assume $E = 10^5$ MPa and $G = 3.846 \cdot 10^4$ as material parameters.

In this example, the beam centerline and section height are defined as

$$c(x) := -\frac{1}{100}x^2 + \frac{1}{10}x; \qquad h(x) := \frac{1}{50}x^2 - \frac{1}{5}x + 1 \tag{28}$$

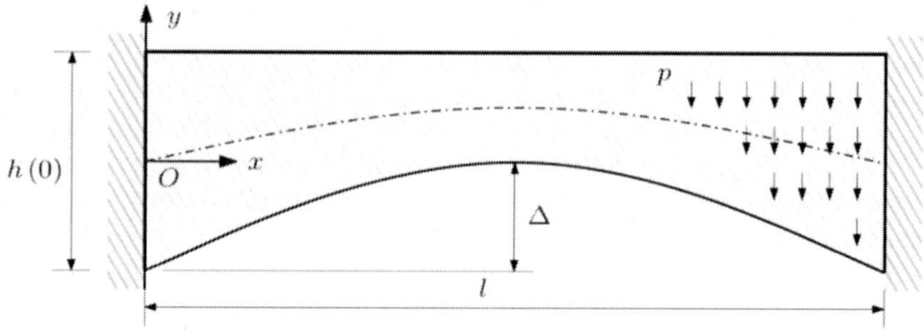

Figure. 7. Statically indeterminate arch-shaped beam: $l = 10$ m, $\Delta = 0.5$ m, $h(l) = h(0) = 1$ m, $p = 50$ kN/m^2, $E = 10^5$ MPa, and $G = 3.846 \cdot 10^4$ MPa.

As shown in Fig. 7, the beam is clamped at both extreme cross sections and subjected to self-weight load p equal to the artificial value of 50 kN/m^2 As a consequence, the vertical load is defined as $p(x) = -50\, h(x)$ and the BCs read

$$\phi(0) = \phi(l) = 0; \qquad v(0) = v(l) = 0; \qquad u(0) = u(l) = 0 \tag{29}$$

In order to provide a reference solution we model the 2D beam body with 2D FEs, using the commercial software Abaqus (Dassault Systémes, Paris, France). Specifically, we use quadrilateral bilinear elements with a characteristic length of 0.001 m leading to a structured (overkill) mesh of 6 513 396 elements.

Fig. 8 reports the numerical solution for the problem under investigation using the proposed IGA collocation method with $n = 8$ and $p = 4$ for each field. The reference FE solution is reported at 21 sections, equally distributed along the beam length.

It is worth noting that, already for $n = 8$, an accurate numerical solution is attained in terms of both internal forces and displacements, with negligible computational costs as compared with 2D FE analysis. Finally, Eqs. (10) allow to accurately recover the cross-section distribution of stresses (as extensively discussed in [11][14]) and therefore to perform accurate analysis of the cross-section strength. Therefore, Fig. 8 demonstrates that the herein proposed method is a promising analysis tool allowing to estimate all the quantities of interest for practitioners also for complex structural elements with a computational effort similar to that required by standard 1D FEs.

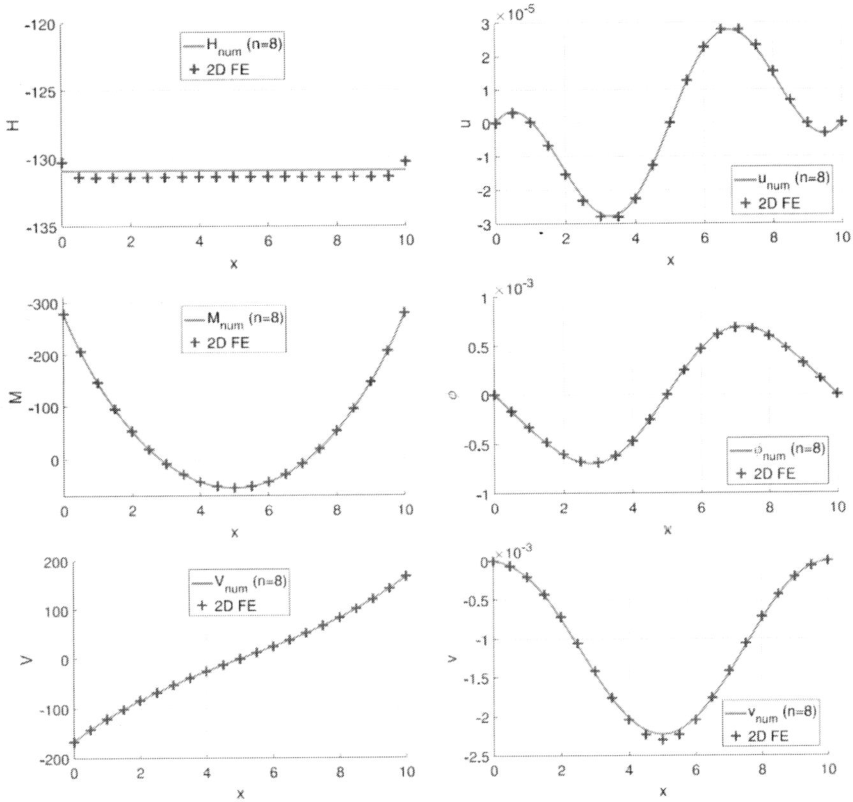

Figure. 8. Statically indeterminate arch-shaped beam: numerical results.

5. CONCLUSIONS

This paper presents an innovative numerical approach for the solution of the ODEs governing the problem of planar non-prismatic Timoshenko-like beams that naturally gives rise to a mixed formulation. The proposed scheme is based on mixed isogeometric collocation, where B-splines of the same order are used for the approximation of all (six) unknown variables, and the governing equations of the problem are solved in strong form. The method is simple, cost-effective, and robust. Finally, several numerical experiments have confirmed its good accuracy, even in the case of coarse meshes. If compared with FEs, the most diffused numerical tools for structural analysis, the herein considered numerical approach presents the following main advantages: (i) it avoids the possible locking effects typical of mixed FEs resulting to be more robust and simple to implement, and (ii) it requires a computational effort smaller than (at most similar to) standard 1D FEs.

Further developments will include the generalization of the proposed combination of the beam model and the collocation method to more complex situations like multilayered and 3D beams.

ACKNOWLEDGMENTS

This work was partially funded by the Austrian Science Found (FWF) [M 2009-N32], as well as by Fondazione Cariplo—Regione Lombardia through the project "Verso nuovi strumenti di simulazione super veloci ed accurati basati sull'analisi isogeometrica", within the program RST—rafforzamento.

REFERENCES

1. G. Balduzzi, G. Hochreiner, J. Füssl, F. Auricchio, Performance evaluation of new straightforward formulas for the serviceability analysis of cambered timber beams, in: Proceedings of the Word Conference on Timber Engineering, 2016.
2. K.G. Vinod, S. Gopalakrishnan, R. Ganguli, **Free vibration and wave propagation analisis of uniform and tapered rotating beams using spectrally formulated finite elements** Internat. J. Solids Structures, 44 (2007), pp. 5875–5893
3. F. Romano, G. Zingone, **Deflections of beams with varying rectangular cross section** J. Eng. Mech., 118 (10) (1992), pp. 2128–2134
4. G. Balduzzi, G. Hochreiner, J. Füssl, F. Auricchio, **Serviceability analysis of non-prismatic timber beams: derivation and validation of new and effective straightforward formulas** Open J. Civ. Eng., 7 (2017), pp. 32–62
5. G. Failla, N. Impollonia, **General finite element description for non-uniform and discontinuous beam elements** Arch. Appl. Mech., 82 (1) (2012), pp. 43–67
6. Z. Friedman, J.B. Kosmatka, **Exact stiffness matrix of a nonuniform beam - II bending of a Timoshenko beam** Comput. Struct., 49 (3) (1993), pp. 545–555
7. N.V. Ramesh Maganti, M.R. Nalluri, **Flapwise bending vibration analysis of functionally graded rotating double-tapered beams** Int. J. Mech. Mater. Eng., 10 (1) (2015), pp. 1–10
8. A.Shooshtari, R. Khajavi, **An efficent procedure to find shape functions and stiffness matrices of nonprismatic Euler–Bernoulli and Timoshenko beam elements** Eur. J. Mech, A/Solids, 29 (2010), pp. 826–836
9. T.H. Trinh, B.S. Gan, **Development of consistent shape functions for linearly solid tapered Timoshenko beam** J. Struct. Constr. Eng., 80 (2015), pp. 1103–1111
10. F. Auricchio, G. Balduzzi, C. Lovadina, **The dimensional reduction approach for 2D non-prismatic beam modelling: a solution based on Hellinger-Reissner principle** Internat. J. Solids Structures, 15 (2015), pp. 264–276
11. A.Beltempo, G. Balduzzi, G. Alfano, F. Auricchi, **Analytical derivation of a general 2D non-prismatic beam model based on the Hellinger-Reissner principl** Eng. Struct., 101 (2015), pp. 88–98
12. D.H. Hodges, A. Rajagopal, J.C. Ho, W. Yu, **Stress and strain recovery for the in-plane deformation of an isotropic tapered strip-beam** J. Mech. Mater. Struct., 5 (2010), pp. 963–975

13. B.A. Boley, **On the accuracy of the Bernoulli–Euler theory for beams of variable section** J. Appl. Mech., 30 (1963), pp. 374–378
14. G. Balduzzi, M. Aminbaghai, E. Sacco, J. Füssl, J. Eberhardsteiner, F. Auricchio, **Non-prismatic beams: a simple and effective Timoshenko-like model** Internat. J. Solids Structures, 90 (2016), pp. 236–250
15. J.A. Cottrell, T.J.R. Hughes, Y. Bazilevs, **Isogeometric Analysis: Toward Integration of CAD and FEA** John Wiley & Sons (2009)
16. F. Auricchio, L. Beirao Da Veiga, T.J.R. Hughes, A. Reali, G. Sangalli, **Isogeometric collocation methods** Math. Models Methods Appl. Sci., 20 (11) (2010), pp. 2075–2107
17. A.Reali, T.J.R. Hughes, **An introduction to isogeometric collocation methods** Isogeometric Methods for Numerical Simulation, Springer (2015), pp. 173–204
18. A.Reali, H. Gomez, **An isogeometric collocation approach for Bernoulli–Euler beams and Kirchhoff plates** Comput. Methods Appl. Mech. Engrg., 284 (2015), pp. 623–636
19. L. Beirao da Veiga, C. Lovadina, A. Reali, **Avoiding shear locking for the Timoshenko beam problem via isogeometric collocation methods** Comput. Methods Appl. Mech. Engrg., 241 (2012), pp. 38–51
20. F. Auricchio, L. Beirao da Veiga, J. Kiendl, C. Lovadina, A. Reali, **Locking-free isogeometric collocation methods for spatial Timoshenko rods**Comput. Methods Appl. Mech. Engrg., 263 (2013), pp. 113–126
21. O. Weeger, S.K. Yeung, M.L. Dun, **Isogeometric collocation methods for Cosserat rods and rod structures** Comput. Methods Appl. Mech. Engrg. (2016)
22. J. Kiendl, F. Auricchio, L. Beirao da Veiga, C. Lovadina, A. Reali, **Isogeometric collocation methods for the Reissner–Mindlin plate problem** Comput. Methods Appl. Mech. Engrg., 284 (2015), pp. 489–507
23. J. Kiendl, F. Auricchio, T.J.R. Hughes, A. Reali, **Single-variable formulations and isogeometric discretizations for shear deformable beams** Comput. Methods Appl. Mech. Engrg., 284 (2015), pp. 988–1004
24. S.P. Timoshenko, D.H. Young, **Theory of Structures** McGraw-Hill (1965)
25. G. Balduzzi, M. Aminbaghai, F. Auricchio, J. Füssl, **Planar Timoshenko-like model for multilayer non-prismatic beams** Int. J. Mech. Mater. Des. (2017) https://doi.org/10.1007/s10999-016-9360-3 in press
26. E.H. Atkin, **Tapered beams: suggested solutions for some typical aircraft cases** Aircr. Eng., 10 (1938), pp. 371–374
27. P. Cicala, **Sulle travi di altezza variabile** Atti Reale Accad. Sci. Torino, 74 (1939), pp. 392–402
28. S. Timoshenko, J.N. Goodier, **Theory of Elasticity** (second ed.)McGraw-Hill (1951)
29. J.L. Krahula, **Shear formula for beams of variable cross section** AIAA (Amer. Inst. Aeronaut. Astronaut.) J., 13 (1975), pp. 1390–1391
30. F. Bleich, **Stahlhochbauten** Verlag von Julius Springer (1932), pp. 80–85 (Chapter 16)
31. M. Aminbaghai, R. Binder, **Analytische Berechnung von Voutenstäben nach Theorie II. Ordnung unter Berücksichtigung der M- und Q- Verformungen** Bautechnik, 83 (2006), pp. 770–776
32. H. Rubin, **Analytische Berechnung von Stäben mit linear veränderlicher Höhe unter Berücksichtigung von M-, Q- und N- Verformungen** Stahlbau, 68 (1999), pp. 112–119
33. O.T. Bruhns, **Advanced Mechanics of Solids** Springer (2003)
34. G. Zhang, R. Alberdi, K. Khandelwal, **Analysis of three-dimensional curved beams using isogeometric approach** Eng. Struct., 117 (2016), pp. 560–574
35. L. Gimena, F.N. Gimena, P. Gonzaga, **Structural analysis of a curved beam element defined in global coordinates** Eng. Struct., 30 (2008), pp. 3355–3364
36. F. Auricchio, G. Balduzzi, C. Lovadina, **A new modeling approach for planar beams: Finite-element solutions based on mixed variational derivations** J. Mech. Mater. Struct., 5 (2010), pp. 771–794

CHAPTER 3

3-Homogeneous Groups and Block-Transitive 7–(v, k, 3) Designs

Xiaolian Liao[1,*], Guohua Chen[1] and Shangzhao Li[2]

[1] *Department of Mathematics Hunan, University of Humanities Science and Technology, Loudi 417000, China*

[2] *School of Mathematics and Statistics, Changshu Institute of Technology, Changshu 215500, China*

ABSTRACT

The classification of a block-transitive designs is an important subject on algebraic combinatorics. With the aid of MATLAB software, using the classification theorem of 3-homogeneous permutation groups, we look at the classification problem of block-transitive 7–(v, k, 3) design and prove our main theorem: If the automorphism group of a 7–(v, k, 3) design is block-transitive, then it is neither isomorphic to Affine Type Groups nor Almost Simple Type Groups.

Keywords: block-transitive; 3-homogeneous groups; permutation group; Affine Type Groups; Almost Simple Type Groups

1. INTRODUCTION

A t–design is a finite incidence structure D=(X,B), where X is a set of points and B a set of blocks, such that (1) each block is incident with k points and (2) each t-subset of X is incident with λ blocks. If $|X|=v$, then we call D a $t-(v, k, \lambda)$ design [1].

Usually we denote $|B|=b$. A t-design D is trivial, if each t-subset of X is a block and all t-subsets of X are contained in B. If any two blocks of D are different, then D is called simple. If a permutation of X preserves a block of D to a block of itself, the permutation is called an automorphism of D, and all the automorphisms of D form a group G, called the automorphism group of D, and we denote it $G \leq Aut(D)$. A group of automorphism of D is block-transitive if G acts transitively on the blocks of D. This is equivalent to that group G is transitive on the blocks and a block stable subgroup of G is also transitive on the blocks. Here we are interested in a design that is nontrivial and simple.

How to construct a block design with given parameters is one of the most important topics of combinatorial mathematics. It is especially difficult to construct a t–design with larger parameters. By [2], we have the following result: if D is a nontrivial $t-(v, k, \lambda)$ design with a block-transitive automorphism group, then $t \leq 7$. Thus, it is necessary to discuss block-transitive designs with $t \leq 7$.

Praeger and Cameron proved a very meaningful theorem in 1993 [2]: when $t > 8$, there is no non-trivial block-transitive t-design, and when $t > 7$, there is no non-trivial flag-transitive t-design. At present, the research results of flag-transitive design are relatively perfect. However, the research on block-transitive t-designs is scarce. In 2010, Huber completed the proof that there is no block-transitive Steiner 6-design (unless $G=P\Gamma L(2,p^e)$, p=2,3, and e is odd prime) [3]. However, when $\lambda \geq 2$, the current research progress is slow and has yielded few results. In this paper, we are going to study the existence of block-transitive $7-(v, k, 3)$ designs. The main results are as follows.

Theorem. *Let* D *be a non-trivial* $7-(v, k, 3)$ *design and* G *be an automorphism group of D. If G acts block-transitively on D, then G is neither isomorphic to Affine Type Groups nor Almost Simple Type Groups.*

2. PRELIMINARY RESULTS

Lemmas 1–5 can be found in the results of Beth et al. [4].

Lemma 1. *Let* D *be a t−(v, k, λ) design, where t ≥ 2 and G ≤ Aut(D)* [4]. *Therefore, the following holds:*

1. *If G acts block-transitively on D , then G acts point* [t/2] *-homogeneously on D.*

2. *If G acts flag-transitively on D , then* G *acts point* [(t+1)/2]*-homogeneously on D.*

In particular, when *t*=7, λ=3 and *G* acts block-transitively on *D*, then *G* acts point 3-homogeneously on *D*. We can use the classification of finite 3-homogeneous permutation groups to discuss a block-transitive 7−(*v*, *k*, 3) design.

Lemma 2. *Let D be a t−(v, k, λ) design. Therefore, the following holds:*

1. *bk=vr*

2. $\binom{v}{t}\lambda = b\binom{k}{t}$

3. *For any* 1 ≤ *s* < *t* , *a t−(v, k, λ) design is also a s−(v, k, λs) design, where:*

$$\lambda_s = \lambda\frac{(v-s)(v-s-1)\ldots(v-t+1)}{(k-s)(k-s-1)\ldots(k-t+1)}$$

4. *If t = 7, then*

$$r(k-1)(k-2)(k-3)(k-4)(k-5)(k-6)=\lambda(v-1)(v-2)(v-3)(v-4)(v-5)(v-6)$$

Lemma 3. *If D is a non-trivial t−(v, k, λ) design, then*

$$\lambda\binom{v-s}{t-s} \equiv 0\left(\bmod\binom{k-s}{t-s}\right),\ 0 \leq s \leq t$$

Lemma 4. *If* D *is a non-trivial t−(v, k, λ) design, then v>k + t.*

Lemma 5. *If D is a t−(v, k, λ) design, then*

$$\lambda(v-t+1)\geq(k-t+1)(k-t+2), t > 2.$$

In this case, when *t*=7, we deduce from Lemma 5 the following upper bound for the positive integer *k*.

Lemma 6. *Let D be a non-trivial* 7−(*v*, *k*, 3) *design, then*

$$k \le \left[\sqrt{3v - \frac{71}{4}} + \frac{11}{2}\right]$$

Proof. By Lemma 5, when $t=7,\lambda=3$, we have $3(v-7+1)\ge(k-7+1)(k-7+2)$, then

$$k \le \left[\sqrt{3v - \frac{71}{4}} + \frac{11}{2}\right]$$

Lemma 7. *Let D be a non-trivial t−(v, k, λ) design and* G *be an automorphism group of* D *[2]. If G acts block-transitively on D, then* $b = \frac{|G|}{|G_B|}$.

Lemma 8. *Let G be a finite 3-homogeneous permutation group on a set X with* $|X| \ge 4$ *, then G is either of Affine Type or Almost Simple Type [5].*

Lemma 9. *In finite 3-homogeneous permutation groups, the classification of Affine Type Group is one of the following [5]:*

1. $G \cong AGL(1,8)$, $A\Gamma L(1,8)$ or $A\Gamma L(1,32)$
2. $G \cong SL(d,2)$, $d\ge 2$
3. $G \cong A_7$, $v=2^4$

Lemma 10. *In finite 3-homogeneous permutation groups on a set X with* $|X|\ge 4$*, let G be of Almost Simple Type [4]. Therefore, G contains a simple normal subgroup N, where N is the socle of group G and* $N \le G \le Aut(N)$*. Thus, N and* $v=|X|$ *are given as follows:*

1. A_v, $v \ge 5$
2. $PLS(2,q)$, $v=q+1$, $q>3$
3. M_v, $v=11,12,22,23,24$
4. M_{11}, $v=12$

Lemma 11. *Let ε be a 3-dimensional subspace in vector space* $V=V(d,2)$*, then* $GL(d,2)=SL(d,2)$ *acts point-transitively on* $V\backslash\varepsilon$ *([6]).*

3. PROOF OF THE MAIN THEOREM

Let *D* be a non-trivial 7−(*v*, *k*, 3) design, the automorphism group *G* of *D* acts block-transitively on *D*, then *G* is a finite 3-homogeneous permutation group. Using Lemma 8, we know that a permutation group of a 7−(*v*, *k*, 3) design is either Affine Type or Almost Simple Type. For *D* is non-trivial, then we can suppose $k>7$. Now we are going to discuss the problem in two cases.

3.1. G Is an Affine Type Group

Corollary 1. *G is not isomorphic to* $AGL(1,8)$, $A\Gamma L(1,8)$ or $A\Gamma L(1,32)$.

If $v=8$, then $k<v-t=8-7=1$, which is a contradiction to the condition of $k>7$.

If $v=32$ and $|G|=|A\Gamma L(1,32)|=4960$, by Lemma 6, we have $k \leq \left[\sqrt{3v-\frac{71}{4}}+\frac{11}{2}\right] \leq 14$, and combining the condition of $k>7$, the parameter k satisfies condition $8\leq k\leq 14$. It is clear here that these are not possible if $10\leq k\leq 14$. Because of Lemma 2 (2), we have $29|b$, but $29\perp|G|$ (where $29\perp|G|$ means that $|G|$ cannot be divisible by 29), which leads to a contradiction. Corollary 1 is impossible.

Corollary 2. *G is not isomorphic to* $SL(d,2)$, $d\geq 2$.

Here $|V|=|V(d,2)|=2^d$. If $d=2$, 3, then $v=|V|=4$, 8, and by the proof of the above Corollary 1, none of the designs satisfying the above conditions exist. Now we assume $d>3$. Let $e_1,e_2,\cdots,e_d$ be a set of bases of vector space $V(d,2)$. Therefore, the dimension of the subspace generated by any 7 points in vector space $V(d,2)$ is at least 3. Let $\varepsilon=<e_1,e_2,e_3>$ be a vector subspace generated by the base vectors e_1,e_2,e_3 and $S=\{0,e_1,e_2, e_3,e_1+e_2,e_1+e_3,e_2+e_3\}$ be any 7-subset of ε. By the definition of t-design, for a 7-design, each 7-subset is contained in exactly 3 blocks and we record these three blocks as B_1,B_2,B_3. Thus, $S\subseteq B_1\cap B_2\cap B_3$. If B_1contains a vector α and $\alpha\in V(d,2)\backslash\varepsilon$, then by the transitivity of $SL(d,2)\varepsilon$ on the vector space $V(d,2)$, we have $\alpha^{SL(d,2)\varepsilon}=V(d,2)\backslash S$ and $\varepsilon\cup V(d,2)\backslash S\subseteq B_1^{SL(d,2)_\varepsilon}\subseteq B_1\cup B_2\cup B_3$.

Therefore, we have $2d-8\leq 3(k-7)$ or $v=2d\leq 3k-13$, on the other hand, by Lemma 5, we have $3(v-6)\geq (k-6)(k-5)$, so $k<14$. As the same proof method of Corollary 1, we can rule out this case.

Corollary 3. *G is not isomorphic to* A_7, $v=24$.

Here $v=2^4=16$, and for $k \leq \left[\sqrt{3v-\frac{71}{4}}+\frac{11}{2}\right] \leq 11$ and $k\geq 8$, the possible value of k is 8, 9, 10, or 11 by calculation. The corresponding r are not positive integers. This is impossible.

Thus, Corollary 3 is not possible.

3.2. G Is an Almost Simple Type

Corollary 4. *G is not isomorphic to* A_v, $v\geq 5$.

Since D is a non-trivial 7-design, then, by Lemma 4, $k<v-7$. Of course, we have $k\leq v-2$, so $A_v(v\geq 5)$ acts v-2-transitively on D, and then G is k-transitive on D. It means that D contains all k-subsets and D is a trivial design, a contradiction.

Corollary 5. *G is not isomorphic to $N=PSL(2,q), v=q+1, q=p^e\geq 3$.*

Here, $N\leq G\leq Aut(N)$ and $Aut(N)=P\Gamma L(2,q)$. For $|N|=|PSL(2,q)|=(q+1)q(q-1)n$, $n=(2,q-1)$.

$$|PGL(2,q)|=(q+1)q(q-1),\ |P\Gamma L(2,q)|=|PGL(2,q)|\cdot e=e(q+1)q(q-1)$$

Then

$$|G|=\frac{a(q+1)q(q-1)}{n},\ q=p^e,\ a|ne$$

For $v=q+1>k\geq 8$, then $q\geq 8$. By Lemmas 2 (1) and 7, we have

$$b=\frac{|G|}{|G_B|}=\lambda\frac{\binom{v}{t}}{\binom{k}{t}}$$

and

$$\frac{a(q+1)(q-1)q}{|G_B|n}=\frac{3(v-1)(v-2)(v-3)(v-4)(v-5)(v-6)}{k(k-1)(k-2)(k-3)(k-4)(k-5)(k-6)} \tag{1}$$

For $v = q + 1$, we have

$$\frac{a(q+1)(q-1)q}{|G_B|n}=\frac{3(q-1)(q-2)(q-3)(q-4)(q-5)(q+1)q}{k(k-1)(k-2)(k-3)(k-4)(k-5)(k-6)} \tag{2}$$

After simplification, we obtain the following:

$$3(q-2)(q-3)(q-4)(q-5)|G_B|n=ak(k-1)(k-2)(k-3)(k-4)(k-5)(k-6) \tag{3}$$

Using Lemma 5 again, then

$$3(q-5)\geq(k-6)(k-5) \tag{4}$$

Add Equation (4) into Equation (3), we have

$$(q-2)(q-3)(q-4)|G_B|n \leq ak(k-1)(k-2)(k-3)(k-4) \quad (5)$$

Additionally, by Equation (4), we can obtain an Inequality (6) under the conditions of $k \geq 27$,

$$k(k-1)(k-2)(k-3) \leq 2[(k-6)(k-5)]2 \quad (6)$$

By Equations (5) and (6) and Lemma 6, we have

$$|G_B|n < \frac{18a(q-5)^2(\sqrt{3q-\frac{59}{4}}+\frac{3}{2})}{(q-2)(q-3)(q-4)} \quad (7)$$

Now we are going to discuss it in three steps.

- $p=2$, $q=2^e$.

Here $n=(2,q-1)=1$. By $a|ne$, we know $a \leq e$, so

$$|G_B| < \frac{18e(2^e-5)^2(\sqrt{3\cdot 2^e-\frac{59}{4}}+\frac{3}{2})}{(2^e-2)(2^e-3)(2^e-4)} \quad (8)$$

Now, we construct an auxiliary function as follows:

$$y=f(e)=\frac{18e(2^e-5)^2(\sqrt{3\cdot 2^e-\frac{59}{4}}+\frac{3}{2})}{(2^e-2)(2^e-3)(2^e-4)} \quad (9)$$

Equation (9) is a decreasing function of e ($e \geq 3$). Using a computer to calculate, we find that $f(18) \approx 1.0979006$, $f(19) \approx 0.8190221 < 1$. Using MATLAB software, we map Figure 1 and Figure 2 as follows (see Appendix A and Appendix B):

For $|G_B| \geq 1$, by properties of a decreasing function, we obtain $e \leq 18$. As a result, the corresponding values of q and v are as shown in Table 1.

Since $8 \leq k \leq \left[\sqrt{3v-\frac{71}{4}}+\frac{11}{2}\right]$ and $v=q+1 \geq 15$. By Equation (3), the possible values of v and k are only one of the following three kinds $(v,k)=(65537,8)$, $(131073,8)$, and $(262145,8)$. They are all in contradiction with the hypothesis $k \geq 26$.

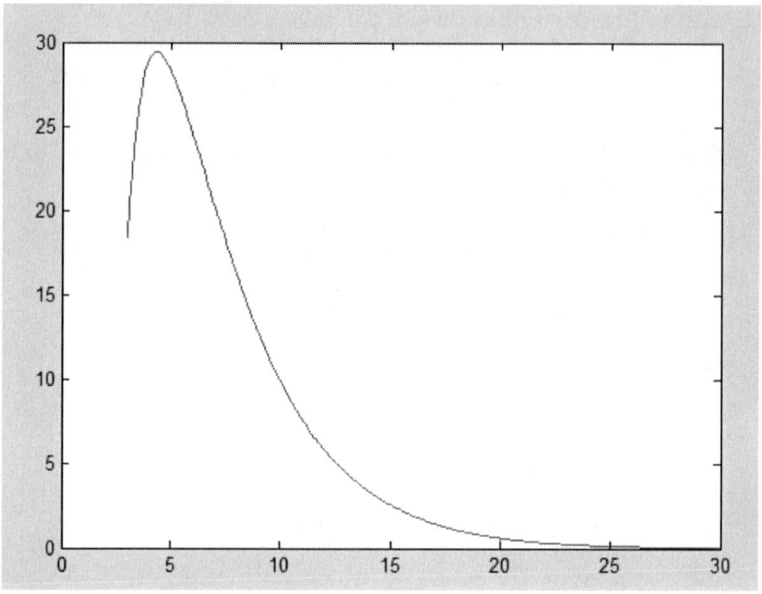

Figure 1. Partial graph of *f*(*e*) (3≤e≤30).

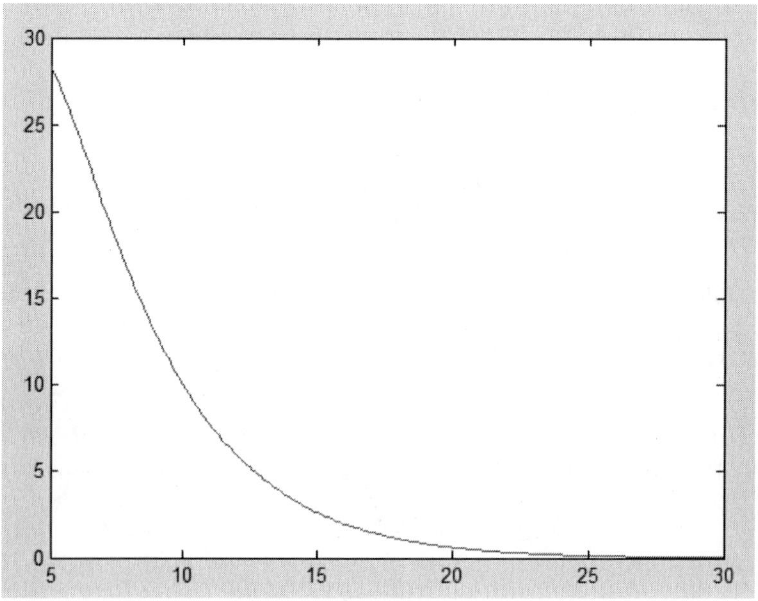

Figure 2. Partial graph of *f*(*e*) (5≤e≤30).

Table 1. Values of q and v.

e	q	v
3	8	9
4	16	17
5	32	33
6	64	65
7	128	129
8	256	257
9	512	513
10	1024	1025
11	2048	2049
12	4096	4097
13	8192	8193
14	16,384	16,385
15	32,768	32,769
16	65,536	65,537
17	131,072	131,073
18	262,144	262,145

Now, we are going to discuss the case that k is less than 27. We can introduce Inequality (10) with Equation (3) and $|G_B|\geq 1$:

$$\frac{3(2^e-2)(2^e-3)(2^e-4)(2^e-5)}{e} \leq k(k-1)(k-2)(k-3)(k-4)(k-5)(k-6). \quad (10)$$

Let

$$f(e)=\frac{3(2^e-2)(2^e-3)(2^e-4)(2^e-5)}{e}$$

and

$$h(k)=k(k-1)(k-2)(k-3)(k-4)(k-5)(k-6)$$

Then, f(e) is an increasing function of e, and the maximum value of $h(k)$ is $h(k)_{max}=h(26)=552{,}552{,}000$. It can be calculated that the maximum value of e is $e_{max}=9$. Due to $k\geq 8$ and $v=2^e+1>k+t\geq 15$, the minimum value of e is emin=4.

Again, with Equation (3), we have

$$(q-2)(q-3)(q-4)(q-5) \mid k(k-1)(k-2)(k-3)(k-4)(k-5)(k-6)e, \tag{11}$$

and

$$(q-2)(q-3)(q-4)(q-5) \leq k(k-1)(k-2)(k-3)(k-4)(k-5)(k-6)e \tag{12}$$

The admissible parameter sets (with Inequality (12) and Lemmas 3–6) are shown in Table 2.

Table 2. Values of q, v and k.

e	q	v	k
4	16	17	8, 9
5	32	33	8, 9, 10, 11, 12, 13, 14
6	64	65	12, 13, 14, 15, 16, 17, 18, 19, 20, 21, 22, 23, 24
7	128	129	16, 17, 18, 19, 20, 21, 22, 23, 24
8	256	257	21, 22, 23, 24, 25, 26
9	512	513	k is at least equal to 29, contradiction.

At last, the admissible parameter sets (v, k) in Table 2 do not satisfy Equation (11). Therefore, we show that it does not occur.

- $p=3$, $q=3^e$.

The proof is similar to the above. However, here $n=(2, q-1)=2$, and by $a|ne$, we have $a\leq 2_e$. Correspondingly, we can construct the following auxiliary function:

$$y = f(e) = \frac{36e(3^e-5)^2\left(\sqrt{3\cdot 3^e - \frac{59}{4}} + \frac{3}{2}\right)}{(3^e-2)(3^e-3)(3^e-4)} \tag{13}$$

Similar to the proof method of the above, we can rule out it.

- $p\geq 5$, $q=p^e$ and p is a prime.

Since $n=(2,q-1)=2$ and $a|ne$, then $a\leq 2e$. If $p\geq 5$, $q=p^e\geq 5^e$, then $q=p^e\geq 5^e\geq 5^{\frac{a}{2}}>2^a$, and $a<\log_2 q$. By Inequality (7), we have

$$2 \leq |G_B|n < \frac{18e(q-5)^2(\sqrt{3q-\frac{59}{4}}+\frac{3}{2})\log_2 q}{(q-2)(q-3)(q-4)} \tag{14}$$

Let

$$f(q) = \frac{18(q-5)^2(\sqrt{3q-\frac{59}{4}}+\frac{3}{2})\log_2 q}{(q-2)(q-3)(q-4)} \tag{15}$$

since $f(q)$ is a reduced function when q is greater than 28 (Figure 3 and Figure 4) (see Appendix C and Appendix D).

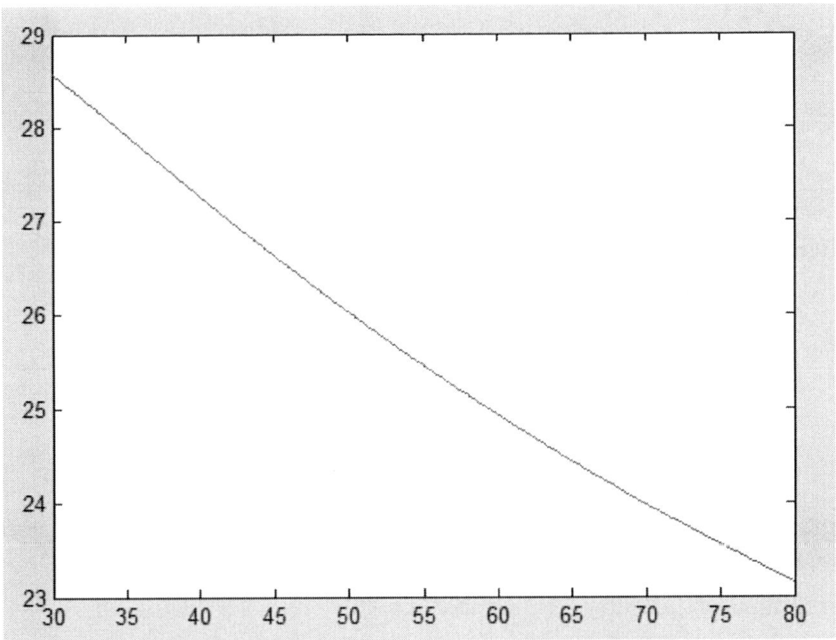

Figure 3. Partial graph of $f(q)$.

For $f(65000)=1.9617$, $f(60000)=2.0273$, binding Inequality (11), the range of possible values of q is $28<q<60000$. Accordingly, the values of k satisfy the condition $13<k<430$. For each pair (q, k), there is no corresponding $7-(q+1, k, 3)$ design by Lemma 2.

In a word, if $N=PLS(2, q)$, $v=q+1$, $q=p^e \geq 3$, and $k \geq 26$, G cannot act block-transitively on any $7-(v, k, 3)$ designs.

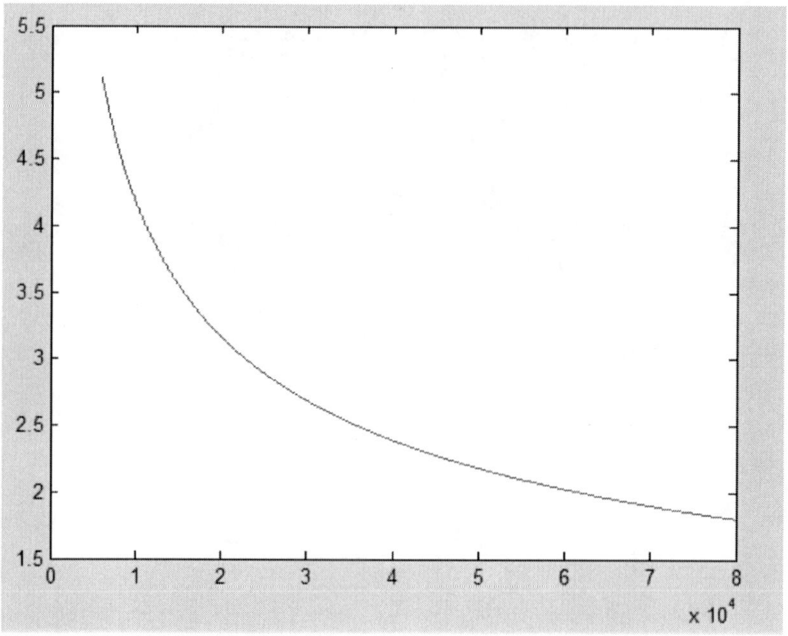

Figure 4. Partial graph of *f*(*q*).

Now, we discuss the case of 8≤*k*<26. By Equation (3),

$$\frac{3(q-2)(q-3)(q-4)(q-5)}{\log_2 q} \leq k(k-1)(k-2)(k-3)(k-4)(k-5)(k-6)$$

After calculating, the prime number that is suitable for the above inequality does not exist.

In summary, Corollary 2 is not possible.

Corollary 6. *G is not isomorphic to N*=M_v, *v*=11,12,22,23,24.

By inequality $8 \leq k \leq \left[\sqrt{3v - \frac{71}{4}} + \frac{11}{2}\right]$ and Lemma 2 (4), we know that admissible parameter sets are 7−(11, 8, 3), 7−(12, 8, 3), 7−(22, 8, 3), 7−(23, 8, 3), 7−(24, 8, 3), and 7−(22, 9, 3), 7−(22, 10, 3).

By Lemma 3, if *t*=7, *λ*=3, we have

$$3\binom{v-s}{7-s} \equiv 0\left(\bmod\binom{k-s}{7-s}\right),\ 0 \leq s \leq 7 \tag{16}$$

- For parameter set 7–(11, 8, 3), Equation (16) does not hold if we take , and 7–(11, 8, 3) design does not exist.
- For parameter sets 7–(12, 8, 3), 7–(22, 8, 3), 7–(22, 9, 3), and 7–(22, 10, 3), Equation (16) does not hold if we take s=3 , thus neither of these four designs exist.
- For parameter sets 7–(23, 8, 3), Equation (16) does not hold when s=2, and this design does not exist.

At last, using Lemma 2, we have

$$bk(k-1)(k-2)(k-3)(k-4)(k-5)(k-6)=3v(v-1)(v-2)(v-3)(v-4)(v-5)(v-6) \tag{17}$$

For parameter sets 7–(24, 8, 3), the right side of Equation (17) can be divisible by 19, so b can be divisible by 19. By Lemma 7, $|G|$ can be divisible by 19, but if $|G|$=244823040a (where a = 1 or 2), this is impossible. Therefore, the 7–(24, 8, 3) design does not exist.

Corollary 7. *G is not isomorphic to N=* M_{11}, v=12.

By the proof of **Corollary 3,** we know that this case will not occur. In this way, we have completed the proof of the main theorem.

4. CONCLUSIONS

With the aid of the MATLAB software, using the classification theorem of 3-homogeneous permutation groups, we have proved that a block-transitive automorphism group of a 7–(v, k, 3) design is neither isomorphic to Affine Type Groups nor Almost Simple Type Groups.

ACKNOWLEDGMENTS

The authors thank the referees for their valuable comments and suggestions on this paper. In particular, the first author thanks Weijun Liu and Huiling Li for their guidance and help. This research was supported by Science Research Project of Hunan Provincial Department of Education (Xiang Jiao Tong(2016)No365).

APPENDIX A

```
e = 3:1/10:30;

y = (18.*e.*(2.^e-5).^2.*((3.*2.^e-59./4).^(1./2) + (3./2)))./((2.^e-2).*(2.^e-3).*(2.^e-4));

plot(e,y);
```

APPENDIX B

```
e = 5:1/10:30;

y = (18.*e.*(2.^e-5).^2.*((3.*2.^e-59./4).^(1./2) + (3./2)))./((2.^e-2).*(2.^e-3).*(2.^e-4));

plot(e,y);
```

APPENDIX C

```
q = 30:1/10:80;

y = (18.* (q-5).^2.*((3.*q-59./4).^(1./2) + (3./2))).*log2(q)./((q2).*(q-3).*(q-4));

plot(q,y);
```

APPENDIX D

```
q = 6000:1/100:80000;

y = (18.*(q-5).^2.*((3.*q-59./4).^(1./2) + (3./2))).*log2(q)./((q2).*(q-3).*(q-4));

plot(q,y);
```

REFERENCES

1. Biggs, N.L.; White, A.T. *Permutation Groups and Combinatorial Structures*; Peking University Press: Beijing, China, 1979.

2. Cameron, P.J.; Praeger, C.E. Block-transitive t-designs II. In *Finite Geometry and Combinatorics*; de Clerck, F., Ed.; Cambridge University Press: Cambridge, UK, 1993; pp. 103–119.
3. Huber, M. On the Cameron Praeger conjecture. *J. Comb. Theory Ser. A* **2010**, *117*, 196–203.
4. Beth, T.; Jungnickel, D.; Lenz, H. *Design Theory*, 2nd ed.; Cambridge University Press: Cambridge, UK, 1999.
5. Kantor, W.M. K-homogeneous groups. *Math. Z.* **1972**, *124*, 261–265
6. Xu, X.; Zhang, J. 3-Homogeneous Groups and 5-(v,k,3) Designs. *Math. Theory Appl.* **2012**, *32*, 5–11.

CHAPTER 4

On the identification of symmetric quadrature rules for finite element methods

F.D. Witherden*, P.E. Vincent

Department of Aeronautics, Imperial College London, SW7 2AZ, United Kingdom

ABSTRACT

In this paper we describe a methodology for the identification of symmetric quadrature rules inside of quadrilaterals, triangles, tetrahedra, prisms, pyramids, and hexahedra. The methodology is free from manual intervention and is capable of identifying a set of rules with a given strength and a given number of points. We also present *polyquad* which is an implementation of our methodology. Using polyquad v1.0 we proceed to derive a complete set of symmetric rules on the aforementioned domains. All rules possess purely positive weights and have all points inside the domain. Many of the rules appear to be new, and an improvement over those tabulated in the literature.

Keywords: Numerical integration, Gaussian quadrature, Finite elements, Cubature

1. INTRODUCTION

When using the finite element method to solve a system of partial differential equations it is often necessary to evaluate surface and volume integrals inside of a standardised domain Ω [1–3]. A popular numerical integration technique is that of Gaussian quadrature in which

$$\int_{\Omega} f(\mathbf{x})\,\mathrm{d}\mathbf{x} \approx \sum_{i}^{N_p} \omega_i f(\mathbf{x}_i), \tag{1}$$

where $f(\mathbf{x})$ is the function to be integrated, $\{\mathbf{x}_i\}$ are a set of N_p points, and $\{\omega_i\}$ the set of associated weights. The points and weights are said to define a *quadrature rule*. A rule is said to be of strength ϕ if it is capable of exactly integrating any polynomial of maximal degree ϕ over Ω. A degree ϕ polynomial $p(\mathbf{x})$ with $\mathbf{x}\in\Omega$ can be expressed as a linear combination of basis polynomials

$$p(\mathbf{x}) = \sum_{i}^{|\mathcal{P}^{\phi}|} \alpha_i \mathcal{P}_i^{\phi}(\mathbf{x}), \quad \alpha_i = \int_{\Omega} p(\mathbf{x}) \mathcal{P}_i^{\phi}(\mathbf{x})\,\mathrm{d}\mathbf{x}, \tag{2}$$

where P^{ϕ} is the set of basis polynomials of degree $\leq\phi$ whose cardinality is given by $|P^{\phi}|$. From the linearity of integration it therefore follows that a strength ϕ quadrature rule is one which can exactly integrate the basis. Taking $f\in P^{\phi}$ the task of obtaining an N_p point quadrature rule of strength ϕ is hence reduced to finding a solution to a system of $|P^{\phi}|$ nonlinear equations. This system can be seen to possess $(N_D+1)N_p$ degrees of freedom where $N_D\geq2$ corresponds to the number of spatial dimensions.

In the case of $N_p\lesssim10$ the above system can often be solved analytically using a computer algebra package. However, beyond this it is usually necessary to solve the above system–or a simplification thereof–numerically. Much of the research into multidimensional quadrature over the past five decades has been directed towards the development of such numerical methods. The traditional objective when constructing quadrature rules is to obtain a rule of strength ϕ inside of a domain Ω using the fewest number of points. To this end efficient quadrature rules have been derived for a variety of domains: triangles[4–13], quadrilaterals[11,14,15], tetrahedra[7,9,16,17], prisms[18], pyramids[19], and hexahedra[11,20–22]. For finite element applications it is desirable that (i) points are arranged symmetrically inside of the domain, (ii) all of the points are strictly inside of the domain, and (iii) all of the weights are positive. The consideration given to these criteria in the literature cited above depends strongly on the intended field of application—not all rules are derived with finite element methods in mind.

Much of the existing literature is predicated on the assumption that the integrand sits in the space of P^{ϕ}. Under this assumption there is little, other than the criteria listed above, to distinguish two N_p rules of strength ϕ; both can be expected to compute the integral exactly with the same number of functional evaluations. It is therefore common practice to terminate the rule discovery process as soon as a rule is found. However, there are cases when either the integrand is inherently non-polynomial in nature, e.g. the quotient of two polynomials, or of a high degree, e.g. a polynomial raised to a high power. In these circumstances the above assumption no longer holds and it is necessary to consider the truncation term associated with each rule. Hence, within this context it is no longer clear that the traditional objective of minimising the number of points required to obtain a rule of given strength is suitable: it is possible that the addition of an extra point will permit the integration of several of the basis functions of degree ϕ+1.

Over the past five or so years there has also been an increased interest in numerical schemes where the same set of points are used for both integration and interpolation. One example of such a scheme is the flux reconstruction (FR) approach introduced by Huynh[23]. In the FR approach there is a need for quadrature rules that (i) are symmetric, (ii) remain strictly inside of the domain, (iii) have a prescribed number of points, and (iv) are associated with a well conditioned nodal basis for polynomial interpolation. These last two requirements exclude many of the points tabulated in the literature. Consequently, there is a need for *bespoke* or *designer* quadrature rules with non-standard properties.

This paper describes a methodology for the derivation of symmetric quadrature rules inside of a variety of computational domains. The method accepts both the number of points and the desired quadrature strength as free parameters and–if successful–yields a set of rules. Traits, such as the positivity of the weights, can then be assessed and rules binned according to their suitability for various applications. The remainder of this paper is structured as follows. In Section2we introduce the six reference domains and enumerate their symmetries. Our methodology is presented in Section3. Based on the approach of Witherden and Vincent[12] the methodology requires no manual intervention and avoids issues relating to ill-conditioning. In Section4 we proceed to describe our open-source implementation, *polyquad*. Using polyquad a variety of truncation-optimised rules, many of which appear to improve over those tabulated in the literature, are obtained and presented in Section5. Finally, conclusions are drawn in Section6.

2. BASES, SYMMETRIES, AND DOMAINS

2.1. Basis polynomials

The defining property of a quadrature rule for a domain Ω is its ability to exactly integrate the set of basis polynomials, P^{ϕ}. This set has an infinite number of representations the simplest of which being the monomials. In two dimensions we can express the monomials as

$$\mathcal{P}^{\phi} = \left\{x^i y^j \mid 0 \leq i \leq \phi,\ 0 \leq j \leq \phi - i\right\}, \tag{3}$$

where ϕ is the maximal degree. Unfortunately, at higher degrees the monomials become extremely sensitive to small perturbations in the inputs. This gives rise to polynomial systems which are poorly conditioned and hence difficult to solve numerically[9,16]. A solution to this is to switch to an *orthonormal basis set*defined in two dimensions as

$$\mathcal{P}^{\phi} = \left\{\psi_{ij}(\mathbf{x}) \mid 0 \leq i \leq \phi,\ 0 \leq j \leq \phi - i\right\}, \tag{4}$$

where $x=(x,y)^T$ and $\psi_{ij}(x)$ satisfies $\forall \mu,\nu$

$$\int_{\Omega} \psi_{ij}(\mathbf{x}) \psi_{\mu\nu}(\mathbf{x})\, \mathrm{d}\mathbf{x} = \delta_{i\mu}\delta_{j\nu}, \tag{5}$$

where $\delta_{i\mu}$ is the Kronecker delta. In addition to being exceptionally well conditioned orthonormal polynomial bases have other useful properties. Taking the constant mode of the basis to be $\psi_{00}(\mathbf{x})=1/c$ we see that

$$\int_{\Omega} \psi_{ij}(\mathbf{x})\, \mathrm{d}\mathbf{x} = c \int_{\Omega} \psi_{00}(\mathbf{x}) \psi_{ij}(\mathbf{x})\, \mathrm{d}\mathbf{x} = c\delta_{i0}\delta_{j0}, \tag{6}$$

from which we conclude that all non-constant modes of the basis integrate up to zero. Following Witherden and Vincent[12] we will use this property to define the truncation error associated with an N_p point rule

$$\xi^2(\phi) = \sum_{i,j} \left\{ \sum_{k}^{N_p} \omega_k \psi_{ij}(\mathbf{x}_k) - c\delta_{i0}\delta_{j0} \right\}^2. \tag{7}$$

This definition is convenient as it is free from both integrals and normalisation factors. The task of constructing an N_p point quadrature rule of strength ϕ is synonymous with finding a set of points and weights that minimise $\xi(\phi)$.

Although the above discussion has been presented primarily in two dimensions all of the ideas and relations carry over into three dimensions.

2.2. Symmetry orbits

A symmetric arrangement of N_p points inside of a reference domain can be decomposed into a linear combination of *symmetry orbits*. This concept is best elucidated with an example. Consider a line segment defined by $[-1,1]$. The segment possesses two symmetries: an identity transformation and a reflection about the origin. For an arrangement of distinct points to be symmetric it follows that if there is a point at α where $0<\alpha\leq 1$ there must also be a point at $-\alpha$. We can codify this by writing $S_2(\alpha)=\pm\alpha$ with $|S_2|=2$. The function S_2 is an example of a *symmetry orbit* that takes a single *orbital parameter*, α, and generates two distinct points. In the limit of $\alpha\to 0$ the two points become degenerate. We handle this degeneracy by introducing a second orbit, $S_1=0$, with $|S_1|=1$. Having identified the symmetries we may now decompose a symmetric arrangement of points as

$$N_p = n_1|\mathcal{S}_1| + n_2|\mathcal{S}_2| = n_1 + 2n_2,$$

where $n_1\in\{0,1\}$ and $n_2\geq 0$ with the constraint on n_1 being necessary to ensure uniqueness. This is a constrained linear Diophantine equation; albeit one that is trivially solvable and admits only a single solution. As a concrete example we take $N_p=11$. Solving the above equation we find $n_1=1$ and $n_2=5$. The n_1 orbit does not take any arguments and so does not contribute any degrees of freedom. Each n_2 orbit takes a single parameter, α, and so contributes one degree of freedom for a grand total of five. This is less than half that associated with the asymmetrical case. Hence, by parameterising the problem in terms of symmetry orbits it is possible to simultaneously reduce the number of degrees of freedom while guaranteeing a symmetric distribution of points.

Symmetries also serve to reduce the number of basis polynomials that must be considered when computing $\xi(\phi)$. Consider the following two monomials

$$p_1(x,y) = x^i y^j, \quad \text{and} \quad p_2(x,y) = x^j y^i,$$

defined inside of a square domain with vertices $(-1,-1)$ and $(1,1)$. We note that $p_1(x,y)=p_2(y,x)$. As this is a symmetry which is expressed by the domain it is clear that any symmetric quadrature rule capable of integrating p_1 is also capable of integrating p_2. Further, the index i is odd we have $p_1(x,y)=-p_1(-x,y)$. Similarly, when j is odd we have $p_1(x,y)=-p_1(x,-y)$. In both cases it follows that the integral of p_1 is zero over the domain. More importantly, it also follows that *any* set of symmetric points are also capable of obtaining this result. This is due to terms on the right hand side of Eq. (1) pairing up and cancelling out. A consequence of this is that not all of equations in the system specified by Eq. (1) are independent. Having identified such polynomials for a given domain it is legitimate to exclude them from our definition of $\xi(\phi)$. Although this exclusion does change the value of $\xi(\phi)$ in the case of a non-zero truncation error the effect is not significant. We shall denote the set of basis polynomials which *are* included as the *objective basis*, and denote this by $\tilde{P}^{\phi}$.

2.3. Reference domains

In the paragraphs which follow we will take $\hat{P}_i^{(\alpha,\beta)}(x)$ to refer to a *normalised*Jacobi polynomial as specified in Section 18.3 of[24]. In two dimensions we take the coordinate axes to be $\mathbf{x}=(x,y)$ and $x=(x,y,z)$ in three dimensions.

Triangle. Our reference triangle can be seen in Fig. 1 and has an area given by $\int_{-1}^{1}\int_{-1}^{-y}\mathrm{d}x\,\mathrm{d}y = 2$. A triangle has six symmetries: two rotations, three reflections, and the identity transformation. A simple means of realising these symmetries is to transform into barycentric coordinates

$$\boldsymbol{\lambda} = (\lambda_1, \lambda_2, \lambda_3)^T \quad 0 \le \lambda_i \le 1,\ \lambda_1 + \lambda_2 + \lambda_3 = 1, \tag{8}$$

which are related to Cartesian coordinates via

$$\mathbf{x} = \begin{pmatrix} -1 & 1 & -1 \\ -1 & -1 & 1 \end{pmatrix} \boldsymbol{\lambda}, \tag{9}$$

where the columns of the matrix can be seen to be the vertices of our reference triangle. The utility of barycentric coordinates is that the symmetric counterparts to a point λ are given by its unique permutations. The number of unique permutations depends on the number of distinct components of λ and leads us to the following three symmetry orbits

$$\begin{aligned} \mathcal{S}_1 &= \left(\tfrac{1}{3}, \tfrac{1}{3}, \tfrac{1}{3}\right), & |\mathcal{S}_1| &= 1, \\ \mathcal{S}_2(\alpha) &= \mathrm{Perm}(\alpha, \alpha, 1-2\alpha), & |\mathcal{S}_2| &= 3, \\ \mathcal{S}_3(\alpha, \beta) &= \mathrm{Perm}(\alpha, \beta, 1-\alpha-\beta), & |\mathcal{S}_3| &= 6, \end{aligned}$$

where α and β are suitably constrained as to ensure that the resulting coordinates are inside of the domain.

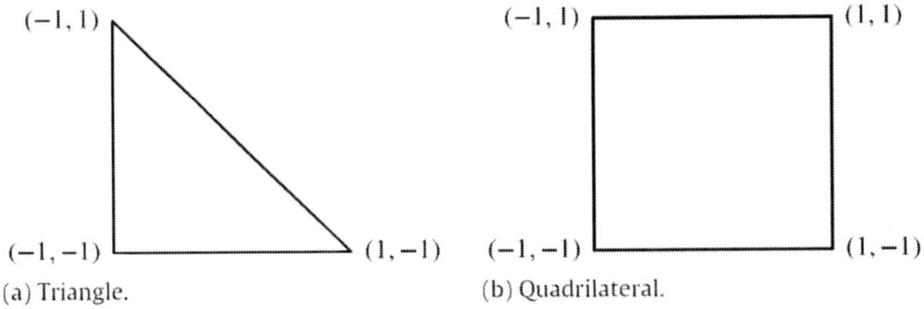

Figure. 1. Reference domains in two dimensions.

It can be easily verified that the orthonormal polynomial basis inside of our reference triangle is given by

$$\psi_{ij}(\mathbf{x}) = \sqrt{2}\hat{P}_i(a)\hat{P}_j^{(2i+1,0)}(b)(1-b)^i, \tag{10}$$

where $a=2(1+x)/(1-y)-1$, and $b=y$ with the objective basis being given by

$$\tilde{\mathcal{P}}^{\phi} = \left\{\psi_{ij}(\mathbf{x}) \mid 0 \le i \le \phi,\ i \le j \le \phi - i\right\}. \tag{11}$$

In the asymptotic limit the cardinality of the objective basis is half that of the complete basis. However, the modes of this objective basis are known not to be completely independent. Several authors have investigated the derivation of an optimal quadrature basis on the triangle. Details can be found in the papers of Lyness[4] and Dunavant[5].

Quadrilateral. Our reference quadrilateral can be seen in Fig. 1. The area is simply $\int_{-1}^{1}\int_{-1}^{1}$. A square has eight symmetries: three rotations, four reflections and the identity transformation. Applying these symmetries to a point (α,β) with $0\le(\alpha,\beta)\le1$ will yield a set $\chi(\alpha,\beta)$ containing its counterparts. The cardinality of χ depends on if any of the symmetries give rise to identical points.

This can be seen to occur when either $\beta=\alpha$ or $\beta=0$. Enumerating the possible combinations of the above conditions gives rise to the following four symmetry orbits

$$\begin{aligned} \mathcal{S}_1 &= (0, 0), & |\mathcal{S}_1| &= 1, \\ \mathcal{S}_2(\alpha) &= \chi(\alpha, 0), & |\mathcal{S}_2| &= 4, \\ \mathcal{S}_3(\alpha) &= \chi(\alpha, \alpha), & |\mathcal{S}_3| &= 4, \\ \mathcal{S}_4(\alpha, \beta) &= \chi(\alpha, \beta), & |\mathcal{S}_4| &= 8. \end{aligned}$$

Trivially, the orthonormal basis inside of our quadrilateral is given by

$$\psi_{ij}(\mathbf{x}) = \hat{P}_i(a)\hat{P}_j(b), \tag{12}$$

where a=x, and b=y. The objective basis is found to be

$$\tilde{\mathcal{P}}^{\phi} = \left\{\psi_{ij}(\mathbf{x}) \mid 0 \le i \le \phi,\ i \le j \le \phi - i,\ (i, j) \text{ even}\right\}, \tag{13}$$

with a cardinality one eighth that of the complete basis.

Tetrahedron. Our reference tetrahedron is a right-tetrahedron as depicted in Fig. 2. Integrating up the volume we find $\int_{-1}^{-1}\int_{-1}^{-z}\int_{-1}^{-1-y-z} \mathrm{d}x\,\mathrm{d}y\,\mathrm{d}z = 4/3$. A tetrahedron has a total of 24 symmetries. Once again it is convenient to work in terms of barycentric coordinates which are specified for a tetrahedron as

$$\boldsymbol{\lambda} = (\lambda_1, \lambda_2, \lambda_3, \lambda_4)^T \quad 0 \le \lambda_i \le 1,\ \lambda_1 + \lambda_2 + \lambda_3 + \lambda_4 = 1, \tag{14}$$

and related to Cartesian coordinates via

$$\mathbf{x} = \begin{pmatrix} -1 & 1 & -1 & -1 \\ -1 & -1 & 1 & -1 \\ -1 & -1 & -1 & 1 \end{pmatrix} \boldsymbol{\lambda}, \tag{15}$$

where as with the triangle the columns of the matrix correspond to vertices of the reference tetrahedron. Similarly the symmetric counterparts of λ are given by its unique permutations. This leads us to the following five symmetry orbits

$$\begin{aligned} \mathcal{S}_1 &= \left(\tfrac{1}{4}, \tfrac{1}{4}, \tfrac{1}{4}, \tfrac{1}{4}\right), & |\mathcal{S}_1| &= 1, \\ \mathcal{S}_2(\alpha) &= \mathrm{Perm}(\alpha, \alpha, \alpha, 1 - 3\alpha), & |\mathcal{S}_2| &= 4, \\ \mathcal{S}_3(\alpha) &= \mathrm{Perm}\left(\alpha, \alpha, \tfrac{1}{2} - \alpha, \tfrac{1}{2} - \alpha\right), & |\mathcal{S}_3| &= 6, \\ \mathcal{S}_4(\alpha, \beta) &= \mathrm{Perm}(\alpha, \alpha, \beta, 1 - 2\alpha - \beta), & |\mathcal{S}_4| &= 12, \\ \mathcal{S}_5(\alpha, \beta, \gamma) &= \mathrm{Perm}(\alpha, \beta, \gamma, 1 - \alpha - \beta - \gamma), & |\mathcal{S}_5| &= 24, \end{aligned}$$

where α, β, and γ are constrained to ensure that all of the resulting coordinates are inside of the domain.

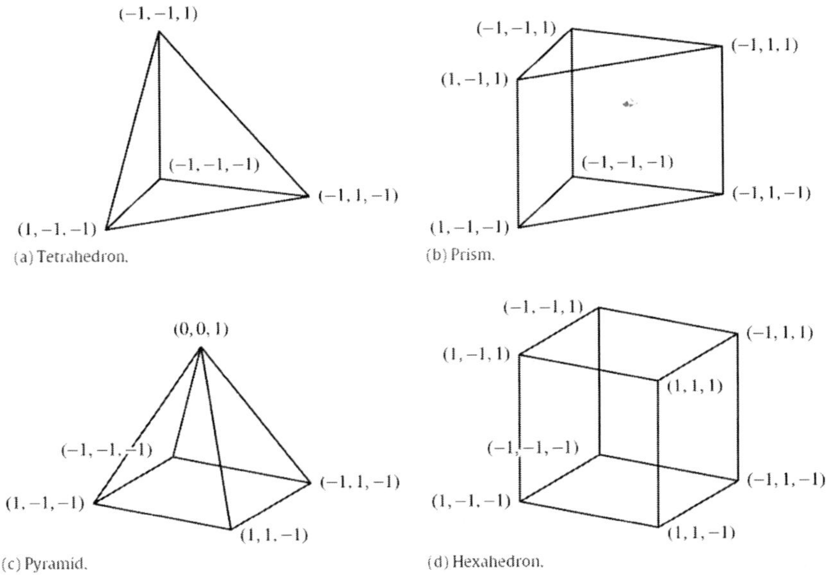

Figure. 2. Reference domains in three dimensions.

With some manipulation it can be verified that the orthonormal polynomial basis inside of our reference tetrahedron is given by

$$\psi_{ijk}(\mathbf{x}) = \sqrt{8}\hat{P}_i(a)\hat{P}_j^{(2i+1,0)}(b)\hat{P}_k^{(2i+2j+2,0)}(c)(1-b)^i(1-c)^{i+j}, \tag{16}$$

where $a=-2(1+x)/(y+z)-1$, $b=2(1+y)/(1-z)$, and $c=z$. The objective basis is given by

$$\tilde{\mathcal{P}}^{\phi} = \left\{\psi_{ijk}(\mathbf{x}) \mid 0 \le i \le \phi, i \le j \le \phi - i, j \le k \le \phi - i - j\right\}. \tag{17}$$

Prism. Extruding the reference triangle along the z-axis gives our reference prism of Fig. 2. It follows that the volume is $\int_{-1}^{1}\int_{-1}^{1}\int_{-1}^{-y} \mathrm{d}x\,\mathrm{d}y\,\mathrm{d}z = 4$. There are a total of 12 symmetries. On account of the extrusion the most natural coordinate system is a combination of barycentric and Cartesian coordinates: $(\lambda_1,\lambda_2,\lambda_3,z)$. Let Perm3 generate all of the unique permutations of its first three arguments. Using this the six symmetry groups of the prism can be expressed as

$$\begin{aligned}
\mathcal{S}_1 &= \left(\tfrac{1}{3}, \tfrac{1}{3}, \tfrac{1}{3}, 0\right), & |\mathcal{S}_1| &= 1,\\
\mathcal{S}_2(\gamma) &= \left(\tfrac{1}{3}, \tfrac{1}{3}, \tfrac{1}{3}, \pm\gamma\right), & |\mathcal{S}_2| &= 2,\\
\mathcal{S}_3(\alpha) &= \mathrm{Perm}_3(\alpha, \alpha, 1-2\alpha, 0), & |\mathcal{S}_3| &= 3,\\
\mathcal{S}_4(\alpha, \gamma) &= \mathrm{Perm}_3(\alpha, \alpha, 1-2\alpha, \pm\gamma), & |\mathcal{S}_4| &= 6,\\
\mathcal{S}_5(\alpha, \beta) &= \mathrm{Perm}_3(\alpha, \beta, 1-\alpha-\beta, 0), & |\mathcal{S}_5| &= 6,\\
\mathcal{S}_6(\alpha, \beta, \gamma) &= \mathrm{Perm}_3(\alpha, \beta, 1-\alpha-\beta, \pm\gamma), & |\mathcal{S}_6| &= 12,
\end{aligned}$$

where the constraints on α and β are identical to those in a triangle and $0<\gamma\leq 1$.

Combining the orthonormal polynomial bases for a right-triangle and line segment yields the orthonormal prism basis

$$\psi_{ijk}(\mathbf{x}) = \sqrt{2}\hat{P}_i(a)\hat{P}_j^{(2i+1,0)}(b)\hat{P}_k(c)(1-b)^i, \tag{18}$$

where $a=2(1+x)/(1-y)-1$, $b=y$, and $c=z$. The objective basis is given by

$$\tilde{\mathcal{P}}^{\phi} = \left\{\psi_{ijk}(\mathbf{x}) \mid 0 \leq i \leq \phi,\ i \leq j \leq \phi - i,\ 0 \leq k \leq \phi - i - j,\ k \text{ even}\right\} \tag{19}$$

Pyramid. Our reference pyramid can be seen in Fig. 2 with a volume determined by $\int_{-1}^{1}\int_{(z-1)/2}^{(1-z)/2}\int_{(z-1)/2}^{(1-z)/2} \mathrm{d}x\,\mathrm{d}y\,\mathrm{d}z = 8/3$. The symmetries are identical to those of a quadrilateral. Extending the notation employed for the quadrilateral we obtain the following symmetry orbits

$$\begin{aligned}
\mathcal{S}_1(\gamma) &= (0, 0, \gamma), & |\mathcal{S}_1| &= 1,\\
\mathcal{S}_2(\alpha, \gamma) &= \chi(\alpha, 0, \gamma), & |\mathcal{S}_2| &= 4,\\
\mathcal{S}_3(\alpha, \gamma) &= \chi(\alpha, \alpha, \gamma), & |\mathcal{S}_3| &= 4,\\
\mathcal{S}_4(\alpha, \beta, \gamma) &= \chi(\alpha, \beta, \gamma), & |\mathcal{S}_4| &= 8,
\end{aligned}$$

subject to the constraints that $0<(\alpha,\beta)\leq(1-\gamma)/2$ and $-1\leq\gamma\leq 1$.

Inside of the reference pyramid the orthonormal polynomial basis is found to be

$$\psi_{ijk}(\mathbf{x}) = 2\hat{P}_i(a)\hat{P}_j(b)\hat{P}_k^{(2i+2j+2,0)}(c)(1-c)^{i+j}, \tag{20}$$

where $a=2x/(1-z)$, $b=2y/(1-z)$, and $c=z$. The objective basis is

$$\tilde{\mathcal{P}}^{\phi} = \left\{\psi_{ijk}(\mathbf{x}) \mid 0 \le i \le \phi,\ i \le j \le \phi - i,\ 0 \le k \le \phi - i - j,\ (i,j)\ \text{even}\right\}. \tag{21}$$

Hexahedron. Our choice of reference hexahedron can be seen in Fig. 2. The volume is, trivially, $\int_{-1}^{1}\int_{-1}^{1}\int_{-1}^{1} \mathrm{d}x\,\mathrm{d}y\,\mathrm{d}z = 8$. A hexahedron exhibits octahedral symmetry with a symmetry number of 48. The procedure for determining the orbits is similar to that used for the quadrilateral. We consider applying these symmetries to a point (α,β,γ) with $0 \le (\alpha,\beta,\gamma) \le 1$ and let the resulting set of points be given by $\Xi(\alpha,\beta,\gamma)$. When α, β, and γ are all distinct and greater than zero the set has a cardinality of 48, as expected. However, when one or more parameters are either identical to one another or equal to zero some symmetries give rise to equivalent points. This reduces the cardinality of the set. Enumerating the various combinations we obtain seven symmetry orbits

$$\begin{aligned}
\mathcal{S}_1 &= \Xi(0,0,0), & |\mathcal{S}_1| &= 1,\\
\mathcal{S}_2(\alpha) &= \Xi(\alpha,0,0), & |\mathcal{S}_2| &= 6,\\
\mathcal{S}_3(\alpha) &= \Xi(\alpha,\alpha,\alpha), & |\mathcal{S}_3| &= 8,\\
\mathcal{S}_4(\alpha) &= \Xi(\alpha,\alpha,0), & |\mathcal{S}_4| &= 12,\\
\mathcal{S}_5(\alpha,\beta) &= \Xi(\alpha,\beta,0), & |\mathcal{S}_5| &= 24,\\
\mathcal{S}_6(\alpha,\beta) &= \Xi(\alpha,\alpha,\beta), & |\mathcal{S}_6| &= 24,\\
\mathcal{S}_7(\alpha,\beta,\gamma) &= \Xi(\alpha,\beta,\gamma), & |\mathcal{S}_7| &= 48.
\end{aligned}$$

Trivially, the orthonormal basis inside of our reference hexahedron is given by

$$\psi_{ijk}(\mathbf{x}) = \hat{P}_i(a)\hat{P}_j(b)\hat{P}_k(c), \tag{22}$$

where $a=x$, $b=y$, and $c=z$. The objective basis is

$$\tilde{\mathcal{P}}^{\phi} = \left\{\psi_{ijk}(\mathbf{x}) \mid 0 \le i \le \phi,\ i \le j \le \phi - i,\ j \le k \le \phi - i - j,\ (i,j,k)\ \text{even}\right\}. \tag{23}$$

3. METHODOLOGY

Our methodology for identifying symmetric quadrature rules is a refinement of that described by Witherden and Vincent[12] for triangles. This method is, in turn, a refinement of that of Zhang et al.[9].

To derive a quadrature rule four input parameters are required: the reference domain, Ω, the number of quadrature points N_p, the target rule strength, ϕ, and a desired runtime, t. The algorithm begins by computing all of the possible symmetric decompositions of N_p. The result is a set of vectors satisfying the relation

$$N_p = \sum_{j=1}^{N_s} n_{ij}|\mathcal{S}_j|, \tag{24}$$

where N_s is the number of symmetry orbits associated with the domain Ω, and n_{ij} is the number of orbits of type j in the ith decomposition. Finding these involves solving the constrained linear Diophantine equation outlined in Section2. It is possible for this equation to have no solutions. As an example we consider the case when N_p=44 for a triangular domain. From the symmetry orbits we have

$$N_p = n_1|\mathcal{S}_1| + n_2|\mathcal{S}_2| + n_3|\mathcal{S}_3| = n_1 + 3n_2 + 6n_3,$$

subject to the constraint that $n_1 \in \{0,1\}$. This restricts N_p to be either a multiple of three or one greater. Since forty-four is neither of these we find the equation to have no solutions. Therefore, we conclude that there can be no symmetric quadrature rules inside of a triangle with forty-four points.

Given a decomposition we are interested in finding a set of orbital parameters and weights that minimise the error associated with integrating the objective basis on Ω. This is an example of a nonlinear least squares problem. A suitable method for solving such problems is the Levenberg–Marquardt algorithm (LMA). The LMA is an iterative procedure for finding a set of parameters that correspond to a local minima of a set of functions. The minimisation process is not always successful and is dependent on an initial guess of the parameters. Within the context of quadrature rule derivation minimisation can be regarded as successful if $\xi(\phi) \sim \epsilon$ where ϵ represents machine precision.

Let us denote the number of parameters associated with symmetry orbit S_i as $[\![S_i]\!]$. Using this we can express the total number of degrees of freedom associated with decomposition i as

$$\sum_{j=1}^{N_s} \left\{ n_{ij}[\![\mathcal{S}_i]\!] + n_{ij} \right\}, \tag{25}$$

with the second term accounting for the presence of one quadrature weight associated with each symmetry orbit. From the list of orbits given in Section2we expect the weights contribute approximately one third of the degrees of freedom. This is not an insignificant fraction. One way of eliminating the weights is to treat them as dependent variables. When the points are prescribed the right hand side of Eq. (1) becomes linear with respect to the unknowns—the weights. In general, however, the number of weights will be different from the number of polynomials in the objective basis. It is therefore necessary to obtain a least squares solution to the system. Linear least squares problems can be solved directly through a variety of techniques. Perhaps the most robust numerical scheme is that of singular value decomposition (SVD). Thus, at the cost of solving a small linear least squares problem at each LMA iteration we are able to reduce the number of free parameters to

$$\sum_{j=1}^{N_S} n_{ij} [\![\mathcal{S}_i]\!]. \tag{26}$$

Such a modification has been found to greatly reduce the number of iterations required for convergence. This reduction more than offsets the marginally greater computational cost associated with each iteration.

Previous works[9,10,18] have emphasised the importance of picking a 'good' initial guess to seed the LMA. To this end several methodologies for seeding orbital parameters have been proposed. The degree of complexity associated with such strategies is not insignificant. Further, it is necessary to devise a separate strategy for each symmetry orbit. Our experience, however, suggests that the choice of decomposition is far more important than the initial guess in determining whether minimisation will be successful. Orbits can therefore be seeded independently using uniform random deviates. Let U_1 be a deviate between [0,1], U_2 between [0,1/2], U_3 between [0,1/3], U_4 between [0,1/4], U_{11} between [−1,1] and, U_γ between [0,(1−γ)/2]. Using these we can seed the various orbital parameters as follows.

Triangle.

$S_2(\alpha{\sim}U_2)$

$S_3(\alpha{\sim}U_2,\beta{\sim}U_3)$.

Quadrilateral.

$S_2(\alpha{\sim}U_1)$

$S_3(\alpha{\sim}U_1)$

$S_4(\alpha{\sim}U_1,\beta{\sim}U_1)$.

Tetrahedron.

$S_2(\alpha{\sim}U_3)$

$S_3(\alpha{\sim}U_2)$

$S_4(\alpha{\sim}U_3,\beta{\sim}U_3)$

$S_5(\alpha{\sim}U_4,\beta{\sim}U_4,\gamma{\sim}U_4)$.

Prism.

$S_2(\gamma{\sim}U_1)$

$S_3(\alpha{\sim}U_2)$

$S_4(\alpha{\sim}U_2,\gamma{\sim}U_1)$

$S_5(\alpha{\sim}U_2,\beta{\sim}U_2)$

$S_6(\alpha{\sim}U_2,\beta{\sim}U_2,\gamma{\sim}U_1)$.

Pyramid.

$S_1(\gamma{\sim}U_{11})$

$S_2(\alpha{\sim}U_\gamma,\gamma{\sim}U_{11})$

$S_3(\alpha{\sim}U_\gamma,\gamma{\sim}U_{11})$

$S_4(\alpha{\sim}U_\gamma,\beta{\sim}U_\gamma,\gamma{\sim}U_{11})$.

Hexahedron.

$S_2(\alpha{\sim}U_1)$

$S_3(\alpha{\sim}U_1)$

$S_4(\alpha{\sim}U_1)$

$S_5(\alpha{\sim}U_1,\beta{\sim}U_1)$

$S_6(\alpha{\sim}U_1,\beta{\sim}U_1)$

$S_7(\alpha{\sim}U_1,\beta{\sim}U_1,\gamma{\sim}U_1)$.

For larger values of N_p we note that many decompositions–especially those for prisms and pyramids–are pathological. As an example of this we consider searching for an N_p=80 point rule inside of a prism where there are 2380 distinct symmetrical decompositions. One such decomposition is N_p=40|S2|where all points lie in a single column down the middle of the prism. Since there is no variation in either x or y it is not possible to obtain a rule of strength $\phi \geq 1$. Hence, the decomposition can be dismissed without further consideration.

A presentation of our method in pseudocode can be seen in Algorithm 1. When the objective basis functions in $\tilde{P}^{\phi}$ are orthonormal Eq. (6) states that the integrand of all non-constant modes is zero. We can exploit this to simplify the computation of b_i. The purpose of CLAMPORBIT is to enforce the constraints associated with a given orbit to ensure that all points remain inside of the domain.

Algorithm 1 Procedure for generating symmetric quadrature rules of strength ϕ with N_p points inside of a domain.

```
procedure FINDRULES(N_p, φ, t)
    for all decompositions of N_p do
        t_0 ← CURRENTTIME()
        repeat
            ℛ ← SEEDORBITS()                          ▷ Initial guess of points
            ξ ← LMA(RULERESID, ℛ)
            if ξ ~ ε then                             ▷ If minimisation was successful
                save ℛ
            end if
        until CURRENTTIME() − t_0 > t
    end for
end procedure

function RULERESID(ℛ)
    for all p_i ∈ P̃^φ do                             ▷ For each basis function
        b_i ← ∫_Ω p_i(x⃗) dx⃗
        for all r_j ∈ ℛ do                            ▷ For each orbit
            r_j ← CLAMPORBIT(r_j)                     ▷ Ensure orbital parameters are valid
            A_ij ← 0
            for all x⃗_k ∈ EXPANDORBIT(r_j) do
                A_ij ← A_ij + p_i(x⃗_k)
            end for
        end for
    end for
    ω ← b/A                                           ▷ Use SVD to determine the weights
    return Aω − b                                     ▷ Compute the residual
end function
```

4. IMPLEMENTATION

We have implemented the algorithms outlined above in a C++11 program called *polyquad*. The program is built on top of the Eigen template library[25] and is parallelised using MPI. It is capable of searching for quadrature rules on triangles, quadrilaterals, tetrahedra, prisms, pyramids, and hexahedra. All rules are guaranteed to be symmetric having all points inside of the domain. Polyquad can also, optionally, filter out rules possessing negative weights.

Further, functionality exists, courtesy of MPFR[26], for refining rules to an arbitrary degree of numerical precision and for evaluating the truncation error of a ruleset.

As a point of reference we consider the case of using polyquad to identify ϕ=10 rules with 81 points inside of a tetrahedra. Running polyquad for one hour on a quad-core Intel i7-4820K CPU we were able to find a total of 50 distinct rules. These rules were split across four distinct orbital decompositions.

The source code for polyquad is available under the terms of the GNU General Public License v3.0 and can be downloaded from https://github.com/vincentlab/Polyquad.

Table 1. Number of points N_p required for a fully symmetric quadrature rule with positive weights of strength ϕ inside of the six reference domains. Rules with underlines represent improvements over those found in the literature (see text).

ϕ	N_p					
	Tri	Quad	Tet	Pri	Pyr	Hex
1	1	1	1	1	1	1
2	3	4	4	5	5	6
3	6	4	8	8	6	6
4	6	8	14	11	10	14
5	7	8	14	16	<u>15</u>	14
6	12	12	24	<u>28</u>	<u>24</u>	<u>34</u>
7	15	12	<u>35</u>	<u>35</u>	<u>31</u>	<u>34</u>
8	16	20	46	<u>46</u>	<u>47</u>	58
9	19	20	<u>59</u>	<u>60</u>	<u>62</u>	58
10	25	<u>28</u>	81	<u>85</u>	<u>83</u>	<u>90</u>
11	28	<u>28</u>				
12	33	<u>37</u>				
13	37	<u>37</u>				
14	42	<u>48</u>				
15	49	<u>48</u>				
16	55	60				
17	60	60				
18	67	<u>72</u>				
19	73	<u>72</u>				
20	79	<u>85</u>				

5. RULES

Using polyquad v1.0 we have derived a set of quadrature rules for each of the reference domains in Section2. All rules are completely symmetric, possess only positive weights, and have all points inside of the domain. It is customary in the literature to refer to quadratures with the last two attributes as being "PI" rules. As polyquad attempts to find a set of rules it is necessary to have a means of differentiating between otherwise equivalent formulae. In constructing this collection the truncation term $\xi(\phi+1)$ was employed with the rule possessing the smallest such term being chosen. The number of points Nprequired for a rule of strength ϕ can be seen in Table 1. The rules themselves are provided as electronic supplementary material (see Appendix A) and have been refined to 38 decimal places.

From the table we note that several of the rules appear to improve over those in the literature. We consider a rule to be an improvement when it either (i) requires fewer points than any fully symmetric rule described in literature or, (ii) when existing fully symmetric rules of this strength are not PI. We note that many of the rules presented by Dunavant for quadrilaterals[14] and hexahedra[21] possess either negative weights or have points outside of the domain. Using polyquad in quadrilaterals we were able to identify PI rules with point counts less than or equal to those of Dunavant at strengths ϕ=8,9,18,19,20. In tetrahedra we were able to reduce the number of points required for ϕ=7and ϕ=9 by one and two, respectively, compared with Zhang et al.[9]. Furthermore, in prisms and pyramids rules requiring significantly fewer points than those in the literature were identified. As an example, the ϕ=9 rule of[18] inside of a prism requires 71 points compared with just 60 for the rule identified by polyquad. Additionally, both of the ϕ=10 rules for prisms and pyramids appear to be new.

6. CONCLUSIONS

We have presented a methodology for identifying symmetric quadrature rules on a variety of domains in two and three dimensions. Our scheme does not require any manual intervention and is not restricted to any particular topological configuration inside of a domain. Additionally, it is also capable of generating a set of rules. We have further provided an open source implementation of our method in C++11, and used it to generate a complete set of symmetric quadrature rules that are suitable for use in finite element solvers. All rules possess purely positive weights and have all points inside the domain. Many of the rules appear to be new, and an improvement over those tabulated in the literature.

ACKNOWLEDGEMENT

The authors would like to thank the Engineering and Physical Sciences Research Council for their support via a Doctoral Training Grant and an Early Career Fellowship (EP/K027379/1).

REFERENCES

1. Jan S. Hesthaven, Tim Warburton, Nodal Discontinuous Galerkin Methods: Algorithms, Analysis, and Applications, Vol. 54 Springer (2008)
2. Pavel Solin, Karel Segeth, Ivo Dolezel, Higher-Order Finite Element Methods CRC Press (2003)
3. George Karniadakis, Spencer Sherwin, Spectral/hp Element Methods for Computational Fluid Dynamics Oxford University Press (2005)
4. J.N. Lyness, D. Jespersen, Moderate degree symmetric quadrature rules for the triangle IMA J. Appl. Math., 15 (1) (1975), pp. 19-32
5. D.A. Dunavant, High degree efficient symmetrical Gaussian quadrature rules for the triangle Internat. J. Numer. Methods Engrg., 21 (6) (1985), pp. 1129-1148
6. James N. Lyness, Ronald Cools, A survey of numerical cubature over triangles Proceedings of Symposia in Applied Mathematics, Vol. 48 (1994), pp. 127-150
7. J.Scott Savage, Andrew F. Peterson, Quadrature rules for numerical integration over triangles and tetrahedral IEEE Antennas Propag. Mag., 38 (3) (1996), pp. 100-102
8. S. Wandzurat, H. Xiao, Symmetric quadrature rules on a triangle Comput. Math. Appl., 45 (12) (2003), pp. 1829-1840
9. Linbo Zhang, Tao Cui, Hui Liu, A set of symmetric quadrature rules on triangles and tetrahedral J. Comput. Math., 27 (1) (2009), pp. 89-96
10. M.A. Taylor, B.A. Wingate, L.P. Bos, Several new quadrature formulas for polynomial integration in the triangle, January 2005. ArXiv Mathematics e-prints.
11. Hong Xiao, Zydrunas Gimbutas, A numerical algorithm for the construction of efficient quadrature rules in two and higher dimensions Comput. Math. Appl., 59 (2) (2010), pp. 663-676
12. F.D. Witherden, P.E. Vincent, An analysis of solution point coordinates for flux reconstruction schemes on triangular elements J. Sci. Comput. (2013), pp. 1-26
13. D.M. Williams, L. Shunn, A. Jameson, Symmetric quadrature rules for simplexes based on sphere close packed lattice arrangements J. Comput. Appl. Math., 266 (2014), pp. 18-38
14. D.A. Dunavant, Economical symmetrical quadrature rules for complete polynomials over a square domain Internat. J. Numer. Methods Engrg., 21 (10) (1985), pp. 1777-1784
15. Ronald Cools, Ann Haegemans, Another step forward in searching for cubature formulae with a minimal number of knots for the square Computing, 40 (2) (1988), pp. 139-146
16. Lee Shunn, Frank Ham, Symmetric quadrature rules for tetrahedra based on a cubic close-packed lattice arrangement J. Comput. Appl. Math., 236 (17) (2012), pp. 4348-4364
17. Patrick Keast, Moderate-degree tetrahedral quadrature formulas Comput. Methods Appl. Mech. Engrg., 55 (3) (1986), pp. 339-348
18. Ethan J. Kubatko, Benjamin A. Yeager, Ashley L. Maggi, New computationally efficient quadrature formulas for triangular prism elements Comput. & Fluids, 73 (2013), pp. 187-201
19. Ethan J. Kubatko, Benjamin A. Yeager, Ashley L. Maggi, New computationally efficient quadrature formulas for pyramidal elements Finite Elem. Anal. Des., 65 (2013), pp. 63-75
20. Arthur H. Stroud, Approximate Calculation of Multiple Integrals Prentice-Hall (1971)
21. D.A. Dunavant, Efficient symmetrical cubature rules for complete polynomials of high degree over the unit cube Internat. J. Numer. Methods Engrg., 23 (3) (1986), pp. 397-407

22. Ronald Cools, Kyung Joong Kim, Rotation invariant cubature formulas over the n-dimensional unit cube J. Comput. Appl. Math., 132 (1) (2001), pp. 15-32
23. H.T. Huynh, A flux reconstruction approach to high-order schemes including discontinuous Galerkin methods, AIAA Paper, 4079:2007, 2007.
24. Frank W.J. Olver, NIST Handbook of Mathematical Functions Cambridge University Press (2010)
25. Gaël Guennebaud, Benoît Jacob, et al. Eigen v3, 2010. http://eigen.tuxfamily.org.
26. Laurent Fousse, Guillaume Hanrot, Vincent Lefèvre, Patrick Pélissier, Paul Zimmermann, MPFR: a multiple-precision binary floating-point library with correct rounding ACM Trans. Math. Softw., 33 (2) (2007), pp. 13:1-13:15

CHAPTER 5

Image Interpolation via Scanning Line Algorithm and Discontinuous B-Spline

Cheng-ming Liu[1], Ze-kun Wang[2], Hai-bo Pang[1] and Jun-xiao Xue[1,*]

[1]*School of Software and Applied Technology, Zhengzhou University, Zhengzhou 450002, China*

[2]*Department of Automation, Tsinghua University, Beijing 100084, China*

ABSTRACT

Image interpolation is a basic operation in image processing. Lots of methods have been proposed, including convolution-based methods, edge modeling methods, point spread function (PSF)-based methods or learning-based methods. Most of them, however, present a high computational complexity and are not suitable for real time applications. However, fast methods are not able to provide artifacts-free images. In this paper we describe a new image interpolation method by using scanning line algorithm which can generate C^{-1} curves or surfaces. The C^{-1}interpolation can truncate the interpolation curve at big skipping; hence, the image edge can be kept. Numerical experiments illustrate the efficiency of the novel method.

Keywords: image interpolation; C^{-1}; scanning line; B-spline

1. INTRODUCTION

Image interpolation, also known as image super resolution, has recently become a hot topic in the field of computer vision and computer graphics due to the increasing number of practical applications of the algorithms proposed. The aim is to improve the resolution of a low resolution (LR) image/video to obtain a high-resolution (HR) one which is able to preserve the characteristics of natural images/videos. The interpolation methods are implemented in a variety of computer tools like printers, digital TV, media players, image processing packages, graphics renderers, and so on. In this paper, we propose a method to generate high-resolution image from a single low-resolution image by a simple C^{-1} interpolation, which runs very fast.

In recent years, many image interpolation or super resolution algorithms have been proposed [1,2], and they can be classified into five categories: based on the point spread function (PSF) method, learning-based method, edge-directed method, geometry-based method or polynomial-based method.

1.1. PSF-Based Interpolation

These methods are constructed based on the PSF, and it is assumed that the LR image is generated by down-sampling from the HR image according to a convolution model as described in Equation (1) where Y denotes the LR image and Xthe unknown HR image, D is the down-sampling matrix, and N is the noise. The image interpolation is regarded as an inverse problem to solve the unknown HR image data [3,4].

$$\mathbf{Y=DX+N}. \tag{1}$$

But usually this inverse problem is ill-posed, so we can only find a optimized solution. An extra regular term is usually required to ensure the smoothness of the HR image and it makes the question more complex. Due to the large amount of image data, the inverse problem solution is usually time-consuming. Qi Shan et al. [5] proposed a fast image/video upsampling method by a feedback control framework based on graphics processing unit (GPU).

1.2. Learning-Based Interpolation

By this method, the HR image patches are recovered from the counterpart of LR patches, and the down-sampling matrix D in Equation (1) is not predefined, but is learned from a training set [6]. The training set is a database of LR and HR image pairs, usually with a relative scale factor of 2. Then we can recover a most likely HR image according to the training set. Under this framework, Markov random field [7] and sparse representation [8] are also introduced. Recently, deep learning based image super resolution has become a hot topic in image processing [9].

1.3. Edge-Directed Interpolation

Since edges are visually attractive to the human perceptual system, many algorithms focus on edge-directed interpolation methods [10,11]. The main idea of these methods is to preserve the edge sharpness during the image interpolation process. The intuitive way is to explicitly estimate the edge orientation and then interpolate along the edge orientation. Some adaptive interpolation methods focus on preserving sharp edges of images, these adaptive and edge-oriented algorithms [12] are also classified into this category.

1.4. Geometry-Based Method

In recent years, geometry-based image processing methods [13,14,15] become more and more popular, some geometric tools or computer graphics tools, such as gradient meshes [16], Delauney triangulations [17] and subdivision are introduced to image processing. In our previous work, we proposed a subdivision based image interpolation method [18]. The subdivision method possessed a tangent vector, by adjusting the tangent vector, we can control the sharpness at image edges. This method is also based on a continuous model, and its tangent vector may be affected by image noises.

1.5. Polynomial-Based Interpolation

Polynomial-based interpolation methods are simple and most often used. The nearest neighbor interpolation, bi-linear interpolation, bi-cubic interpolation and cubic B-spline interpolation belong to this category. They are usually implemented by convolving an image with a convolution kernel as the weighting function [19]. These methods run very fast, but they usually cause blurring on image edges because the kernels are continuous functions. Blending kernels [20] and two-dimensional cubic convolution kernels [21] have been proposed to improve it.

The PSF-based method, learning-based method, edge-directed method and geometry-based method mentioned above are very efficient in keeping the edge sharping of HR images, but most of them are time-consuming, especially the learning based method. The polynomial-based methods are almost real-time, but they do not handle the image edges specially. In this paper, we propose a novel image interpolation algorithm based on discontinuous B-spline, which we called C^{-1}interpolation. It can generate interpolation curves with discontinuous points at image edges, hence it can preserve the sharpness of images from the theoretical foundation. While in flat area, our interpolation becomes the classical B-spline interpolation. In general, our method runs as the B-spline interpolation in most of the image area except image edges which are processed specially by C^{-1} interpolation.

2. C^{-1} INTERPOLATION

Interpolation is a general tool in geometric design, it aims to generate fairing (piecewise) polynomial curves/surfaces while keeping smoothness as high as possible. While in some practical applications such as computer aided design (CAD), simulating deformations of objects, animation, etc., only interpolation and smoothness are not enough, and some geometrical or physical constraints are necessary, such as arc length constrained curve design [22,23], subdivision surfaces with boundary curves and cross boundary derivatives [24], modified Catmull-Clark or Loop subdivision, which can interpolate given normals [25], or constrained subdivision surfaces interpolating a given curve [26,27]. These methods may not be smooth near some extraordinary points, but they are all continuous everywhere. In image interpolation, the interpolation should be interrupted at big data skipping to maintain image edge sharping. In this paper, we describe a new interpolation method with some discontinuous points, which we called C^{-1} interpolation, because its smoothness is less than C^0 continuous.

Discontinuous interpolation may be implemented by combining several piecewise interpolation curves/surfaces, but it is not convenient for real application. We adopt a kind of B-spline interpolation with replicative knots, and the C^{-1}interpolation is a kind of modified B-spline that is discontinuous at some knots. A B-Spline curve is constituted of some piecewise polynomials defined on some knots, and it is formulated as

$$p(t) = \sum_{i=0}^{n} p_i N_{i,k}(t). \tag{2}$$

where $\{p_i\}$ are control vertices, and $N_{i,k}(t)$ is the i–th basis function of a k order B-Spline [28] defined on knots vector T which is defined as

$$T = [\overbrace{0, \cdots, 0}, \cdots, \overbrace{b, \cdots, b}, \cdots, \overbrace{1, \cdots, 1}]$$

where $b(0<b<1)$ is the inner knot with replicative number k. For a inner knot with replicative number r, the smoothness of the B-Spline curve at this knot is $k–1–r$. Hence, the curve will be discontinuous. In this paper, we just modify the quasi-uniform B-spline knot by setting some inner knots with replicative number k. Figure 1 illustrates a C^{-1}interpolation with two discontinuous points, Figure 1a is the traditional B-spline curve, and Figure 1b is discontinuous B-spline interpolation.

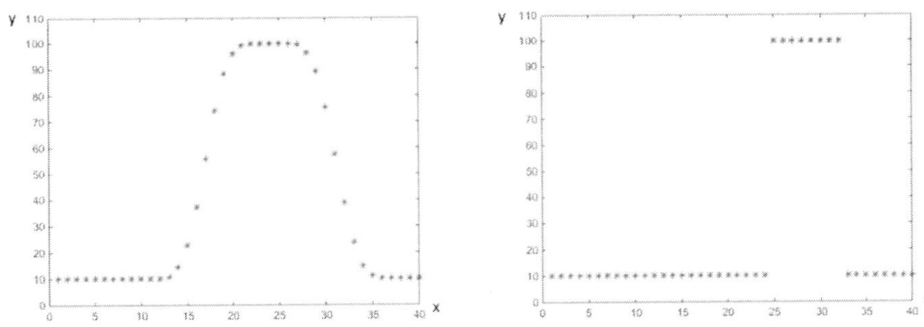

(a) (b)

Figure 1. B-Spline interpolation with two discontinuous points. (**a**) is the traditional B-spline; (**b**) is the discontinuous B-spline.

3. ALGORITHM AND EXPERIMENT RESULTS

The key point of image interpolation method base on C^{-1} is to construct knot vectors with replicative inner knots according to the image big skip. Hence, the first step is to determine the image edge points, we adopt the scanning line algorithm here to detect image edges.

For a scanning line $y=i$, which denotes the i–th line of an image, we set a threshold $thres=(max(I_i)-min(I_i))/4$. If $\|\Delta I_i(j)\|$>thres, then a node with j is added to a linked list, where $\Delta I_i(j)=I_i(j+1)-I_i(j)$.

According to the analysis above, our algorithm is described as follows.

For each line of the LR image,

Step1. For i–th line of an image, determine the edge point with the scanning line algorithm. The big skip points are stored in a linked list.

Step2. Construct a knot vector T according to the linked list. For node j, let $t_j = t_j + 1 = \cdots = t_j + k - 1$. Other knots are determined uniformly.

Step3. Interpolate the i–th line with a C^{-1} B-Spline determined on knot vector T, where k is set to 3.

For each column of the LR image, replicate step1–step3, and we will get the HR image.

In the next, we will illustrate the efficiency of our new image interpolation algorithm by comparing some experiments. For convenience, we assume that the scale factor stays the same both horizontally and vertically. We will compare our method with the bilinear interpolation, the new edge directed interpolation (NEDI) algorithm [10] , the fast image upsampling [5]. The bilinear algorithm and the C−1 interpolation is implemented on Matlab2014 (MathWorks, Natick, MS, United States), programs of the NEDI algorithm and fast upsampling algorithm are obtained from the homepage of the authors [29,30].

For a color image, it is usually interpolated through three channels separately and is finally combined to a color image. In this paper, we convert the RGB model to YUV model, and then interpolate only on the Y-channel. We test these methods on a variety of images. All the experiments were done on a Thinkpad laptop (Lenovo, Beijing, China) with Core i3 CPU @1.70 GHz and 4 GB main memory. 2×2 times enlargement of a color image with resolution 100×100typically takes 1 s by our method, while the NEDI and upsampling method take over 8 seconds CPU time.

In the following, we show the ability of our C^{-1} interpolation method numerically by calculating the peak signal-to-noise ratio (PSNR) and the mean structural similarity (MSSIM) [31]. In our experiments, the test data are obtained as follows. For an original image, we down-sample it to $\frac{1}{2} \times \frac{1}{2}$ of its original size by bilinear interpolation, and then up-sample it by the mentioned image interpolation algorithms and finally get the HR images with the same size as the original ones.

Here we choose the Kodak lossless true color image suite [32] with resolution 512×768 as the test images and the scale factor is 2×2. The PSNR values and the MSSIM values of the mentioned methods on the test images are shown in Table 1 and Table 2, respectively. The test images are the baboon (Figure 2) , kodim05 (Figure 3a) and kodim23 (Figure 3b). Here, we can see that the performance of our methods are better than the others both in PSNR and MSSIM.

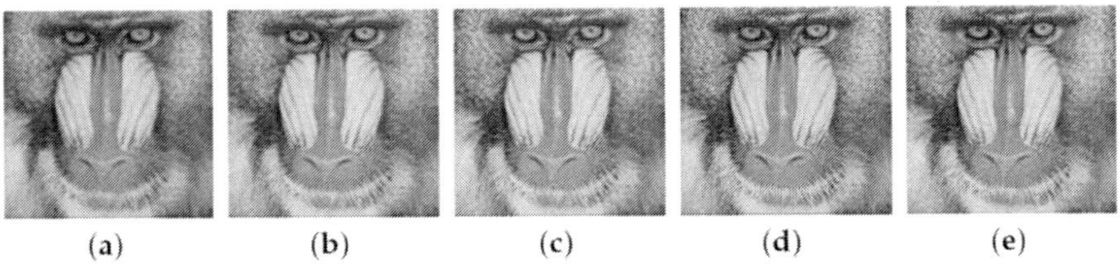

Figure 2. Results of image interpolation. From left to right are: (a) original image; (b) bi-linear interpolation; (c) new edge directed interpolation (NEDI) interpolation; (d) fast upsampling interpolation; (e) C^{-1} interpolation.

Figure 3. 4×4 enlargement results of our image interpolation. (a) 4×4 enlargement result of Kodim05; (b) 4×4 enlargement result of Kodim23.

Table 1. Peak signal-to-noise ratio (PSNR) values.

	Bilinear	NEDI	Upsampling	C^{-1} Interpolation
baboon	24.684	24.072	24.576	25.168
kodim05	23.817	23.545	23.878	24.269
kodim23	31.334	30.828	31.039	32.234

Table 2. Mean structural similarity (MSSIM) values.

	Bilinear	NEDI	Upsampling	C^{-1} Interpolation
baboon	0.7245	0.7041	0.7448	0.7670
kodim05	0.7370	0.7281	0.7534	0.7689
kodim23	0.9249	0.9207	0.9185	0.9335

4. CONCLUSIONS

In this paper, we propose a simple but efficient image interpolation algorithm. The algorithm can automatically generate discontinuous interpolation at image edges, and it can maintain sharpness at the image edges from the theoretical basis. Some numerical experiments illustrate the efficiency of the novel algorithm. Compared with other methods, our algorithm is simple. Hence, it is suitable for hardware implementation and runs very fast.

ACKNOWLEDGMENTS

We thank all the anonymous reviewers for their valuable comments. We also thank the authors of NEDI, MSSIM and the fast upsampling algorithms for they kindly provide their programs on web. This work is supported by NSFC. 61402420.

REFERENCES

1. Lehmann, T.M.; Gönner, C.; Spitzer, K. Survey: Interpolation Methods in Medical Image Processing. *IEEE Trans. Med. Imaging* **1999**, *18*, 1049–1075.
2. Acharya, T.; Tsai, P.S. Computational Foundations of Image Interpolation Algorithms. *ACM Ubiquity* **2007**, *8*, 1–17.
3. Chan, R.H.; Riemenschneider, S.D.; Shen, L.X.; Shen, Z.W. Tight frame: An Efficient Way for High-resolution Image Reconstruction. *Appl. Comput. Harmonic Anal.* **2004**, *17*, 91–115.
4. El-Khamy, S.; Hadhoud, M.; Dessouky, M.; Salam, B.; El-Samie, F.A. Efficient Implementation of Image Interpolation as an Inverse Problem. *Digit. Signal Process.* **2005**, *15*, 137–152.
5. Shan, Q.; Li, Z.R.; Jia, J.Y.; Tang, C.K. Fast Image/Video Upsampling. *ACM Trans. Graph.* **2008**, *27*, 1–7.
6. Chang, H.; Yeung, D.Y.; Xiong, Y. Super-Resolution through Neighbor Embedding. In Proceedings of the IEEE Computer Society Conference on Computer Vision and Pattern Recognition, Columbus, OH, USA, 23–28 June 2004; Volume 1, pp. 275–282.
7. Freeman, W.T.; Pasztor, E.C.; Carmichael, O.T. Learning Low-Level Vision. *Int. J. Comput. Vis.* **2000**, *40*, 25–47.
8. Kim, K.I.; Kwon, Y. Single-Image Super-Resolution Using Sparse Regression and Natural Image Prior. *IEEE Trans. Pattern Anal. Mach. Intell.* **2010**, *32*, 1127–1133.
9. Dong, C.; Loy, C.C.; He, K.; Tang, X. Image Super-Resolution Using Deep Convolutional Networks. *IEEE Trans. Pattern Anal. Mach. Intell.* **2016**, *38*, 295–307.
10. Li, X.; Orchard, M.T. New Edge-Directed Interpolation. *IEEE Trans. Image Process.* **2001**, *10*, 1521–1527.
11. Akhtar, P.; Azhar, F. A Single Image Interpolation Scheme for Enhanced Super Resolution in Bio-Medical Imaging. In Proceedings of the 2010 4th International Conference on Bioinformatics and Biomedical Engineering (iCBBE), Chengdu, China, 18–20 June 2010; pp. 1–5.

12. Chen, M.J.; Huang, C.H.; Lee, W.L. A Fast Edge-oriented Algorithm for Image Interpolation. *Image Vis. Comput.* **2005**, *23*, 791–798.
13. Su, D.; Willis, P. Image Interpolation by Pixel-Level Data-Dependent Triangulation. *Comput. Graph. Forum* **2004**, *23*, 189–201.
14. Liang, L.M.; Zou, B.J.; Zhao, H.X.; Qiu, X. Image Interpolation via Tangent-Control Subdivision. In Proceedings of the 2008 Congress on Image and Signal Processing, Sanya, China, 27–30 May 2008; Volume 4, pp. 102–106.
15. Pan, Q.; Luo, X.N.; Zhu, J.W. A Medical Image Magnification Based on Local Geometric Similarity. *J. Softw.* **2009**, *20*, 1146–1155.
16. Lai, Y.K.; Hu, S.M.; Martin, R.R. Automatic and Topology-Preserving Gradient Mesh Generation for Image Vectorization. *ACM Trans. Graph. (SIGGRAPH)* **2009**, *28*, 1–8.
17. Demaret, L.; Dyn, N.; Iske, A. Image Compression by Linear Splines Over Adaptive Triangulations. *Signal Process.* **2006**, *86*, 1604–1616.
18. Liu, C.M.; Luo, X.N. Image enlargement via interpolatory subdivision. *IET Image Process.* **2011**, *5*, 567–571.
19. Keys, R.G. Cubic Convolution Interpolation for Digital Image Processing. *IEEE Trans. Acoust. Speech Signal Process.* **1981**, *29*, 1153–1160.
20. Liang, L.M. Image Interpolation by Blending Kernels. *IEEE Signal Process. Lett.* **2008**, *15*, 805–808.
21. Shi, J.Z.; Reichenbach, S.E. Image Interpolation by Two-Dimensional Parametric Cubic Convolution. *IEEE Trans. Image Process.* **2006**, *15*, 1857–1870.
22. Van Damme, R.; Wang, R.H. Curve Interpolation with Constrained Length. *Computing* **1995**, *54*, 69–81.
23. Roulier, J.A.; Piper, B. Prescribing the Length of Parametric Curves. *Comput. Aided Geom. Des.* **1996**, *13*, 3–22.
24. Levin, A. Combined subdivision schemes for the design of surfaces satisfying boundary conditions. *Comput. Aided Geom. Des.* **1999**, *16*, 345–354.
25. Biermann, H.; Levin, A.; Zorin, D. Piecewise smooth subdivision surfaces with normal control. In Proceedings of the 27th annual conference on computer graphics and interactive techniques, New Orleans, LA, USA, 23–28 July 2000; pp. 113–120.
26. Nasri, A.H. Recursive subdivision of polygonal complexes and its applications in computer-aided geometric design. *Comput. Aided Geom. Des.* **2000**, *17*, 595–619.
27. Nasri, A.H.; Abbas, A. Designing Catmull-Clark subdivision surfaces with curve interpolation constraints. *Comput. Graph.* **2002**, *26*, 393–400.
28. Piegl, L.; Tiller, W. *The NURBS Book*, 2nd ed.; Springer: New York, NY, USA, 1997.
29. Li, X. New Edge Direction Interpolation. 2001. Available online: http://www.csee.wvu.edu/~xinl/publications.html(accessed on 19 July 2013).
30. Shan, Q.; Li, Z.; Jia, J.; Tang, C.K. Fast Image/Video Upsampling. 2008. Available online: http://www.cse.cuhk.edu.hk/~leojia/projects/upsampling/index.html (accessed on 11 August 2011).
31. Wang, Z.; Bovik, A.C.; Sheikh, H.R.; Simoncelli, E.P. Image Quality Assessment: From Error Visibility to Structural Similarity. *IEEE Trans. Image Process.* **2004**, *13*, 600–612.
32. Kodak. Kodak Lossless True Color Image Suite. Available online: http://r0k.us/graphics/kodak/ (accessed on 1 June 2011).

CHAPTER 6

How many Fourier samples are needed for real function reconstruction?

Gerlind Plonka Marius Wischerhoff

Institute for Numerical and Applied ematics, University of Göttingen, Lotzestr. 16-18, 37083 Göttingen, Germany

ABSTRACT

In this paper we present some new results on the reconstruction of structured functions by a small number of equidistantly distributed Fourier samples. In particular, we show that real spline functions of order m with non-uniform knots containing N terms can be uniquely reconstructed by only $m+N$ Fourier samples. Further, linear combinations of N non-equispaced shifts of a known low-pass function Φ can be reconstructed by $N+1$ Fourier samples. In the bivariate case, we consider the problem of function recovering by a small amount of Fourier samples on different lines through the origin. Our methods are based on the Prony method. The proofs given in this paper are constructive. Some numerical examples show the applicability of the proposed approach.

Keywords: Sparse Fourier reconstruction, Prony method, B-spline functions, Radial functions

1 INTRODUCTION

The reconstruction of structured functions from the knowledge of samples of its Fourier transform is a common problem in several scientific areas as radioastronomy, computed tomography and magnet resonance imaging, [1]. In this paper, we aim to recover specially structured functions uniquely from the smallest possible number of equidistantly distributed Fourier samples.

Within the last years, there has been an increasing interest in exploiting special properties of functions that have to be reconstructed. Usually, the central issue is the recovery of signals possessing a sparse representation in a given basis or frame from a rather small set of determining points. Particularly, compressive sensing has triggered significant research activity. For example, a trigonometric polynomial of degree N with only $s \ll N$ active terms has been shown to be recovered by $O(s\log^4(N))$ sampling points that are randomly chosen from a discrete set $\{j/N\}_{j=0}^{N-1}$, [5], or from the uniform measure on [0,1], [17]. The recovery algorithms in compressed sensing are usually based on suitable l_1-minimization methods, and exact recovery can be ensured only with a certain probability. In contrast, there exist also deterministic methods for the recovery of sparse trigonometric functions, based on the classical Prony method or the annihilating filter method, [7, 21].

In [15] and [14], the so-called approximate Prony method has been studied, and a stable algorithm was derived that works also for noisy input data while the original Prony method suffers from its numerical instabilities. Other modifications of the Prony method aiming at a more stable behavior are e.g. the Least-Squares Prony method [10], the Total-Least-Squares Prony method [10], pencil based methods [11, 12, 18] and the method in [3] using an iterative quadratic maximum likelihood approach. In [8], a pencil based approach for Prony's method is combined with a maximum a posteriori probability estimator for stable recovery of polygon shapes from moments. In [9], a stabilization of Prony's method is proposed, where instead of using the (perturbed) Fourier samples directly, a windowed average of their autocorrelation sequence is applied. The unknown frequency parameters are then obtained as the zeros of a suitably defined orthogonal polynomial.

Vetterli et al. [21] introduced signals with finite rate of innovation, i.e., signals with special structure having a finite number of degrees of freedom per unit of time. Using the annihilating filter method (that is equivalent to Prony's method) they showed that finite length signals with finite rate of innovation can be completely reconstructed using a generalized Shannon sampling theorem although these signals are not bandlimited.

In the present paper, we apply the Prony method for the reconstruction of real structured functions from a small number of equidistantly distributed Fourier samples. Here, the Fourier transform $\hat{f}$ of a function $f\in L^1(\mathbb{R}^d)$ is defined by $\hat{f}(\omega)=\int_{\mathbb{R}^d} f(x)e^{-i\omega\cdot x}\,dx$. In the univariate case, we particularly consider B-spline functions with non-uniform knots and linear combinations of non-equispaced shifts of a known "low-pass" function Φ satisfying $\hat{\Phi}(\omega)\neq 0$ for $\omega\in(-T,T)$, where $T>0$.

In the bivariate case, we want to recover the functions from only a small amount of Fourier samples on different lines through the origin. In case of separable functions as tensor products of non-uniform B-spline functions the recovery problem can be treated similarly as in the univariate case. For the non-separable case the problem is more involved. In [13], the so-called algebraic coupling of matrix pencils (ACMP) algorithm is used for recovery of bivariate exponentials, where $O(N^2)$ samples are needed to recover a series of the form $\sum_{k=1}^{N} a_k \exp(i\omega_1 T_k)\exp(i\omega_2 S_k)$, see also [19, 20].

We will study linear combinations of non-uniform shifts of bivariate functions Φ of the form $f(x_1,x_2)=\sum_{j=1}^{N} c_j\Phi(x_1-v_{j,1},x_2-v_{j,2})$ with unknowns $c_j>0$, $v_{j,1}$, $v_{j,2}$, $j=1,\ldots,N$, and where $\hat{\Phi}(\omega_1,\omega_2)$ is bounded away from zero for $\omega_1^2+\omega_2^2<T^2$ and $T>0$. We show that function recovery is possible using $3N+1$ Fourier samples on only three lines through the origin, where the third line is chosen dependently on the candidates for shifts found from the first two lines.

Moreover, we conjecture that one can always reconstruct the function f from $4N+1$ Fourier samples given on four predetermined lines whose choice does not depend on the data. The idea of our method is related to a recent preprint, [16], where the authors propose to take sufficiently many lines for complete recovery of multivariate exponentials.

The paper is organized as follows. In Sect. 2, we shortly summarize the Prony method that will be frequently used in the remaining paper. Section 3 is devoted to univariate function recovery. We start with real step functions with compact support of the form $f(x)=\sum_{j=1}^{N} c_j^1 \mathbf{1}_{[T_j,T_{j+1})}(x)$with arbitrary knots $T_1,\ldots,T_{N+1}$, and show that f can be recovered by $N+1$ Fourier samples. The method transfers to non-uniform B-spline functions in Sect. 3.2. Moreover, we consider the reconstruction of linear combinations of non-uniform shifts of a given low-pass function Φ and its derivatives in Sect. 3.3. In Sect. 4, we study the bivariate case. We start with tensor-products of non-uniform spline functions. The non-separable case of non-uniform translates of a suitable bivariate function Φ is considered in Sect. 4.2. All recovery results are constructive. In Sect. 5we present some numerical examples for the univariate and the bivariate case showing that the algorithms are stable for exact input data.

2 PRONY METHOD

Consider a function $P(\omega)$ of the special form

$$P(\omega) = \sum_{j=1}^{N} c_j \mathrm{e}^{-\mathrm{i}\omega T_j} \qquad (2.1)$$

with non-zero coefficients $c_j \in \mathbb{R}$ and real frequencies $T_1 < T_2 < \cdots < T_N$.

We want to evaluate all frequencies $T_1,\ldots,T_N$ and all coefficients c_j, $j=1,\ldots,N$, from the function values $P(\ell h)$, $\ell=0,\ldots,N$, where h is assumed to be a positive constant with $hT_j \in [-\pi,\pi)$ for all $j \in \{1,\ldots,N\}$. For this purpose, the Prony method can be applied as follows.

Let us consider the complex polynomial $\Lambda : \mathbb{C} \to \mathbb{C}$,

$$\Lambda(z) := \prod_{j=1}^{N} \left(z - \mathrm{e}^{-\mathrm{i}hT_j}\right) = \sum_{\ell=0}^{N} \lambda_\ell z^\ell . \qquad (2.2)$$

with the unknown frequencies T_j from (2.1), where λ_ℓ are the coefficients of Λ in the monomial basis. Particularly, we have $\lambda_N = 1$.

Then we observe that for $m=0,\ldots,N$,

$$\sum_{\ell=0}^{N} \lambda_\ell P(h(\ell - m)) = \sum_{\ell=0}^{N} \lambda_\ell \sum_{j=1}^{N} c_j \mathrm{e}^{-\mathrm{i}h(\ell-m)T_j} = \sum_{j=1}^{N} c_j \mathrm{e}^{\mathrm{i}hmT_j} \sum_{\ell=0}^{N} \lambda_\ell \mathrm{e}^{-\mathrm{i}h\ell T_j}$$

$$= \sum_{j=1}^{N} c_j \mathrm{e}^{\mathrm{i}hmT_j} \Lambda\left(\mathrm{e}^{-\mathrm{i}hT_j}\right) = 0$$

Hence, the coefficient vector $\boldsymbol{\lambda} = (\lambda_0,\ldots,\lambda_N)^T$ is the solution of the linear system

$\mathbf{T}_{N+1}\boldsymbol{\lambda} = \mathbf{0}$ (2.3)

with the Toeplitz matrix $\mathbf{T}_{N+1} := (P(h(\ell - m)))_{m,\ell=0}^{N} \in \mathbb{R}^{(N+1)\times(N+1)}$. Observe that by $P(-\omega) = \sum_{j=1}^{N} c_j \mathrm{e}^{\mathrm{i}\omega T_j} = \overline{P(\omega)}$ all entries of $\mathbf{T}_{N+1}$ are given. With the Vandermonde matrix $\mathbf{V}_{N,N+1} := (\exp(-\mathrm{i}hkT_j))_{j=1,k=0}^{N}$ we have

$$\mathbf{T}_{N+1} = \mathbf{V}_{N,N+1}^{*} \operatorname{diag}(c_1, c_2, \ldots, c_N) \mathbf{V}_{N,N+1}$$

Since $\mathbf{V}_{N,N+1}$ has rank N, and $c_j \neq 0$ for $j=1,\ldots,N$, we get rank($\mathbf{T}_{N+1}$)=N. Hence, the eigenvector $\boldsymbol{\lambda}$ of $\mathbf{T}_{N+1}$ corresponding to the eigenvalue 0 is uniquely determined by (2.3) and $\lambda_N=1$.

Knowing $\boldsymbol{\lambda}$, we can compute the zeros $z_j := \mathrm{e}^{-\mathrm{i}hT_j}$ $(j=1,\ldots,N)$ of the polynomial Λ and hence find the frequencies $T_1,\ldots,T_N$.

Finally, the coefficients c_j, $j=1,\ldots,N$ are obtained from the linear system

$$P(\ell h) = \sum_{j=1}^{N} c_j \mathrm{e}^{-\mathrm{i}\ell h T_j}, \quad \ell = 0,\ldots,N$$

We summarize the algorithm as follows.

Algorithm 2.1

Input: $P(\ell h)$, $\ell=0,\ldots,N$, step size h.

1. Form the Toeplitz matrix $\mathbf{T}_{N+1} = (P(h(\ell-m)))_{m,\ell=0}^{N} \in \mathbb{R}^{(N+1)\times(N+1)}$ using that $P(-\ell h) = \overline{P(\ell h)}$.

2. Solve the system $\mathbf{T}_{N+1}\boldsymbol{\lambda}=\mathbf{0}$, where $\lambda_N=1$.

3. Compute the zeros of the polynomial $\Lambda(z) = \sum_{\ell=0}^{N} \lambda_\ell z^\ell$ on the unit circle and extract the frequencies T_j from the zeros $z_j = \mathrm{e}^{-\mathrm{i}hT_j}$, $j=1,\ldots,N$.

4. Compute the coefficients c_j from the system $P(\ell h) = \sum_{j=1}^{N} c_j \mathrm{e}^{-\mathrm{i}\ell h T_j}$, $\ell = 0,\ldots,N$.

Output: Frequencies T_j and coefficients c_j, $j=1,\ldots,N$, determining $P(\omega)$ in (2.1).

The procedure is not numerically stable with respect to inexact Fourier measurements. For improving the stability of the Prony method we refer to the ESPRIT method [18], the matrix pencil method [12] and the approximate Prony method [9, 15].

Remarks 2.2

1. For a unique computation of the knots T_j we need to ensure that $hT_j \in [-\pi,\pi)$, since $\mathrm{e}^{-\mathrm{i}\omega}$ is 2π-periodic. Otherwise, we will not be able to extract the values T_j from the zeros $z_j = \mathrm{e}^{-\mathrm{i}hT_j}$ of Λon the unit circle uniquely.

2. While the frequencies T_j are not known, one only needs to find a suitable upper bound for $|T_j|$ in order to fix a suitable step size h.

3. In applications, also the number N of terms in (2.1) is usually unknown. Having given at least an upper bound $M \geq N$ and $M+1$ function values $P(\ell h)$,

$\ell=0,\ldots,M$, one can also apply the above procedure (replacing N by M) and obtains N by examining rank($\mathbf{T}_{M+1}$). In this case, (2.3) cannot longer be solved uniquely, but each zero-eigenvector will serve for the determination of the zeros of Λ on the unit circle and hence of T_j, $j=1,\ldots,N$, see e.g. [15].

3 RECOVERY OF SPECIAL UNIVARIATE FUNCTIONS

3.1 Step functions

Let us consider a piecewise step function with compact support of the form

$$f(x) = \sum_{j=1}^{N} c_j^1 \mathbf{1}_{[T_j, T_{j+1})}(x) \tag{3.1}$$

where $\mathbf{1}_{[a,b)}$ denotes the characteristic function of the interval $[a,b)$, and c_j^1 are real coefficients with $c_j^1 \neq c_{j+1}^1$ for all $j\in\{1,\ldots,N-1\}$.

We want to answer the question, how many Fourier samples are needed to recover the function f.

Theorem 3.1 *Let* $-\infty<T_1<T_2<\cdots<T_{N+1}<\infty$ *and let* $c_j^1 \in \mathbb{R}$ *for* $j=1,\ldots,N$ *with* $c_j^1 \neq c_{j+1}^1$ *for* $j=1,\ldots,N-1$. *Assume that the constant* $h>0$ *satisfies* $hT_j\in[-\pi,\pi)$ *for* $j=1,\ldots,N+1$. *Then the function* f *in (3.1) can be completely recovered by the* $N+1$ *Fourier samples* $\widehat{f}(\ell h)$, $\ell=1,\ldots,N+1$.

Proof We observe from (3.1) that for $\omega\neq0$

$$\widehat{f}(\omega) = \sum_{j=1}^{N} \frac{c_j^1}{\mathrm{i}\omega}\left(\mathrm{e}^{-\mathrm{i}\omega T_j} - \mathrm{e}^{-\mathrm{i}\omega T_{j+1}}\right) = \frac{1}{\mathrm{i}\omega}\sum_{j=1}^{N+1} c_j^0 \mathrm{e}^{-\mathrm{i}\omega T_j}$$

with $c_j^0 := c_j^1 - c_{j-1}^1$, and with the convention that $c_0^1 = c_{N+1}^1 = 0$. Observe that $c_j^0 \neq 0$ by assumption. Hence,

$$(\mathrm{i}\omega)\widehat{f}(\omega) = \sum_{j=1}^{N+1} c_j^0 \mathrm{e}^{-\mathrm{i}\omega T_j},$$

and we can apply the Prony method described in Sect. 2 to $P(\omega):=(i\omega)$ $\widehat{f}(\omega)$, where we use the known values

$$P(\ell h) = (i\ell h) \cdot \widehat{f}(\ell h), \quad \ell = 1, \dots, N+1,$$
$$P(-\ell h) = \overline{P(\ell h)}, \quad \ell = 1, \dots, N+1,$$
$$P(0) = 0.$$

In this way, we determine all values $T_1,\dots,T_{N+1}$ and the corresponding coefficients c_j^0,j=1,...,N+1, uniquely. Finally, the coefficients c_j^1 are obtained using the recursion

$$c_1^1 = c_1^0,$$
$$c_j^1 = c_{j-1}^1 + c_j^0, \quad j = 2, \dots, N \quad \square$$

3.2 Non-uniform spline functions

The above approach can easily be transferred to higher order non-uniform spline functions of the form

$$f(x) = \sum_{j=1}^{N} c_j^m B_j^m(x), \tag{3.2}$$

where B_j^m is the B-spline of order m determined by the knots $T_j,\dots,T_{j+m}$. The B-spline functions B_j^m satisfy the recurrence relation

$$B_j^m(x) = \frac{x - T_j}{T_{j+m-1} - T_j} B_j^{m-1}(x) + \frac{T_{j+m} - x}{T_{j+m} - T_{j+1}} B_{j+1}^{m-1}(x)$$

with $B_j^1(x) := \mathbf{1}_{[T_j,T_{j+1})}(x)$. For the first derivative of B_j^m we find for $m \geq 3$

$$\left(B_j^m\right)'(x) = (m-1) \cdot \left(\frac{B_j^{m-1}(x)}{T_{j+m-1} - T_j} - \frac{B_{j+1}^{m-1}(x)}{T_{j+m} - T_{j+1}} \right) \tag{3.3}$$

see [6, p. 115]. Replacing the usual differentiation by the differentiation from the right, the above formula is applicable for m=2, too. For k=1,...,m−1 we get

$$f^{(k)}(x)=\sum_{j=1}^{N} c_j^m \left(B_j^m\right)^{(k)}(x)=\sum_{j=1}^{N+k} c_j^{m-k} B_j^{m-k}(x) \tag{3.4}$$

where the coefficients c_j^{m-k} can be recursively evaluated from c_j^m using (3.3). Finally, taking the distributional derivative we have

$$(B_j^1)'(x)=(\mathbf{1}_{[T_j,T_{j+1})})'(x)=\delta(x-T_j)-\delta(x-T_{j+1}), \tag{3.5}$$

where δ denotes the Dirac distribution with $\widehat{\delta}(\omega)=1$ for all $\omega\in\mathbb{R}$. Hence, the m-th derivative of f in (3.2) is a linear combination of weighted Dirac distributions,

$$f^{(m)}(x)=\sum_{j=1}^{N+m} c_j^0\delta(x-T_j)$$

Application of the Fourier transform yields

$$(\mathrm{i}\omega)^m\widehat{f}(\omega)=\sum_{j=1}^{N+m} c_j^0 \mathrm{e}^{-\mathrm{i}\omega T_j}. \tag{3.6}$$

Theorem 3.2 *Suppose that there exist a knot sequence* $-\infty<T_1<T_2<\cdots<T_{N+m}<\infty$ *and values* $c_j^m\in\mathbb{R}$, $j=1,\ldots,N$. *Assume that the constant* $h>0$ *satisfies* $hT_j\in[-\pi,\pi)$ *for all* $j=1,\ldots,N+m$. *Then the spline functionfin* (3.2) *can be completely recovered by theN+mFourier samples* $\widehat{f}(\ell h)$, $\ell=1,\ldots,N+m$.

Proof As shown above, the Fourier transform of the m-th derivative of f is of the form (3.6), and supposing that $c_j^0\neq 0$ for $j=1,\ldots,N+m$, we can compute the knots T_j and the coefficients c_j^0 for $j=1,\ldots,N+m$ uniquely by applying the Prony method given in Sect. 2 to $P(\omega)=(\mathrm{i}\omega)^m\widehat{f}(\omega)$. Further, applying the formulas (3.3) and (3.5) together with (3.4), we obtain the following recursion to compute the coefficients c_j^m,

$$c_j^{k+1}=\begin{cases} c_1^0 & \text{for } k=0,\ j=1,\\ c_j^0+c_{j-1}^1 & \text{for } k=0,\ j=2,\ldots,N+m-1,\\ \left(\frac{T_{m+1-k}-T_1}{m-k}\right)c_1^k & \text{for } k=1,\ldots,m-1,\ j=1,\\ \left(\frac{T_{m+j-k}-T_j}{m-k}\right)c_j^k+c_{j-1}^{k+1} & \text{for } k=1,\ldots,m-1,\ j=2,\ldots,N+m-k-1 \end{cases}$$

Remarks 3.3

1) The above proof of Theorem 3.2 is constructive. In particular, if N is not known, but we have an upper bound $M \geq N$, then the Prony method will also find the correct knots T_j and the corresponding coefficients c0jcj0 from $M+m$ Fourier samples, and the numerical procedure will be more stable, see e.g. [9, 14, 15].

2) In the above proof we rely upon the fact that $c_j^0 \neq 0$ for $j=1,\ldots,N+m$. If we have the situation that $c_{j_0}^0=0$ for an index $j_0 \in \{1,\ldots,N+m\}$, then we will not be able to reconstruct the knot T_{j0}. But this situation will only occur if the representation of f in (3.2) is redundant, i.e., if f in (3.2) can be represented by less than N summands, so we will still be able to recover the exact function f. Observe that the above recovery procedure always results in the simplest representation of f so that the reconstructed representation of f of the form (3.2) does not possess redundant terms.

3) Considering the non-linear problem to approximate a continuous univariate function f from given samples by a spline function with free knots, one wants to find optimal knots as well as optimal coefficients of the B-spline expansion f in (3.2) such that $g-f$ is small in a given norm. This problem is very challenging but of high interest for sparse signal approximation. While the above Theorems 3.1 and 3.2 yield a reconstruction of spline functions with free knots from Fourier samples, the above problem uses sampling values of g itself. The question whether Prony-like methods may be helpful to solve this non-linear approximation problem will be subject of our further research.

3.3 Non-uniform translates

Let us consider functions that have a sparse representation of the form

$$f(x) = \sum_{j=1}^{N} c_j \Phi(x - T_j). \tag{3.7}$$

with $c_j \in \mathbb{R} \setminus \{0\}$ for all $j=1,\ldots,N$, the knot sequence $-\infty < T_1 < \cdots < T_N < \infty$, and where $\Phi \in C(\mathbb{R}) \cap L_1(\mathbb{R})$ is a real low-pass filter function with a Fourier transform that is bounded away from zero, i.e. $|\hat{\Phi}(\omega)| > C_0$ for $\omega \in (-T,T)$ for some constants $C_0>0$ and $T>0$. As a low-pass filter function Φ we can take

- the centered cardinal B-spline of order m, $\Phi = N_m$, with

$$\widehat{N}_m(\omega) = \left(\operatorname{sinc}\left(\frac{\omega}{2}\right)\right)^m \neq 0 \quad \text{for all } \omega \in (-2\pi, 2\pi)$$
;

- the Gaussian function, $\Phi(x) = \exp(-\frac{x^2}{\sigma^2}), \sigma > 0$, with

$$\widehat{\Phi}(\omega) = \sqrt{\pi} \cdot \sigma \cdot \exp\left(-\frac{\sigma^2\omega^2}{4}\right) > 0 \quad \text{for all } \omega \in \mathbb{R};$$

- the Meyer window $\Phi(x)$ with $T = \frac{2}{3}$ and

$$\widehat{\Phi}(\omega) = \begin{cases} 1 & \text{for } |\omega| \leq \frac{1}{3}, \\ \cos\left(\frac{\pi}{2}(3|\omega| - 1)\right) & \text{for } \frac{1}{3} < |\omega| \leq \frac{2}{3} \\ 0 & \text{otherwise;} \end{cases}$$
,

- a real valued Gabor function $\Phi(x)=e^{-\alpha x^2}\cos(\beta x)$, $\alpha>0$, $\beta>0$, with

$$\widehat{\Phi}(\omega) = \frac{1}{2}\sqrt{\frac{\pi}{\alpha}}\left(\exp\left(-\frac{(\beta-\omega)^2}{4\alpha}\right) + \exp\left(-\frac{(\omega+\beta)^2}{4\alpha}\right)\right) > 0 \quad \text{for all } \omega \in \mathbb{R}$$

Fourier transform of (3.7) yields

$$\widehat{f}(\omega) = \left(\sum_{j=1}^{N} c_j e^{-i\omega T_j}\right)\widehat{\Phi}(\omega) \tag{3.8}$$

Theorem 3.4 *Let* $-\infty<T_1<\cdots<T_N<\infty$ *be a real sequence and* $c_j \in \mathbb{R}\setminus\{0\}$ *for* $j=1,\ldots,N$. *Further, let* $\Phi \in C(\mathbb{R}) \cap L_1(\mathbb{R})$ *be a given function with* $|\widehat{\Phi}(\omega)| > C_0|$ *for all* $\omega \in (-T,T)$ *and some* $C_0>0$. *Let* $h>0$ *be a constant satisfying* $|hT_j|<\min\{\pi,T\}$ *for all* $j=1,\ldots,N$. *Then the function* f *of the form* (3.7) *can be uniquely recovered by the Fourier samples* $\widehat{f}(\ell h)$, $\ell=0,\ldots,N$.

Proof Using the assumption on $\widehat{\Phi}$ we find from (3.8)

$$\frac{\widehat{f}(\omega)}{\widehat{\Phi}(\omega)} = \sum_{j=1}^{N} c_j e^{-i\omega T_j}$$

and hence we can compute all T_j and c_j by Prony's method given in Sect. 2

The above idea can be generalized to functions f of the form

$$f(x) = \sum_{j=1}^{N} \sum_{r=0}^{R-1} c_{j,r} \Phi^{(r)}(x - T_j) \tag{3.9}$$

with $c_{j,r} \in \mathbb{R}$ and $T_j \in \mathbb{R}$ as before, where $\Phi^{(r)}$ denotes the r-th derivative of Φ. Fourier transform now yields

$$\widehat{f}(\omega) = \left(\sum_{j=1}^{N} \sum_{r=0}^{R-1} c_{j,r} (\mathrm{i}\omega)^r \mathrm{e}^{-\mathrm{i}\omega T_j} \right) \widehat{\Phi}(\omega) \tag{3.10}$$

Theorem 3.5 *Let* $-\infty < T_1 < \cdots < T_N < \infty$ *be a real sequence and* $c_{j,r} \in \mathbb{R}$ *for* $j=1,\ldots,N$, $r=0,\ldots,R-1$, *where we assume that* $\sum_{r=0}^{R-1} |c_{j,r}| > 0$, *i.e., the coefficients* $c_{j,r}$ *corresponding to one frequency* T_j *do not all vanish at the same time. Further, let* $\Phi \in C(\mathbb{R}) \cap L_1(\mathbb{R})$ *be a given function with* $|\widehat{\Phi}(\omega)| > C_0$ *for all* $\omega \in (-T,T)$ *and some* $C_0 > 0$. *Let* $h > 0$ *be a constant satisfying* $|hT_j| < \min\{\pi, T\}$ *for all* $j=1,\ldots,N$. *Then the function* f *in* (3.9) *can be uniquely recovered by the Fourier samples* $\widehat{f}(\ell h)$, $\ell=0,\ldots,NR$.

Proof Regarding (3.10), we now want to apply Prony's method to a function of the form

$$Q(\omega) := \sum_{j=1}^{N} \sum_{r=0}^{R-1} c_{j,r} (\mathrm{i}\omega)^r \mathrm{e}^{-\mathrm{i}\omega T_j},$$

and this function structure is different from (2.1) for $R>1$. We remark that functions $Q(\omega)$ of the above form are called *extended exponential sums*, see [2, p. 169]. We consider now the polynomial

$$\Lambda(z) := \prod_{j=1}^{N} \left(z - \mathrm{e}^{-\mathrm{i}hT_j}\right)^R = \sum_{\ell=0}^{NR} \lambda_\ell z^\ell$$

with unknown shifts T_j. Then we observe that for $m=0,\ldots,NR$

$$\begin{aligned}
\sum_{\ell=0}^{NR} \lambda_\ell\, Q(h(\ell-m)) &= \sum_{\ell=0}^{NR} \lambda_\ell \sum_{j=1}^{N} \sum_{r=0}^{R-1} c_{j,r} \left(\mathrm{i}h(\ell-m)\right)^r \mathrm{e}^{-\mathrm{i}h(\ell-m)T_j} \\
&= \sum_{j=1}^{N} \sum_{r=0}^{R-1} c_{j,r} \mathrm{e}^{\mathrm{i}hmT_j} \sum_{\ell=0}^{NR} \lambda_\ell \left(\mathrm{i}h(\ell-m)\right)^r \mathrm{e}^{-\mathrm{i}h\ell T_j} \\
&= \sum_{j=1}^{N} \sum_{r=0}^{R-1} c_{j,r} \mathrm{e}^{\mathrm{i}hmT_j} (\mathrm{i}h)^r \sum_{\nu=0}^{r} \binom{r}{\nu} (-m)^{r-\nu} \sum_{\ell=0}^{NR} \lambda_\ell \ell^\nu \mathrm{e}^{-\mathrm{i}h\ell T_j}
\end{aligned}$$

Using the notation $S_\nu := \sum_{\ell=0}^{NR} \lambda_\ell \ell^\nu e^{-ih\ell T_j}$, we observe that S_ν can be written as a linear combination of the derivatives $\Lambda^{(\mu)}(z) = \sum_{\ell=\mu}^{NR} \lambda_\ell \frac{\ell!}{(\ell-\mu)!} z^{\ell-\mu}$, $\mu = 0, \ldots, \nu$, i.e., there exist coefficients $\alpha_\mu^\nu \in \mathbb{N}$ so that

$$S_\nu = \sum_{\mu=0}^{\nu} \alpha_\mu^\nu \Lambda^{(\mu)}(e^{-ihT_j}) e^{-i\mu h T_j}$$

and because of $\Lambda(\mu)(e^{-ihTj})=0$ for $\mu=0,\ldots,R-1$ we finally get

$$\sum_{\ell=0}^{NR} \lambda_\ell Q(h(\ell - m)) = 0$$

Hence, the coefficient vector $\boldsymbol{\lambda}=(\lambda_0,\ldots,\lambda_{NR})^T$ with $\lambda_{NR}=1$ is a zero-eigenvector of the Toeplitz matrix

$$\mathbf{T}_{NR+1} := \left(Q(h(\ell - m))\right)_{m,\ell=0}^{NR} \in \mathbb{R}^{(NR+1)\times(NR+1)}$$

Observe that all entries of $\mathbf{T}_{NR+1}$ are given, since we have $Q(-\omega) = \overline{Q(\omega)}$ and $Q(0)=0$. The method now applies along the same lines as given in Sect. 2□.

Remarks 3.6

1) The special functions f regarded in Sects. 3.1–3.3 are so-called functions of finite rate of innovation, as introduced for example in [21].
2) Similarly as in (3.9) we can also generalize the method to sums of B-splines and their derivatives, i.e., we can consider non-uniform translates of B-splines of different order,

$$f(x) = \sum_{j=1}^{N} \sum_{r=1}^{m} c_{j,r} B_j^r(x)$$
,

and $f(x)$ can be recovered by the Fourier samples $\hat{f}(\ell h)$, $\ell=1,\ldots,(N+m)m$.

4 RECOVERY OF SPECIAL BIVARIATE FUNCTIONS

4.1 Tensor products of non-uniform spline functions

Let us consider now a non-uniform tensor product spline representation

$$f(x_1,x_2)=\sum_{j=1}^{N_1}\sum_{k=1}^{N_2} c_{j,k}^{m_1,m_2} B_j^{m_1}(x_1) B_k^{m_2}(x_2), \tag{4.1}$$

where $B_j^{m_1}$ and $B_k^{m_2}$ are B-splines of order m_1 and m_2, respectively, determined by the knot sequences $T_j,\ldots,T_{j+m1}$ and $S_k,\ldots,S_{k+m2}$, respectively. Analogously as in Sect. 3.2, differentiation yields

$$\frac{\partial^{m_1}}{\partial x_1^{m_1}}\frac{\partial^{m_2}}{\partial x_2^{m_2}} f(x_1,x_2)=\sum_{j=1}^{N_1+m_1}\sum_{k=1}^{N_2+m_2} c_{j,k}^{0,0}\cdot\delta(x_1-T_j)\cdot\delta(x_2-S_k)$$

.

Fourier transform gives

$$(\mathrm{i}\omega_1)^{m_1}(\mathrm{i}\omega_2)^{m_2}\widehat{f}(\omega_1,\omega_2)=\sum_{j=1}^{N_1+m_1}\left(\sum_{k=1}^{N_2+m_2} c_{j,k}^{0,0}\mathrm{e}^{-\mathrm{i}\omega_2 S_k}\right)\mathrm{e}^{-\mathrm{i}\omega_1 T_j}. \tag{4.2}$$

Theorem 4.1 *Le tm$_1$,m$_2$∈ℕ be given integers, and letfbe a bivariate spline function of the form* (4.1) *with knot sequences*$-\infty<T_1<\cdots<T_{N1+m1}<\infty$ *and* $-\infty<S_1<\cdots<S_{N2+m2}<\infty$, *and with real coefficients* $c_{j,k}$,$j=1,\ldots,N_1$, $k=1,\ldots,N_2$. *Leth*$_1$*and* h_2 *be two positive constants satisfying* $|h_1T_j|<\pi$ *for all* $j=1,\ldots,N_1+m_1$ *and* $|h_2S_k|<\pi$ *for all* $k=1,\ldots,N_2+m_2$. *Thenfcan be uniquely recovered by the* $(N_1+m_1)\cdot(N_2+m_2)$ *Fourier samples* $\widehat{f}$ $(\mu h_1,\nu h_2)$, $\mu=1,\ldots,N_1+m_1$, $\nu=1,\ldots,N_2+m_2$.

Proof Set $p_j(\omega_2):=\sum_{k=1}^{N_2+m_2} c_{j,k}^{0,0}\mathrm{e}^{-\mathrm{i}\omega_2 S_k}$. Then the equality (4.2) reads

$$(\mathrm{i}\omega_1)^{m_1}(\mathrm{i}\omega_2)^{m_2}\widehat{f}(\omega_1,\omega_2)=\sum_{j=1}^{N_1+m_1} p_j(\omega_2)\mathrm{e}^{-\mathrm{i}\omega_1 T_j}. \tag{4.3}$$

Fixing $\omega_2:=h_2$, we apply Prony's method from Sect. 2 to the function

$$P(\omega_1) := (\mathrm{i}\omega_1)^{m_1}(\mathrm{i}h_2)^{m_2}\widehat{f}(\omega_1, h_2) = \sum_{j=1}^{N_1+m_1} p_j(h_2)\mathrm{e}^{-\mathrm{i}\omega_1 T_j}$$

and obtain the knot sequence $T_1,...,T_{N1+m1}$ as well as the coefficients $p_j(h_2)$, $j=1,...,N_1+m_1$, using the Fourier samples $\widehat{f}$ $(\mu h_1,h_2)$, $\mu=1,...,N_1+m_1$. In the unlucky case that not all values $p_j(h_2), j=1,...,N_1+m_1$ are non-zero, we do not find all values T_j by this procedure and have to repeat the method for $\omega_2=2h_2,3h_2,...$ etc. in order to complete the knot sequence $\{T_j, j=1,...,N_1+m_1\}$.

Next, knowing the T_j, we compute all further coefficients $p_j(\nu h_2)$, $j=1,...,N_1+m_1$, $\nu=2,...,N_2+m_2$, from the Fourier samples $\widehat{f}$ $(\mu h_1,\nu h_2)$, $\mu=1,...,N_1+m_1$, $\nu=2,...,N_2+m_2$, using (4.3). Afterwards, we apply the Prony method to

$$p_1(\omega_2) = \sum_{k=1}^{N_2+m_2} c_{1,k}^{0,0}\mathrm{e}^{-\mathrm{i}\omega_2 S_k}$$

and use $p_1(h_2),...,p_1((N_2+m_2)h_2)$ in order to determine the knot sequence $S_1,...,S_{N2+m2}$ and the coefficients $c_{1,k}^{0,0}$, $k=1,...,N_2+m_2$, uniquely. Again, in case that $c_{1,k}^{0,0}=0$ for some $k\in\{1,...,N_2+m_2\}$ we do not obtain all S_k and need to apply Prony's method also to $p_j(\omega_2)$ for $j>1$ in order to complete the knot sequence $\{S_k, k=1,...,N_2+m_2\}$.

All further coefficients $c_{j,k}^{0,0}$ are obtained from the linear systems

$$p_j(\nu h_2) = \sum_{k=1}^{N_2+m_2} c_{j,k}^{0,0}\mathrm{e}^{-\mathrm{i}\nu h_2 S_k}, \quad \nu = 1,\dots,N_2+m_2$$

for each $j=2,3,...,N_1+m_1$. Finally, we have to evaluate the original coefficients $c_{j,k}^{m_1,m_2}$ from $c_{j,k}^{0,0}$ using the recursions

$$c_{j,k}^{r_1+1,r_2} = \begin{cases} c_{1,k}^{0,r_2} & \text{for } r_1=0,\ j=1, \\ c_{j,k}^{0,r_2} + c_{j-1,k}^{1,r_2} & \text{for } r_1=0,\ j=2,\dots,N_1+m_1-1, \\ \left(\frac{T_{m_1+1-r_1}-T_1}{m_1-r_1}\right)c_{1,k}^{r_1,r_2} & \text{for } r_1=1,\dots,m_1-1,\ j=1, \\ \left(\frac{T_{m_1+j-r_1}-T_j}{m_1-r_1}\right)c_{j,k}^{r_1,r_2} + c_{j-1,k}^{r_1+1,r_2} & \text{for } r_1=1,\dots,m_1-1, \\ & \quad j=2,\dots,N_1+m_1-r_1-1, \end{cases}$$

where $r_2=0,...,m_2$, $k=1,...,N_2+m_2-r_2$, and

$$c_{j,k}^{r_1,r_2+1} = \begin{cases} c_{j,1}^{r_1,0} & \text{for } r_2=0,\ k=1, \\ c_{j,k}^{r_1,0} + c_{j,k-1}^{r_1,1} & \text{for } r_2=0,\ k=2,\dots,N_2+m_2-1, \\ \left(\frac{S_{m_2+1-r_2}-S_1}{m_2-r_2}\right) c_{j,1}^{r_1,r_2} & \text{for } r_2=1,\dots,m_2-1,\ k=1, \\ \left(\frac{S_{m_2+k-r_2}-S_k}{m_2-r_2}\right) c_{j,k}^{r_1,r_2} + c_{j,k-1}^{r_1,r_2+1} & \text{for } r_2=1,\dots,m_2-1, \\ & \quad k=2,\dots,N_2+m_2-r_2-1, \end{cases}$$

where $r_1=0,\dots,m_1$, $j=1,\dots,N_1+m_1-r_1$□ .

Remarks 4.2

1) Observe that in the tensor product case we usually need to apply the Prony method only twice in order to obtain the two knot sequences $\{T_j\}_{j=1,\dots,N1+m1}$ and $\{S_k\}_{k=1,\dots,N2+m2}$. All coefficients $c_{j,k}^{0,0}$ can afterwards be computed by a linear system of equations. As in the univariate case, the problem of vanishing terms $p_j(kh_2)$ or vanishing coefficients $c_{j,k}^{0,0}$ only occurs if the function f in (4.1) contains local redundancies.

2) A tensor product of the form

$$f(x_1,x_2) := \sum_{j=1}^{N_1}\sum_{k=1}^{N_2} c_{j,k}\Phi_1(x_1-T_j)\Phi_2(x_2-S_k) \tag{4.4}$$

with two low-pass filter functions Φ_1 and Φ_2 satisfying $\widehat{\Phi}_\nu(\omega)\neq 0$ for $\omega\in(-T,T)$ for ome $T>0$ ($\nu=1,2$) can be similarly handled by generalizing the results of Sect. 3.3. Fourier transform of (4.4) yields

$$\widehat{f}(\omega_1,\omega_2) = \left(\sum_{j=1}^{N_1}\sum_{k=1}^{N_2} c_{j,k}\mathrm{e}^{-\mathrm{i}\omega_1 T_j}\mathrm{e}^{-\mathrm{i}\omega_2 S_k}\right)\widehat{\Phi}_1(\omega_1)\widehat{\Phi}_2(\omega_2) .$$

Hence, for given functions Φ_1,Φ_2 we can recover f completely using the Fourier samples $\widehat{f}\,(\ell_1 h_1,\ell_2 h_2)$, $\ell_1=0,\dots,N_1$, $\ell_2=0,\dots,N_2$ by following the same lines as in the proof of Theorem 4.1. Here, h_1,h_2 have to satisfy $|h_1T_j|<\min\{\pi,T\}$ and $|h_2S_k|<\min\{\pi,T\}$ for all $j=1,\dots,N_1$, $k=1,\dots,N_2$.

4.2 Non-uniform translates of radial functions

For a given bivariate radial function $\Phi(x_1,x_2)\in C(\mathbb{R}^2)\cap L^1(\mathbb{R}^2)$ we assume that $\widehat{\Phi}(\omega_1,\omega_2)$ is bounded and satisfies $|\widehat{\Phi}(\omega_1,\omega_2)|>C_0>0|$ for $\omega:=(\omega_1,\omega_2)^T$ with $\|\omega\|_2=(\omega_1^2+\omega_2^2)^{\frac{1}{2}}<T$ and a suitable constant $T>0$. Such a function Φ

can be simply constructed with the help of a univariate low-pass function as given in Sect. 3.3 with

$$\Phi(x_1, x_2) := \Phi(r), \quad r := \left(x_1^2 + x_2^2\right)^{\frac{1}{2}}$$

Let us consider now a function $f(x_1,x_2)$ with the sparse representation

$$f(x_1, x_2) = \sum_{j=1}^{N} c_j \Phi(x_1 - v_{j,1}, x_2 - v_{j,2}). \tag{4.5}$$

As before, we would like to answer the questions, how many Fourier samples are needed to recover f if Φ and N are known, and how to compute the real shifts $v_j:=(v_j,1,v_j,2)$ and the real coefficients c_j, $j=1,\dots,N$, from these samples. Observe that this problem is completely different from the separable case considered in Sect. 4.1.

Fourier transform of (4.5) yields

$$\hat{f}(\omega_1, \omega_2) = \left(\sum_{j=1}^{N} c_j \mathrm{e}^{-\mathrm{i}\cdot(\omega_1 v_{j,1} + \omega_2 v_{j,2})}\right) \hat{\Phi}(\omega_1, \omega_2). \tag{4.6}$$

In the following, we consider only the case $c_j>0$ for all $j=1,\dots,N$.

Theorem 4.3 *Let $\Phi \in C(\mathbb{R}^2) \cap L^1(\mathbb{R}^2)$ be a given, real, bivariate function with $|\hat{\Phi}(\omega_1,\omega_2)|>C_0>0$ for $\|\omega\|_2<T$ for some $T>0$. Further, let f be a bivariate function with the sparse representation* (4.5), *where $c_j, v_{j,1}, v_{j,2}$, $j=1,\dots,N$, are real numbers and $c_j>0$ for $j=1,\dots,N$. Assume that the constant $h>0$ satisfies $h\|\mathbf{v}_j\|_2<\min\{\pi,T\}$ with $\|\mathbf{v}_j\|_2:=(v_{j,1}^2+v_{j,2}^2)^{\frac{1}{2}}$ for $j=1,\dots,N$. Then f can be uniquely recovered from the set of* $3N+1$ *Fourier samples given by*

$$\left\{\hat{f}(0,0), \hat{f}(\ell h, 0), \hat{f}(0, \ell h), \hat{f}(\cos(\alpha\pi)\ell h, \sin(\alpha\pi)\ell h), \ \ell = 1, \dots, N\right\},$$

Where $\alpha \in (0,1)\setminus\{\frac{1}{2}\}$ needs to be chosen suitably.

Proof We give a constructive proof. From (4.6) we obtain for $\omega_2=0$

$$\frac{\hat{f}(\omega_1, 0)}{\hat{\Phi}(\omega_1, 0)} = \sum_{j=1}^{N} c_j \mathrm{e}^{-\mathrm{i}\omega_1 v_{j,1}}$$

However, we are faced with the problem that two or more shifts $\mathbf{v}_j=(v_{j,1},v_{j,2})$ may possess the same first coordinate. Let us assume that the wanted set

$\{v_{1,1},...,v_{N,1}\}$ of first coordinates contains $N_1 \le N$ distinct values $\widetilde{v}_{1,1}, \dots, \widetilde{v}_{N_1,1}$. Then we find

$$\frac{\widehat{f}(\omega_1, 0)}{\widehat{\Phi}(\omega_1, 0)} = \sum_{k=1}^{N_1} c_k^1 \mathrm{e}^{-\mathrm{i}\omega_1 \widetilde{v}_{k,1}}, \tag{4.7}$$

where for the true first coordinates of the wanted shifts it follows that $v_{j,1} \in \widetilde{V}_1 := \{\widetilde{v}_{1,1}, \dots, \widetilde{v}_{N_1,1}\}$ for each $j=1,...,N$, and where c_k^1 is the sum of all coefficients belonging to shift vectors with the same first coordinate $\widetilde{v}_{k,1}$,

$$c_k^1 := \sum_{\substack{j \\ v_{j,1}=\widetilde{v}_{k,1}}} c_j, \quad k = 1, \dots, N_1 \tag{4.8}$$

Observe that $c_k^1 > 0$ for all $k=1,...,N_1$, since we consider only the case $c_j>0$ for all $j=1,...,N$. Applying Prony's method in Sect. 2 to (4.7) using the Fourier samples $\widehat{f}$ $(\ell h,0)$, $\ell=0,...,N$, provides us the values $\widetilde{v}_{1,1}, \dots, \widetilde{v}_{N_1,1}$ and the corresponding coefficients c_k^1, $k=1,...,N_1$.

Analogously, we observe from (4.6) with $\omega_1=0$ that

$$\frac{\widehat{f}(0, \omega_2)}{\widehat{\Phi}(0, \omega_2)} = \sum_{j=1}^{N} c_j \mathrm{e}^{-\mathrm{i}\omega_2 v_{j,2}} = \sum_{k=1}^{N_2} c_k^2 \mathrm{e}^{-\mathrm{i}\omega_2 \widetilde{v}_{k,2}},$$

where $\widetilde{v}_{k,2}$ are the distinct values of the set $\{v_{1,2},...,v_{N,2}\}$ and c_k^2 are the corresponding coefficients for $k=1,...,N_2$, $N_2 \le N$. The values $\widetilde{v}_{k,2}, c_k^2$, $k=1,...,N_2$, are computed by Prony's method from the samples $\widehat{f}$ $(0,\ell h)$, $\ell=0,...,N$.

Hence, the true shift vectors $\mathbf{v}_j$ have to be contained in the set

$$G := \left\{\mathbf{v} = (v_1, v_2) : v_1 \in \widetilde{V}_1,\ v_2 \in \widetilde{V}_2\right\},$$

where $\widetilde{V}_\nu := \{\widetilde{v}_{k,\nu} : k = 1, \dots, N_\nu\}$, $\nu=1,2$. In order to find the true shift vectors $\mathbf{v}_j$ we now determine an angle $\alpha\pi$, such that the orthogonal projections of all $\mathbf{v} \in G$ onto the line $y=\tan(\alpha\pi)x$ are distinct, i.e. that $(\cos\alpha\pi)v_1+(\sin\alpha\pi)v_2$ are distinct for all $\mathbf{v} \in G$. Since G contains $N_1N_2 \le N^2$ entries, such a number $\alpha \in (0,1)\backslash\{\frac{1}{2}\}$ can always be found.

Now, we consider

$$\frac{\hat{f}(\omega_1 \cos(\alpha\pi), \omega_1 \sin(\alpha\pi))}{\hat{\Phi}(\omega_1 \cos(\alpha\pi), \omega_1 \sin(\alpha\pi))} = \sum_{k=1}^{N_3} c_k^3 e^{-i\omega_1 \tilde{v}_{k,3}},$$

where $\tilde{v}_{k,3}$, $k=1,\ldots,N_3$ with $N_3 \le N$ are the distinct values of the set $\{v_{j,1}\cos(\alpha\pi)+v_{j,2}\sin(\alpha\pi): j=1,\ldots,N\}$. However, the construction of α yields that $N_3=N$ since all possible shift vectors yield different projections onto the third line $y=\tan(\alpha\pi)x$.

Let $\tilde{V}_3 := \{\tilde{v}_{k,3} : k = 1,\ldots,N\}$ be the set of distinct frequencies, and let c_k^3 be the corresponding coefficients obtained by applying the Prony method to the samples $f(\cos(\alpha\pi)\ell h, \sin(\alpha\pi)\ell h)$, $\ell = 0,\ldots,N$. Hence, the point set

$$\tilde{G} := \left\{ \mathbf{v} = (v_1, v_2) : v_1 \in \tilde{V}_1,\ v_2 \in \tilde{V}_2,\ v_1 \cos(\alpha\pi) + v_2 \sin(\alpha\pi) \in \tilde{V}_3 \right\}$$

contains now only the N wanted shifts $\mathbf{v}_j$, and the corresponding coefficients c_j are given by the set $\{c_j^3, j=1,\ldots,N\}$.□

In order to improve the robustness of the reconstruction method, the angle α should be chosen such that the minimal distance between two orthogonal projections of elements from G onto the line $y=\tan(\alpha\pi)x$ is maximized. With $\theta_\alpha:=(\cos(\alpha\pi),\sin(\alpha\pi))^T$, the projection point $\mathbf{p_v}$ of $\mathbf{v}$onto this line is

$$\mathbf{p_v} = \langle \mathbf{v}, \theta_\alpha \rangle \theta_\alpha = \left(\cos(\alpha\pi)v_1 + \sin(\alpha\pi)v_2\right)\theta_\alpha$$

Hence, we need to maximize the minimal distance of two projection points with respect to α, i.e., we have to solve the max-min problem

$$\max_{\alpha \in (0,1)\setminus\{\frac{1}{2}\}} \min_{\substack{\mathbf{v},\mathbf{w}\in G \\ \mathbf{v}\neq\mathbf{w}}} \left(\langle \mathbf{v} - \mathbf{w}, \theta_\alpha \rangle\right)^2$$

Remarks 4.4

1. In the reconstruction scheme given in Theorem 4.3, the angle α of the third line of Fourier samples has to be taken dependently on the set G, i.e., dependently on the candidates for shifts in G found from the first two lines. For practical purposes it would be of great interest to compute the wanted shifts and coefficients of f in (4.5) from given Fourier samples taken beforehand independently from the shifts in f. In fact, for most practical cases, the consideration of the point set $\tilde{G}$ (with a priori given angle $\alpha\pi$) already yields a sufficiently small set of candidates, such that the true shifts can be found using the $N_1+N_2+N_3$ conditions of the form (4.8) (or

similar to (4.8)) for the coefficients. However, counterexamples can be found for certain sets of shifts with special symmetry properties, where a complete reconstruction of f is not possible. We conjecture that the set of Fourier samples on four lines of the form

$$\{\hat{f}(0,0), \hat{f}(\ell h, 0), \hat{f}(0, \ell h), \hat{f}(\cos(\alpha\pi)\ell h, \sin(\alpha\pi)\ell h), \hat{f}(-\sin(\alpha\pi)\ell h, \cos(\alpha\pi)\ell h), \ \ell = 1, \ldots, N\},$$

where α satisfies $\tan(\alpha\pi) \neq \frac{1}{n}$ for $n \in \mathbb{N}$, always suffices for a unique reconstruction of f. Here, we consider the Fourier samples on four lines where the first two lines are orthogonal and the last two are also orthogonal. In this case, the true shift vectors $\mathbf{v}_j$ have to be contained in the set

$$G := \{\mathbf{v} = (v_1, v_2) : v_1 \in \widetilde{V}_1, \ v_2 \in \widetilde{V}_2, \ v_1 \cos(\alpha\pi) + v_2 \sin(\alpha\pi) \in \widetilde{V}_3, -v_1 \sin(\alpha\pi) + v_2 \cos(\alpha\pi) \in \widetilde{V}_4\},$$

where $\widetilde{V}_\nu := \{\widetilde{v}_{k,\nu} : k = 1, \ldots, N_\nu\}, \ \nu = 1, 2, 3, 4$. Moreover, the Prony method provides $N_1+N_2+N_3+N_4$ conditions for the coefficients of the form (4.8) (or similar to (4.8)) that can be applied for determining all true shifts of f.

2. The considered idea of function reconstruction can also be generalized to d-variate functions ($d>2$).

5 NUMERICAL RESULTS

We want to apply the described reconstruction methods to examples of step functions, non-uniform spline functions and non-uniform translates of radial functions. All examples considered in this section have been computed using MATLAB 7.11 with double precision arithmetic on a MacBook Pro with a 2.4 GHz Intel Core 2 Duo processor.

In the first two examples we consider the reconstruction of univariate functions. Figure 1presents a step function that is determined by the knot sequence $\{T_j\}_{j=1,\ldots,7}$ and the coefficient sequence $\{c_j\}_{j=1,\ldots,6}$ given in Table 1. Observe that the knots $T_1=-11.5$ and $T_2=-11.43$ are very close, and that the difference of the two successive coefficients $c_3=1.2$ and $c_4=1.1$ is rather small. To show the exactness of the reconstruction we have displayed the absolute reconstruction errors $|T_j^* - T_j|, j = 1, \ldots, 7$, and $|c_j^* - c_j|, j = 1, \ldots, 6$, where T_j^* and c_j^* denote the reconstructed knot values and coefficient values, respectively.

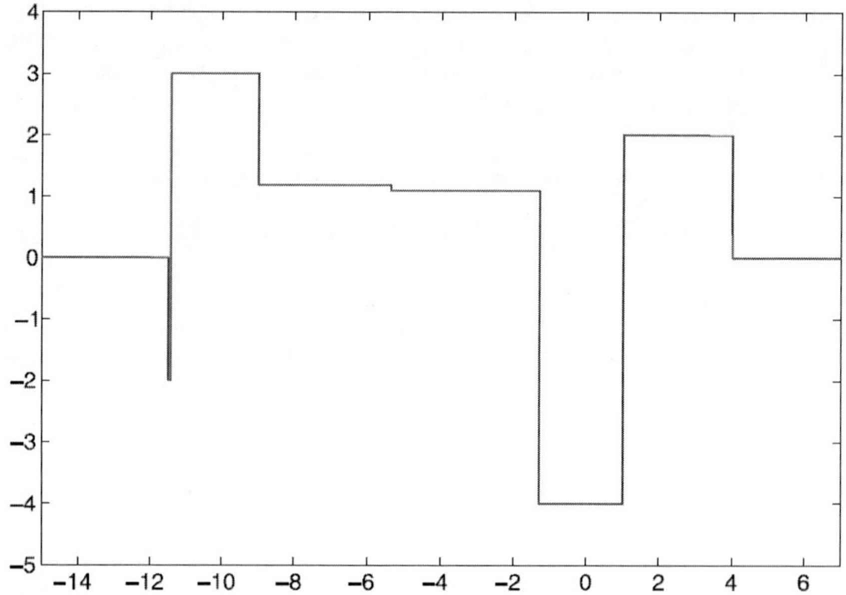

Figure. 1 Original function of the form (3.1) with N=6 determined by $\{T_j\}$ and $\{c_j\}$ given in Table 1

Table 1 Parameters for the original function in Fig. 1 and reconstruction errors, where h=0.27

j	T_j	$\|T_j^* - T_j\| \approx$	c_j	$\|c_j^* - c_j\| \approx$
1	−11.5	$9.81 \cdot 10^{-13}$	−2	$6.24 \cdot 10^{-11}$
2	−11.43	$4.867 \cdot 10^{-13}$	3	$1.91 \cdot 10^{-14}$
3	−9	$5.329 \cdot 10^{-15}$	1.2	$2.864 \cdot 10^{-14}$
4	−5.37	$1.51 \cdot 10^{-14}$	1.1	$3.153 \cdot 10^{-14}$
5	−1.3	$1.554 \cdot 10^{-15}$	−4	$4.441 \cdot 10^{-14}$
6	1	$1.998 \cdot 10^{-15}$	2	$6.306 \cdot 10^{-14}$
7	4	$3.997 \cdot 10^{-15}$		

The second example shows the results for the reconstruction of a non-uniform spline function of the form (3.2), see Fig. 2. We have taken N=5 and non-uniform B-splines of order m=5. The original parameters T_j and c_j are listed in Table 2, and we also compare them with the reconstructed values T_j^* and c_j^*, respectively.

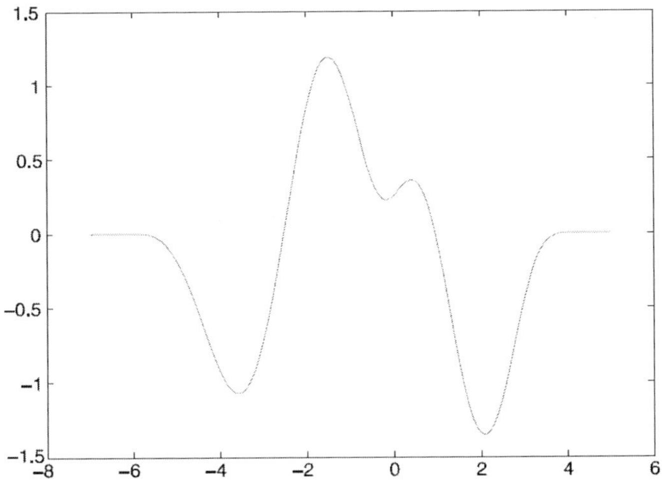

Figure. 2 Original function of the form (3.2) determined by $\{T_j\}$ and $\{c_j\}$ (see Table 2) with N=5, m=5

In the last two examples, we want to show how our proposed algorithm works for the case of non-uniform translates of bivariate radial functions. Therefore, we have taken the radial function $\Phi(x_1, x_2) := \exp(-\alpha \cdot (x_1^2 + x_2^2))$ with α=0.05 and a discrete grid setting with 128×128 points where the values for the first and the second coordinate are ranging from −64 to 63 and from −63 to 64, respectively.

First, we have taken an original function which consists only of four summands, but where three shift vectors are lying closely to each other on the same vertical line, see Fig. 3. The determining parameters are listed in Table 3. In addition, also the absolute reconstruction errors between the original parameters and the reconstructed parameters $v_{j,1}^*$, $v_{j,2}^*$ and c_j^*, respectively, are listed in Table 3. We have used these parameters to evaluate the reconstructed function on the discrete grid and to compare it with the original function on this grid. In this way we get a maximal absolute error between the original and the reconstructed function of approximately $1.175 \cdot 10^{-8}$.

Table 2 Parameters for the original function in Fig. 2 and reconstruction errors, where h=0.5

j	T_j	$\lvert T_j^* - T_j \rvert \approx$	c_j	$\lvert c_j^* - c_j \rvert \approx$
1	−6	0	−3.2	$8.66 \cdot 10^{-14}$
2	−5.8	$3.553 \cdot 10^{-15}$	3.1	$2.576 \cdot 10^{-14}$
3	−4	$8.882 \cdot 10^{-16}$	−0.8	$7.996 \cdot 10^{-13}$
4	−2.25	$1.332 \cdot 10^{-15}$	1.5	$2.783 \cdot 10^{-12}$
5	−0.6	$2.887 \cdot 10^{-15}$	−3	$5.799 \cdot 10^{-12}$
6	0	$1.337 \cdot 10^{-15}$		
7	1.3	$3.109 \cdot 10^{-15}$		
8	2.73	$4.441 \cdot 10^{-16}$		
9	3.5	$4.441 \cdot 10^{-15}$		
10	4.2	$4.441 \cdot 10^{-15}$		

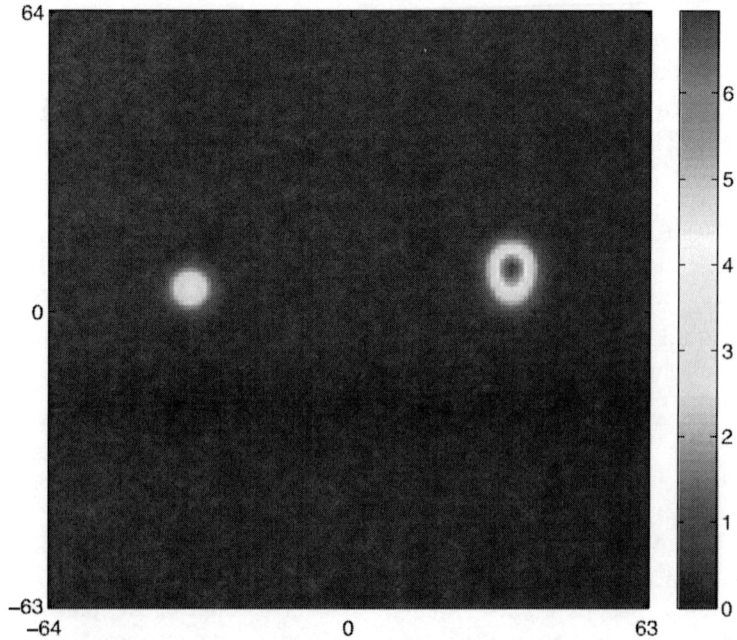

Figure. 3 Original function of the form (4.5) determined by $\{\mathbf{v}_j\}$ and $\{c_j\}$ given in Table 3

Table 3 Parameters for the original function in Fig. 3 and reconstruction errors, where $\alpha = \frac{4}{9}$

j	$v_{j,1}$	$\lvert v^*_{j,1} - v_{j,1}\rvert \approx$	$v_{j,2}$	$\lvert v^*_{j,2} - v_{j,2}\rvert \approx$	c_j	$\lvert c^*_j - c_j\rvert \approx$
1	34	0	5	$1.194 \cdot 10^{-11}$	3	$1.862 \cdot 10^{-10}$
2	−34	0	5	$1.194 \cdot 10^{-11}$	4	$1.408 \cdot 10^{-12}$
3	34	0	10	$1.779 \cdot 10^{-8}$	2	$5.141 \cdot 10^{-7}$
4	34	0	10.25	$7.993 \cdot 10^{-9}$	4	$5.143 \cdot 10^{-7}$

The second bivariate function, where we have applied our algorithm, is displayed in Fig. 4. Considering only the shift vectors and not the coefficients, this function has an 8-fold rotation symmetry. For the original parameters and the reconstruction errors see Table 4. Again, we have used the reconstructed parameters to evaluate the function on the discrete grid. Comparison with the original function yields a maximal absolute error of approximately $5.193 \cdot 10^{-10}$.

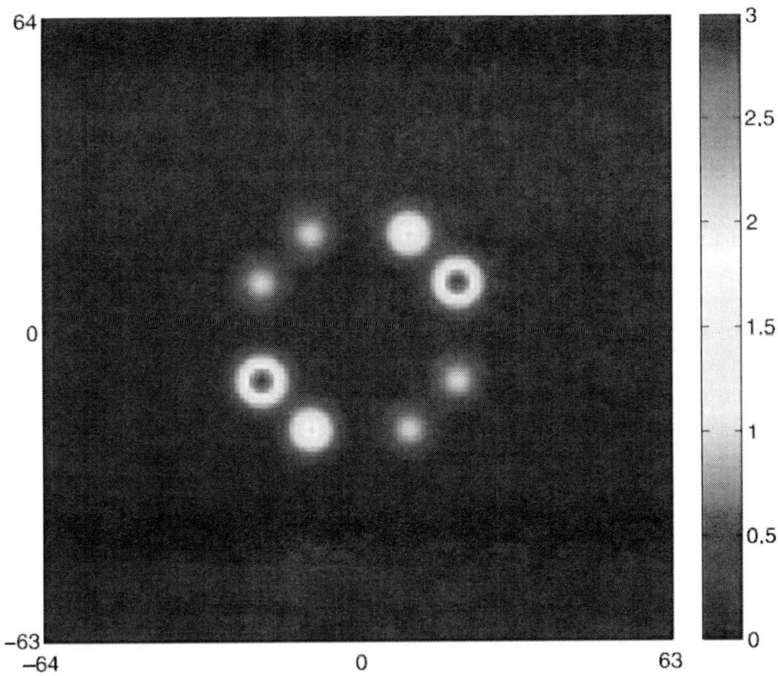

Figure. 4 Original function of the form (4.5) determined by $\{\mathbf{v}_j\}$ and $\{c_j\}$ given in Table 4

Table 4 Parameters for the original function in Fig. 4 and reconstruction errors, where α=0.4375

j	$v_{j,1}$	$\lvert v^*_{j,1} - v_{j,1}\rvert \approx$	$v_{j,2}$	$\lvert v^*_{j,2} - v_{j,2}\rvert \approx$	c_j	$\lvert c^*_j - c_j\rvert \approx$
1	-10	$5.329 \cdot 10^{-15}$	20	$1.066 \cdot 10^{-14}$	1	$4.545 \cdot 10^{-10}$
2	10	$1.776 \cdot 10^{-15}$	20	$1.066 \cdot 10^{-14}$	2	$1.506 \cdot 10^{-10}$
3	20	$1.776 \cdot 10^{-14}$	10	$7.105 \cdot 10^{-15}$	3	$5.193 \cdot 10^{-10}$
4	20	$1.776 \cdot 10^{-14}$	-10	0	1	$1.907 \cdot 10^{-12}$
5	10	$1.776 \cdot 10^{-15}$	-20	$2.132 \cdot 10^{-14}$	1	$4.962 \cdot 10^{-11}$
6	-10	$5.329 \cdot 10^{-15}$	-20	$2.132 \cdot 10^{-14}$	2	$5.203 \cdot 10^{-11}$
7	-20	$3.553 \cdot 10^{-15}$	-10	0	3	$1.12 \cdot 10^{-10}$
8	-20	$3.553 \cdot 10^{-15}$	10	$7.105 \cdot 10^{-15}$	1	$7.349 \cdot 10^{-11}$

6 CONCLUSION

In this paper, we have emphasized the question of how to reconstruct structured functions by means of a smallest number of Fourier data. However, in case of noisy Fourier measurements, the performance of reconstruction can be greatly improved if a larger number of Fourier data is available, see e.g. [9, 12, 15, 18]. In particular, for small data sets we recommend the preprocessing step of data filtering presented in [9]. In that reference, one can also find error estimates for the obtained function parameters.

Recently, Candès et al. [4] proposed the reconstruction of functions of the form (2.1) using a total variation minimization formulation. To tackle this minimization problem, a semidefinite program is applied to solve the dual problem in a first step. The obtained vector is used to define a special polynomial whose zeros on the unit circle are related to the wanted parameters T_j. The exact connections between the minimization approach in the context of super-resolution and the direct algorithms for the Prony method will be subject of further research.

ACKNOWLEDGEMENTS

We thank the referees for their helpful comments in order to improve the representation of the results in this paper. This work is supported by the German Research Foundation (DFG) in the framework of SFB 755.

REFERENCES

1. Bracewell, R.N.: The Fourier Transform and Its Applications. McGraw-Hill, New York (2000)
2. Braess, D.: Nonlinear Approximation Theory. Springer, Berlin (1986)
3. Bresler, Y., Macovski, A.: Exact maximum likelihood parameter estimation of superimposed exponential signals in noise. IEEE Trans. Acoust. Speech Signal Process.. **ASSAP-34**, 1081–1089 (1986)
4. Candès, E., Fernandez-Granda, C.: Towards a ematical theory of super-resolution. Comm. Pure Appl. . (to appear)
5. Candès, E., Romberg, J., Tao, T.: Robust uncertainty principles: exact signal reconstruction from highly incomplete frequency information. IEEE Trans. Inf. Theory **52**(2), 489–509 (2006)
6. de Boor, C.: A Practical Guide to Splines. Springer, New York (2001)
7. Dragotti, P.L., Vetterli, M., Blu, T.: Sampling moments and reconstructing signals of finite rate of innovation: Shannon meets Strang-Fix. IEEE Trans. Signal Process. **50**(6), 1417–1428 (2002)
8. Elad, M., Milanfar, P., Golub, G.H.: Shape from moments—an estimation theory perspective. IEEE Trans. Signal Process. **52**(7), 1814–1829 (2004)
9. Filbir, F., Mhaskar, H., Prestin, J.: On the problem of parameter estimation in exponential sums. Constr. Approx. **35**, 323–343 (2012)
10. Golub, G.H., Van Loan, C.: Matrix Computations, 3rd edn. Johns Hopkins University Press, Baltimore (1996)
11. Golub, G.H., Milanfar, P., Varah, J.: A stable numerical method for inverting shape from moments. SIAM J. Sci. Comput. **21**(4), 1222–1243 (1999)
12. Hua, Y., Sarkar, T.K.: On SVD for estimating generalized eigenvalues of singular matrix pencil in noise. IEEE Trans. Signal Process. **39**, 892–900 (1991)
13. Maravic, I., Vetterli, M.: Exact sampling results for some classes of parametric nonbandlimited 2-D signals. IEEE Trans. Signal Process. **52**(1), 175–198 (2004)
14. Peter, T., Potts, D., Tasche, M.: Nonlinear approximation by sums of exponentials and translates. SIAM J. Sci. Comput. **33**(4), 1920–1944 (2011)
15. Potts, D., Tasche, M.: Parameter estimation for exponential sums by approximate Prony method. Signal Process. **90**(5), 1631–1642 (2010)
16. Potts, D., Tasche, M.: Parameter estimation for multivariate exponential sums. Preprint (2011)
17. Rauhut, H.: Random sampling of sparse trigonometric polynomials. Appl. Comput. Harmon. Anal. **22**(1), 16–42 (2007)
18. Roy, R., Kailath, T.: ESPRIT—estimation of signal parameters via rotational invariance techniques. IEEE Trans. Acoust. Speech Signal Process. **37**, 984–995 (1989)
19. Shukla, P., Dragotti, P.L.: Sampling schemes for 2-d signals with finite rate of innovation using kernels that reproduce polynomials. In: Proc. of IEEE Int. Conf. on Image Processing (ICIP) (2005)
20. Vanpoucke, F., Moonen, M., Berthoumieu, Y.: An efficient subspace algorithm for 2-D harmonic retrieval. In: Proc. of IEEE Int. Conf. Acoust., Speech, Signal Processing, vol. 4, pp. 461–464 (1994)
21. Vetterli, M., Marziliano, P., Blu, T.: Sampling signals with finite rate of innovation. IEEE Trans. Signal Process. **50**(6), 1417–1428 (2002)

CHAPTER 7

On the error propagation of semi-Lagrange and Fourier methods for advection problems☆

Lukas Einkemmer*, Alexander Ostermann

Department of Mathematics, University of Innsbruck, Austria

ABSTRACT

In this paper we study the error propagation of numerical schemes for the advection equation in the case where high precision is desired. The numerical methods considered are based on the fast Fourier transform, polynomial interpolation (semi-Lagrangian methods using a Lagrange or spline interpolation), and a discontinuous Galerkin semi-Lagrangian approach (which is conservative and has to store more than a single value per cell).

We demonstrate, by carrying out numerical experiments, that the worst case error estimates given in the literature provide a good explanation for the error propagation of the interpolation-based semi-Lagrangian methods. For the discontinuous Galerkin semi-Lagrangian method, however, we find that the characteristic property of semi-Lagrangian error estimates (namely the fact that the error increases proportionally to the number of time steps) is not observed. We provide an explanation for this behavior and conduct numerical simulations that corroborate the different qualitative features of the error in the two respective types of semi-Lagrangian methods.

The method based on the fast Fourier transform is exact but, due to round-off errors, susceptible to a linear increase of the error in the number of time steps. We show how to modify the Cooley–Tukey algorithm in order to obtain an error growth that is proportional to the square root of the number of time steps.

Finally, we show, for a simple model, that our conclusions hold true if the advection solver is used as part of a splitting scheme.

Keywords: Semi-Lagrange methods, FFT, Error propagation, High-precision, computations

1. INTRODUCTION

The accurate numerical simulation of advection dominated problems is an important problem in many scientific applications. However, due to the non-dissipative nature of the equations considered, care has to be taken to obtain a stable numerical scheme (see, for example, [1]). A large body of research has been accumulated that describes finite difference, finite volume, and finite element discretizations of such problems. However, for advection-dominated problems so-called semi-Lagrangian methods offer a competitive alternative. These methods integrate the characteristics back in time and consequently have to use some interpolation scheme to reconstruct the desired value at the grid points. Strictly speaking, semi-Lagrangian methods can only be applied to systems of first-order differential equations. However, in many instances, first-order systems arise from the splitting of more complicated equations or constitute the linear part of an evolution equation (which is then treated separately from the nonlinearity). Consequently, semi-Lagrangian methods have been used extensively in applications ranging from fluid dynamics to plasma physics (see e.g. [2,3]). Such an approach is especially promising, if the characteristics (of a sub-problem) can be computed analytically; this can be done, for example, in context of the Vlasov–Poisson equations. In addition, semi-Lagrangian methods do not impose a Courant–Friedrichs–Lewy (CFL) condition.

In some problems, methods based on the FFT (fast Fourier transform) can also be employed; this is the case for tensor product domains (see e.g. [4]). Compared to FFT based methods, the semi-Lagrangian methods provide a local approximation (which is important in the context of parallelization). They are more easily applicable to non-periodic boundary conditions (due to the absence of Gibbs' phenomenon) and usually are better suited to handle nonlinearities. Using the fast Fourier transform, on the other hand, allows us to solve the linear advection equation exactly (in infinite precision arithmetics).

In most scientific applications a tolerance of say 10^{-3} is sufficient. In this case, the main research goal is to construct more efficient algorithms and to implement better step size control mechanism. Also methods that preserve certain invariants of the continuous system are of interest in that context.

However, a number of applications have been identified where double precision floating point numbers are not sufficient. A proposed remedy is to (selectively) use 128-bit floating point numbers. Note, however, that this procedure is accompanied by a significant reduction in performance. Examples of such problems range from the investigation of vortex sheet roll-ups in fluid dynamics to electromagnetic scattering phenomena (for an excellent review article see [5]).

Also, concern has been raised in recent years with regard to the reproducibility of numerical simulations; especially if such simulations are conducted on different computer systems. In [6], for example, it is demonstrated that climate codes show significantly different results depending on the number of processors that are employed in the simulation. One popular choice of numerical methods for atmospheric modeling are semi-Lagrangian methods.

Furthermore, due to the diminishing gain in per core CPU (central processing unit) performance, massively parallel computing architectures, such as GPUs and the Xeon Phi, have become more and more common. Usually in such situations the memory per core is significantly smaller than in more traditional cluster systems. In addition, single precision floating point performance is usually faster than double precision floating point performance (for example, the CUDA FFT single precision implementation achieves a speedup of about 2.5 compared to the double precision implementation [7]). Such considerations make the use of single precision floating point numbers attractive for some applications.

Therefore, our goal in this paper is to study the error propagation in a context where results close to machine precision are of interest or where the error has to be tightly controlled. We will limit ourselves to the advection equation (on a finite spatial interval)

$$\partial_t u(t,x) + v\partial_x u(t,x)=0, \tag{1}$$

where u is a continuously differentiable function and v is a given constant.

For this model problem, we consider the time evolution of the interplay of round-off and discretization errors for semi-Lagrangian and FFT based methods. The discretization of (1) is important in itself as it is a building block for many more involved schemes (for example, in the context of splitting methods or for methods where the linear part is treated differently). Such schemes are applied, for example, in fluid dynamics or to solve the Vlasov equation. Note, however, that problems where v is a function of space and time can be treated as well within the semi-Lagrangian approach. In this case the characteristics have to be integrated backward in time by a suitable ordinary differential equation solver. In certain situations a function v which depends on the unknown function u can be handled as well (see, for example, [8]).

For future reference, we note that the analytic solution of (1) can be easily written down as

$$u(t,x) = u(0,x - vt),$$

where in this paper we always assume that v is a constant independent of x and t.

2. DESCRIPTION AND ERROR BOUNDS

In this section we will describe how to use the semi-Lagrangian method (Section 2.1) and the fast Fourier transform (Section 2.2). Furthermore, we will discuss some theoretical results concerning the discretization error of these schemes.

2.1. The semi-Lagrangian method

A time step in the semi-Lagrangian method for the ith grid point is computed as follows:

$$u_n(x_i) = u_{n-1}\left(X_{xi}(\tau)\right),$$

where u_n is the numerical solution after n time steps, τ is the time step size, and the characteristics of Eq. (1) are given by $X_x(\tau) = x - v\tau$. Note that $X_{xi}(\tau)$ does not necessarily coincide with any grid point. Therefore, a sufficiently accurate interpolation procedure has to be used in order to extend the values stored at the grid to the entire domain. Both (continuous) spline interpolation as well as (discontinuous) Legendre or Lagrange interpolation are popular choices. Furthermore, similar to discontinuous Galerkin methods, multiple coefficients can be stored for each cell (which yields a local reconstruction at the expense of additional memory demands).

It is well known (see e.g. [9,10]) that in the case of semi-Lagrangian methods the error of the fully discretized problem can be estimated by

$$\|u(n\tau, x) - u_n(x)\| \leq C\left(h^q + \frac{h^q}{\tau}\right) \tag{2}$$

where h is the grid size, and q is the order of the space discretization (for example, the order of the Lagrange interpolation). Note that C is a constant that is independent of n, τ, and h. Such estimates are usually derived in one (or all) of the L^p norms. Note that there is no term proportional to τ as the characteristics are known analytically. However, results can be derived that take time discretization errors into account (see e.g. [9,10]).

The first term on the right-hand side in Eq. (2) is the usual spatial error term. The disturbing implication, however, is that the second term is directly proportional to the number of time steps taken. This, however, is to be expected, as in each projection an error proportional to h^q is made. In the worst case these errors accumulate to give the above mentioned bound. Note that the second term is usually not present if Eulerian discretization methods (for example finite difference schemes) are employed.

Similarly how the discontinuous Galerkin (dG) method considers a polynomial reconstruction that only uses data attached to the corresponding cell, it is possible to formulate a semi-Lagrangian method based on this reconstruction. This dG semi-Lagrangian method also requires only the data from neighboring cells in order to perform a time step (for arbitrary order in space). The scheme is described in some detail in [11,10]. Since there is no ambiguity, in this paper, we will refer to this scheme as the dG approximation.

Let us duly note that the second term in Eq. (2) is a worst case estimate that is valid for all the interpolation and projection schemes discussed here. Thus, in the next section we will investigate the actual numerical behavior for the spline interpolation, the Lagrange interpolation, and the discontinuous Galerkin approximation.

2.2. The fast Fourier transform

In case of the FFT based scheme we compute the Fourier transform of (1)which gives

$$\partial_t \hat{u}(t, k) + ikv\hat{u}(t, k) = 0 \tag{3}$$

where we have denoted the Fourier component with frequency $k \in Z$ by $\hat{u}(t,k)$. We can easily solve (3) to get

$$\hat{u}(t,k) = e^{-ikvt}\,\hat{u}(0,k).$$

Therefore, the advection in Fourier space is described by the multiplication with an appropriate phase factor. The numerical scheme truncates the Fourier series. Therefore, we only consider $-m \leq k \leq m$. Note that in the numerical implementation we employ the so-called discrete Fourier transform (DFT). The DFT replaces the integral necessary to determine the Fourier coefficient by a quadrature formula. It can alternatively be interpreted as a (trigonometric) polynomial interpolation.

Since $u(t,k)$ is a real function, only the non-negative frequencies have to be stored in memory. If exact arithmetics is used, we obtain an error bound that depends on the spatial regularity of the solution. For $u(t,\cdot) \in C^q(a,b)$, with $a < b$, and $u(t,\cdot)$ periodic in the first q derivatives we have

$$\|u(n\tau,x) - un(x)\| \leq Ch^{q-1},$$

where $h = (b - a)/m$ is the grid size. In particular, for periodic $u(t,\cdot) \in C^\infty(a,b)$ the convergence is super-polynomial in the number of grid points. This is the only discretization error provided that exact arithmetics is employed.

3. NUMERICAL INVESTIGATION

The purpose of this section is to present the results from a number of numerical simulations conducted. It will soon be apparent that the actual computations display a more complicated behavior as would be expected from the error estimates discussed in the previous section. Note that in all the numerical simulations conducted we have chosen to discretize problem (1) using $v = 1$.

In Fig. 1, we compare the error propagation for a Lagrange interpolation, a discontinuous Galerkin method, and the Fourier approximation using the initial value

$$u(0,x) = \frac{1}{2 + \cos \pi x}$$

on the interval $[-1,1]$ with periodic boundary conditions (the same interval and periodic boundary conditions are used for all simulations in this paper). As expected, initially the FFT method achieves a performance close to machine precision. Note, however, that the error growth is linear in the number of time steps. However, from a stochastic description of the round-off error one would expect an error growth proportional to the square root in the number of time steps. Let us postpone the detailed investigation of this issue until Section 5.

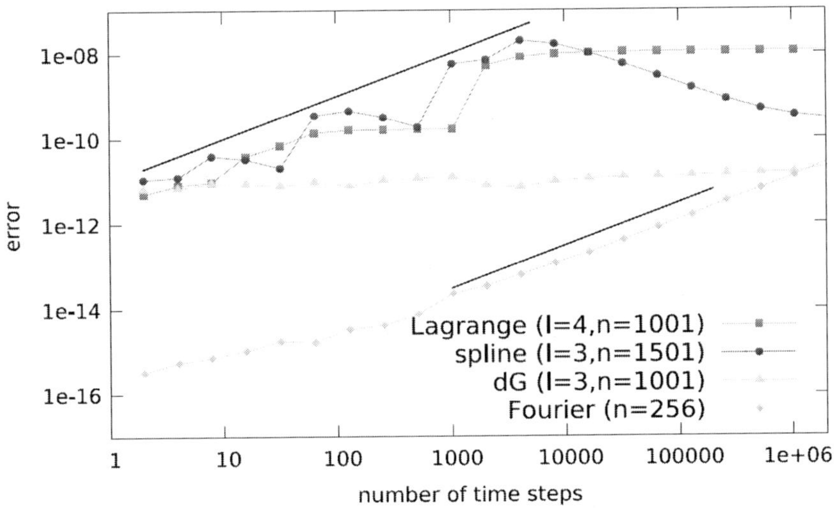

Figure. 1. The L^∞ error of the Lagrange, spline, dG, and FFT based methods, as a function of the number of time steps, is shown. The FFT routine from the FFTW library is used. The polynomial degree is denoted by l and the number of cells/grid points is denoted by n. As a reference two black lines of slope 1 are drawn.

Furthermore, even though the worst case error estimate for a general semi-Lagrangian method does include the term proportional to the number of steps, this is only observed for the Lagrange and the spline interpolation (see Fig. 1). However, the dG method does not exhibit such a behavior. In fact, there is almost no error propagation even after more than 10^6 steps in time have been conduced. In this instance, an error in the initial value that is orders of magnitude away from machine precision can still be competitive with the FFT based scheme (which shows a linear propagation of the error).

For both the Lagrange and the spline interpolation some oscillations do occur. In general, however, a linear error propagation is observed.

In Fig. 2 we compare different polynomial degrees for both the Lagrange and dG based methods with the initial value

$$u(0,x) = \cos 4\pi x. \tag{5}$$

As before, we initially observe a linear error growth, which yields a reduction in accuracy of at least three orders of magnitude for the Lagrange interpolation. No such behavior is observed for the dG method.

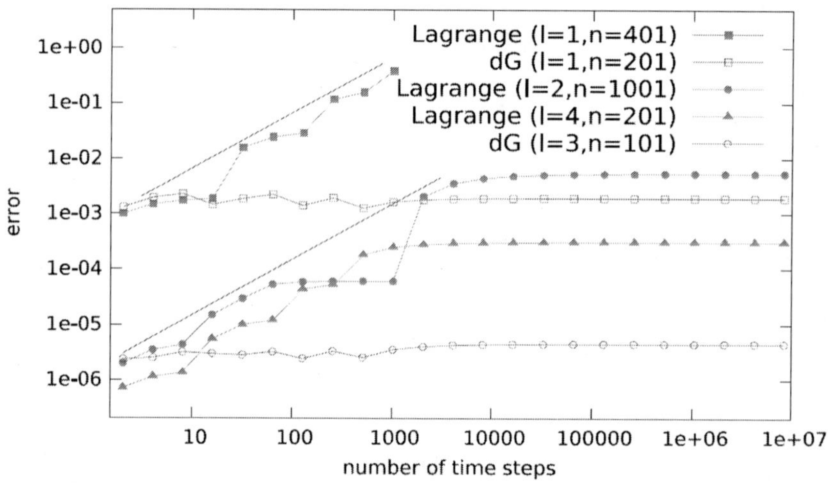

Figure. 2. The L^∞ error as a function of the number of time steps is shown for a number of different configurations (the interpolation degree l and the number of grid points/cells n of the Lagrange and dG interpolation methods are varied). The initial value given in (5) is used. As a reference two black lines of slope 1 are shown.

4. A THEORETICAL INVESTIGATION OF THE SEMI-LAGRANGIAN METHODS

In the previous section we observed a remarkable difference in the error propagation for the semi-Lagrangian methods employing Lagrange or spline interpolation on the one hand and the discontinuous Galerkin method on the other hand. The conjecture is that in case of the discontinuous Galerkin scheme the errors made in each step average to zero over the course of many time steps, while for the interpolation methods they are in fact well described by the worst case estimate stated in the introduction.

It is our goal now to provide an explanation for this behavior in the case of the linear Lagrange interpolation. For simplicity, let us choose $v = 1$ in Eq. (1). In addition, in this section, we employ a notation which drops the time dependence of u. Thus, we denote the initial value for a given time step by $u(x)$ and the ith grid point by x_i. A single time step of size τ (and with $v = 1$) then gives the new value at the ith grid point (which we denote by $\tilde{u}(x_i)$)

$$\tilde{u}(x_i) = \frac{1}{h}\left(\tau u(x_{i-1}) + (h - \tau)u(x_i)\right) \tag{6}$$

Note that we have restricted ourselves to $\tau < h$. This is justified as each advection with $\tau > h$ can be decomposed into an advection that can be solved exactly, where τ is a multiple of h, and an advection for which $\tau<h$ holds true.

The corresponding extension to the entire domain is then given by (where $\xi\in[0,h]$ is restricted to the cell under consideration)

$$\tilde{u}(x_i + \xi) = \frac{1}{h}\left((h - \xi)\tilde{u}(x_i) + \xi\tilde{u}(x_{i+1})\right) \tag{7}$$

Before we proceed, let us make two remarks. First, in what follows, we compute the error as compared to the advected initial value which lies in the space of piecewise linear functions (and not to the analytic initial value). This is in fact the correct choice as we are interested in the error propagation and not in the initial projection error (which clearly is bounded by Ch2 in this case). Second, the error is a function of two variables; the position $x = x_i + \zeta$ and the size of the time step τ.

Let us consider the average (with respect to the spatial variable in a single cell, which is denoted by ξ) for the exact advection

$$\begin{aligned}\frac{1}{h}\int_0^h u(x_i + \xi - \tau)\,d\xi &= \frac{1}{h}\int_{h-\tau}^h u(x_{i-1} + \xi)\,d\xi + \frac{1}{h}\int_0^{h-\tau} u(x_i + \xi)\,d\xi \\ &= \frac{\tau^2}{2h^2}u(x_{i-1}) + \frac{(h+\tau)^2 - 3\tau^2}{2h^2}u(x_i) + \frac{(h-\tau)^2}{2h^2}u(x_{i+1})\end{aligned}$$

and for the linear Lagrangian interpolation (using (7) and (6))

$$\frac{1}{h}\int_0^h \tilde{u}(x_i+\xi)\,\mathrm{d}\xi = \frac{\tau}{2h}u(x_{i-1}) + \frac{1}{2}u(x_i) + \frac{h-\tau}{2h}u(x_{i+1})$$

Now, since we are interested in simulations where a large number of steps has to be conducted it is reasonable to assume that for a fixed cell in the computational grid the step size $\tau \in [0,h]$ is uniformly distributed across that interval. Thus, the average in a single cell (averaged in both space as well as step size) for the exact solution is given by

$$\frac{1}{h}\int_0^h \frac{1}{h}\int_0^h u(x_i+\xi-\tau)\,\mathrm{d}\xi\,\mathrm{d}\tau = \frac{1}{6}\left(u(x_{i-1}) + 4u(x_i) + u(x_{i+1})\right)$$

whereas for the linear Lagrangian interpolation we get

$$\frac{1}{h}\int_0^h \frac{1}{h}\int_0^h \tilde{u}(x_i+\xi)\,\mathrm{d}\xi\,\mathrm{d}\tau = \frac{1}{4}\left(u(x_{i-1}) + 2u(x_i) + u(x_{i+1})\right)$$

The double averaged error $\bar{\bar{e}}$ in a single cell is therefore given by

$$\bar{\bar{e}} = \frac{1}{12}\left(u(x_{i-1}) - 2u(x_i) + u(x_{i+1})\right) \approx \frac{h^2}{12}u''(x_i)$$

Since there is a non-zero average error this error is amplified in each time step and gives a linear error propagation. Similarly to this computation we can also derive results for higher degree Lagrange interpolation. For the case of piecewise quadratic polynomials, for example, we get

$$\begin{aligned}\bar{\bar{e}} &= \frac{1}{144}\left(u(x_{i-2}) + 2u(x_{i-1}) - 12u(x_i) + 14u(x_{i+1}) - 5u(x_{i+2})\right)\\ &\approx -\frac{h^3}{24}u^{(3)}(x_i).\end{aligned}$$

In contrast, the discontinuous Galerkin method by construction preserves the average exactly. This is a necessary condition (but not a sufficient one) in order for the errors to cancel out on average. This is, of course, a different way of stating that the dG scheme is locally conservative for any step size while the Lagrange interpolation is not. The fact that most semi-Lagrangian schemes are not conservative is well established in the literature. To remedy this deficiency usually high-order methods are employed which provide sufficient accuracy to keep the violation in mass conservation to an acceptable level.

However, in our context this is not a remedy since, as we have observed in the previous section, even a Lagrange interpolation that is of high accuracy will loose at least three orders of magnitude in precision after approximately 10^3time steps. This is no concern if an approximation correct to three digits is desired. However, it is a significant drawback if we are interested in accuracies close to machine precision.

Note that since the average error is proportional to the second derivative we would expect that this behavior can be observed in numerical simulations. To that end we consider the convex initial value

$$u(0,x) = (x - 1)(x + 1) \tag{8}$$

and the concave initial value

$$u(0,x) = -(x - 1)(x + 1). \tag{9}$$

In fact Fig. 3 shows the expected behavior. Note that the errors made do depend on both the step size τ as well as the position x.

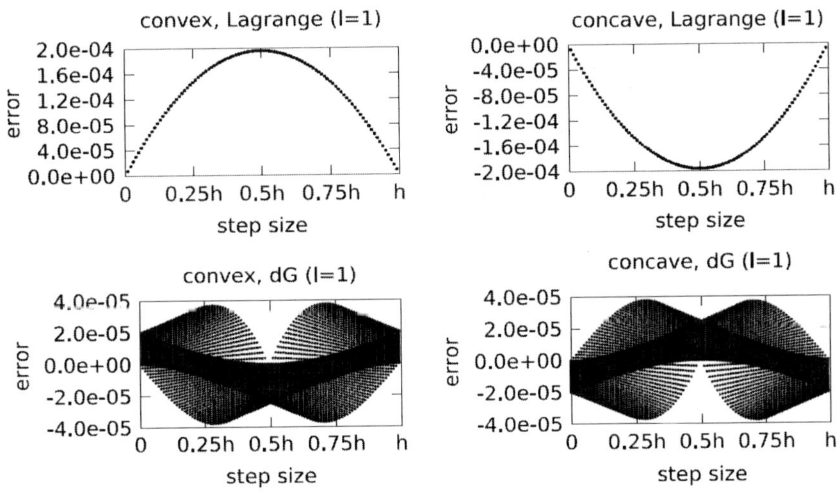

Figure. 3. The error, after a single time step of size $\tau \in [0,h]$, where h is the cell size, is shown for the convex (8) and concave (9) initial values. In case of the Lagrangian interpolation the error at the different grid points is plotted at the same position on the x-axis (the value of which corresponds to the step size τ). Since the errors are almost identical they lie on a point. For the dG method the errors computed at different (equidistant) positions (within a single cell) are displayed at the corresponding τ value.

For the Lagrange interpolation we have plotted the error at the different grid points at the same τ value (these points are almost identical and thus indistinguishable in the plot). In the case of the discontinuous Galerkin method we want to demonstrate that the error inside a single cell cancels out. Therefore, we have plotted the error at different points (but inside the same cell) at the same τ value.

In addition, we show the error as a function of the spatial variable in Fig. 4. As would be expected we observe an error that is similar to the second derivative of (4) for the Lagrange interpolation and an oscillatory error for the dG method.

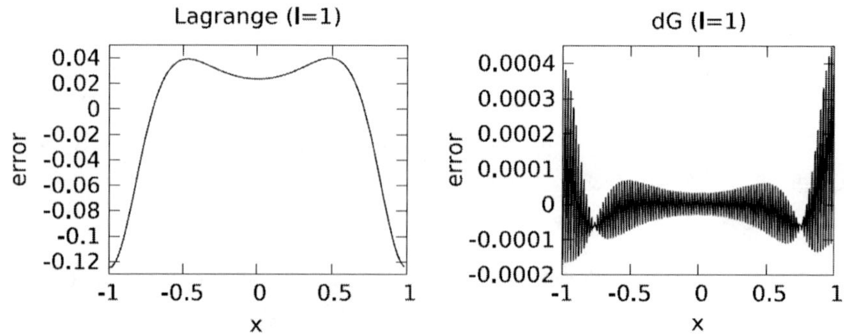

Figure. 4. The pointwise error after 10^4 steps of size $\tau = 2 \cdot 10^{-4}$ for the Lagrange and dG method (with 101 grid points) is shown. The left plot (Lagrange interpolation) matches the second derivative of (4) (the initial value used in this simulation). In case of the discontinuous Galerkin approximation the error displays small oscillations of high frequency.

5. FAST FOURIER TRANSFORM ROUND-OFF ERROR PROPAGATION

In the numerical simulations conducted in Section 3 we observed that the error growth is linear in the number of time steps (and not proportional to the square root as we would expect from a pure propagation of round-off errors). This behavior is consistent across numerical libraries; in Fig. 5 results using the FFTW (Fastest Fourier Transform in the West) library and the radix-2 implementation found in GSL (GNU Scientific Library) are shown.

An obvious explanation is to suggest that the phase factor used to compute the advection incurs some additional round-off errors. This phenomenon is well known in the context of reducing the round-off errors introduced by FFT routines (see e.g. [12]). In that context, care has to be taken that the twiddle factors are computed to sufficient accuracy. A similar approach can be used to compute the phase factor in the advection. However, Fig. 6 clearly shows that the error growth is still linear in the number of time steps.

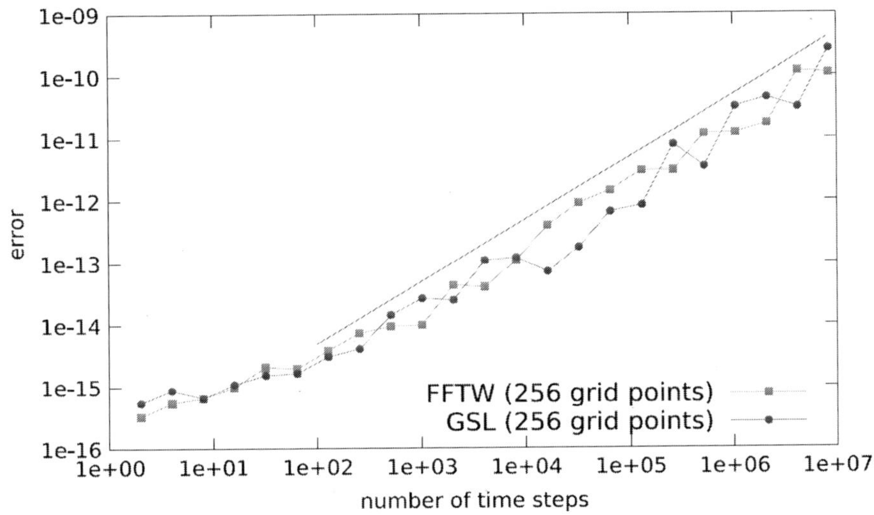

Figure. 5. The L^∞ error of the FFT based advection as a function of the number of time steps. Results for the FFTW and GSL library are shown. As a reference a black line with slope 1 is also displayed.

Note that the FFT algorithm as originally proposed by Cooley and Tukey is usually not implemented in high-performance FFT libraries (such as FFTW). A number of additional optimizations are performed. For the FFTW library a discussion can be found in [13]. These optimizations often have a significant impact on accuracy. Therefore, accuracy benchmarks are performed in order to verify that the round-off errors are reasonable (see, for example, [13]). However, in this paper we are interested in error propagation for a large number of time steps and not primarily with the scaling of the round-off error for large problem sizes.

In Fig. 7 the error propagation for the plain Cooley–Tukey algorithm is shown for the initial value

$$u(0,x) = \frac{1}{2+\cos(\pi x + \varphi)} \tag{10}$$

where φ is chosen at random. Even though the error propagation is significantly reduced compared to the FFTW implementation, at least four orders of magnitude are lost and the initial error growth is still linear.

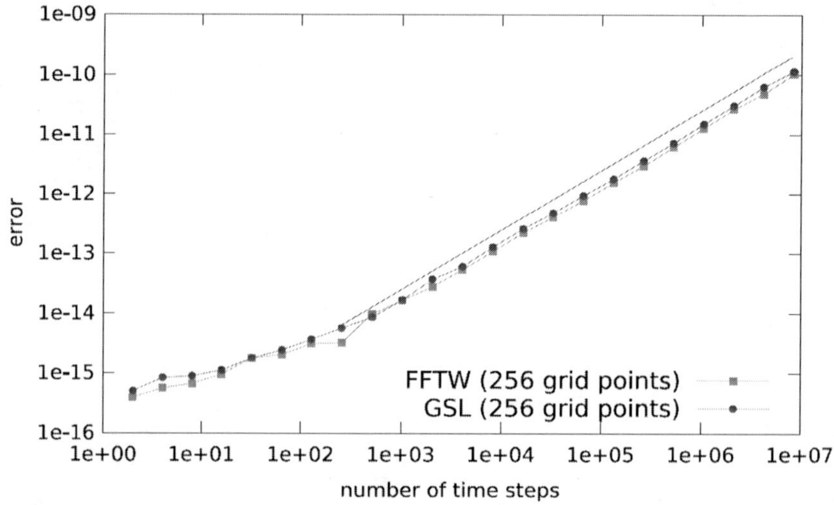

Figure. 6. L^∞ error of the FFT based advection as a function of the number of time steps. The phase factor needed for the translation and the corresponding combination with the signal is computed in high precision arithmetics and then rounded down to double precision. As a reference a black line with slope 1 is also shown.

If, in addition, the multiplications in the fast Fourier transform are computed to a higher precision, the error growth shows a behavior that is roughly proportional to the square root of the number of steps. In Fig. 7 the multiplications have been implemented in the 80 bit extended precision type[1] implemented in the x86 hardware.

In the naive implementation used here we observe a reduction in performance of about 10%–15%. Note, however, that if vectorization is used such procedures can result in a more severe reduction in performance.

On the other hand, this approach would also be advantageous, if double precision floating point computations significantly impact performance (such as commonly found on GPU systems). In this case the input and the output would be stored as single precision floating point numbers and multiplications would be performed as double precision (with appropriately computed twiddle factors) and then correctly rounded to single precision.

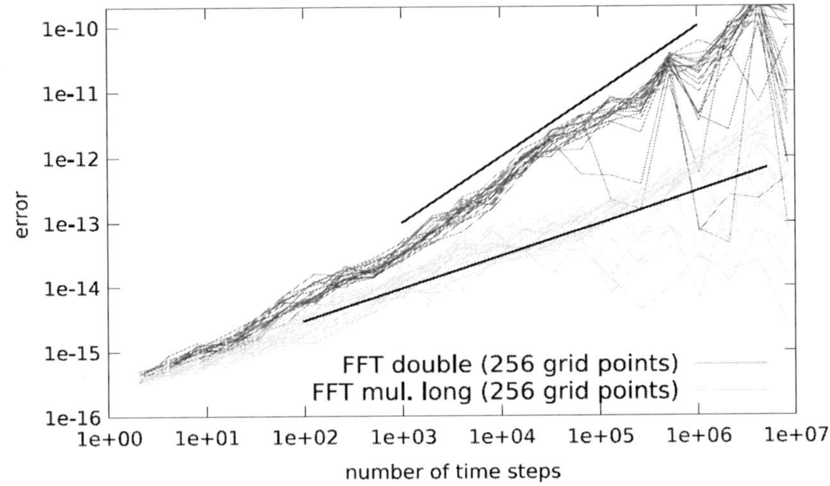

Figure. 7. The L^∞ error of the FFT based advection as a function of the number of time steps is shown for a number of different initial values as given in Eq. (10). The plain FFT implementation following the Cooley–Tukey algorithm (blue) and a plain FFT algorithm where the multiplications for the phase factor as well as in the Cooley–Tukey algorithm are carried out in 80-bit arithmetics (green) are compared. Note that in the latter case the storage requirement is still essentially the same (that is we do only have to store the input and output vector, in double precision, as well as the twiddle factors). As a reference two black lines with slope 1 (upper line) and slope 1/2 (lower line) are shown. (For interpretation of the references to color in this figure legend, the reader is referred to the web version of this article.)

6. SPLITTING OF AN ADVECTION EQUATION WITH SOURCE TERM

In this section we consider the advection equation supplemented by a (position dependent) source term. That is, we consider

$$\partial_t u(t,x) + \partial_x u(t,x) = s(x), \tag{11}$$

where the source term is chosen as $s(x) = (1 + \cos \pi x)\cos 5\pi x$ and periodic boundary conditions are imposed. The solution can be easily determined by the method of characteristics

$$u(t,x) = u_0(x-t) + \int_0^t s(x-t+\sigma)\,\mathrm{d}\sigma$$

which for the initial value given in (4) is plotted in Fig. 8 (top left).

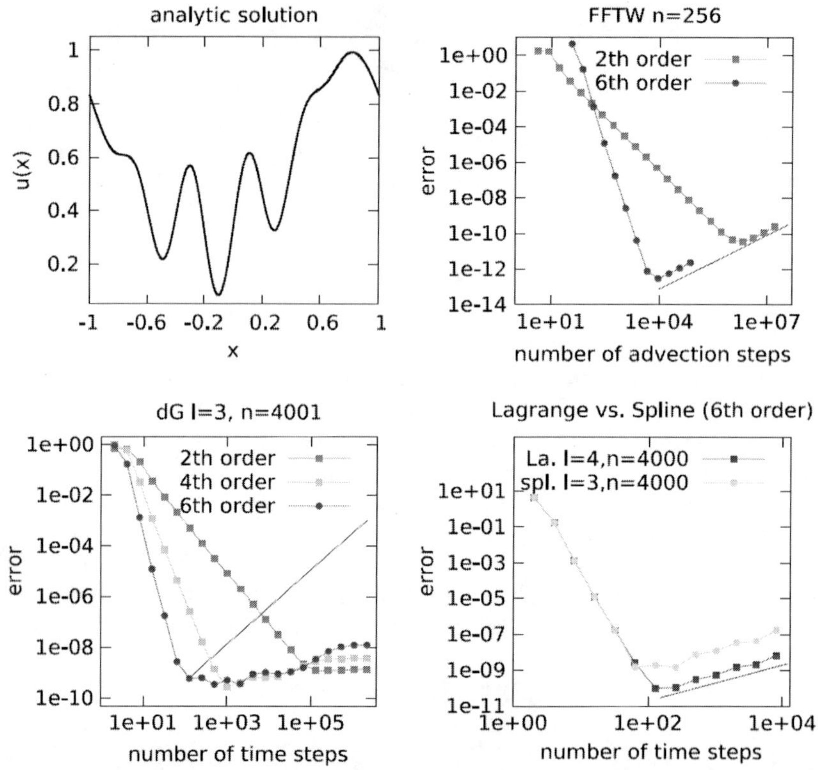

Figure. 8. The solution of (11) is computed for the final time $t = 1.8$. The analytical solution is shown on the top left. The numerical solution is computed using a splitting approach. The results for the FFT based method (top right), the discontinuous Galerkin (dG) method (bottom left), and the Lagrange and spline interpolations (bottom right) are shown. The black lines have slope 1 and are shown for comparison.

For the time integration we employ the second order Strang splitting scheme as well as the 6th order scheme constructed from it by composition (see, for example, [14]). An approximation to the solution of the first sub-problem (the advection equation) can be computed as described in the previous sections. The remaining sub-problem (corresponding to the source term) is easily solved analytically. Note, however, that in the case of the dG method only the coefficients (in the Legendre expansion) are stored in memory. Thus, in each cell, we evaluate the approximation at the Gauss–Legendre points. We then compute the solution of the sub-problem on these points and use the result to reconstruct the coefficients.

The numerical simulations conducted confirm the observations made in the previous sections. For the FFT based method (using the FFTW library) we see, after a decrease in the error due to the time discretization error, the characteristic linear increase in the error (see Fig. 8 top right). Furthermore, we observe that, as expected, the lowest error we can achieve for a given time discretization is only dependent on the number of advection steps that have to be made in order to reach that tolerance (thus the method of order six is clearly the preferred choice in this case). All these phenomena are due to round-off errors only.

The spline and Lagrange interpolations show a similar behavior. However, in this case the linear increase in the error (for further decreasing step size) is dependent on the space discretization (see Fig. 8 bottom right).

For the dG method, on the other hand, the minimal error that can be achieved (for a given space discretization) is almost independent of the numerical method used in time. Of course, the 6th order method is usually more efficient if high precision is desired. However, if a large number of time steps are taken with the Strang splitting scheme, a similar accuracy than for the 6th order method can be achieved (without changing the space discretization). Furthermore, there is no linear increase in the error. All these observations are in line with the observations made in Sections 3 and 4.

7. CONCLUSION

In this paper we have considered the error propagation for the advection equation in the case where high precision is desired. The numerical methods considered exhibit a variety of different phenomena.

In case of the fast Fourier transform method round-off errors are the primary concern. A number of libraries that implement the FFT show a linear error growth in the number of time steps. However, if the multiplication of the Fourier coefficients with the twiddle factors is performed to sufficient accuracy the growth in the error is only proportional to the square root in the number of time steps.

Furthermore, we have shown that the term proportional to the number of time steps, that is routinely obtained in error estimates for semi-Lagrangian methods, is not observed for all semi-Lagrangian schemes. In fact it is true that the qualitative features of the error are markedly different for the interpolation (Lagrange as well as spline) and the discontinuous Galerkin based semi-Lagrangian schemes considered in this paper.

REFERENCES

1. K. Morton, A. Priestley, E. Süli **Stability of the Lagrange–Galerkin method with non-exact integration** Modél. Math. Anal. Numér., 22 (4) (1988), pp. 625-653
2. Staniforth, J. Côté **Semi-Lagrangian integration schemes for atmospheric models—a review** Mon. Weather Rev., 119 (9) (1991), pp. 2206-2223
3. F. Filbet, E. Sonnendrücker **Comparison of Eulerian Vlasov solvers** Comput. Phys. Comm., 150 (3) (2003), pp. 247-266

A. Klimas, W. Farrell **A splitting algorithm for Vlasov simulation with filamentation filtration** J. Comput. Phys., 110 (1) (1994), pp. 150-163

4. D. Bailey **High-precision floating-point arithmetic in scientific computation** Comput. Sci. Eng., 7 (3) (2005), pp. 54-61
5. Y. He, C. Ding, Using accurate arithmetics to improve numerical reproducibility and stability in parallel applications, in: Proceedings of the 14th International Conference on Supercomputing, ICS'00, New York, NY, USA, 2000, pp. 225–234.
6. NVIDIA cuFFT Library. https://developer.nvidia.com/cufft (Last retrieved November 11, 2014).
7. L. Einkemmer, A. Ostermann, A splitting approach for the Kadomtsev–Petviashvili equation, 2014. ArXiv Preprint, arXiv:1407.8154.
8. N. Besse **Convergence of a semi-Lagrangian scheme for the one-dimensional Vlasov–Poisson system** SIAM J. Numer. Anal., 42 (1) (2004), pp. 350-382
9. L. Einkemmer, A. Ostermann **Convergence analysis of a discontinuous Galerkin/Strang splitting approximation for the Vlasov–Poisson equations** SIAM J. Numer. Anal., 52 (2) (2014), pp. 757-778
10. L. Einkemmer, A. Ostermann **Convergence analysis of Strang splitting for Vlasov-type equations** SIAM J. Numer. Anal., 52 (1) (2014), pp. 140-155
11. J. Schatzman **Accuracy of the discrete Fourier transform and the fast Fourier transform** SIAM J. Sci. Comput., 17 (5) (1996), pp. 1150-1166
12. FFT Accuracy Benchmark Comments. http://www.fftw.org/accuracy/comments.html (Last retrieved November 11, 2014).
13. E. Hairer, C. Lubich, G. Wanner **Geometric Numerical Integration: Structure-Preserving Algorithms for Ordinary Differential Equations** Springer, Berlin, Heidelberg (2006)

CHAPTER 8

Surface Roughness Modeling Using Q-Sequence

A.M.M. Sharif Ullah

Kitami Institute of Technology, 165 Koen-cho, Kitami, Hokkaido 090-8507, Japan

ABSTRACT

Dynamical systems play a vital role in studying highly non-linear phenomena. One of the families of the dynamical systems is integer sequences. There is an integer sequence called Q-sequence: $Q(n) = Q(n - Q(n - 1)) + Q(n - Q(n - 2))$; for $n = 3, 4, \ldots$; and $Q(1) = Q(2) = 1$. It exhibits a unique chaotic-order that might help develop approximate models of highly nonlinear phenomena. We explore this possibility and show how to modify a segment of the Q-sequence so that the modified segment becomes an approximate model of surface roughness (a highly non-linear phenomena that results from the material removal processes (e.g., turning, milling, grinding, and so on). The Q-sequence-based models of surface roughness can be used to recreate the surface heights whenever necessary. As such, it is a helpful means for developing simulation systems for virtual manufacturing.

Keywords: dynamical systems; integer sequence; chaos; surface roughness; modeling

1. INTRODUCTION

We often measure the dimensions, forms, and surfaces of artificial artifacts and see whether they are consistent with the given specifications. This has created a discipline of study called metrology. International standards have been developed to systematize the activities underlying this discipline [1]. A great deal of research has been conducted to develop reliable electro-mechanical devices for dimensional, form, and surface metrology [2,3,4,5]. Particularly in surface metrology [6], we deal with the heights of a machined surfaces measured by contact or non-contact instruments [4,5,6]. International standards provide a set of standards to measure the surface heights and then to process (filter [7], and quantify) them for surface characterization [1]. According to these standards, for example, the roughness of a machined surface is often quantified by such standard parameters as arithmetic average height R_a, peak-to-valley height R_z, fractal dimension, and so on [8]. Sometimes, non-conventional parameters, e.g., entropy [8], are also used for quantifying the surface roughness. Some authors have worked on the uncertainty modeling of surface roughness using probability-distribution-neutral representation, e.g., possibility distributions and fuzzy numbers [8]. Nowadays, we have Web-based systems, e.g., the system developed by the National Institute of Standards and Technology (NIST, Gaithersburg, MD, USA) [9], by which one can determine the standard roughness parameters online [1]. In addition, to share the evaluated surface roughness, efforts have been made to create web-based data, e.g., XML data incorporating the information of R_a [10]. Even though we characterized a surface by using R_a, R_z, entropy, fractal dimension, and possibility distribution, an individual/system who/that receives this information will not be able to recreate the surface heights. This means that we lose the surface height dynamics if we use the conventional quantification process described above. Thus, we need another means to capture the *dynamics* of surface roughness so that the individual/system) who/that) receives it can recreate it whenever necessary. It has been stressed that the manufacturing phenomena (e.g., the cutting force and even the surface roughness) are highly non-linear and can be modeled, in principle, by stationary and non-stationary Gaussian processes [11,12,13]. A surface roughness profile, in particular, consists of certain stochastic features [11], and to recreate the heights of a surface roughness profile, i.e., to capture the dynamics underlying a surface roughness profile, one needs to model these features using stochastic formulations [11,14]. This issue of dynamic representation of surface roughness has become even more important due to the advent of Internet of Things (IoT) [15], as schematically illustrated in Figure 1.

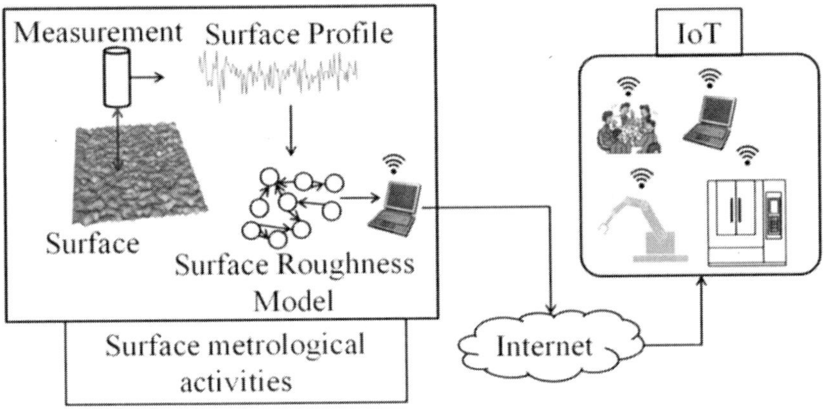

Figure 1. Surface metrological activities from the viewpoint of Internet of Things (IoT).

IoT involved in the manufacturing systems requires cyber-physical systems [15,16,17,18] where the hardware and software systems will not only share the static data of non-linear phenomena of manufacturing activities but also the models that are capable of storing and sharing the underlying dynamics. A scenario of such futuristic systems is schematically shown in Figure 1 where the surface metrology activities are considered as an example. As seen from Figure 1, as far as the IoT is concerned, not only surface roughness quantification but also the modeling of surface heights is important for surface metrology. The model must capture the dynamics of the surface roughness so that it (the model) can recreate the surface heights whenever necessary in IoT-based systems, as schematically illustrated in Figure 1.

However, numerous authors have developed methods and tools to capture the dynamics of machined surface heights. For example, Wu [19] developed a methodology to simulate engineered surfaces using Fast Fourier Transform (FFT) where a given spectral density or auto-correlation function (ACF) is used as a means to model the irregular heights of a surface. Higuchi et al. [20] applied the concept of fractional Brownian motion (fBm) to simulate the surface heights of grinding wheels. Ullah et al. [21] developed a dynamical system that operates on some fuzzy if–then rules to simulate the surface roughness heights. Here, the fuzzy if–then rules are extracted from a given surface roughness profile. Ullah et al. [11] considered that the surface heights of a machined surface consist of four features, namely, trend, cycle, irregularities, and burst. They developed a stochastic model to organize these features and to recreate surface heights. Uchidate et al. [22] introduced an autoregression based model to create surface heights for the sake of soft-calibration. Sharif Ullah et al. [23] modeled the microscopic interactions between workpiece and tool (e.g., a grinding wheel) that are stochastic in nature to simulate the surface heights of a machined surface for several passes. Nevertheless, the methodologies developed so far to capture the dynamics of surface roughness, e.g., the methodologies described in [11,19,20,21,22,23] and in the references therein, are parameter-dependent, requiring a great deal of efforts of the users to set the right values of a relatively large number of parameters. Therefore, a simpler but user-friendly methodology is needed to model the dynamics of the surface roughness. From this contemplation, this article is written. In particular, an integer sequence called the Q-sequence [24] will be employed to create a model of a surface profile. The remainder of this article is organized as follows:

Section 2 describes the main features of the Q-sequence. Section 3 describes a modification process of the Q-sequence. Section 4 describes how to create an approximate model of surface profile heights using a modified Q-sequence. Section 5provides the discussions and concluding remarks of this article.

2. Q-SEQUENCE

This section describes the main features of Q-sequence. Hofstadter introduced a dynamical system consisting of integers called Q-sequence [24] as follows:

$$Q(n) = \begin{cases} 1 & n = 1, 2 \\ Q(n - Q(n-1)) + Q(n - Q(n-2)) & Otherwise \end{cases} \quad (1)$$

In Equation (1), n is a natural number, i.e., n = 1, 2, 3, 4, etc. The first 100 values of $Q(n)$ are as follows: 1, 1, 2, 3, 3, 4, 5, 5, 6, 6, 6, 8, 8, 8, 10, 9, 10, 11, 11, 12, 12, 12, 12, 16, 14, 14, 16, 16, 16, 16, 20, 17, 17, 20, 21, 19, 20, 22, 21, 22, 23, 23, 24, 24, 24, 24, 24, 32, 24, 25, 30, 28, 26, 30, 30, 28, 32, 30, 32, 32, 32, 32, 40, 33, 31, 38, 35, 33, 39, 40, 37, 38, 40, 39, 40, 39, 42, 40, 41, 43, 44, 43, 43, 46, 44, 45, 47, 47, 46, 48, 48, 48, 48, 48, 48, 64, 41, 52, 54, and 56. Figure 2 shows the nature of $Q(n) \in \aleph^{+}$ for $n \leq 2000$ (i.e., relatively small values of n). Pinn [25] studied the chaotic behavior that $Q(n)$ exhibits for both small and large values of n. Some of the characteristics reported in [25] are as follows: (1) On short scales, $Q(n)$ looks chaotic having groups of generations of sequences. (2) The k-th generation has $2k$ members which have "parents" mostly in the generation $k - 1$, and a few from the generation $k - 2$. In other words, in a short scale, a segment of $Q(n)$ consists of integers that are close to each other. (3) $Q(n)$ has bursts with increasing amplitude and length. (4) The trend in $Q(n)$ disappears if the integer part of $n/2$ is subtracted. This is true if n is relatively small.

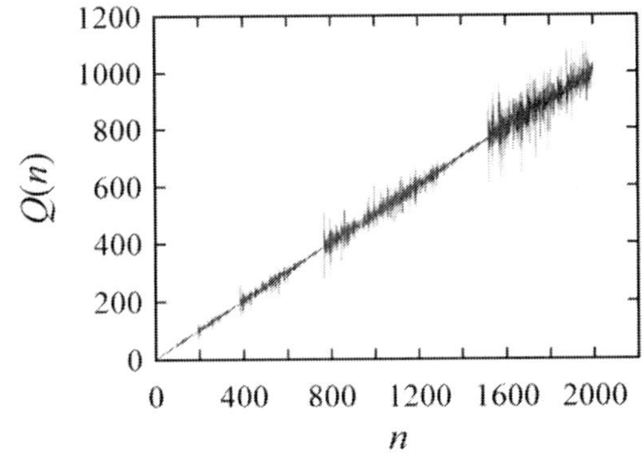

Figure 2. The nature of the Q-sequence for small values of n.

This results in another integer sequence denoted as $S(n) \in \mathfrak{I}$ and given as

$$S(n) = Q(n) - Int\left(\frac{n}{2}\right). \tag{2}$$

Figure 3 shows the time series plot of $S(n)$ for the small values of n. As seen from Figure 3, similar to $Q(n)$, $S(n)$ also shows bursts at intervals n = 3, 6, 12, 24, 48, 96, etc.

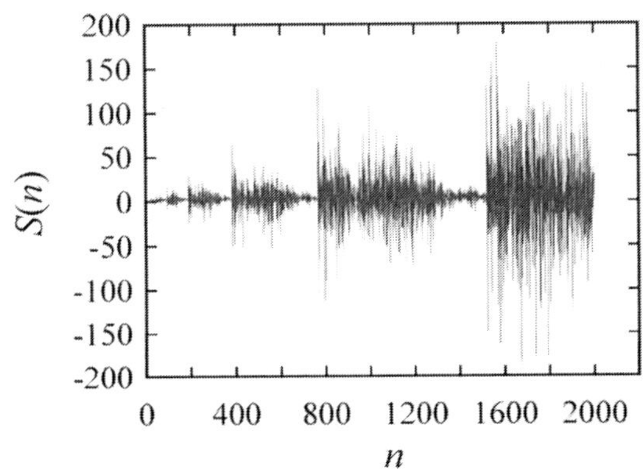

Figure 3. The nature of $S(n)$ for small values of n.

However, the trend seen in $Q(n)$ disappears in the case of $S(n)$. It can be modified in different ways to model non-linear signals. This issue is elaborated in the subsequent sections taking the case of surface roughness modeling.

3. MODIFYING THE Q-SEQUENCE

This section shows a simple but useful modification technique of Q-sequence for the sake of modeling non-linear signals. Here, the Q-sequence refers to its trendless counterpart, i.e., $S(n)$. In particular, a small segment of $S(n)$ between two consecutive bursts can be used to create an approximate model of highly nonlinear signals, e.g., cutting force and surface roughness. The modification process uses successive linear interpolations that gradually expand a small segment of $S(n)$. The formal description of this modification process is as follows.

Let $S(n1,n2)$ be a segment of $S(n)$, where $n2 > n1$, as follows:

$$S(n1,n2)=[S(n1),S(n1+1)...S(n2)]. \tag{3}$$

Let us consider a segment of $S(n)$, $S(n1 = 1000,\ n2 = 1200)$. This segment is taken between two consecutive bursts of $S(n)$. The time series plot and the return-map of this segment are shown in Figure 4.

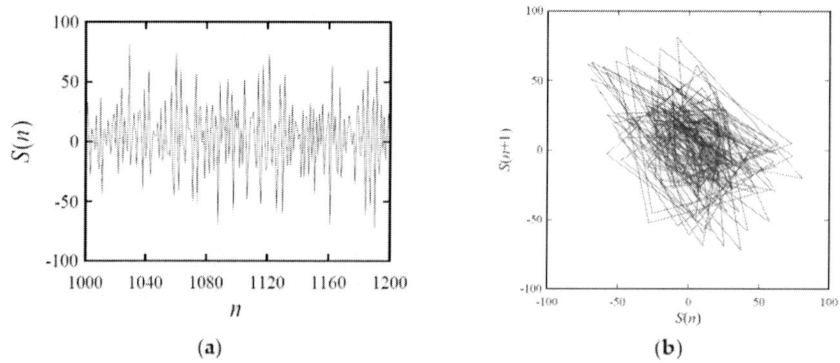

Figure 4. The time series and return-map of $S(1000,1200)$: (**a**) time series; (**b**) return-map.

In general, a return-map (or delay map) is a point-cloud that consists of a set of ordered-pairs or points of the nature $\{(y(t),y(t+j)) \in \Re^2 \mid t = 0,1, ...,$

$\exists j \in \{1, 2, ...\}\}$ created from a time series $y(t) \in \Re$, $t = 0, 1$, etc. It can represent the hidden order underlying the parameter considered, which is difficult to grasp from the time series plot alone. For this reason, when one studies a non-linear behavior or dynamical system, e.g., $S(n)$, return-maps are prepared along with the time series to attain more insights into it [26]. This role of the return-map can be understood clearly when one compares the time series plots and the return-maps shown in the remainder of this article.

However, one can modify $S(n1,n2)$ by adding more integers without destroying its apparent look. The easiest way to achieve this is to add an integer at the middle of every two consecutive integers of $S(n1,n2)$. To be more specific, let $R(t,1)$ be an integer sequence wherein all integers of $S(n1,n2)$ are included in addition to the integers that are the integer parts of the average of every two consecutive points of $S(n1,n2)$. Therefore, the following formulation holds:

$$R(t,1) = \begin{cases} S(n1+t) & t = 0,2,4,\ldots,a \\ Int\left(\frac{S(n1+t)+S(n1+t+1)}{2}\right) & Otherwise. \end{cases} \quad (4)$$

In Equation (4), $a = n2 - n1$ or $n2 - n1 - 1$, if it is an even or odd number, respectively.

Figure 5 shows the time series plot and the return map of $R(t,1)$ corresponding to $S(n1 = 1000, n2 = 1200)$.

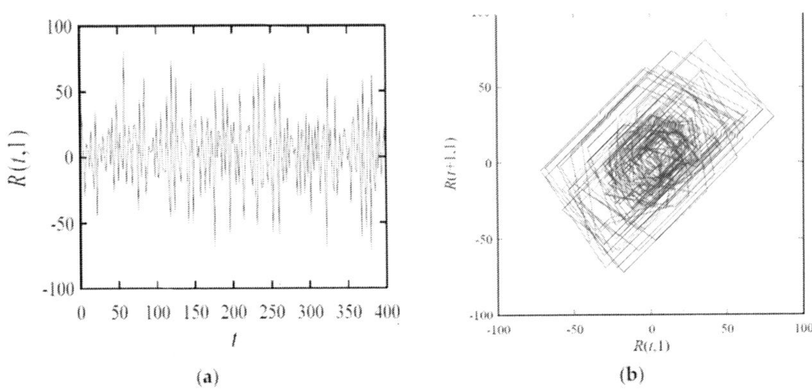

Figure 5. The time series and return-map of $R(t,1)$ corresponding to $S(1000,1200)$: (**a**) time series; (**b**) return-map.

The difference between $S(1000,1200)$ and $R(t,1)$ is not visible from their time series plots as shown in Figure 4 and Figure 5, respectively, whereas their difference is visible when the return-maps as shown in Figure 4 and Figure 5 are compared. In particular, the return-map shown in Figure 4 is more scattered compared to that shown in Figure 5. This means that the gap between two consecutive points in Figure 5 is smaller than that in Figure 4, which is expected.

If needed, $R(t,1)$ can be expanded further, as follows:

$$R(t,i+1) = \begin{cases} R(t,i) & t = 0,2,4,\ldots \\ Int\left(\frac{R(t,i)+R(t+1,i)}{2}\right) & Otherwise \end{cases} \quad (5)$$

In Equation (5), $\forall i \in \{1, 2, ...\}$. For example, Figure 6 and Figure 7 show the time series plots and return-maps of the integer sequences $R(t,2)$ and $R(t,3)$ found after applying the linear interpolation, as defined in Equation (5), to $R(t,1)$ and $R(t,2)$, respectively.

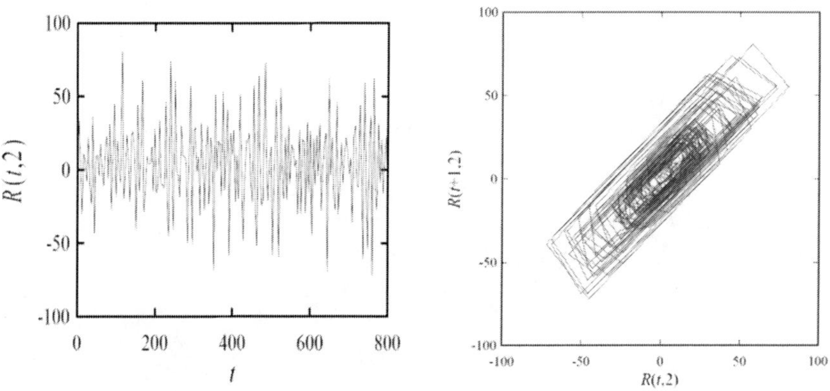

(a) (b)

Figure 6. The time series and return-map of $R(t,2)$ corresponding to $S(1000,1200)$: (**a**) time series; (**b**) return-map.

As a synopsis, the following remarks can be made: (a) All return maps of $R(t,i)$, i = 1, 2, 3, follow a trend—a straight line with a unit slope. (b) The spread of the points in all return-maps decreases with the increase in the number of points in the sequence or decreases with the increase in i. (c) Most of the points in the return maps are located at the middle portion and relatively fewer points are located at two extremes. (d) The return-maps of two nearby $R(t,i)$, i.e., $R(t,1)$ and $R(t,2)$ or $R(t,2)$ and $R(t,3)$, are somewhat similar but the return-maps of the sequences that are relatively far from each other in terms of i(here, $R(t,1)$ and $R(t,3)$) look significantly different. Therefore, while modeling a highly irregular set of data points (e.g., the data points representing the heights of a processed surface), one must consult both the time series plot and its return-map. This strategy will be used to model a surface roughness profile, as described in the next section.

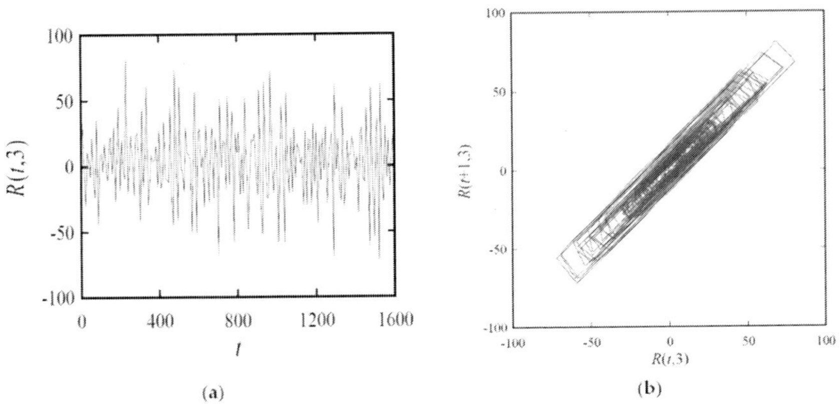

Figure 7. The time series plot and return-map of $R(t,3)$ corresponding to $S(1000,1200)$: (**a**) time series; (**b**) return-map.

4. MODELING SURFACE ROUGHNESS

This section describes how to model a surface roughness profile using the integer sequences, $R(t,i)$, $i = 1, 2, \ldots$

First, consider a surface roughness profile denoted as $z(t) \in \Re$, $i = 0, 1, \ldots, 250$, and its return-map $\{(z(t),z(t + 1)) \mid i = 0, \ldots, 250\}$, as shown in Figure 8. This surface roughness profile is one of the surface roughness profiles found while (surface) grinding a specimen made of glass using a Cubic Boron Nitride (cBN) grinding wheel in different grinding conditions. The experiments were performed at the Kitami Institute of Technology under the supervision of the author. A non-contact surface metrology instrument measures the primary profile of the ground surfaces. The NIST Surface Metrology Algorithm Testing System [27] removes the form error from the primary profile. No other filtering was applied to remove the waviness from the surface heights obtained after removing the form error. One can calculate the standard roughness parameters as prescribed in the ISO standard [1] using the surface heights shown in Figure 8.

Calculating the values of these parameters does not preserve the dynamics of the roughness profile. Instead, if one can establish a model of the dynamics of the roughness profile, then it (the established model) can be used within the framework of IoT [14,15,16,17,18], or any other means, to recreate the profile heights. From the recreated profile heights, the standard roughness parameters can be calculated, if needed. This means that to achieve the cyber-physical system [14,15,16,17,18] of the surface metrology, it is more meaningful to create a model of the dynamic of the roughness profile than to just calculate the values of the roughness parameter. From this viewpoint, this section describes a procedure to modify the integer sequences, particularly, the ones given by $R(t,i)$. The goal is to make it a model of the surface roughness heights or to store the dynamics of the surface roughness for the sake of recreation.

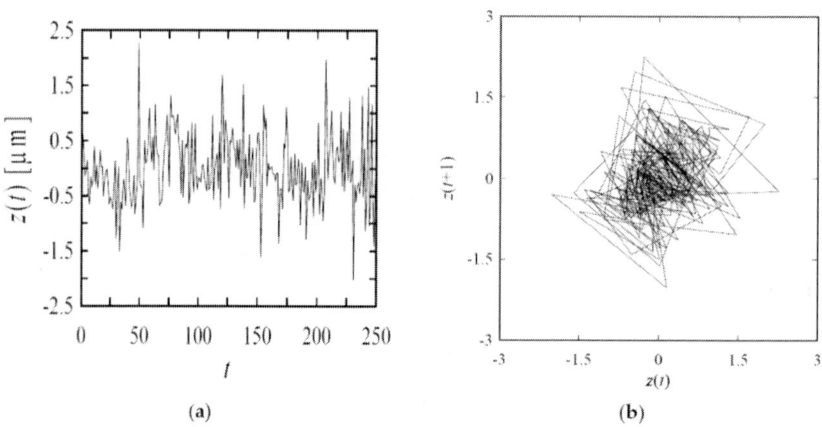

Figure 8. A surface profile and its return-map: (**a**) surface heights; (**b**) return-map.

For the sake of modeling, the surface roughness profile shown in Figure 8 has been expanded by the linear interpolation using the procedure defined in Equations (4) and (5). (Note that the operation denoted as *Int* is not performed this time). The profile after the second linear interpolation denoted as $z(t,2)$ is shown in Figure 9 in terms of the time series plot and return-map. The return-map shown in Figure 9 exhibits similar irregularities compared to that of $R(t,3)$ (Figure 7). This means that $R(t,3)$ has a potential to become a model of the interpolated roughness profile $z(t,2)$.

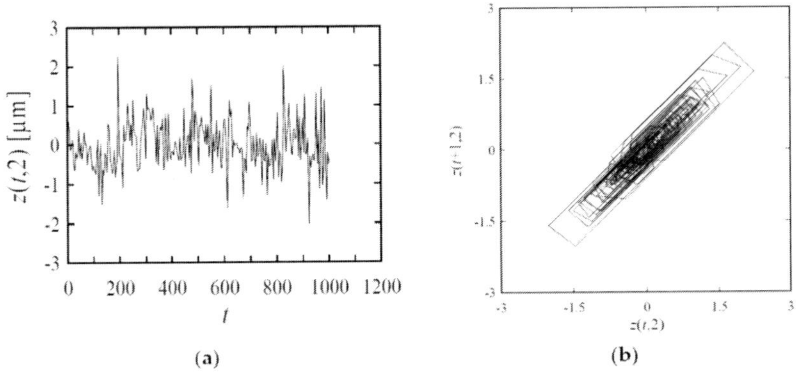

Figure 9. The time series plot and return-map of the linear interpolated roughness profile: (**a**) time series; (**b**) return-map.

To make the comparison between $R(t,3)$ and $z(t,2)$ even more meaningful, $R(t,3)$ can be scaled to $z(t)$ and then shifted by an amount $\alpha \in \Re$ (a small real number), resulting in a time series $V(t)$ as follows:

$$V(t) = z_{\text{max}} - \frac{r_{\text{max}} - R(t,3)}{r_{\text{max}} - r_{\text{min}}}(z_{\text{max}} - z_{\text{min}}) + \alpha. \tag{6}$$

In Equation (6), $z_{\text{max}} = \max(z(t) \mid t = 0, 1, \ldots)$, $z_{\text{min}} = \min(z(t) \mid t = 0, 1, \ldots)$, $r_{\text{max}} = \max(R(t,3) \mid t = 0, 1, \ldots)$, and $r_{\text{min}} = \min(R(t,3) \mid t = 0, 1, \ldots)$. If needed, one can add noises using a stochastic process, e.g., a noise that follows normal distribution [28], to $V(t)$ to make it even more meaningful. The idea of adding such a stochastic noise is kept out of the scope of this article, however.

For the sake of visual inspection, the segments of $V(t)$ and $z(t,2)$ for $t = 0$, 1, ..., 500, are shown in the same plot (Figure 10), where z_{max} = 2.260563913, $z_{\text{min}} = -2.020452268$, $r_{\text{max}} = 81$, $r_{\text{min}} = -72$, and $\alpha = -0.1$. As seen from time series plots in Figure 10, both segments show a similar kind of variability. The similarity between the variability is more evident in the plot of the return-maps. In particular, both return-maps overlap and have almost the identical returns from one point to another.

How about the quantitative similarities between $V(t)$ (the model) and $z(t,2)$ (real surface roughness)? To answer this question, the values of R_a, R_z, and Entropy are calculated as described in [8]. The results are summarized in Table 1. As seen from Table 1, R_z is the same for both model and real surface roughness profiles, whereas R_a of the model surface roughness is greater than that of the real surface roughness profile, and Entropy of the model surface roughness is less than that of the real surface roughness profile. This difference in Entropy refers to the fact that the real surface roughness heights exhibit more complexity than those of the model.

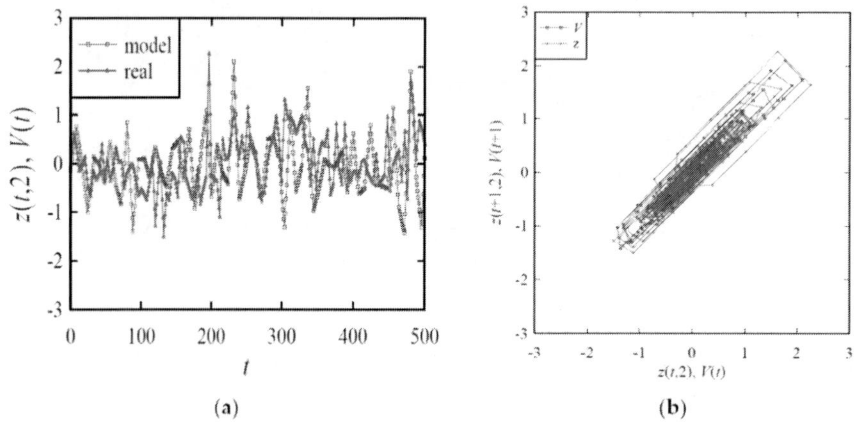

Figure 10. Comparison between the model and real surface roughness profiles: (**a**) time series; (**b**) return-map.

Table 1. Comparison between real and model surface roughness profiles.

Parameters	Model ($V(t)$)	Real ($z(t,2)$)
R_a (μm)	0.471	0.419
R_z (μm)	4.281	4.281
Entropy (Bits)	3.209	4.063

To gain more insight into the quantitative similarities between $V(t)$ and $z(t,2)$, possibility distributions can be constructed using the respective point-clouds (return-maps), as shown in Figure 10. A possibility distribution (or a fuzzy number) is a probability-distribution-neutral representation of the irregularity associated with a variable [28]. It helps compare two roughness profiles, too, as shown in [8]. Thus, the possibility distributions of the return-maps of $V(t)$ and $z(t,2)$ have been constructed using the procedure described in [28]. The results are shown in Figure 11. It is worth mentioning that the possibility distribution produces a more reliable quantification of uncertainties associated with physical quantities, e.g., the works described in [29,30] where possibility distributions have been used to quantify the uncertainties associated with materials properties of some natural materials..

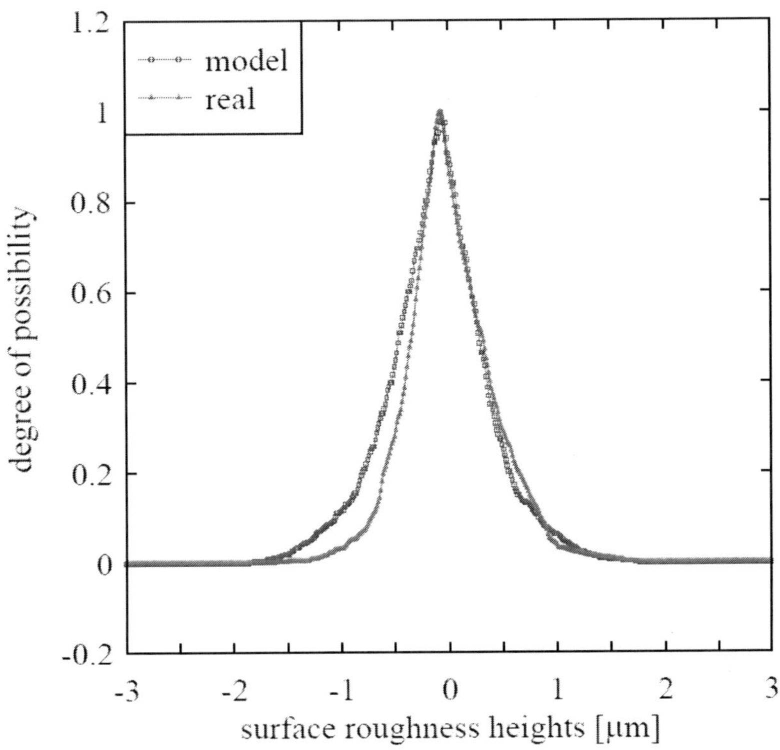

Figure 11. Comparison between real surface roughness and its model in terms of the degree of possibility.

As seen from Figure 11, the shapes of the possibility distributions are identical except for surface roughness heights in the range [−1.5, −0.5] μm, i.e., in the range located on the left hand side of the pick. For both cases, on the other hand, the picks are at about 0 μm.

The above descriptions collectively refer to the fact that a signal $V(t)$ derived from Q-sequence approximately models the dynamics of a surface roughness profile.

5. DISCUSSION AND CONCLUDING REMARKS

The results reported in Section 2, Section 3 and Section 4 collectively refer to a procedure of modeling the heights of a surface profile, as schematically illustrated in Figure 12. As seen from Figure 12, the following steps can be exhausted for modeling.

Step 1 Generate $Q(n)$ (Equation (1)).

Step 2 Generate $S(n)$ (Equation (2)).

Step 3 Select a segment of $S(n)$, $S(n1,n2)$ (Equation (3)).

Step 4 Expand $S(n1,n2)$ by a linear interpolation operation and generate $R(t,1)$ (Equation (4)).

Step 5 Expand $R(t,1)$ by successive linear interpolation and generate $R(t,i)$, $i = 1, 2, \ldots$ (Equation (5)).

Step 6 Select one of the $R(t,i)$, $\exists i \in \{1, 2, \ldots\}$.

Step 7 Scale and shift $R(t,i)$ selected in Step 6 and generate $V(t)$ (Equation (6)).

Step 8 Compare $V(t)$ with the given surface profile $z(t)$ or with one of its ($z(t)$'s) linear interpolated profiles, $z(t,j)$, $j = 1, 2$, etc.

Step 9 If the comparison is satisfactory in terms of qualitative and quantitative measures, then accept $V(t)$ as a model of the roughness profile. Create semantic web to use $V(t)$ in the framework of IoT. Otherwise, go back to Step 3 and continue.

Although the above procedure is applied to surface roughness only, it can also be applied to model other nonlinear signals such as cutting force. This issue can be explored further. Nevertheless, when one has the models that mimic the dynamics of various non-linear phenomena of the manufacturing process, it would not be difficult to build the cyber-physical systems for the seamless transfer of knowledge and information of the manufacturing processes from one system to another within the framework of IoT. This means that the methodologies like the one described here will become the valuable constituents of the manufacturing systems in the years to come, i.e., in the era of Industry 4.0. This also means that the devices developed for forms and surface metrology, e.g., the ones described in [2,3,4,5], require systems aided by the methodology described here to make them compatible with Industry 4.0.

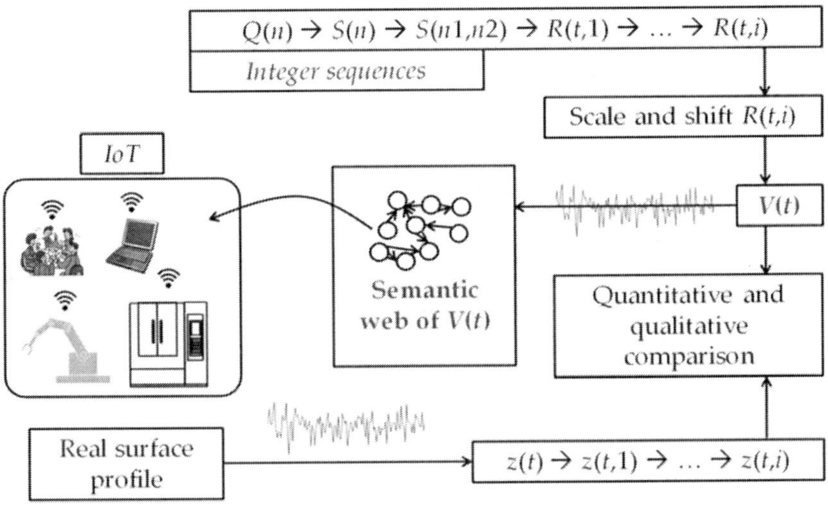

Figure 12. Schematic diagram of dynamic modeling of surface profile using Q-sequence.

ACKNOWLEDGMENTS

An initial short version of the work presented here has been published in the Proceedings of the Ninth CIRP Workshop on Modeling of Machining Operations, 11–12 May 2006, Bled, Slovenia (pp. 431–437).

REFERENCES

1. ISO TC 213. Available online: http://www.iso.org/iso/home/ store/ catalogue_tc/catalogue_tc_browse.htm?commid=54924&published=on
2. Jusko, O.; Neugebauer, M.; Reimann, H.; Bernhardt, R. Recent progress in CMM-based form measurement. *Int. J. Autom. Technol.* **2015**, *9*, 170–175.
3. Woźniak, A.; Krajewski, G. CMM dynamic properties of the scanning measurement of a 2D profile. *Int. J. Autom. Technol.* **2015**, *9*, 530–533.
4. Ito, S.; Jia, Z.; Goto, S.; Hosobuchi, K.; Shimizu, Y.; He, G.; Gao, W. An electrostatic force probe for surface profile measurement in noncontact condition. *Int. J. Autom. Technol.* **2013**, *7*, 714–719.
5. Elrawemi, M.; Blunt, L.; Muhamedsalih, H.; Gao, F.; Fleming, L. Implementation of in Process Surface Metrology for R2R flexible PV barrier films. *Int. J. Autom. Technol.* **2015**, *9*, 312–321.
6. Whitehouse, D. A new look at surface metrology. *Wear* **2009**, *266*, 560–565.
7. Wang, X.; Shi, T.; Liao, G.; Zhang, Y.; Hong, Y.; Chen, K. Using Wavelet Packet Transform for Surface Roughness Evaluation and Texture Extraction. *Sensors* **2017**, *17*, 933.

8. Sharif Ullah, A.M.M.; Fuji, A.; Kubo, A.; Tamaki, J.; Kimura, M. On the surface metrology of bimetallic components. *Mach. Sci. Technol.* **2015**, *19*, 339–359.
9. Bui, S.H.; Vorburger, T.V. Surface metrology algorithm testing system. *Precis. Eng.* **2007**, *31*, 218–225.
10. Li, T.; Blunt, L.A.; Jiang, X.; Zeng, W. An Information Model for Surface Metrology. *Procedia CIRP* **2013**, *10*, 251–258.
11. Sharif Ullah, A.M.M.; Tamaki, J.; Kubo, A. Modeling and Simulation of 3D Surface Finish of Grinding. *Adv. Mater. Res.* **2010**, *126–128*, 672–677.
12. Sharif Ullah, A.M.M.; Harib, K.H. Simulation of Cutting Force using Nonstationary Gaussian Process. *J. Intell. Manuf.***2010**, *21*, 681–691.
13. Pawlus, P. Simulation of Stratified Surface Topographies. *Wear* **2008**, *264*, 457–463.
14. Sharif Ullah, A.M.M.; Arai, N.; Watanabe, M. Concept Map and Internet-aided Manufacturing. *Procedia CIRP* **2013**, *12*, 378–383.
15. Weyer, S.; Schmitt, M.; Ohmer, M.; Gorecky, D. Towards Industry 4.0—Standardization as the crucial challenge for highly modular, multi-vendor production systems. *IFAC-PapersOnLine* **2015**, *48*, 579–584.
16. Monostori, L. Cyber-physical Production Systems: Roots, Expectations and R&D challenges. *Procedia CIRP* **2014**, *17*, 9–13.
17. Ramos, L. Semantic Web for manufacturing, trends and open issues: Toward a state of the art. *Comput. Ind. Eng.* **2015**, *90*, 444–460.
18. Lee, J.; Bagheri, B.; Kao, H.-A. A Cyber-Physical Systems architecture for Industry 4.0-based manufacturing systems. *Manuf. Lett.* **2015**, *3*, 18–23.
19. Wu, J.-J. Simulation of rough surfaces with FFT. *Tribol. Int.* **2000**, *33*, 47–58.
20. Higuchi, M.; Yamaguchi, T.; Yano, A.; Yamamoto, N.; Ueshima, R.; Matumori, N.; Yoshizawa, I. Development of Design Technology of Porous Superfinishing Stone Using Fractal Geometry (2nd Report)—Geometric Modeling of Stone Topography and Design Support System. *J. Jpn. Soc. Precis. Eng.* **2001**, *67*, 428–432. (In Japanese).
21. Ullah, A.M.M.S.; Harib, K.H. Knowledge extraction from time series and its application to surface roughness simulation. *Inf. Knowl. Syst. Manag.* **2006**, *5*, 117–134.
22. Uchidate, M.; Yanagi, K.; Yoshida, I.; Shimizu, T.; Iwabuchi, A. Generation of 3D random topography datasets with periodic boundaries for surface metrology algorithms and measurement standards. *Wear* **2011**, *271*, 565–570.
23. Sharif Ullah, A.M.M.; Chowdhury, M.A.K.; Kubo, A. A Surface Generation Mechanism of Grinding. *Appl. Mech. Mater.* **2017**, *860*, 13–18.
24. Hofstadter, D.R. *Gödel, Escher, Bach: An Eternal Golden Braid*; Vintage Books: New York, NY, USA, 1980; pp. 137–138.
25. Pinn, K. Order and chaos in Hofstadter's Q(n) sequence. *Complexity* **1999**, *4*, 41–46.
26. Kantz, H.; Schreiber, T. *Nonlinear Time Series Analysis*; Cambridge University Press: Cambridge, UK, 2002.
27. NIST Surface Roughness Database. Available online: http://physics. nist.gov/ VSC/jsp/Database.jsp (accessed on 12 January 2017).
28. Sharif Ullah, A.M.M.; Shamsuzzaman, M. Fuzzy Monte Carlo Simulation using point-cloud-based probability-possibility transformation. *Simulation* **2013**, *89*, 860–875.
29. Ullah, A.M.M.S.; Shahinur, S.; Haniu, H. On the Mechanical Properties and Uncertainties of Jute Yarns. *Materials***2017**, *10*, 450.
30. Shahinur, S.; Ullah, A.M.M.S. Quantifying the Uncertainty Associated with the Material Properties of a Natural Fiber. *Procedia CIRP* **2017**, *61*, 541–546.

CHAPTER 9

Nonexistence and existence results for a class of fourth-order difference mixed boundary value problems

Xiaoqing Deng

School of Mathematics and Statistics, Hunan University of Commerce, Changsha 410205, China

ABSTRACT

In this paper, a class of fourth-order nonlinear difference equations are considered. By making use of the critical point method, we establish various sets of sufficient conditions for the nonexistence and existence of solutions for mixed boundary value problems and give some new results. Our results successfully complement the existing results in the literature.

Keywords: Nonexistence and existence, Mixed boundary value problems, Fourth-order, Mountain, Pass lemma, Discrete variational theory

1. INTRODUCTION

Below **N**, **Z** and **R** denote the sets of all natural numbers, integers and real numbers respectively. k is a positive integer. For any a, $b \in \mathbf{Z}$, define $\mathbf{Z}(a) = \{a, a+1, \ldots\}$, $\mathbf{Z}(a,b) = \{a, a+1, \ldots, b\}$ when $a < b$. Δ is the forward difference operator $\Delta u_n = u_{n+1} - u_n$, $\Delta^2 u_n = \Delta(\Delta u_n)$. Besides, * denotes the transpose of a vector.

Recently, difference equations have attracted the interest of many researchers since they provided a natural description of several discrete models. Such discrete models are often investigated in various fields of science and technology such as computer science, economics, neural networks, ecology, cybernetics, biological systems, optimal control, and population dynamics. These studies cover many of the branches of difference equations, such as stability, attractivity, periodicity, oscillation, and boundary value problems, see [8, 17, 18, 19, 23, 26, 27, 29, 34, 42] and the references therein.

The present paper considers the fourth-order nonlinear difference equation

$$\Delta^2(p_{n-1}\Delta^2 u_{n-2}) - \Delta(q_n(\Delta u_{n-1})^{\delta}) + r_n u^{\delta}_n = f(n,u_n),\ \mathrm{n} \in Z(1,k), \qquad (1.1)$$

with boundary value conditions

$$\Delta u - 1 = \Delta u_0 = 0,\ u_{k+1} = u_k + 2 = 0, \qquad (1.2)$$

where p_n is nonzero and real valued for each $n \in \mathbf{Z}(0,k+1)$, $\{q_n\}_{n \in \mathbf{Z}(1,k+1)}$ and $\{r_n\}_{n \in \mathbf{Z}(1,k)}$ are real sequences, δ is the ratio of odd positive integers, $f \in C(\mathbf{R}^2,\mathbf{R})$.

We may think of (1.1) with (1.2) as being a discrete analogue of the following fourth-order nonlinear differential equation

$$[p(t)u''(t)]'' - [q(t)u'(t)]' = f(t,u(t)),\ t \in [a,b], \qquad (1.3)$$

with boundary value conditions

$$u(a) = u'(a) = 0,\ u(b) = u'(b) = 0. \qquad (1.4)$$

Equation (1.3) includes the following equation

$$u^{(4)}(t) = f(t,u(t)),\ t \in R, \qquad (1.5)$$

which is used to describe the bending of an elastic beam; see, for example, [5, 16, 20, 22, 25, 39] and the references therein. Owing to its importance in physics, many methods are applied to study fourth-order boundary value problems by many authors.

In recent years, the study of boundary value problems for differential equations develops at relatively rapid rate. By using various methods and techniques, such as fixed point theory, topological degree theory, coincidence degree theory, a series of existence results of nontrivial solutions for differential equations have been obtained in literatures, we refer to [2, 3, 4, 7, 21, 37]. And critical point theory is also an important tool to deal with problems on differential equations [11, 14, 15, 28, 33, 43]. Only since 2003, critical point theory has been employed to establish sufficient conditions on the existence of periodic solutions of difference equations. By using the critical point theory, Guo and Yu [17, 18, 19] and Shi *et al.* [35] have successfully proved the existence of periodic solutions of second-order nonlinear difference equations. We also refer to [40, 41] for the discrete boundary value problems. Compared to first-order or second-order difference equations, the study of higher-order equations, and in particular, fourth-order equations, has received considerably less attention (see, for example, [9, 10, 13, 31, 32, 36, 38] and the references contained therein). Yan, Liu [38] in 1997 and Thandapani, Arockiasamy [36] in 2001 studied the following fourth-order difference equation of form,

$$\Delta^2 (p_n \Delta^2 u_n) + f(n,u_n) = 0, n \in Z \tag{1.6}$$

The authors obtain criteria for the oscillation and nonoscillation of solutions for equation (1.6). In 2005, Cai, Yu and Guo [6] have obtained some criteria for the existence of periodic solutions of the fourth-order difference equation

$$\Delta^2(p_{n-2}\Delta^2 u_{n-2}) + f(n,u_n) = 0, n \in Z. \tag{1.7}$$

In 1995, Peterson and Ridenhour considered the disconjugacy of equation (1.7) when $p_n \equiv 1$ and $f(n,u_n) = q_n u_n$ (see [31]).

The boundary value problem (BVP) for determining the existence of solutions of difference equations has been a very active area of research in the last twenty years, and for surveys of recent results, we refer the reader to the monographs by Agarwal *et al.* [1, 1 2, 24, 29, 34]. We use the critical point theory to give some sufficient conditions for the nonexistence and existence of solutions for the BVP (1.1) with (1.2). We shall study the suplinear and sublinear cases. The main idea in this paper is to transfer the existence of the BVP (1.1) with (1.2) into the existence of the critical points of some functional. The proof is based on the notable Mountain Pass lemma in combination with variational technique. The purpose of this paper is two-folded. On one hand, we shall further demonstrate the powerfulness of critical point theory in the study of solutions for boundary value problems of difference equations. On the other hand, we shall complement existing ones. The motivation for the present work stems from the recent paper in [11].

Let

$$\bar{p} = \max\{p_n : n \in \mathbf{Z}(1, k+1)\}, \qquad \underline{p} = \min\{p_n : n \in \mathbf{Z}(1, k+1)\},$$
$$\bar{q} = \max\{q_n : n \in \mathbf{Z}(2, k+1)\}, \qquad \underline{q} = \min\{q_n : n \in \mathbf{Z}(2, k+1)\},$$
$$\bar{r} = \max\{r_n : n \in \mathbf{Z}(1, k)\}, \qquad \underline{r} = \min\{r_n : n \in \mathbf{Z}(1, k)\}.$$

Our main results are as follows.

Theorem 1.1

Assume that the following hypotheses are satisfied:

(p) for any $n \in \mathbf{Z}(1,k+1)$, $p_n < 0$;

(q) for any $n \in \mathbf{Z}(2,k+1)$, $q_n \leq 0$;

(r) for any $n \in \mathbf{Z}(1,k)$, $r_n \leq 0$;

(F_1) there exists a functional $F(n,v) \in C^1(\mathbf{Z} \times \mathbf{R},\mathbf{R})$ *with* $F(0,\cdot) = 0$ *such that*

$$\frac{\partial F(n, v)}{\partial v} = f(n, v), \quad \forall n \in \mathbf{Z}(1, k)$$

(F_2) there exists a constant $M_0 > 0$ *for all* $(n,v) \in \mathbf{Z}(1,k) \times \mathbf{R}$ *such that* $|f(n,v)| \leq M_0$.

Then the BVP (1.1) *with* (1.2) *possesses at least one solution.*

Remark 1.1

Assumption (F_2) implies that there exists a constant $M_1 > 0$ such that (F'_2) $|F(n,v)| \leq M_1 + M_0|v|$, $\forall (n,v) \in \mathbf{Z}(1,k) \times \mathbf{R}$.

Theorem 1.2

Suppose that (F_1) *and the following hypotheses are satisfied:*

(p′) for any $n \in \mathbf{Z}(1,k+1)$, $p_n > 0$;

(q′) for any $n \in \mathbf{Z}(2,k+1)$, $q_n \geq 0$;

(r′) for any $n \in \mathbf{Z}(1,k)$, $r_n \geq 0$;

(F_3) there exists a functional $F(n,v) \in C^1(\mathbf{Z} \times \mathbf{R},\mathbf{R})$ *such that*

$$\lim_{v \to 0} \frac{F(n,v)}{|v|} = 0, \quad \forall n \in \mathbf{Z}(1,k)$$

(F_4) there exists a constant $\beta > \max\{2, \delta + 1\}$ such that for any $n \in \mathbf{Z}(1,k)$,

$$0 < vf(n,v) < \beta F(n,v), \forall_v \neq 0.$$

Then the BVP (1.1) *with* (1.2) *possesses at least two nontrivial solutions.*

Remark 1.2 Assumption (F_4) implies that there exist constants $a_1 > 0$ and $a_2 > 0$ such that (F'_4) $F(n,v) > a_1|v|^{\beta} - a_2, \forall n \in \mathrm{Z}(1,k)$.

Theorem 1.3 *Suppose that* (p'),(q'),(r'),(F_1) *and the following assumption are satisfied*:

(F_5) there exist constants $R > 0$ and $1 < \alpha < 2$ such that for $n \in \mathbf{Z}(1,k)$ and $|v| \geq R$,

$$0 < f(n,v) \leq \alpha F(n,v).$$

Then the BVP (1.1) *with* (1.2) *possesses at least one solution.*

Remark 1.3 Assumption (F_5) implies that for each $n \in \mathrm{Z}(1,k)$ there exist constants $a_3 > 0$ and $a_4 > 0$ such that

($F'5$) $F(n,v) \leq a_3|v|^{\alpha} + a_4, \forall (n,v) \in \mathbf{Z}(1,k) \times \mathbf{R}$.

Theorem 1.4 *Suppose that* (p),(q),(r),(F_1) *and the following assumption are satisfied*:

$$(F_6)\ vf(n,v) > 0, \text{ for } v \neq 0, \forall n \in \mathbf{Z}(1,k).$$

Then the BVP (1.1) *with* (1.2) *has no nontrivial solutions.*

Remark 1.4 In the existing literature, results on the nonexistence of solutions of discrete boundary value problems are very scarce. Hence, Theorem 1.4 complements existing ones.

The remainder of this paper is organized as follows. First, in Sect. 2, we shall establish the variational framework for the BVP (1.1) with (1.2) and transfer the problem of the existence of the BVP (1.1) with (1.2) into that of the existence of critical points of the corresponding functional. Some related fundamental results will also be recalled. Then, in Sect. 3, we shall complete the proof of the results by using the critical point method. Finally, in Sect. 4, we shall give three examples to illustrate the main results.

About the basic knowledge for variational methods, we refer the reader to [28, 30, 33, 43].

2. VARIATIONAL STRUCTURE AND SOME LEMMAS

In order to apply the critical point theory, we shall establish the corresponding variational framework for the BVP (1.1) with (1.2) and give some lemmas which will be of fundamental importance in proving our main results. First, we state some basic notations.

Let $\mathbf{R}^k$ be the real Euclidean space with dimension k. Define the inner product on $\mathbf{R}^k$ as follows:

$$\langle u, v\rangle = \sum_{j=1}^{k} u_j v_j, \quad \forall u, v \in \mathbf{R}^k \tag{2.1}$$

by which the norm $\|\cdot\|$ can be induced by

$$\|u\| = \left(\sum_{j=1}^{k} u_j^2\right)^{\frac{1}{2}}, \quad \forall u \in \mathbf{R}^k \tag{2.2}$$

On the other hand, we define the norm $\|\cdot\|_r$ on $\mathbf{R}^k$ as follows:

$$\|u\|_r = \left(\sum_{j=1}^{k} |u_j|^r\right)^{\frac{1}{r}} \tag{2.3}$$

for all $u \in \mathbf{R}^k$ and $r>1$.

Since $\|u\|_r$ and $\|u\|_2$ are equivalent, there exist constants c_1, c_2 such that $c_2 \geq c_1 > 0$, and

$$c_1\|u\|_2 \leq \|u\|_r \leq c_2\|u\|_2, \forall u \in R^k. \tag{2.4}$$

Clearly, $\|u\| = \|u\|_2$. For any $u = (u_1, u_2, \ldots, u_k)^* \in \mathbf{R}^k$, for the BVP (1.1) with (1.2), consider the functional J defined on $\mathbf{R}^k$ as follows:

$$J(u) = \frac{1}{2}\sum_{n=1}^{k} p_{n+1}(\Delta^2 u_n)^2 + \frac{1}{\delta+1}\sum_{n=1}^{k} q_{n+1}(\Delta u_n)^{\delta+1} + \frac{1}{\delta+1}\sum_{n=1}^{k} r_n u_n^{\delta+1}$$

$$-\sum_{n=1}^{k} F(n, u_n) + \frac{1}{2}p_1(\Delta u_1)^2 \tag{2.5}$$

where

$$\frac{\partial F(n, v)}{\partial v} = f(n, v), \qquad \Delta u_{-1} = \Delta u_0 = 0, \qquad u_{k+1} = u_{k+2} = 0$$

Clearly, $J \in C^1(\mathbf{R}^k, \mathbf{R})$ and for any $u = \{u_n\}_{n=1}^{k} = (u_1, u_2, \ldots, u_k)^*$, by using $\Delta u_{-1} = \Delta u_0 = 0$, $u_{k+1} = u_{k+2} = 0$, we can compute the partial derivative as

$$\frac{\partial J}{\partial u_n} = \Delta^2\left(p_{n-1}\Delta^2 u_{n-2}\right) - \Delta\left(q_n(\Delta u_{n-1})^{\delta}\right) + r_n u_n^{\delta} - f(n, u_n), \quad \forall n \in \mathbf{Z}(1, k)$$

Thus, u is a critical point of J on $\mathbf{R}^k$ if and only if

$$\Delta^2\left(p_{n-1}\Delta^2 u_{n-2}\right) - \Delta\left(q_n(\Delta u_{n-1})^{\delta}\right) + r_n u_n^{\delta} = f(n, u_n), \quad \forall n \in \mathbf{Z}(1, k)$$

We reduce the existence of the BVP (1.1) with (1.2) to the existence of critical points of J on $\mathbf{R}^k$. That is, the functional J is just the variational framework of the BVP (1.1) with (1.2).

Let P and Q be the $k \times k$ matrices defined by

$$P = \begin{pmatrix} 6 & -4 & 1 & 0 & 0 & \cdots & 0 & 0 & 0 \\ -4 & 6 & -4 & 1 & 0 & \cdots & 0 & 0 & 0 \\ 1 & -4 & 6 & -4 & 1 & \cdots & 0 & 0 & 0 \\ 0 & 1 & -4 & 6 & -4 & \cdots & 0 & 0 & 0 \\ \vdots & \vdots & \vdots & \vdots & \vdots & \ddots & \vdots & \vdots & \vdots \\ 0 & 0 & 0 & 0 & 0 & \cdots & 6 & -4 & 1 \\ 0 & 0 & 0 & 0 & 0 & \cdots & -4 & 6 & -4 \\ 0 & 0 & 0 & 0 & 0 & \cdots & 1 & -4 & 6 \end{pmatrix}.$$

$$Q = \begin{pmatrix} 2 & -1 & 0 & \cdots & 0 & 0 \\ -1 & 2 & -1 & \cdots & 0 & 0 \\ 0 & -1 & 2 & \cdots & 0 & 0 \\ \vdots & \vdots & \vdots & \ddots & \vdots & \vdots \\ 0 & 0 & 0 & \cdots & 2 & -1 \\ 0 & 0 & 0 & \cdots & -1 & 2 \end{pmatrix}.$$

Clearly, P and Q are positive definite. Let $\lambda_1, \lambda_2, \ldots, \lambda_k$ be the eigenvalues of P, $\tilde{\lambda}_1, \tilde{\lambda}_2, \ldots, \tilde{\lambda}_k$ be the eigenvalues of Q. Applying matrix theory, we know λj>0,λ~j>0,j=1,2,...,kλj>0,λ~j>0,j=1,2,...,k. Without loss of generality, we may assume that

$$0 < \lambda_1 \leq \lambda_2 \leq \ldots \leq \lambda_k, \tag{2.6}$$

$$0 < \tilde{\lambda}_1 \leq \tilde{\lambda}_2 \leq \ldots \leq \tilde{\lambda}_k. \tag{2.7}$$

Let E be a real Banach space, $J \in C^1(E,\mathbf{R})$, i.e., J is a continuously Fréchet-differentiable functional defined on E. J is said to satisfy the Palais-Smale condition (P.S. condition for short) if any sequence $\{u^{(l)}\} \subset E$ for which $\{J(u^{(l)})\}$ is bounded and $J'(u^{(l)}) \to 0 (l \to \infty)$ possesses a convergent subsequence in E.

Let B_ρ denote the open ball in E about 0 of radius ρ and let ∂B_ρ denote its boundary.

Lemma 2.1 (Mountain Pass lemma [33]) *Let E be a real Banach space and J* $\in C^1(E,R)$ *satisfy the P.S. condition. If* $J(0) = 0$ *and*

(J_1) there exist constants $\rho, a > 0$ *such that* $J|_{\partial B_\rho} \geq a$*, and*

(J_2) there exists $e \in E \setminus B_\rho$ *such that* $J(e) \leq 0$.

Then J possesses a critical value $c \geq a$ *given by*

$$c = \inf_{g \in \Gamma} \max_{s \in [0,1]} J(g(s)) \tag{2.8}$$

where

$$\Gamma = \{g \in C([0,1], E) | g(0) = 0, g(1) = e\} \tag{2.9}$$

Lemma 2.2 *Suppose that* $(p'),(q'),(r'),(F_1),(F_3)$ *and* (F_4) *are satisfied. Then the functionalJsatisfies the P.S. condition.*

Proof Let $u^{(l)} \in R^k$, $l \in Z(1)$ be such that $\{J(u^{(l)})\}$ is bounded. Then there exists a positive constant M_2 such that

$$-M_2 \leq J(u^{(l)}) \leq M_2, \forall l \in N.$$

By (F'_4), we have

$$
\begin{aligned}
-M_2 &\le J(u^{(l)}) \\
&= \frac{1}{2}\sum_{n=1}^{k} p_{n+1}(\Delta^2 u_n^{(l)})^2 + \frac{1}{\delta+1}\sum_{n=1}^{k} q_{n+1}(\Delta u_n^{(l)})^{\delta+1} \\
&\quad + \frac{1}{\delta+1}\sum_{n=1}^{k} r_n (u_n^{(l)})^{\delta+1} - \sum_{n=1}^{k} F(n, u_n^{(l)}) + \frac{1}{2}p_1(\Delta u_1^{(l)})^2 \\
&\le \frac{\bar{p}}{2}\sum_{n=1}^{k}(u_{n+2}^{(l)} - 2u_{n+1}^{(l)} + u_n^{(l)})^2 + \frac{\bar{q}c_2^{\delta+1}}{\delta+1}\left\{\left[\sum_{n=1}^{k}(u_{n+1}^{(l)} - u_n^{(l)})^2\right]^{\frac{1}{2}}\right\}^{\delta+1} \\
&\quad + \frac{\bar{r}c_2^{\delta+1}}{\delta+1}\|u^{(l)}\|^{\delta+1} - a_1\sum_{n=1}^{k}|u_n^{(l)}|^{\beta} + a_2 k + \bar{p}\|u^{(l)}\|^2 \\
&\le \frac{\bar{p}}{2}(u^{(l)})^* P u^{(l)} + \frac{\bar{q}c_2^{\delta+1}}{\delta+1}[(u^{(l)})^* Q u^{(l)}]^{\frac{\delta+1}{2}} + \frac{\bar{r}c_2^{\delta+1}}{\delta+1}\|u^{(l)}\|^{\delta+1} \\
&\quad - a_1 c_1^{\beta}\|u^{(l)}\|^{\beta} + a_2 k + \bar{p}\|u^{(l)}\|^2 \\
&\le \left(\frac{\lambda_k}{2}+1\right)\bar{p}\|u^{(l)}\|^2 + \frac{\bar{q}c_2^{\delta+1}\tilde{\lambda}_k^{\frac{\delta+1}{2}}}{\delta+1}\|u^{(l)}\|^{\delta+1} + \frac{\bar{r}c_2^{\delta+1}}{\delta+1}\|u^{(l)}\|^{\delta+1} \\
&\quad - a_1 c_1^{\beta}\|u^{(l)}\|^{\beta} + a_2 k,
\end{aligned}
$$

where $u^{(l)} = (u_1^{(l)}, u_2^{(l)}, \ldots, u_k^{(l)})^*,\ u^{(l)} \in \mathbf{R}^k$. That is,

$$
\begin{aligned}
&a_1 c_1^{\beta}\|u^{(l)}\|^{\beta} - \left(\frac{\lambda_k}{2}+1\right)\bar{p}\|u^{(l)}\|^2 - \frac{\bar{q}c_2^{\delta+1}\tilde{\lambda}_k^{\frac{\delta+1}{2}}}{\delta+1}\|u^{(l)}\|^{\delta+1} - \frac{\bar{r}c_2^{\delta+1}}{\delta+1}\|u^{(l)}\|^{\delta+1} \\
&\le M_2 + a_2 k.
\end{aligned}
$$

Since $\beta > \max\{2, \delta+1\}$, there exists a constant $M_3 > 0$ such that

$$\|\|u^{(l)}\|\| \le M_3,\ \forall l \in \mathrm{N}.$$

Therefore, $\{u^{(l)}\}$ is bounded on $\mathbf{R}^k$. As a consequence, $\{u^{(l)}\}$ possesses a convergence subsequence in $\mathbf{R}^k$. Thus the P.S. condition is verified.

3. PROOF OF THE MAIN RESULTS

In this section, we shall prove our main results by using the critical point theory.

Proof of Theorem 1.1 By (F′2)(F2′), for any $u = (u_1,u_2,...,u_k)^* \in R^k$, we have

$$
\begin{aligned}
J(u) &= \frac{1}{2}\sum_{n=1}^{k} p_{n+1}\left(\Delta^2 u_n\right)^2 + \frac{1}{\delta+1}\sum_{n=1}^{k} q_{n+1}(\Delta u_n)^{\delta+1} + \frac{1}{\delta+1}\sum_{n=1}^{k} r_n u_n^{\delta+1} \\
&\quad - \sum_{n=1}^{k} F(n,u_n) + \frac{1}{2}p_1(\Delta u_1)^2 \\
&\le \frac{\bar{p}}{2}\sum_{n=1}^{k}(u_{n+2} - 2u_{n+1} + u_n)^2 + M_0\sum_{n=1}^{k}|u_n| + M_1 k \\
&\le \frac{\bar{p}}{2}u^* P u + M_0\sqrt{k}\|u\| + M_1 k \\
&\le \frac{\bar{p}\lambda_1}{2}\|u\|^2 + M_0\sqrt{k}\|u\| + M_1 k \to -\infty
\end{aligned}
$$

as $\|u\| \to +\infty$.

The above inequality means that $-J(u)$ is coercive. By the continuity of $J(u)$, J attains its maximum at some point, and we denote it $\hat{u}$, that is,

$$J(\hat{u}) = \max\{J(u) | u \in R^k\}.$$

Clearly, $\hat{u}$ is a critical point of the functional J. This completes the proof of Theorem 1.1.

Proof of Theorem 1.2 By (F_3), for any $\epsilon = \frac{p\lambda_1}{4}$ (λ_1 can be referred to (2.6)), there exists $\rho > 0$, such that

$$|F(n,v)| \le \frac{p\lambda_1}{4}|v|, \quad \forall n \in \mathbf{Z}(1,k)$$

for $|v| \le \rho$.

For any $u = (u_1,u_2,...,u_k)^* \in \mathbf{R}^k$ and $\|u\| \le \rho$, we have $|u_n| \le \rho$, $n \in \mathbf{Z}(1,k)$.

For any $n \in \mathbf{Z}(1,k)$,

$$
\begin{aligned}
J(u) &= \frac{1}{2}\sum_{n=1}^{k} p_{n+1}(\Delta^2 u_n)^2 + \frac{1}{\delta+1}\sum_{n=1}^{k} q_{n+1}(\Delta u_n)^{\delta+1} + \frac{1}{\delta+1}\sum_{n=1}^{k} r_n u_n^{\delta+1} \\
&\quad - \sum_{n=1}^{k} F(n, u_n) + \frac{1}{2} p_1 (\Delta u_1)^2 \\
&\geq \frac{p}{2}\sum_{n=1}^{k}(u_{n+2} - 2u_{n+1} + u_n)^2 - \frac{p\lambda_1}{4}\sum_{n=1}^{k}|u_n| \\
&\geq \frac{p}{2}u^* P u - \frac{p\lambda_1}{4}\|u\|^2 \\
&\geq \frac{p\lambda_1}{2}\|u\|^2 - \frac{p\lambda_1}{4}\|u\|^2 \\
&= \frac{p\lambda_1}{4}\|u\|^2.
\end{aligned}
$$

where $u = (u_1, u_2, \ldots, u_k)^*$, $u \in \mathbf{R}^k$.

Take $a = \frac{p\lambda_1}{4}\rho^2 > 0$. Therefore,

$J(u) \geq a > 0, \forall u \in \partial B\rho$.

At the same time, we have also proved that there exist constants $a > 0$ and $\rho > 0$ such that $J|_{\partial B\rho} \geq a$. That is to say, J satisfies the condition (J_1) of the Mountain Pass lemma.

For our setting, clearly $J(0)=0$. In order to exploit the Mountain Pass lemma in critical point theory, we need to verify other conditions of the Mountain Pass lemma. By Lemma 2.2, J satisfies the P.S. condition. So it suffices to verify the condition (J_2).

From the proof of the P.S. condition, we know

$$
J(u) \leq \left(\frac{\lambda_k}{2} + 1\right)\bar{p}\|u\|^2 + \frac{\bar{q}c_2^{\delta+1}\tilde{\lambda}_k^{\frac{\delta+1}{2}}}{\delta+1}\|u\|^{\delta+1} + \frac{\bar{r}c_2^{\delta+1}}{\delta+1}\|u\|^{\delta+1} - a_1 c_1^{\beta}\|u\|^{\beta} + a_2 k
$$

Since $\beta > \max\{2, \delta + 1\}$, we can choose $\bar{u}$ large enough to ensure that $J(\bar{u}) < 0$.

By the Mountain Pass lemma, J possesses a critical value $c \geq a > 0$, where

$$c = \inf_{h \in \Gamma} \sup_{s \in [0,1]} J(h(s))$$

and

$$\Gamma = \{h \in C([0,1], R_k) \mid h(0) = 0, h(1) = \bar{u}\}.$$

Let $\tilde{u} \in R_k$ be a critical point associated to the critical value c of J, i.e., $J(\hat{u}) =$ c. Similar to the proof of the P.S. condition, we know that there exists $\hat{u} \in R_k$ such that

$$J(\hat{u}) = c_{\max} = \max_{s \in [0,1]} J(h(s))$$

Clearly, $\hat{u} \neq 0$. If $\hat{u} \neq \hat{u}$, then the conclusion of Theorem 1.2 holds. Otherwise, $\tilde{u} = \hat{u}$. Then $c = J(\tilde{u}) = c_{max} = \max_{s \in [0,1]} J(h(s))$. That is,

$$\sup_{u \in \mathbf{R}^k} J(u) = \inf_{h \in \Gamma} \sup_{s \in [0,1]} J(h(s))$$

Therefore,

$$c_{\max} = \max_{s \in [0,1]} J(h(s)), \quad \forall h \in \Gamma$$

By the continuity of $J(h(s))$ with respect to s, $J(0) = 0$ and $J(\bar{u}) < 0$ imply that there exists $s_0 \in (0,1)$ such that

$$J(h(s_0)) = c_{\max}.$$

Choose h_1, $h_2 \in \Gamma$ such that $\{h_1(s) \mid s \in (0,1)\} \cap \{h_1(s) \mid s \in (0,1)\}$ is empty, then there exists $s_1, s_2 \in (0,1)$ such that

$$J(h_1(s_1)) = J(h_2(s_2)) = c_{\max}.$$

Thus, we get two different critical points of J on $\mathbf{R}^k$ denoted by

$$u^1 = h_1(s_1),\ u^2 = h_2(s_2).$$

The above argument implies that the BVP (1.1) with (1.2) possesses at least two nontrivial solutions. The proof of Theorem 1.2 is finished.

Proof of Theorem 1.3 We only need to find at least one critical point of the functional J defined as in (2.5).

By (F'_5), for any $u = (u_1,u_2,\ldots,u_k)^* \in \mathbf{R}^k$, we have

$$\geq \frac{p\lambda_1}{2}\|u\|^2 - a_3 c_2^{\alpha}\left[\left(\sum_{n=1}^{k} u_n^2\right)^{\frac{1}{2}}\right]^{\alpha} - a_4 k$$

$$\geq \frac{p\lambda_1}{2}\|u\|^2 - a_3 c_2^{\alpha}\|u\|^{\alpha} - a_4 k \to +\infty$$

$$J(u) = \frac{1}{2}\sum_{n=1}^{k} p_{n+1}(\Delta^2 u_n)^2 + \frac{1}{\delta+1}\sum_{n=1}^{k} q_{n+1}(\Delta u_n)^{\delta+1} + \frac{1}{\delta+1}\sum_{n=1}^{k} r_n u_n^{\delta+1}$$

$$-\sum_{n=1}^{k} F(n,u_n) + \frac{1}{2}p_1(\Delta u_1)^2$$

$$\geq \frac{p}{2}\sum_{n=1}^{k}(u_{n+2} - 2u_{n+1} + u_n)^2 - a_3\sum_{n=1}^{k}|u_n|^{\alpha} - a_4 k$$

$$= \frac{p}{2}u^* P u - a_3\left[\left(\sum_{n=1}^{k}|u_n|^{\alpha}\right)^{\frac{1}{\alpha}}\right]^{\alpha} - a_4 k$$

as $\|u\| \to +\infty$.

By the continuity of J, we know from the above inequality that there exist lower bounds of values of the functional. And this means that J attains its minimal value at some point which is just the critical point of J with the finite norm. □

Proof of Theorem 1.4 Assume, for the sake of contradiction, that the BVP (1.1) with (1.2) has a nontrivial solution. Then J has a nonzero critical point $u^{\star}$. Since

$$\frac{\partial J}{\partial u_n} = \Delta^2\left(p_{n-1}\Delta^2 u_{n-2}\right) - \Delta\left(q_n(\Delta u_{n-1})^{\delta}\right) + r_n u_n^{\delta} - f(n,u_n)$$

we get

$$\begin{aligned}
&\sum_{n=1}^{k} f(n,u_n^{\star})u_n^{\star} \\
&= \sum_{n=1}^{k}[\Delta^2(p_{n-1}\Delta^2 u_{n-2}^{\star}) - \Delta(q_n(\Delta u_{n-1}^{\star})^{\delta}) + r_n(u_n^{\star})^{\delta}]u_n^{\star} \qquad (3.1) \\
&= \sum_{n=1}^{k} p_{n+1}(\Delta^2 u_n^{\star})^2 + \sum_{n=1}^{k} q_{n+1}(\Delta u_n^{\star})^{\delta+1} + \sum_{n=1}^{k} r_n(u_n^{\star})^{\delta+1} + p_1(\Delta u_1^{\star})^2 \le 0.
\end{aligned}$$

On the other hand, it follows from (F_6) that

$$\sum_{n=1}^{k} f(n,u_n^{\star})u_n^{\star} > 0 \qquad (3.2)$$

This contradicts (3.1) and hence the proof is complete. □

4. EXAMPLES

As an application of Theorems 1.2, 1.3 and 1.4, we give four examples to illustrate our main results.

Example 4.1

For $n \in \mathbf{Z}(1,k)$, assume that

$$\Delta^4 u_{n-2} - \Delta(9^n(\Delta u_{n-1})^{\delta}) + 3^n u^{\delta}_n = \beta\varphi(n)u_n|u_n|^{\beta-2}, \qquad (4.1)$$

with boundary value conditions (1.2), δ is the ratio of odd positive integers, $\beta > \max\{2,\delta+1\}$, φ is continuously differentiable and $\varphi(n) > 0$, $n \in \mathbf{Z}(1,k)$ with $\varphi(0) = 0$. We have

$$p_n \equiv 1, \qquad q_n = 9^n, \qquad r_n = 3^n, \qquad f(n,v) = \beta\varphi(n)v|v|^{\beta-2}$$

and

$$F(n,v) = \varphi(n)|v|^{\beta}.$$

It is easy to verify all the assumptions of Theorem 1.2 are satisfied and then the BVP (4.1) with (1.2) possesses at least two nontrivial solutions.

Example 4.2 For $n \in Z(1,k)$, assume that

$$\Delta^2(8^{n-1}\Delta^2 u_{n-2}) - \Delta(6^n(\Delta u_{n-1})^\delta) + 5^n u^\delta_n = \alpha\psi(n)u_n|u_n|^{\alpha-2}, \tag{4.2}$$

with boundary value conditions (1.2), δ is the ratio of odd positive integers, $1 < \alpha < 2$, ψ is continuously differentiable and $\psi(n) > 0$, $n \in \mathbf{Z}(1,k)$ with $\psi(0) = 0$. We have

$$p_n = 8^n,\ q_n = 6^n,\ r_n = 5_n,\ f(n,v) = \alpha\psi(n)v|v|^{\alpha-2}$$

and

$$F(n,v) = \psi(n)|v|\alpha.$$

It is easy to verify all the assumptions of Theorem 1.3 are satisfied and then the BVP (4.2) with (1.2) possesses at least one solution.

Example 4.3

For $n \in \mathbf{Z}(1,k)$, assume that

$$-\Delta^4 u_{n-2} + \Delta(9^n(\Delta u_{n-1})^\delta) - 8^n u_n^\delta = \frac{4}{3}u_n^{\frac{1}{3}} \tag{4.3}$$

with boundary value conditions (1.2), δ is the ratio of odd positive integers. We have

$$p_n \equiv -1,\ q_n = -9^n,\ r_n = -8^n,\ f(n,v) = \frac{4}{3}v^{\frac{1}{3}}$$

and

$$F(n,v) = v^{\frac{4}{3}}$$

It is easy to verify all the assumptions of Theorem 1.4 are satisfied and then the BVP (4.3) with (1.2) has no nontrivial solutions.

Example 4.4

For $n \in \mathbf{Z}(1,k)$, assume that

$$\Delta^4 u_{n-2} = 4u_n|u_n|^3 \quad (4.4)$$

with boundary value conditions (1.2). We have

$$\delta = 1, \beta = 5, p_n \equiv 1, q_n = r_n \equiv 0,$$

$$f(n,v) = 4v|v|^3,\ F(n,v) = \frac{4}{5}|v|^5.$$

It is easy to verify all the assumptions of Theorem 1.2 are satisfied and then the BVP (4.4) with (1.2) possesses two nontrivial solutions $u_n = \sin(\frac{\pi}{2}n)$ and $u_n = \cos(\frac{\pi}{2}n)$.

REFERENCES

1. Agarwal, R.P.: Difference Equations and Inequalities: Theory, Methods and Applications. Marcel Dekker, New York (2000)
2. Ahlbrandt, C.D.: Dominant and recessive solutions of symmetric three term recurrences. J. Differ. Equ. **107**(2), 238–258 (1994)
3. Anuradha, V., Maya, C., Shivaji, R.: Positive solutions for a class of nonlinear boundary value problems with Neumann-Robin boundary conditions. J. Math. Anal. Appl. **236**(1), 94–124 (1999)
4. Arcoya, D.: Positive solutions for semilinear Dirichlet problems in an annulus. J. Differ. Equ. **94**(2), 217–227 (1991)
5. Bai, Z., Wang, H.: On positive solutions of some nonlinear fourth-order beam equations. J. Math. Anal. Appl. **270**(2), 357–368 (2002)
6. Cai, X.C., Yu, J.S., Guo, Z.M.: Existence of periodic solutions for fourth-order difference equations. Comput. Math. Appl. **50**(1–2), 49–55 (2005)
7. Cecchi, M., Marini, M., Villari, G.: On the monotonicity property for a certain class of second order differential equations. J. Differ. Equ. **82**(1), 15–27 (1989)
8. Chen, S.Z.: Disconjugacy, disfocality, and oscillation of second order difference equations. J. Differ. Equ. **107**(2), 383–394 (1994)
9. Chen, P., Fang, H.: Existence of periodic and subharmonic solutions for second-order p-Laplacian difference equations. Adv. Differ. Equ. **2007**, 1–9 (2007)
10. Chen, P., Tang, X.H.: Existence of infinitely many homoclinic orbits for fourth-order difference systems containing both advance and retardation. Appl. Math. Comput. **217**(9), 4408–4415 (2011)
11. Chen, P., Tang, X.H.: New existence and multiplicity of solutions for some Dirichlet problems with impulsive effects. Math. Comput. Model. **55**(3–4), 723–739 (2012)
12. Cull, P., Flahive, M., Robson, R.: Difference Equations: From Rabbits to Chaos. Springer, New York (2005)
13. Fang, H., Zhao, D.P.: Existence of nontrivial homoclinic orbits for fourth-order difference equations. Appl. Math. Comput. **214**(1), 163–170 (2009)
14. Guo, C.J., O'Regan, D., Xu, Y.T., Agarwal, R.P.: Existence of subharmonic solutions and homoclinic orbits for a class of even higher order differential equations. Appl. Anal. **90**(7), 1169–1183 (2011)

15. Guo, C.J., O'Regan, D., Xu, Y.T., Agarwal, R.P.: Existence and multiplicity of homoclinic orbits of a second-order differential difference equation via variational methods. Appl. Math. Inf. Mech. **4**(1), 1–15 (2012)
16. Guo, C.J., Xu, Y.T.: Existence of periodic solutions for a class of second order differential equation with deviating argument. J. Appl. Math. Comput. **28**(1–2), 425–433 (2008)
17. Guo, Z.M., Yu, J.S.: Applications of critical point theory to difference equations. Fields Inst. Commun. **42**, 187–200 (2004)
18. Guo, Z.M., Yu, J.S.: Existence of periodic and subharmonic solutions for second-order superlinear difference equations. Sci. China Math. **46**(4), 506–515 (2003)
19. Guo, Z.M., Yu, J.S.: The existence of periodic and subharmonic solutions of subquadratic second order difference equations. J. Lond. Math. Soc. **68**(2), 419–430 (2003)
20. Gupta, C.P.: Existence and uniqueness theorems for the bending of an elastic beam equation. Appl. Anal. **26**(4), 289–304 (1988)
21. Hale, J.K., Mawhin, J.: Coincidence degree and periodic solutions of neutral equations. J. Differ. Equ. **15**(2), 295–307 (1974)
22. Han, G., Xu, Z.: Multiple solutions of some nonlinear fourth-order beam equations. Nonlinear Anal. **68**(12), 3646–3656 (2008)
23. Henderson, J., Thompson, H.B.: Existence of multiple solutions for second-order discrete boundary value problems. Comput. Math. Appl. **43**(10–11), 1239–1248 (2002)
24. Kocic, V.L., Ladas, G.: Global Behavior of Nonlinear Difference Equations of Higher Order with Applications. Kluwer Academic, Dordrecht (1993)
25. Li, F., Zhang, Q., Liang, Z.: Existence and multiplicity of solutions of a kind of fourth-order boundary value problem. Nonlinear Anal. **62**(5), 803–816 (2005)
26. Liu, Y.J., Ge, W.G.: Twin positive solutions of boundary value problems for finite difference equations with p-Laplacian operator. J. Math. Anal. Appl. **278**(2), 551–561 (2003)
27. Matsunaga, H., Hara, T., Sakata, S.: Global attractivity for a nonlinear difference equation with variable delay. Comput. Math. Appl. **41**(5–6), 543–551 (2001)
28. Mawhin, J., Willem, M.: Critical Point Theory and Hamiltonian Systems. Springer, New York (1989)
29. Mickens, R.E.: Difference Equations: Theory and Application. Van Nostrand Reinhold, New York (1990)
30. Pankov, A., Zakhrchenko, N.: On some discrete variational problems. Acta Appl. Math. **65**(1–3), 295–303 (2001)
31. Peterson, A., Ridenhour, J.: The (2, 2)-disconjugacy of a fourth order difference equation. J. Differ. Equ. Appl. **1**(1), 87–93 (1995)
32. Popenda, J., Schmeidel, E.: On the solutions of fourth order difference equations. Rocky Mt. J. Math. **25**(4), 1485–1499 (1995)
33. Rabinowitz, P.H.: Minimax Methods in Critical Point Theory with Applications to Differential Equations. Amer. Math. Soc., Providence (1986)
34. Sharkovsky, A.N., Maistrenko, Y.L., Romanenko, E.Y.: Difference Equations and Their Applications. Kluwer Academic, Dordrecht (1993)
35. Shi, H.P., Ling, W.P., Long, Y.H., Zhang, H.Q.: Periodic and subharmonic solutions for second order nonlinear functional difference equations. Commun. Math. Anal. **5**(2), 50–59 (2008)
36. Thandapani, E., Arockiasamy, I.M.: Fourth-order nonlinear oscillations of difference equations. Comput. Math. Appl. **42**(3–5), 357–368 (2001)
37. Wang, H.Y.: On the existence of positive solutions for semilinear elliptic equations in the annulus. J. Differ. Equ. **109**(1), 1–7 (1994)
38. Yan, J., Liu, B.: Oscillatory and asymptotic behavior of fourth order nonlinear difference equations. Acta Math. Sin. **13**(1), 105–115 (1997)
39. Yao, Q.: Positive solutions of a nonlinear elastic beam equation rigidly fastened on the left and simply supported on the right. Nonlinear Anal. **69**(5–6), 1570–1580 (2008)
40. Yu, J.S., Guo, Z.M.: Boundary value problems of discrete generalized Emden-Fowler equation. Sci. China Math. **49**(10), 1303–1314 (2006)
41. Yu, J.S., Guo, Z.M.: On boundary value problems for a discrete generalized Emden-Fowler equation. J. Differ. Equ. **231**(1), 18–31 (2006)

42. Zhou, Z., Yu, J.S., Chen, Y.M.: Periodic solutions of a $2n$th-order nonlinear difference equation. Sci. China Math. **53**(1), 41–50 (2010)
43. Zou, W.M., Schechter, M.: Critical Point Theory and Its Applications. Springer, New York (2006)

CHAPTER 10

A New Smoothing Nonlinear Penalty Function for Constrained Optimization

Touna Yang[1], Nguyen Thanh Binh[2,3,*], Tran Manh Thang[4] and Duong Thi Hoa[3]

[1] *School of Mathematical Sciences, Dalian University of Technology, Dalian 116024, China*

[2] *Department of Mathematics, Shanghai University, Shanghai 200444, China*

[3] *Yen Bai Teacher's Training College, Yen Bai City 320000, Vietnam*

[4] *Department of Education and Training Yen Bai, Yen Bai City 320000, Vietnam*

ABSTRACT

In this study, a new smoothing nonlinear penalty function for constrained optimization problems is presented. It is proved that the optimal solution of the smoothed penalty problem is an approximate optimal solution of the original problem. Based on the smoothed penalty function, we develop an algorithm for finding an optimal solution of the optimization problems with inequality constraints. We further discuss the convergence of this algorithm and test this algorithm with three numerical examples. The numerical examples show that the proposed algorithm is feasible and effective for solving some nonlinear constrained optimization problems.

Keywords: penalty function; smoothing method; constrained optimization

1. INTRODUCTION

Consider the following constrained optimization problem:

$$
\begin{aligned}
(P) \qquad & \min \ f(x) \\
& \text{s.t. } g_i(x) \leq 0, \ i = 1, 2, \ldots, m, \\
& x \in \mathbb{R}^n,
\end{aligned}
$$

where the functions $f, g_i: R^n \to R, i \in I = \{1, 2, \ldots, m\}$, are continuously differentiable functions.

Let $X_0 = \{x \in R^n | g_i(x) \leq 0, i \in I\}$ be the feasible solution set and we assume that X_0 is not empty.

For a general constrained optimization problem, the penalty function method has attracted many researchers in both theoretical and practical aspects. However, to obtain an optimal solution for the original problem, the conventional quadratic penalty function method usually requires that the penalty parameter tends to infinity, which is undesirable in practical computation. In order to overcome the drawbacks of the quadratic penalty function method, exact penalty functions were proposed to solve problem (P). Zangwill [1] first proposed the l1 exact penalty function

$$F^1(x, \rho) = f(x) + \rho \sum_{i=1}^{m} g_i^+(x), \tag{1}$$

where $\rho > 0$ is a penalty parameter, and $g_i^+(x) = \max\{0, g_i(x)\}, i = 1, 2, \ldots, m$. It was proved that there exists a fixed constant $\rho_0 > 0$, for any $\rho > \rho_0$, and any global solution of the exact penalty problem is also a global solution of the original problem. Therefore, the exact penalty function methods have been widely used for solving constrained optimization problems (see, e.g., [2,3,4,5,6,7,8,9]).

Recently, the nonlinear penalty function of the following form has been investigated in [10,11,12,13]:

$$F^k(x, \rho) = \left[f(x)^k + \rho \sum_{i=1}^{m} (g_i^+(x))^k \right]^{\frac{1}{k}}, \tag{2}$$

where $f(x)$ is assumed to be positive and $k \in (0, +\infty)$. It is called the k-th power penalty function in [14,15]. Obviously, if $k=1$, the nonlinear penalty function $F^k(x, \rho)$ is reduced to the l1 exact penalty function. In [12], it was shown that the exact penalty parameter corresponding to $k\in[0,1]$ is substantially smaller than that of the l1 exact penalty function. Rubinov and Yang [13] also studied a penalty function as follows:

$$\psi_\rho^k(x,c) = [f(x) - c]^k + \rho \sum_{i=1}^{m} g_i^+(x), \tag{3}$$

where $c\in R$ such that $f(x)-c>0$ for any $x\in R^n$, and $k\in(0,+\infty)$. The corresponding penalty problem of (P) is defined as

$$(P_\rho) \qquad \min\ \psi_\rho^k(x,c) \qquad \text{s.t. } x \in \mathbb{R}^n.$$

In fact, the original problem (P) is equivalent to the problem as follows:

$$\begin{aligned} (P') \qquad & \min\ [f(x) - c]^k \\ & \text{s.t. } g_i(x) \le 0,\ i = 1,2,\ldots,m, \\ & \quad\ x \in \mathbb{R}^n. \end{aligned}$$

Obviously, the penalty problem (P_ρ) is the l_1 exact penalty problem of problem (P') defined as (1).

It is noted that these penalty functions $F^1(x,\rho)$,$F^k(x,\rho)$($0<k\le1$) and $\psi_\rho^k(x,c)$ are not differentiable at x such that $g_i(x)=0$for some $i\in I$, which prevents the use of gradient-based methods and causes some numerical instability problems in its implementation, when the value of the penalty parameter becomes large [3,5,6,8]. In order to use existing gradient-based algorithms, such as a Newton method, it is necessary to smooth the exact penalty function. Thus, the smoothing of the exact penalty function attracts much attention [16,17,18,19,20,21,22,23,24]. Pinar and Zenios [21] and Wu et al. [22] discussed a quadratic smoothing approximation to nondifferentiable exact penalty functions for constrained optimization. Binh [17] and Xu et al. [23] proposed a second-order differentiability technique to the l_1 exact penalty function. It is shown that the optimal solution of the smoothed penalty problem is an approximate optimal solution of the original optimization problem. Zenios et al. [24] discussed an algorithm for the solution of large-scale optimization problems.

In this study, we aim to develop the smoothing technique for the nonlinear penalty function (3). First, we define the following smoothing function $q_{\epsilon,\rho}^k(t)$ by

$$q^k_{\epsilon,\rho}(t) = \begin{cases} 0 & \text{if } t \le 0, \\ \frac{2m^2\rho^2}{9\epsilon^2} t^{3k} & \text{if } 0 \le t \le \left(\frac{\epsilon}{m\rho}\right)^{\frac{1}{k}}, \\ t^k + \frac{\epsilon}{3m\rho} e^{-\frac{m\rho}{\epsilon} t^k + 1} - \frac{10\epsilon}{9m\rho} & \text{if } t \ge \left(\frac{\epsilon}{m\rho}\right)^{\frac{1}{k}}, \end{cases}$$

where $0<k<+\infty, \rho>0$ and $\epsilon>0$. By considering this smoothing function, a new smoothing nonlinear penalty function is obtained. We use this smoothing nonlinear penalty function that is able to convert a constrained optimization problem into minimizations of a sequence of continuously differentiable functions and propose a corresponding algorithm for solving constrained optimization problems.

The rest of this paper is organized as follows. In Section 2, we propose a new smoothing penalty function for inequality constrained optimization problems, and some fundamental properties of its are proved. In Section 3, an algorithm based on the smoothed penalty function is presented and its global convergence is proved. In Section 4, we report results on application of this algorithm to three test problems and compare the results obtained with other similar algorithms. Finally, conclusions are discussed in Section 5.

2. SMOOTHING NONLINEAR PENALTY FUNCTIONS

In this section, we first construct a new smoothing function. Then, we introduce our smoothing nonlinear penalty function and discuss its properties.

Let $q^k(t)$:R→R be as follows:

$$q^k(t) = \begin{cases} 0 & \text{if } t \le 0, \\ t^k & \text{if } t \ge 0, \end{cases}$$

where $0<k<+\infty$. Obviously, the function $q^k(t)$ is C^1 on R for $k>1$, but it is not C^1 for $0<k\le 1$. It is useful in defining exact penalty functions for constrained optimization problems (see, e.g., [14,15,21]). Consider the nonlinear penalty function

$$F^k_\rho(x,c) = [f(x) - c]^k + \rho \sum_{i=1}^{m} q^k(g_i(x)), \tag{4}$$

and the corresponding penalty problem

$$(NP_\rho) \qquad \min \ F_\rho^k(x,c) \qquad \text{s.t. } x \in \mathbb{R}^n.$$

As previously mentioned, for any $\epsilon>0$ and $\rho>0$, the function $q_{\epsilon,\rho}^k(t)$ is defined as:

$$q_{\epsilon,\rho}^k(t) = \begin{cases} 0 & \text{if } t \le 0, \\ \dfrac{2m^2\rho^2}{9\epsilon^2}t^{3k} & \text{if } 0 \le t \le \left(\frac{\epsilon}{m\rho}\right)^{\frac{1}{k}}, \\ t^k + \dfrac{\epsilon}{3m\rho}e^{-\frac{m\rho}{\epsilon}t^k+1} - \dfrac{10\epsilon}{9m\rho} & \text{if } t \ge \left(\frac{\epsilon}{m\rho}\right)^{\frac{1}{k}}, \end{cases}$$

where $0<k<+\infty$.

Figure 1 shows the behavior of $q^k(t)$ and $q_{\epsilon,\rho}^k(t)$.

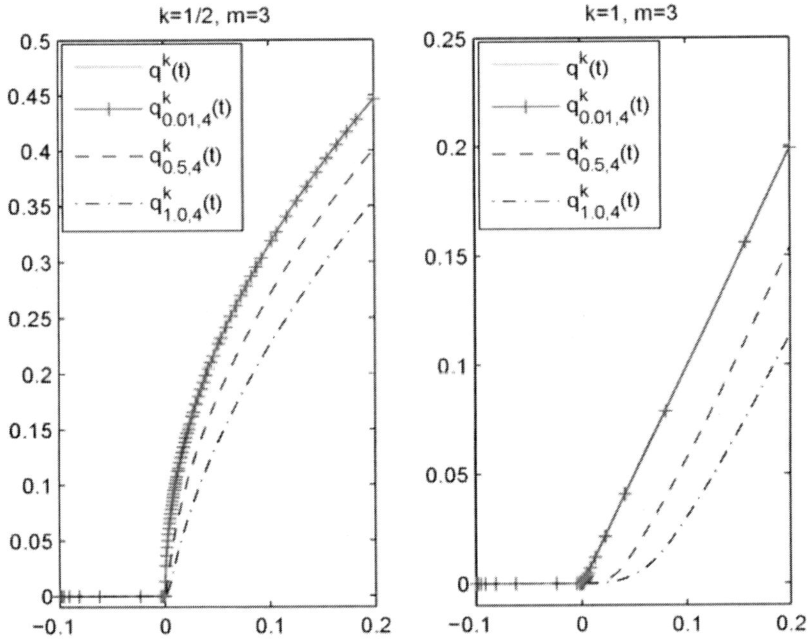

Figure 1. The behavior of $q^k(t)$ and $q_{\epsilon,\rho}^k(t)$.

In the following, we discuss the properties of $q^k_{\epsilon,\rho}(t)$.

Lemma 1.

For $0<k<+\infty$ *and any* $\epsilon>0$*, we have*

(i) $q^k_{\epsilon,\rho}(t)$ *is continuously differentiable for* $k>\frac{1}{3}$ *on* R*, where*

$$[q^k_{\epsilon,\rho}(t)]' = \begin{cases} 0 & \text{if} \quad t \le 0, \\ \dfrac{2km^2\rho^2}{3\epsilon^2} t^{3k-1} & \text{if} \quad 0 \le t \le \left(\frac{\epsilon}{m\rho}\right)^{\frac{1}{k}}, \\ kt^{k-1} - \dfrac{1}{3}kt^{k-1}e^{-\frac{m\rho}{\epsilon}t^k+1} & \text{if} \quad t \ge \left(\frac{\epsilon}{m\rho}\right)^{\frac{1}{k}}. \end{cases}$$

(ii) $\lim\limits_{\epsilon\to 0} q^k_{\epsilon,\rho}(t) = q^k(t)$.

(iii) $q^k(t) \ge q^k_{\epsilon,\rho}(t), \ \forall t \in \mathbb{R}$.

Proof. (i) First, we prove that $q^k_{\epsilon,\rho}(t)$ is continuous. Obviously, the function $q^k_{\epsilon,\rho}(t)$ is continuous at any $t \in \mathbb{R}\backslash\left\{0, \left(\frac{\epsilon}{m\rho}\right)^{\frac{1}{k}}\right\}$. We only need to prove that $q^k_{\epsilon,\rho}(t)$ continuous at the separating points: 0 and $\left(\frac{\epsilon}{m\rho}\right)^{\frac{1}{k}}$.

(1) For t=0, we have

$$\lim_{t\to 0^-} q^k_{\epsilon,\rho}(t) = \lim_{t\to 0^-} 0 = 0, \quad \lim_{t\to 0^+} q^k_{\epsilon,\rho}(t) = \lim_{t\to 0^+} \frac{2m^2\rho^2}{9\epsilon^2}t^{3k} = 0,$$

which implies

$$\lim_{t\to 0^-} q^k_{\epsilon,\rho}(t) = \lim_{t\to 0^+} q^k_{\epsilon,\rho}(t) = 0 = q^k_{\epsilon,\rho}(0).$$

Thus, $q^k_{\epsilon,\rho}(t)$ is continuous at t=0.

(2) For $t = \left(\frac{\epsilon}{m\rho}\right)^{\frac{1}{k}}$, we have

$$\lim_{t\to\left[\left(\frac{\epsilon}{m\rho}\right)^{\frac{1}{k}}\right]^-} q^k_{\epsilon,\rho}(t) = \lim_{t\to\left[\left(\frac{\epsilon}{m\rho}\right)^{\frac{1}{k}}\right]^-} \frac{2m^2\rho^2}{9\epsilon^2}t^{3k} = \frac{2\epsilon}{9m\rho},$$

$$\lim_{t\to\left[\left(\frac{\epsilon}{m\rho}\right)^{\frac{1}{k}}\right]^+} q^k_{\epsilon,\rho}(t) = \lim_{t\to\left[\left(\frac{\epsilon}{m\rho}\right)^{\frac{1}{k}}\right]^+} \left[t^k + \frac{\epsilon}{3m\rho}e^{-\frac{m\rho}{\epsilon}t^k+1} - \frac{10\epsilon}{9m\rho}\right] = \frac{2\epsilon}{9m\rho},$$

which implies

$$\lim_{t\to\left[\left(\frac{\epsilon}{m\rho}\right)^{\frac{1}{k}}\right]^-} q^k_{\epsilon,\rho}(t) = \lim_{t\to\left[\left(\frac{\epsilon}{m\rho}\right)^{\frac{1}{k}}\right]^+} q^k_{\epsilon,\rho}(t) = \frac{2\epsilon}{9m\rho} = q^k_{\epsilon,\rho}\left(\left(\frac{\epsilon}{m\rho}\right)^{\frac{1}{k}}\right).$$

Thus, $q^k_{\epsilon,\rho}(t)$ is continuous at $t = \left(\frac{\epsilon}{m\rho}\right)^{\frac{1}{k}}$.

Next, we will show that $q^k_{\epsilon,\rho}(t)$ is continuously differentiable, i.e., $[q^k_{\epsilon,\rho}(t)]'$ is continuous. Actually, we only need to prove that $[q^k_{\epsilon,\rho}(t)]'$ is continuous at the separating points: 0 and $\left(\frac{\epsilon}{m\rho}\right)^{\frac{1}{k}}$.

(1) For t=0, we have

$$\lim_{t\to 0^-}[q^k_{\epsilon,\rho}(t)]' = \lim_{t\to 0^-} 0 = 0, \quad \lim_{t\to 0^+}[q^k_{\epsilon,\rho}(t)]' = \lim_{t\to 0^+} \frac{2km^2\rho^2}{3\epsilon^2}t^{3k-1} = 0,$$

which implies

$$\lim_{t\to 0^-}[q^k_{\epsilon,\rho}(t)]' = \lim_{t\to 0^+}[q^k_{\epsilon,\rho}(t)]' = 0 = [q^k_{\epsilon,\rho}(0)]'.$$

Thus, $[q^k_{\epsilon,\rho}(t)]'$ is continuous at t=0.

(2) For $t = \left(\frac{\epsilon}{m\rho}\right)^{\frac{1}{k}}$, we have

$$\lim_{t\to\left[\left(\frac{\epsilon}{m\rho}\right)^{\frac{1}{k}}\right]^-}[q^k_{\epsilon,\rho}(t)]' = \lim_{t\to\left[\left(\frac{\epsilon}{m\rho}\right)^{\frac{1}{k}}\right]^-} \frac{2km^2\rho^2}{3\epsilon^2}t^{3k-1} = \frac{2k}{3}\left(\frac{\epsilon}{m\rho}\right)^{\frac{k-1}{k}},$$

$$\lim_{t\to\left[\left(\frac{\epsilon}{m\rho}\right)^{\frac{1}{k}}\right]^+}[q^k_{\epsilon,\rho}(t)]' = \lim_{t\to\left[\left(\frac{\epsilon}{m\rho}\right)^{\frac{1}{k}}\right]^+}\left(kt^{k-1} - \frac{1}{3}kt^{k-1}e^{-\frac{m\rho}{\epsilon}t^k+1}\right) = \frac{2k}{3}\left(\frac{\epsilon}{m\rho}\right)^{\frac{k-1}{k}},$$

which implies

$$\lim_{t\to\left[\left(\frac{\epsilon}{m\rho}\right)^{\frac{1}{k}}\right]^-}[q^k_{\epsilon,\rho}(t)]' = \lim_{t\to\left[\left(\frac{\epsilon}{m\rho}\right)^{\frac{1}{k}}\right]^+}[q^k_{\epsilon,\rho}(t)]' = \frac{2k}{3}\left(\frac{\epsilon}{m\rho}\right)^{\frac{k-1}{k}} = \left[q^k_{\epsilon,\rho}\left(\left(\frac{\epsilon}{m\rho}\right)^{\frac{1}{k}}\right)\right]'.$$

Thus, $[q^k_{\epsilon,\rho}(t)]'$ is continuous at $t=(\frac{\epsilon}{m\rho})^{\frac{1}{k}}$.

(ii) For ∀t∈R, by the definition of $q^k(t)$ and $q^k_{\epsilon,\rho}(t)$, we have

$$q^k(t)-q^k_{\epsilon,\rho}(t)=\begin{cases}0 & \text{if } t\le 0,\\ t^k-\dfrac{2m^2\rho^2}{9\epsilon^2}t^{3k} & \text{if } 0\le t\le\left(\frac{\epsilon}{m\rho}\right)^{\frac{1}{k}},\\ \dfrac{10\epsilon}{9m\rho}-\dfrac{\epsilon}{3m\rho}e^{-\frac{m\rho}{\epsilon}t^k+1} & \text{if } t\ge\left(\frac{\epsilon}{m\rho}\right)^{\frac{1}{k}}.\end{cases}$$

When $0\le t\le\left(\frac{\epsilon}{m\rho}\right)^{\frac{1}{k}}$, let u=t^k. Then, we have $0\le u\le\frac{\epsilon}{m\rho}$. Consider the function:

$$G(u)=u-\frac{2m^2\rho^2}{9\epsilon^2}u^3,\quad 0\le u\le\frac{\epsilon}{m\rho},$$

and we have

$$G'(u)=1-\frac{2m^2\rho^2}{3\epsilon^2}u^2,\quad 0\le u\le\frac{\epsilon}{m\rho}.$$

Obviously, $G'(u)>0 \text{ for } 0\le u\le\frac{\epsilon}{m\rho}$. Moreover, G(0)=0 and $G(\frac{\epsilon}{m\rho})=\frac{7\epsilon}{9m\rho}$. Hence, we have

$$0\le q^k(t)-q^k_{\epsilon,\rho}(t)\le\frac{7\epsilon}{9m\rho}.$$

When $t\ge\left(\frac{\epsilon}{m\rho}\right)^{\frac{1}{k}}$, we have

$$0<q^k(t)-q^k_{\epsilon,\rho}(t)=\frac{10\epsilon}{9m\rho}-\frac{\epsilon}{3m\rho}e^{-\frac{m\rho}{\epsilon}t^k+1}\le\frac{10\epsilon}{9m\rho}.$$

Thus, we have

$$0\le q^k(t)-q^k_{\epsilon,\rho}(t)\le\frac{10\epsilon}{9m\rho}.$$

That is,

$$\lim_{\epsilon \to 0} q^k_{\epsilon,\rho}(t) = q^k(t).$$

(iii) For ∀t∈R, from (ii), we have

$$q^k(t) - q^k_{\epsilon,\rho}(t) \geq 0,$$

which is $q^k(t) \geq q^k_{\epsilon,\rho}(t)$.

This completes the proof. □

In this study, we always assume that $c<0$ and $|c|$ is large enough, such that $f(x)-c>0$ for all $x \in R^n$. Let

$$F^k_{\epsilon,\rho}(x,c) = [f(x) - c]^k + \rho \sum_{i=1}^{m} q^k_{\epsilon,\rho}(g_i(x)), \quad 0 < k < +\infty. \tag{5}$$

Then, $F^k_{\epsilon,\rho}(x,c)$ is continuously differentiable at any $x \in R^n$ and is a smooth approximation of $F^k_\rho(x,c)$. We have the following smoothed penalty problem:

$$(NP_{\epsilon,\rho}) \qquad \min \ F^k_{\epsilon,\rho}(x,c) \qquad \text{s.t. } x \in \mathbb{R}^n.$$

Lemma 2. *We have that*

$$0 \leq F^k_\rho(x,c) - F^k_{\epsilon,\rho}(x,c) \leq \frac{10\epsilon}{9}, \quad 0 < k < +\infty \tag{6}$$

for any $x \in R^n, \epsilon>0$ *and* $\rho>0$.

Proof. For any $x \in Rn, \epsilon>0, \rho>0$, we have

$$F^k_\rho(x,c) - F^k_{\epsilon,\rho}(x,c) = \rho \sum_{i=1}^{m} \left(q^k(g_i(x)) - q^k_{\epsilon,\rho}(g_i(x)) \right).$$

Note that

$$q^k(g_i(x)) - q^k_{\epsilon,\rho}(g_i(x)) = \begin{cases} 0 & \text{if } g_i(x) \leq 0, \\ [g_i(x)]^k - \dfrac{2m^2\rho^2}{9\epsilon^2}[g_i(x)]^{3k} & \text{if } 0 \leq g_i(x) \leq \left(\frac{\epsilon}{m\rho}\right)^{\frac{1}{k}}, \\ \dfrac{10\epsilon}{9m\rho} - \dfrac{\epsilon}{3m\rho} e^{-\frac{m\rho}{\epsilon}[g_i(x)]^k + 1} & \text{if } g_i(x) \geq \left(\frac{\epsilon}{m\rho}\right)^{\frac{1}{k}}, \end{cases}$$

for any $i \in I$.

By Lemma 1, we have

$$0 \leq \sum_{i=1}^{m} (q^k(g_i(x)) - q^k_{\epsilon,\rho}(g_i(x))) \leq \frac{10\epsilon}{9\rho},$$

which implies

$$0 \leq \rho \sum_{i=1}^{m} (q^k(g_i(x)) - q^k_{\epsilon,\rho}(g_i(x))) \leq \frac{10\epsilon}{9}.$$

Hence,

$$0 \leq F^k_\rho(x,c) - F^k_{\epsilon,\rho}(x,c) \leq \frac{10\epsilon}{9}.$$

This completes the proof. □

Lemma 3. *Let* x^* *and* x^*_ρ *be optimal solutions of problem* (P) *and problem* (NP_ρ), *respectively. If* x^*_ρ *is a feasible solution to problem* (P), *then* x^*_ρ *is an optimal solution for problem* (P).

Proof. Under the given conditions, we have that

$$0 < [f(x^*_\rho) - c]^k = F^k_\rho(x^*_\rho, c) \leq F^k_\rho(x^*, c) = [f(x^*) - c]^k, \quad 0 < k < +\infty.$$

Therefore, $f(x^*_\rho) - c \leq f(x^*) - c$, which is $f(x^*_\rho) \leq f(x^*)$.

Since x^* is an optimal solution and x^*_ρ is feasible to problem (P), which is

$$f(x^*_\rho) \geq f(x^*).$$

Therefore, x^*_ρ is an optimal solution for problem (P).

This completes the proof.

Theorem 1. *Let* x^*_ρ *and* $x^*_{\epsilon,\rho}$ *be the optimal solutions of problem* (NP_ρ) *and problem* ($NP_{\epsilon,\rho}$), *respectively, for some* $\rho>0$ *and* $\epsilon>0$. *Then, we have that*

$$0 \leq F^k_\rho(x^*_\rho, c) - F^k_{\epsilon,\rho}(x^*_{\epsilon,\rho}, c) \leq \frac{10\epsilon}{9}, \quad 0 < k < +\infty. \tag{7}$$

Furthermore, if x_ρ^* satisfies the conditions of Lemma 3 and $x_{\epsilon,\rho}^*$ is feasible to problem (P), then $x_{\epsilon,\rho}^*$ is an optimal solution for problem (P).

Proof. By Lemma 2, for $\rho>0$ and $\epsilon>0$, we obtain

$$\begin{aligned} 0 &\le F_\rho^k(x_\rho^*, c) - F_{\epsilon,\rho}^k(x_\rho^*, c) \\ &\le F_\rho^k(x_\rho^*, c) - F_{\epsilon,\rho}^k(x_{\epsilon,\rho}^*, c) \\ &\le F_\rho^k(x_{\epsilon,\rho}^*, c) - F_{\epsilon,\rho}^k(x_{\epsilon,\rho}^*, c) \\ &\le \frac{10\epsilon}{9}. \end{aligned}$$

That is,

$$0 \le F_\rho^k(x_\rho^*, c) - F_{\epsilon,\rho}^k(x_{\epsilon,\rho}^*, c) \le \frac{10\epsilon}{9},$$

and

$$\begin{aligned} 0 \le &\left\{ [f(x_\rho^*) - c]^k + \rho \sum_{i=1}^m q^k(g_i(x_\rho^*)) \right\} - \left\{ [f(x_{\epsilon,\rho}^*) - c]^k + \rho \sum_{i=1}^m q_{\epsilon,\rho}^k(g_i(x_{\epsilon,\rho}^*)) \right\} \\ \le &\frac{10\epsilon}{9}. \end{aligned} \quad (8)$$

From the definition of $q^k(t)$, $q_{\epsilon,\rho}^k(t)$ and the fact that x_ρ^*, $x_{\epsilon,\rho}^*$ are feasible for problem (P), we have

$$\sum_{i=1}^m q^k(g_i(x_\rho^*)) = \sum_{i=1}^m q_{\epsilon,\rho}^k(g_i(x_{\epsilon,\rho}^*)) = 0.$$

Note that $f(x_{\epsilon,\rho}^*) - c > 0$, and from (8), we have

$$0 < [f(x_{\epsilon,\rho}^*) - c]^k \le [f(x_\rho^*) - c]^k.$$

Therefore, $f(x_{\epsilon,\rho}^*) - c \le f(x_\rho^*) - c$, which is $f(x_{\epsilon,\rho}^*) \le f(x_\rho^*)$.

As $x_{\epsilon,\rho}^*$ is feasible to (P) and by Lemma 3, x_ρ^* is an optimal solution to (P), we have

$$f(x^*_{\epsilon,\rho}) \geq f(x^*_\rho).$$

Thus, $x^*_{\epsilon,\rho}$ is an optimal solution for problem (*P*).

This completes the proof.

Definition 1. *A feasible solution* x^* *of problem* (*P*) *is called a KKT point, if there exists a* $\mu^* \in R^m$ *such that the solution pair* (x^*, μ^*) *satisfies the following conditions:*

$$\nabla f(x^*) + \sum_{i=1}^{m} \mu_i^* \nabla g_i(x^*) = 0, \tag{9}$$

$$\mu_i^* g_i(x^*) = 0,\ g_i(x^*) \leq 0,\ \mu_i^* \geq 0,\ \ i \in I. \tag{10}$$

Theorem 2. *Suppose the functions* $f, g_i (i \in I)$ *in problem (P) are convex. Let* x^* *and* $x^*_{\epsilon,\rho}$ *be the optimal solutions of problem* (*P*)*and problem* ($NP_{\epsilon,\rho}$), *respectively. If* $x^*_{\epsilon,\rho}$ *is feasible to problem* (P), *and there exists a* $\mu^* \in R^m$ *such that the pair* $(x^*_{\epsilon,\rho}, \mu^*)$ *satisfies the conditions in Equations (9) and (10), then we have that*

$$0 \leq [f(x^*_{\epsilon,\rho}) - c]^k - [f(x^*) - c]^k \leq \frac{10\epsilon}{9}, \quad 0 < k < +\infty. \tag{11}$$

Proof. Since the functions $f, g_i (i \in I)$ are continuously differentiable and convex, we see that

$$f(x^*) \geq f(x^*_{\epsilon,\rho}) + \nabla f(x^*_{\epsilon,\rho})^T (x^* - x^*_{\epsilon,\rho}), \tag{12}$$

$$g_i(x^*) \geq g_i(x^*_{\epsilon,\rho}) + \nabla g_i(x^*_{\epsilon,\rho})^T (x^* - x^*_{\epsilon,\rho}), \quad i = 1, 2, \ldots, m. \tag{13}$$

After applying the conditions given in Equations (9), (10), (12) and (13), we see that

$$
\begin{aligned}
f(x^*) &\geq f(x^*_{\epsilon,\rho}) + \nabla f(x^*_{\epsilon,\rho})^T (x^* - x^*_{\epsilon,\rho}) \\
&= f(x^*_{\epsilon,\rho}) - \sum_{i=1}^{m} \mu_i^* \nabla g_i(x^*_{\epsilon,\rho})^T (x^* - x^*_{\epsilon,\rho}) \\
&\geq f(x^*_{\epsilon,\rho}) - \sum_{i=1}^{m} \mu_i^* \left[g_i(x^*) - g_i(x^*_{\epsilon,\rho}) \right] \\
&= f(x^*_{\epsilon,\rho}) - \sum_{i=1}^{m} \mu_i^* g_i(x^*) \\
&\geq f(x^*_{\epsilon,\rho}).
\end{aligned}
$$

Therefore, $f(x^*) - c \geq f(x^*_{\epsilon,\rho}) - c > 0$. Thus,

$$
[f(x^*_{\epsilon,\rho}) - c]^k \leq [f(x^*) - c]^k \leq [f(x^*) - c]^k + \rho \sum_{i=1}^{m} q^k(g_i(x^*)) = F_\rho^k(x^*, c).
$$

By Lemma 2, we have

$$
F_\rho^k(x^*, c) \leq F_{\epsilon,\rho}^k(x^*, c) + \frac{10\epsilon}{9}.
$$

It follows that

$$
\begin{aligned}
[f(x^*_{\epsilon,\rho}) - c]^k &\leq F_{\epsilon,\rho}^k(x^*, c) + \frac{10\epsilon}{9} \\
&= [f(x^*) - c]^k + \rho \sum_{i=1}^{m} q_{\epsilon,\rho}^k(g_i(x^*)) + \frac{10\epsilon}{9} \qquad (14) \\
&= [f(x^*) - c]^k + \frac{10\epsilon}{9}.
\end{aligned}
$$

Since $x^*_{\epsilon,\rho}$ is feasible to (*P*), which is

$$
f(x^*) \leq f(x^*_{\epsilon,\rho}),
$$

then

$$
f(x^*) - c \leq f(x^*_{\epsilon,\rho}) - c,
$$

and, by $f(x^{⍰})-c>0$, we have

$$0 < [f(x^*) - c]^k \leq [f(x^*_{\epsilon,\rho}) - c]^k. \tag{15}$$

Combining Equations (14) and (15), we have that

$$[f(x^*) - c]^k \leq [f(x^*_{\epsilon,\rho}) - c]^k \leq [f(x^*) - c]^k + \frac{10\epsilon}{9},$$

which is

$$0 \leq [f(x^*_{\epsilon,\rho}) - c]^k - [f(x^*) - c]^k \leq \frac{10\epsilon}{9}, \quad 0 < k < +\infty.$$

This completes the proof.

3. ALGORITHM

In this section, by considering the above smoothed penalty function, we propose an algorithm to find an optimal solution of problem (*P*), defined as Algorithm 1.

Definition 2. *For $\epsilon>0$, a point $x^*_\epsilon \in X_0$ is called an ϵ-feasible solution to (P), if it satisfies $g_i(x^*_\epsilon) \leq \epsilon, \forall i \in I$.*

Algorithm 1: Algorithm for solving problem (P)

Step 1: Let the initial point x_1^0. Let $\epsilon_1 > 0$, $\rho_1 > 0$, $0 < \gamma < 1$, $\beta > 1$ and choose a constant $c < 0$ such that $f(x) - c > 0$, $\forall x \in X_0$, let $j = 1$ and go to Step 2.

Step 2: Use x_j^0 as the starting point to solve the following problem:

$$(NP_{\epsilon_j,\rho_j}) \qquad \min_{x \in \mathbb{R}^n} F^k_{\epsilon_j,\rho_j}(x,c) = [f(x) - c]^k + \rho_j \sum_{i=1}^{m} q^k_{\epsilon_j,\rho_j}(g_i(x)).$$

Let $x^*_{\epsilon_j,\rho_j}$ be an optimal solution of (NP_{ϵ_j,ρ_j}) (the solution of (NP_{ϵ_j,ρ_j}) we obtained by the BFGS method given in [25]).

Step 3: If $x^*_{\epsilon_j,\rho_j}$ is ϵ-feasible for problem (P), then the algorithm stops and $x^*_{\epsilon_j,\rho_j}$ is an approximate optimal solution of problem (P). Otherwise, let $\rho_{j+1} = \beta\rho_j$, $\epsilon_{j+1} = \gamma\epsilon_j$, $x^0_{j+1} = x^*_{\epsilon_j,\rho_j}$ and $j = j + 1$. Then, go to Step 2.

Remark 1. *From 0 < ⍰ < 1, ⍰ > 1, we can easily see that as* j → +∞, *the sequence* {⍰$_j$}→0 *and the sequence* $\{\rho_j\} \to +\infty$.

Theorem 3. *For $k > \frac{1}{3}$, suppose that for $\epsilon \in (0, \epsilon_1]$ and $\rho \in [\rho_1, +\infty)$, the set*

$$\arg\min_{x \in \mathbb{R}^n} F^k_{\epsilon,\rho}(x, c) \neq \emptyset. \quad (16)$$

Let $\{x^*_{\epsilon_j,\rho_j}\}$ be the sequence generated by Algorithm 1. If $\lim_{\|x\| \to +\infty} f(x) = +\infty$ and the sequence $\{F^k_{\epsilon_j,\rho_j}(x^*_{\epsilon_j,\rho_j}, c)\}$ is bounded, then $\{x^*_{\epsilon_j,\rho_j}\}$ is bounded and the limit point of $\{x^*_{\epsilon_j,\rho_j}\}$ is the solution of (P).

Proof. First, we prove that $\{x^*_{\epsilon_j,\rho_j}\}$ is bounded. Note that

$$F^k_{\epsilon_j,\rho_j}(x^*_{\epsilon_j,\rho_j}, c) = [f(x^*_{\epsilon_j,\rho_j}) - c]^k + \rho_j \sum_{i=1}^{m} q^k_{\epsilon_j,\rho_j}(g_i(x^*_{\epsilon_j,\rho_j})), \quad j = 0, 1, \ldots. \quad (17)$$

From the definition of $q^k_{\epsilon,\rho}(t)$, we have

$$\rho_j \sum_{i=1}^{m} q^k_{\epsilon_j,\rho_j}(g_i(x^*_{\epsilon_j,\rho_j})) \geq 0. \quad (18)$$

Suppose, on the contrary, that the sequence $\{x^*_{\epsilon_j,\rho_j}\}$ is unbounded and without loss of generality $\|x^*_{\epsilon_j,\rho_j}\| \to +\infty$ as $j \to +\infty$, and $f(x^*_{\epsilon_j,\rho_j}) - c > 0$. Then, $\lim_{j \to +\infty} [f(x^*_{\epsilon_j,\rho_j}) - c]^k = +\infty$, and from Equations (17) and (18), we have

$$F^k_{\epsilon_j,\rho_j}(x^*_{\epsilon_j,\rho_j}, c) \geq [f(x^*_{\epsilon_j,\rho_j}) - c]^k \to +\infty, \quad j = 0, 1, \ldots,$$

which contradicts with the sequence $\{F^k_{\epsilon_j,\rho_j}(x^*_{\epsilon_j,\rho_j}, c)\}$ being bounded. Thus, $\{x^*_{\epsilon_j,\rho_j}\}$ is bounded.

Next, we prove that the limit point of $\{x^*_{\epsilon_j,\rho_j}\}$ is the solution of problem (*P*). Let x^* be a limit point of $\{x^*_{\epsilon_j,\rho_j}\}$. Then, there exists the subset $J \subset N$ such that $x^*_{\epsilon_j,\rho_j} \to x^*$ for $j \in J$, where N is the set of natural numbers. We have to show that x^* is an optimal solution of problem (P). Thus, it is sufficient to show (i) $x^* \in X_0$ and (ii) $f(x^*) \leq \inf_{x \in X_0} f(x)$

(i) Suppose $x^* \notin X_0$. Then, there exists $\theta_0 > 0$ and the subset $J' \subset J$, such that $g_{i'}(x^*_{\epsilon_j,\rho_j}) \geq \theta_0 > 0$ for any $j \in J'$ and some $i' \in I$.

If $\theta_0 \leq g_{i'}(x^*_{\epsilon_j,\rho_j}) < \left(\frac{\epsilon_j}{m\rho_j}\right)^{\frac{1}{k}}$, from the definition of $q^k_{\epsilon,\rho}(t)$ and $x^*_{\epsilon_j,\rho_j}$ is the optimal solution according j-th values of the parameters ϵ_j,ρ_j for any $x \in X_0$, we have

$$[f(x^*_{\epsilon_j,\rho_j}) - c]^k + \frac{2m^2\rho_j^3\theta_0^{3k}}{9\epsilon_j^2} \leq F^k_{\epsilon_j,\rho_j}(x^*_{\epsilon_j,\rho_j}, c)$$
$$\leq F^k_{\epsilon_j,\rho_j}(x, c) = [f(x) - c]^k,$$

which contradicts with $\rho_j \to +\infty$ and $\epsilon_j \to 0$.

If $g_{i'}(x^*_{\epsilon_j,\rho_j}) \geq \theta_0 \geq \left(\frac{\epsilon_j}{m\rho_j}\right)^{\frac{1}{k}}$ or $g_{i'}(x^*_{\epsilon_j,\rho_j}) \geq \left(\frac{\epsilon_j}{m\rho_j}\right)^{\frac{1}{k}} \geq \theta_0$, from the definition of $q^k_{\epsilon,\rho}(t)$ and $x^*_{\epsilon_j,\rho_j}$ is the optimal solution according j-th values of the parameters ϵ_j,ρ_j for any $x \in X_0$, we have

$$[f(x^*_{\epsilon_j,\rho_j}) - c]^k + \rho_j\theta_0^k + \frac{\epsilon_j}{3m}e^{-\frac{m\rho_j}{\epsilon_j}\theta_0^k+1} - \frac{10\epsilon_j}{9m} \leq F^k_{\epsilon_j,\rho_j}(x^*_{\epsilon_j,\rho_j}, c)$$
$$\leq F^k_{\epsilon_j,\rho_j}(x, c) = [f(x) - c]^k,$$

which contradicts with $\rho_j \to +\infty$ and $\epsilon_j \to 0$.

Thus, $x^* \in X_0$.

(ii) For any $x \in X_0$, we have

$$[f(x^*_{\epsilon_j,\rho_j}) - c]^k \leq F^k_{\epsilon_j,\rho_j}(x^*_{\epsilon_j,\rho_j}, c) \leq F^k_{\epsilon_j,\rho_j}(x, c) = [f(x) - c]^k.$$

We know that $f(x^*_{\epsilon_j,\rho_j}) - c > 0$, so $f(x^*_{\epsilon_j,\rho_j}) - c \leq f(x) - c$. Therefore, $f(x^*) \leq \inf_{x \in X_0} f(x)$ holds.

This completes the proof.

4. NUMERICAL EXAMPLES

In this section, we apply the Algorithm 1 to three test problems. The proposed algorithm is implemented in Matlab (R2011A, The MathWorks Inc., Natick, MA, USA).

In each example, we take $\epsilon=10^{-6}$. Then, it is expected to get an ϵ-solution to problem (P) with Algorithm 1, and the numerical results are presented in the following tables.

Example 1. *Consider the following problem ([20], Example 4.1)*

$$\begin{aligned} \min\ & f(x) = x_1^2 + x_2^2 + 2x_3^2 + x_4^2 - 5x_1 - 5x_2 - 21x_3 + 7x_4 \\ s.t.\ & g_1(x) = 2x_1^2 + x_2^2 + x_3^2 + 2x_1 + x_2 + x_4 - 5 \leq 0, \\ & g_2(x) = x_1^2 + x_2^2 + x_3^2 + x_4^2 + x_1 - x_2 + x_3 - x_4 - 8 \leq 0, \\ & g_3(x) = x_1^2 + 2x_2^2 + x_3^2 + 2x_4^2 - x_1 - x_4 - 10 \leq 0. \end{aligned}$$

For $k = \frac{2}{3}$, let $x_1^0 = (0, 0, 0, 0)$, $\rho_1=6, \beta=10, \epsilon_1=0.01, \gamma=0.01$ and choose $c=-100$. The results are shown in Table 1.

Table 1. Results of Algorithm 1 with $k = \frac{2}{3}, x_1^0 = (0, 0, 0, 0)$ for Example 1.

j	ρ_j	ϵ_j	$x^*_{\epsilon_j,\rho_j}$	$f(x^*_{\epsilon_j,\rho_j})$	$g_1(x^*_{\epsilon_j,\rho_j})$	$g_2(x^*_{\epsilon_j,\rho_j})$	$g_3(x^*_{\epsilon_j,\rho_j})$
1	6	0.01	(0.214257, 0.952510, 1.934008, −1.051001)	−44.266455	0.069500	0.044928	−1.353205
2	60	0.0001	(0.166332, 0.828748, 2.013798, −0.959021)	−44.233325	−0.000071	−0.000006	−1.911178

For k=1, let $x_1^0 = (5, 5, 5, 5)$, $\rho_1=10, \beta=4, \epsilon_1=0.01, \gamma=0.1$ and choose $c=-100$. The results are shown in Table 2.

Table 2. Results of Algorithm 1 with k=1, $x_1^0 = (5, 5, 5, 5)$ for Example 1.

j	ρ_j	ϵ_j	$x^*_{\epsilon_j,\rho_j}$	$f(x^*_{\epsilon_j,\rho_j})$	$g_1(x^*_{\epsilon_j,\rho_j})$	$g_2(x^*_{\epsilon_j,\rho_j})$	$g_3(x^*_{\epsilon_j,\rho_j})$
1	10	0.01	(0.049915, 1.064341, 1.936277, −1.083612)	−44.010514	−0.032469	0.064160	−0.600569
2	40	0.001	(0.161485, 0.837434, 2.012060, −0.962236)	−44.233462	0.000003	0.000003	−1.870398
3	160	0.0001	(0.169837, 0.833494, 2.009512, −0.963710)	−44.233813	0.000000	0.000000	−1.892242

The results in Table 1 and Table 2 show that the convergence of Algorithm 1 and the objective function values are almost the same. By Table 1, we obtain that an approximate optimal solution $x^*=(0.166332, 0.828748, 2.013798, -0.959021)$ after two iterations with function value $f(x^*)=-44.233325$. In [20], the obtained approximate optimal solution is $x^*=(0.170056, 0.841066, 2.004907, -0.968785)$ with function value $f(x^*)=-44.225989$. Numerical results obtained by our algorithm are slightly better than the results in [20].

Example 2. *Consider the following problem ([22], Example 3.2)*

$$\begin{aligned} \min\ & f(x) = -x_1 - x_2 \\ \text{s.t.}\ & g_1(x) = -2x_1^4 + 8x_1^3 - 8x_1^2 + x_1 - 2 \le 0, \\ & g_2(x) = -4x_1^4 + 32x_1^3 - 88x_1^2 + 96x_1 + x_2 - 36 \le 0, \\ & 0 \le x_1 \le 3, \\ & 0 \le x_2 \le 4. \end{aligned}$$

For $k = \frac{3}{4}$, let $x_1^0 = (3,\ 1)$,$\rho1$=5,β=10,$\epsilon1$=0.1,γ=0.1, and choose c=−10. The results are shown in Table 3.

Table 3. Results of Algorithm 1 with $k = \frac{3}{4}, x_1^0 = (3,\ 1)$ for Example 2.

j	ρ_j	ϵ_j	$x^*_{\epsilon_j,\rho_j}$	$f(x^*_{\epsilon_j,\rho_j})$	$g_1(x^*_{\epsilon_j,\rho_j})$	$g_2(x^*_{\epsilon_j,\rho_j})$
1	5	0.1	(2.112050, 3.900242)	−6.012292	0.000039	0.000052
2	50	0.01	(2.112103, 3.900086)	−6.012190	−0.000020	−0.000008

For k=1, let $x_1^0 = (0,\ 1)$,$\rho1$=6,β=10,$\epsilon1$=0.02,γ=0.01 and choose c=−10. The results are shown in Table 4.

Table 4. Results of Algorithm 1 with k=1, $x_1^0 = (0,\ 1)$ for Example 2.

j	ρ_j	ϵ_j	$x^*_{\epsilon_j,\rho_j}$	$f(x^*_{\epsilon_j,\rho_j})$	$g_1(x^*_{\epsilon_j,\rho_j})$	$g_2(x^*_{\epsilon_j,\rho_j})$
1	6	0.02	(2.111875, 3.900776)	−6.012651	0.000232	0.000278
2	60	0.0002	(2.112763, 3.898814)	−6.011577	−0.000755	−0.000109

The results in Table 3 and Table 4 show that the convergence of Algorithm 1 and the objective function values are almost the same. By Table 3, we obtain an approximate optimal solution is x^*=(2.112103,3.900086) after 2 iterations with function value $f(x^*)$=−6.012190. In [22], the obtained global solution is x^*=(2.3295,3.1784) with function value $f(x^*)$=−5.5080.

Numerical results obtained by our algorithm are much better than the results in [22].

Example 3. *Consider the following problem ([26], Example 4.1)*

$$\begin{aligned} \min\ & f(x) = x_1^2 + x_2^2 - \cos(17x_1) - \cos(17x_2) + 3 \\ s.t.\ & g_1(x) = (x_1 - 2)^2 + x_2^2 - 1.6^2 \le 0, \\ & g_2(x) = x_1^2 + (x_2 - 3)^2 - 2.7^2 \le 0, \\ & 0 \le x_1 \le 2, \\ & 0 \le x_2 \le 2. \end{aligned}$$

For $k = \frac{2}{3}$, let $x_1^0 = (0, 1)$,ρ_1=1,β=3,ϵ_1=0.01,γ=0.01 and choose c=−2. The results are shown in Table 5.

Table 5. Results of Algorithm 1 with $k = \frac{2}{3}$, $x_1^0 = (0, 1)$ for Example 3.

j	ρ_j	ϵ_j	$x^*_{\epsilon_j,\rho_j}$	$f(x^*_{\epsilon_j,\rho_j})$	$g_1(x^*_{\epsilon_j,\rho_j})$	$g_2(x^*_{\epsilon_j,\rho_j})$
1	1	0.01	(0.016363, 1.092060)	2.271514	2.567409	−3.649496
2	3	0.0001	(0.725355, 0.399258)	1.837548	−0.775873	−0.000000

For $k = \frac{3}{4}$, let $x_1^0 = (0, 0)$,ρ_1=1,β=9,ϵ_1=0.01,γ=0.01, and choose c=−2. The results are

Table 6. Results of Algorithm 1 with $k = \frac{3}{4}$,$x_1^0 = (0, 0)$ for Example 3.

j	ρ_j	ϵ_j	$x^*_{\epsilon_j,\rho_j}$	$f(x^*_{\epsilon_j,\rho_j})$	$g_1(x^*_{\epsilon_j,\rho_j})$	$g_2(x^*_{\epsilon_j,\rho_j})$
1	1	0.01	(0.387905, 1.086812)	2.448684	1.220019	−3.479255
2	9	0.0001	(0.725356, 0.399258)	1.837548	−0.775876	−0.000000

The results in Table 5 and Table 6 show that the convergence of Algorithm 1 and the objective function values are almost the same. By Table 5, we obtain that an approximate optimal solution is x^*=(0.725355,0.399258) after two iterations with function value $f(x^*)$=1.837548. In [26], the obtained approximate optimal solution is x^*=(0.7255,0.3993)with function value $f(x^*)$=1.8376.

Numerical results obtained by our algorithm are slightly better than the results in [26].

5. CONCLUSIONS

In this study, we have proposed a new smoothing approach to the nonsmooth penalty function and developed a corresponding algorithm to solve constrained optimization with inequality constraints. It is shown that any optimal solution of the smoothed penalty problem is shown to be an approximate optimal solution or a global solution of the original optimization problem. Furthermore, the numerical results given in Section 4 show that the Algorithm 1 has a good convergence for an approximate optimal solution.

ACKNOWLEDGMENTS

The authors would like to express their gratitude to anonymous referees' detailed comments and remarks that help us improve our presentation of this paper considerably. This work is supported by grants from the National Natural Science Foundation of China (No. 11371242 and 61572099).

REFERENCES

1. Zangwill, W.I. Nonlinear programming via penalty function. *Manag. Sci.* **1967**, *13*, 334–358.
2. Bazaraa, M.S.; Goode, J.J. Sufficient conditions for a globally exact penalty function without convexity. *Math. Program. Study* **1982**, *19*, 1–15.
3. Di Pillo, G.; Grippo, L. An exact penalty function method with global conergence properties for nonlinear programming problems. *Math. Program.* **1986**, *36*, 1–18.
4. Di Pillo, G.; Grippo, L. Exact penalty functions in constrained optimization. *SIAM J. Control. Optim.* **1989**, *27*, 1333–1360.
5. Han, S.P.; Mangasrian, O.L. Exact penalty function in nonlinear programming. *Math. Program.* **1979**, *17*, 251–269.
6. Lasserre, J.B. A globally convergent algorithm for exact penalty functions. *Eur. J. Oper. Res.* **1981**, *7*, 389–395.
7. Mangasarian, O.L. Sufficiency of exact penalty minimization. *SIAM J. Control. Optim.* **1985**, *23*, 30–37.
8. Rosenberg, E. Exact penalty functions and stability in locally Lipschitz programming. *Math. Program.* **1984**, *30*, 340–356.
9. Yu, C.J.; Teo, K.L.; Zhang, L.S.; Bai, Y.Q. A new exact penalty function method for continuous inequality constrained optimization problems. *J. Indus. Mgmt. Optimiz.* **2010**, *6*, 895–910.
10. Huang, X.X.; Yang, X.Q. Convergence analysis of a class of nonlinear penalization methods for constrained optimization via first-order necessary optimality conditions. *J. Optim. Theory Appl.* **2003**, *116*, 311–332.
11. Rubinov, A.M.; Glover, B.M.; Yang, X.Q. Extended Lagrange and penalty functions in continuous optimization. *Optimization* **1999**, *46*, 327–351.

12. Rubinov, A.M.; Yang, X.Q.; Bagirov, A.M. Penalty functions with a small penalty parameter. *Optim. Methods Softw.* **2002**, *17*, 931–964.
13. Rubinov, A.M.; Yang, X.Q. *Lagrange-Type Functions in Constrained Non-Convex Optimization*; Kluwer Academic Publishers: Dordrecht, Netherlands, 2003.
14. Binh, N.T.; Yan, W.L. Smoothing approximation to the *k*-th power nonlinear penalty function for constrained optimization problems. *J. Appl. Math. Bioinform.* **2015**, *5*, 1–19.
15. Yang, X.Q.; Meng, Z.Q.; Huang, X.X.; Pong, G.T.Y. Smoothing nonlinear penalty functions for constrained optimization. *Numer. Funct. Anal. Optimiz.* **2003**, *24*, 351–364.
16. Binh, N.T. Smoothing approximation to l_1 exact penalty function for constrained optimization problems. *J. Appl. Math. Inform.***2015**, *33*, 387–399.
17. Binh, N.T. Second-order smoothing approximation to l_1 exact penalty function for nonlinear constrained optimization problems. *Theor. Math. Appl.* **2015**, *5*, 1–17.
18. Binh, N.T. Smoothed lower order penalty function for constrained optimization problems. *IAENG Int. J. Appl. Math.* **2016**, *46*, 76–81.
19. Chen, C.H.; Mangasarian, O.L. Smoothing methods for convex inequalities and linear complementarity problems. *Math. Program.* **1995**, *71*, 51–69.
20. Meng, Z.Q.; Dang, C.Y.; Jiang, M.; Shen, R. A smoothing objective penalty function algorithm for inequality constrained optimization problems. *Numer. Funct. Anal. Optimiz.* **2011**, *32*, 806–820.
21. Pinar, M.C.; Zenios, S.A. On smoothing exact penalty function for convex constrained optimization. *SIAM J. Optim.* **1994**, *4*, 486–511.
22. Wu, Z.Y.; Lee, H.W.J.; Bai, F.S.; Zhang, L.S. Quadratic smoothing approximation to l_1 exact penalty function in global optimization. *J. Ind. Manag. Optim.* **2005**, *1*, 533–547.
23. Xu, X.S.; Meng, Z.Q.; Sun, J.W.; Huang, L.G.; Shen, R. A second-order smooth penalty function algorithm for constrained optimization problems. *Comput. Optim. Appl.* **2013**, *55*, 155–172.
24. Zenios, S.A.; Pinar, M.C.; Dembo, R.S. A smooth penalty function algorithm for network-structured problems. *Eur. J. Oper. Res.***1995**, *83*, 220–236.
25. Nocedal, J.; Wright, S.T. *Numerical Optimization*; Springer: New York, NY, USA, 1999.
26. Sun, X.L.; Li, D. Value-estimation function method for constrained global optimization. *J. Optim. Theory Appl.* **1999**, *102*, 385–409.

CHAPTER 11

A global convergent quasi-Newton method for systems of monotone equations

Zixin Chen[1], Wanyou Cheng[2], Xiaoliang Li[2]

College of City, Dongguan University of Technology, Dongguan 523808, China

College of Computer, Dongguan University of Technology, Dongguan 523808, China

ABSTRACT

In this paper, we propose a quasi-Newton method for solving systems of monotone equations. The method is a combination of the Broyden method and the hyperplane projection method. Under appropriate conditions, we prove that the proposed method is globally convergent. Preliminary numerical results show that the proposed method is promising.

Keywords: Monotone equations, Hyperplane projection method, Global convergence

1. INTRODUCTION

In this paper, we consider the problem of finding a solution of the nonlinear system of equations

$$F(x) = 0, \tag{1.1}$$

where $F:R^n \to R^n$ is continuous and monotone. By monotonicity, we mean

$$\langle F(x) - F(y), x - y\rangle \geq 0, \forall x,y \in R^n.$$

Nonlinear monotone equations have many practical background such as the first order necessary condition of the unconstrained convex optimization problem and the subproblems in the generalized proximal algorithms with Bregman distances [9]. Some monotone variational inequality problems can also be converted into the form of the problem by means of fixed point maps or normal maps if the underlying function satisfies some coercive conditions [12].

Many methods for solving (1.1) fall into the class of the quasi-Newton methods since they converge rapidly from sufficiently good initial guess. Since Boryden [1] proposed the first quasi-Newton method for solving nonlinear equations, there has been significant progress in the theoretical study on quasi-Newton methods, especially in local convergence analysis [2, 3]. To ensure global convergence, some line search strategy for some merit function are used. Recently, Solodov and Svaiter [10] presented a Newton-type algorithm for solving systems of monotone equations. By using hybrid projection method, they showed that their method converges globally. For nonlinear equations, Griewank [4] obtained a global convergence results for Broyden's rank one method. By introduce a new line search process, Li and Fukushima [7] have developed a globally convergent Broyden-like method for solving nonlinear equations and [6] presented a globally convergent Gauss-Newton-based BFGS method for solving symmetric nonlinear equations. The method in [6, 7] is not norm descent. Gu, Li, Qi and Zhou [5] generalized the method in [6] and proposed a globally convergent and norm descent BFGS method for solving symmetirc equations. Quite recently, Zhou and Li [13] proposed a global convergence BFGS method for systems of monotone equations without use of merit functions. We refer to papers [8, 11] for a review on recent advances in this area.

In this paper, based on the hyperplane projection method [10], we propose a quasi-Newton method for solving systems of monotone equations without use of merit functions. The method is a combination of the Broyden method and the hyperplane projection method [10]. Under appropriate conditions, we show that the proposed method is globally convergent. Preliminary numerical results show that the method is promising.

The paper is organized as follows. In Sect. 2, after simply recalling hyperplane projection method, we present the algorithm. In Sect. 3, we establish the global convergence of the algorithm. We report some numerical results in the last section.

2. ALGORITHM

In this section, we describe the method in detail. Firstly, let us first recall the hyperplane projection method in [10]. Note that by the monotonicity of F, for any x¯x¯ such that $F(\bar{x}) = 0$, we have

$$\langle F(z_k), \bar{x} - z_k\rangle \leq 0.$$

Let x_k be the current iterate. By performing some kind of line search procedure along a direction $\bar{d}_k$, a point $z_k = x_k + \alpha k \bar{d} k$ can be computed such that

$$\langle F(z_k), x_k - z_k\rangle > 0.$$

Thus the hyperplane

$$H_k = \{x \in R^n || \langle F(z_k), x - z_k\rangle = 0\}$$

strictly separates the current iterate x_k from zeros of (1.1). Therefore, it is reasonable to let the next iterate x_{k+1} be the projection of x_k onto the hyperplane.

Now, we state the steps of the algorithm as follow.

Algorithm 2.1 (Broyden method)

- **STEP 1**. Given an initial point $x_0 \in R^n$ and constants $\beta \in (0,1)$, $\eta \in (0,1)$, $\xi \in (0,1)$ and $0 < \sigma_{\min} < \sigma_{\max}$. Given the initial steplength $\sigma_0 = 1$, $B_0 = I$ (the identity matrix) and $d_0 = -F(x_0)$. Let $k := 0$.
- **STEP 2**. Stop if $\|F(x_k)\| = 0$.
- **STEP 3**. Determine steplength $\alpha k = \sigma_k \beta^{mk}$ such that m_k is the smallest nonnegative integer m satisfying

$$-\langle F(x_k + \sigma_k\beta^m d_k), d_k\rangle \geq \eta\sigma_k\beta^m \| F(x_k + \sigma_k\beta^m d_k)\| \| \|d_k\|^2. \quad (2.1)$$

Let $z_k = x_k + \alpha_k d_k$. Stop if $\|F(z_k)\| = 0$.

- **STEP 4**. Compute the projection of x_k on H_k by

$$x_{k+1} = x_k - \frac{\langle F(z_k), x_k - z_k\rangle}{\|F(z_k)\|^2} F(z_k) \quad (2.2)$$

Stop if $\|F(x_{k+1})\| = 0$.

- **STEP 5**. Compute B_{k+1} by the following Broyden update formula

$$B_{k+1} = B_k + \frac{(y_k - B_k s_k)s_k^T}{\|s_k\|^2} \tag{2.3}$$

where $s_k = x_k - x_{k-1}$ and $y_k = F(x_k) - F(x_{k-1})$.

- **STEP 6**. Compute d_{k+1} by solving the linear equation

$$B_{k+1}d_{k+1} = -F(x_{k+1}). \tag{2.4}$$

If the system (2.4) is not solvable or the condition

$$d_{k+1}^T F(x_{k+1}) < -\xi \left\| F(x_{k+1}) \right\|^2$$

is not satisfied, set $d_{k+1} = -F(x_{k+1})$ and $\sigma_{k+1} = \max\{\sigma_{\min}, \min\{\frac{\|s_k\|^2}{s_k^T y_k}, \sigma_{\max}\}\}$; else set $\sigma_{k+1} = 1$.

- **STEP 7**. Let $k := k + 1$. Go to Step 3.

Remark

It is easy to see from Step 6 of Algorithm 2.1 that

−FTkdk≥ξ‖Fk‖2.−FkTdk≥ξ||Fk||2.

$$-F_k^T d_k \geq \xi \| F_k \|^2 \tag{2.5}$$

Therefore after a finite number of reductions of α_k, the line search condition (2.1) necessarily holds. Consequently, Algorithm 2.1 is well-defined.

3. CONVERGENCE PROPERTY

This section is devoted to the global convergence of Algorithm 2.1. To establish global convergence of Algorithm 2.1, we need the following assumption.

Assumption 3.1 (1) ∇F is Lipschitz continuous on R^n, i.e., there is a constant $L>0$ such that

$$|||\nabla F(x) - \nabla F(y)\| \leq L\ \|x - y\|,\ \forall x,y \in R^n,$$

where ∇F denotes the Jacobian of F.

(2) $\nabla F(x)$ in nonsingular for every $x \in R^n$.

Before proving global convergence of Algorithm 2.1, we first give three preliminary lemmas. The following lemma is from [10].

Lemma 3.1 *Let F be monotone and* $x,y \in R^n$ *satisfy* $\langle F(y), x-y \rangle > 0$. *Let*

$$x^{+} = x - \frac{\langle F(y), x - y\rangle}{\|F(y)\|^2} F(y)$$

Then for any $\bar{x} \in R^n$ *such that* $F(\bar{x})=0$, *it holds that*

$$\|x^{+} - \bar{x}\|^2 \leq \|x - \bar{x}\|^2 - \|x^{+} - x\|^2.$$

Define

$$\delta_k = \frac{\|y_k - B_k s_k\|}{\|s_k\|} \quad \text{and} \quad A_{k+1} = \int_0^1 \nabla F(x_k + \tau s_k) d\tau$$

Then by the mean-value theorem, we have $y_k = A_{k+1} s_k$ and hence

$$\delta_k = \frac{\|(A_{k+1} - B_k) s_k\|}{\|s_k\|}$$

Moreover, by the update formula (2.3), we have

$$B_{k+1} = B_k + \frac{(A_{k+1} - B_k) s_k s_k^T}{\|s_k\|^2}$$

In a similar way to Lemma 2.6 in [7], it is not difficult to prove the following useful lemma.

Lemma 3.2

Suppose that Assumption 3.1 *holds and the sequence* $\{x_k\}$ *generated by Algorithm* 2.1 *is bounded. If*

$$\sum_{k=0}^{\infty} \|s_k\|^2 < \infty \tag{3.1}$$

then there is a subsequence of $\{\delta_k\}$ *tending to zero.*

Lemma 3.3

Suppose that Assumption 3.1 holds and the sequence $\{x_k\}$ *generated by Algorithm 2.1 is bounded. If* (3.1) *holds, then there exist an infinite set* K_1 *and a constant* $C_1>0$ *such that*

$$\xi\|F(x_k)\| \leq \|d_k\| \leq C_1\|F(x_k)\| \tag{3.2}$$

for all $k \in K_1$ *large enough.*

Proof

By Lemma 3.2, there is a subsequence $\{\delta_k\}_{k\in K}$ of $\{\delta_k\}$ converging to zero. Since $\{x_k\}_{k\in K}$ is bounded, there exists an infinite set $K_1 \subset K$ such that $\lim_{k\in K_1} x_k = \bar{x}$. By (3.1) and the definition of A_{k+1}, it is clear that $\{A_{k+1}\}_{k\in K_1}$ tends to $\nabla F(\bar{x})$. By the nonsingularity of $\nabla F(\bar{x})$, there exists a constant $M_1 > 0$ such that $\|A_{k+1}^{-1}\| \leq M_1$ for all $k \in K_1$ sufficiently large. Thus by Step 6 of Algorithm 2.1 and the definition of δ_k, we have

$$\begin{aligned}\|d_k\| &\leq \max\left\{\left\|F(x_k)\right\|, \left\|A_{k+1}^{-1}\left((A_{k+1} - B_k)d_k - F(x_k)\right)\right\|\right\}\\ &\leq \max\left\{\left\|F(x_k)\right\|, M_1\left(\delta_k\|d_k\| + \left\|F(x_k)\right\|\right)\right\}.\end{aligned}$$

Since $\lim_{k\in K_1} \delta_k = 0$, the last inequality implies that there is a constant $C_1 > 0$ such that for all $k \in K_1$ sufficiently large

$$\|d_k\| \leq C_1\left\|F(x_k)\right\| \tag{3.3}$$

On the other hand, applying Cauchy-Schwarz inequality to (2.5), we obtain

$$\|d_k\| \geq \xi\|F_k\|$$

The last inequality together with (3.3) implies (3.2). □

Now we establish a global convergence theorem for Algorithm 2.1.

Theorem 3.1 *Suppose that Assumption* 3.1 *holds. Let* $\{x_k\}$ *be generated by Algorithm* 2.1. *Suppose that F is monotone and that the solution set of* (1.1) *is not empty. Then for any* $\bar{x}$ *such that* $F(\bar{x}) = 0$, *it holds that*

$$\|x_{k+1} - \bar{x}\|^2 \leq \|x_k - \bar{x}\|^2 - \|x_k + 1 - x_k\|^2.$$

In particular, $\{x_k\}$ *is bounded. Furthermore, it holds that either* $\{x_k\}$ *is finite and the last iterate is a solution, or the sequence is infinite and* $\lim_{k\to\infty}\|x_{k+1} - x_k\| = 0$. *Moreover,* $\{x_k\}$ *converges to some solution of* (1.1).

Proof

We first note that if the algorithm terminates at some iteration k, then $\|F(z_k)\| = 0$ or $\|F(x_k)\| = 0$. This means that x_k or z_k is a solution of (1.1).

Suppose that $\|F(z_k)\|\neq 0$ and $\|F(x_k)\|\neq 0$ for all k. Then an infinite sequence $\{x_k\}$ is generated. It follows from (2.1) that

$$\langle F(z_k), x_k - z_k\rangle = -\alpha_k\langle F(z_k), d_k\rangle \geq \eta\|F(z_k)\|\alpha_k^2\|d_k\|^2 > 0 \tag{3.4}$$

Let $\bar{x}$ be any solution such that $F(\bar{x}) = 0$. By (2.2), (3.4) and Lemma 3.1, we obtain

$$\|x_{k+1} - \bar{x}\|^2 \leq \|x_k - \bar{x}\|^2 - \|x_{k+1} - x_k\|^2 \tag{3.5}$$

Hence the sequence $\{\|xk - \bar{x}\|2\}$ is decreasing and convergent. In particular, the sequence $\{\|x_k - \bar{x}\|\}$ is convergent and the sequence $\{x_k\}$ is bounded. Again by (3.5), we have

$$\|x_{k+1} - x_k\|^2 \leq \|x_k - \bar{x}\|^2 - \|x_{k+1} - \bar{x}\|^2 \tag{3.6}$$

Summing both side of (3.6), since the sequence $\{\|x_k - \bar{x}\|2\}$ is convergent, we have (3.1). In particular, we have

$$\lim_{k\to\infty}\|x_{k+1} - x_k\| = 0 \tag{3.7}$$

By (2.2) and (3.4), we obtain

$$\|x_{k+1} - x_k\| = \frac{\langle F(z_k), x_k - z_k \rangle}{\|F(z_k)\|} \geq \eta \alpha_k^2 \|d_k\|^2$$

The last inequality together with (3.7) implies

$$\lim_{k \to \infty} \alpha_k \|d_k\| = 0 \tag{3.8}$$

Now we consider the following two possible cases:

1) $\lim_{k\to\infty} \inf\|F(x_k)\| = 0$.

2) $\lim_{k\to\infty} \inf\|F(x_k)\| = \epsilon > 0$.

If (i) holds, by the continuity of F and the boundedness of $\{x_k\}$, it is clear that the sequence $\{x_k\}$ has some accumulation point $\hat{x}$ such that $F(\hat{x}) = 0$. From (3.5), it holds that the sequence $\{\|x_k - \hat{x}\|\}$ is convergent, and since $\hat{x}$ is an accumulation point of $\{x_k\}$, it must hold that $\{x_k\}$ converges to $\hat{x}$.

If (ii) holds. In this case, by the boundedness of $\{x_k\}$ and the continuity of F, there exists a positive constant C such that

$$\frac{\epsilon}{2} \leq \|F(x_k)\| \leq C \tag{3.9}$$

On the other hand, by Assumption 3.1, the boundedness of $\{x_k\}$ and (3.1), then Lemma 3.3 holds. Lemma 3.3 and (3.2) and (3.9) implies that $\{d_k\}_{k\in K1}$ is bounded from below. Hence, from (3.8) we get that

$$\lim_{k \in K_1, k \to \infty} \alpha_k = 0$$

By the line search rule, we have for all $k \in K_1$ sufficiently large, $\sigma_k \beta^{mk-1}$ will not satisfy (2.1). This means

$$-\langle F(x_k + \sigma_k \beta^{m_k - 1} d_k), d_k \rangle < \eta \sigma_k \beta^{m_k - 1} \|F(x_k + \sigma_k \beta^{m_k - 1} d_k)\| \|d_k\|^2 \tag{3.10}$$

The boundedness of $\{x_k\}k\in K_1$ implies that there exist an accumulation point $\hat{x}$ and an infinite index set $K_2 \subset K_1$ such that $\lim_{k\in K2} x_k = \hat{x}$. Since the sequence $\{d_k\}_{k\in K2}$ is also bounded, there exist an infinite index set $K_3 \subset K_2$

and an accumulation point $\hat{d}$ such that $\lim_{k \in K3} d_k = \hat{d}$. Taking limit in (3.10) for $k \in K_3$, we obtain

$$-\langle F(\hat{x}), \hat{d} \rangle \leq 0.$$

However, it is easy to see from (2.5) that

$$-\langle F(\hat{x}), \hat{d} \rangle > 0.$$

This yields a contradiction. Consequently, the case (ii) is not possible. The proof is complete. □

4. NUMERICAL RESULTS

In this section, we tested Algorithm 2.1 and compared it with the BFGS method in [13] and the INM method in [10]. We implemented Algorithm 2.1 with the following parameters: $\beta = 0.6$, $\xi = 10^{-8}$ and $\eta = 10^{-4}$. If $\sigma_k \notin [\sigma_{min}, \sigma_{max}]$, we replace it by

$$\sigma_k = \begin{cases} 1 & \text{if } \|F(x_k)\| > 1, \\ \|F(x_k)\|^{-1} & \text{if } 10^{-5} \leq \|F(x_k)\| \leq 1, \\ 10^5 & \text{if } \|F(x_k)\| < 10^{-5}, \end{cases}$$

where $\sigma_{min} = 10^{-10}$ and $\sigma_{max} = 10^{10}$. We stop the iteration if the iteration number exceeds 500 or the inequality

$$\|\|F(x_k)\|\| \leq 10^{-4} \text{ or} \|\|F(z_k)\|\| \leq 10^{-4}$$

is satisfied. The BFGS method in [13] was implemented with the following parameters: $\beta = 0.6$, $\sigma = 10^{-5}$, $h = 10^{-4}$ and $r = 0$. For the INM method in [10], we set $\mu_k = \|F(x_k)\|$, $\rho_k = 0$, $\beta = 0.4$, $\lambda = 0.0001$. The stop criterion is $\|F(x_k)\| \leq 10^{-4}$ or the iteration number exceeds 500. The codes were written in FORTRAN 90 with double precision arithmetic and carried out on a PC (CPU 3.0 GHz, 512M memory) with Windows operation system.

The efficiency of the proposed method was tested on the following two problems with various dimensions and different initial points.

Problem 1

Function F is given by

$$F(x) = Ax + g(x),$$

where $g(x) = (2e^{x1} - 1, 3e^{x2} - 1,\ldots,3e^{xn-1} - 1,2e^{xn-1})^T$ and

$$A = \begin{pmatrix} 2 & -1 & & & \\ -1 & 2 & -1 & & \\ & \ddots & \ddots & \ddots & \\ & & \ddots & \ddots & -1 \\ & & & -1 & 2 \end{pmatrix}$$

Problem 2

Function F is given by

$$F_1(x) = 2x_1 + sin(x_1) - 1$$
$$F_i(x) = -2x_{i-1} + 2x_i + sin(x_i) - 1.0, \quad i = 2, \ldots, n-1$$
$$F_n(x) = 2x_n + sin(x_n) - 1.$$

We note that Problem 1 is symmetric while Problem 2 is nonsymmetric. The results are listed in Tables 1–2 where $x_1 = (0.1,0.1,\ldots,0.1)^T$, $x_2 = (1,1,\ldots,1)^T$, $x_3 = (\frac{1}{n}, \frac{2}{n}, \ldots, 1)^T$, $x_4 = (-10, -10, \ldots, -10)^T$, $x_5 = (-0.1, -0.1, \ldots, -0.1)^T$, $x_6 = (-1, -1, \ldots, -1)^T$, $x_7 = (1 - \frac{1}{n}, 1 - \frac{2}{n}, \ldots, 0)^T$, $x_8 = (-0.01, -0.01, \ldots, -0.01)^T$, $x_9 = (\frac{n}{n-1}, \frac{n}{n-1}, \ldots, \frac{n}{n-1})$, $x_{10} = (\frac{1}{n}, \frac{1}{n}, \ldots, \frac{1}{n})$, $x_{11} = (\frac{n}{n+1}, \frac{n}{n+1}, \ldots, \frac{n}{n+1})$ $x_{12} = (\frac{1}{3}, \frac{1}{3}, \ldots, \frac{1}{3})$ In Tables 1–2, we report the problem number along with the initial point number (Pro(initial)), the dimension of each test problem (dim), the number of iterations (iter), the number of function evaluations (fun) and the CPU time in seconds (time). We claim that two method fails, and use the symbol 'F', when some of the following options hold:

a) the number of iterations is greater than or equal to 500; or

b) the number of backtracking required by the line search along a step is greater than or equal to 20.

We tested each problem 100 times with the same initial point. The CPU time reported in Tables 1–2 is the average value. In the tables, "method 1" and "method 2" represent Algorithm 2.1 and the BFGS method in [13] respectively.

From Tables 1–2, we observe that method 1 performed much better than method 2 and in most cases the INM method performs best.

Table 1 Test results for Problem 1

Method 1				Method 2		INM	
Pro(initial)	**Dim**	**Iter**	**Time**	**Iter**	**Time**	**Iter**	**Time**
1(1)	(50)	33	0.31250D−02	53	0.78125D−02	26	0.26875D−02
1(2)	(50)	26	0.46875D−02	59	0.10937D−01	21	0.33750D−02
1(3)	(50)	36	0.46875D−02	65	0.93750D−02	25	0.31250D−02
1(4)	(50)	77	0.78125D−02	72	0.12500D−01	101	0.10594D+00
1(5)	(50)	36	0.62500D−02	50	0.93750D−02	35	0.55313D−02
1(6)	(50)	20	0.31250D−02	44	0.46875D−02	121	0.19687D+00
1(7)	(50)	29	0.46875D−02	64	0.10937D−01	24	0.35938D−02
1(8)	(50)	37	0.62500D−02	48	0.78125D−02	92	0.11563D+00
1(9)	(50)	34	0.46875D−02	55	0.10937D−01	32	0.40625D−02
1(10)	(50)	32	0.46875D−02	50	0.93750D−02	36	0.51250D−02
1(11)	(50)	36	0.46875D−02	53	0.78125D−02	30	0.30312D−02
1(12)	(50)	30	0.62500D−02	51	0.93750D−02	23	0.53750D−02
1(1)	(100)	36	0.25000D−01	61	0.40625D−01	23	0.18750D−01
1(2)	(100)	34	0.20313D−01	68	0.45312D−01	26	0.19687D−01
1(3)	(100)	32	0.20313D−01	68	0.42188D−01	23	0.18875D−01
1(4)	(100)	89	0.54688D−01	81	0.54688D−01	121	0.24781D+01
1(5)	(100)	36	0.23438D−01	63	0.39062D−01	28	0.19688D−01
1(6)	(100)	22	0.12500D−01	49	0.31250D−01	116	0.22687D+01
1(7)	(100)	29	0.17188D−01	69	0.42188D−01	22	0.16188D−01
1(8)	(100)	38	0.23438D−01	66	0.42188D−01	99	0.21250D+00
1(9)	(100)	34	0.20313D−01	69	0.45312D−01	27	0.19375D−01
1(10)	(100)	36	0.17188D−01	64	0.40625D−01	27	0.16375D−01
1(11)	(100)	38	0.25000D−01	66	0.40625D−01	36	0.23750D−01
1(12)	(100)	29	0.17188D−01	63	0.39062D−01	22	0.14562D−01
1(1)	(200)	37	0.85938D−01	67	0.16406D+00	28	0.65562D−01
1(2)	(200)	42	0.98437D−01	71	0.19219D+00	23	0.48469D−01
1(3)	(200)	39	0.95312D−01	80	0.20156D+00	24	0.72250D−01
1(4)	(200)	92	0.21563D+00	93	0.23438D+00	113	0.28844D+01
1(5)	(200)	40	0.92188D−01	57	0.14219D+00	47	0.98125D−01
1(6)	(200)	31	0.71875D−01	56	0.14062D+00	91	0.17631D+01
1(7)	(200)	29	0.67187D−01	81	0.20625D+00	18	0.58625D−01

1(8)	(200)	38	0.84375D−01	67	0.16719D+00	85	0.16719D+01
1(9)	(200)	37	0.84375D−01	71	0.18125D+00	43	0.98031D−01
1(10)	(200)	42	0.95312D−01	64	0.16094D+00	24	0.46469D−01
1(11)	(200)	29	0.65625D−01	67	0.17188D+00	17	0.48094D−01
1(12)	(200)	35	0.81250D−01	67	0.17969D+00	22	0.65688D−01

Table 2 Test results for Problem 2

Method 1				**Method 2**		**INM**	
Pro(initial)	**Dim**	**Iter**	**Time**	**Iter**	**Time**	**Iter**	**Time**
2(1)	(20)	105	0.31250D−02	96	0.46875D−02	123	0.25000D−01
2(2)	(20)	95	0.31250D−02	80	0.31250D−02	134	0.25000D−01
2(3)	(20)	82	0.00000D+00	95	0.31250D−02	73	0.15625D−01
2(4)	(20)	120	0.31250D−02	121	0.31250D−02	F	F
2(5)	(20)	94	0.31250D−02	98	0.31250D−02	314	0.46875D−01
2(6)	(20)	91	0.31250D−02	103	0.31250D−02	F	F
2(7)	(20)	75	0.31250D−02	84	0.31250D−02	145	0.25000D−01
2(8)	(20)	96	0.46875D−02	95	0.31250D−02	183	0.31250D−01
2(9)	(20)	65	0.31250D−02	77	0.15625D−02	142	0.21875D−01
2(10)	(20)	74	0.31250D−02	91	0.31250D−02	141	0.18750D−01
2(11)	(20)	73	0.31250D−02	83	0.15625D−02	127	0.21875D−01
2(12)	(20)	87	0.31250D−02	88	0.31250D−02	95	0.18750D−01
2(1)	(50)	227	0.34375D−01	223	0.40625D−01	150	0.24750D−01
2(2)	(50)	177	0.28125D−01	206	0.35937D−01	236	0.23438D+00
2(3)	(50)	175	0.28125D−01	220	0.37500D−01	122	0.15313D−01
2(4)	(50)	F	F	F	F	F	F
2(5)	(50)	170	0.26562D−01	216	0.34375D−01	227	0.40063D−01
2(6)	(50)	197	0.29687D−01	226	0.32813D−01	F	F
2(7)	(50)	311	0.50000D−01	211	0.35937D−01	249	0.43750D−01
2(8)	(50)	170	0.25000D−01	226	0.34375D−01	167	0.19375D−01
2(9)	(50)	164	0.25000D−01	203	0.32813D−01	238	0.22812D+00
2(10)	(50)	209	0.34375D−01	225	0.35937D−01	159	0.18750D−01
2(11)	(50)	273	0.40625D−01	201	0.32813D−01	237	0.35812D−01

2(12)	(50)	210	0.31250D−01	218	0.35937D−01	160	0.27813D−01
2(1)	(100)	F	F	F	F	230	0.10656D+01
2(2)	(100)	F	F	421	0.26719D+00	451	0.30219D+01
2(3)	(100)	460	0.26562D+00	F	F	206	0.18750D+00
2(4)	(100)	174	0.10312D+00	F	F	F	F
2(5)	(100)	378	0.21719D+00	F	F	239	0.14719D+01
2(6)	(100)	483	0.27813D+00	F	F	F	F
2(7)	(100)	F	F	418	0.25938D+00	454	0.27687D+01
2(8)	(100)	365	0.20938D+00	F	F	224	0.10469D+01
2(9)	(100)	F	F	431	0.26875D+00	455	0.36375D+01
2(10)	(100)	370	0.21250D+00	F	F	224	0.10469D+01
2(11)	(100)	F	F	413	0.25469D+00	448	0.29187D+01
2(12)	(100)	379	0.21563D+00	F	F	267	0.11281D+01

Simultaneously, during the numerical experiments, it is interesting to note that the step $d_k=-F(x_k)$ never appeared when $k>0$ in method 1. In other words, the condition $d_k^T F_k \le -\xi \| F_k \|^2$ was always satisfied.

5. CONCLUSION

In this paper, we propose an algorithm for solving nonlinear monotone equations, which combines the Broyden method and the hyperplane projection method. Under appropriate conditions, we prove that the proposed method is globally convergent. We also report some numerical results to show efficiency of the proposed method.

REFERENCES

1. Broyden, C.G.: A class of methods for solving nonlinear simultaneous equations. Math. Comput. **19**, 577–593 (1965)
2. Dennis, J.E., More, J.J. Jr.: A characterization of superlinear convergence and its application to quasi-Newton methods. Math. Comput. **28**, 549–560 (1974)
3. Dennis, J.E., More, J.J. Jr.: Quasi-Newton method, motivation and theory. SIAM Rev. **19**, 46–89 (1977)
4. Griewank, A.: The global convergence of Broyden-like methods with suitable line search. J. Aust. Math. Soc. Ser. B **28**, 75–92 (1986)

5. Gu, G.Z., Li, D.H., Qi, L.Q., Zhou, S.Z.: Desecent direction of quasi-Newton methods for symmetric nonlinear equations. SIAM J. Numer. Anal. **40**, 1763–1774 (2002)
6. Li, D.H., Fukushima, M.: A globally and superlinear convergent Gauss-Newton based BFGS methods for symmetric nonlinear equations. SIAM J. Numer. Anal. **37**, 152–172 (1999)
7. Li, D.H., Fukushima, M.: A derivative-free line search and global convergence of Broyden-like method for nonlinear equations. Optim. Methods Softw. **13**, 583–599 (2000)
8. Li, D.H., Cheng, W.Y.: Recent progress in the global convergence of quasi-Newton methods for nonlinear equations. Hokkaido Math. J. **36**, 729–743 (2007)
9. Iusem, A.N., Solodov, M.V.: Newton-type methods with generalized distances for constrained optimization. Optimization **41**, 257–278 (1997)
10. Solodov, M.V., Svaiter, B.F.: A globally convergent inexact Newton method for systems of monotone equations. In: Fukushima, M., Qi, L. (eds.) Reformulation: Nonsmooth, Piecewise Smooth, Semismooth and Smoothing Methods, pp. 355–369. Kluwer Academic, Norwell (1998)
11. Martínez, J.M.: Practical quasi-Newton methods for solving nonlinear systems. J. Comput. Appl. Math. **124**, 97–121 (2000)
12. Zhao, Y.B., Li, D.: Monotonicity of fixed point and normal mapping associated with variational inequality and its application. SIAM J. Optim. **4**, 962–973 (2001)
13. Zhou, W., Li, D.H.: A globally convergent BFGS method for nonlinear monotone equations without any merit functions. Math. Comput. **77**, 2231–2240 (2008)

CHAPTER 12

Damping Characteristics of Viscoelastic Damping Structure under Coupled Condition

Jun Wang, Dagang Sun *, Shizhong Liu and Xin Zhang

College of Mechanical Engineering, Taiyuan University of Science and Technology, Taiyuan 030024, China

ABSTRACT

Temperature has an influence on damping characteristics of the viscoelastic damping structure. The change of the damping characteristics of the structure under the cycle load is a dynamic and coupled process. The hyperelastic-viscoelastic model was used to describe nonlinear deformation and viscoelasticity simultaneously. The temperature distribution and change of the damping characteristics under the coupled condition was analyzed by finite element method (FEM). The maximum value of the simulation results was in agreement with the one calculated by the formula in the literature. Dynamic stiffness and dissipated energy were obtained based on the hysteresis loop. Dynamic stiffness and dissipated energy gradually decreased with the increase of the temperature.

Keywords: viscoelastic damping structure; hyper-viscoelasticity; damping characteristics; thermal-mechanical coupling

1. INTRODUCTION

The viscoelastic damping structure is widely applying for vibration and noise reduction. The viscoelastic damping layer, most of which is rubber or rubberlike polymers, represents hysteresis under a dynamic load. Part of the mechanical energy is absorbed and finally dissipated as heat due to the internal friction of the molecular chains. Continuous cyclic load and poor conduction of heat may cause extensive heat to build up in the structure. The mechanical response of the viscoelastic materials is often highly sensitive to temperature [1,2,3]. Heat may change the mechanical characteristics of the structure and the damping capability [4,5,6]. Excessive heat may lead to early fatigue failure or even explosive rupture. Therefore, it is essential to evaluate the temperature distribution and damping characteristics of the viscoelastic damping structure due to the mechanical energy dissipation during cyclic loading.

Numerous analyses have been proposed to estimate the temperature distribution and damping characteristics of viscoelastic material and its structure. Macro-mechanical or micro-mechanical material models were proposed to describe thermo-viscoelastic behavior [7,8,9,10]. The complexity of the theory restricts their engineering application. Habibi et al. investigated structural bamboo at the microscopic and macroscopic level [11]. Two kinds of biological cells separately have the responsibility of viscoelasticity at lower or higher frequencies. David I. G. Jones introduced simple and effective approaches for describing the damping-related properties of viscoelastic materials, with emphasis on the effects of frequency and temperature, and proceeded to illustrate simple techniques for measuring the desired properties and for selecting and applying the materials [12]. Johnson and Chen employed a linear viscoelastic model (the Maxwell solid model) to solve the coupled thermal and large strain history integral. Due to under-prediction of the size of the hysteresis loop in the linear viscoelasticity, the error in dissipated energy prediction at large strain is unacceptable [13]. Shah et al. studied the coupled problem of deformation of a linear-viscoelastic composite cylinder by applying the correspondence principle [14]. Pesek et al. proposed a mathematical model based on a weak formulation of the partial differential equation by FEMLAB (original release of COMSOL Multiphysics) to investigate the thermo-mechanical interaction in a pre-stressed rubber block used for resilient elements of composed tram wheels. A proportional damping model and the equality of the heat energy density and the dissipation energy density were computed to perform coupling between the mechanical and thermal equations under selected simple stress states [15]. Banic et al. investigated the temperature of a rubber damper under cyclic loading due to hysteresis losses by finite element analysis (FEA). The visco-plastic constitutive model established by Bergstrom-Boyce was used to predict the heat generation and hysteresis in the rubber-metal spring of railway draw gear [16]. Luo et al. predicted the heat generation of a rubber spring instrument during the spring-accelerated fatigue test. A static hysteresis loop was obtained via the FEA approach experimentally [17]. Kamran and Anastasia used a non-linear visco-elastic constitutive model (proposed by Schapery) to analyze the effect of coupling between the thermal and mechanical response, which was attributed to the dissipation of energy, heat conduction and temperature-dependent material parameters on the overall response of visco-elastic solids [18]. Hwang and Yeong analyzed the temperature distribution of a coupled 3D dynamic rolling simulation of a tire by finite element method (FEM) [19]. The heat generation rate was assumed to be equal to the strain energy density function multiplied by the hysteresis coefficient. Fenza et al. investigated the damping characteristics of a viscoelastic embedded composite fuselage structure by experiments at different temperatures [20]. Kerchman and Cheng [21] evaluated the heat generation and transient temperature using linearized constitutive model and FEM. Frequency-dependence on the Viscoelastic Damping VED structure is also a matter of major concern. The sandwich viscoelastic damping structure is analyzed by the method of model reduction to reduce the high-order finite element models to a smaller size in direct dynamic analysis [22]. The frequency response analysis of viscoelastic beams and plane frames with an arbitrary number of Kelvin-Voigt viscoelastic dampers was concerned. The exact frequency response in all frame members was also obtained in closed analytical form [23].

Since the damping characteristics of viscoelastic material are sensitive to temperature, also due to the low conductivity of the material, the damping ability is a dynamic coupled process. Some works treated the coupled problem with a one-way coupling approach, especially common in the rolling resistance field of rubber tires. Some coupled thermo-mechanical constitutive models need to user-defined material (UMAT) subroutine by support. Meanwhile, due to the coupled effect, the temperature distribution of the viscoelastic damping structure may not be constant or homogeneous. In this paper, a fully coupled analysis of the viscoelastic damping structure will be investigated to describe the change of the damping characteristics more accurately. The investigation by commercial finite code ABAQUS (Dassault Systèmes, Vélizy-Villacoublay, France) will be validated by comparing it with the available field data in the present literature.

2. SIMULATION METHOD

2.1. Hyper-Viscoelastic Model

Viscoelastic materials usually represent large deformation and dynamic characteristics simultaneously. The linear viscoelastic models do a poor job of replicating the hysteresis loop in a load/unload cycle of deformation because the hysteresis loops generated are narrow. Therefore, the combined usage of the hyperelasticity and linear viscoelasticity (usually described as a Prony series) is used for the hysteresis analysis. The stress response of the hyper-viscoelastic model consists of a nonlinear elastic part and a viscous part. The elastic response is instantaneous while the viscous part is prolonged over time. More details of the constitutive model as formulations and implementation are available in the literature [24,25]. The hyperelastic response (time-independent) is generally derived from stress-strain data by tensile, compression, shear and/or biaxial tests. There stress-strain data may be fitted as a particular strain energy function by the linear or nonlinear least squares method. The dynamic mechanical characteristics may be obtained by the dynamic mechanical analyzer (DMA). The Prony series parameters were fitted by the optimization method. For simplicity, the constitutive parameters of the material were from the example in the ABAQUS Example Problem Manual article [26,27]. All units of British thermal units (BTU) parameters were translated into the international system of units (SI).

The hyperelastic response is described as the Neo Hooke model:

$$U = C_{10}(\bar{I}_1 - 3) + \frac{1}{D_1}(J_{el} - 1)^2 \tag{1}$$

where C_{10} is the positive material parameter, C_{10}=1.0423×10^3, psi = 7.1864 × 10^6 Pa, and D_1 controls compressibility, D^1=9.6267×10^{-6}.

The N-term Prony series:

$$g(t) = g_\infty + \sum_{i=1}^{N} g_i \exp(-t/\tau_i) \tag{2}$$

where g_∞ and g_i are normalize dimensionless constants and $g_\infty + \sum_{i=1}^{N} g_i = 1$.

The Prony parameters were as follows: g_1=0.0396, t_1=1.766. g_2=0.1018, t_2=0.1536. g_3=0.858, t3=0.0127.

2.2. Finite Element Method (FEM) Implementation

For temperature dependence, most viscoelastic materials are usually assumed as thermal rheological simple (TRS) material near or above the glass transition temperature. The TRS translation function is expressed by the Williams–Landel–Ferry (WLF) equation [28]:

$$\log A = -\frac{C_1(\theta - \theta_0)}{C_2 + (\theta - \theta_0)} \tag{3}$$

where the values are defined as θ_0 = 21.7 °C, $C^0{}_1$ = 56.1 °C, and $C^0{}_2$ = 1000 °C.

By means of the backward difference method, the temperature is integrated into the Newton method for solving nonlinear equations. Its exact solution algorithm [28]:

$$\begin{bmatrix} K_{uu} & K_{u\theta} \\ K_{\theta u} & K_{\theta\theta} \end{bmatrix} \begin{Bmatrix} \Delta u \\ \Delta\theta \end{Bmatrix} = \begin{Bmatrix} R_u \\ R_\theta \end{Bmatrix} \tag{4}$$

where Δu and $\Delta\theta$ are the respective corrections to the incremental displacement and temperature, K_{ij} are sub-matrices of the fully coupled Jacobian matrix, R_u and R_θ are the mechanical and thermal residual vectors, respectively.

A viscoelastic damping structure consisting of two elastic constrained layers and one viscoelastic damping layer was accomplished by the solution of temperature displacement in ABAQUS. The length was 0.09 m with 45 elements. The thickness of the elastic constrained layer and the viscoelastic damping layer was 0.01 m with eight elements. The elastic constrained layer was discretized into 4-node plane strain thermally coupled quadrilateral (CPE4T) elements and 4-node plane strain thermally coupled quadrilateral (CPE4HT) elements for the viscoelastic damping layer. A sinusoidal displacement U=0.0064sinωt (ω=2πf, f = 1 Hz) in the x direction was applied on the top left-hand corner. The bottom side was completely fixed (Figure 1). Heat generation by hysteresis is associated with intrinsic dissipation due to plasticity, which is usually described by inelastic heat friction (IHF). IHF is defined by the ratio of the dissipated energy to the plastic work [29]. For viscoelastic materials, the IHF is assumed to be 1.071×10^{-4} in the ABAQUS help documentation. The properties of materials refer to the ABAQUS Example Problem Manual article (Table 1). The initial temperature was 21.7 °C. An adaptive time stepping was determined with a creep strain error tolerance of 5×10^{-3}.

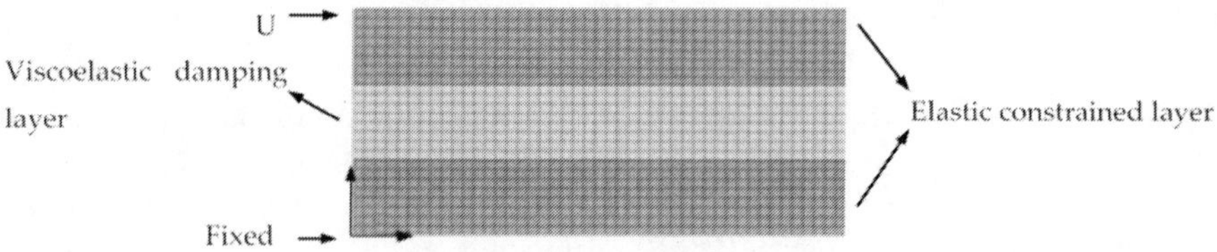

Figure 1. Finite Element (FE) model of viscoelastic structure.

Table 1. Properties of materials.

Property	Elastic Constrained Layer	Viscoelastic Damping Layer
Density (kg/m^3)	7850	1130
Modulus of elasticity (Pa)	2.1×10^{11}	-
Poisson ratio	0.3	-
Thermal expansion coefficient (10^{-6}(m/m·K))	10.8	220
Specific heat capacity (J/kg·°C)	502	1900
Heat conduction (W/(m·°C)	70	0.14
Non-elastic thermal friction coefficient	-	1.071×10^{-4}

3. RESULTS AND DISCUSSION

3.1. Temperature Distribution

The temperature distribution in the end was contoured on a postprocessor (Figure 2). The temperature adjacent to the elastic constrained layer nearly maintained the ambient temperature (21.7 °C) due to pure elasticity and excellent thermal conductivity. The temperature was increased from the outside to the inside as concentric circle in the viscoelastic damping layer. The maximal value θmax appeared in the center, and reached 28.1 °C. The same result could be found in the ABAQUS Example Problem Manual article.

The value for θmax can also be calculated by the next formula [30]:

$$\theta_{\max} = \theta + \frac{fU_d H^2}{8K} \tag{5}$$

where θ is the initial temperature, f is the frequency of the loading cycles, H is the thickness of the viscoelastic component, K is the heat conduction of the viscoelastic material, and U_d is the amount of energy generated per cycle:

$$U_d = \pi E_2 \varepsilon_0^2 \quad (6)$$

where E_2 is the loss modulus of the viscoelastic material and ε_0 is the amplitude of the strain.

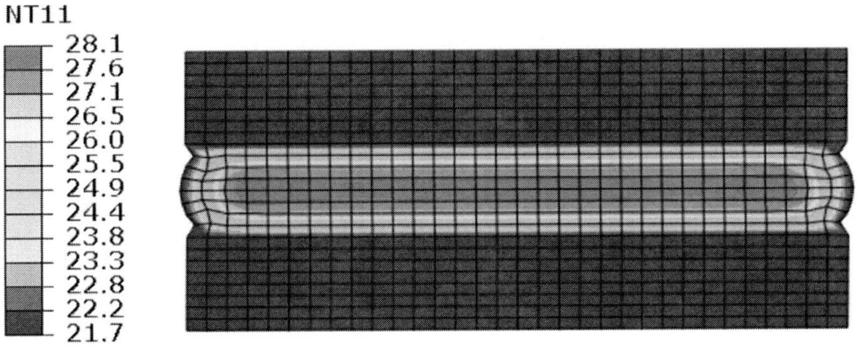

Figure 2. Temperature (°C) contour in the end.

Further, θ_{max} calculated at 28.9 °C by Equation (5) matched well with the simulation (28.1 °C). The simulation error was 2.7%, so it is clear that the proposed method has the advantages of high accuracy to evaluate the maximal value of the temperature distribution.

3.2. Dynamic Damping Characteristics

In this part, the change of the dissipated energy and dynamic stiffness were discussed. The hysteresis loop is generated by load and displacement due to hysteresis behavior. The integration area of the hysteresis loop is the dissipated energy E_d, which represents the ability of the viscoelastic damping structure. The reaction force of every node R_{Fn} on the bottom and displacement x of left corner on the top were extracted separately on the postprocessor. The reaction force of the structure RF was summed by RF_n. The combined RF with x the hysteresis curve was drawn (Figure 3a). The hysteresis loop did not form completely in the first period, so E_d was calculated from the second period to the end. E_d was reduced with the increase of the temperature. With the temperature increased, the relaxation time of the intermolecular motion was shortened. The dissipated energy was decreasing because the motion of the molecule gradually kept up with the external force [13]. Dynamic stiffness is defined as GB/T 15168-2013 [31]

$$F_d = \frac{F_0}{X_0} \cdot \frac{y'}{x'} \tag{7}$$

where F_0 is double amplitude in maximal displacement, X_0 is double amplitude corresponding to the transmitting force, x' is the displacement per unit length on the x-axis, and y' is the force per unit length on the y-axis (Figure 3b). Thirty percent of the dynamic stiffness was decreased in the period of loading. A similar result was found by Liu [23]. Both the stiffness and damping coefficient decreased with the temperature increasing. Creep was aggravated by the temperature rising while the carrying capacity of the viscoelastic damping structure decreased.

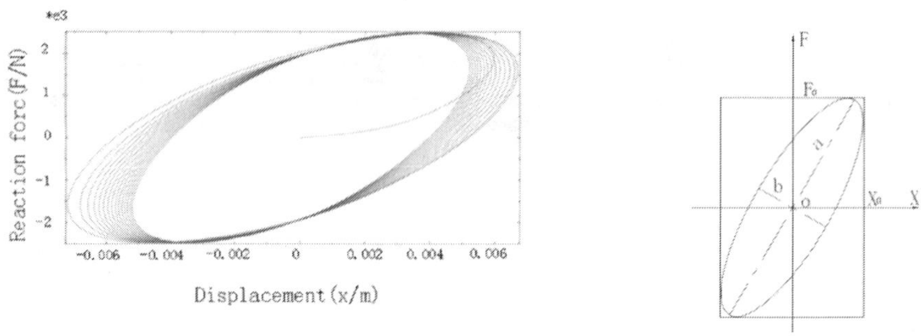

(a) (b)

Figure 3. Hysteresis loops (**a**) Coupled hysteresis loop; (**b**) Schematic diagram.

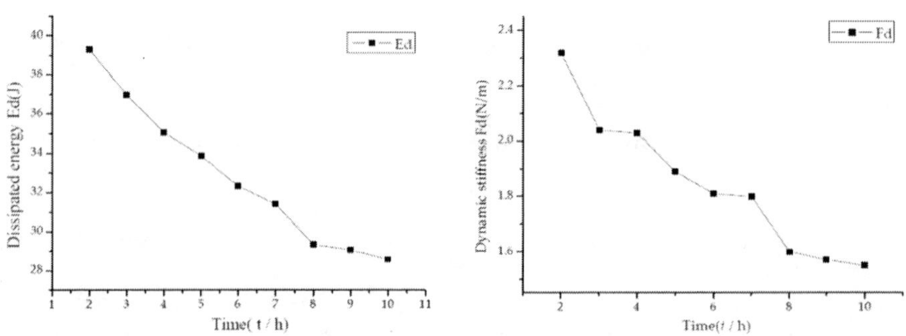

(a) (b)

Figure 4. Change of dynamic damping characteristics. (**a**) Dissipated energy (E_d); (**b**) Dynamic stiffness (F_d).

With the increase of the total number of cycles, the elastic modulus or stiffness of the material decreases. It is a common phenomenon that the structural stiffness cannot bear external load before the material has been destroyed. The ability of the dissipated energy will strongly decline. The change of E_d and F_d were seen in Figure 4.

4. CONCLUSIONS

The aim of this research was to investigate the temperature distribution and change of the damping characteristics of the viscoelastic damping structure under a coupled condition. A hyper-viscoelastic constitutive model was employed to describe the hyperelastic response and viscoelastic response. A two-dimensional planar FEM model was analyzed in the coupled temperature-displacement solver in ABAQUS. The temperature distribution at the end of the load illustrated that built-up heat appeared in the center of the structure. The maximal temperature is in agreement with the one calculated by the empirical formula. With the increase of the temperature caused by inelastic dissipation comes a reduction in the dissipated energy and dynamic stiffness. Since viscoelastic materials exhibit better dissipation behavior when subjected to shear load, in the future research the analysis will be implemented in more styles of load such as bend, compression and hybrid condition. Besides, the IHF coefficient is a key factor for determining the dissipated energy due to the inelastic deform. The value of the IHF will be evaluated precisely by an experiment in the next step.

ACKNOWLEDGMENTS

The work was funded by the National Natural Science Foundation for Young Scientists of China (Grant No. 51405323), the National Natural Science Foundation for Young Scientists of China (Grant No. 51305288).

REFERENCES

1. Ward, I.M.; Sweeney, J. Chapter 2 The mechanical properties of polymers: General considerations. In *Mechanical Properties of Solid Polymers*, 2nd ed.; Wiley: Hoboken, NJ, USA, 2013.
2. Christensen, R. Chapter 3 Thermoviscoelasticity. In *Theory of Viscoelasticity*, 2nd ed.; Academic Press: Waltham, MA, USA, 1982.
3. Ferry, J.D. Chapter 11 Dependence of viscoelastic behavior on temperature and pressure. In *Viscoelastic Properties of Polymers*; Wiley: Hoboken, NJ, USA, 1970.

4. Chang, K.C.; Soong, T.T.; Oh, S.; Lai, M.L. Effect of Ambient Temperature on Viscoelastically Damped Structure. *J. Struct. Eng.* **1992**, *118*, 1955–1973.
5. Fang, Q.H.; Zhang, F.P.; Huang, B.Z. Study on Extension Characteristics of Vulcanized Rubber at Different Temperatures. *J. Build. Mater.* **2005**, *8*, 383–386.
6. Liu, D.H.; Fan, D.; Ouyang, Y.F.; Wu, C.P. Temperature Effect on Mechanical Properties of Rubber Isolators. *Noise Vib. Control* **2014**, *3*, 203–206.
7. Boukamel, A.; Méo, S.; Débordes, O.; Jaeger, M. A Thermo-viscoelastic Model for Elastomeric Behaviour and Its Numerical Application. *Arch. Appl. Mech.* **2001**, *71*, 785–801.
8. Rodas, C.O.; Zaïri, F.; Naït-abdelaziz, M. A Finite Strain Thermo-viscoelastic Constitutive Model to Describe the Self-heating in Elastomeric Materials during Low-cycle Fatigue. *J. Mech. Phys. Solids* **2013**, *64*, 396–410.
9. Stefanie, R. A Micromechanically Motivated Material Model for the Thermo-viscoelastic Material Behaviour of Rubber-like Polymers. *Int. J. Plast.* **2003**, *19*, 909–940.
10. Holzapfel, G.A.; Simo, J.C. A New Viscoelastic Constitutive Model for Continuous Media at Finite Thermomechanical Changes. *Int. J. Solids Struct.* **1996**, *33*, 3019–3034.
11. Habibi, M.K.; Tam, L.H.; Lau, D.; Yang, L. Viscoelastic Damping Behavior of Structural Bamboo Material and Its Microstructural Origins. *Mech. Mater.* **2016**, *97*, 184–198.
12. Jones, D.I.G. *Handbook of Viscoelastic Vibration Damping*, 1st ed.; Wiley: Hoboken, NJ, USA, 2001.
13. Johnson, A.R.; Chen, T.K. Approximating Thermo-viscoelastic Heating of Largely Strained Solid Rubber Components. *Comput. Methods Appl. Mech. Engrg.* **2005**, *194*, 313–325.
14. Shah, S.; Muliana, A.; Rajagopal, K.R. Coupled Heat Conduction and Deformation in a viscoelastic Composite Cylinder. *Mech. Time-Depend. Mater.* **2009**, *13*, 121–147.
15. Pešek, L.; Půst, L.; Šulc, P. FEM Modeling of Thermo-Mechanical Interaction in Pre-pressed Rubber Block. *Eng. Mech.***2007**, *14*, 3–11. Available online: http://www. im.fme. vutbr.cz/pdf/14_1_003.pdf (accessed on 13 March 2017).
16. Banic, M.S.; Stamenkovic, D.S.; Miltenovic, V.D.; Milosevi, M.S.; Miltenovi, A.V.; Djeki, P.S.; Rackov, M.J. Prediction of Heat Generation in Rubber or Rubber-metal Springs. *Therm. Sci.* **2012**, *16*, 527–539.
17. Luo, R.K.; Wu, W.X. A Method to Predict the Heat Generation in a Rubber Spring Used in the Railway Industry. *Proc. Inst. Mech. Eng. Part F. J. Rail Rapid Transit* **2005**, *219*, 239–244.
18. Khan, A.M. Fully Coupled Heat Conduction and Deformation Analyses of Nonlinear Viscoelastic Composites. *Mech. Time Depend. Mater.* **2012**, *16*, 461–489.
19. Lin, Y.J.; Hwang, S.J. Temperature Prediction of Rolling Tires by Computer Simulation. *Math. Comput. Simul.* **2004**, *67*, 235–249.
20. Fenza, A.D.; Monaco, E.; Amoroso, F.; Lecce, L. Experimental Approach in Studying Temperature Effects on Composite Material Structures Realized with Viscoelastic Damping Treatments. *J. Vib. Control* **2014**, *22*, 358–370.
21. Kerchman, V.; Cheng, S. Experimental Study and Finite Element Simulation of Heat Build-up in Rubber Compounds with Application to Fracture. *Rubber Chem. Technol.* **2003**, *76*, 386–405.
22. Zghal, S.; Bouazizi, M.L.; Bouhaddi, N.; Nasri, R. Model Reduction Methods for Viscoelastic Sandwich Structures in Frequency and Time Domains. *Finite Elements Anal. Des.* **2015**, *93*, 12–29.
23. Failla, G. An Exact Generalised Function Approach to Frequency Response Analysis of Beams and Plane Frames with the Inclusion of Viscoelastic Damping. *J. Sound Vib.* **2016**, *360*, 171–202.
24. Johnson, A.R.; Quigley, C.J.; Mead, J.L. Large Strain Viscoelastic Constitutive Models for Rubber, Part I: Formulations. *Rubber Chem. Technol.* **1994**, *67*, 904–917.
25. Quigley, C.J.; Mead, J.; Johnson, A.R. Large Strain Viscoelastic Constitutive Models for Rubber, Part II: Determination of Material Constants. *Rubber Chem. Technol.* **1995**, *68*, 230–247.
26. Systèmes, D. ABAQUS 6.14. Available online: http://abaqus.software.polimi.it/v6.14/ index.html (accessed on 10 March 2017).

27. Ghazaly, N.M. ABAQUS Analysis User's Manual, Vol 2-abaqus 6.10.
28. Holzapfel, G.A.; Reiter, G. Fully Coupled Thermomechanical Behaviour of Viscoelastic Solids Treated with Finite Elements. *Int. J. Eng. Sci.* **1995**, *33*, 1037–1058.
29. Rittel, D. On the Conversion of Plastic Work to Heat during High Strain Rate Deformation of Glassy Polymers. *Mech. Mater.* **1999**, *31*, 131–139.
30. Gent, A.N.; Hertz, D.L.; Hamed, G.R. Chapter 4 Dynamic mechanical properties. In *Engineering with Rubber—How to Design Rubber Components*, 2nd ed.; Hanser Gardner Publications, Carl Hanser Publishers: Cincinnati, OH, USA, 2001.
31. GB/T 15168-2013. Vibration and shock isolators measuring method for its static and dynamic characteristics. Available online: http://www.sac.gov.cn/was5/web/ search?channelid=97779&templet=gjcxjg_detail.jsp&searchword=STANDARD_CODE='GB/T 15168-2013'&XZ=T&STANDARD_CODE=GB/T 15168-2013 (accessed on 10 March 2017).

CHAPTER 13

Spin-polarized transport in ferromagnetic multilayers: An unconditionally convergent FEM integrator

Claas Abert[a], Gino Hrkac[b], Marcus Page[c], Dirk Praetorius[c], Michele Ruggeri[c],*, Dieter Suess[a]

[a] *Institute of Solid State Physics, Vienna University of Technology, Austria*

[b] *College of Engineering, Mathematics and Physical Sciences, University of Exeter, United Kingdom*

[c] *Institute for Analysis and Scientific Computing, Vienna University of Technology, Austria*

ABSTRACT

We propose and analyze a decoupled time-marching scheme for the coupling of the Landau–Lifshitz–Gilbert equation with a quasilinear diffusion equation for the spin accumulation. This model describes the interplay of magnetization and electron spin accumulation in magnetic and nonmagnetic multilayer structures. Despite the strong nonlinearity of the overall PDE system, the proposed integrator requires only the solution of two linear systems per time-step. Unconditional convergence of the integrator towards weak solutions is proved.

Keywords: Micromagnetics, Landau–Lifshitz–Gilbert equation, Spin accumulation, Finite element method

1. INTRODUCTION

The interaction between electric current and magnetization in magnetic nanostructure devices and the control of this interaction have been realized through the prediction of the spin-transfer torque by Slonczewski and Berger [1,2]. The transfer of spin angular momentum between the spin-polarized electrical current and the local magnetization has been observed in various magnetic devices, such as metallic spin-valves systems, magnetic tunnel junctions, and magnetic domain walls in permalloy nanowires [3,4]. Based on these experiments, a number of technological applications have been proposed, e.g., STT-MRAMs, racetrack memories, and magnetic vortex oscillators [5,6].

The fundamental physics underlying these phenomena is understood as due to a spin torque that arises from the transfer of the spin angular momentum between conduction free electrons and magnetization. In the original works of Berger and Slonczewski [1,2], a homogeneous spin accumulation is assumed due to a current which flows through a first magnetic layer perpendicular to the interface into a second magnetic layer. The spin torque effect leads to an interaction between the spin-polarized current and the magnetization in the second layer. For magnetic multilayers it has been shown that a proper description of the magnetoresistance is essential to take into account the interplay between successive interfaces [7–9]. In order to calculate the spin torque transfer, the spin transport properties have to be calculated far beyond the interface.

The original model of Berger and Slonczewski has been extended by taking into account the diffusion process of the spin accumulation by Shpiro et al. for one-dimensional systems [10] and by García-Cervera and Wang [11,12] for three-dimensional systems. There, the overall system of PDEs (SDLLG) is a quasilinear diffusion equation for the evolution of the spin accumulation coupled to the Landau–Lifshitz–Gilbert equation (LLG) for the magnetization dynamics. Existence of global weak solutions to LLG goes back to [13], while, in the same spirit, existence of global weak solutions to SDLLG is proved in [11].

The reliable numerical integration of LLG (and, in particular, SDLLG) faces several challenges due to the nonuniqueness of weak solutions, the explicit nonlinearity, and an inherent nonconvex modulus constraint. Numerical approximation schemes for weak solutions of LLG are first proposed in [14,15]. First unconditional convergence results can be found in [16,17], which consider the small-particle limit of LLG with exchange only. On the one hand, the integrator of [16] relies on the midpoint rule and reduced integration, and thus has to solve one nonlinear system of equations per time-step. On the other hand, the tangent plane integrator of [17], which extends the prior works [14,15], relies on a reformulation of LLG which is solved for the discrete time derivative. Each time-step consists of the solution of one linear system of equations plus nodal projection. It has been generalized to linear-implicit time integration and full effective field in [18,19].

Numerical integration of the coupling of LLG to other time-dependent PDEs has been analyzed in [20,21] for the full Maxwell equations (MLLG), in [22,23] for the eddy current formulation, and in [24] for LLG with magnetostriction. While [20] analyzes an extension of the midpoint scheme of [16], the works [21–24]extend the tangent plane scheme from [17], and emphasis is on the decoupling of the time-marching scheme in [21,23,24].

In the models and works mentioned, e.g., MLLG, the coupling of LLG and Maxwell equations is weak in the sense that the magnetization of LLG only contributes to the right-hand side of the Maxwell system, while the magnetic field from the Maxwell equations gives a contribution to the effective field of LLG. In SDLLG the principal part of the differential operator of the spin diffusion equation depends nonlinearly on the magnetization. A first numerical integrator for SDLLG is proposed and empirically validated in [12]. While this scheme appears to be unconditionally stable, the work does not prove convergence of the discrete solution towards a weak solution of SDLLG.

In our work, we extend the tangent plane integrator to SDLLG and prove unconditional convergence. Altogether, the contributions of the current work can be summarized as follows:

- The proposed integrator is proven to converge (at least for a subsequence) towards a weak solution of SDLLG. This convergence is unconditional, i.e., there is no CFL-type coupling of the time and space discretizations. Despite the nonlinearity of SDLLG, each time-step requires only the solution of two successive linear systems, one for (the discrete time derivative of) the magnetization and one for the spin accumulation.
- Our analysis thus provides, in particular, an alternate proof for the existence of (global) weak solutions of SDLLG, which has first been proved in [11]. In addition to [11], we prove that any weak limit of the proposed integrator satisfies an energy estimate similar to the theoretical behavior of (formal) strong solutions of SDLLG.

- Unlike prior work on the tangent plane integrator, we adopt an idea from [25] and show that the nodal projection step of the tangent plane scheme is *not* necessary. In particular and unlike the cited works, our analysis can therefore avoid a technical angle condition on the triangulations used. This result also transfers to the models and analysis of [17–19,21,24,23] and simplifies their (extended) tangent plane integrators.

1.1. Outline

The paper is organized as follows: In Section 2, we introduce and accurately describe the mathematical model, see (9) for the nondimensional formulation of SDLLG. In Section 3, we formulate a decoupled time-marching scheme (Algorithm 6) for the numerical integration of SDLLG and prove its well-posedness (Proposition 9). Section 4 contains the main result of our work (Theorem 12), which states unconditional convergence of the scheme towards weak solutions of SDLLG. Following [11], weak solutions of SDLLG have finite energy. In Section 5, we prove that any weak limit obtained by the proposed numerical integrator shows the same energy behavior as formal strong solutions of SDLLG (Theorem 24). Numerical examples as well as the empirical validation of the proposed algorithm are postponed to a forthcoming paper [26].

1.2. Notation

We use the standard notation [27] for Lebesgue and Sobolev spaces and norms. For any domain D, we denote the L^2 scalar product by $(r,s)D = \int_D rs$ for all $r,s \in L^2(D)$. In the case of (spaces of) vector-valued functions, we use bold letters. For a sequence $\{x_n\}n \geq 1$ in a Banach space X and $x \in X$, we write $x_n \to x$ (resp. $x_n \rightharpoonup x$) in X if the sequence converges strongly (resp. weakly) to x in X. Similarly, we write $x_n \overset{\text{sub}}{\to} x$ (resp. $x_n \overset{\text{sub}}{\rightharpoonup} x$) in X if there exists a subsequence of $\{x_n\}n \geq 1$ which converges strongly (resp. weakly) to x in X. Throughout the paper, C denotes a generic positive constant, independent of the discretization parameters, not necessarily the same at each occurrence. Alternatively, we write $A \lesssim B$ to abbreviate $A \leq C\,B$. Given $a,b \in R^3$, we denote by $a \otimes b \in R^{3\times 3}$ the tensor product defined by $(a \otimes b)j_k = a_j b_k$ for all $1 \leq j$, $k \leq 3$. By $|\cdot|$, we denote both the Frobenius norm of a matrix and the Euclidean norm of a vector. Since the meaning is clear from the argument, this does not lead to any ambiguity.

2. MODEL PROBLEM

In this section, we present the mathematical model, for which we introduce a nondimensional formulation, as well as the notion of a weak solution. We use physical units in the International System of Units (SI).

2.1. Physical background

We consider a magnetic multilayer. Let $\omega \subset \Omega$ be polyhedral Lipschitz domains in R^3, where Ω corresponds to the volume occupied by the multilayer, and ω corresponds to the ferromagnetic part. A possible experimental setup is shown in Fig. 1. Given some finite time $T > 0$, we consider the time-space domains $\omega_T := (0,T) \times \omega$ and $\Omega_T := (0,T) \times \Omega$.

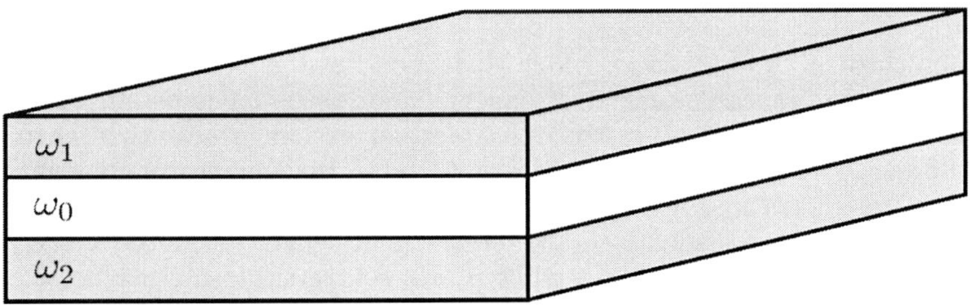

Figure. 1. Schematic of a magnetic nanopillar structure (trilayer) consisting of two ferromagnetic films, ω_1 and ω_2, separated by a nonmagnetic interlayer ω_0. The current is assumed to flow perpendicularly from ω_1 to a bottom electrode connected to ω_2. In this case, $\omega = \omega_1 \cup \omega_2$ and $\Omega = \omega_1 \cup \omega_0 \cup \omega_2$.

In micromagnetics, the quantity of interest is the magnetization $M : \omega_T \rightarrow R^3$, measured in ampere per meter (A/m). If the temperature is constant and far below from the Curie temperature of the ferromagnetic material, M is a vector field of constant modulus $|M| = Ms$, with Ms being the saturation magnetization (in A/m). In the absence of spin currents, the dynamics of M is described by the Landau–Lifshitz–Gilbert equation (LLG), which, in the so-called Gilbert form, reads

$$\frac{\partial \mathbf{M}}{\partial t} = -\gamma \mu_0 \mathbf{M} \times \mathbf{H}_{\text{eff}} + \frac{\alpha}{M_s} \mathbf{M} \times \frac{\partial \mathbf{M}}{\partial t} \quad \text{in } \omega_T \tag{1}$$

Here, $\gamma = 1.76\times10^{11}$ rad/(sT) (radian per second per tesla) and $\mu_0 = 4\pi \times 10^{-7} N/A^2$ (Newton per square ampere) are the gyromagnetic ratio and the permeability of vacuum, respectively, while $\alpha > 0$ is the nondimensional empiric Gilbert damping parameter. The effective field $H_{eff} : \Omega_T \rightarrow R^3$, measured in A/m, depends on M and is proportional to the negative functional derivative of the total magnetic Gibbs free energy with respect to M, i.e.,

$$\mu_0 \mathbf{H}_{\text{eff}}(\mathbf{M}) = -\frac{\delta \mathcal{E}(\mathbf{M})}{\delta \mathbf{M}} \tag{2}$$

In (2) the energy functional reads

$$\mathcal{E}(\mathbf{M}) = \frac{A}{M_s^2}\int_\omega |\nabla \mathbf{M}|^2 + K\int_\omega \phi(\mathbf{M}/M_s) - \mu_0\int_\omega \mathbf{H}_e \cdot \mathbf{M} + \frac{\mu_0}{2}\int_{\mathbb{R}^3} |\nabla u|^2 \tag{3}$$

and consists of four terms, which correspond to the exchange energy, the anisotropy energy, Zeeman's energy, and the magnetostatic energy, respectively. In (3), $A > 0$ is the so-called exchange stiffness constant, measured in joule per meter (J/m), and $K > 0$ is the anisotropic constant (in J/m^3), while $\phi : S^2 \rightarrow R$ is a (nondimensional) smooth function, which takes into account the anisotropy of the ferromagnetic material. Moreover, H_e is a given external field (in A/m), while $u : R^3 \rightarrow R$ refers to the magnetostatic potential, which is the unique solution of the full-space transmission problem

$\Delta u = \nabla\cdot \mathrm{M} \text{in } \omega,$

$\Delta u = 0 \ in \ R^3\backslash\overline{\omega},$

$[u] = 0 \text{on } \partial\omega,$

$[\partial_n u] = -\mathrm{M}\cdot\mathrm{n} \text{ on } \partial\omega,$

$u(x) = O(1/|x|) \text{as } |x|\rightarrow\infty.$

Combining (2) and (3), we obtain the following expression for the effective field:

$$\mathbf{H}_{\text{eff}}(\mathbf{M}) = \frac{2A}{\mu_0 M_s^2}\Delta\mathbf{M} - \frac{K}{\mu_0 M_s}\nabla\phi(\mathbf{M}/M_s) + \mathbf{H}_e + \mathbf{H}_s \tag{4}$$

where $H_s = -\nabla u$ denotes the stray field (in A/m).

The dynamics of the spin accumulation $S : \Omega_T \to R_3$, measured in A/m, is described by the diffusion equation

$$\frac{\partial \mathbf{S}}{\partial t} = -\nabla \cdot \mathbf{J}_S - \frac{2\widetilde{D}_0}{\lambda_{sf}^2}\mathbf{S} - \frac{2\widetilde{D}_0}{M_s\lambda_J^2}\mathbf{S} \times \mathbf{M} \quad \text{in } \Omega_T \tag{5}$$

where $\widetilde{D}_0 : \Omega \to R$ is the diffusion coefficient (in m^2/s), λ_{sf} is the characteristic length of the spin-flip relaxation, and λ_J is related to the mean free path of an electron (both measured in m). The spin current $J_S : \Omega^T \to R^{3\times3}$, measured in A/s, is defined by

$$\mathbf{J}_S = \frac{\beta\mu_B}{eM_s}\mathbf{M} \otimes \mathbf{J}_e - 2\widetilde{D}_0\left(\nabla\mathbf{S} - \frac{\beta\beta'}{M_s^2}\mathbf{M} \otimes (\nabla\mathbf{S} \cdot \mathbf{M})\right) \quad \text{in } \Omega_T \tag{6}$$

where $\mu_B = 9.2741 \times 10^{-24}$Am^2 is the Bohr magneton, $e = -1.602\times10^{-19}$ As is the charge of the electron, and $J_e : \Omega^T \to R^3$ is the applied current density field (in A/m^2), while the constants $0 < \beta, \beta' < 1$ are the nondimensional spin polarization parameters of the magnetic layers. In (6) we denote by $\nabla S \cdot M \in R^3$ the matrix–vector product between the transpose of the Jacobian ∇S and M, i.e., $\nabla S \cdot M = M_1\nabla S_1 + M_2\nabla S_2 + M_3\nabla S_3$. In (5)–(6), it is implicitly assumed that M = 0 in the nonmagnetic but conducting material $\Omega\backslash\overline{\omega}$.

To describe the dynamics of the magnetization, we take into account the interaction between the spin accumulation and the magnetization. Thus, we consider an augmented version of (1), namely

$$\frac{\partial \mathbf{M}}{\partial t} = -\gamma\mathbf{M} \times (\mu_0\mathbf{H}_{\text{eff}}(\mathbf{M}) + J\mathbf{S}) + \frac{\alpha}{M_s}\mathbf{M} \times \frac{\partial \mathbf{M}}{\partial t} \quad \text{in } \omega_T \tag{7}$$

where the constant J in N/A^2 is the strength of the interaction between the spin accumulation and the magnetization. Finally, to complete the setting, (5)–(7) are supplemented by initial conditions

$$M(0) = M^0 \text{ in } \omega \text{ and } S(0) = S^0 \text{ in } \Omega,$$

for some given initial states $M^0 : \omega \to R^3$ and $S^0 : \Omega \to R^3$ with $|M^0| = M_s$, and homogeneous Neumann boundary conditions

$$\frac{\partial \mathbf{M}}{\partial \mathbf{n}} = 0 \quad \text{on } (0, T) \times \partial\omega \quad \text{and} \quad \frac{\partial \mathbf{S}}{\partial \mathbf{n}} = 0 \quad \text{on } (0, T) \times \partial\Omega$$

2.2. Nondimensional form of the problem

We introduce a nondimensional form of the system (5)–(7). We perform the substitution $t' = \gamma\ \mu_0 M_s t$, with t' being the so-called (nondimensional) reduced time, and set $T' = \gamma\mu_0 M_s T$. We rescale the spatial variable by $x' = x/L$, with L being a characteristic length of the problem (measured in m), e.g., the intrinsic length scale $L = \sqrt{2A/\mu_0 M_s^2}$. However, to simplify our notation, we write t,T,x,ω, and Ω, instead of t',T',x',ω/L, and Ω/L, respectively. We introduce the nondimensional vector unknowns $m = M/M_s$, so that the modulus constraint becomes $|m| = 1$, and $s = S/M_s$. Furthermore, we set $\mathbf{h}_{eff} = \mathbf{H}_{eff}/M_s, \mathbf{f} = \mathbf{H}_e/M_s$, $h_s = H_s/M_s$, $c = J/\mu_0$, $j = \mu B_{Je}/(Le\gamma\mu_0 M_s^2)$, $D_0 = 2\widetilde{D}_0/(\gamma\ \mu_0 M_s L^2)$, $m^0 = M^0/M_s$ and $s^0 = S^0/Ms$. With these substitutions, the nondimensional augmented form of LLG becomes

$$\partial_t m = -m \times (h_{eff}(m) + cs) + \alpha m \times \partial tm \text{ in } \omega_T,$$

where the effective field is given by

$$\mathbf{h}_{eff}(\mathbf{m}) = C_{exch}\Delta\mathbf{m} - C_{ani}\nabla\phi(\mathbf{m}) + \mathbf{f} + \mathbf{h}_s(\mathbf{m}) \tag{8}$$

with $C_{exch} = 2A/(\mu_0 L^2 M_s^2)$ and Cani $= K/(\mu_0 M_s^2)$, while the diffusion equation (5) reads

$$\partial_t \mathbf{s} = -\nabla\cdot\left(\beta\mathbf{m}\otimes\mathbf{j} - D_0\left(\nabla\mathbf{s} - \beta\beta'\mathbf{m}\otimes(\nabla\mathbf{s}\cdot\mathbf{m})\right)\right) - \frac{L^2 D_0}{\lambda_{sf}^2}\mathbf{s} - \frac{L^2 D_0}{\lambda_J^2}\mathbf{s}\times\mathbf{m} \quad \text{in } \Omega_T$$

To simplify our notation and without loss of generality, we assume that $L = \lambda_{sf} = \lambda_J$.

To sum up, we seek for $m : \omega_T \rightarrow R^3$ with $|m| = 1$ and $s : \Omega_T \rightarrow R^3$ such that

$$\partial_t m = -m \times (h_{eff}(m) + cs) + \alpha m \times \partial_t m \text{ in } \omega_T, \tag{9a}$$

$$\partial_t s = -\nabla\cdot(\beta m\otimes j - D_0(\nabla s - \beta\beta' m\otimes(\nabla s\cdot m))) - D_0 s - D_0(s \times m) \text{ in } \Omega_T, \tag{9b}$$

$$\partial_n m = 0 \text{ on } (0,T) \times \partial\omega, \tag{9c}$$

$$\partial_n s = 0 \text{ on } (0,T) \times \partial\Omega, \tag{9d}$$

$$m(0) = m^0 \text{ in } \omega, \tag{9e}$$

$$s(0) = s^0 \text{ in } \Omega. \tag{9f}$$

Here, $c,\alpha > 0$ and $0 < \beta,\beta' < 1$ are constants. For the diffusion coefficient $D_0 \in L^\infty(\Omega)$, we assume that there exists a positive constant D_* such that $D_0 \geq D_*$ a.e. in Ω. We also assume that $f \in L^2(\omega_T)$ and $j \in L^2(0,T; H^1(\Omega))$. Moreover, in (9a) we allow a more general effective field of the form

$$h_{eff}(m) = C_{exch}\Delta m + \pi(m) + f, \tag{10}$$

where $\pi : L^2(\omega) \to L^2(\omega)$ is a general time-independent field contribution. We emphasize that (10) in particular covers (8) with $\pi(m) = -C_{ani}\nabla\phi(m) + h_s(m)$.

Remark 1 The constraint $|m| = 1$ directly follows from the PDE formulation, provided $|m^0| = 1$ in ω_T. Indeed, from (9a), we deduce that $\partial_t|m|^2 = 2m\cdot\partial_t m = 0$ in ω_T.

2.3. Weak solution of the problem

Let $\tilde{H}^{-1}(\Omega) = H^1(\Omega)^*$ be the dual space of $H^1(\Omega)$ and denote by $\langle\cdot,\cdot\rangle$ the corresponding duality pairing, understood in the sense of the Gelfand triple $H^1(\Omega) \subset L^2(\Omega) \subset \tilde{H}^{-1}(\Omega)$. In view of the weak formulation of (9b), we consider the time-dependent bilinear form $a(t,\cdot,\cdot): H^1(\Omega) \times H^1(\Omega) \to \mathbb{R}$defined by

$$a(t,\zeta_1,\zeta_2) = (D_0\nabla\zeta_1,\nabla\zeta_2)_\Omega - \beta\beta'(D_0 m(t)\otimes(\nabla\zeta_1\cdot m(t)),\nabla\zeta_2)_\omega + (D_0\zeta_1,\zeta_2)_\Omega + (D_0(\zeta_1 \times m(t)),\zeta_2)_\omega,$$

for all $t \in [0,T]$ and $\zeta^1,\zeta^2 \in H^1(\Omega)$.

We recall from [11, Definition 1] the notion of a weak solution of the SDLLG system (9), which extends the definition of weak solutions of LLG from [13].

Definition 2

Let $m^0 \in H^1(\omega)$ with $|m^0| = 1$ a.e. in ω, and $s^0 \in H^1(\Omega)$. The pair (m,s) is called a weak solution of SDLLG if the following properties (i)–(iv) are satisfied:

1) $m \in H^1(\omega_T)$ with $|m| = 1$ a.e. in ω_T and $m(0) = m^0$ in the sense of traces,

2) $s \in L^2(0, T; H^1(\Omega)) \cap L^\infty(0, T; L^2(\Omega))$, $\partial_t s \in L^2(0, T; \tilde{H}^{-1}(\Omega))$ and $s(0) = s^0$ in the sense of traces,

3) for all $\varphi \in H^1(\omega_T)$, it holds

$$(\partial_t \mathbf{m}, \boldsymbol{\varphi})_{\omega_T} + \alpha (\partial_t \mathbf{m} \times \mathbf{m}, \boldsymbol{\varphi})_{\omega_T} = -C_{\text{exch}} (\nabla \mathbf{m} \times \mathbf{m}, \nabla \boldsymbol{\varphi})_{\omega_T} + (\pi(\mathbf{m}) \times \mathbf{m}, \boldsymbol{\varphi})_{\omega_T} + (\mathbf{f} \times \mathbf{m}, \boldsymbol{\varphi})_{\omega_T} + c(\mathbf{s} \times \mathbf{m}, \boldsymbol{\varphi})_{\omega_T}. \tag{11a}$$

4) for almost all $t \in [0, T]$ and all $\zeta \in H^1(\Omega)$, it holds

$$\langle \partial_t s(t), \zeta \rangle + a(t, s(t), \zeta) = \beta\, (m(t) \otimes j(t), \nabla \zeta)\omega - \beta\, (j(t) \cdot n, m(t) \cdot \zeta)_{\partial\Omega \cap \partial\omega}. \tag{11b}$$

Remark 3

If (m,s) is a weak solution of SDLLG, then it holds $m \in C(0, T; L^2(\omega))$ and $s \in C(0, T; L^2(\Omega))$, cf., e.g., [27, Section 5.9.2, Theorems 2 and 3].

Remark 4

The boundary term in (11b) is missing in [11]. This error has recently been noticed and corrected, so that the overall result of [11] remains valid [28]. The present analysis provides an alternate proof for the existence of solutions and hence validity of the results of [11,28].

The following lemma highlights the parabolic nature of Eq. (9b).

Lemma 5

The time-dependent bilinear form $a(t,\cdot,\cdot)$ *is continuous and positive definite. Indeed, it holds*

$$a(t, \boldsymbol{\zeta}, \boldsymbol{\zeta}) \geq (1 - \beta\beta') D_* \|\boldsymbol{\zeta}\|^2_{\mathbf{H}^1(\Omega)} \tag{12}$$

for almost all $t \in [0,T]$.

Proof

The continuity directly follows from the regularity assumptions on the data, as $|m|=1$ a.e. in ΩT. As for the positive definiteness, we note

$$|\mathbf{m}(t) \otimes (\nabla \boldsymbol{\zeta} \cdot \mathbf{m}(t)) \cdot \nabla \boldsymbol{\zeta}| \leq |\nabla \boldsymbol{\zeta}|^2 \quad \text{for all } \boldsymbol{\zeta} \in \mathbf{H}^1(\Omega)$$

As a consequence, since $D0 \geq D*$ and $0 < \beta\beta' < 1$, we get

$$\begin{aligned} a(t, \boldsymbol{\zeta}, \boldsymbol{\zeta}) &= (D_0 \nabla \boldsymbol{\zeta}, \nabla \boldsymbol{\zeta})_\Omega - \beta\beta' (D_0 \mathbf{m}(t) \otimes (\nabla \boldsymbol{\zeta} \cdot \mathbf{m}(t)), \nabla \boldsymbol{\zeta})_\omega + (D_0 \boldsymbol{\zeta}, \boldsymbol{\zeta})_\Omega \\ &\geq (D_0 \nabla \boldsymbol{\zeta}, \nabla \boldsymbol{\zeta})_\Omega - \beta\beta' (D_0 |\mathbf{m}(t) \otimes (\nabla \boldsymbol{\zeta} \cdot \mathbf{m}(t))|, |\nabla \boldsymbol{\zeta}|)_\omega + (D_0 \boldsymbol{\zeta}, \boldsymbol{\zeta})_\Omega \\ &\geq (1 - \beta\beta') D_* \|\nabla \boldsymbol{\zeta}\|^2_{\mathbf{L}^2(\Omega)} + D_* \|\boldsymbol{\zeta}\|^2_{\mathbf{L}^2(\Omega)}. \end{aligned}$$

This establishes (12) and concludes the proof. □

3. NUMERICAL ALGORITHM

For the time discretization, we consider a uniform partition $0 = t_0 < t_1 < \cdots < t_N = T$ of the time interval [0,T] with time-step size k=T/N, i.e., tj=jk for 0≤j≤N.

Given a sequence of functions $\{\varphi^j\}_{0 \le j \le N}$, such that any φ^j is associated with the time-step t_j, for $0 \le j \le N-1$ we define the difference quotient := $d_t\varphi^{j+1} := (\varphi^{j+1} - \varphi^j)/k$. We consider the piecewise linear and the two piecewise constant time-approximations defined as follows: for 0 ≤ j ≤ N – 1and $t \in [t_j, t_j + 1)$, we have

$$\varphi_k(t) := \frac{t - t_j}{k}\varphi^{j+1} + \frac{t_{j+1} - t}{k}\varphi^j, \qquad \varphi_k^-(t) := \varphi^j, \qquad \varphi^+(t) := \varphi^{j+1} \tag{13}$$

Obviously, it holds $\partial_t\varphi_k(t) = d_t\varphi^{j+1}$ for all $t \in [t_j, t_j + 1)$.

For the spatial discretization, let $\{\mathcal{T}_h^\Omega\}_{h>0}$h>0 be a shape-regular and (globally) quasi-uniform family of regular tetrahedral triangulations of Ω, parameterized by the mesh size $h = \max h_K$, where $h_K = \mathrm{diam}(K)$ for all $K \in T_h^\Omega$. By T_h^ω, we denote the restriction of T_h^Ω to $^\omega$. We assume that ω is resolved, i.e.,

$$\mathcal{T}_h^\omega = \mathcal{T}_h^\Omega|_\omega = \{K \in \mathcal{T}_h^\Omega : K \cap \omega \neq \emptyset\} \quad \text{and} \quad \overline{\omega} = \bigcup_{K \in \mathcal{T}_h^\omega} K$$

Let us denote by $\mathcal{S}^1(\mathcal{T}_h^\Omega)^3$ the standard finite element space of globally continuous and piecewise affine functions from Ω to R^3. Correspondingly, we also consider S1(Thω)3.

By $\mathcal{S}^1(\mathcal{T}_h^\omega)^3$. By $\mathcal{I}_h^\Omega : \mathbf{C}(\overline{\Omega}) \to \mathcal{S}^1(\mathcal{T}_h^\Omega)^3$ and $\mathcal{I}_h^\omega : \mathbf{C}(\overline{\omega}) \to \mathcal{S}^1(\mathcal{T}_h^\omega)^3$, we denote the nodal interpolation operators onto these spaces. Since ω is resolved, these operators coincide on ω, i.e., $\mathcal{I}_h^\Omega(\boldsymbol{\varphi})|_\omega = \mathcal{I}_h^\omega(\boldsymbol{\varphi}|_\omega)$ for $\boldsymbol{\varphi} \in \mathbf{C}(\overline{\Omega})$. In particular, there is no ambiguity, if we denote both operators by *lh*. The set of nodes of the triangulation T^h_ω is denoted by N^h_ω.

We recall that, under the constraint |m| = 1, the strong form of (9a) can equivalently be stated as

$$\alpha\partial_t\mathbf{m} + \mathbf{m} \times \partial_t\mathbf{m} = \mathbf{h}_{\text{eff}}(\mathbf{m}) + c\mathbf{s} - ((\mathbf{h}_{\text{eff}}(\mathbf{m}) + c\mathbf{s}) \cdot \mathbf{m})\,\mathbf{m}$$

This formulation is used to construct the upcoming numerical scheme. Since (14) is linear in ∂_tm, the main idea is to introduce an additional free variable $v = \partial_t$m. To discretize v, we introduce the discrete tangent space defined by

$$\mathcal{K}_{\phi_h} := \left\{\boldsymbol{\psi}_h \in \mathcal{S}^1(\mathcal{T}_h^{\omega})^3 : \boldsymbol{\psi}_h(\mathbf{z}) \cdot \boldsymbol{\phi}_h(\mathbf{z}) = 0 \text{ for all } \mathbf{z} \in \mathcal{N}_h^{\omega}\right\}$$

for any $\phi_h \in S^1(T^{\omega}{}_h)^3$. Moreover, we consider the set

$$\mathcal{M}_h := \left\{\boldsymbol{\phi}_h \in \mathcal{S}^1(\mathcal{T}_h^{\omega})^3 : \left|\boldsymbol{\phi}_h(\mathbf{z})\right| = 1 \text{ for all } \mathbf{z} \in \mathcal{N}_h^{\omega}\right\}$$

These sets reflect two main properties of m and v, namely the orthogonality $m \cdot v = 0$ and the unit-length constraint $|m| = 1$.

Let $\mathcal{U}_h = \left\{\boldsymbol{\phi}_h \in \mathcal{S}^1(\mathcal{T}_h^{\omega})^3 : \left|\boldsymbol{\phi}_h(\mathbf{z})\right| \geq 1 \text{ for all } \mathbf{z} \in \mathcal{N}_h^{\omega}\right\}$. We consider the nodal projection map $\Pi_h : \mathcal{U}_h \to \mathcal{M}_h$ defined by $\Pi_h\boldsymbol{\phi}_h(\mathbf{z}) = \boldsymbol{\phi}_h(\mathbf{z})/\left|\boldsymbol{\phi}_h(\mathbf{z})\right|$ for all $\mathbf{z} \in \mathcal{N}_h^{\omega}$ and $\boldsymbol{\phi}_h \in \mathcal{U}_h$. A simple argument based on the elementwise use of barycentric coordinates shows that $\left\|\Pi_h\boldsymbol{\phi}_h\right\|_{\mathbf{L}^{\infty}(\omega)} = 1$ for all $\boldsymbol{\phi}_h \in \mathcal{U}_h$. Moreover, we have the estimate

$$\left\|\nabla \Pi_h\boldsymbol{\phi}_h\right\|_{\mathbf{L}^2(\omega)} \leq c_{\Pi} \left\|\nabla\boldsymbol{\phi}_h\right\|_{\mathbf{L}^2(\omega)} \quad \text{for all } \boldsymbol{\phi}_h \in \mathcal{U}_h \tag{15}$$

where the constant $c_{\Pi} > 0$ depends only on the shape-regularity of the triangulation, cf., e.g., [25, Lemma 2.2]. With an additional angle condition on $\mathcal{T}_h^{\omega}$, it is well known that (15) holds even with $c_{\Pi} = 1$, cf. [29].

Let $\mathbf{m}_h^0 \in \mathcal{M}_h$ and $\mathbf{s}_h^0 \in \mathcal{S}^1(\mathcal{T}_h^{\Omega})^3$ be suitable approximations of the initial conditions. Moreover, we consider a numerical realization $\pi_h : L^2(\omega) \to L^2(\omega)$of π, which is assumed to fulfill a certain set of properties, see (H2)–(H3) below. This allows us to include the approximation errors, e.g., those which arise from the numerical computation of the stray field, into the overall convergence analysis. For ease of presentation, we assume that f and j are continuous in time, i.e., $f \in C(0, T; L^2(\omega))$ and $j \in C(0, T; H^1(\Omega))$, so that the expressions $f^j = f(t_j)$ and $j_j = j(t_j)$ are meaningful for all $0 \leq j \leq N$. It is even possible to replace f_j and j_j by some numerical approximation $\mathbf{f}_h^j$ and $\mathbf{j}_h^j$ as long as some weak convergence properties are fulfilled, cf. [19].

Analogously to what we have done in Section 2 for the continuous problem, for $0 \leq I \leq N^{-1}$ we define the bilinear form $a_h^{i+1} : \mathcal{S}^1(\mathcal{T}_h^{\Omega})^3 \times \mathcal{S}^1(\mathcal{T}_h^{\Omega})^3 \to \mathbb{R}$ by

$$\begin{aligned} a_h^{i+1}(\zeta_1, \zeta_2) = {} & \left(D_0\nabla\zeta_1, \nabla\zeta_2\right)_{\Omega} - \beta\beta'\left(D_0\Pi_h\mathbf{m}_h^{i+1} \otimes \left(\nabla\zeta_1 \cdot \Pi_h\mathbf{m}_h^{i+1}\right), \nabla\zeta_2\right)_{\omega} \\ & + \left(D_0\zeta_1, \zeta_2\right)_{\Omega} + \left(D_0\left(\zeta_1 \times \Pi_h\mathbf{m}_h^{i+1}\right), \zeta_2\right)_{\omega} \end{aligned}$$

for all $\zeta_1,\zeta_2 \in S1(\mathcal{T}_h^{\Omega})^3$. For the numerical integration of the SDLLG system (9), we propose the following algorithm.

Algorithm 6

Input: $\mathbf{m}_h^0, \mathbf{s}_h^0, \{\mathbf{f}^i\}_{0\le i\le N-1}, \{\mathbf{j}^{i+1}\}_{0\le i\le N-1}$, parameter $0 \le \theta \le 1$.

For all $0 \le i \le N^{-1}$ iterate:

- compute $\mathbf{v}_h^i \in \mathcal{K}_{\mathbf{m}_h^i}$ such that

$$\alpha\left(\mathbf{v}_h^i, \boldsymbol{\phi}_h\right)_\omega + \left(\mathbf{m}_h^i \times \mathbf{v}_h^i, \boldsymbol{\phi}_h\right)_\omega + C_{\text{exch}}\theta k\left(\nabla \mathbf{v}_h^i, \nabla \boldsymbol{\phi}_h\right)_\omega$$
$$= -C_{\text{exch}}\left(\nabla \mathbf{m}_h^i, \nabla \boldsymbol{\phi}_h\right)_\omega + \left(\boldsymbol{\pi}_h(\mathbf{m}_h^i), \boldsymbol{\phi}_h\right)_\omega + \left(\mathbf{f}^i, \boldsymbol{\phi}_h\right)_\omega + c\left(\mathbf{s}_h^i, \boldsymbol{\phi}_h\right)_\omega \quad (16a)$$

for all $\boldsymbol{\phi}_h \in \mathcal{K}_{\mathbf{m}_h^i}$;

- define $\mathbf{m}_h^{i+1} \in \mathcal{S}^1(\mathcal{T}_h)^3$

$$\mathbf{m}_h^{i+1} = \mathbf{m}_h^i + k\mathbf{v}_h^i \quad (16b)$$

- compute $\mathbf{s}_h^{i+1} \in \mathcal{S}^1(\mathcal{T}_h^{\Omega})^3$ such that

$$(d_t \mathbf{s}_h^{i+1}, \zeta_h)_\Omega + a_h^{i+1}(\mathbf{s}_h^{i+1}, \zeta_h) = \beta\left(\Pi_h \mathbf{m}_h^{i+1} \otimes \mathbf{j}^{i+1}, \nabla \zeta_h\right)_\omega - \beta\left(\mathbf{j}^{i+1} \cdot \mathbf{n}, \Pi_h \mathbf{m}_h^{i+1} \cdot \zeta_h\right)_{\partial\Omega\cap\partial\omega}$$

for all $\zeta_h \in \mathcal{S}^1(\mathcal{T}_h^{\Omega})^3$.

Output: Sequence of discrete functions $\left\{\left(\mathbf{v}_h^i, \mathbf{m}_h^{i+1}, \mathbf{s}_h^{i+1}\right)\right\}_{0\le i\le N-1}$.

The overall system (9) is a nonlinearly coupled system of a linear diffusion equation for s with the nonlinear LLG equation for m. However, our scheme only requires the solution of two linear systems per time-step, since the treatment of the micromagnetic part and the spin diffusion part is completely decoupled for the time-integration. This greatly simplifies an actual numerical implementation as well as the possible preconditioning of iterative solvers.

Remark 7 Unlike this work, earlier results on the tangent plane integrator [17–24] define $\mathbf{m}_h^{i+1} := \Pi_h(\mathbf{m}_h^i + k\mathbf{v}_h^i)$ in (16b). Unconditional convergence in the sense of Theorem 12 can then be achieved with an additional angle condition on the triangulation $\mathcal{T}_h^{\omega}$, which ensures (15) with $c_\Pi = 1$. This assumption is avoided in the present work.

The following result follows from standard scaling arguments.

Lemma 8

Let {Th}h > 0 be a quasi-uniform family of triangulations of Ω *and* r ∈ [1,∞). *Then,*

$$C^{-1} \|w_h\|^r_{L^r(\Omega)} \leq h^3 \sum_{z \in \mathcal{N}_h} |w_h(z)|^r \leq C \|w_h\|^r_{L^r(\Omega)} \quad \text{for all } w_h \in \mathcal{S}^1(\mathcal{T}_h)$$

The constant C > 0 *depends only on* r, *but is independent of the mesh size* h. □

The following proposition states that the above algorithm is well defined, cf. [25, Propositions 3.1 and 4.1] for corresponding results in the frame of harmonic maps and the harmonic map heat flow.

Proposition 9 *Algorithm 6 is well defined in the following sense: for each time-step* 0 ≤ *i* ≤ N−1, *there exists a unique solution* $(\mathbf{v}_h^i, \mathbf{m}_h^{i+1}, \mathbf{s}_h^{i+1})$. *Moreover, it holds*

$$\left|\mathbf{m}_h^{i+1}(\mathbf{z})\right|^2 = 1 + k^2 \sum_{\ell=0}^{i} \left|\mathbf{v}_h^\ell(\mathbf{z})\right|^2 \geq 1 \quad \text{for all } \mathbf{z} \in \mathcal{N}_h^{\omega} \qquad (17)$$

as well as

$$C_*^{-1} \left\|\mathbf{m}_h^{i+1}\right\|^2_{\mathbf{L}^2(\omega)} \leq 1 + k^2 \sum_{\ell=0}^{i} \left\|\mathbf{v}_h^\ell\right\|^2_{\mathbf{L}^2(\omega)} \qquad (18)$$

where the constant C* > 0 *depends only on the shape-regularity of* $\{\mathcal{T}_h^{\omega}\}_{h>0}$, *but is independent of h and k.*

Proof Let 0 ≤ *i* ≤ N−1. For step (i) of the algorithm, it is straightforward to show that problem (16a) is characterized by a positive definite bilinear form. Unique solvability thus follows from linearity and finite space dimension. Step (ii) is clearly well defined. For all z ∈ Nh, the nodewise orthogonality from $\mathcal{K}_{\mathbf{m}_h^i}$ proves

$$\left|\mathbf{m}_h^{i+1}(\mathbf{z})\right|^2 = \left|\mathbf{m}_h^i(\mathbf{z}) + k\mathbf{v}_h^i(\mathbf{z})\right|^2 = \left|\mathbf{m}_h^i(\mathbf{z})\right|^2 + k^2 \left|\mathbf{v}_h^i(\mathbf{z})\right|^2$$

Since $\mathbf{m}_h^0 \in \mathcal{M}_h$, mathematical induction proves

$$\left|\mathbf{m}_h^{i+1}(\mathbf{z})\right|^2 = \left|\mathbf{m}_h^0(\mathbf{z})\right|^2 + k^2 \sum_{\ell=0}^{i} \left|\mathbf{v}_h^\ell(\mathbf{z})\right|^2 = 1 + k^2 \sum_{\ell=0}^{i} \left|\mathbf{v}_h^\ell(\mathbf{z})\right|^2 \geq 1$$

This proves (17). The norm equivalence from Lemma 8 in the case $r = 2$ yields

$$\begin{aligned}\left\|\mathbf{m}_h^{i+1}\right\|_{\mathbf{L}^2(\omega)}^2 &\lesssim h^3 \sum_{\mathbf{z}\in\mathcal{N}_h^\omega} \left|\mathbf{m}_h^{i+1}(\mathbf{z})\right|^2 = h^3 \sum_{\mathbf{z}\in\mathcal{N}_h^\omega} \left(1 + k^2 \sum_{\ell=0}^{i} \left|\mathbf{v}_h^\ell(\mathbf{z})\right|^2\right) \\ &= h^3(\#\mathcal{N}_h^\omega) + k^2 \sum_{\ell=0}^{i} h^3 \sum_{\mathbf{z}\in\mathcal{N}_h^\omega} \left|\mathbf{v}_h^\ell(\mathbf{z})\right|^2 \lesssim 1 + k^2 \sum_{\ell=0}^{i} \left\|\mathbf{v}_h^\ell\right\|_{\mathbf{L}^2(\omega)}^2\end{aligned}$$

This establishes (18). For step (iii), we use the same argument as for step (i). Due to (17), the nodewise projections in (16c) are well defined. Let $b_h^i : \mathcal{S}^1(\mathcal{T}_h^\Omega)^3 \times \mathcal{S}^1(\mathcal{T}_h^\Omega)^3 \to \mathbb{R}$ be the bilinear form associated to problem (16c), i.e.,

$$\begin{aligned}b_h^i(\zeta_1, \zeta_2) = \frac{1}{k}\left(\zeta_1, \zeta_2\right)_\Omega + \left(D_0\nabla\zeta_1, \nabla\zeta_2\right)_\Omega - \beta\beta'\left(D_0\Pi_h\mathbf{m}_h^{i+1} \otimes \left(\nabla\zeta_1 \cdot \Pi_h\mathbf{m}_h^{i+1}\right), \nabla\zeta_2\right)_\Omega \\ + \left(D_0\zeta_1, \zeta_2\right)_\Omega + \left(D_0\left(\zeta_1 \times \Pi_h\mathbf{m}_h^{i+1}\right), \zeta_2\right)_\Omega.\end{aligned}$$

Since $\left\|\Pi_h\mathbf{m}_h^{i+1}\right\|_{\mathbf{L}^\infty(\omega)} = 1$, we see

$$\left(D_0\Pi_h\mathbf{m}_h^{i+1} \otimes \left(\nabla\boldsymbol{\zeta}_1 \cdot \Pi_h\mathbf{m}_h^{i+1}\right), \nabla\boldsymbol{\zeta}_2\right)_\Omega \leq \left(D_0\left|\nabla\boldsymbol{\zeta}_1\right|, \left|\nabla\boldsymbol{\zeta}_2\right|\right)_\Omega$$

It follows that

$$\begin{aligned}b_h^i(\boldsymbol{\zeta}, \boldsymbol{\zeta}) &\geq \frac{1}{k}\left\|\boldsymbol{\zeta}\right\|_{\mathbf{L}^2(\Omega)}^2 + (1 - \beta\beta')\left(D_0\nabla\boldsymbol{\zeta}, \nabla\boldsymbol{\zeta}\right)_\Omega + \left(D_0\boldsymbol{\zeta}, \boldsymbol{\zeta}\right)_\Omega \\ &\geq \frac{1 + kD_*}{k}\left\|\boldsymbol{\zeta}\right\|_{\mathbf{L}^2(\Omega)}^2 + D_*(1 - \beta\beta')\left\|\nabla\boldsymbol{\zeta}\right\|_{\mathbf{L}^2(\Omega)}^2.\end{aligned}$$

As $0 < \beta\beta' < 1$ and $D_* > 0$, $b_h^i(\cdot,\cdot)$ is positive definite and problem (16c) is thus well posed. □

4. CONVERGENCE ANALYSIS

In this section, we consider the convergence properties of Algorithm 6 and show that it is indeed unconditionally convergent towards a weak solution of SDLLG in the sense of Definition 2. We emphasize that the proof is constructive in the sense that it even shows existence of weak solutions. We start by collecting some general assumptions:

(H1) The discrete initial data $m^0 \in M_h$ and $s^0 \in S^1(T_h^{\omega})3$ satisfy

$$\mathbf{m}_h^0 \rightharpoonup \mathbf{m}^0 \quad \text{in } \mathbf{H}^1(\omega) \quad \text{and} \quad \mathbf{s}_h^0 \rightharpoonup \mathbf{s}^0 \quad \text{in } \mathbf{L}^2(\Omega)$$

(H2) The general field contribution π_h is bounded, i.e.,

$$\|\boldsymbol{\pi}_h(\mathbf{w})\|_{\mathbf{L}^2(\omega)} \le C_{\pi} \|\mathbf{w}\|_{\mathbf{L}^2(\omega)} \quad \text{for all } \mathbf{w} \in \mathbf{L}^2(\omega)$$

with a constant $C_{\pi} > 0$ which depends only on $|\omega|$.

(H3) It holds

$$\boldsymbol{\pi}_h(\mathbf{w}_{hk}) \rightharpoonup \boldsymbol{\pi}(\mathbf{w}) \quad \text{in } \mathbf{L}^2(\omega_T) \text{ as } (h, k) \to 0$$

for any sequence $w_{hk} \to w$ in $L^2(\omega_T)$.

Remark 10 Usual stray field discretizations by hybrid FEM–BEM methods, e.g., the Fredkin–Koehler approach from [30], or FEM–BEM coupling methods satisfy (H2)–(H3), see [19].

Remark 11 For a discrete operator $\pi_h : H^1(\omega) \to L^2(\omega)$, assumption (H2) can be relaxed to

$$\|\boldsymbol{\pi}_h(\mathbf{w})\|_{\mathbf{L}^2(\omega)} \le C_{\pi} \|\mathbf{w}\|_{\mathbf{H}^1(\omega)} \quad \text{for all } \mathbf{w} \in \mathbf{H}^1(\omega)$$

Within this setting, and with an appropriate modification of assumption (H3), the hybrid FEM–BEM method from [31] for the computation of the stray field can also be included into our analysis. Then, the proof of Proposition 19 becomes more technical, but the assertion remains true. We refer to the argument of [19]which can be adapted accordingly.

From now on, we consider the time-approximations $\mathbf{m}_{hk}, \mathbf{m}_{hk}^{\pm}, \mathbf{s}_{hk}, \mathbf{s}_{hk}^{\pm}$ defined by (13). The next theorem is the main result of this work.

Theorem 12

Let $\{\mathcal{T}_h^\Omega\}_{h>0}$ *be a shape-regular and quasi-uniform family of triangulations.*

- *Suppose* $1/2 < \theta \leq 1$ *and that assumptions* (H1)–(H2) *are satisfied.*

Then, there exist $\mathrm{m} \in L^2(\omega_T)$ *and* $\mathrm{s} \in L^2(0, T; H^1(\Omega))$ *such that*

$$\mathbf{m}_{hk}^{-} \overset{\text{sub}}{\rightharpoonup} \mathbf{m} \quad in\, \mathbf{L}^2(\omega_T) \quad and \quad \mathbf{s}_{hk}^{-} \overset{\text{sub}}{\rightharpoonup} \mathbf{s} \quad in\, L^2(0, T; \mathbf{H}^1(\Omega))$$

- *In addition to the above, let assumption* (H3) *be satisfied. Then, it holds*

$$(\mathbf{m}_{hk}, \mathbf{s}_{hk}) \overset{\text{sub}}{\rightharpoonup} (\mathbf{m}, \mathbf{s}) \quad in\, \mathbf{H}^1(\omega_T) \times \left[L^2(0, T; \mathbf{H}^1(\Omega)) \cap H^1(0, T; \widetilde{\mathbf{H}}^{-1}(\Omega))\right]$$

Where (m,s) *is a weak solution of SDLLG.*

Remark 13

In particular, Theorem 12 yields existence of weak solutions, and each accumulation point of (mhk,shk) is a weak solution of SDLLG in the sense of Definition 2.

The proof of Theorem 12 will roughly be done in three steps, namely

1) boundedness of the discrete quantities and energies,
2) existence of weakly convergent subsequences via compactness,
3) identification of the limits with weak solutions of SDLLG.

For the sake of readability, we split our argument into several lemmata.

To start with, we recall the following result, which states a well-known and simple algebraic trick which often simplifies the computation and the estimation of sums.

Lemma 14 Abel's Summation by Parts

Let X be a vector space endowed with a symmetric bilinear form $(\cdot,\cdot)$. *Given an integer* $j \geq 1$, *let* $\{v_i\}_{0 \leq i \leq j} \subset X$. *Then, it holds*

$$\sum_{i=0}^{j-1} (v_{i+1} - v_i, v_{i+1}) = \frac{1}{2}(v_j, v_j) - \frac{1}{2}(v_0, v_0) + \frac{1}{2}\sum_{i=0}^{j-1}(v_{i+1} - v_i, v_{i+1} - v_i)$$

□

The first ingredient for step (i) is the following proposition.

Proposition 15

Let $1 \leq j \leq N$ *and suppose that the assumptions of Theorem* 12(a) *are satisfied. Then, the discrete functions* $\{\mathbf{s}_h^{i+1}\}_{0 \leq i \leq j-1}$ *obtained through Algorithm* 6 *fulfill*

$$\left\|\mathbf{s}_h^j\right\|_{\mathbf{L}^2(\Omega)}^2 + k\sum_{i=0}^{j-1}\left\|\mathbf{s}_h^{i+1}\right\|_{\mathbf{H}^1(\Omega)}^2 + \sum_{i=0}^{j-1}\left\|\mathbf{s}_h^{i+1} - \mathbf{s}_h^i\right\|_{\mathbf{L}^2(\Omega)}^2 \leq C \tag{19}$$

The constant $C > 0$ *depends only on the data, but is in particular independent of the discretization parameters* h *and* k.

Proof

Let $0 \leq i \leq j - 1$. For (16c), we choose $\zeta_h = \mathbf{s}_h^{i+1}$ as test function. After multiplication by k, we obtain

$$\begin{aligned}&\left(\mathbf{s}_h^{i+1} - \mathbf{s}_h^i, \mathbf{s}_h^{i+1}\right)_\Omega + k\left(D_0\nabla\mathbf{s}_h^{i+1}, \nabla\mathbf{s}_h^{i+1}\right)_\Omega - k\beta\beta'\left(D_0\Pi_h\mathbf{m}_h^{i+1}\otimes\left(\nabla\mathbf{s}_h^{i+1}\cdot\Pi_h\mathbf{m}_h^{i+1}\right), \nabla\mathbf{s}_h^{i+1}\right)_\Omega + k\left(D_0\mathbf{s}_h^{i+1}, \mathbf{s}_h^{i+1}\right)_\Omega \\ &= k\beta\left(\Pi_h\mathbf{m}_h^{i+1}\otimes\mathbf{j}^{i+1}, \nabla\mathbf{s}_h^{i+1}\right)_\omega - k\beta\left(\mathbf{j}^{i+1}\cdot\mathbf{n}, \Pi_h\mathbf{m}_h^{i+1}\cdot\mathbf{s}_h^{i+1}\right)_{\partial\Omega\cap\partial\omega}.\end{aligned}$$

Since $D^0 \geq D_*$ and $\left\|\Pi_h\mathbf{m}_h^{i+1}\right\|_{\mathbf{L}^\infty(\omega)} = 1$, it follows that

$$\begin{aligned}&\left(\mathbf{s}_h^{i+1} - \mathbf{s}_h^i, \mathbf{s}_h^{i+1}\right)_\Omega + kD_*\left(1 - \beta\beta'\right)\left(\nabla\mathbf{s}_h^{i+1}, \nabla\mathbf{s}_h^{i+1}\right)_\Omega + kD_*\left(\mathbf{s}_h^{i+1}, \mathbf{s}_h^{i+1}\right)_\Omega \\ &\leq k\beta\left(\Pi_h\mathbf{m}_h^{i+1}\otimes\mathbf{j}^{i+1}, \nabla\mathbf{s}_h^{i+1}\right)_\omega - k\beta\left(\mathbf{j}^{i+1}\cdot\mathbf{n}, \Pi_h\mathbf{m}_h^{i+1}\cdot\mathbf{s}_h^{i+1}\right)_{\partial\Omega\cap\partial\omega},\end{aligned}$$

cf. the proof of Lemma 5. Summing up over $i = 0,\ldots,j - 1$, and exploiting Abel's summation by parts from Lemma 14 for the term $\sum_{i=0}^{j-1}\left(\mathbf{s}_h^{i+1} - \mathbf{s}_h^i, \mathbf{s}_h^{i+1}\right)_\Omega$, we get

$$\begin{aligned}&\frac{1}{2}\left\|\mathbf{s}_h^j\right\|_{\mathbf{L}^2(\Omega)}^2 + \frac{1}{2}\sum_{i=0}^{j-1}\left\|\mathbf{s}_h^{i+1} - \mathbf{s}_h^i\right\|_{\mathbf{L}^2(\Omega)}^2 + kD_*\left(1 - \beta\beta'\right)\sum_{i=0}^{j-1}\left\|\nabla\mathbf{s}_h^{i+1}\right\|_{\mathbf{L}^2(\Omega)}^2 + kD_*\sum_{i=0}^{j-1}\left\|\mathbf{s}_h^{i+1}\right\|_{\mathbf{L}^2(\Omega)}^2 \\ &\leq \frac{1}{2}\left\|\mathbf{s}_h^0\right\|_{\mathbf{L}^2(\Omega)}^2 + k\beta\sum_{i=0}^{j-1}\left[\left(\Pi_h\mathbf{m}_h^{i+1}\otimes\mathbf{j}^{i+1}, \nabla\mathbf{s}_h^{i+1}\right)_\omega - \left(\mathbf{j}^{i+1}\cdot\mathbf{n}, \Pi_h\mathbf{m}_h^{i+1}\cdot\mathbf{s}_h^{i+1}\right)_{\partial\Omega\cap\partial\omega}\right].\end{aligned}$$

Exploiting $0 < 1 - \beta\beta' < 1$ on the left-hand side, the Cauchy–Schwarz inequality and the Young inequality on the right-hand side, we obtain, for any choice of $\varepsilon > 0$,

$$\frac{1}{2}\left\|\mathbf{s}_h^j\right\|_{\mathbf{L}^2(\Omega)}^2+\frac{1}{2}\sum_{i=0}^{j-1}\left\|\mathbf{s}_h^{i+1}-\mathbf{s}_h^i\right\|_{\mathbf{L}^2(\Omega)}^2+kD_*\left(1-\beta\beta'\right)\sum_{i=0}^{j-1}\left\|\mathbf{s}_h^{i+1}\right\|_{\mathbf{H}^1(\Omega)}^2$$
$$\leq\frac{1}{2}\left\|\mathbf{s}_h^0\right\|_{\mathbf{L}^2(\Omega)}^2+\frac{Ck\beta}{2\varepsilon}\sum_{i=0}^{j-1}\left\|\mathbf{j}^{i+1}\right\|_{\mathbf{H}^1(\Omega)}^2+\frac{Ck\beta\varepsilon}{2}\sum_{i=0}^{j-1}\left\|\mathbf{s}_h^{i+1}\right\|_{\mathbf{H}^1(\Omega)}^2.$$

Here the constant $C > 0$ is the stability constant of the trace operator. It follows that

$$\frac{1}{2}\left\|\mathbf{s}_h^j\right\|_{\mathbf{L}^2(\Omega)}^2+\frac{1}{2}\sum_{i=0}^{j-1}\left\|\mathbf{s}_h^{i+1}-\mathbf{s}_h^i\right\|_{\mathbf{L}^2(\Omega)}^2+k\left[D_*\left(1-\beta\beta'\right)-\frac{C\beta\varepsilon}{2}\right]\sum_{i=0}^{j-1}\left\|\mathbf{s}_h^{i+1}\right\|_{\mathbf{H}^1(\Omega)}^2$$
$$\leq\frac{1}{2}\left\|\mathbf{s}_h^0\right\|_{\mathbf{L}^2(\Omega)}^2+\frac{Ck\beta}{2\varepsilon}\sum_{i=0}^{j-1}\left\|\mathbf{j}^{i+1}\right\|_{\mathbf{H}^1(\Omega)}^2.$$

If we choose $\varepsilon < 2_{D*}(1 - \beta\beta')/C\beta$, then all the coefficients on the left-hand side are positive. From (H1) and the regularity of j, we know that the right-hand side is uniformly bounded with respect to h and k. This yields the estimate (19). □

Corollary 16

Under the assumptions of Proposition 15, *the sequences*{shk}*and*{shk±}*are uniformly bounded in*L2(0, *T*; H¹(*Ω*))*and in* $L^\infty(0, T; L^2(\Omega))$, *i.e.,*

$$\|\mathbf{s}_{hk}\|_{L^2(0,T;\mathbf{H}^1(\Omega))}+\left\|\mathbf{s}_{hk}^{\pm}\right\|_{L^2(0,T;\mathbf{H}^1(\Omega))}+\|\mathbf{s}_{hk}\|_{L^\infty(0,T;\mathbf{L}^2(\Omega))}+\left\|\mathbf{s}_{hk}^{\pm}\right\|_{L^\infty(0,T;\mathbf{L}^2(\Omega))}\leq C$$

where the constant C > 0 *depends only on the data, but is in particular independent of the discretization parameters*h*and*k.

Proof The result follows from the boundedness of the discrete functions $\{\mathbf{s}_h^{i+1}\}_{0\leq i\leq N-1}$ from Proposition 15. □

Let $\mathcal{P}_h:\mathbf{L}^2(\Omega)\to\mathcal{S}^1(\mathcal{T}_h^\Omega)^3$ be the $L^2(\Omega)$-orthogonal projection onto $\mathcal{S}^1(\mathcal{T}_h^\Omega)^3$, i.e.,

$$\left(\mathcal{P}_h\eta-\eta,\eta_h\right)_\Omega=0\quad\text{for all }\eta\in\mathbf{L}^2(\Omega),\ \eta_h\in\mathcal{S}^1(\mathcal{T}_h^\Omega)^3$$

Since $\{\mathcal{T}_h^\Omega\}_{h>0}$is quasi-uniform, it is well known that P_h is stable in $H^1(\Omega)$, i.e.,

$$\|\mathcal{P}_h\eta\|_{\mathbf{H}^1(\Omega)}\lesssim\|\eta\|_{\mathbf{H}^1(\Omega)}\quad\text{for all }\eta\in\mathbf{H}^1(\Omega)\tag{20}$$

We also refer to [32,33] for recent results on H^1-stability on locally refined meshes. With this, we obtain uniform boundedness of $\partial_t s_{hk}$.

Proposition 17 *The sequence* $\{\partial_t s_{hk}\}$*is uniformly bounded in* $L^2(0, T; \widetilde{H}^{-1}(\Omega))$, *i.e.,*

$$\|\partial_t \mathbf{s}_{hk}\|_{L^2(0,T;\widetilde{\mathbf{H}}^{-1}(\Omega))} \le C$$

where the constant $C>0$ *depends only on the data, but is in particular independent of the discretization parameters* h *and* k.

Proof

Let $w \in H^1(\Omega)\setminus\{0\}$, $0 \le i \le N - 1$, and $t \in [t_i, t_i + 1)$. From (16c) and the H^1-stability (20) of P_h, we get

$$\begin{aligned}\langle \partial_t \mathbf{s}_{hk}(t), \mathbf{w}\rangle &= (\partial_t \mathbf{s}_{hk}(t), \mathbf{w})_\Omega = \left(d_t \mathbf{s}_h^{i+1}, \mathbf{w}\right)_\Omega = \left(d_t \mathbf{s}_h^{i+1}, \mathcal{P}_h \mathbf{w}\right)_\Omega \\ &= \beta\left(\Pi_h \mathbf{m}_h^{i+1} \otimes \mathbf{j}^{i+1}, \nabla \mathcal{P}_h \mathbf{w}\right)_\omega - \beta\left(\mathbf{j}^{i+1}\cdot \mathbf{n}, \Pi_h \mathbf{m}_h^{i+1}\cdot \mathcal{P}_h \mathbf{w}\right)_{\partial\Omega\cap\partial\omega} - a_h^{i+1}(\mathbf{s}_h^{i+1}, \mathcal{P}_h \mathbf{w}) \\ &\lesssim \left(\left\|\mathbf{j}^{i+1}\right\|_{\mathbf{H}^1(\Omega)} + \left\|\mathbf{s}_h^{i+1}\right\|_{\mathbf{H}^1(\Omega)}\right)\|\mathcal{P}_h \mathbf{w}\|_{\mathbf{H}^1(\Omega)} \lesssim \left(\left\|\mathbf{j}^{i+1}\right\|_{\mathbf{H}^1(\Omega)} + \left\|\mathbf{s}_h^{i+1}\right\|_{\mathbf{H}^1(\Omega)}\right)\|\mathbf{w}\|_{\mathbf{H}^1(\Omega)}\end{aligned}$$

Dividing by $\|w\|_{H^1(\Omega)}$ and taking the supremum over $w \in H^1(\Omega)\setminus\{0\}$, we obtain

$$\|\partial_t \mathbf{s}_{hk}(t)\|_{\widetilde{\mathbf{H}}^{-1}(\Omega)} \lesssim \left\|\mathbf{j}^{i+1}\right\|_{\mathbf{H}^1(\Omega)} + \left\|\mathbf{s}_h^{i+1}\right\|_{\mathbf{H}^1(\Omega)}$$

Squaring, integrating over (t_i, t_{i+1}), and summing up over $0 \le i \le N - 1$, we get

$$\|\partial_t \mathbf{s}_{hk}\|^2_{L^2(0,T;\widetilde{\mathbf{H}}^{-1}(\Omega))} \lesssim k\sum_{i=0}^{N-1}\left\|\mathbf{j}^{i+1}\right\|^2_{\mathbf{H}^1(\Omega)} + k\sum_{i=0}^{N-1}\left\|\mathbf{s}_h^{i+1}\right\|^2_{\mathbf{H}^1(\Omega)}$$

The boundedness from Proposition 15 thus yields (21). □

We derive the corresponding estimates for the discrete quantities $\left\{\left(\mathbf{v}_h^i, \mathbf{m}_h^{i+1}\right)\right\}_{0\le i\le N-1}$.

Lemma 18

Let $0 \le i \le N - 1$. *The discrete functions* (v_h^i, m_h^{i+1}) *obtained through Algorithm 6 fulfill*

$$\alpha \left\|\mathbf{v}_h^i\right\|_{\mathbf{L}^2(\omega)}^2 + \frac{C_{\mathrm{exch}}}{2k}\left(\left\|\nabla \mathbf{m}_h^{i+1}\right\|_{\mathbf{L}^2(\omega)}^2 - \left\|\nabla \mathbf{m}_h^i\right\|_{\mathbf{L}^2(\omega)}^2\right) + C_{\mathrm{exch}} k\left(\theta - \frac{1}{2}\right)\left\|\nabla \mathbf{v}_h^i\right\|_{\mathbf{L}^2(\omega)}^2$$
$$= \left(\pi_h(\mathbf{m}_h^i), \mathbf{v}_h^i\right)_\omega + \left(\mathbf{f}^i, \mathbf{v}_h^i\right)_\omega + c\left(\mathbf{s}_h^i, \mathbf{v}_h^i\right)_\omega . \tag{22}$$

Proof

We test (16a) with $\boldsymbol{\phi}_h = \mathbf{v}_h^i \in \mathcal{K}_{\mathbf{m}_h^i}$ to get

$$\alpha \left\|\mathbf{v}_h^i\right\|_{\mathbf{L}^2(\omega)}^2 + \frac{C_{\mathrm{exch}}}{2k}\left(\left\|\nabla \mathbf{m}_h^{i+1}\right\|_{\mathbf{L}^2(\omega)}^2 - \left\|\nabla \mathbf{m}_h^i\right\|_{\mathbf{L}^2(\omega)}^2\right) + C_{\mathrm{exch}} k\left(\theta - \frac{1}{2}\right)\left\|\nabla \mathbf{v}_h^i\right\|_{\mathbf{L}^2(\omega)}^2$$
$$= \left(\pi_h(\mathbf{m}_h^i), \mathbf{v}_h^i\right)_\omega + \left(\mathbf{f}^i, \mathbf{v}_h^i\right)_\omega + c\left(\mathbf{s}_h^i, \mathbf{v}_h^i\right)_\omega .$$

Exploiting the vector identity

$$2\,(a + b) \cdot a = |a|^2 + |a + b|^2 - |b|^2 \text{ for all } a,b \in R^3$$

with the choice $\mathbf{a} = k\nabla \mathbf{v}_h^i$ and $\mathbf{b} = \nabla \mathbf{m}_h^i$, and taking into account (16b), we obtain (22). □

Proposition 19

Suppose that the assumptions of Theorem 12(a) are satisfied. Then, there exists $k_0 > 0$ *such that for all time-step sizes* $0 < k < k_0$ *and* $1 \le j \le N$ *the discrete functions* $\{(\mathbf{v}_h^i, \mathbf{m}_h^{i+1})\}_{0\le i\le j-1}$ *obtained through Algorithm 6 fulfill*

$$\left\|\nabla \mathbf{m}_h^j\right\|_{\mathbf{L}^2(\omega)}^2 + k\sum_{i=0}^{j-1}\left\|\mathbf{v}_h^i\right\|_{\mathbf{L}^2(\omega)}^2 + \left(\theta - \frac{1}{2}\right)k^2\sum_{i=0}^{j-1}\left\|\nabla \mathbf{v}_h^i\right\|_{\mathbf{L}^2(\omega)}^2 \le C \tag{23}$$

The constant $C > 0$ *depends only on the data and* k_0*, but is otherwise independent of the discretization parameters h and k.*

Proof

Let $1 \le j \le N$. From Lemma 18, multiplying (22) by k/C_{exch}, summing up over $0 \le i \le j - 1$ and exploiting the telescopic sum, we obtain

$$\frac{1}{2}\left\|\nabla \mathbf{m}_h^j\right\|_{\mathbf{L}^2(\omega)}^2 + \frac{\alpha k}{C_{\mathrm{exch}}}\sum_{i=0}^{j-1}\left\|\mathbf{v}_h^i\right\|_{\mathbf{L}^2(\omega)}^2 + k^2\left(\theta - \frac{1}{2}\right)\sum_{i=0}^{j-1}\left\|\nabla \mathbf{v}_h^i\right\|_{\mathbf{L}^2(\omega)}^2$$
$$= \frac{1}{2}\left\|\nabla \mathbf{m}_h^0\right\|_{\mathbf{L}^2(\omega)}^2 + \frac{k}{C_{\mathrm{exch}}}\sum_{i=0}^{j-1}\left[\left(\pi_h(\mathbf{m}_h^i), \mathbf{v}_h^i\right)_\omega + \left(\mathbf{f}^i, \mathbf{v}_h^i\right)_\omega + c\left(\mathbf{s}_h^i, \mathbf{v}_h^i\right)_\omega\right]$$

The Cauchy–Schwarz inequality and the Young inequality, together with assumption (H2), yield for any $\varepsilon > 0$

$$\frac{1}{2}\left\|\nabla \mathbf{m}_h^j\right\|_{\mathbf{L}^2(\omega)}^2 + \frac{k}{C_{\text{exch}}}\left(\alpha - \frac{2+c}{2}\varepsilon\right)\sum_{i=0}^{j-1}\left\|\mathbf{v}_h^i\right\|_{\mathbf{L}^2(\omega)}^2 + k^2\left(\theta - \frac{1}{2}\right)\sum_{i=0}^{j-1}\left\|\nabla \mathbf{v}_h^i\right\|_{\mathbf{L}^2(\omega)}^2$$
$$\leq \frac{1}{2}\left\|\nabla \mathbf{m}_h^0\right\|_{\mathbf{L}^2(\omega)}^2 + \frac{k}{2\varepsilon C_{\text{exch}}}\sum_{i=0}^{j-1}\left[C_\pi^2\left\|\mathbf{m}_h^i\right\|_{\mathbf{L}^2(\omega)}^2 + \left\|\mathbf{f}^i\right\|_{\mathbf{L}^2(\omega)}^2 + c\left\|\mathbf{s}_h^i\right\|_{\mathbf{L}^2(\omega)}^2\right].$$

From Proposition 9, we deduce

$$k\sum_{i=0}^{j-1}\left\|\mathbf{m}_h^i\right\|_{\mathbf{L}^2(\omega)}^2 \leq C'\left(1 + k^2\sum_{i=0}^{j-1}\left\|\mathbf{v}_h^i\right\|_{\mathbf{L}^2(\omega)}^2\right)$$

where the constant $C' > 0$ depends only on $|\omega|$,T and C_*. We thus obtain

$$\frac{1}{2}\left\|\nabla \mathbf{m}_h^j\right\|_{\mathbf{L}^2(\omega)}^2 + \frac{k}{C_{\text{exch}}}\left(\alpha - \frac{2+c}{2}\varepsilon - \frac{kC_\pi^2 C'}{2\varepsilon}\right)\sum_{i=0}^{j-1}\left\|\mathbf{v}_h^i\right\|_{\mathbf{L}^2(\omega)}^2 + k^2\left(\theta - \frac{1}{2}\right)\sum_{i=0}^{j-1}\left\|\nabla \mathbf{v}_h^i\right\|_{\mathbf{L}^2(\omega)}^2$$
$$\leq \frac{1}{2}\left\|\nabla \mathbf{m}_h^0\right\|_{\mathbf{L}^2(\omega)}^2 + \frac{C' C_\pi^2}{2\varepsilon C_{\text{exch}}} + \frac{k}{2\varepsilon C_{\text{exch}}}\sum_{i=0}^{j-1}\left[\left\|\mathbf{f}^i\right\|_{\mathbf{L}^2(\omega)}^2 + c\left\|\mathbf{s}_h^i\right\|_{\mathbf{L}^2(\omega)}^2\right].$$

Note that $\theta > 1/2$. If we choose $\varepsilon < 2\alpha/(2 + c)$, for $k < k_0 := \varepsilon(2\alpha - (2 + c)\varepsilon)/(C_\pi^2 C')$ all the coefficients on the left-hand side are positive. From the regularity of f, assumption (H1), and the boundedness from Proposition 15, we know that the right-hand side is uniformly bounded. This yields the estimate (23). □

Corollary 20

Under the assumptions of Proposition 19, and if $k < k_0$*, the sequences* $\{\mathbf{m}_{hk}\}$, $\{\mathbf{m}_{hk}^\pm\}$, $\{\Pi_h \mathbf{m}_{hk}^+\}$ *and* $\{\mathbf{v}_{hk}^-\}$ *are uniformly bounded. In particular, it holds*

$$\|\mathbf{m}_{hk}\|_{\mathbf{H}^1(\omega_T)} + \left\|\mathbf{m}_{hk}^\pm\right\|_{L^2(0,T;\mathbf{H}^1(\omega))} + \left\|\Pi_h \mathbf{m}_{hk}^+\right\|_{L^2(0,T;\mathbf{H}^1(\omega))} + \left\|\mathbf{v}_{hk}^-\right\|_{\mathbf{L}^2(\omega_T)} \leq C$$

where the constant $C > 0$ *depends only on the data and* k_0*, but is independent of the discretization parameters h and k.*

Proof

The result follows from the boundedness of the discrete functions $\{(\mathbf{v}_h^i, \mathbf{m}_h^{i+1})\}_{0\leq i\leq N-1}$ from Propositions 9 and 19, and from (15). □

We can now proceed with step (ii) of the proof and conclude the existence of weakly convergent subsequences.

Proposition 21

Suppose that the assumptions of Theorem 12(a) *are satisfied. Then, there exist* m $\in H^1(\omega^T) \cap L^\infty(0, T; H^1(\omega))$ *and* s $\in L^2(0, T; H^1(\Omega)) \cap L^\infty(0, T; L^2(\Omega)) \cap H^1(0, T; \widetilde{H}^{-1}(\Omega))$, *with* $|m| = 1$ *a.e. in* ω^T, *such that there holds*

$$\mathbf{m}_{hk} \overset{\text{sub}}{\rightharpoonup} \mathbf{m} \quad \textit{in}\, \mathbf{H}^1(\omega_T), \tag{24a}$$

$$\mathbf{m}_{hk}, \mathbf{m}_{hk}^{\pm}, \Pi_h \mathbf{m}_{hk}^{+} \overset{\text{sub}}{\rightharpoonup} \mathbf{m} \quad \textit{in}\, L^2(0, T; \mathbf{H}^1(\omega)), \tag{24b}$$

$$\mathbf{m}_{hk}, \mathbf{m}_{hk}^{\pm}, \Pi_h \mathbf{m}_{hk}^{+} \overset{\text{sub}}{\rightarrow} \mathbf{m} \quad \textit{in}\, \mathbf{L}^2(\omega_T), \tag{24c}$$

$$\mathbf{v}_{hk}^{-} \overset{\text{sub}}{\rightharpoonup} \partial_t \mathbf{m} \quad \textit{in}\, \mathbf{L}^2(\omega_T), \tag{24d}$$

$$\mathbf{s}_{hk}, \mathbf{s}_{hk}^{\pm} \overset{\text{sub}}{\rightharpoonup} \mathbf{s} \quad \textit{in}\, L^2(0, T; \mathbf{H}^1(\Omega)), \tag{24e}$$

$$\partial_t \mathbf{s}_{hk} \overset{\text{sub}}{\rightharpoonup} \partial_t \mathbf{s} \quad \textit{in}\, L^2(0, T; \widetilde{\mathbf{H}}^{-1}(\Omega)) \tag{24f}$$

For $(h, k) \to (0,0)$. *Moreover, there exists one subsequence for which* (24) *holds simultaneously.*

Proof

The boundedness results from Corollary 20, in combination with the Eberlein–Šmulian theorem, allow us to extract weakly convergent subsequences of $\{\mathbf{m}_{hk}\}, \{\mathbf{m}_{hk}^{\pm}\}, \{\Pi_h \mathbf{m}_{hk}^{+}\}$ and $\{\mathbf{v}_{hk}^{-}\}$ and $\{\mathbf{v}_{hk}^{-}\}$. Let $m \in H^1(\omega_T)$ be such that $\mathbf{m}_{hk} \overset{\text{sub}}{\rightharpoonup} \mathbf{m}$ in $\mathbf{H}^1(\omega_T)$. From the continuous inclusions $H^1(\omega_T) \subset L^2(0, T; H^1(\omega)) \subset L^2(\omega_T)$ and the compact embedding $H^1(\omega_T) \Subset L^2(\omega_T)$, we deduce

$$\mathbf{m}_{hk} \overset{\text{sub}}{\rightharpoonup} \mathbf{m} \quad \text{in}\, L^2(0, T; \mathbf{H}^1(\omega)) \quad \text{and} \quad \mathbf{m}_{hk} \overset{\text{sub}}{\rightarrow} \mathbf{m} \quad \text{in}\, \mathbf{L}^2(\omega_T)$$

With $\|\mathbf{m}_{hk} - \mathbf{m}_{hk}^{\pm}\|_{\mathbf{L}^2(\omega_T)} \leq k \|\mathbf{v}_{hk}^{-}\|_{\mathbf{L}^2(\omega_T)}$, we can identify the limits of the subsequences of $\{\mathbf{m}_{hk}\}$ and $\{\mathbf{m}_{hk}^{\pm}\}$. As $\partial_t \mathbf{m}_{hk} = \mathbf{v}_{hk}^{-}$, it clearly holds that $v = \partial_t m$ a.e. in ω_T.

We now prove that the limiting function m satisfies the unit-length constraint. First, we observe that

$$\left\| |\mathbf{m}|^2 - |\mathbf{m}_{hk}^+|^2 \right\|_{L^1(\omega_T)} \leq \left\| \mathbf{m} + \mathbf{m}_{hk}^+ \right\|_{\mathbf{L}^2(\omega_T)} \left\| \mathbf{m} - \mathbf{m}_{hk}^+ \right\|_{\mathbf{L}^2(\omega_T)} \xrightarrow{\text{sub}} 0 \tag{25}$$

for $(h, k) \to 0$. For $0 \le i \le N - 1$ and $K \in \mathcal{T}_h^{\omega}$, a standard interpolation estimate for the piecewise linear function $\mathbf{m}_h^{i+1} \in \mathcal{S}^1(\mathcal{T}_h^{\omega})^3$ yields

$$\left\| |\mathbf{m}_h^{i+1}|^2 - \mathcal{I}_h\left(|\mathbf{m}_h^{i+1}|^2\right) \right\|_{L^2(K)} \lesssim h_K^2 \left\| D^2 |\mathbf{m}_h^{i+1}|^2 \right\|_{L^2(K)} \lesssim h_K^2 \left\| \nabla \mathbf{m}_h^{i+1} \right\|_{\mathbf{L}^4(K)}^2 \lesssim h_K^{1/2} \left\| \nabla \mathbf{m}_h^{i+1} \right\|_{\mathbf{L}^2(K)}^2$$

From Proposition 19, we obtain

$$\left\| |\mathbf{m}_{hk}^+|^2 - \mathcal{I}_h\left(|\mathbf{m}_{hk}^+|^2\right) \right\|_{L^2(\omega_T)} \lesssim h^{1/2}.$$

For all $1 \le j \le N$, Proposition 9 and the discrete norm equivalence of Lemma 8with $r = 2$ yield

$$\left\| \mathcal{I}_h\left(|\mathbf{m}_h^j|^2\right) - 1 \right\|_{L^1(\omega)} \lesssim \sum_{\mathbf{z} \in \mathcal{N}_h^{\omega}} h^3 \left| |\mathbf{m}_h^j(\mathbf{z})|^2 - 1 \right| \le k^2 \sum_{i=0}^{j-1} h^3 \sum_{\mathbf{z} \in \mathcal{N}_h^{\omega}} |\mathbf{v}_h^i(\mathbf{z})|^2 \lesssim k^2 \sum_{i=0}^{j-1} \left\| \mathbf{v}_h^i \right\|_{\mathbf{L}^2(\omega)}^2$$

Then, from Proposition 19, we deduce

$$\left\| \mathcal{I}_h\left(|\mathbf{m}_{hk}^+|^2\right) - 1 \right\|_{L^1(\omega_T)} \lesssim k \tag{27}$$

Combining (26)–(27), the triangle inequality thus yields that $|\mathbf{m}_{hk}^+|^2 \xrightarrow{\text{sub}} 1$ in $\mathbf{L}^1(\omega_T)$ for $(h, k) \to 0$, whence $|\mathrm{m}| = 1$ a.e. in ω_T follows from (25).

For $x \in \mathbb{R}^3$ with $|\mathrm{x}| \ge 1$, it holds that

$$\left| \mathbf{x} - \frac{\mathbf{x}}{|\mathbf{x}|} \right| = |\mathbf{x}| - 1 = \frac{|\mathbf{x}|^2 - 1}{|\mathbf{x}| + 1} \le \frac{1}{2}\left(|\mathbf{x}|^2 - 1\right)$$

Due to (17), this yields for all $1 \le j \le \mathrm{N}$

$$\left|\mathbf{m}_h^j(\mathbf{z}) - \Pi_h \mathbf{m}_h^j(\mathbf{z})\right| \leq \frac{1}{2}\left(\left|\mathbf{m}_h^j(\mathbf{z})\right|^2 - 1\right) = \frac{1}{2}k^2 \sum_{i=0}^{j-1} \left|\mathbf{v}_h^i(\mathbf{z})\right|^2$$

whence by virtue of Proposition 19

$$\left\|\mathbf{m}_h^j - \Pi_h \mathbf{m}_h^j\right\|_{\mathbf{L}^1(\omega)} \lesssim k^2 \sum_{i=0}^{j-1} \left\|\mathbf{v}_h^j\right\|_{\mathbf{L}^2(\omega)}^2 \lesssim k$$

This implies $\Pi_h \mathbf{m}_{hk}^+ \overset{\text{sub}}{\to} \mathbf{m}$ in $\mathbf{L}^1(\omega_T)$ as $(h,k) \to (0,0)$. Since $\|\Pi_h \mathbf{m}_{hk}^+\|_{\mathbf{L}^\infty(\omega_T)} + \|\mathbf{m}\|_{\mathbf{L}^\infty(\omega_T)} = 2$, we have $\Pi_h \mathbf{m}_{hk}^+ \overset{\text{sub}}{\to} \mathbf{m}$ even in $L_2(\omega_T)$ as well as $\Pi_h \mathbf{m}_{hk}^+ \overset{\text{sub}}{\rightharpoonup} \mathbf{m}$ in $L^2(0, T; H^1(\omega))$.

From Corollary 16, we similarly deduce the existence of weakly convergent subsequences of $\{\mathbf{s}_{hk}\}$ and $\{\mathbf{s}_{hk}^\pm\}$. Due to Proposition 15, the quantity $\sum_{i=0}^{N-1} \|\mathbf{s}_h^{i+1} - \mathbf{s}_h^i\|_{\mathbf{L}^2(\Omega)}^2$ is bounded. This allows to identify the weak limits, since

$$\left\|\mathbf{s}_{hk} - \mathbf{s}_{hk}^\pm\right\|_{\mathbf{L}^2(\Omega_T)} \lesssim k \sum_{i=0}^{N-1} \left\|\mathbf{s}_h^{i+1} - \mathbf{s}_h^i\right\|_{\mathbf{L}^2(\Omega)}^2 \longrightarrow 0 \quad \text{for } (h,k) \to 0$$

Finally, from Proposition 17, we deduce the existence of a weakly convergent subsequence of $\{\partial_t \mathbf{s}_{hk}\}$, and it is easy to see that its limit is precisely $\partial_t \mathbf{s}$, cf. [27, Section 7.1.2, Theorem 3]. This establishes (24e)–(24f) and thus concludes the proof. □

Remark 22

As the constants which guarantee the boundedness of Proposition 15, Corollary 16 and Proposition 17, are independent of T, we deduce that s ∈ $L^2(\mathbb{R}^+; H^1(\Omega)) \cap L^2(\mathbb{R}^+; L^2(\Omega)) \cap H^1(\mathbb{R}^+; \widetilde{H}^{-1}(\Omega))$.

We have collected all the ingredients for the proof of our main theorem.

Proof of Theorem 12

The result of part (a) follows directly from Proposition 21. To conclude the proof of part (b), it remains to identify the limiting functions (m,s) with a weak solution of SDLLG in the sense of Definition 2.

To check (11a), we essentially proceed as in [17]. Let $\varphi \in C^\infty(\overline{\omega T})$. For $0 \leq i \leq N - 1$, we test (16a) with respect to $\mathcal{I}_h\left((\mathbf{m}_{hk}^- \times \boldsymbol{\varphi})(t_i)\right) \in \mathcal{K}_{\mathbf{m}_h^i}$, with Ih being the nodal interpolation operator onto $\mathcal{S}^1(\mathcal{T}_h^\omega)^3$. Multiplication with k and summation over $0 \leq i \leq N - 1$ yield

$$\left(\alpha\mathbf{v}_{hk}^- + \mathbf{m}_{hk}^- \times \mathbf{v}_{hk}^-, \mathcal{I}_h\left(\mathbf{m}_{hk}^- \times \varphi_k^-\right)\right)_{\omega_T} = -C_{\text{exch}}\left(\nabla\left(\mathbf{m}_{hk}^- + \theta k\mathbf{v}_{hk}^-\right), \nabla\mathcal{I}_h\left(\mathbf{m}_{hk}^- \times \varphi_k^-\right)\right)_{\omega_T}$$
$$+ \left(\pi_h(\mathbf{m}_{hk}^-), \mathcal{I}_h\left(\mathbf{m}_{hk}^- \times \varphi_k^-\right)\right)_{\omega_T}$$
$$+ \left(\mathbf{f}_k^-, \mathcal{I}_h\left(\mathbf{m}_{hk}^- \times \varphi_k^-\right)\right)_{\omega_T} + c\left(\mathbf{s}_{hk}^-, \mathcal{I}_h\left(\mathbf{m}_{hk}^- \times \varphi_k^-\right)\right)_{\omega_T}$$

where $\mathcal{I}_h\left(\mathbf{m}_{hk}^- \times \varphi_k^-\right)(t) = \mathcal{I}_h\left(\left(\mathbf{m}_{hk}^- \times \varphi\right)(t_i)\right)$ for all $t \in [t_i, t_i + 1)$. From the well-known approximation properties of Ih and the boundedness of $\sqrt{k}\left\|\nabla\mathbf{v}_{hk}^-\right\|_{\mathbf{L}^2(\omega_T)}$ from Proposition 19 for $\theta \in (1/2,1]$, we deduce

$$\left(\alpha\mathbf{v}_{hk}^- + \mathbf{m}_{hk}^- \times \mathbf{v}_{hk}^-, \mathbf{m}_{hk}^- \times \varphi_k^-\right)_{\omega_T} + C_{\text{exch}}\left(\nabla\left(\mathbf{m}_{hk}^- + \theta k\mathbf{v}_{hk}^-\right), \nabla\left(\mathbf{m}_{hk}^- \times \varphi_k^-\right)\right)_{\omega_T}$$
$$- \left(\pi_h(\mathbf{m}_{hk}^-), \mathbf{m}_{hk}^- \times \varphi_k^-\right)_{\omega_T} - \left(\mathbf{f}_k^-, \mathbf{m}_{hk}^- \times \varphi_k^-\right)_{\omega_T} - c\left(\mathbf{s}_{hk}^-, \mathbf{m}_{hk}^- \times \varphi_k^-\right)_{\omega_T} = \mathcal{O}(h)$$

Passing to the limit for $(h,k) \to (0,0)$, we obtain

$$(\alpha\partial_t\mathbf{m} + \mathbf{m} \times \partial_t\mathbf{m}, \mathbf{m} \times \varphi)_{\omega_T} = -C_{\text{exch}}(\nabla\mathbf{m}, \nabla(\mathbf{m} \times \varphi))_{\omega_T} + (\pi(\mathbf{m}) + \mathbf{f} + c\mathbf{s}, \mathbf{m} \times \varphi)_{\omega_T}$$

In the latter, we have used the convergence properties from Proposition 21, assumption (H3) for the general field contribution, as well as $\mathbf{f}_k^- \rightharpoonup \mathbf{f}$ and $\mathbf{m}_{hk}^- \times \varphi_k^- \overset{\text{sub}}{\to} \mathbf{m} \times \varphi$ in $\mathbf{L}^2(\omega_T)$.

Direct calculations and standard properties of the cross product yield the identities

$$(\nabla\mathbf{m}, \nabla(\mathbf{m} \times \varphi))_{\omega_T} = (\nabla\mathbf{m} \times \mathbf{m}, \nabla\varphi)_{\omega_T}, \qquad (\partial_t\mathbf{m}, \mathbf{m} \times \varphi)_{\omega_T} = (\partial_t\mathbf{m} \times \mathbf{m}, \varphi)_{\omega_T},$$
$$(\mathbf{m} \times \partial_t\mathbf{m}, \mathbf{m} \times \varphi)_{\omega_T} = (\partial_t\mathbf{m}, \varphi)_{\omega_T}, \qquad (\pi(\mathbf{m}), \mathbf{m} \times \varphi)_{\omega_T} = (\pi(\mathbf{m}) \times \mathbf{m}, \varphi)_{\omega_T},$$
$$(\mathbf{f}, \mathbf{m} \times \varphi)_{\omega_T} = (\mathbf{f} \times \mathbf{m}, \varphi)_{\omega_T}, \qquad (\mathbf{s}, \mathbf{m} \times \varphi)_{\omega_T} = (\mathbf{s} \times \mathbf{m}, \varphi)_{\omega_T},$$

from which, by density, we deduce (11a).

To check (11b), let $\varphi \in C^\infty(0, T; \mathbf{C}^\infty(\overline{\Omega}))$. Given $0 \le i \le N - 1$, let $t \in [t_i, t_i + 1)$. In (16c) we choose the test function $\zeta_h = \mathcal{I}_h(\varphi(t)) \in \mathcal{S}^1(\mathcal{T}_h^\Omega)^3$. Integration in time over $(t_i, t_i + 1)$ and summation over $0 \le i \le N - 1$ yield

$$(\partial_t\mathbf{s}_{hk}, \mathcal{I}_h\varphi)_{\Omega_T} + \left(D_0\nabla\mathbf{s}_{hk}^+, \nabla\mathcal{I}_h\varphi\right)_{\Omega_T} - \beta\beta'\left(D_0\Pi_h\mathbf{m}_{hk}^+ \otimes \left(\nabla\mathbf{s}_{hk}^+ \cdot \Pi_h\mathbf{m}_{hk}^+\right), \nabla\mathcal{I}_h\varphi\right)_{\omega_T}$$
$$+ \left(D_0\mathbf{s}_{hk}^+, \mathcal{I}_h\varphi\right)_{\Omega_T} + \left(D_0\left(\mathbf{s}_{hk}^+ \times \Pi_h\mathbf{m}_{hk}^+\right), \mathcal{I}_h\varphi\right)_{\omega_T}$$
$$= \beta\left(\Pi_h\mathbf{m}_{hk}^+ \otimes \mathbf{j}_k^+, \nabla\mathcal{I}_h\varphi\right)_{\omega_T} - \beta\left(\mathbf{j}_k^+ \cdot \mathbf{n}, \Pi_h\mathbf{m}_{hk}^+ \cdot \mathcal{I}_h\varphi\right)_{(0,T)\times(\partial\Omega\cap\partial\omega)}, \tag{28}$$

where $\mathcal{I}_h\varphi(t) = \mathcal{I}_h(\varphi(t))$ for all $t \in (0, T)$. Passing (28) to the limit for $(h,k) \to 0$, due to the convergence properties stated in Proposition 21, in combination with the standard approximation properties of Ih, we deduce

$$\int_0^T \langle \partial_t \mathbf{s}(t), \varphi(t) \rangle + (D_0 \nabla \mathbf{s}, \nabla \varphi)_{\Omega_T} - \beta\beta' (D_0 \mathbf{m} \otimes (\nabla \mathbf{s} \cdot \mathbf{m}), \nabla \varphi)_{\omega_T} + (D_0 \mathbf{s}, \varphi)_{\Omega_T} + (D_0 (\mathbf{s} \times \mathbf{m}), \varphi)_{\omega_T}$$
$$= \beta (\mathbf{m} \otimes \mathbf{j}, \nabla \varphi)_{\omega_T} - \beta (\mathbf{j} \cdot \mathbf{n}, \mathbf{m} \cdot \varphi)_{(0,T) \times (\partial\Omega \cap \partial\omega)} .$$

By density, this is also true for all $\varphi \in C^\infty(0, T; H^1(\Omega))$. Hence in particular for each $\zeta \in H^1(\Omega)$ and a.e. $t \in (0,T)$ we have (11b).

Since $\mathbf{m}_{hk} \overset{\text{sub}}{\rightharpoonup} \mathbf{m}$ in $\mathbf{H}^1(\omega_T)$ with $\mathbf{m}_{hk}(0) = \mathbf{m}_h^0$, and $\mathbf{s}_{hk} \overset{\text{sub}}{\rightharpoonup} \mathbf{s}$ $H^1(0, T; \widetilde{\mathbf{H}}^{-1}(\Omega))$ with $\mathbf{s}_{hk}(0) = \mathbf{s}_h^0$, assumption ($H^1$) allows to deduce $m(0) = m^0$ and $s(0) = s^0$ in the sense of traces. □

5. ENERGY ESTIMATE

In this section, we exploit our constructive convergence proof to derive an energy estimate for weak solutions of SDLLG, which is also meaningful from a physical point of view. The total magnetic Gibbs free energy from (3) is strongly related to the standard form (1) of LLG and does not take into account the interaction between the magnetization and spin accumulation. As we are dealing with the augmented form (7) of LLG, we extend (3) and define the free energy of the system by

$$\mathcal{E}(\mathbf{M}, \mathbf{S}) = \frac{A}{M_s^2} \int_\omega |\nabla \mathbf{M}|^2 + K \int_\omega \phi(\mathbf{M}/M_s) - \mu_0 \int_\omega \mathbf{H}_e \cdot \mathbf{M} - \frac{\mu_0}{2} \int_\omega \mathbf{H}_s(\mathbf{M}) \cdot \mathbf{M} - J \int_\omega \mathbf{S} \cdot \mathbf{M}. \tag{29}$$

This definition is in agreement with (7), since in this case it is easy to see that

$$-\frac{\delta \mathcal{E}(\mathbf{M}, \mathbf{S})}{\delta \mathbf{M}} = \mu_0 \mathbf{H}_{\text{eff}}(\mathbf{M}) + J\mathbf{S}$$

where the effective field is given by (4). A simple formal computation shows that strong solutions to (7) satisfy

$$\frac{d\mathcal{E}}{dt} = -\frac{\alpha}{\gamma M_s} \int_\omega \left| \frac{\partial \mathbf{M}}{\partial t} \right|^2 - \mu_0 \int_\omega \frac{\partial \mathbf{H}_e}{\partial t} \cdot \mathbf{M} - J \int_\omega \frac{\partial \mathbf{S}}{\partial t} \cdot \mathbf{M}. \tag{30}$$

Neglecting the spin accumulation term and assuming that H_e is constant in time, Eq. (30) reduces to

$$\frac{d\mathcal{E}}{dt} = -\frac{\alpha}{\gamma M_s}\int_{\omega}\left|\frac{\partial \mathbf{M}}{\partial t}\right|^2 \leq 0$$

which reveals the well-known dissipative behavior of solutions to the standard form (1) of LLG.

The main aim of this section is to prove a property corresponding to (30) in the context of weak solutions. To this end, we move to the nondimensional framework introduced in Section 2 and consider the following assumptions:

(H4) the operator $\pi : L^2(\omega) \to L^2(\omega)$ from (10) is linear, self-adjoint, and bounded;

(H5) it holds

$$\pi_h(\mathbf{w}_{hk}) \to \pi(\mathbf{w}) \quad \text{in } \mathbf{L}^2(\omega_T) \text{ as } (h,k) \to 0$$

for any sequence $w_{hk} \to w$ in $L^2(\omega_T)$, which is slightly stronger than (H3);

(H6) the applied field f belongs to $H^1(0, T; L^2(\omega))$.

Remark 23

For some fixed easy axis $e \in S^2$ and the corresponding uniaxial anisotropy density function $\phi(\mathbf{m}) = 1-(\mathbf{m}\cdot\mathbf{e})^2$, the operator

$$\pi(\mathbf{m}) = \mathbf{h}_s(\mathbf{m}) - C_{\text{ani}}\nabla\phi(\mathbf{m}) = \mathbf{h}_s(\mathbf{m}) + 2C_{\text{ani}}(\mathbf{e}\cdot\mathbf{m})\mathbf{m} \tag{31}$$

satisfies (H4). Moreover, all the stray field discretizations mentioned in Remark 10 satisfy (H5), see [19]. The operator π from (31) is even well defined and bounded as operator $\pi : \mathbf{L}^p(\omega) \to \mathbf{L}^p(\omega)$ for all $1 < p < \infty$, see [34]. Unlike [18], the proof of our energy estimate, see Theorem 24, avoids this additional regularity, but only relies on the energy setting $p = 2$.

Up to an additive constant, the nondimensional counterpart of (29) reads

$$\mathcal{E}(\mathbf{m},\mathbf{s}) = \frac{1}{2}C_{\text{exch}}\int_{\omega}|\nabla\mathbf{m}|^2 - \int_{\omega}\mathbf{f}\cdot\mathbf{m} - \frac{1}{2}\int_{\omega}\pi(\mathbf{m})\cdot\mathbf{m} - c\int_{\omega}\mathbf{s}\cdot\mathbf{m}. \tag{32}$$

The following theorem proves an energy estimate which generalizes (30) to weak solutions.

Theorem 24

Suppose that assumptions (H1)–(H2) *and* (H4)–(H6) *are satisfied. Let* (m,s) *be a weak solution of SDLLG obtained as a weak limit of the finite element solutions from Algorithm* 6 *for* ½ < θ ≤ 1. *Then, the energy functional from* (32) *satisfies*

$$\mathcal{E}(\mathbf{m}(t),\mathbf{s}(t)) + \alpha\int_{t'=0}^{t}\left\|\partial_t\mathbf{m}(t')\right\|_{\mathbf{L}^2(\omega)}^2 + \int_{t'=0}^{t}\left(\partial_t\mathbf{f}(t'),\mathbf{m}(t')\right)_\omega + c\int_{t'=0}^{t}\left\langle\partial_t\mathbf{s}(t'),\mathbf{m}(t')\right\rangle \le \mathcal{E}(\mathbf{m}_0,\mathbf{s}_0)$$

for almost all $t \in (0,T)$.

Proof

Given $t \in (0,T)$, let $0 \le j \le N - 1$ such that $t \in [t_j, t_j + 1)$. Let $0 \le i \le j$. From Lemma 18, we get

$$\begin{aligned}\mathcal{E}(\mathbf{m}_h^{i+1},\mathbf{s}_h^{i+1}) - \mathcal{E}(\mathbf{m}_h^{i},\mathbf{s}_h^{i}) &= \frac{1}{2}C_{\text{exch}}\left(\left\|\nabla\mathbf{m}_h^{i+1}\right\|_{\mathbf{L}^2(\omega)}^2 - \left\|\nabla\mathbf{m}_h^{i}\right\|_{\mathbf{L}^2(\omega)}^2\right) - \left(\mathbf{f}^{i+1},\mathbf{m}_h^{i+1}\right)_\omega + \left(\mathbf{f}^{i},\mathbf{m}_h^{i}\right)_\omega \\ &\quad - \frac{1}{2}\left(\pi(\mathbf{m}_h^{i+1}),\mathbf{m}_h^{i+1}\right)_\omega + \frac{1}{2}\left(\pi(\mathbf{m}_h^{i}),\mathbf{m}_h^{i}\right)_\omega - c\left(\mathbf{s}_h^{i+1},\mathbf{m}_h^{i+1}\right)_\omega + c\left(\mathbf{s}_h^{i},\mathbf{m}_h^{i}\right)_\omega \\ &= -\alpha k\left\|\mathbf{v}_h^i\right\|_{\mathbf{L}^2(\omega)}^2 - C_{\text{exch}}k^2\left(\theta - \frac{1}{2}\right)\left\|\nabla\mathbf{v}_h^i\right\|_{\mathbf{L}^2(\omega)}^2 \underbrace{- \left(\mathbf{f}^{i+1},\mathbf{m}_h^{i+1}\right)_\omega + \left(\mathbf{f}^{i},\mathbf{m}_h^{i} + k\mathbf{v}_h^i\right)_\omega}_{=T_1} \\ &\quad \underbrace{+k\left(\pi_h(\mathbf{m}_h^i),\mathbf{v}_h^i\right)_\omega - \frac{1}{2}\left(\pi(\mathbf{m}_h^{i+1}),\mathbf{m}_h^{i+1}\right)_\omega + \frac{1}{2}\left(\pi(\mathbf{m}_h^{i}),\mathbf{m}_h^{i}\right)_\omega}_{=T_2} \\ &\quad \underbrace{-c\left(\mathbf{s}_h^{i+1},\mathbf{m}_h^{i+1}\right)_\omega + c\left(\mathbf{s}_h^{i},\mathbf{m}_h^{i} + k\mathbf{v}_h^i\right)_\omega}_{=T_3}.\end{aligned}$$

By definition (16b), it holds $\mathbf{m}_h^{i+1} = \mathbf{m}_h^i + k\mathbf{v}_h^i$. We thus obtain

$$T_1 = -\left(\mathbf{f}^{i+1} - \mathbf{f}^{i},\mathbf{m}_h^{i+1}\right)_\omega - \left(\mathbf{f}^{i},\mathbf{m}_h^{i+1} - \mathbf{m}_h^{i} - k\mathbf{v}_h^i\right)_\omega = -k\left(d_t\mathbf{f}^{i+1},\mathbf{m}_h^{i+1}\right)_\omega$$

Analogously, we see that $T_3 = -ck\left(d_t\mathbf{s}_h^{i+1},\mathbf{m}_h^{i+1}\right)_\omega$. Since π is linear and self-adjoint, (16b) also reveals

$$\begin{aligned}T_2 &= -k\left(\pi(\mathbf{m}_h^i) - \pi_h(\mathbf{m}_h^i),\mathbf{v}_h^i\right)_\omega + k\left(\pi(\mathbf{m}_h^i),\mathbf{v}_h^i\right)_\omega \\ &\quad - \frac{1}{2}\left(\pi(\mathbf{m}_h^{i+1}) - \pi(\mathbf{m}_h^{i}),\mathbf{m}_h^{i+1}\right)_\omega - \frac{1}{2}\left(\pi(\mathbf{m}_h^{i}),\mathbf{m}_h^{i+1} - \mathbf{m}_h^{i}\right)_\omega \\ &= -k\left(\pi(\mathbf{m}_h^i) - \pi_h(\mathbf{m}_h^i),\mathbf{v}_h^i\right)_\omega + \frac{1}{2}k\left(\pi(\mathbf{m}_h^i),\mathbf{v}_h^i\right)_\omega - \frac{1}{2}k\left(\pi(\mathbf{v}_h^i),\mathbf{m}_h^{i+1}\right)_\omega \\ &= -k\left(\pi(\mathbf{m}_h^i) - \pi_h(\mathbf{m}_h^i),\mathbf{v}_h^i\right)_\omega - \frac{1}{2}k^2\left(\pi(\mathbf{v}_h^i),\mathbf{v}_h^i\right)_\omega.\end{aligned}$$

Altogether, we thus obtain

$$\mathcal{E}(\mathbf{m}_h^{i+1}, \mathbf{s}_h^{i+1}) - \mathcal{E}(\mathbf{m}_h^i, \mathbf{s}_h^i) + \alpha k \left\|\mathbf{v}_h^i\right\|_{\mathbf{L}^2(\omega)}^2 + k\left(d_t \mathbf{f}^{i+1}, \mathbf{m}_h^{i+1}\right)_\omega + ck\left(d_t \mathbf{s}_h^{i+1}, \mathbf{m}_h^{i+1}\right)_\omega$$
$$= -C_{\text{exch}} k^2 \left(\theta - \frac{1}{2}\right) \left\|\nabla \mathbf{v}_h^i\right\|_{\mathbf{L}^2(\omega)}^2 - k\left(\pi(\mathbf{m}_h^i) - \pi_h(\mathbf{m}_h^i), \mathbf{v}_h^i\right)_\omega - \frac{1}{2}k^2\left(\pi(\mathbf{v}_h^i), \mathbf{v}_h^i\right)_\omega.$$

Since π is a bounded operator, it follows that

$$\mathcal{E}(\mathbf{m}_h^{i+1}, \mathbf{s}_h^{i+1}) - \mathcal{E}(\mathbf{m}_h^i, \mathbf{s}_h^i) + \alpha k \left\|\mathbf{v}_h^i\right\|_{\mathbf{L}^2(\omega)}^2 + k\left(d_t \mathbf{f}^{i+1}, \mathbf{m}_h^{i+1}\right)_\omega + ck\left(d_t \mathbf{s}_h^{i+1}, \mathbf{m}_h^{i+1}\right)_\omega$$
$$+ k\left(\pi(\mathbf{m}_h^i) - \pi_h(\mathbf{m}_h^i), \mathbf{v}_h^i\right)_\omega \lesssim k^2 \left\|\mathbf{v}_h^i\right\|_{\mathbf{L}^2(\omega)}^2.$$

Summation over $0 \leq i \leq j$ and the boundedness from Proposition 19 yield

$$\mathcal{E}(\mathbf{m}_{hk}^+(t_{j+1}), \mathbf{s}_{hk}^+(t_{j+1})) - \mathcal{E}(\mathbf{m}_h^0, \mathbf{s}_h^0) + \alpha \int_{t'=0}^{t_{j+1}} \left\|\mathbf{v}_{hk}^-(t')\right\|_{\mathbf{L}^2(\omega)}^2 + \int_{t'=0}^{t_{j+1}} \left(\partial_t \mathbf{f}_k(t'), \mathbf{m}_{hk}^+(t')\right)_\omega$$
$$+ c\int_{t'=0}^{t_{j+1}} \left\langle \partial_t \mathbf{s}_{hk}(t'), \mathbf{m}_h^+(t')\right\rangle + \int_{t'=0}^{t_{j+1}} \left(\pi(\mathbf{m}_{hk}^-(t')) - \pi_h(\mathbf{m}_{hk}^-(t')), \mathbf{v}_{hk}^-(t')\right)_\omega$$
$$\lesssim k \int_{t'=0}^{t_{j+1}} \left\|\mathbf{v}_{hk}^-(t')\right\|_{\mathbf{L}^2(\omega)}^2 \lesssim k.$$

The available convergence results on $\mathbf{m}_{hk}^{\pm}$, $\mathbf{s}_{hk}^+$, $\mathbf{s}_{hk}$, $\mathbf{v}_{hk}^-$, and $\mathbf{f}_k$, and f_k, as well as assumption (H5), allow us to employ standard arguments with weakly lower semicontinuity for the limit (h, k) → 0. This concludes the proof of (33). □

ACKNOWLEDGMENTS

The research of GH, MP, DP, and DS is supported by the Vienna Science and Technology Fund (WWTF) under grant MA09-029. The research of DP and MR is supported through the doctoral school *Dissipation and Dispersion in Nonlinear PDEs*, funded by the Austrian Science Fund (FWF) under grant W1245, and through the innovative projects initiative of Vienna University of Technology. Additionally, CA and DS acknowledge financial support of the Austrian Federal Ministry of Science, Research and Economy and the National Foundation for Research, Technology and Development (Christian Doppler Laboratory *Advanced Magnetic Sensing and Materials*). GH would like to thank the EPSRC (grant EP/K008412/1) and the Royal Society (grant UF080837) for financial support.

REFERENCES

1. L. Berger, Emission of spin waves by a magnetic multilayer traversed by a current Phys. Rev. B, 54 (1996), pp. 9353-9358
2. J.C. Slonczewski, Current-driven excitation of magnetic multilayers, J. Magn. Magn. Mater., 159 (1996), pp. L1-L7
3. D.C. Ralph, M.D. Stiles, Spin transfer torques, J. Magn. Magn. Mater., 320 (2008), pp. 1190-1216
4. J.Z. Sun, D.C. Ralph, Magnetoresistance and spin-transfer torque in magnetic tunnel junctions, J. Magn. Magn. Mater., 320 (2008), pp. 1190-1216
5. Q. Mistral, M. vanKampen, G. Hrkac, J.V. Kim, T. Devolder, P. Crozat, C. Chappert, L. Lagae, T.Schrefl, Current-driven vortex oscillations in metallic nanocontacts, Phys. Rev. Lett., 100 (2008), p. 257201
6. S.S.P. Parkin, M. Hayashi, L. Thomas, Magnetic domain-wall racetrack memory, Science, 320 (2008), pp. 190-194
7. M. Johnson, R.H. Silsbee, Coupling of electronic charge and spin at a ferromagnetic–paramagnetic metal interface, Phys. Rev. B, 37 (1988), pp. 5312-5325
8. T. Valet, A. Fert, Theory of the perpendicular magnetoresistance in magnetic multilayers, Phys. Rev. B, 48 (1993), pp. 7099-7113
9. P.C. van Son, H. van Kempen, P. Wyder, Boundary resistance of the ferromagnetic–nonferromagnetic metal interface, Phys. Rev. Lett., 58 (1987), pp. 2271-2273
10. Shpiro, P.M. Levy, S. Zhang, Self-consistent treatment of nonequilibrium spin torques in magnetic multilayers, Phys. Rev. B, 67 (2003), p. 104430
11. C.J. García-Cervera, X.P. Wang, Spin-polarized transport: existence of weak solutions, Discrete Contin. Dyn. Syst. Ser. B, 7 (2007), pp. 87-100
12. C.J. García-Cervera, X.P. Wang, Spin-polarized currents in ferromagnetic multilayers, J. Comput. Phys., 224 (2007), pp. 699-711
13. F. Alouges, A. Soyeur, On global weak solutions for Landau–Lifshitz equations: existence and nonuniqueness, Nonlinear Anal., 18 (1992), pp. 1071-1084
14. F. Alouges, P. Jaisson, Convergence of a finite element discretization for the Landau–Lifshitz equation in micromagnetism, Math. Models Methods Appl. Sci., 16 (2006), pp. 299-316
15. S. Bartels, J. Ko, A. Prohl, Numerical analysis of an explicit approximation scheme for the Landau–Lifshitz–Gilbert equation, Math. Comp., 77 (2008), pp. 773-788
16. S. Bartels, A. Prohl, Convergence of an implicit finite element method for the Landau–Lifshitz–Gilbert equation, SIAM J. Numer. Anal., 44 (2006), pp. 1405-1419
17. F. Alouges, A new finite element scheme for Landau–Lifchitz equations, Discrete Contin. Dyn. Syst. Ser. S, 1 (2008), pp. 187-196
18. F. Alouges, E. Kritsikis, J.C. Toussaint, A convergent finite element approximation for Landau–Lifschitz–Gilbert equation, Physica B, 407 (2012), pp. 1345-1349
19. F. Bruckner, M. Feischl, T. Führer, P. Goldenits, M. Page, D. Praetorius, M. Ruggeri, D. Suess, Multiscale modeling in micromagnetics: existence of solutions and numerical integration, Math. Models Methods Appl. Sci. (2014), 10.1142/S0218202514500328
20. L. Baňas, S. Bartels, A. Prohl, A convergent implicit finite element discretization of the Maxwell–Landau–Lifshitz–Gilbert equation, SIAM J. Numer. Anal., 46 (2008), pp. 1399-1422
21. L. Baňas, M. Page, D. Praetorius, A convergent linear finite-element scheme for the Maxwell–Landau–Lifshitz–Gilbert equation, 2013, Preprint Available at: http://arxiv.org/abs/1303.4009 (submitted for publication).
22. K.N. Le, T. Tran, A convergent finite element approximation for the quasi-static Maxwell–Landau–Lifshitz–Gilbert equations, Comput. Math. Appl., 66 (2013), pp. 1389-1402
23. K.N. Le, M. Page, D. Praetorius, T. Tran, On a decoupled linear FEM integrator for eddy-current-LLG, Appl. Anal. (2014), 10.1080/00036811.2014.916401

24. L. Baňas, M. Page, D. Praetorius, J. Rochat, A decoupled and unconditionally convergent linear FEM integrator for the Landau–Lifshitz–Gilbert equation with magnetostriction, IMA J. Numer. Anal. (2013) http://dx.doi.org/10.1093/imanum/drt050
25. S. Bartels, Projection-free approximation of geometrically constrained partial differential equations, 2013. Preprint.
26. Abert, M. Ruggeri, F. Bruckner, C. Vogler, G. Hrkac, D. Praetorius, D. Suess, Spin transport and magnetization dynamics in magnetic and multiferroic systems, 2014 (in preparation).
27. L.C. Evans, Partial Differential Equations (second ed.), Graduate Studies in Mathematics, vol. 19, American Mathematical Society (2010)
28. C.J. García-Cervera, 2014 (private communication).
29. S. Bartels, Stability and convergence of finite-element approximation schemes for harmonic maps, SIAM J. Numer. Anal., 43 (2005), pp. 220-238
30. D.R. Fredkin, T.R. Koehler, Hybrid method for computing demagnetization fields, IEEE Trans. Magn., 26 (1990), pp. 415-417
31. C.J. García-Cervera, A. Roma, Adaptive mesh-refinement for micromagnetic simulations, IEEE Trans. Magn., 42 (2006), pp. 1648-1654
32. R.E. Bank, H. Yserentant, On the H1-stability of the L2-projection onto finite element spaces, Numer. Math., 126 (2014), pp. 361-381
33. M. Karkulik, C. Pfeiler, D. Praetorius, L2-orthogonal projections onto finite elements on locally refined meshes are H1-stable, 2013. Preprint Available at: http://arxiv.org/abs/1307.0917 (submitted for publication).
34. Praetorius, Analysis of the operator Δ^{-1}div arising in magnetic models, Z. Anal. Anwend., 23 (2004), pp. 589-605

CHAPTER 14

A Weakly Pareto Compliant Quality Indicator

Emanuele Dilettoso, Santi Agatino Rizzo* and Nunzio Salerno

Department of Electrical, Electronics and Computer Engineering, University of Catania, Catania 95125, Italy

ABSTRACT

In multi- and many-objective optimization problems, the optimization target is to obtain a set of non-dominated solutions close to the Pareto-optimal front, well-distributed, maximally extended and fully filled. Comparing solution sets is crucial in evaluating the performance of different optimization algorithms. The use of performance indicators is common in comparing those sets and, subsequently, optimization algorithms. Therefore, an effective performance indicator must encompass these features as a whole and, above all, it must be Pareto dominance compliant. Unfortunately, some of the known indicators often fail to properly reflect the quality of a solution set or cost a lot to compute. This paper demonstrates that the Degree of Approximation (DOA) quality indicator is a weakly Pareto compliant unary indicator that gives a good estimation of the match between the approximated front and the Pareto-optimal front.

Keywords: multi-objective optimization; many-objective optimization; distance indicator; algorithms performance; Pareto optimality; quality indicator

1. INTRODUCTION

The optimized design of industrial applications is often problematic because of the simultaneous occurrence of many conflicting targets [1,2,3]. In real-world optimization problems, the decision maker needs to have a wide range of solutions to choose from [4]. Some optimization methods solve a single function obtained by aggregating different objective functions [5,6,7]. The choice of weights is the major weakness to this approach [5]. Other multi- and many-objective optimization algorithms (MOOAs) search for a non-dominated solution set [8,9,10], i.e., a set of multiple alternative solutions. This set is the Approximation Set in the decision space and the Approximated Pareto Front (APF) in the objective functions space. The main goal of such algorithms is to provide an APF matching the Pareto-optimal front (POF). The problem is to assess how well the approximated front fits the optimal one [11]. The notion of optimization algorithms performance involves evaluating the quality of the solution and the required computational effort [12]. This proves troublesome in the case of multi- and many-objective optimization problems (MOOPs): a good approach would be to use a quality indicator (QI), i.e., a function of the APF that simplifies the quantitative performance comparison of different optimization algorithms. The simplest comparison method would be to check whether one APF is better than another with respect to the Pareto dominance relations [11]. Thus, a QI must be able to account for Pareto dominance to properly compare two different algorithms. This is known as *completeness* with respect to Pareto dominance relations, and is the most desired property of a QI. More specifically, assuming there are two MOOAs providing, respectively, two non-dominated set A and B, a (weakly) Pareto compliant QI must comply with the following relation: *if A dominates B then QI(A) must be better than QI(B)*. On the other hand, if there exists a scenario where A dominates B, but the QI(A) is worse than QI(B), then the QI is not Pareto compliant, therefore it could provide misleading results when it is used to compare MOOAs.

Moreover, when APFs are *incomparable* with respect to Pareto dominance relations, more information is needed to compare the APFs provided by different MOOAs. Generally, a good MOOA should [13,14,15]:

1) minimize the APF distance from the POF;
2) obtain a good (usually uniform) distribution of the solutions found;
3) maximize the APF extension i.e., for each objective the non-dominated solutions should cover a wide range of values (best case: the global optimum of each objective function must be found);

4) maximize the APF density, i.e., high cardinality for the approximation set is desirable.

Each goal represents a desired feature of the APF: in the following we refer to them as *closeness*, *distribution*, *extension* and *cardinality*, respectively. It is worth noticing that, given a scenario where:

1) A is closer to the POF than B;
2) the solutions in A are better distributed than the ones in B;
3) A is more extended than B;
4) the size of A is greater than the size of B,

it is very probable that A dominates B, or, at least B does not dominate A.

Although it is improbable that the two APFs will be incomparable with respect to Pareto dominance relations, when this event occurs (an example is shown in Figure 1) QI(A) should be better than QI(B). In other words, the QI should reveal that A outperforms B with respect to all features and, consequently, A is preferable to B even though the two APFs are incomparable.

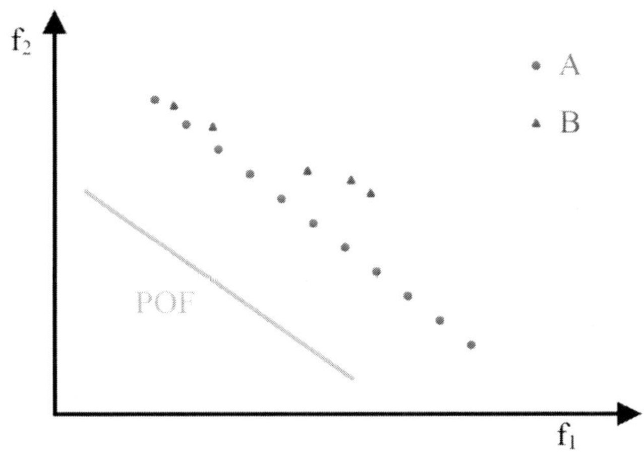

Figure 1. In this case A and B are incomparable in terms of Pareto dominance, but A is preferable to B because A is closer to the Pareto-optimal front (POF), more extended, more populated, and better distributed.

A unary QI (UQI) estimates a non-dominated solution set quality by means of a real number [16]; then it is useful to estimate the effectiveness of a MOOA. Several known UQIs have no or limited completeness as regards Pareto dominance relations and are unable to take into account all the features listed previously. Few UQIs overcome these limitations despite needing much computational effort.

This paper demonstrates the $\succ$-completeness of the UQI, called Degree of Approximation (DOA) [17]. Moreover, it proves its ability to take into account all four features.

To our knowledge, Hypervolume [1] is the only $\rhd$-complete UQI (then Hypervolume is a *Pareto compliant* UQI), and for this reason it is considered the best UQI for comparing optimization algorithms. Nevertheless, the relation $A \lhd B$ differs from $A < B$ since the former accounts for the case in which A contains some solutions of B but the probability of this specific event is very low, and it can be considered null when the objective functions' space belongs to the set of real numbers. Therefore, DOA can be used to evaluate the performance of optimization algorithms instead of the Hypervolume since it is proven that DOA is $\succ$-complete (then DOA is a *weakly Pareto compliant* UQI). Note that the calculation of Hypervolume is difficult as the number of objective functions increases, while the calculation of DOA is usually very simple and fast even in the case of many-objective optimization. DOA calculation needs the knowledge of the POF, while the Hypervolume indicator needs to know the reference point. However, it is not a limitation when they are applied to compare the performance of different MOOAs. In fact, the best way to perform the comparisons is using properly designed benchmark problems for which the POF is known [18]: Schaffer's benchmark [19], Fonseca's benchmark [20], Poloni's benchmark [21], Kursawe's benchmark [22], ZDT1-6 [13], and DTLZ1-7 [23].

In the Evolutionary Multi-Objective community, UQIs are also adopted as the guidance mechanism during the optimization process, e.g., SMS-EMOEA [24] exploits the Hypervolume indicator during optimization. The use of a given UQI in indicator-based optimization algorithms enables one to implicitly scalarize the multi-objective problem. In this case, the compliance with the dominance relation of the indicator is one reason for the slow convergence rates of elitist multi- and many-objective evolutionary algorithms (MOEAs) [25]. On the other hand, DOA is devised to evaluate the performance of the final set of non-dominated solutions and it is not devised to be included as guidance mechanism of a MOOA. Hence, in the DOA's application field, Pareto compliance is a suitable and necessary feature.

The paper is organized as follows. Section 2 recalls the definitions and terminology typically used in multi-objective optimization related to the Pareto dominance concept. Section 3 outlines the characteristics of a QI and presents a review of the most common UQIs. Section 4 describes DOA in detail, while Section 5 and Section 6 mathematically demonstrate its $\succ\succ$-completeness and $\succ$-completeness, respectively. Section 7 proves DOA *compatibility* with respect to the *not better*dominance relation. Finally, Section 8 validates DOA with some examples to highlight its accounting for closeness, distribution, extension and cardinality. Conclusions and future works are drawn in Section 9 and minor details of the proof in Section 6 have been reported in the appendices.

2. DEFINITIONS AND TERMINOLOGY

2.1. Multi- and Many-Objective Optimization Problem

Solving a MOOP means finding the optimal and feasible parameter configurations. A feasible solution (configuration) is called *decision vector* ($x = x_1, x_2, \ldots, x_m$) and is a point in the *decision space*(X). An *objective vector*($y = y_1, y_2, \ldots, y_m$), that is a point in the *objective space* (Y), is linked to each decision vector by means of evaluating function f. So, a MOOP, with m decision variables (parameters to be set), n targets (objective functions to be optimized), and c constraints (ℓ equality and c-ℓ are inequality constraints), can be mathematically represented as follows.

Maximize or minimize:

$$y = f(x) = (f_1(x),\ f_2(x), \ldots,\ f_n(x)) \tag{1}$$

subject to:

$$\begin{aligned} g_i(x) &= 0 \quad i = 1, 2, \ldots, \ell \\ g_i(x) &\geq 0 \quad i = \ell + 1, \ell + 2, \ldots, c \end{aligned} \tag{2}$$

where:

$$\begin{aligned} x &= (x_1, x_2, \ldots, x_m) \in X \\ y &= (y_1, y_2, \ldots, y_n) \in Y \\ y_i &= f_i(x) \quad i = 1, 2, \ldots, n \end{aligned} \tag{3}$$

Without loss of generality, in the following it is assumed that each objective function has to be minimized.

2.2. Pareto Dominance

Usually, in real-world MOOPs, there is no single parameter configuration that simultaneously optimizes all objective functions, i.e., a point does not exist in the decision space that is a global optimum. Thus, solving a real-world MOOP means offering the designer a set of alternative optimal solutions in the *Pareto dominance* sense.

Pareto dominance—A decision vector x^1*dominates* another decision vector x^2 iff:

$$f_i\left(x^1\right) \leq f_i\left(x^2\right) \quad i = 1, 2, \ldots, n \quad \text{and} \quad \exists i : f_i\left(x^1\right) < f_i\left(x^2\right) \tag{4}$$

This relation is denoted as $x^1 \prec x^2$. When one or more of these relations is not satisfied, x^1 does not dominate x^2; this condition is denoted as $x^1 \nprec x^2$. It is worth noticing that, for a single objective function, the standard relation *less than* is generally used to define the corresponding minimization problem, while the symbol $\prec$ represents a natural extension of $<$ in the case of MOOPs [26].

Pareto optimality—A decision vector x' is said to be Pareto-optimal iff:

$$\nexists x \in X : x \prec x' \tag{5}$$

The set that groups this kind of solution is known as a Pareto-optimal set, and all the solutions of this set are alternative, with no one solution being dominated by the other solutions.

In addition to dominance, other types of relation between the solutions can be defined:

strictly dominance: a decision vector x^1 *strictly dominates* another decision vector x^2 (denoted as $x^1 \prec\prec x^2$) iff:

$$f_i\left(x^1\right) < f_i\left(x^2\right) \quad i = 1, 2, \ldots, n \tag{6}$$

weakly dominance: a decision vector x^1 *weakly dominates* the decision vector x^2 (denoted as $x^1 \preccurlyeq x^2$) iff:

$$f_i\left(x^1\right) \leq f_i\left(x^2\right) \quad i = 1, 2, \ldots, n \tag{7}$$

Finally, when x^1 is better than x^2 with respect to a subset of objective functions but x^2 is better than x^1 with respect to another subset, the two solutions are said *incomparable*, denoted as $x^1||x^2$ (or $x^2||x^1$):

$$\begin{aligned} & x^1 \npreceq x^2 \;\wedge\; x^2 \npreceq x^1 \\ \Rightarrow\quad & x^1||x^2 \; (or\; x^2||x^1) \end{aligned} \tag{8}$$

Table 1. Dominance relations between two solutions [11].

Symbol	Relation	Description
$x^1 \prec\prec x^2$	*strictly dominance* x^1 strictly dominates x^2	x^1 is better than x^2 with respect to each objective function
$x^1 \prec x^2$	*dominance* x^1 dominates x^2	x^1 is not worse than x^2 with respect to each objective function and x^1 is better than x^2 by at least one objective function
$x^1 \preceq x^2$	*weakly dominance* x^1 weakly dominates x^2	x^1 is not worse than x^2 with respect to each objective function
$x^1 \parallel x^2$	*incomparability* x^1 and x^2 are incomparable	x^1 and x^2 do not weakly dominate each other

Table 2. Dominance relations between two APFs [11].

Symbol	Relation	Description
$A \prec\prec B$	A strictly dominates B	each solution belonging to B is strictly dominated by a solution belonging to A
$A \prec B$	A dominates B	each solution belonging to B is dominated by a solution belonging to A
$A \lhd B$	A is better than B	each solution belonging to B is weakly dominated by a solution belonging to A, and $A \neq B$
$A \preceq B$	A weakly dominates B	each solution belonging to B is weakly dominated by a solution belonging to A
$A \,\|\|\, B$	A and B are incomparable	A and B do not weakly dominate each other

Table 1 resumes the dominance relations. It is worth to note that a relation may imply other relations:

$$x^1 \prec\prec x^2 \Rightarrow x^1 \prec x^2 \Rightarrow x^1 \preceq x^2 \tag{9}$$

$$x^1 \npreceq x^2 \Rightarrow x^1 \nprec x^2 \Rightarrow x^1 \nprec\nprec x^2. \tag{10}$$

By relating the solutions of one APF A to those of another APF B it is possible to extend the dominance relations between two solutions to two APFs. Table 2 shows the relations between two APFs.

3. QUALITY INDICATOR

3.1. Definitions

A quality indicator QI is a function q: $S \rightarrow \mathbb{R}$, where S is the objective functions space, that assigns a real value to a set of APFs belonging to S related to a MOOP. When the function q has just one argument (i.e., one APF), the quality indicator is called *unary*, when it has two arguments (i.e., two APFs) it is called *binary*, and so on.

The aim of a QI is to compare APFs and so QIs are mainly used to indicate if a MOOA works any better than others. Some QIs can also be applied as the acceptance criterion to the selection operator of the stochastic search algorithms [27], but DOA is not devised for such a scope.

3.2. Comparison Methods

This paper focuses on the use of QIs for evaluating the performances of different optimization algorithms. To do this the QI results must be interpreted by means of an interpretation function E: $\mathbb{R}^q \rightarrow$ Bool, where q depends on the size of the QI set. Figure 2 shows some examples of interpretation functions (A and B are two APFs).

Finally, the combination of a quality indicator, I, and an interpretation function, E, is called a comparison method [11], and is referred to as $C_{I,E}$: $C_{I,E}(\text{A},\text{B}) = E(I(\text{A}),I(\text{B}))$.

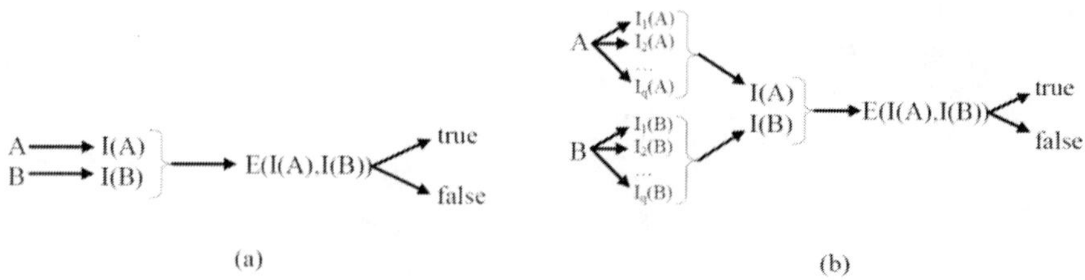

Figure 2. Comparison method in case of one QI (**a**) and in case of a vector of q QIs (**b**).

3.3. Compatibility and Completeness

Usually, one or a set of QIs can be useful to compare different optimization algorithms to figure out which works better on a particular class of problems.

Non–dominated solutions are preferred to the dominated ones from the designer's point of view. Then, when a comparison method shows that APF A is preferable to APF B, A must be better than B. In a similar way, when A is better than B, a comparison method must indicate that A is preferable to B. Such features are known as ⊳-compatibility and ⊳-completeness [11].

Let ▶ be an arbitrary dominance relation among those defined in Table 2 (≻≻ or ≻ or ⊳). A comparison method $C_{I,E}$ is said ▶*-compatible* if for each possible pair of APFs A and B:

$$C_{I,E}(A,B) \text{ is true} \Rightarrow A \blacktriangleleft B \tag{11}$$

A comparison method $C_{I,E}$ is said ▶*-complete* if for each possible pair of APFs A and B:

$$A \blacktriangleleft B \Rightarrow C_{I,E}(A,B) \text{ is true.} \tag{12}$$

It has been demonstrated [11] that a comparison method based on a UQI (or on a finite combination of UQIs) that is both ⊳-compatible and ⊳-complete cannot exist. Moreover, Pareto dominance is sufficient but not necessary to consider an APF preferable to another: there are pairs of APFs with considerable quality difference which are considered, by Pareto dominance relations, as not comparable [16]. Hence, if a comparison method based on UQI were ⊳-compatible, the indicator could not provide any preference in the case of two incomparable APFs. Therefore, it would be better if the UQI were only compatible with $\ntriangleright$ [28] and it should take into account all the features (closeness, distribution, extension, cardinality) that are desirable for an APF.

Finally, while a comparison method $\triangleright$-complete is necessary (i.e., when APF A is better than APF B the comparison method must highlight it), when a comparison method shows that A is preferable to B, one of the following two cases must hold:

- A is *better* than B ($A \lhd B$);
- A and B are incomparable and A outperforms B with respect to closeness, distribution, extension and cardinality.

3.4. Closeness, Distribution, Extension, and Cardinality

The main target of an optimization algorithm to solve a MOOP is to find an APF as similar as possible to the POF. Hence, as said before, the APF must be:

- close to the POF; Figure 3 represents the extreme cases: an APF exhibiting good closeness only, and an APF with all good features but not close to the POF;
- well distributed (usually uniform); Figure 4 shows an APF exhibiting a uniform distribution only and an APF with all good features but not uniformly distributed;
- very extended (in the best case the global optimum of each objective function belongs to the APF); Figure 5 shows an APF with only a good extension and one with all good features but not extended;
- of high cardinality; Figure 6 shows an APF with good cardinality only and an APF with all good features but poor cardinality.

Table 3 points out if a specific feature partially ◒ or totally ● affects the value of some UQIs. A heuristic approach has been applied to determine whether a feature (closeness, distribution, extension, cardinality) affects the QI value. In particular, an APF B obtained by improving a given feature of another APF A is expected to have an indicator value better than that of A when the indicator is sensitive to this feature. For example, if an APF is gradually moved towards the POF and the indicator increasingly improves, then the indicator is influenced by the closeness feature. An indicator is *partially*affected by a feature when it sometimes improves and other times does not change.

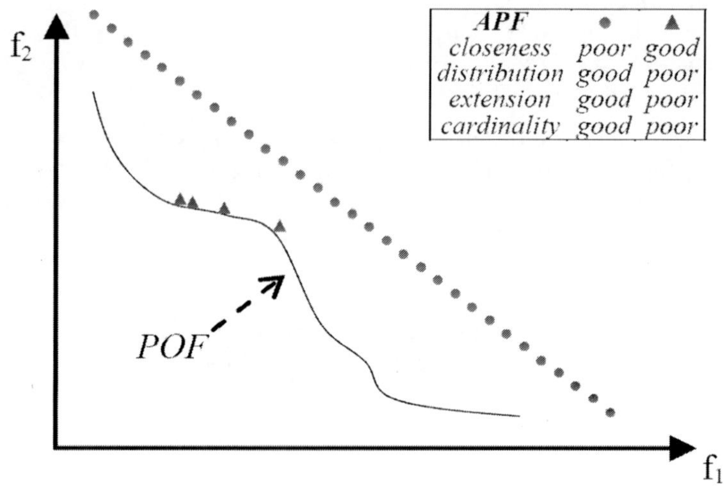

Figure 3. An APF (blue dots) with all good features but not close to the POF and another (red triangles) that is only close to the POF.

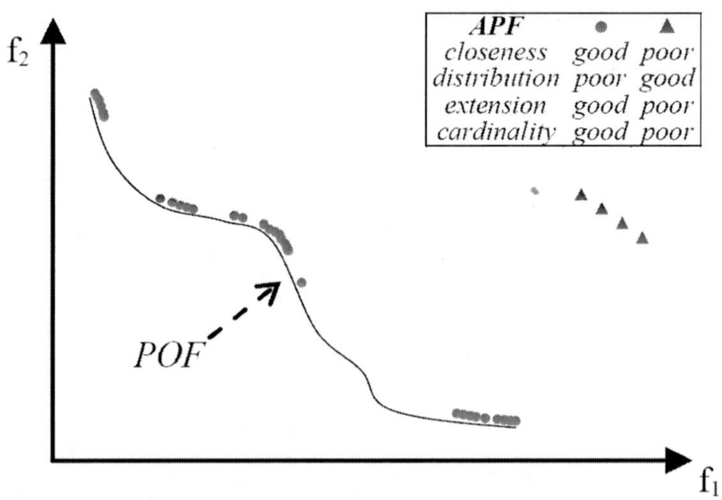

Figure 4. An APF (blue dots) with all good features but not uniformly distributed and another (red triangles) that is only uniformly distributed.

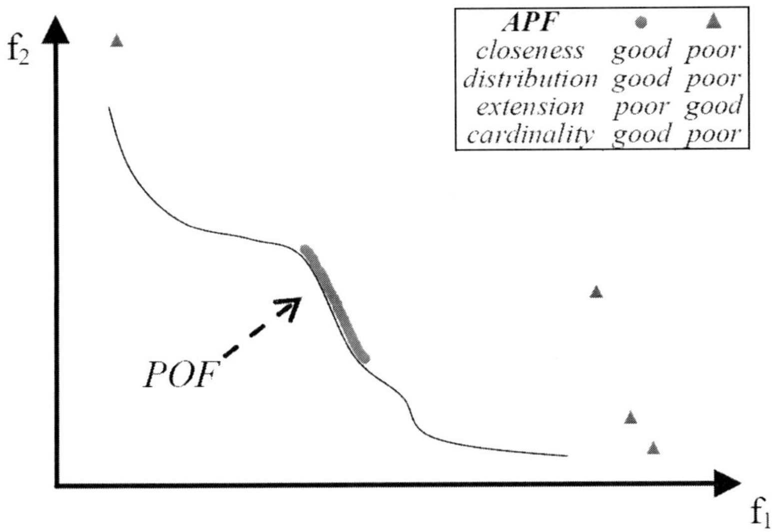

Figure 5. An APF blue dots) with all good features but not extended and another (red triangles) that is only extended.

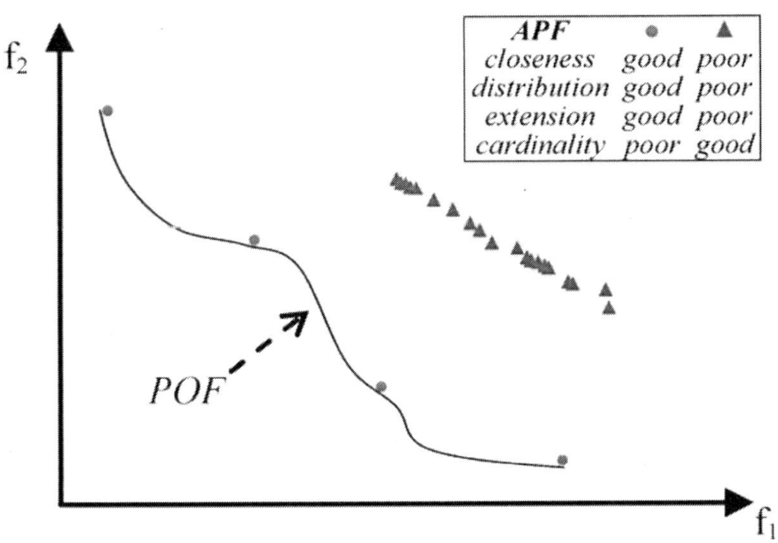

Figure 6. An APF (blue dots) with all good features but with poor cardinality and another (red triangles) that has only high cardinality.

Table 3. Summary of selected UQIs and features that influence their value.

Indicator	Closeness	Distribution	Extension	Cardinality
Average Distance from Reference Set [30]	●	●	●	●
Chi-Square-Like Deviation Measure [33]	◐	●	◐	
Completeness Indicator [31,32]	●	●	●	●
Enclosing Hypercube [11]	◐		●	
Generational Distance [34]	●			
Hypervolume [1]	●	●	●	●
Inverted Generational Distance [29]	●	●	●	●
M_1* [13]	●			
M_2* [13]		●		◐
M_3* [13]			●	
Maximum Pareto Front Error [34]	●			
Outer Diameter [26]			●	
Overall Nondominated Vector Generation [34]				●
Overall Pareto Spread [35]			●	
Potential Function [27]	●	●	●	●
Seven Points Average Distance [36]	●	◐	●	
Spacing [37]		●		
Unary ε-Indicator [11,26]	●			
Uniform Distribution [38]		●		
Worst Distance from Reference Set [30]	●			
Δ [8]		●	●	
Δ_p [39,40]	●	●	●	●

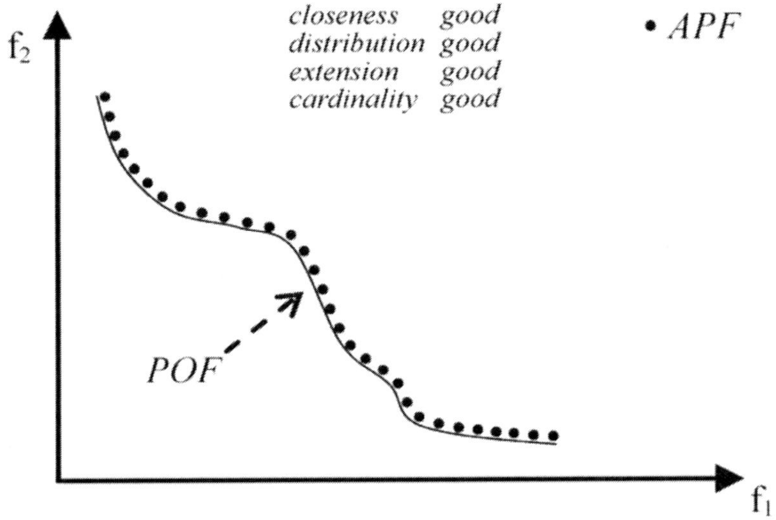

Figure 7. An APF with all the desired features.

Figure 7 shows an APF with all the desired features. A good QI must take into account all these features to give a correct measure of APF quality.

The Inverted Generational Distance indicator (IGD) [29] and a similar indicator using a weighted-scalar distance function called Average Distance from Reference Set indicator (ADRS) [30], the Completeness indicator [31,32], the Potential Function indicator [27] and the Hypervolume indicator [1] account for all the features but they present some drawbacks.

The IGD and ADRS indicators have the same complexity of DOA, but they are ≻≻-complete only [11]. The Δ_p indicator [39] can be considered as the combination of slight variations of the Generational Distance and the IGD indicator [25]. Therefore, it presents the advantage and limitations of these indicators, that is it accounts for all the features but it is ≻≻-complete only.

The Completeness and Potential Function indicators are as ≻-complete as the DOA indicator. Nevertheless, the Completeness indicator cannot be directly computed, but can be estimated by drawing samples from the feasible set and computing completeness for these samples. The confidence interval for the true value can be evaluated with any reliability value, given sufficiently large samples [26]. For the Potential Function indicator similar considerations hold. Hence, the drawback of both indicators is the high computational cost.

To our knowledge, Hypervolume is the only ⊳-complete UQI, and so is considered the best UQI for comparing optimization algorithms. Nevertheless, the relation A⊲B differs from A≺B since the former accounts for the case in which B contains some solutions of A but the probability of this specific event is very low, and it can be considered null when the objective functions' space belongs to the set of real numbers.

Moreover, Hypervolume running time grows exponentially with the number of objective functions [41,42,43,44]. The most obvious method for calculating Hypervolume is the inclusion-exclusion algorithm, with complexity $O(n2^m)$, where $n$is the number of objectives and m is the number of APF points. The fastest methods for calculating Hypervolume (e.g., LebMeasure [45], Hypervolume by Slicing Objectives algorithm [46]) lead to a $O(m^2n^3)$complexity. The DOA indicator has a lower computational cost, presenting a $O(nMm)$ complexity, where M is the number of POF points.

4. THE WEAKLY PARETO COMPLIANT QUALITY INDICATOR

The comparison method based on DOA and its associated interpretation function is ≻-complete. In detail, for a given POF and an APF A, DOA is computed as follows.

First, given a solution i belonging to the POF, $D_{i,A}$, is determined from the sub-set of A containing the solutions dominated by i (Figure 8). Hence, if the number of solutions belonging to $D_{i,A}$ is not null, for each approximated solution $a \in D_{i,A}$ the Euclidean distance $df_{i,a}$ between a and i is computed as:

$$df_{i,a} = \sqrt{\sum_{k=1}^{n} \left[f_{k,a} - f_{k,i}\right]^2}, \tag{13}$$

with:

n number of objective functions,

$f_{k,a}$ value of k-th objective function of the approximated solution a,

$f_{k,i}$ value of k-th objective function of optimal solution i.

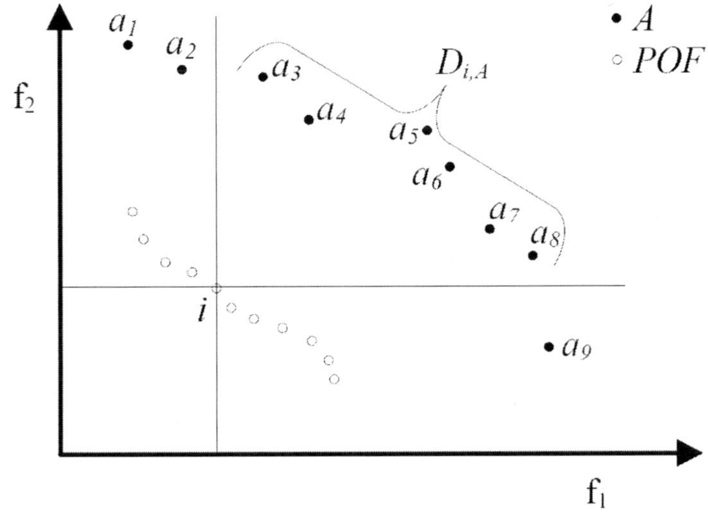

Figure 8. $D_{i,A}$ of a point i belonging to the POF (example with $n = 2$).

Euclidean distance $d_{i,A}$ (Figure 9) between i and the nearest approximated solution belonging to $D_{i,A}$ is computed in the objective function space as:

$$d_{i,A} = \begin{cases} \min(df_{i,a}) & a \in D_{i,A} \quad if\ |D_{i,A}| > 0 \\ \infty & if\ |D_{i,A}| = 0 \end{cases}, \tag{14}$$

where $|D_{i,A}|$ is the number of solutions belonging to $D_{i,A}$.

Another quantity $r_{i,A}$ (similarly to $d_{i,A}$) is computed for i considering the solutions of A not dominated by i (i.e., $A\backslash D_{i,A}$):

$$r_{i,A} = \begin{cases} \min(rf_{i,a}) & a \in A\backslash D_{i,A} \quad if\ |A\backslash D_{i,A}| > 0 \\ \infty & if\ |A\backslash D_{i,A}| = 0 \end{cases}, \tag{15}$$

where $rf_{i,a}$ is a *reduced distance* (Figure 10) between i and a non-dominated solution a of A (i.e., $\forall a \in$ A: $i \parallel a$), i.e., computed only for objectives k with $f_{k,a} \geq f_{k,i}$:

$$rf_{i,a} = \sqrt{\sum_{k=1}^{n} [\max(0, f_{k,a} - f_{k,i})]^2}. \tag{16}$$

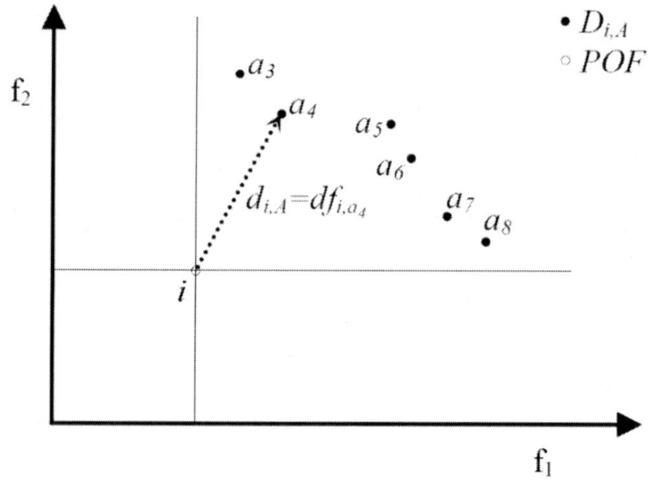

Figure 9. $d_{i,A}$ of a point i belonging to the POF.

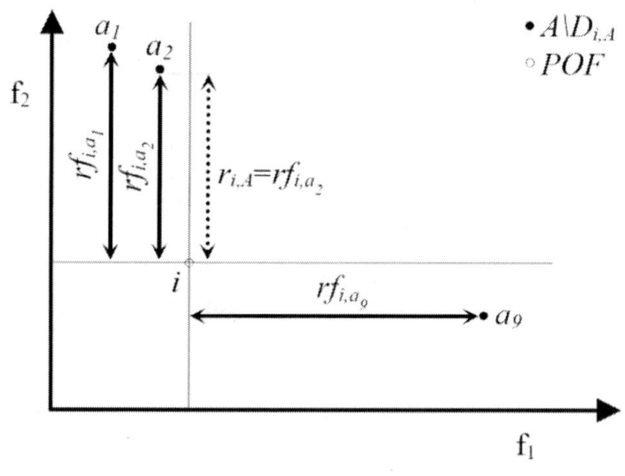

Figure 10. $r_{i,A}$ of a point i belonging to the POF.

Note that, $rf_{i,a}$ is equal to $df_{i,a}$ when $a \in D_{i,A}$. Moreover, defining n_a ($n_a < n$) as the number of functions for which the $f_{k,a} - f_{k,i} \geq 0$ ($f_{k,a} \geq f_{k,i}$, $k = 1,..,n_a$ and $f_{k,a} < f_{k,i}$, $k = n_a + 1,..,n$) expression (16) can be rewritten as:

$$rf_{i,a} = \sqrt{\sum_{k=1}^{n_a} [f_a(k) - f_i(k)]^2 + \sum_{k=n_a+1}^{n} 0}. \tag{17}$$

Finally, defining

$$s_{i,A} = \min(d_{i,A}, r_{i,A}) \quad (18)$$

the DOA indicator for the APF A is computed as:

$$DOA(A) = \frac{1}{|POF|} \sum_{i=1}^{|POF|} s_{i,A}. \quad (19)$$

DOA and IGD present some similarities. More specifically, if $d_{i,A}$, Equation (14), is computed considering all solutions in A regardless of the dominance relation with i, and only this quantity is considered then the IGD indicator is obtained, that is:

$$IGD(A) = \frac{1}{|POF|} \sum_{i=1}^{|POF|} d_{i,A}. \quad (20)$$

The IGD indicator is not $\succ$-complete while DOA is $\succ$-complete, as will be proved in the following. Therefore, the use of $r_{i,A}$ is the enabling key for DOA $\succ$-completeness.

While the Hypervolume indicator needs to know the reference point, the DOA calculation needs the knowledge of the POF, like the IGD indicator. This is not a drawback in MOOA benchmarking which is usually carried out for problems with known POF. More specifically, the Pareto optimal solutions and the analytical expression of the objective functions are usually known. Therefore, the POF is obtained by points uniformly discretizing the decision parameter intervals where the Pareto optimal solutions are located. The value of DOA does not depend on the number of points in the POF if |POF|>>|APF|.

Considering two APFs A and B, the proposed quality indicator needs interpreting [11] to affirm either that *A is preferable to B* or *B is preferable to A* or *A and B are equivalent*: the proposed obvious interpretation function is illustrated in Figure 11. Moreover, DOA changes with arbitrary scaling of the objective functions, since the DOA indicator is a distance-based metric, while the relationship between DOA(A) and DOA(B) does not change.

In the following, it is demonstrated that A$\prec$B implies *A is preferable to B*, that is DOA(A) $<$ DOA(B), in order to affirm that DOA is a $\succ$-complete quality indicator.

For the sake of clarity, the ≻≻-completeness of DOA is demonstrated before proving its ≻-completeness.

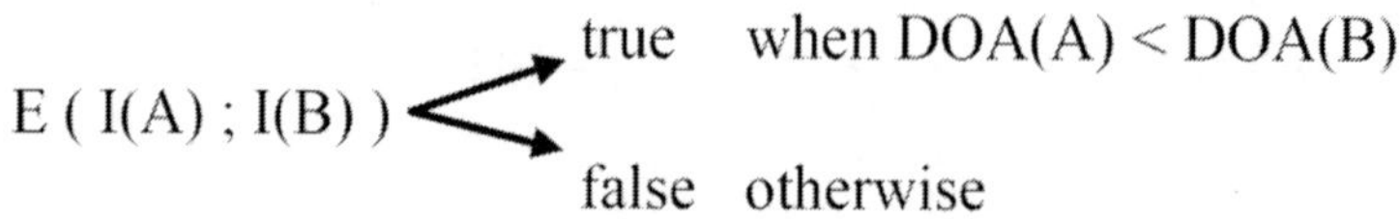

Figure 11. Interpretation function: pseudo-code to compare A and B by means of DOA(A) and DOA(B).

5. ≻≻-COMPLETENESS

DOA is a ≻≻-complete quality indicator if DOA(A)<DOA(B) for any pair of APF A and B, with A≺≺B.

In the hypothesis that A≺≺B, each solution of B is strictly dominated by, at least, one solution of A. To demonstrate that DOA(A)<DOA(B) is sufficient to prove that $s_{i,A}$ is always lesser than $s_{i,B}$ for each point $i \in$ POF. In other words,

if

$$s_{i,A} < s_{i,B} \quad \forall\, i \in \mathrm{POF}, \tag{21}$$

then

$$DOA(A) = \frac{1}{|POF|}\sum_{i=1}^{|POF|} s_{i,A} < \frac{1}{|POF|}\sum_{i=1}^{|POF|} s_{i,B} = DOA(B). \tag{22}$$

Considering a point i ∈POF, in the following, b indicates the solution belonging to B which provides $s_{i,B}$ and a a solution of A that strictly dominates b ($a \prec\prec b$); only four scenarios are possible (see Figure 12):

- A1. $i \prec\prec b \wedge i \preccurlyeq a$
- B1. $i \prec\prec b \wedge i // a$
- C1. $i \prec b \wedge i // a$
- D1. $i // b \wedge i // a$

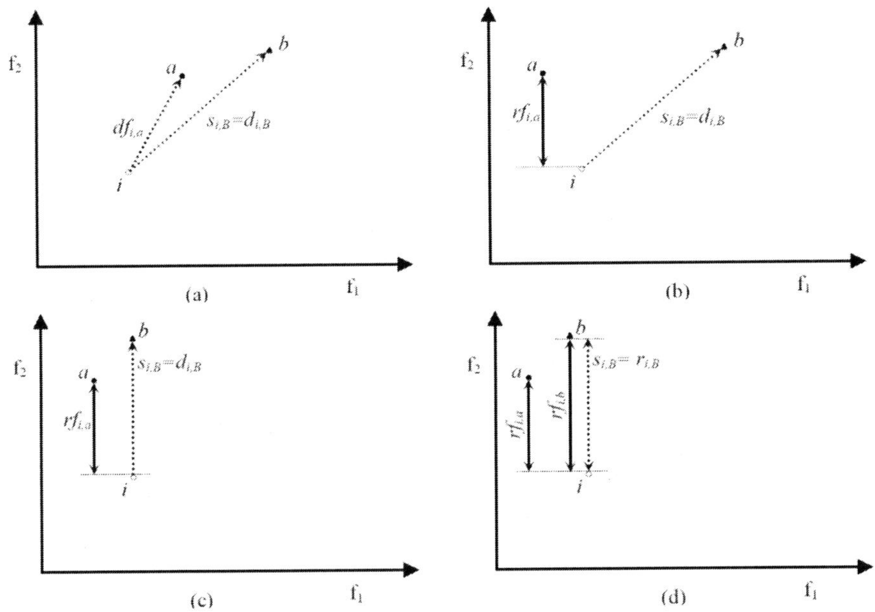

Figure 12. Possible scenarios for A$\succ\succ$B.(**a**) scenario A1: most relevant case; (**b**) scenario B1 or C1; (**c**) scenario C1: limit case; (**d**) scenario D1.

Note that the other scenarios $i \preccurlyeq b \wedge i \preccurlyeq a$ and $i // b \wedge i \preccurlyeq a$ are not possible because $a \prec\prec b$: in fact, from either $i \preccurlyeq b \wedge a \prec\prec b$ and $i // b \wedge a \prec\prec b$ follows $i \npreccurlyeq a$.

Moreover, it is worth mentioning the following:

Remark 1. *$i \preccurlyeq a$ implies that $s_{i,A} \leq df_{i,a}$, in detail:*

- $s_{i,A} = df_{i,a}$ *iff* $s_{i,A} = d_{i,A} \wedge d_{i,A} = df_{i,a}$;
- $s_{i,A} < df_{i,a}$ *either if* $s_{i,A} = d_{i,A} \wedge d_{i,A} = df_{i,a^*} < df_{i,a}$ *(where $a^* \in$ A and $a^* \neq a$) or if* $s_{i,A} = r_{i,A}$ *(this implies that $r_{i,A} < d_{i,A} \leq df_{i,a}$).*

Remark 2. *$i//a$ implies that $s_{i,A} \leq rf_{i,a}$, in detail:*

- $s_{i,A} = rf_{i,a}$ *iff* $s_{i,A} = r_{i,A} \wedge r_{i,A} = rf_{i,a}$;
- $s_{i,A} < rf_{i,a}$ *either if* $s_{i,A} = r_{i,A} \wedge r_{i,A} = rf_{i,a^*} < rf_{i,a}$ *(where $a^* \in A$ and $a^* \neq a$) or if* $s_{i,A} = d_{i,A}$ *(this implies that $d_{i,A} < r_{i,A} \leq rf_{i,a}$).*

Finally, the inequality $s_{i,A} < s_{i,B}$ will be proved for the four scenarios A1–D1: this inequality naturally implies the $\succ\succ$-completeness of the DOA indicator.

5.1. A1. i≺≺b ∧ i≼a

In this case, i strictly dominates b then $s_{i,B} = d_{i,B} = df_{i,b}$, because b is the solution which provides $s_{i,B}$. Moreover, $i \preccurlyeq a$implies that $s_{i,A} \leq df_{i,a}$ (see Remark 1).

So, in order to demonstrate that $s_{i,A} < s_{i,B}$ it is sufficient to demonstrate that $df_{i,a} < df_{i,b}$.

Recalling that

i▯a▯ $f_{k,i} \leq f_{k,a}, \forall\ k = 1,\ldots, n$

a▯▯b ▯$f_{k,a} < f_{k,b}, \forall\ k = 1,\ldots, n$

the following inequalities hold:

$$\begin{gathered} 0 \leq f_{k,a} - f_{k,i} < f_{k,b} - f_{k,i} \quad \forall k = 1,..,n \\ \Rightarrow \\ df_{i,a} = \sqrt{\sum_{k=1}^{n} [f_{k,a} - f_{k,i}]^2} < \sqrt{\sum_{k=1}^{n} [f_{k,b} - f_{k,i}]^2} = df_{i,b} \\ \Rightarrow \\ s_{i,A} \leq df_{i,a} < df_{i,b} = s_{i,B} \end{gathered} \tag{23}$$

5.2. B1. i≺≺b ∧ i||a

In this case, i strictly dominates b then $s_{i,B} = d_{i,B} = df_{i,b}$, because b is the solution which provides $s_{i,B}$. Moreover, $i // a$implies that $s_{i,A} \leq rf_{i,a}$ (see Remark 2).

So, in order to demonstrate that $s_{i,A} < s_{i,B}$ it is sufficient to demonstrate that $rf_{i,a} < df_{i,b}$. Proof is given in the next section because scenario C encompasses scenario B.

5.3. C1. i≺b ∧ i||a

In this case, i dominates b then $s_{i,B} = d_{i,B} = df_{i,b}$, because b is the solution which provides $s_{i,B}$. Moreover, $i // a$ implies that $s_{i,A} \leq rf_{i,a}$ (see Remark 2).

So, in order to demonstrate that $s_{i,A} < s_{i,B}$ it is sufficient to demonstrate that $rf_{i,a} < df_{i,b}$. Ordering the n objective functions of solution a in such a way that the first n_a (with $n_a < n$) are greater than those of i and recalling that:

$\boldsymbol{i||a}$ □ $f_{k,i} < f_{k,a}$, $\forall\ k = 1,\ldots, n_a$

$f_{k,i} \geq f_{k,a}$, $\forall\ k = n_a + 1,\ldots, n$

$\boldsymbol{i}$□$\boldsymbol{b}$□ $f_{k,i} \leq f_{k,b}$, $\forall\ k = 1,\ldots, n$

$\boldsymbol{a}$□□$\boldsymbol{b}$ □$f_{k,a} < f_{k,b}$, $\forall\ k = 1,\ldots, n$

then the following inequalities hold:

$$
\begin{aligned}
&0 < f_{k,a} - f_{k,i} < f_{k,b} - f_{k,i} \quad \forall k = 1,..,n_a \\
&0 \leq f_{k,b} - f_{k,i} \quad \forall k = n_a + 1,..,n \\
&\Rightarrow \\
&rf_{i,a} = \sqrt{\sum_{k=1}^{n_a} [f_{k,a} - f_{k,i}]^2 + \sum_{k=n_a+1}^{n} 0} < \\
&\sqrt{\sum_{k=1}^{n_a} [f_{k,b} - f_{k,i}]^2 + \sum_{k=n_a+1}^{n} [f_{k,b} - f_{k,i}]^2} = df_{i,b} \\
&\Rightarrow \\
&s_{i,A} \leq rf_{i,a} < df_{i,b} = s_{i,B}.
\end{aligned}
\tag{24}
$$

5.4. D1. i||b Λ i||a

In this case, i and b are incomparable then $s_{i,B} = r_{i,B} = rf_{i,b}$, because b is the solution which provides $s_{i,B}$. Moreover, $i//a$implies that $s_{i,A} \leq rf_{i,a}$ (see Remark 2).

So, in order to demonstrate that $s_{i,A} < s_{i,B}$ it is sufficient to demonstrate that $rf_{i,a} < rf_{i,b}$.

Ordering the n objective functions of solution a in such a way that the first n_a are greater than those of i, ordering the $n$objective functions of solution b in such a way that the first n_b are greater than those of i (with $n_a \leq n_b < n$, since $a \gg b$ Λ $i//a$implies $n_a \leq n_b$, while $i//b$ implies $n_b < n$) and recalling that:

$\boldsymbol{i||a}$□ $f_{k,i} < f_{k,a}$, $\forall\ k = 1,\ldots, n_a$

$f_{k,i} \geq f_{k,a}$, $\forall\ k = n_a + 1,\ldots, n$

$\boldsymbol{i||b}$□ $f_{k,i} < f_{k,b}$, $\forall\ k = 1,\ldots, n_b$

$$f_{k,i} \geq f_{k,b}, \forall\, k = n_b + 1,\dots, n$$

a⍰⍰***b*** ⍰ $f_{k,a} < f_{k,b}, \forall\, k = 1,\dots, n$

then the following inequalities hold:

$$\begin{array}{ll} 0 < f_{k,a} - f_{k,i} < f_{k,b} - f_{k,i} & \forall k = 1,..,n_a \\ \quad 0 < f_{k,b} - f_{k,i} & \forall k = n_a + 1,..,n_b \\ \quad 0 \geq f_{k,b} - f_{k,i} & \forall k = n_b + 1,..,n \end{array}$$
$$\Rightarrow$$
$$rf_{i,a} = \sqrt{\sum_{k=1}^{n_a} [f_{k,a} - f_{k,i}]^2 + \sum_{k=n_a+1}^{n_b} 0 + \sum_{k=n_b+1}^{n} 0} < \tag{25}$$
$$\sqrt{\sum_{k=1}^{n_a} [f_{k,b} - f_{k,i}]^2 + \sum_{k=n_a+1}^{n_b} [f_{k,b} - f_{k,i}]^2 + \sum_{k=n_b+1}^{n} 0} = rf_{i,b}$$
$$\Rightarrow \quad s_{i,A} \leq rf_{i,a} < rf_{i,b} = s_{i,B}$$

6. ≻-COMPLETENESS

In this section is proved that DOA is a ≻-complete quality indicator. Consider any pair of APF A and B, with A≺B, the ≻-completeness of DOAis demonstrated by proving that $s_{i,A}$ is never greater than $s_{i,B}$ (for each point i∈POF) and always exists a point i*∈ POF for which $s_{i^*,A}$ is lesser than $s_{i^*,B}$:

if

$$s_{i,A} \leq s_{i,B}\ \forall\, i \in \text{POF} \wedge \exists\, i^* \in \text{POF}: s_{i^*,A} < s_{i^*,B} \tag{26}$$

then

$$\text{DOA(A)} = \frac{1}{|\text{POF}|}\left(s_{i*,A} + \sum_{i=2}^{|\text{POF}|} s_{i,A}\right) < \frac{1}{|\text{POF}|}\left(s_{i*,B} + \sum_{i=2}^{|\text{POF}|} s_{i,B}\right) = \text{DOA(B)}. \tag{27}$$

In the following, b indicates the solution belonging to B which provides $s_{i,B}$ for a point i ∈ POF and a a solution of A that dominates b (a≺b). Moreover, the ≻-completeness of DOA is proved in the worst and most general case, i.e., when ∀ b∈B ∄ a∈A: a≺≺b (i.e., a≺b ∧ a⊀⊀b, limit case); only five scenarios are possible (see Figure 13):

- A2. $i \prec\prec b \wedge i \prec a$
- B2. $i \prec\prec b \wedge i // a$
- C2. $i \prec b \wedge i \preccurlyeq a$
- D2. $i \prec b \wedge i // a$
- E2. $i // b \wedge i // a$

Note that the scenario $i // b \wedge i \preccurlyeq a$ is not possible because $a \prec b$: in fact, from $i // b \wedge a \prec b$ follows $i \npreccurlyeq a$. Moreover, scenario A2 does not include $i = a$, differently from section 5, because in this case $i \prec\prec b$ while $a \prec b \wedge a \nprec\nprec b$. Analogously, differently from section 5, when $i \prec b$ the scenario $i \preccurlyeq a$ is possible. Finally, the scenario $i \preccurlyeq b$ is not considered because A≺B, in fact $i = b$ would lead to the absurd $a \prec b = i$.

In order to demonstrate the ≻-completeness of DOA, it is proved that the inequality $s_{i,A} < s_{i,B}$ is verified $\forall i$ for the three scenarios A2, B2 and C2. While for the remaining two scenarios D2 and E2 we will prove that the following two sufficient conditions hold:

α. $s_{i,A} \leq s_{i,B}$

β. $\exists\ i^* \in$ POF: $s_{i^*,A} < s_{i^*,B}$.

For the sake of simplicity, the proof of β will be given in Appendix A.

6.1. A2. i≺≺b ∧ i≺a

In this case, i strictly dominates b then $s_{i,B} = d_{i,B} = df_{i,b}$, because b is the solution which provides $s_{i,B}$. Moreover, $i \prec a$implies that $s_{i,A} \leq df_{i,a}$ (see Remark 1).

So, in order to demonstrate that $s_{i,A} < s_{i,B}$ it is sufficient to demonstrate that $df_{i,a} < df_{i,b}$.

Recalling that:

$$\boldsymbol{i} \square \boldsymbol{a} \square \quad f_{k,i} \leq f_{k,a},\ \forall\ k = 1,\ldots,n$$

$$\boldsymbol{a} \square \boldsymbol{b} \square \quad f_{k,a} \leq f_{k,b},\ \forall\ k = 1,\ldots,n \wedge \exists\ j: f_{j,a} < f_{j,b}$$

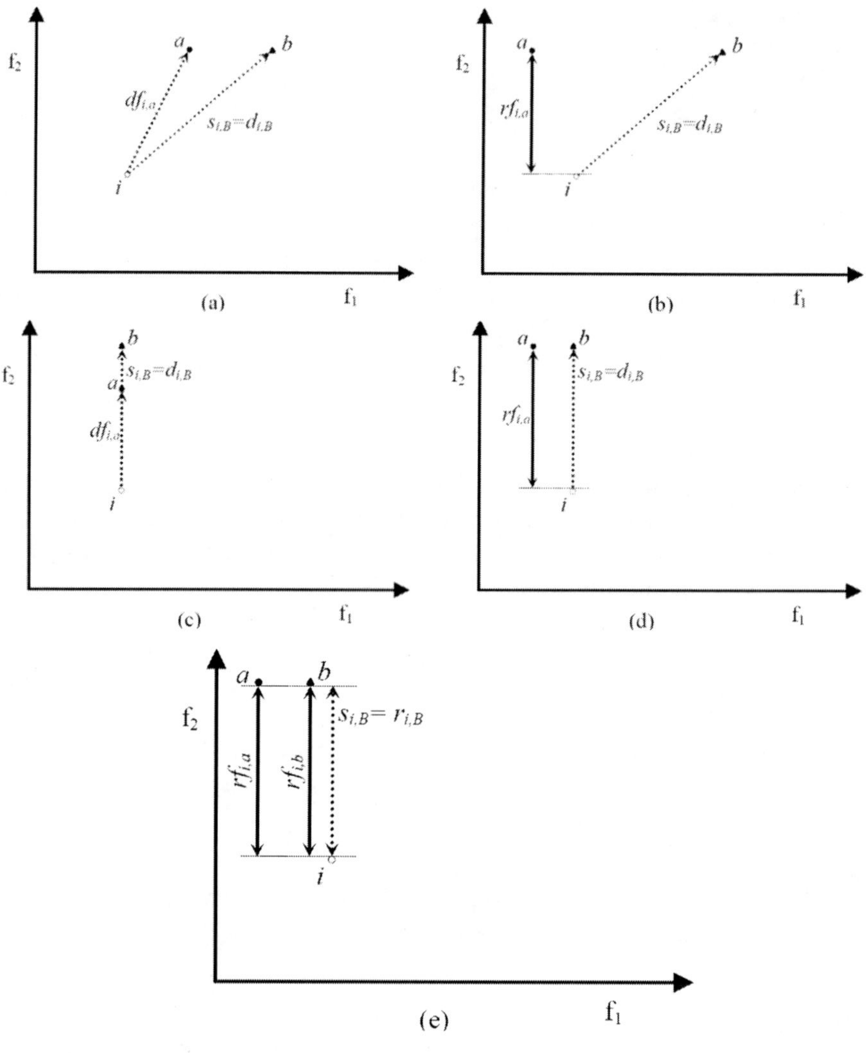

Figure 13. Possible scenarios for A≻B. (**a**) scenario A2 or C2; (**b**) scenario B2 or D2; (**c**) scenario C2: limit case; (**d**) scenario D2: limit case; (**e**) scenario E2.

the following inequalities hold:

$$
\begin{aligned}
&0 \le f_{k,a} - f_{k,i} \le f_{k,b} - f_{k,i} \quad \forall k = 1,..,n \\
&0 \le f_{k,a} - f_{k,i} < f_{k,b} - f_{k,i} \qquad k = j \\
&\Rightarrow \\
&df_{i,a} = \sqrt{\sum_{\substack{k=1 \\ k \ne j}}^{n} [f_{k,a} - f_{k,i}]^2 + [f_{j,a} - f_{j,i}]^2} < \\
&\sqrt{\sum_{\substack{k=1 \\ k \ne j}}^{n} [f_{k,b} - f_{k,i}]^2 + \left[f_{j,b} - f_{j,i}\right]^2} = df_{i,b} \\
&\Rightarrow \\
&s_{i,A} \le df_{i,a} < df_{i,b} = s_{i,B}.
\end{aligned}
\tag{28}
$$

6.2. B2. i≺≺b Λ i||a

In this case, i strictly dominates b then $s_{i,B} = d_{i,B} = df_{i,b}$, because b is the solution which provides $s_{i,B}$. Moreover, $i//a$implies that $s_{i,A} \le rf_{i,a}$ (see Remark 2).

So, in order to demonstrate that $s_{i,A} < s_{i,B}$ it is sufficient to demonstrate that $rf_{i,a} < df_{i,b}$.

Ordering the n objectives f of solution a in such a way that the first n_a (with $n_a < n$) are greater than those of i and recalling that:

$$\boldsymbol{i||a} \Rightarrow \quad f_{k,i} < f_{k,a},\ \forall\ k = 1,\dots,n_a$$

$$f_{k,i} \ge f_{k,a},\ \forall\ k = n_a + 1,\dots,n$$

$$\boldsymbol{i \prec\prec b} \Rightarrow f_{k,i} < f_{k,b},\ \forall\ k = 1,\dots,n$$

$$\boldsymbol{a \prec b} \Rightarrow \quad f_{k,a} \le f_{k,b},\ \forall\ k = 1,\dots,n$$

then the following inequalities hold:

$$
\begin{gathered}
0 < f_{k,a} - f_{k,i} \leq f_{k,b} - f_{k,i} \quad \forall k = 1, .., n_a \\
0 < f_{k,b} - f_{k,i} \qquad \forall k = n_a + 1, .., n \\
\Rightarrow \\
rf_{i,a} = \sqrt{\sum_{k=1}^{n_a} \left[f_{k,a} - f_{k,i}\right]^2 + \sum_{k=n_a+1}^{n} 0} < \\
\sqrt{\sum_{k=1}^{n_a} \left[f_{k,b} - f_{k,i}\right]^2 + \sum_{k=n_a+1}^{n} \left[f_{k,b} - f_{k,i}\right]^2} = df_{i,b} \\
\Rightarrow \\
s_{i,A} \leq rf_{i,a} < df_{i,b} = s_{i,B}.
\end{gathered}
\tag{29}
$$

6.3. C2. i≺b ∧ i≼a

In this case, i dominates b then $s_{i,B} = d_{i,B} = df_{i,b}$, because b is the solution which provides $s_{i,B}$. Moreover, $i \preccurlyeq a$ implies that $s_{i,A} \leq df_{i,a}$ (see Remark 1).

So, in order to demonstrate that $s_{i,A} < s_{i,B}$ it is sufficient to demonstrate that $df_{i,a} < df_{i,b}$.

Recalling that:

$$\boldsymbol{i} \preccurlyeq \boldsymbol{a} \Leftrightarrow \quad f_{k,i} \leq f_{k,a},\ \forall\ k = 1, \ldots, n$$

$$\boldsymbol{a} \prec \boldsymbol{b} \Leftrightarrow \quad f_{k,a} \leq f_{k,b},\ \forall\ k = 1, \ldots, n\ \wedge\ \exists\ j\text{: } f_{j,a} < f_{j,b}$$

then the following inequalities hold:

$$
\begin{aligned}
&0 \leq f_{k,a} - f_{k,i} \leq f_{k,b} - f_{k,i} \quad \forall k = 1, .., n \\
&0 \leq f_{k,a} - f_{k,i} < f_{k,b} - f_{k,i} \quad \forall k = j \\
&\Rightarrow \\
&df_{i,a} = \sqrt{\sum_{\substack{k=1 \\ k \neq j}}^{n} \left[f_{k,a} - f_{k,i}\right]^2 + \left[f_{j,a} - f_{j,i}\right]^2} < \\
&\sqrt{\sum_{\substack{k=1 \\ k \neq j}}^{n} \left[f_{k,b} - f_{k,i}\right]^2 + \left[f_{j,b} - f_{j,i}\right]^2} = df_{i,b} \\
&\Rightarrow \\
&s_{i,A} \leq df_{i,a} < df_{i,b} = s_{i,B}
\end{aligned}
\tag{30}
$$

6.4. D2. i≺b Λ i||a

In this case, i dominates b then $s_{i,B} = d_{i,B} = df_{i,b}$, because b is the solution which provides $s_{i,B}$. Moreover, $i//a$ implies that $s_{i,A} \leq rf_{i,a}$ (see Remark 2).

So, in order to demonstrate that $s_{i,A} \leq s_{i,B}$ it is sufficient to demonstrate that $rf_{i,a} \leq df_{i,b}$.

Ordering the n objectives f of solution a in such a way that the first n_a (with $n_a < n$) are greater than those of i and recalling that:

$i//a$□ $f_{k,i} < f_{k,a}, \forall\ k = 1,\ldots, n_a$

$f_{k,i} \geq f_{k,a}, \forall\ k = n_a + 1,\ldots, n$

i□b□ $f_{k,i} \leq f_{k,b}, \forall\ k = 1,\ldots, n\ \Lambda\ \exists\ h\text{: } f_{h,i} < f_{h,b}$

a□b□ $f_{k,a} \leq f_{k,b}, \forall\ k = 1,\ldots, n\ \Lambda\ \exists\ j\text{: } f_{j,a} < f_{j,b}$

then the following inequalities hold

$$
\begin{aligned}
&0 < f_{k,a} - f_{k,i} \leq f_{k,b} - f_{k,i} \quad \forall k = 1,..,n_a \\
&0 \leq f_{k,b} - f_{k,i} \qquad \forall k = n_a + 1,..,n \\
&\Rightarrow \\
&rf_{i,a} = \sqrt{\sum_{k=1}^{n_a} [f_{k,a} - f_{k,i}]^2 + \sum_{k=n_a+1}^{n} 0} \leq \\
&\sqrt{\sum_{k=1}^{n_a} [f_{k,b} - f_{k,i}]^2 + \sum_{k=n_a+1}^{n} [f_{k,b} - f_{k,i}]^2} = df_{i,b} \\
&\Rightarrow \\
&s_{i,A} \leq rf_{i,a} \leq df_{i,b} = s_{i,B}.
\end{aligned}
\tag{31}
$$

Note that $rf_{i,a}$ is strictly lesser than $df_{i,b}$ when $1 \leq j \leq n_a$, since

$$
\sum_{k=1}^{n_a} [f_{k,a} - f_{k,i}]^2 < \sum_{k=1}^{n_a} [f_{k,b} - f_{k,i}]^2. \tag{32}
$$

Otherwise $s_{i,A} \leq s_{i,B}$. In particular, $rf_{i,a} = df_{i,b}$ iff $f_{k,a} = f_{k,b}\ \forall\ k = 1,\ldots,n_a\ \Lambda\ f_{k,i} = f_{k,b}\ \forall\ k = n_a + 1,\ldots,n$. In this case, obviously, $f_{h,i} < f_{h,a} = f_{h,b}$ with $1 \leq h \leq n_a$ and

$f_{j,a} < f_{j,i} = f_{j,b}$ with $j > n_a$. As said before, the proof that $\exists\ i^* \in$POF: $s_{i^*,A} < s_{i^*,B}$ has been reported in Appendix A.

6.5. E2. i||b Λ i||a

In this case, i and b are incomparable then $s_{i,B} = r_{i,B} = rf_{i,b}$, because b is the solution which provides $s_{i,B}$. Moreover, $i//a$implies that $s_{i,A} \le rf_{i,a}$ (see Remark 2).

So, in order to demonstrate that $s_{i,A} \le s_{i,B}$, it is sufficient to demonstrate that $rf_{i,a} \le rf_{i,b}$. Ordering the n objectives f of solution a in such a way that the first n_a are greater than those of i, ordering the n objectives f of solution b in such a way that the first n_b are greater than those of i (with $n_a \le n_b < n$, since $a \prec b \wedge i//a$ implies $n_a \le n_b$, while $i//b$ implies $n_b < n$) and recalling that:

$$\textbf{\textit{i}}||\textbf{\textit{a}}⃞ \quad f_{k,i} < f_{k,a},\ \forall\ k = 1,\dots,n_a$$

$$f_{k,i} \ge f_{k,a},\ \forall\ k = n_a + 1,\dots,n$$

$$\textbf{\textit{i}}||\textbf{\textit{b}}⃞ \quad f_{k,i} < f_{k,b},\ \forall\ k = 1,\dots,n_b$$

$$f_{k,i} \ge f_{k,b},\ \forall\ k = n_b + 1,..,n$$

$$\textbf{\textit{a}}⃞\textbf{\textit{b}}⃞ \quad f_{k,a} \le f_{k,b},\ \forall\ k = 1,\dots,n\ \wedge\ \exists\ j: f_{j,a} < f_{j,b}$$

then the following inequalities hold:

$$\begin{array}{ll} 0 < f_{k,a} - f_{k,i} \le f_{k,b} - f_{k,i} & \forall k = 1,..,n_a \\ 0 < f_{k,b} - f_{k,i} & \forall k = n_a + 1,..,n_b \\ 0 \ge f_{k,b} - f_{k,i} & \forall k = n_b + 1,..,n \end{array}$$
$$\Rightarrow$$
$$rf_{i,a} = \sqrt{\sum_{k=1}^{n_a} [f_{k,a} - f_{k,i}]^2 + \sum_{k=n_a+1}^{n_b} 0 + \sum_{k=n_b+1}^{n} 0} \le \tag{33}$$
$$\sqrt{\sum_{k=1}^{n_a} [f_{k,b} - f_{k,i}]^2 + \sum_{k=n_a+1}^{n_b} [f_{k,b} - f_{k,i}]^2 + \sum_{k=n_b+1}^{n} 0} = rf_{i,b}$$
$$\Rightarrow$$
$$s_{i,A} \le rf_{i,a} \le rf_{i,b} = s_{i,B}.$$

It is worth noting that:

$$rf_{i,a} < rf_{i,b} \text{ if } n_b \neq n_a;$$

$$rf_{i,a} \leq rf_{i,b} \text{ if } n_b = n_a.$$

In the last case, $rf_{i,a} = rf_{i,b}$ iff $f_{k,a} = f_{k,b}$ $\forall$ k = 1,..,n_a. In this case, obviously, $f_{j,a} < f_{j,b} \leq f_{j,i}$ whit $j > n_a$. As said before, the proof that $\exists$ i^*∈POF: $s_{i^*,A} < s_{i^*,B}$ has been reported in Appendix A.

7. ⋫-COMPATIBILITY

In this section it is proved that DOA is a ⋫-compatible quality indicator. The following remarks are necessary.

Remark 3.

A solution a' belonging to A does not influence DOA(A) if, □ *i∈POF:*

- $s_{i,A} < df_{i,a'}$ *when a' is dominated by i;*
- $s_{i,A} < rf_{i,a'}$ *when a' is not dominated by i.*

In fact, in this case $s_{i,A} \neq df_{i,a'}$ and $s_{i,A} \neq rf_{i,a'}$, by which follows that DOA(A) does not change its value if *a'* is moved off from A. These means that an APF B = A\\{*a'*} has the same quality indicator value, i.e., DOA(A) = DOA(B). Using DOA seems *B equivalent to A* while A, having one more solution, is *better* than B [11]. Then the proposed method is not a ⊳-complete quality indicator. On the other hand, DOA together with its interpretation function is a ≻-complete comparison method, as it is demonstrated before.

Remark 4.

The relation A□B is equivalent to assume that B = C ∪ D, where C □ A, D ∩ A = Ø and □ b∈D ∃ a∈A: a□b. Note that, when C = Ø then A□B. Hence, the difference between case A□B and A□B is that in the latter B could contains some solutions of A. Moreover, obviously, only the last case includes B □ A (i.e., D = Ø). For these reasons when A□B, DOA(A) is never greater than DOA(B).

Remark 5.

The relation A||B involves that DOA(A) can be greater or less than or equal to DOA(B).

For two generic APF A and B, the $\succ$-completeness of DOA, together with Remarks 3–5, imply that if DOA(A) < DOA(B) then $A \prec B$ or $A \triangleleft B$ or $A || B$, i.e., it is sure that $B \ntriangleleft A$. Then DOA is a $\ntriangleright$-compatible unary quality indicator.

8. DOA VALIDATION

To demonstrate that DOA takes into account all features (closeness, distribution, extension, and cardinality) three typical POFs have been considered:

- convex and connected;
- non-convex and connected;
- convex and disconnected.

In particular, the DOA unary quality indicator has been computed for different examples of APFs. Both POFs and APFs are drawn in Figure 14, Figure 15 and Figure 16. Table 4 shows the values of DOA for the APFs considered.

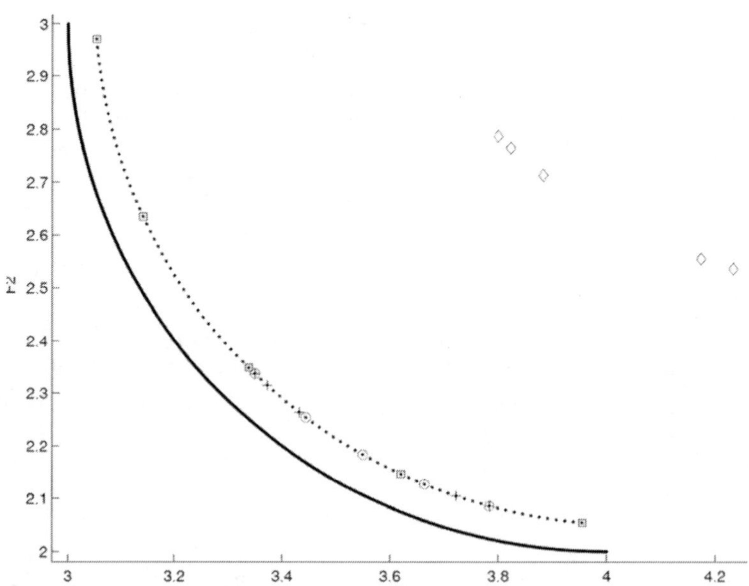

Figure 14. Convex and connected POF (solid line), APF1 (◊), APF2 (+), APF3 (○), APF4 (□) and APF5 (●).

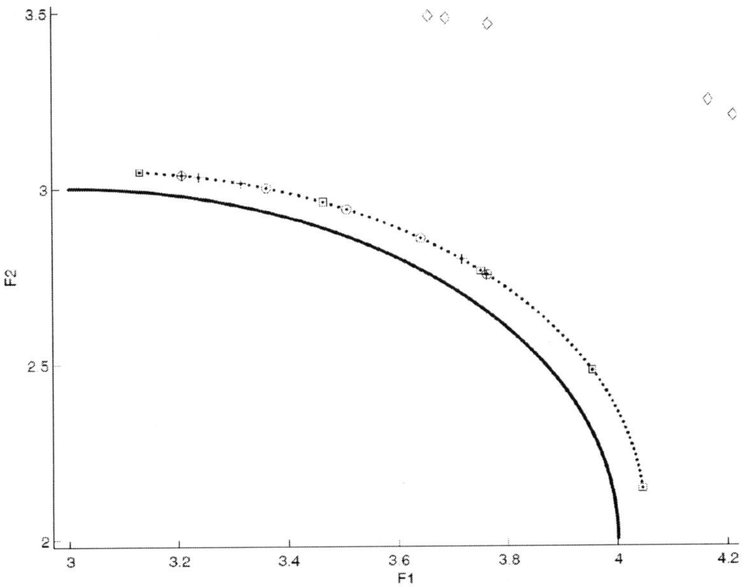

Figure 15. Non-convex and connected POF (solid line), APF1 (◊), APF2 (+), APF3 (○), APF4 (□) and APF5 (●).

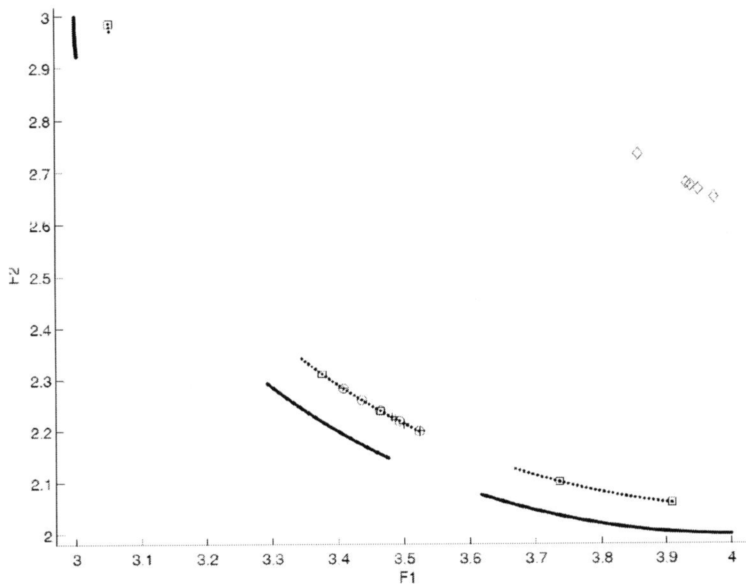

Figure 16. Convex and disconnected POF (solid line), APF1 (◊), APF2 (+), APF3 (○), APF4 (□) and APF5 (●).

Table 4. DOA Evaluation for some typical POF (symbol in brackets is the marker associated to the APF in Figure 14, Figure 15 and Figure 16).

POF	APF	Closeness	Distribution	Extension	Cardinality	DOA
Convex and connected (see Figure 14)	APF1(◇)	poor	poor	poor	poor	0.71040
	APF2(+)	good	poor	poor	poor	0.16940
	APF3(○)	good	good	poor	poor	0.16287
	APF4(□)	good	good	good	poor	0.10253
	APF5(●)	good	good	good	good	0.06431
Non-convex and connected (see Figure 15)	APF1(◇)	poor	poor	poor	poor	0.79167
	APF2(+)	good	poor	poor	poor	0.24303
	APF3(○)	good	good	poor	poor	0.23465
	APF4(□)	good	good	good	poor	0.09301
	APF5(●)	good	good	good	good	0.06993
Convex and disconnected (see Figure 16)	APF1(◇)	poor	poor	poor	poor	0.69510
	APF2(+)	good	poor	poor	poor	0.16866
	APF3(○)	good	good	poor	poor	0.16810
	APF4(□)	good	good	good	poor	0.07254
	APF5(●)	good	good	good	good	0.06331

Let us examine the strategy adopted to choose the examples of APF for each POF: the APF B obtained by improving a given feature of APF A is expected to have a better indicator value than that of A if the indicator is sensitive to this feature. For example, if an APF is gradually moved towards the POF and the indicator increasingly improves, then the indicator is influenced by the closeness feature. The validation was performed according to these considerations. Hence, from an APF (APF1, indicated in the figures by symbol◊) with only poor features, the second APF (APF2, indicated by +) is created by improving APF1 closeness that is by converging APF1 on the POF. Therefore, APF2 has better closeness than APF1 but the same distribution, extension and cardinality. The third APF (APF3, indicated by ○) is obtained by improving the distribution of APF2 by uniformly distributing the solutions of APF2. APF3 has better distribution than APF2 but the same closeness, extension and cardinality. The fourth APF (APF4, indicated by □) is created by improving the extension of APF3, preserving the other features. Finally, the fifth APF (APF5, indicated by •) is created by adding new points to APF4, and hence improving the cardinality of APF5 with respect to the fourth APF. It is worth noting that it does not matter in which order the different features are added to the initial APF1, and the order used in Table 4 simply follows the features' description given in the Introduction.

Whatever the characteristics of the POF, such a strategy highlights that the value of DOA decreases when one feature improves.

The results in Table 4 highlight the ≻-completeness of DOA too. In fact, the first APF is dominated by the others and it has a DOA value worse than those of the other APFs.

9. CONCLUSIONS AND FUTURE WORK

Evaluating the performance of MOOAs is very difficult because their comparison involves comparing APFs. QIs are used to measure the goodness of the APF provided by different optimization algorithms to highlight which works better.

Therefore, a QI must be able to account for Pareto dominance to properly compare two different algorithms. Moreover, when APFs are incomparable, further data (closeness, distribution, extension and cardinality) must be taken into account to compare the APFs provided by different MOOAs. Few UQIs are ≻-complete and able to account for the aforementioned features, yet they require great computational effort.

This paper has described the DOA unary quality indicator, which could be very useful in assessing the performance of an MOOA by estimating the match between the approximation front found by the MOOA and the optimal one. It has been proven that it is $\succ$-complete, $\ntriangleright$-compatible, and requires little computational cost. Moreover, a numerical validation was carried out to demonstrate that it accounts for closeness, distribution, extension, and cardinality. An implementation of the DOA indicator is available online: http://wwwelfin.diees.unict.it/esg/DOA.html.

The major drawback of the proposed indicator is that it is not $\triangleright$-complete. Even though the dominance relation A $\triangleleft$ B differs from A $\prec$ B since the former accounts for the case in which B contains some solutions of A, the probability of this specific event is next to nil. Nevertheless, a future development of this work is to properly modify DOA to make it $\triangleright$-complete, maintaining low computational complexity. In this perspective, the underlying reasons leading from a not $\succ$-complete indicator, IGD, to the similar one proposed in this paper, DOA, having $\succ$-completeness can be the enabling keys.

Moreover, an integral formulation of DOA can be developed to deal with continuous POFs that can be expressed by an analytical function.

Finally, innovative studies have proposed interesting strategies to use UQIs requiring the knowledge of the POF as the guidance mechanism for indicator-based MOEAs. Therefore, the use of DOA for indicator-based evolutionary algorithms is another attractive development of the work.

AUTHOR CONTRIBUTIONS

The authors contributed equally to this work.

APPENDIX A.

Hypothesis. A$\prec$B.

Thesis. $\exists\, i^* \in$ POF: $s_{i^*,A} = d_{i^*,A} < s_{i^*,B}$.

Proof by Reductio ad absurdum.

In this proof some remarks must be taken into account:

1) $df_{i^*,a^*} = d_{i^*,A} \Rightarrow df_{i^*,a^*} \leq df_{i^*,a'}\ \forall\, a' \in D_{i^*,A}$

2) $df_{i^*,a^*} < r_{i^*,A} \Rightarrow df_{i^*,a^*} < rf_{i^*,a''}\ \forall\, a'' \in A \setminus D_{i^*,A}$

3) when $i \preccurlyeq a \prec b \Rightarrow df_{i,a} < df_{i,b}$ (see Section C2)

4) when $i//a \wedge i \prec b \wedge a \prec b \Rightarrow rf_{i,a} \leq df_{i,b}$ (see Section D2)

5) when $i//a \wedge i//b \wedge a \prec b \Rightarrow rf_{i,a} \leq rf_{i,b}$ (see Section E2)

6) $\exists\, i^* \in$ POF and $\exists\, a^* \in A$: $s_{i^*,A} = d_{i^*,A} = df_{i^*,a^*} < r_{i^*,A}$ (proved in Appendix B).

Assume the opposite of the thesis:

$$s_{i^*,B} \leq s_{i^*,A}; \tag{A1}$$

from(A1) and Remark (VI), it follows that:

$$\exists\, b' \in D_{i^*,B}:\ s_{i^*,B} = df_{i^*,b'}\ (\leq df_{i^*,a^*} = s_{i^*,A}) \tag{A2}$$

or

$$\exists\, b'' \in B \backslash D_{i^*,B}:\ s_{i^*,B} = rf_{i^*,b''}\ (\leq df_{i^*,a^*} = s_{i^*,A}). \tag{A3}$$

Considering inequality (A2), three scenarios are to be analyzed:

(a) $a^* \prec b'$

(b) $a' \prec b'$, where $a' \in D_{i^*,A}$

(c) $a'' \prec b'$, where $a'' \in A \backslash D_{i^*,A}$.

In Scenario (a), from Remark (III), follows:

$$s_{i*,A} = d_{i*,A} = df_{i*,a*} < df_{i*,b\prime} = s_{i*,B} \Rightarrow s_{i*,B} > s_{i*,A}, \tag{A4}$$

which is in contradiction with (A1).

In Scenario (b), considering Remarks (I) and (III), follows:

$$s_{i*,A} = d_{i*,A} = df_{i*,a*} \leq df_{i*,a\prime} < df_{i*,b\prime} = s_{i*,B} \Rightarrow s_{i*,B} > s_{i*,A}, \tag{A5}$$

which is in contradiction with (A1).

In Scenario (c), by considering Remarks (II) and (IV), follows:

$$s_{i*,A} = d_{i*,A} = df_{i*,a*} < rf_{i*,a''} \leq df_{i*,b\prime} = s_{i*,B} \Rightarrow s_{i*,B} > s_{i*,A}, \tag{A6}$$

which is in contradiction with (A1).

Considering (A3), $s_{i^*,B} = rf_{i^*,b''}$ implies $i^*//b''$, i.e., $\nexists\ a \in D_{i^*,A}$: $a \prec b''$. Hence only one scenario has to be analyzed: $a'' \prec b''$, where $a'' \in A \backslash D_{i^*,A}$.

By considering Remarks (II) and (V), follows:

$$s_{i*,A} = d_{i*,A} = df_{i*,a*} < rf_{i*,a''} \leq rf_{i*,b''} = s_{i*,B} \Rightarrow s_{i*,B} > s_{i*,A}, \quad \text{(A7)}$$

which is in contradiction with (A1). □

APPENDIX B.

Hypothesis. A is a generic APF.

Thesis. $\exists\ i \in$ POF and $\exists\ a \in$ A: $s_{i,A} = d_{i,A} = df_{i,a} < r_{i,A}$.

Proof. The proof is given by induction, starting from |A| = 1 and adding to A other solutions recursively. First, only two objective functions (n = 2) are considered, then the same procedure is used for the general case (n > 2).

B.1. Proof by Induction with n = 2

Hypothesis. |A| = 1.

Proof. Being A = $\{a\}$ and recalling that POF$\preccurlyeq$A, follows that there exist a solution $i \in$POF for which $i \preccurlyeq a$, then $a \in D_{i,A}$ and $|A \backslash D_{i,A}| = 0$. This implies that:

$$\begin{aligned} &d_{i,A} = df_{i,a} < \infty \\ &r_{i,A} = \infty \\ &\Rightarrow \\ &s_{i,A} = d_{i,A} = df_{i,a} < r_{i,A} \end{aligned} \quad \text{(A8)}$$

Hypothesis. |A| = 2.

Proof. Being A = $\{a_1,a_2\}$, if $\exists\ i \in$POF: $i \preccurlyeq a_1 \wedge i \preccurlyeq a_2$, then a_1 and a_2 belong to $D_{i,A}$ and $|A \backslash D_{i,A}| = 0$:

$$\begin{aligned} &d_{i,A} = df_{i,a} = \min(df_{i,a1}, df_{i,a2}) < \infty \\ &r_{i,A} = \infty \\ &\Rightarrow \\ &s_{i,A} = d_{i,A} = df_{i,a} < r_{i,A}, \end{aligned} \quad \text{(A9)}$$

where a is equal to the solution which provides $s_{i,A}$ between a_1 and a_2.

On the other hand, when there does not exist such a solution i, recalling that POF$\preccurlyeq$A, then there exist two solutions i_1, $i_2$belonging to the POF for which $i_1 \preccurlyeq a_1$ and $i_2 \preccurlyeq a_2$. Obviously, $i_1 || a_2$ and $i_2 || a_1$. Hence, without loss of generality it is assumed that:

$$\begin{aligned} f_{1,i2} &\leq f_{1,a2} < f_{1,i1} \leq f_{1,a1} \\ f_{2,i1} &\leq f_{2,a1} < f_{2,i2} \leq f_{2,a2}. \end{aligned} \tag{A10}$$

The thesis is proved if $s_{i1,A} = d_{i1,A} = df_{i1,a1} < rf_{i1,a2} = r_{i1,A} \vee s_{i2,A} = d_{i2,A} = df_{i2,a2} < rf_{i2,a1} = r_{i2,A}$. The proof is by *reductio ad absurdum*. Supposing that:

$$s_{i1,A} = r_{i1,A} = rf_{i1,a2} < df_{i1,a1} = d_{i1,A} \wedge s_{i2,A} = r_{i2,A} = rf_{i2,a1} < df_{i2,a2} = d_{i2,A}, \tag{A11}$$

in which:

$$\begin{aligned} rf_{i1,a2} &= f_{2,a2} - f_{2,i1} \\ df_{i1,a1} &= \sqrt{[f_{1,a1} - f_{1,i1}]^2 + [f_{2,a1} - f_{2,i1}]^2} \\ rf_{i2,a1} &= f_{1,a1} - f_{1,i2} \\ df_{i2,a2} &= \sqrt{[f_{1,a2} - f_{1,i2}]^2 + [f_{2,a2} - f_{2,i2}]^2}. \end{aligned} \tag{A12}$$

Note that:

$$\begin{aligned} &\sqrt{[f_{1,a1} - f_{1,i1}]^2 + [f_{2,a1} - f_{2,i1}]^2} < f_{1,a1} - f_{1,i1} + f_{2,a1} - f_{2,i1} \\ &\sqrt{[f_{1,a2} - f_{1,i2}]^2 + [f_{2,a2} - f_{2,i2}]^2} < f_{1,a2} - f_{1,i2} + f_{2,a2} - f_{2,i2}, \end{aligned} \tag{A13}$$

because the quantities in the brackets are not negative. From (A11) and (A13) follows:

$$\begin{aligned} &f_{2,a2} - f_{2,i1} = rf_{i1,a2} < df_{i1,a1} < f_{1,a1} - f_{1,i1} + f_{2,a1} - f_{2,i1} \\ &f_{1,a1} - f_{1,i2} = rf_{i2,a1} < df_{i2,a2} < f_{1,a2} - f_{1,i2} + f_{2,a2} - f_{2,i2} \\ &\Rightarrow \\ &0 < -f_{2,a2} + f_{2,i1} + f_{1,a1} - f_{1,i1} + f_{2,a1} - f_{2,i1} \\ &0 < -f_{1,a1} + f_{1,i2} + f_{1,a2} - f_{1,i2} + f_{2,a2} - f_{2,i2}, \end{aligned} \tag{A14}$$

then

$$\begin{aligned} 0 &< [-f_{1,a1} + f_{1,i2} + f_{1,a1} - f_{1,i1} + f_{1,a2} - f_{1,i2}] + \\ &+ [-f_{2,a2} + f_{2,i1} + f_{2,a1} - f_{2,i1} + f_{2,a2} - f_{2,i2}] = , \\ &= f_{1,a2} - f_{1,i1} + f_{2,a1} - f_{2,i2}, \end{aligned} \quad \text{(A15)}$$

which leads to an absurdity because, according to(A10), it is:

$$\begin{aligned} f_{1,a2} - f_{1,i1} &< 0 \\ f_{2,a1} - f_{2,i2} &< 0 \end{aligned} . \quad \text{(A16)}$$

Adding to A other solutions recursively, the previous procedure can be applied to demonstrate that the thesis is always true whatever |A| is.

B.2. Proof by Induction with n = 3

Hypothesis. |A| = 1.

Proof. The proof is the same provided for $n = 2$ in (A8).

Hypothesis. |A| = 2

Proof. Being A = $\{a_1, a_2\}$, if ∃ i∈POF: $i \preccurlyeq a_1 \wedge i \preccurlyeq a_2$, then a_1 and a_2 belong to $D_{i,A}$ and $|A \backslash D_{i,A}| = 0 \Rightarrow$ The proof is the same provided in (A9).

On the other hand, when does not exist such solution i, recalling that POF≼A then there exist two solutions i_1, $i_2$belonging to the POF for which $i_1 \preccurlyeq a_1$ and $i_2 \preccurlyeq a_2$. Obviously, $i_1 || a_2$ and $i_2 || a_1$. Hence, without loss of generality it is assumed that:

$$\begin{aligned} f_{1,i2} \le f_{1,a2} &< f_{1,i1} \le f_{1,a1} \\ f_{2,i1} \le f_{2,a1} &< f_{2,i2} \le f_{2,a2} \\ f_{3,i1} \le f_{3,a1} &< f_{3,i2} \le f_{3,a2}. \end{aligned} \quad \text{(A17)}$$

Likewise, for the case of two objective functions the thesis it will be proven that $s_{i1,A} = d_{i1,A} = df_{i1,a1} < rf_{i1,a2} = r_{i1,A} \vee s_{i2,A} = d_{i2,A} = df_{i2,a2} < rf_{i2,a1} = r_{i2,A}$.

The proof is by *reductio ad absurdum*.

Assuming that:

$$s_{i1,A} = r_{i1,A} = rf_{i1,a2} < df_{i1,a1} = d_{i1,A} \wedge s_{i2,A} = r_{i2,A} = rf_{i2,a1} < df_{i2,a2} = d_{i2,A}, \quad \text{(A18)}$$

which implies:

$$
\begin{aligned}
&rf_{i1,a2} = \sqrt{[f_{2,a2} - f_{2,i1}]^2 + [f_{3,a2} - f_{3,i1}]^2} < \\
&\sqrt{[f_{1,a1} - f_{1,i1}]^2 + [f_{2,a1} - f_{2,i1}]^2 + [f_{3,a1} - f_{3,i1}]^2} = df_{i1,a1} \\
&\Rightarrow \\
&[f_{2,a2} - f_{2,i1}]^2 + [f_{3,a2} - f_{3,i1}]^2 < \\
&[f_{1,a1} - f_{1,i1}]^2 + [f_{2,a1} - f_{2,i1}]^2 + [f_{3,a1} - f_{3,i1}]^2
\end{aligned} \tag{A19}
$$

and

$$
\begin{aligned}
&rf_{i2,a1} = f_{1,a1} - f_{1,i2} < \\
&\sqrt{[f_{1,a2} - f_{1,i2}]^2 + [f_{2,a2} - f_{2,i2}]^2 + [f_{3,a2} - f_{3,i2}]^2} = df_{i2,a2} \\
&\Rightarrow \\
&[f_{1,a1} - f_{1,i2}]^2 < \\
&[f_{1,a2} - f_{1,i2}]^2 + [f_{2,a2} - f_{2,i2}]^2 + [f_{3,a2} - f_{3,i2}]^2.
\end{aligned} \tag{A20}
$$

Summing each member of (A19) and (A20) follows:

$$
\begin{aligned}
&[f_{1,a1} - f_{1,i2}]^2 + [f_{2,a2} - f_{2,i1}]^2 + [f_{3,a2} - f_{3,i1}]^2 < \\
&[f_{1,a1} - f_{1,i1}]^2 + [f_{2,a1} - f_{2,i1}]^2 + [f_{3,a1} - f_{3,i1}]^2 + \\
&+[f_{1,a2} - f_{1,i2}]^2 + [f_{2,a2} - f_{2,i2}]^2 + [f_{3,a2} - f_{3,i2}]^2 \\
&\Rightarrow \\
&0 < [f_{1,a1} - f_{1,i1}]^2 + [f_{1,a2} - f_{1,i2}]^2 - [f_{1,a1} - f_{1,i2}]^2 + \\
&\quad + [f_{2,a1} - f_{2,i1}]^2 + [f_{2,a2} - f_{2,i2}]^2 - [f_{2,a2} - f_{2,i1}]^2 + \\
&\quad + [f_{3,a1} - f_{3,i1}]^2 + [f_{3,a2} - f_{3,i2}]^2 - [f_{3,a2} - f_{3,i1}]^2.
\end{aligned}
$$

Note that the quantities in the brackets are not negative and hence:

$$
\begin{aligned}
&0 < [f_{1,a1} - f_{1,i1}]^2 + [f_{1,a2} - f_{1,i2}]^2 - [f_{1,a1} - f_{1,i2}]^2 \\
&\quad + [f_{2,a1} - f_{2,i1}]^2 + [f_{2,a2} - f_{2,i2}]^2 - [f_{2,a2} - f_{2,i1}]^2 + \\
&\quad + [f_{3,a1} - f_{3,i1}]^2 + [f_{3,a2} - f_{3,i2}]^2 - [f_{3,a2} - f_{3,i1}]^2 < \\
&< [f_{1,a1} - f_{1,i1} + f_{1,a2} - f_{1,i2}]^2 - [f_{1,a1} - f_{1,i2}]^2 + \\
&\quad + [f_{2,a1} - f_{2,i1} + f_{2,a2} - f_{2,i2}]^2 - [f_{2,a2} - f_{2,i1}]^2 + \\
&\quad + [f_{3,a1} - f_{3,i1} f_{3,a2} - f_{3,i2}]^2 - [f_{3,a2} - f_{3,i1}]^2 < \\
&< f_{1,a1} - f_{1,i1} + f_{1,a2} - f_{1,i2} - f_{1,a1} + f_{1,i2} + \\
&\quad + f_{2,a1} - f_{2,i1} + f_{2,a2} - f_{2,i2} - f_{2,a2} + f_{2,i1} + \\
&\quad + f_{3,a1} - f_{3,i1} f_{3,a2} - f_{3,i2} - f_{3,a2} + f_{3,i1} = \\
&= f_{1,a2} - f_{1,i1} + f_{2,a1} - f_{2,i2} + f_{3,a1} - f_{3,i2},
\end{aligned}
$$

which leads to an absurdity because, according to(A17), it is:

$$f_{1,a2} - f_{1,i1} < 0$$
$$f_{2,a1} - f_{2,i2} < 0$$
$$f_{3,a1} - f_{3,i2} < 0.$$

The cases with $n > 3$ can be proved in a similar way.

REFERENCES

1. Zitzler, E.; Thiele, L. Multiobjective optimization using evolutionary algorithms—A comparative case study. In *Parallel Problem Solving from Nature-PPSN V*; Springer: Heidelberg/Berlin, Germany, 1998; Volume 1498, pp. 292–301.
2. Lei, Y.; Gong, M.; Zhang, J.; Li, W.; Jiao, L. Resource allocation model and double-sphere crowding distance for evolutionary multi-objective optimization. *Eur. J. Oper. Res.* **2014**, *234*, 197–208.
3. Wang, R.; Purshouse, R.C.; Fleming, P.J. Preference-inspired co-evolutionary algorithms using weight vectors. *Eur. J. Oper. Res.* **2015**, *243*, 423–441.
4. Sinha, A.; Korhonen, P.; Wallenius, J.; Deb, K. An interactive evolutionary multi-objective optimization algorithm with a limited number of decision maker calls. *Eur. J. Oper. Res.* **2014**, *233*, 674–688.
5. Ghosh, A.; Dehuri, S. Evolutionary Algorithms for Multi-Criterion Optimization: A Survey. *Int. J. Comput. Inf. Sci.***2004**, *2*, 38–57.
6. Dilettoso, E.; Rizzo, S.A.; Salerno, N. A Parallel Version of the Self-Adaptive Low-High Evaluation Evolutionary-Algorithm for Electromagnetic Device Optimization. *IEEE Trans. Magn.* **2014**, *50*, 633–636.
7. Wilfried, J.; Blume, C. Pareto Optimization or Cascaded Weighted Sum: A Comparison of Concepts. *Algorithms* **2014**, *7*, 166–185.
8. Deb, K. *Multi-Objective Optimization using Evolutionary Algorithms*; John Wiley & Sons: Hoboken, NJ, USA, 2001.
9. Chen, B.; Zeng, W.; Lin, Y.; Zhang, D. A New Local Search-Based Multiobjective Optimization Algorithm. *IEEE Trans. Evol. Comput.* **2015**, *19*, 50–73.
10. Talbi, E.G.; Basseur, M.; Nebro, A.J.; Alba, E. Multi-objective optimization using metaheuristics: Non-standard algorithms. *Int. Trans. Oper. Res.* **2012**, *19*, 283–305.
11. Zitzler, E.; Thiele, L.; Laumanns, M.; Fonseca, C.M.; Fonseca, V.G. Performance assessment of multiobjective optimizers: An analysis and review. *IEEE Trans. Evol. Comput.* **2003**, *7*, 117–132.
12. Fonseca, C.M.; Fleming, P.J. On the performance assessment and comparison of stochastic multiobjective optimizers. In *Parallel Problem Solving from Nature (PPSN-IV)*; Springer: Berlin, Germany, 1996; pp. 584–593.
13. Zitzler, E.; Deb, K.; Thiele, L. Comparison of multiobjective evolutionary algorithms: Empirical results. *Evol. Comput.***2000**, *8*, 173–195.
14. Shukla, P.K.; Deb, K. On finding multiple Pareto-optimal solutions using classical and evolutionary generating methods. *Eur. J. Oper. Res.* **2007**, *181*, 1630–1652.
15. Chen, Y.; Zou, X.; Xie, W. Convergence of multi-objective evolutionary algorithms to a uniformly distributed representation of the Pareto front. *Inf. Sci.* **2011**, *181*, 3336–3355.
16. Lizárraga, G.; Gomez, M.J.; Castañon, M.G.; Acevedo-Davila, J.; Rionda, S.B. Why Unary Quality Indicators Are Not Inferior to Binary Quality Indicators. In *MICAI 2009 Advances in Artificial Intelligence*; Aguirre, A.H., Borja, R.M., Garciá, C.A.R., Eds.; Springer: Berlin, Germany, 2009; Volume 5845, pp. 646–657.
17. Dilettoso, E.; Rizzo, S.A.; Salerno, N. A new indicator to assess the quality of a Pareto approximation set applied to improve the optimization of a magnetic shield. In

Proceedings of the Scientific Computing in Electrical Engineering, Zurich, Switzerland, 11–14 September 2012.
18. Deb, K.; Pratap, A.; Agarwal, S.; Meyariva, T. A Fast and Elitist Multiobjective Genetic Algorithm: NSGA-II. *IEEE Trans.Evol. Comput.* **2002**, *6*, 182–197.
19. Schaffer, J.D. Multiple objective optimization with vector evaluated genetic algorithms. In Proceedings of the First International Conference on Genetic Algorithms, Pittsburgh, PA, USA, 24–26 July 1985; Grefensttete, J.J., Ed.; Lawrence ErlbaumAssociates Inc.: Hillsdale, NJ, USA, 1987; pp. 93–100.
20. Fonseca, C.M.; Fleming, P.J. An overview of evolutionary algorithms in multi-objective optimization. *Evol. Comput. J.***1995**, *3*, 1–16.
21. Poloni, C. Hybrid GA for Multiobjective aerodynamic shape optimization. In *Genetic Algorithms in Engineering and Computer Science*; Winter, G., Periaux, J., Galan, M., Cuesta, P., Eds.; Wiley: New York, NY, USA, 1997; pp. 397–414.
22. Kursawe, F. A variant of evolution strategies for vector optimization. In *Parallel Problem Solving from Nature*; Schwefel, H.-P., Männer, R., Eds.; Springer: Berlin, Germany, 1990; pp. 193–197.
23. Deb, K.; Thiele, L.; Laumanns, M.; Zitzler, E. Scalable multiobjective optimization test problems. In Proceedings of the IEEE Congress on Evolutionary Computation, Honolulu, HI, USA, 12–17 May 2002; pp. 825–830.
24. Beume, N.; Naujoks, B.; Emmerich, M. SMS-EMOA: Multiobjective selection based on dominated hypervolume. *Eur. J. Oper. Res.* **2007**, *181*, 1653–1669.
25. Schütze, O.; Domínguez-Medina, C.; Cruz-Cortés, N.; de la Fraga, L.G.; Sun, J.-Q.; Toscano, G.; Landa, R. A scalar optimization approach for averaged Hausdorff approximations of the Pareto front. *Eng. Optim.* **2016**, *48*, 1593–1617.
26. Zitzler, E.; Knowles, J.D.; Thiele, L. Quality assessment of pareto set approximations. In *Multiobjective Optimization*; Lecture Notes in Computer Science; Springer: Berlin, Germany, 2008; Volume 5252, pp. 373–404.
27. Laumanns, M.; Zenklusen, R. Stochastic convergence of random search methods to fixed size Pareto front approximations. *Eur. J. Oper. Res.* **2011**, *213*, 414–421.
28. Fonseca, C.M.; Knowles, J.D.; Thiele, L.; Zitzler, E. A Tutorial on the Performance Assessment of Stochastic Multiobjective Optimizers. Available online: http://www.tik.ee.ethz.ch/pisa/publications/emo-tutorial-2up.pdf(accessed on 15 December 2016).
29. Coello Coello, C.A.; Sierra, M.R. A Study of the Parallelization of a Coevolutionary Multi-objective Evolutionary Algorithm. *Lect. Notes Comput. Sci.* **2004**, *2972*, 688–697.
30. Czyzak, P.; Jaskiewicz, A. Pareto simulated annealing—a metaheuristic technique for multi-objective combinatorial optimization. *J. MultiCriteria Decis. Anal.* **1998**, *7*, 34–47.
31. Lotov, A.V.; Kamenev, G.K.; Berezkin, V.E. Approximation and Visualization of Pareto-Efficient Frontier for Nonconvex Multiobjective Problems. *Dokl. Math.* **2002**, *66*, 260–262.
32. Lotov, A.V.; Bushenkov, V.A.; Kamenev, G.K. *Interactive Decision Maps: Approximation and Visualization of Pareto Frontier*; Springer: Boston, MA, USA, 2004.
33. Srinivas, N.; Deb, K. Multiobjective optimization using nondominated sorting in genetic algorithms. *Evol. Comput.***1994**, *2*, 221–248.
34. Van Veldhuizen, D.A. Multiobjective Evolutionary Algorithms: Classifications, Analyzes, and New Innovations. Ph.D. Thesis, Engineering of the Air Force Institute of Technology University, Wright-Patterson AFB, OH, USA, 1999.
35. Wu, J.; Azarm, S. Metrics for Quality Assessment of a Multiobjective Design Optimization Solution Set. *J. Mech. Des.***2001**, *123*, 18–25.
36. Schott, J.R. Fault Tolerant Design Using Single and Multicriteria Genetic Algorithm Optimization. Mc.S. Thesis, Department of Aeronautics and Astronautics, Massachusetts Institute of Technology, Boston, MA, USA, 1995.
37. Van Veldhuizen, D.A.; Lamont, G.B. On measuring multiobjective evolutionary algorithm performance. In Proceedings of the 2000 Congress on Evolutionary Computation, La Jolla, CA, USA, 16–19 July 2000; pp. 204–211.
38. Tan, K.C.; Khor, E.F.; Lee, T.H. Evolutionary Algorithms for Multi-Objective Optimization: Performance Assessments and Comparisons. *J. Artif. Intel. Rev.* **2002**, *17*, 253–290.

39. Schutze, O.; Esquivel, X.; Lara, A.; Coello Coello, C.A. Using the Averaged Hausdorff Distance as a Performance Measure in Evolutionary Multi-Objective Optimization. *IEEE Trans. Evol. Comput.* **2012**, *16*, 504–522.
40. Rudolph, G.; Schütze, O.; Grimme, C.; Medina, C.D.; Trautmann, H. Optimal averaged Hausdorff archives for bi-objective problems: Theoretical and numerical results. *Comput. Optim. Appl.* **2016**, *64*, 589–618.
41. While, L. A new analysis of the LebMeasure algorithm for calculating hypervolume. In *Evolutionary Multi-Criterion Optimization*; Lecture Notes in Computer Science; Springer: Heidelberg/Berlin, Germany, 2005; Volume 3410, pp. 326–340.
42. While, L.; Bradstreet, L.; Barone, L.; Hingston, P. Heuristics for optimising the calculation of hypervolume for multi-objective optimisation problems. In Proceedings of the IEEE Congress on Evolutionary Computation, Edinburgh, UK, 2–5 September 2005; pp. 2225–2232.
43. Fonseca, C.M.; Paquete, L.; López-Ibáñez, M. An improved dimension-sweep algorithm for the hypervolume indicator. In Proceedings of the IEEE Congress on Evolutionary Computation, Vancouver, BC, Canada, 16–21 July 2006; pp. 1157–1163.
44. Beume, N.; Rudolph, G. Faster S-Metric calculation by considering dominated hypervolume as Klee's measure problem. In Proceedings of the 2nd IASTED Conference on Computational Intelligence, San Francisco, CA, USA, 20–22 November 2006; pp. 231–236.
45. Knowles, J.; Corne, D.; Fleischer, M. Bounded archiving using the lebesgue measure. In Proceedings of the 2003 Congress on Evolutionary Computation, Canberra, Australia, 8–12 December 2003; Volume 4, pp. 2490–2497.
46. While, L.; Barone, L.; Hingston, P.; Huband, S. A Faster Algorithm for Calculating Hypervolume. *IEEE Trans. Evol.Comput.* **2006**, *10*, 29–38.

CHAPTER 15

Rational Spline Image Upscaling with Constraint Parameters

Xunxiang Yao[1], Yunfeng Zhang[1], Fangxun Bao[2,*] and Caiming Zhang[3]

[1] *School of Computer Science and Technology, Shandong University of Finance and Economics, Jinan 250014, China*

[2] *School of Mathematics, Shandong University, Jinan 250100, China*

[3] *School of Computer Science and Technology, Shandong University, Jinan 250101, China*

ABSTRACT

Image interpolation is one of key contents in image processing. We present an interpolation algorithm based on a rational function model with constraint parameters. Firstly, based on the construction principle of the rational function, the detection threshold is selected through contour analysis. The smooth and non-smooth areas are interpolated by bicubic interpolation and general rational interpolation, respectively. In order to enhance the contrast in non-smooth areas and preserve the details, the parameter optimization technique is applied to get optimal shape parameters. Experimental results on benchmark test images demonstrate that the proposed method achieves competitive performance with the state-of-the-art interpolation algorithms, especially in image details and texture features.

Keywords: rational function; adaptive interpolation; region division; parameters optimization

1. INTRODUCTION

Interpolation acts as a bridge between the continuous world and the discrete one. As an important technique, it pervades many applications [1,2]. A digital image is not an exact snapshot of reality, it is only a discrete approximation. Image interpolation focuses on the issue which obtains a high-resolution image from a low-resolution one. Image interpolation plays an important role in image processing, and it is widely used in various fields, such as aerospace, medical, military, scientific research, communications, remote sensing satellite, television, film production, etc.

Generally speaking, the interpolation technique is used in nearly every geometric transformation, such as translation, scaling, rotation, etc. Such operations are utilized in many commercial digital image processing software [3]. The main issue of image interpolation is to maintain texture details and edge structure, while eliminating blocking artifacts, texture disorder, and other visual artifacts. Quantities of image interpolation methods have been proposed in several articles [4,5,6,7,8,9,10,11,12,13]. In these existing methods, linear filters (as the simplest technique) have been widely used in image interpolation, such as the bilinear, bicubic [4], and cubic spline algorithms [5]. Although these traditional methods are effective, they have disadvantages in ringing artifacts, blurred details, and so forth. Because the image can be affected by many factors, including the light, natural background, and the characteristics of its own texture, all in all, the relationship between pixels is not linear [14].

With ever-increasing capacity of computation power, many image interpolation methods have been proposed in the past few years. Jeong et al. [15] presented a multi-frame example-based super-resolution (SR) algorithm using locally directional self-similarity. Jha et al. [16] proposed a new image interpolation method using adaptive weights based on inverse gradients and distances from the pixels used in prediction. In [17], an edge-guided interpolation approach was proposed, which improved the accuracy of interpolation by detecting edges and fitting them with templates. In [18], predetermined edge patterns were used to obtain optimal parameters. As a consequence, according to the original images' edge structures, high quality interpolated images could be obtained. Edge-Directed interpolation (EDI) methods have been presented [19]. Said and Pearlman [20] proposed a source model which focuses on the integrity of detected edges and modifies the interpolation to adapt to the original one.

Then, a New Edge-Directed Interpolation (NEDI) adaptive method was presented, which obtains better subjective quality than EDI. Based on the geometric duality between the low-resolution covariance and the high-resolution covariance, the relationship of high-resolution covariance and the low-resolution one can be estimated [6]. A soft-decision interpolation technique (SAI) was proposed, which estimates unknown pixels in groups [13].

We dedicated our research to the integration of image interpolation and human visual perception. However, how to design the interpolation algorithm that combines with visual perception for the purpose of getting an "ideal" interpolated image is still a challenge for image interpolation methods. In this paper, a new image interpolation method based on rational function model is proposed. Considering the speed and quality of the interpolated image, the input image will be classified into smooth areas and non-smooth areas. For smooth areas, a bicubic interpolation is used to lower time complexity. For non-smooth areas, the proposed optimal rational interpolation function is used to improve the accuracy of interpolation. The bicubic interpolation function is a special form of the same interpolation function model on the condition that the parameters are chosen with some specific values. Namely, parameters α and β equal 1. The mean value of nine interpolation data points is the threshold, and is used for non-smooth area detection. Image interpolation, processing, region detection, different region interpolation, and visual contrast enhancement are all based on one rational interpolation model. Experimental results show good image quality results in both edges and details. The algorithm framework is shown in Figure 1.

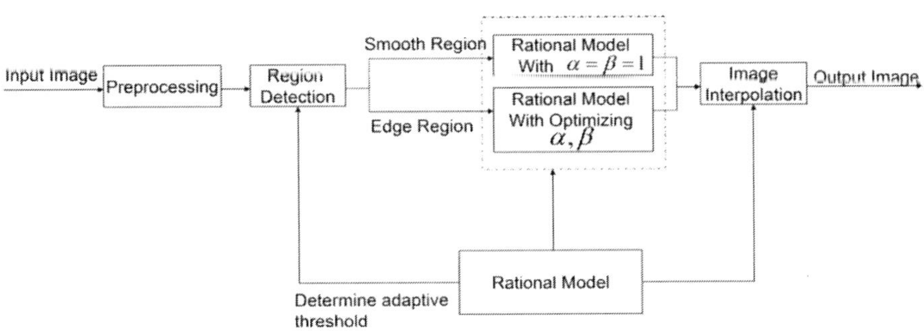

Figure 1. Algorithm framework.

This paper is organized as follows: Section 2 introduces the fundamental principles of the rational function model and its properties. Section 3 presents the proposed interpolation algorithm. Experimental results are shown for demonstration in Section 4. Section 5 concludes this paper.

2. A BIVARIATE RATIONAL INTERPOLATION

In recent years, the univariate rational spline interpolations with parameters have been developed [21,22,23]. These kinds of interpolation splines have a simple mathematical representation and can preserve property of interpolated curve and surface. Motivated by the univariate rational spline interpolation, the bivariate rational interpolation with parameters based on the function values has been studied in [24,25,26,27,28,29]. The interpolation function has a piecewise explicit rational mathematical representation with parameters, and it can be represented by its basis.

Let Ω:[$a,b;c,d$] be the plane region, let $f(x,y)$ be a bivariate function defined in the region Ω, and let $a=x_1<x_2<\cdots<x_n<x_{n+1}=b$ and $c=y_1<y_2<\cdots<ym<y_{m+1}=d$ be the knot sequences. Denote $f(x_i,y_j)$ by $f_{i,j}$; then, $\{(x_i,y_j,f_{i,j}),\ i=1,2,\ldots n,n+1;j=1,2,\ldots m,m+1\}$ are the given set of data points. For any point $(x,y)\in[x_i,x_i+1;y_j,y_j+1]$ in the xy-plane, let $h_i = x_{i+1} - x_i,\ \theta = \frac{x-x_i}{h_i}$, and $l_j = y_{j+1} - y_j,\ \eta = \frac{y-y_j}{l_j}$. For each $y=y_j$,$j=1,2,\cdots m+1$, construct the x-direction interpolation curve; this is given by

$$P^*_{i,j}(x) = \frac{p^*_{i,j}(x)}{q^*_{i,j}(x)},\ x \in [x_i, x_{i+1}],\ i = 1,2,\cdots n-1 \tag{1}$$

Where

$$\begin{aligned} p^*_{i,j}(x) &= (1-\theta)^3\alpha_{i,j}f_{i,j} + \theta(1-\theta)^2 V^*_{i,j} + \theta^2(1-\theta)W^*_{i,j} \\ &+ \theta^3 f_{i+1,j}, \\ q^*_{i,j}(x) &= (1-\theta)\alpha_{i,j} + \theta, \end{aligned} \qquad 1$$

and

$$\begin{aligned} V^*_{i,j} &= (\alpha_{i,j}+1)f_{i,j} + \alpha_{i,j}f_{i+1,j}, \\ W^*_{i,j} &= (\alpha_{i,j}+2)f_{i+1,j} - h_i\Delta^*_{i+1,j}, \end{aligned}$$

with $\alpha_{i,j}>0$, and $\Delta^*_{i,j}=(f_{i+1,j}-f_{i,j})/h_i$. This interpolation is called the rational cubic interpolation based on function values which satisfies

$$p^*_{i,j}(x_i) = f_{i,j},\ p^*_{i,j}(x_{i+1}) = f_{i+1,j},$$

$$p^{*'}_{i,j}(x_i) = \Delta^*_{i,j},\ p^{*'}_{i,j}(x_{i+1}) = \Delta^*_{i+1,j}.$$

Obviously, the interpolation is a local one, it is defined in the interval $[x_i,x_i+1]$ and depends on the data at three points $\{(x_r,y_j,f_{r,j}),r=i,i+1,i+2\}$ and the parameter $\alpha_{i,j}$.

For each pair $(i,j),i=1,2,\cdots n-1$ and $j=1,2,\cdots m-1$, using the x-direction interpolation function $P^*_{i,j}(x)$, define the bivariate rational interpolating function $P_{i,j}(x,y)$ on $[x_i,x_{i+1};y_j,y_{j+1}]$ as follows

$$P_{i,j}(x,y) = \frac{p_{i,j}(x,y)}{q_{i,j}(y)}, \quad i = 1,2,\cdots,n-1;\ j = 1,2,\cdots,m-1 \tag{2}$$

where

$$\begin{aligned} p_{i,j}(x,y) &= (1-\eta)^3\beta_{i,j}P^*_{i,j}(x) + \eta(1-\eta)^2V_{i,j} \\ &+ \eta^2(1-\eta)W_{i,j} + \eta^3P^*_{i,j+1}(x), \\ q_{i,j}(y) &= (1-\eta)\beta_{i,j} + \eta, \end{aligned}$$

and

$$\begin{aligned} V_{i,j} &= (\beta_{i,j}+1)P^*_{i,j}(x) + \beta_{i,j}P^*_{i,j+1}(x), \\ W_{i,j} &= (\beta_{i,j}+2)P^*_{i,j+1}(x) - l_j\Delta_{i,j+1}(x), \end{aligned}$$

with $\beta_{i,j}>0$, and $\Delta_{i,j}(x) = (P^*_{i,j+1}(x) - P^*_{i,j}(x))/l_j$.

In the subregion $[x_i,x_{i+1};y_j,y_{j+1}]$, the function $P_{i,j}(x,y)$ is called a bivariate rational interpolation function based on function values. It depends on the data at nine points $\{(x_r,y_s,f_{r,s}),r=i,i+1,i+2, s=j,j+1,j+2\}$ and which satisfies

$$P_{i,j}(x_r,y_s) = f(x_r,y_s), r = i,i+1, s = j,j+1$$

Consider the equally spaced knots case; namely, for all i=1,2,⋯,n and j=1,2,⋯,m, h_i=h_j and l_i=l_j. The interpolating function $P_{i,j}(x,y)$ is C^1 in the whole interpolating region. The bivariate rational interpolating function $P_{i,j}(x,y)$ can be expressed as follows:

$$P_{i,j}(x,y) = \sum_{r=0}^{2}\sum_{s=0}^{2} \omega_{rs}(\theta,\alpha_i;\eta,\beta_j) f_{i+r,j+s} \tag{3}$$

where

$$\omega_{rs}(\theta,\alpha_i;\eta,\beta_j) = \omega_r(\theta,\alpha_i)\omega_s(\eta,\beta_j)$$

$$\omega_0(\theta,\alpha_i) = \frac{(1-\theta)^2(\alpha_i+\theta)}{(1-\theta)\alpha_i+\theta}$$

$$\omega_1(\theta,\alpha_i) = \frac{\theta(1-\theta)\alpha_i+3\theta^2-2\theta^3}{(1-\theta)\alpha_i+\theta}$$

$$\omega_2(\theta,\alpha_i) = \frac{-\theta^2(1-\theta)}{(1-\theta)\alpha_i+\theta}.$$

The terms $\omega_{rs}(\theta,\alpha_i;\eta,\beta_j)$, r=0,1,2; s=0,1,2 are called the basis of the bivariate interpolation, which satisfy

$$\sum_{r=0}^{2}\sum_{s=0}^{2} \omega_{rs}(\theta,\alpha_i;\eta,\beta_j) = 1$$

From Equation (3), the interpolating function Pi,j(x,y) is defined by a given set of data points $\{f_{i,j}, f_{i+1,j}, f_{i+2,j}; f_{i,j+1}, f_{i+1,j+1}, f_{i+2,j+1}; f_{i,j+2}, f_{i+1,j+2}, f_{i+2,j+2}\}$. Applying the interpolating function, we can construct a patch through points $f_{i,j}, f_{i+1,j}, f_{i,j+1}, f_{i+1,j+1}$.

3. BASIC ALGORITHMS

Generally speaking, there is always a contradiction between the processing speed of interpolation and the resultant quality in image interpolation. The commonly used methods [6,7,13] usually adopt different interpolation functions for different regions Furthermore, the different region detection algorithm is not related to the interpolation. Namely, the used methods are not based on the interpolation function. Because the image has natural attributes, its inherent attributes are inevitably affected by using the commonly used methods. Thus, we present a novel interpolation model to solve this problem. Moreover, the processing speed of interpolation and the resultant quality are all preserved using the new algorithm.

3.1. Image Non-Smooth Areas Detection

In this paper, a variety of textures and edges of the image area are called non-smooth areas. The smooth areas contain abundant detailed information, and have critical effects on the image quality. First of all, the non-smooth areas are detected.

From the rational function, a patch can be constructed given nine data points. All of them have different effects on the patch through their weights $\omega_{rs}(\theta,\alpha;\eta,\beta)$. When the weights present great differences from each other, the patch becomes more and more non-flat, considered as non-smooth area in the interpolated image. As mentioned above, the data points play a different role in the structure processing. The drawing and analyses of contours depends on the decision of the sign. On this basis, contour analysis is used to detect the non-smooth areas. The detection model is based on the interpolation model. As mentioned above, an interpolated patch is constructed using nine data points. The points play different roles in the structure processing. The vertices of the patch are the key points. The other data points are auxiliary. As the detection threshold, the mean value of the nine data points can be used for detecting the non-smooth areas in the interpolated image. Namely, for any given set of data $\sum_{r=0}^{2}\sum_{s=0}^{2} f_{r,s},\ r,s=0,1,2,$, the detection threshold λ is given as follows:

$$\lambda = \frac{\sum_{r=0}^{2}\sum_{s=0}^{2} f_{r,s}}{9}$$

Let $\delta=f_{r,s}-\lambda, r,s=0,1$; from the contours drawing and analyses, if δ are all nonpositive and have nonnegative sign, the region is regarded as non-smooth. Otherwise it is smooth. Basically, the detection threshold is selected based on the rational function construction. The non-smooth detection results are shown in Figure 2.

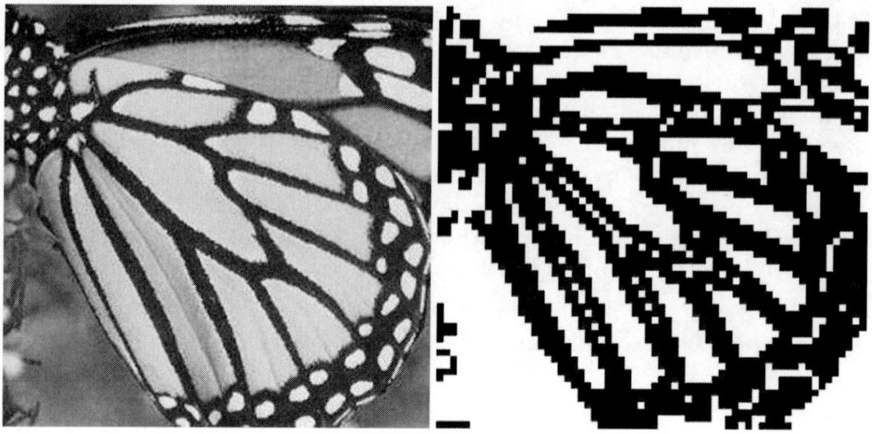

(a) (b)

Figure 2. Region detection. (**a**) Original image; (**b**) Non-smooth areas.

3.2. Image Interpolation

An image is a set of values on a 2D plane. It is affected by the material of the object surface, the physical appearance of background objects , light strength and angle, and noise of the imaging progress. These data are purely random and can be constructed completely. The value of these data are gradually changed. In general, iit is nonlinear. As an nonlinear function, bivariate rational interpolation is a good choice to implement image interpolation. As is well known, interpolation processing speed is an important standard to measure an interpolation algorithm. Bivariate rational interpolation with parameters has nice properties. If the parameters equal to 1, it is a bicubic interpolation function. In this case, it may be written as

$$P_{i,j}(x,y) = \sum_{r=0}^{2}\sum_{s=0}^{2} \omega_{rs}(\theta,\eta) f_{i+r,j+s} \tag{4}$$

where

$$\omega_{rs}(\theta,\eta) = \omega_r(\theta)\omega_s(\eta)$$

and

$$\omega_0(\theta) = \theta^3 - \theta^2 - \theta + 1,$$
$$\omega_1(\theta) = -2\theta^3 + \theta^2 + \theta,$$
$$\omega_2(\theta) = \theta^3 - \theta^2.$$

From Section 3.1, an image should be divided into multiscale edge regions and non-multiscale edge areas by using region detection. In order to reduce computational complexity, the multiscale edge regions and non-multiscale edge areas are interpolated by bicubic interpolation and rational interpolation, respectively. As follows, image interpolation based on the rational function model is introduced.

Given a $m \times n$ image $I_{m,n}$, let $f_{i,j}(0 \le i \le m-1, 0 \le j \le n-1)$ be the gray value of the i line and the j row of $I_{m,n}$. The pixel coordinate is (i,j). Denote a two-dimension discrete signal by $I_{m,n}$. At the integer points it is simple. Denote the data point by the gray value of each pixel. Then, the continuous interpolating surface can be constructed based on a bivariate rational interpolation method for a discrete image. For the random point $f_{i,j}$ in an image, our concern is how to construct the white points in a rectangular cell. First, the interpolation data must be ascertained. The data points are $\sum_{r=0}^{2}\sum_{s=0}^{2} f_{r,s},\ r,s = 0,1,2$. Then, based on the α_i and β_j values, we can obtain the interpolation function $P_1(x,y)$by substitution of the interpolation data into Equation (3). Finally, the function values of the white points are calculated by proper x and y.

3.3. Parameters Optimization

For image interpolation based on the rational function, the following optimal equation is derived from Equation (3).

$$\max grad(P_{i,j}(x,y)) = \max \sqrt{\frac{\partial P^2}{\partial x} + \frac{\partial P^2}{\partial y}}$$

then

$$\max grad(P_{i,j}(x,y)) \doteq \max \left(\left|\frac{\partial P}{\partial x}\right| + \left|\frac{\partial P}{\partial y}\right|\right).$$

Denote

$$F(\theta, \alpha_i; \eta, \beta_j) = |\frac{\partial P}{\partial x}| + |\frac{\partial P}{\partial y}|$$

the following equation is derived.

$$\max\ F(\theta, \alpha_i; \eta, \beta_j) \quad s.t.\ \alpha_i > 0, \beta_j > 0 \tag{5}$$

the parameters α_i, β_j are satisfied with the above equation as the optimal solution. The optimal parameters α_i, β_j are denoted by α_i^*, β_j^*.

It must be pointed out that some interpolated image pixels are varied by selecting parameters α_i^*, β_j^*. $P_{i,j}(x,y)$ defined by 3 should satisfy the boundary property, and the interpolating patch can be modified when the parameters are different.

Furthermore, for the interpolated image, it also satisfies $0 \le P_{i,j}(x,y) \le 255$. For the case of the maximum value of $P_{i,j}(x,y) > 255$, assume that $P_{i,j}(x,y)$ reaches its maximum value $P_{i,j}^*(x,y)$ at point (x^*, y^*) in subregion $[x_i, x_{i+1}; y_j, y_{j+1}]$; i.e., $P_{i,j}(x^*, y^*) > 255$, $P_{i,j}(x,y)$ should be redefined by

$$255 \times \frac{P_{i,j}(x,y)}{P_{i,j}(x^*,y^*)}.$$

4. EXPERIMENTS

Experiments were conducted to evaluate the effectiveness of the interpolation algorithm. We compare three state-of-the-art interpolation algorithms, including NEDI [6], DFDF [7], SAI [13]. All experiments are performed with software provided by the authors of these algorithms. In our experiments, the four gray images shown in Figure 3 are applied to test visual effects.

Table 1 gives the Peak Signal to Noise Ratio (PSNRs) and Structural Similarity Index (SSIMs) generated by all algorithms for the images. It can be seen that the proposed method has a higher average PSNR and SSIM among the compared algorithms.

Figure 3. Images used for quantitative comparison. (**a**) Light-tower; (**b**) Dollar; (**c**) Cliff; (**d**) Barbara.

Figure 4. (**a**) Original Image; (**b**) NEDI; (**c**) DFDF; (**d**) SAI; (**e**) Proposed Method.

Table 1. Peak Signal to Noise Ratio (PSNR) and Structural Similarity Index (SSIM) results of the reconstructed high-resolution (HR) images by different methods.

	NEDI		DFDF		SAI		Our Method	
	PSNR	SSIM	PSNR	SSIM	PSNR	SSIM	PSNR	SSIM
Light-tower	22.78	0.7937	23.25	0.7971	22.86	0.8005	23.37	0.8009
Dollar	19.10	0.8084	19.21	0.8066	19.24	0.8055	19.36	0.8118
Cliff	25.08	0.7115	25.05	0.7184	25.16	0.7233	25.22	0.7268
Barbara	22.35	0.8513	23.64	0.8766	23.54	0.8635	24.12	0.8801
Milkdrop	30.97	0.9156	34.36	0.9196	32.39	0.9176	34.48	0.9216
Couple	28.65	0.9391	29.06	0.9413	29.32	0.9443	29.14	0.9420
Goldhill	26.60	0.7645	26.69	0.7678	26.92	0.7772	26.92	0.7750
Door	33.12	0.9446	33.08	0.9447	31.16	0.9467	33.20	0.9478
Sky	28.41	0.9154	28.95	0.8608	29.05	0.9364	28.96	0.9378
Boat	25.82	0.8941	25.54	0.8378	25.43	0.9120	25.61	0.8973
Average	25.22	0.8207	25.74	0.8225	25.58	0.8326	25.98	0.8384

NEDI: new edge-directed interpolation; SAI: a soft-decision estimationtechnique for adaptive image interpolation; DFDF: directional filtering and data fusion.

We performed tests on natural images to show the improvements of the proposed method in the visual effects. Figure 4, Figure 5 and Figure 6 show the comparison of interpolation in test images. In Figure 5, all of the interpolation algorithms had aliasing in texture, but our method gave less. In Figure 6, we can see that NEDI suffers from some noisy interpolation artifacts.

The SAI method also suffers from noisy artifacts. Our method had better performance in maintaining image features. As shown in Figure 7 and Figure 8, shape loss and noisy points. were introduced in images of a door and fence by the use of NEDI and SAI. The DFDF algorithm also introduced some errors of edge and texture.

In general, experimental results on benchmark test images demonstrate that the proposed method achieved very competitive performance with the state-of-art interpolation algorithms, especially in image details and texture features.

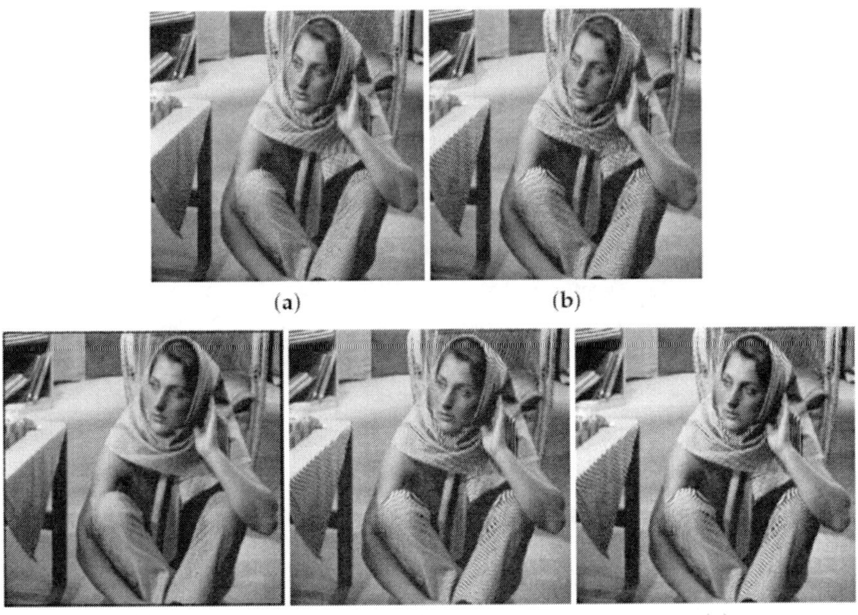

Figure 5. (**a**) Original Image; (**b**) NEDI; (**c**) DFDF; (**d**) SAI; (**e**) Proposed Method.

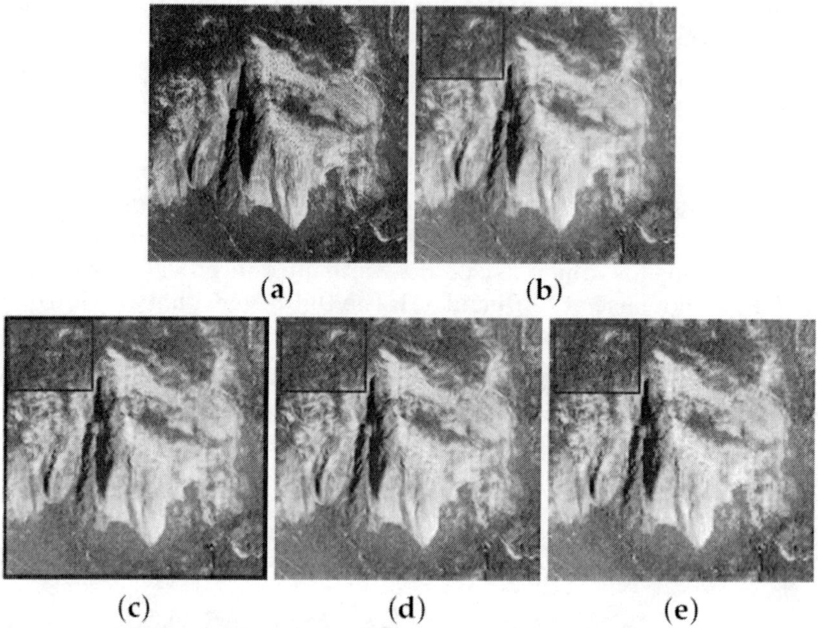

Figure 6. (**a**) Original Image; (**b**) NEDI; (**c**) DFDF; (**d**) SAI; (**e**) Proposed Method.

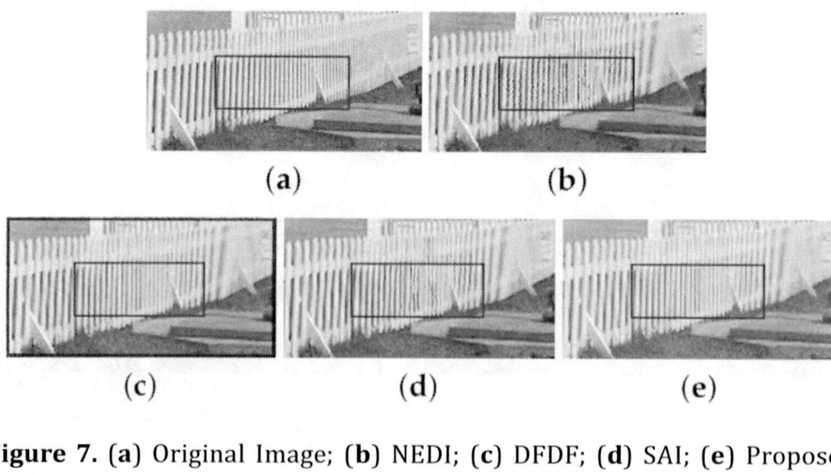

Figure 7. (**a**) Original Image; (**b**) NEDI; (**c**) DFDF; (**d**) SAI; (**e**) Proposed Method.

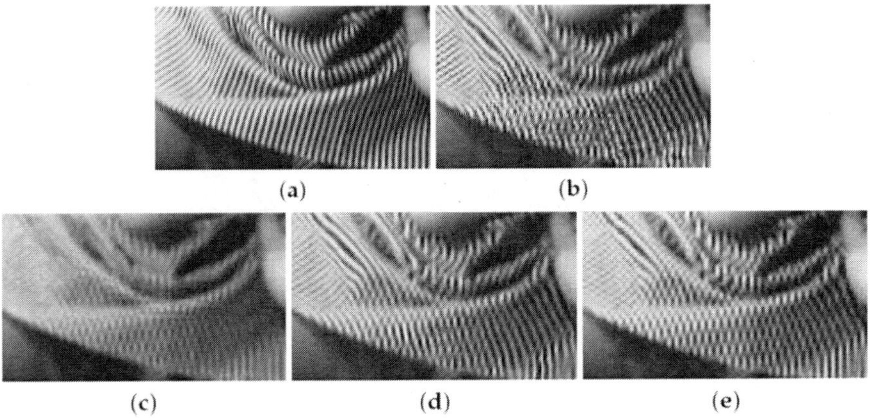

Figure 8. (**a**) Original Image; (**b**) NEDI; (**c**) DFDF; (**d**) SAI; (**e**) Proposed Method.

5. CONCLUSIONS

Although image interpolation is not the most advanced research subject, research results in this field have come forth continuously in recent years. They are usually based on relatively simple theory and have broad applicability However, the interpolation expression forms are various. Therefore, according to the advantages of the different interpolation methods, we can take advantage of these methods and get good results. However, these combination methods have complicated forms, and do not meet the needs of timeliness and practicality. Basically, these methods often neglect the natural image attributes. The main contributions of our method are not combination, but adopting function constructed in Section 2. In this process, non-smooth area detection, image interpolation in different regions, and visual perception are merged into one interpolation function model. The image details and texture features are preserved by using this algorithm, and it can help to describe the image more objectively; hence, more features of the image can be preserved.

ACKNOWLEDGMENTS

This work was supported by National Natural Science Foundation of China (No. 61373080,61672018), the Fostering Project of Dominant Discipline and Talent Team of Shandong Province Higher Education

Institutions and Natural Science Foundation of Shandong Province (No. ZR2015AM007).

REFERENCES

1. Wu, J.; Anisetti, M.; Wu, W.; Damiani, E.; Jeon, G. Bayer demosaicking with polynomial interpolation. *J. IEEE Trans. Image Process.* **2016**, *25*, 5369–5382.
2. Pan, H.; Zou, Z.; Zhang, G.; Zhu, X. A penalized spline-based attitude model for high-resolution satellite imagery. *J. IEEE Trans. Geosci. Remote Sens.* **2016**, *54*, 1849–1959.
3. Su, D.; Willis, P. Image interpolation by pixel-level data-dependent triangulation. *Comput. Graph. Forum* **2004**, *23*, 189–201.
4. Keys, R.G. Cubic convolution interpolation for digital image processing. *IEEE Trans. Acoust. Speech Signal Process.* **1981**, *29*, 1153–1160.
5. Hou, H.; Andrews, H. Cubic splines for image interpolation and digital filtering. *IEEE Trans. Acoust. Speech Signal Process.* **1978**, *26*, 508–517.
6. Li, X.; Orchard, M.T. New edge-directed interpolation. *IEEE Trans. Image Process.* **2001**, *15*, 1521–1527.
7. Zhang, L.; Wu, X. Image interpolation via directional filtering and data fusion. *IEEE Trans. Image Process.* **2001**, *10*, 1521–1527.
8. Battiato, S.; Stanco, F. Alz: Adaptive learning for zooming digital images. In Proceedings of the International Conference on Consumer Electronics (ICCE 2007), Las Vegas, NV, USA, 10–14 January 2007.
9. Takeda, H.; Farsiu, S.; Milanfar, P. Kernel regression for image processing and reconstruction. *IEEE Trans. Image Process.* **2007**, *16*, 349–366.
10. Battiato, S.; Giuffrida, E.U.; Rundo, F. A cellular neural network for zooming digital colour images. In Proceedings of the International Conference on Consumer Electronics (ICCE 2008), Las Vegas, NV, USA, 9–13 January 2008.
11. Giachetti, A.; Asuni, N. Fast artifacts-free image interpolation. In Proceedings of the 2008 British Machine Vision Conference, Leeds, UK, 4–9 September 2008.
12. Asuni, N.; Giachetti, A. Accuracy improvements and artifacts removal in edge based image interpolation. In Proceedings of the 3rd International Conference on Computer Vision Theory and Applications, Funchal, Portugal, 1 July 2008.
13. Zhang, X.; Wu, X. Image interpolation by adaptive 2-d autoregressive modeling and soft-decision estimation. *IEEE Trans. Image Process.* **2008**, *17*, 887–896.
14. Liu, X.; Zhao, D.; Xiong, R.; Ma, S.; Gao, W.; Sun, H. Image interpolation via regularized local linear regression. *IEEE Trans. Image Process.* **2011**, *20*, 3455–3469.
15. Jeong, S.; Yoon, I.; Jeon, J.; Paik, J. Multi-frame example-based super-resolution using locally directional self-similarity. In Proceedings of the IEEE International Conference on Consumer Electronics, Las Vegas, NV, USA, 9–12 January 2015; pp. 353–358.
16. Jha, A.K.; Kumar, A.; Schaefer, G.; Ahad, M.A.R. An adaptive distance-based edge preserving interpolation algorithm for natural images. In Proceedings of the 2015 IEEE International Conference on Informatics, Electronics and Vision, Fukuoka, Japan, 15–18 June 2015.
17. Jensen, K.; Anastassiou, D. Subpixel edge localization and the interpolation of still images. *IEEE Trans. Image Process.* **1995**, *4*, 285–295.
18. Carrato, S.; Tenze, L. A high quality 2 x image interpolator. *IEEE Signal Process. Lett.* **2000**, *7*, 132–135.
19. Woods, J.W. Two-dimensional discrete markovian fields. *IEEE Trans. Inf. Theory* **1972**, *18*, 232–240.
20. Said, A.; Pearlman, W.A. A new, fast and efficient image codec based on set partitioning of hierarchical trees. *IEEE Trans. Circuits Syst. Video Technol.* **1996**, *6*, 243–250.

21. Nyiri, E.; Gibaru, O.; Auquiert, P. Fast L1-ck polynomial spline interpolation algorithm with shape-preserving properties. *Comput. Aided Geom. Des.* **2011**, *28*, 65–74.
22. Zhu, C.; Wang, R.; Shi, X.; Liu, F. Functional splines with different degrees of smoothness and their applications. *Comput. Aided Des.* **2008**, *40*, 616–624.
23. Wang, R.; Lang, F. Special multivariate quadratic spline space. *Math. Comput. Model.* **2009**, *49*, 760–769.
24. Duan, Q.; Zhang, Y.; Twizell, E. A bivariate rational interpolation and the properties. *Appl. Math. Comput.* **2006**, *179*, 190–199.
25. Zhang, Y.; Duan, Q.; Twizell, E. Convexity control of a bivariate rational interpolating spline surfaces. *Comput. Graph.***2007**, *31*, 679–687.
26. Duan, Q.; Bao, F.; Zhang, Y. Shape control of a bivariate interpolating spline surface. *Int. J. Comput. Math.* **2008**, *85*, 813–825.
27. Zhang, Y.; Bao, F.; Zhang, C.; Qi, D. A weighted bivariate blending rational interpolation function and visualization control. *J. Comput. Anal. Appl.* **2012**, *14*, 1303–1321.
28. Zhang, Y.; Bao, F.; Zhang, C.; Duan, Q. Local shape control of a bivariate rational interpolating surface with mixing conditions. In Proceedings of the 2011 Eighth International Symposium on Voronoi Diagrams in Science and Engineering (ISVD), Qing Dao, China, 28–30 June 2011; pp. 200–205.
29. Sun, Q.; Bao, F.; Zhang, Y.; Duan, Q. A bivariate rational interpolation based on scattered data on parallel lines. *J. Vis. Commun. Image Represent.* **2013**, *24*, 75–80.

CHAPTER 16

Design Optimization of the Lines of the Bulbous Bow of a Hull Based on Parametric Modeling and Computational Fluid Dynamics Calculation

Weilin Luo[1,2,*] and Linqiang Lan[1]

[1] *School of Mechanical Engineering and Automation, Fuzhou University, Fuzhou 350116, China*

[2] *Fujian Province Key Laboratory of Structural Performances in Ship and Ocean Engineering, Fuzhou 350116, China*

ABSTRACT

To reduce the ship wave-making resistance, the lines of the bulbous bow of a hull are optimized by an automatic optimization platform at the ship design stage. Parametric modeling was applied to the hull by using non-uniform rational basis spline (NURBS). The Rankine-source panel method was used to calculate the wave-making resistance. A hybrid optimization strategy was applied to achieve the optimization goal. A Ro-Ro ship was taken as an example to illustrate the optimization method adopted, with the objective to minimize the wave-making resistance. The optimization results show that wave-making resistance obviously reduces and the wave-shape of the near bow becomes gentle after the lines of the bulbous bow of the hull are optimized, which demonstrates the validity of the proposed optimization design strategy.

Keywords: hull forms optimization; parametric modeling; computational fluid dynamics calculation; wave-making resistance

1. INTRODUCTION

Design of ship hull forms is one of the most important contents of the general ship design. How to reduce the ship resistance by means of well-designed forms is always the concern for ship designers and/or researchers. The parent ship based design method predominates in the field of ship design, by which the designed hull can inherit some excellent performance from the parent ship. For a long time, designer's experience played an important role in obtaining the desired hull forms. With the development of computer science and technology, the quality of ship design has been improved considerably by introducing some computational numerical calculation methods. For example, computational fluid dynamics (CFD) based numerical simulation can be used to evaluate the hydrodynamic performances of a ship after the hull forms are designed. By modifying the hull forms and repeatedly performing CFD simulation, the satisfactory hull forms can be obtained. To improve the design efficiency, computer aided design (CAD) was proposed to combine with CFD in the optimization design of hull forms [1]. During the past decade, CAD/CFD integrated hull-form design systems have been developed and successfully applied to the drag reduction of ships [2]. For example, Percival et al. combined a simple CFD tool and B-Spline method to the optimization design of a Wigley ship [3]. Yusuke et al. presented the bulbous bow optimization of a container ship based on the naval architectural package (NAPA) system and a Rankine-source panel method [1]. Tahara et al. applied NAPA and a RANS (Reynolds-averaged Navier–Stokes) solver to the optimization design of a container ship [4]. Abt and Harries presented the generic, multi-objective ship design optimization based on software of the Ship Design Laboratory of the National Technical University of Athens (NTUA–SDL) in which well-established naval architectural and optimization software packages are integrated [5]. Harries and Abt distinguished three types of coupling of CAD and CFD [6]. Couser et al. explored the multi-dimensional design-space using first-principle methods within the FRIENDSHIP framework [7]. Brizzolara and Vernengo proposed an integration of a parametric generation module, a multi-objective optimization algorithm and a CFD solver in the optimization of a new unmanned surface vehicle (USV) and small waterplane area twin hull (SWATH) [8]. Biliotti et al. presented a fully automatic optimization chain to the optimization of fast naval vessels by adopting the *ModeFrontier* optimization environment to the FRIENDSHIP framework, the CFD codes and a multi-objective genetic algorithm [9]. Ginnis et al. employed the NURBS (non-uniform rational basis spline) method and Kelvin-source method to the optimization of a container ship [10]. Brenner et al. used the FRIENDSHIP-SHIPFLOW optimization scheme to retrofit the ships in operation [11]. Zakerdoost et al. used the NURBS method and potential theory to the optimization design of a Wigley ship [12]. Vernengo et al. presented the optimization of a Semi-SWATH by a fully parametric model of the unconventional hull form, a 3D linear Rankine-sources panel method, and a multiobjective global convergence genetic algorithm [13]. Combined with the optimization of a high speed round bilge monohull, Brizzolara et al. addressed the significance of parametric hull form definition by comparing it with Free Form Deformation technique [14]. Ang et al. proposed the Free Form Deformation and potential theory to the optimization design of a heavy-lift and pipe-lay vessel [15]. Wang proposed the NURBS method and CFD calculation based on Neumann–Michell theory to the optimization design of several life ships [16].

Besides the parametric modeling of hull forms and calculation of hydrodynamic performances, optimization is another important factor in the hull-form design system. To guarantee the optimum design and the solving efficiency, an appropriate optimization algorithm is vital to the optimizer. During the last several decades, many optimization algorithms have been proposed such as successive quadratic programming (SQP) [17], genetic algorithm (GA) [18], simulated annealing (SA) [19], particle swarm optimization (PSO) [20], infeasibility driven evolutionary algorithm (IDEA) [21], and quasi-Newton method [10], among others. Generally, these algorithms can be categorized into gradient-based and derivative-free methods [22]. For the gradient-based optimization algorithms (e.g., SQP and quasi-Newton approaches), the interest is the fast convergence; however, the limitation is the locally optimal solution. For the derivative-free optimization algorithms (e.g., GA, SA, PSO, and IDEA approaches), the advantage is the global optimization; however, the convergence rate cannot be guaranteed. Since each optimization algorithm has its advantages and disadvantages, a hybrid optimization scheme should be preferable. In this paper, we perform the combination of a global optimization method (Ensemble Investigation) and a local optimization method (T-Search algorithm) to the optimization design of hull forms of a surface ship. The design optimization is carried out in the SHIPFLOW-CAESES (former FRIENDSHIP) DESIGN environment. Based on the automatic optimization platform, the parametric modeling and the CFD calculation are integrated. The NURBS method is employed to the parametric modeling while the Rankine-source panel method is applied to calculate the wave-making resistance. The minimization of the wave-making resistance is taken as the optimization objective while the design variables are form parameters of the lines of the bulbous bow.

The rest of the paper is organized as follows. In Section 2, the parametric modeling method is introduced; in Section 3, the CFD method to calculate the wave-making resistance is described; in Section 4, the hybrid optimization algorithm is addressed; in Section 5, the entire optimization scheme is described; in Section 6, an example is studied to confirm the validity of the optimization strategy proposed in the study; and the final section is the concluding remarks.

2. PARAMETRIC MODELING OF HULL FORMS

In the geometry modeling of a hull, it is often required to obtain the forms rapidly. In addition, a large number of forms should be analyzed so that the optimization can be efficiently performed. In this paper, the NURBS method is employed to meet the mentioned requirements. Based on this method, the high-quality of the lines can be guaranteed with fairly less design variables than conventional design methodology. This method provides the best way to establish the relationship between parameters and hull forms and makes sure that the design variation among the entire optimization process is effective and feasible. The parametric model is generated by CAESES-Modeler. The process of curves generation starts with a set of given data elements that are used to define the complete parametric curve.

Within the modeler, one can define a set of longitudinal lines and express them as basic curves to describe the ship hull by means of differential, integral and topological information. Transversal basic curves are able to be formed as soon as the longitudinal basic curves are defined (by fair B-Spline parametric curves adopted in the study). Then, a series of surfaces can be set up by corresponding transversal sections that stem from the parametric hull model. Generally, the design of the fully parametric hull surfaces makes it possible to transform the hull form efficiently and effectively. Moreover, all of the hull topologies, the hull sections and the whole hull surface can be generated using the basic curves specifically and precisely.

Usually, the hull forms are described by feature curves [23], e.g., the design waterline, flat of side, flat of bottom, etc., which are listed in Table 1 and some of the curves are shown in Figure 1.

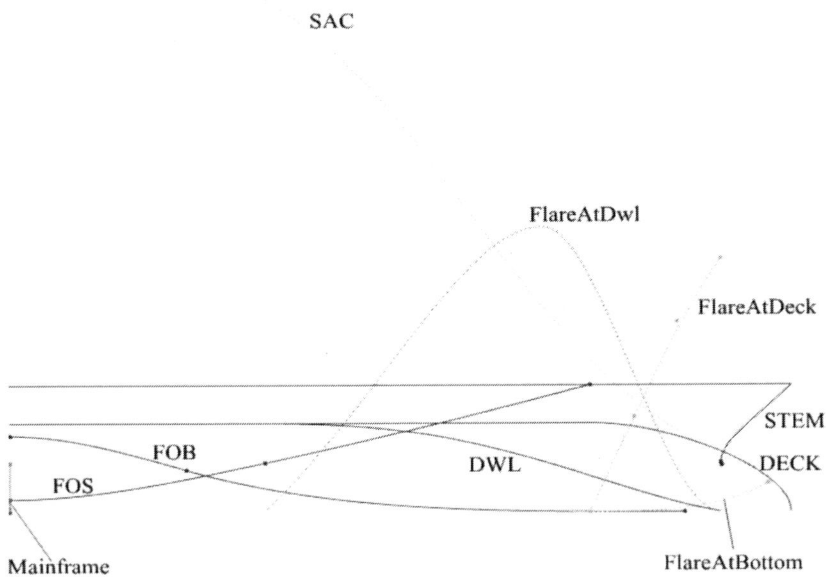

Figure 1. Basic feature curves describing hull forms.

Table 1. Basic feature curves describing hull forms.

Characteristic	Curve	Abbreviation
Position	Design waterline	DWL
	Deck line	DEC
	Flat of side curve	FOS
	Flat of bottom curve	FOB
	Center plane curve	CPC
Tangent angle	Tangent angle at beginning and end	TAB, TAE
Curvature	Curvature at beginning and end	CAB,CAE
Area	Sectional area curve	SAC
Centroid of area	Vertical and Lateral moments of sectional area	VMS, LMS

For the bulbous bow, the basic feature curves include: the top longtitudinal section line, the low longtitudinal section line, the half beam line, and the height line of the maximal breadth, as shown in Figure 2. The shape of the bulbous bow can be modified by changing these basic feature curves that can be achieved by controlling design variables. Figure 3 presents an example of the variation of the shape of a bulbous bow by modifying these feature curves.

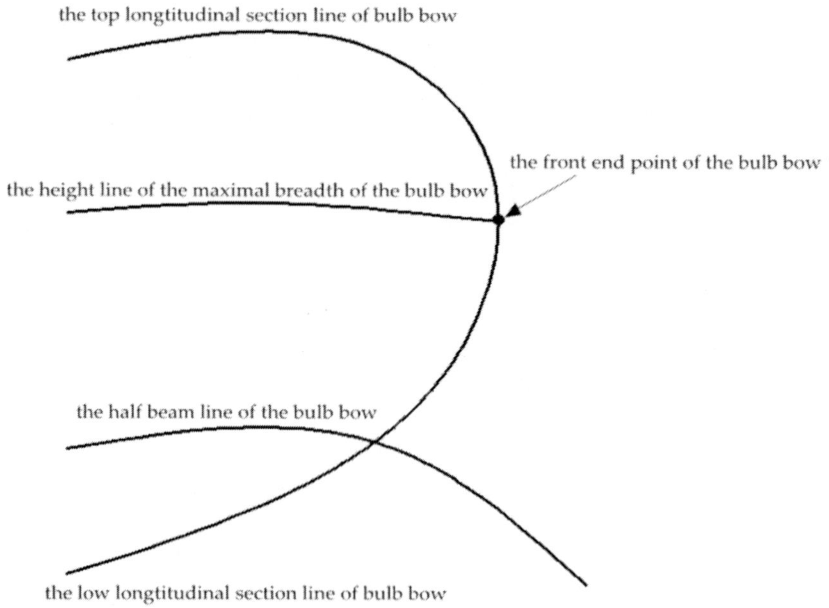

Figure 2. The basic feature curves of a bulbous bow.

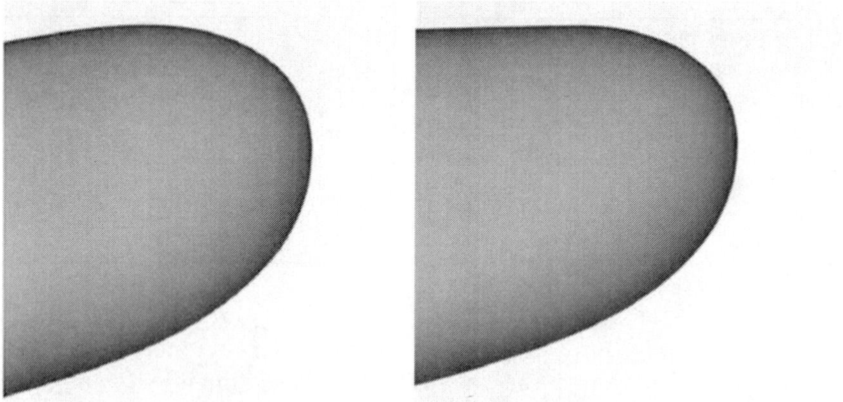

Figure 3. Transformation of a bulb bow: **left**, plot-original; **right**, plot-modified.

Using the NURBS method, curves can be expressed as [24]:

$$Q(t) = \begin{pmatrix} x(t) \\ y(t) \end{pmatrix} = \frac{\sum\limits_{i=0}^{n} w_i N_{i,k}(t) d_i}{\sum\limits_{i=0}^{n} w_i N_{i,k}(t)}, \quad 0 \leq t \leq 1 \tag{1}$$

where n is the number vertex points, w_i is the weight, d_i is the control point, and $N_{i,k}(t)$ is the B-Spline basis function. For the hull forms, a NURBS surface is a bi-variate vector-valued piecewise rational function as [24]:

$$S(u,v) = \begin{pmatrix} x(u,v) \\ y(u,v) \\ z(u,v) \end{pmatrix} = \frac{\sum\limits_{i=0}^{n}\sum\limits_{j=0}^{m} N_{i,p}(u) N_{j,q}(v) w_{i,j} P_{i,j}}{\sum\limits_{i=0}^{n}\sum\limits_{j=0}^{m} N_{i,p}(u) N_{j,q}(v) w_{i,j}}, \quad 0 \leq u, v \leq 1 \tag{2}$$

where $P_{i,j}$ forms a bidirectional control net [12]. $N_{i,p}(u)$ and $N_{j,q}(v)$ are B-Spline basis functions in the direction of $\vec{U} = \{u_0, \cdots, u_{n+p+1}\}$ and $\vec{V} = \{v_0, \cdots, v_{m+q+1}\}$, respectively.

The hull forms can be expressed parametrically by using the form parameters to constitute the feature curves and hull section frames. The general procedure to generate fairing surfaces of the hull form observes four steps, as presented in Figure 4. First, the form parameters should be suitably selected. Second, the parametric design of the longitudinal feature curves is performed. Third, transversal feature curves can be similarly generated and a set of surfaces can be derived by means of interpolation. Finally, fairing form variations can be obtained [23]. It should be noted that the number and the range of the form parameters should be selected carefully to prevent any distortion of the ship. In the study, eight form parameters are selected for the generation of the bulbous bow. More details about these parameters are presented in the Example Study section.

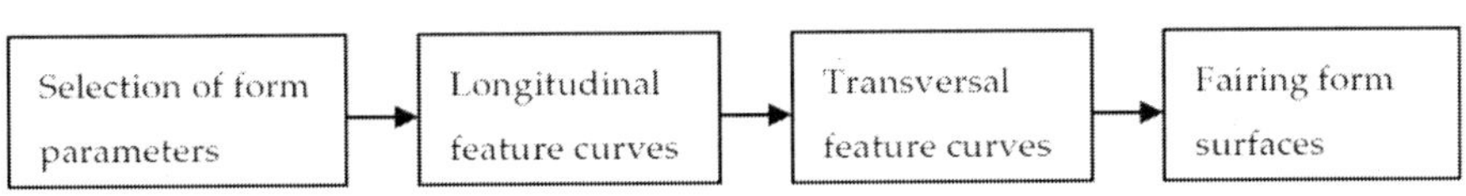

Figure 4. Parametric modeling of a hull form.

3. CALCULATION OF WAVE-MAKING RESISTANCE

In the study, the optimization objective is to minimize the wave-making resistance. Suppose the fluid is inviscid and incompressible, and Rankine-source panel method is employed.

For a ship traveling with a steady forward speed U in the calm water of infinite depth, the wave-making velocity potential $\phi(x,y,z)$ satisfies the following equations:

$$\text{in the fluid domain}: \quad \nabla^2\phi = 0 \tag{3}$$

$$\text{on the free surface}: = \frac{1}{g}\left(-U_s \cdot \nabla\phi + \frac{1}{2}\nabla\phi \cdot \nabla\phi\right) \tag{4}$$

$$\text{on the free surface}: \left(\nabla\phi - U_s \cdot \vec{n}\right) \cdot \nabla\xi = \phi_z \tag{5}$$

$$\text{on the hull surface}: \frac{\partial\phi}{\partial n} = U_s \cdot \vec{n} \tag{6}$$

$$\text{at infinity}: \quad \nabla\phi = (0,0,0) \tag{7}$$

where $U_s = (U,0,0)$, g is the acceleration of gravity, and ξ is the free surface elevation.

The velocity potential at the field point P can be calculated as [25]

$$\phi(P) = -\frac{1}{4\pi}\iint_{SB}\sigma(Q)\left(\frac{1}{r(P,Q)} + \frac{1}{r'(P,Q')}\right)ds - \frac{1}{4\pi}\iint_{SF}\sigma(Q)\left(\frac{1}{r(P,Q)} + \frac{1}{r'(P,Q')}\right)ds \tag{8}$$

where Q and Q' are source points, $\sigma(Q)$ is the source strength, and r and r' are the distances between the field point and source points.

When the ship is sailing, the wave is steep and the floating state cannot be neglected. Therefore, the nonlinear free surface boundary condition should be used. The method of Taylor series expansion is applied to Equations (4) and (5) by making use of the approximate solution $z = Z$ and $\varphi = \phi$. Then, the boundary condition on the approximate free surface can be obtained as:

$$\left[2(\nabla A - U\nabla\varphi_1) + \vec{W}B\right]\cdot\nabla\phi + \vec{W}\cdot\left[\left(\vec{W}\cdot\nabla\right)\nabla\varphi\right] + g\phi_z = 2\nabla\varphi\cdot[\nabla A - U\nabla\varphi_1] + B(A - gZ) \quad (9)$$

$$\xi = Z + \frac{\vec{W}\cdot\nabla\phi - A + gZ}{\vec{W}\cdot\nabla\varphi_z - g} \quad (10)$$

where $\vec{W} = \nabla\phi - U_s$, $A = \frac{1}{2}\nabla\varphi\cdot\nabla\varphi$ and $B = \frac{\left[\vec{W}\cdot(\nabla A - U\nabla\varphi_x) + g\varphi_z\right]_z}{\vec{W}\cdot\nabla\varphi_z - g}$.

The boundary condition on the ship surface is:

$$\nabla\phi\cdot\vec{n} = Un_1 \quad (11)$$

Based on Bernoulli equation, the pressure can be calculated as

$$p = \rho(U\phi_x - (\nabla\phi\cdot\nabla\phi)/2 + gz) \quad (12)$$

where U is the ship velocity, and ρ is the fluid density. By integrating the pressure along the wetted boundary surface, one has the hydrodynamic force on the hull as

$$\vec{F} = (F_1, F_2, F_3) = \iint_{SB} p\vec{n}\,dS \quad (13)$$

Thus, the wave-making resistance and its nondimensional form can be obtained as

$$R_w = -F_1 = -\iint_{SB} pn_1 dS \quad (14)$$

and

$$C_w = \frac{R_w}{0.5\rho U^2 S_0} \quad (15)$$

respectively, where S_0 is the wetted surface area in calm waters. C_w is also named as the coefficient of wave-making resistance.

4. OPTIMIZATION ALGORITHMS

To guarantee the globally optimal solution and solving efficiency as well, a hybrid algorithm is applied in the study. Ensemble Investigation is employed to obtain the globally optimal solution. This algorithm allows permuting a set of design variables and generating DOE (design of experiments) tables, which is very effective to gather information about the optimization problem investigated in the whole design space. Generated DOE tables are useful to detect the trends of the optimization variables with regard to the optimization objectives, irrespective of constraints [26]. This optimization approach is performed by creating several different versions of a proposed new design, and then selecting the option that best fits the design goals. The generation of a systematic series of design options can be completed soon. These options are tested against design goals—for example, the hydrodynamic performance. Computational techniques such as regression analysis can be used to determine the "best" option.

To improve the efficiency of solution-searching, the T-Search algorithm is incorporated. This algorithm is a method of feasible direction. It uses a direct search until some constraint gets violated. At the expense of a little extra effort, T-Search is characterized by efficient operation within the admissible region with satisfactory performance along the boundary of that region [27]. The other two features of the algorithm are the allowance made for small perturbations of the base point and the flexible directions for exploration in the tangent hyperspace [28]. It consists of exploratory moves that start from a so-called base point along the variable axes followed by global moves in the descent search direction found in successful exploratory moves. If a constraint bound is approached, then it returns to the last admissible point and performs a unidirectional optimization along the hyperplane tangent to the active constraint either to keep the search in the feasible domain or to bring it back to the feasible domain. T-Search is able to find the local minimum of an arbitrary, explicitly-stated function of more than one variable, subject to arbitrary, non-linear constraints.

5. OPTIMIZATION SCHEME

5.1. Optimization Goal and Design Variables

The optimization objective in the study is to minimize the wave-making resistance under designed ship velocity, i.e., min$\{C_w\}$. The constraints are set to be subject to (1) $|\Delta_0 - \Delta_p|/\Delta_0 \leq 1\%$ where Δ_0 is the initial displacement, and Δ_p is the displacement of optimized ship; (2) $|LCB_0 - LCB_p|/LCB_0 \leq 1\%$, where LCB_0 is the initial longitudal coordiante of the boyance center while LCB_p is the longitudal coordiante of boyance center of the optimized ship; and (3) the ship length, breadth and draft are constant during the optimization process.

Since the lines of the bulbous bow are vital to the wave-making resistance, the design variables are selected as form control parameters of bulbous bow, including the distance between the center of the bulb bow and the front end of the bulb bow (D_{cf}); the height of the front end of the bulb bow (H_f); the contour fullness of the top longtitudinal section of bulb bow (F_{tl}) and its coefficient (C_{ftl}); the contour fullness of the low longtitudinal section of bulb bow (F_{ll}) and its coefficient (C_{fll}); the contour fullness at the half beam of the bulb bow (F_{hb}); and half of the maximal breadth of the bulb bow (B_h).

These form control parameters are used to generate the basic feature curves of the bulbous bow, as shown in Figure 2.

5.2. Optimization Framework

In the optimization framework, there are mainly three modules: the parametric modeling, CFD calculation and lines modification. The optimization operation is performed in the SHIPFLOW-CAESES DESIGN environment. First, NURBS based parametric modeling is performed in the CAESES and the lines offsets of the given hull can be obtained. Then, the files of the lines of offsets are automatically imported into the SHIPFLOW so that the CFD calculation can be carried out. Afterwards, the CFD results are imported to CAESES as comparison with the optimization objective.

If the optimization goal is achieved, the lines are exported as the optimal lines; otherwise, the design variables are modified based on the hybrid optimization algorithm, and the optimization operation is repeated until the optimization goal is achieved. For general procedure, the optimization design is presented in Figure 5.

It is noted that a batch file is necessary to connect SHIPFLOW and CAESES applications. SHIPFLOW provides the batch file in the installation package. The batch file includes echo commands, pause commands, call commands, start commands, go-to commands, and set commands. There is a boundary of surface between the surface of the bulbous bow and the surface of the front part of hull. This boundary is maintained between optimization circles so that the bulbous bow can connect to the front part of hull smoothly.

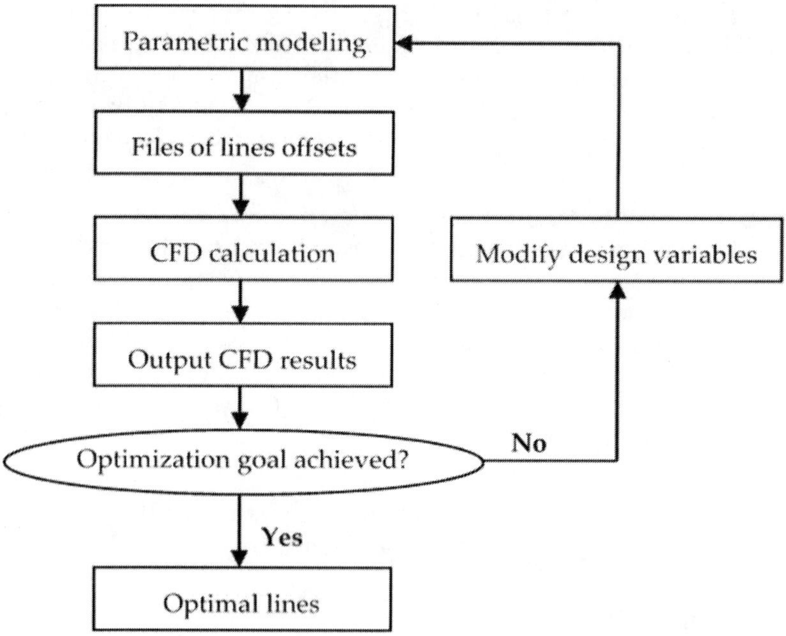

Figure 5. Optimization procedure.

6. EXAMPLE STUDY

A Ro-Ro ship is investigated to verify the optimization scheme proposed in the study. The main particulars of the ship are listed in Table 2. The ship velocity is 22 knots. In terms of Froude number, one has $Fr = 0.28$.

Table 2. Main particulars of a Ro-Ro ship.

Description	Variable	Value
Length (m)	L	165
Breadth (m)	B	24.8
Draft (m)	d	8.7
Block coefficient	C_b	0.65

In the CAESES framework, the form parameters are imported to the curve generator to obtain a set of feature curves. Then, fairing surfaces can be derived automatically through a surface generator. The parameterized hull surfaces are shown in Figure 6.

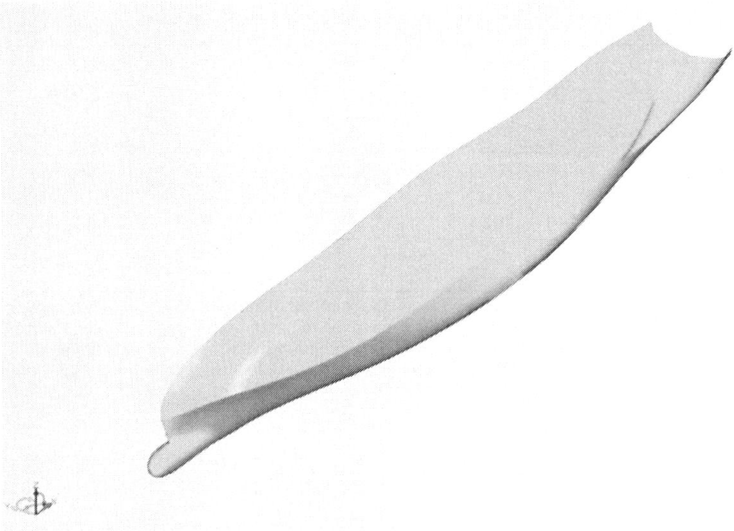

Figure 6. Hull surfaces of the Ro-Ro ship.

Based on the optimization framework shown in Figure 5, the hybrid optimization algorithm is performed. In detail, the Ensemble Investigation is employed to obtain feasible solutions in the whole design space. A set of optimized hull forms that satisfy the constraints are derived. Then, the T-Search algorithm is used within the set to determine the solution with minimal wave-making resistance. The design variables and their variations are listed in Table 3. The results of optimization objective and constraints are presented in Table 4.

As can be seen from the optimization results, the wave-making resistance is reduced by modifying the design variables while the constraints are satisfied. The initial values of design variables are one set of the feasible solutions family. The variation of the design variables indicates that smaller D_{cf} and F_{tl}, against larger H_f, C_{ftl}, F_{ll}, C_{fll}, F_{hb}, and B_h help reduce the wave-making resistance. The comparison of the wave contours on free surfaces before and after optimization is presented in Figure 7. The comparison of the longitudinal wave cuts before and after optimization is given as Figure 8. The right plot in Figure 7 presents the changes of wave contours on the forward part of the ship. Similarly, in Figure 8, the right plot highlights the changes of wave cuts on the area around the bulbous bow.

Table 3. Optimization results of the design variables.

Design Variable	Range	Initial Value	Optimized Value
D_{cf} (m)	[0, 1]	0.624	0.237
H_f (m)	[1, 5.5]	4.287	4.856
F_{tl}	[0.1, 0.6]	0.41	0.34
C_{ftl}	[0.52, 0.91]	0.73	0.842
F_{ll}	[1.12, 1.37]	1.28	1.31
C_{fll}	[0.65, 0.96]	0.85	0.943
F_{hb}	[1.4, 2.0]	1.64	1.873
B_h (m)	[2.1, 2.58]	2.301	2.384

D_{cf}, the distance between the center of the bulb bow and the front end of the bulb bow; H_f, the height of the front end of the bulb bow; F_{tl}, the contour fullness of the top longtitudinal section of the bulb bow; C_{ftl}, the coefficient of the contour fullness of the top longtitudinal section; F_{ll}, the contour fullness of the low longtitudinal section of the bulb bow; C_{fll}, the coefficient of the contour fullness of the low longtitudinal section; F_{hb}, the contour fullness at the half beam of the bulb bow; B_h, half of the maximal breadth of the bulb bow.

Table 4. Optimization results of the objective and constraints.

Description	Initial Value	Optimized Value	Variation
Nondimensional wave-making resistance, C_w	0.0020368	0.0019488	4.32% (↓)
Displacement, Δ(t)	22357.695	22382.706	0.112% (↑)
Longitudal coordiante of boyance center, LCB (m)	0.515798	0.515262	0.104% (↓)

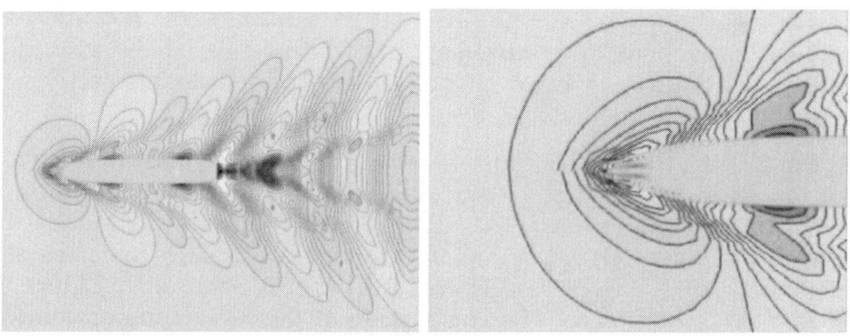

Figure 7. Comparison of the wave contours on free surfaces before and after optimization; upper part,—before optimization; lower part,—after optimization.

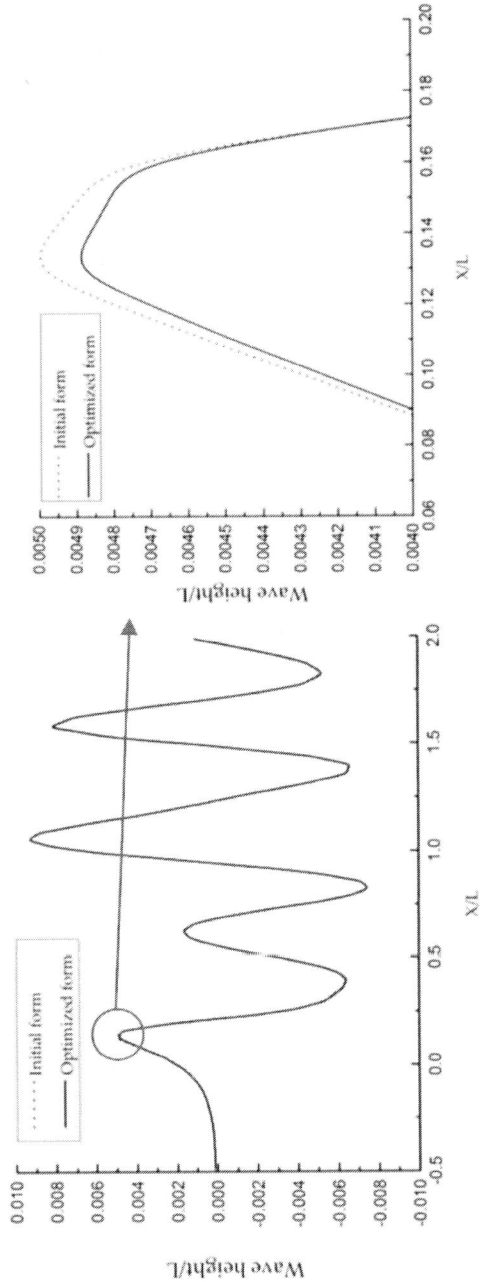

Figure 8. Comparison of the longitudinal wave cuts before and after optimization (y/L= 0.1). L, ship length; units in m/m.

As can be seen from the wave variation, the wave numbers and the wave amplitude decrease obviously around the bow after the lines of the bulb bow are optimized, which implies a decrease of wave-making resistance. Figure 9 and Figure 10present the variation of the lines of the bulb bow. In Figure 9, the left plot is the original form of the bulb bow, while the right plot is the optimized form. In Figure 10, the yellow lines represent the optimized results while the black lines are with the original form. From the comparison results, it can be indicated that a stretch of the bulb bow upwards helps reduce the wave-making resistance.

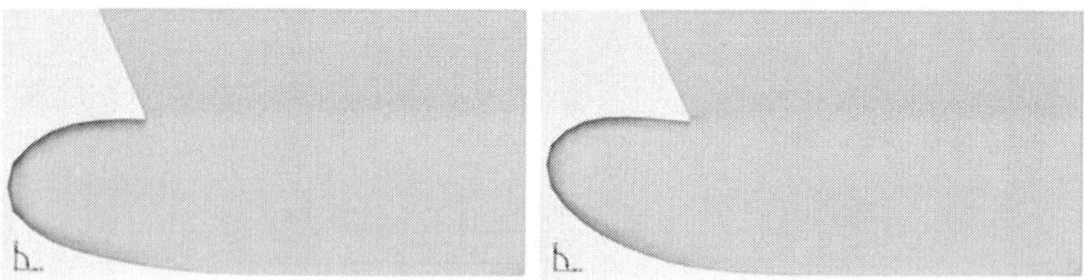

Figure 9. Comparison of the bulbous bows before and after optimization: left,—original; right,—optimized.

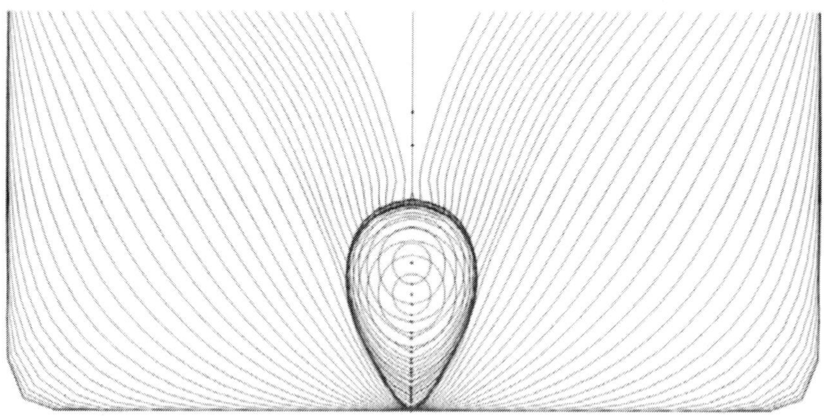

Figure 10. Comparison of the lines before and after optimization.

7. CONCLUSIONS

The combination of CFD and CAD improves the quality of ship hull form design. In this paper, an optimization design strategy is proposed based on SHIPFLOW-CAESES framework. The optimization results demonstrate the feasibility of using successfully different software systems in the optimization process. A fully automatic optimization integration framework is achieved by using CAESES coupled with CFD solver SHIPFLOW. Through the framework, the full parametric modeling of the hull, hydrodynamic calculation, design evaluation and shape variation are implemented effectively, which improves the quality and efficiency of ship design. The NURBS method is employed in the parametric modeling of the hull forms, while potential theory is used to calculate the wave-making resistance of the ship hull. To improve the optimization efficiency, a hybrid optimization scheme is taken. The validity of the proposed optimization design framework is confirmed by applying the optimization framework to a Ro-Ro ship. Based on the simulation results, some recommendations can be summarized as follows: (i) the smaller D_{cf} and F_{tl}, against larger H_f, C_{ftl}, F_{ll}, C_{fll}, F_{hb}, and $B_h$helps reduce the wave-making resistance; and (ii) a stretch of the bulb bow upwards also helps reduce the wave-making resistance.

In this study, only the bulbous bow optimization is concerned. In the next work, the optimization of the entire hull will be studied. Moreover, total resistance will be considered in the optimization design, instead of the only wave-making resistance. In addition, another calculation method for wave resistance, i.e., the wave cut analysis will be studied. As mentioned in literature, wave cut analysis provides a more accurate and robust solution. Moreover, for a planning hull, instead of the displacement hull that is investigated in the study, wave cut analysis might be preferable.

ACKNOWLEDGMENTS

This work was partially supported by the Special Item supported by the Fujian Provincial Department of Ocean and Fisheries (No. MHGX-16), and the Special Item for the University in Fujian Province supported by the Education Department (No. JK15003).

REFERENCES

1. Yusuke, T.; Sugimoto, S.; Shinya, M. Development of CAD/CFD/optimizer-integrated hull-form design system. *J. Kansai Soc. Naval Archit.* **2003**, *240*, 29–36.
2. Ahmadzadehtalatapeh, M.; Mousavi, M. A review on the drag reduction methods of the ship hulls for improving the hydrodynamic performance. *Int. J. Marit. Technol.* **2015**, *4*, 51–64.
3. Percival, S.; Hendix, D.; Noblesse, F. Hydrodynamic optimization of ship hull forms. *Appl. Ocean Res.* **2001**, *23*, 337–355.

4. Tahara, Y.; Tohyama, S.; Katsui, T. CFD-based multi-objective optimization method for ship design. *Int. J. Numer. Methods Fluids* **2006**, *52*, 499–527.
5. Abt, C.; Harries, S. Friendship-Framework—Integrating ship-design modelling, simulation, and optimization. *Naval Archit.* **2007**, *1*, 36–37.
6. Harries, S.; Abt, C. Tight and loose coupling of CAD and CFD—Methods, practical aspects, advantages. In Proceedings of the RINA International Conference-Marine CFD 2008, Southampton, UK, 26–27 March 2008; pp. 35–41.
7. Couser, P.; Harries, S.; Tillig, F. On design-space exploration and design refinement by numerical simulation. In Proceedings of the RINA International Conference in Marine Design, Coventry, UK, 14–15 September 2011; pp. 101–110.
8. Brizzolara, S.; Vernengo, G. Automatic computer driven optimization of innovative hull forms for marine vehicles. In Proceedings of the 10th WSEAS International Conference on Applied Computer and Applied Computational Science, ACACOS'11, Venice, Italy, 8–10 March 2011; pp. 273–278.
9. Biliotti, I.; Brizzolara, S.; Viviani, M.; Vernengo, G.; Ruscelli, D.; Galliussi, M.; Guadalupi, D.; Manfredini, A. Automatic parametric hull form optimization of fast naval vessels. In Proceedings of the 11th International Conference on Fast Sea Transportation, FAST 2011, Honolulu, HI, USA, 26–29 September 2011; pp. 294–301.
10. Ginnis, A.I.; Feurer, C.; Belibassakis, K.A.; Kaklis, P.D.; Kostas, K.V.; Gerostathis, T.P.; Politis, C.G. A CATIA® ship-parametric model for isogeometric hull optimization with respect to wave resistance. In Proceedings of the International Conference on Computer Applications in Shipbuilding, Trieste, Italy, 20–22 September 2011.
11. Brenner, M.; Zagkas, V.; Harries, S.; Stein, T. Optimization using viscous flow computations for retrofitting ships in operation. In Proceedings of the 5th International Conference on Computational Methods in Marine Engineering, MARINE 2013, Hamburg, Germany, 29–31 May 2013; pp. 69–80.
12. Zakerdoost, H.; Ghassemi, H.; Ghiasi, M. An evolutionary optimization technique applied to resistance reduction of the ship hull form. *J. Naval Archit. Mar. Eng.* **2013**, *10*, 1–12.
13. Vernengo, G.; Brizzolara, S.; Bruzzone, D. Resistance and seakeeping optimization of a fast multihull passenger ferry. *Int. J. Offshore Polar Eng.* **2015**, *25*, 26–34.
14. Brizzolara, S.; Vernengo, G.; Pasquinucci, C.A.; Harries, S. Significance of parametric hull form definition on hydrodynamic performance optimization. In Proceedings of the MARINE 2015—Computational Methods in Marine Engineering VI, Rome, Italy, 15–17 June 2015; pp. 254–265.
15. Ang, J.; Goh, C.; Li, Y. Hull form design optimization for improved efficiency and hydrodynamic performance of "ship-shaped" offshore vessels. In Proceedings of the International Conference on Computer Applications in Shipbuilding, Bremen, Germany, 29 September–1 October 2015; pp. 1–10.
16. Wang, J. A NURBS-Based Computational Tool for Hydrodynamic Optimization of Ship Hull Forms. Ph.D. Thesis, George Mason University, Fairfax, VA, USA, 2015.
17. Tahara, Y.; Stern, F.; Himeno, Y. CFD-based optimization of a surface combatant. *J. Ship Res.* **2004**, *48*, 273–287.
18. Campana, E.F.; Peri, D.; Pinto, A.; Stern, F.; Tahara, Y. A comparison of global optimization methods with application to ship design. In Proceedings of the 5th Osaka Colloquium on Advanced Research on Ship Viscous Flow and Hull Form Design by EFD and CFD Approaches, Osaka, Japan, 14–15 March 2005.
19. Wen, A.S.; Mariyam, S.; Shamsuddin, H.; Samian, Y. Optimized NURBS ship hull fitting using simulated annealing. In Proceedings of the International Conference on Computer Graphics, Imaging and Visualisation, Sydney, Australia, 26–28 July 2006; pp. 484–489.
20. Pinto, A.; Peri, D.; Campana, E.F. Multiobjective optimization of a containership using deterministic particle swarm optimization. *J. Ship Res.* **2007**, *51*, 217–228.
21. Ayob, M.; Ahmad, F.; Ray, T.; Smith, W. A hydrodynamic preliminary design optimization framework for high speed planing craft. *J. Ship Res.* **2012**, *56*, 35–47.
22. Takai, T. Simulation Based Design for High Speed Sea Lift with Waterjets by High Fidelity URANS Approach. Master's Thesis, University of Iowa, Iowa City, IA, USA, 2010.

23. Han, S.; Lee, Y.; Choi, Y.B. Hydrodynamic hull form optimization using parametric models. *J. Mar. Sci. Technol.* **2012**, *17*, 1–17.
24. Zhang, P.; Zhu, D.; He, S. The parametric design method of hull form. *Ship Build. China* **2008**, *49*, 26–34.
25. Liu, Y. *Theory of Ship Wave Making Resistance*; National Defense Industry Press: Beijing, China, 2003.
26. Koutroukis, G. Parametric Design and Multi-Objective Optimization-Study of an Ellipsoidal Containership. Master's Thesis, National Technical University of Athens, Athens, Greece, 2012.
27. Save, M.; Prager, W. *Structural Optimization: Volume 2: Mathematical Programming*; Springer: New York, NY, USA, 1990.
28. Hilleary, R.R. *The Tangent Search Method of Constrained Minimization*; U.S. Naval Postgraduate School: Monterey, CA, USA, 1966.

CHAPTER 17

Multiphase cascaded lattice Boltzmann method

Daniel Lycett-Brown *, Kai H. Luo

Energy Technology Research Group, Faculty of Engineering and the Environment, University of Southampton, Southampton, SO17 1BJ, UK

ABSTRACT

To improve the stability of the lattice Boltzmann method (LBM) at high Reynolds number the cascaded LBM has recently been introduced. As in the multiple relaxation time (MRT) method the cascaded LBM introduces additional relaxation times into the collision operator, but does so in a co-moving reference frame. This has been shown to significantly increase stability at low viscosity in the single phase case. Here the cascaded LBM is further developed to include multiphase flow. For this the force term is calculated by the interaction potential method, and introduced into the collision operator via the exact difference method (EDM). Comparisons are made with the lattice Bhatnagar–Gross–Krook (LBGK) method, and an MRT implementation. Both the cascaded and MRT methods are shown to significantly reduce spurious velocities over the LBGK method. For the particular case of the Shan–Chen interparticle force term calculation with the EDM, the cascaded LBM is successfully combined with a multiphase method, and shown to perform as well as the more established MRT method. The cascaded LBM is found to be a considerably improved approach to the simulation of multiphase flow over the LBGK, significantly increasing the stability range of both density ratio and Reynolds number. Additionally the importance of including third order velocity terms in the equilibria of both the cascaded and MRT methods is discussed.

Keywords: Lattice Boltzmann, Cascaded LBM, Multiphase, Spurious velocities

1. INTRODUCTION

The lattice Boltzmann method (LBM) is a rapidly developing approach to computational fluid dynamics (CFD). It has been successfully applied to a variety of problems, including (but not limited to) turbulence, micro flows, flows through porous media, magnetohydrodynamics and both multiphase and multi-component systems (see e.g. [1–3] and references therein). Instead of solving the macroscopic Navier–Stokes equations as in traditional CFD, the LBM works on the mesoscopic scale, solving a discretised Boltzmann equation, designed to recover the Navier–Stokes equations in the macroscopic limit. As the LBM works with particle distribution functions, complex macroscopic fluid behaviors which occur as a result of particle interactions, such as phase separation, can be easily included. As interfaces between high and low density phases arise naturally, no interface tracking is required, representing a significant advantage over traditional CFD methods for multiphase flows.

A number of methods for including multiphase behavior into the LBM have been proposed, including the free-energy models [4–6], those based on the kinetic theory of dense fluids [7–9], and the interaction potential models [10–12] which are used here. Originally proposed by Shan and Chen [10] these models calculate a force through a local interaction potential, which then modifies the equilibrium distribution functions. Despite the success of the multiphase LBM, simulating flows with both a high density ratio between the liquid and gas phases and low viscosity remains challenging, a major problem being the well known formation of spurious velocities around curved interfaces. A number of improvements to the interaction potential model have been proposed, and can be divided into two categories; those that modify the force calculation, such as increasing the order of isotropy [13] or modifying the equation of state [14], and those that improve the incorporation of the force into the equilibrium distribution functions, such as the exact difference method (EDM) [15], and the method by Guo et al. [16]. Lee and Fischer [17] have recently introduced a new model which recasts the force calculation from the pressure form used in the interaction potential models, to a potential form, so as to eliminate discretization errors responsible for the spurious velocities. The scheme is shown to remove spurious velocities from interfaces at equilibrium, however compromises conservation of mass and momentum [18].

In its simplest form the LBM uses a single relaxation time Bhatnagar–Gross–Krook (BGK) collision operator. It has been extensively shown in the single phase case that a significant improvement in attainable Reynolds number can be obtained through the use of a multiple relaxation time collision operator [19–22]. Instead of relaxing particle distribution functions towards their equilibrium distribution functions, a transformation is made into moment space, where individual moments can be relaxed independently, and the relaxation rates of higher order moments can be used to increase stability. Attempts have been made to apply this to the various multiphase schemes, leading in some cases to an increase in attainable Reynolds number [23–27]. A decrease in spurious velocities has also been observed. Recently Geier et al. [28] proposed the cascaded LBM, in which the collision operator relaxes moments in a co-moving reference frame, and showed improvements over results obtained using the MRT collision operator. Here, this cascaded LBM is applied to the multiphase case, with results compared to an MRT implementation. The EDM is used (in both cases), as this gives significant improvement over the original Shan–Chen implementation of the interaction potential model, and does not modify the collision operator (as is the case in the method of Guo et al.).

Here an alternative derivation of the cascaded LBM is presented in Section 2, and the MRT method used for comparison is described in Section 3. The multiphase method using the EDM, is introduced in Section 4. Results and comparisons are then given in Section 5, and conclusions drawn.

2. CASCADED LBM

Although the MRT method significantly enhances stability over the LBGK method as viscosity decreases, it still becomes unstable for sufficiently low viscosities. Geier et al. offered an explanation for this instability, and derived the cascaded LBM in an attempt to overcome it [28]. The two main problems with the MRT method were identified as insufficient Galilean invariance, and a so-called 'crosstalk' between moments. The Galilean invariance arises as a result of relaxing raw moments, defined in the reference frame of a fixed lattice, and can be overcome by instead relaxing central moments, defined in a reference frame moving with the fluid. These central moments can be expressed in terms of raw moments, with central moments of a certain order only containing terms of raw moments of that order and below. Relaxing a raw moment therefore effects higher order central moments, and it is this crosstalk between central moments that is suggested as a source of instability. This is overcome through relaxing moments in a cascade from lowest to highest order moment, the effect of the relaxation of a raw moment on a higher order central moment being known and removed before that higher moment is itself relaxed.

Here we follow a slightly different derivation to that given by Geier et al. and begin with the raw moment representation of populations (see e.g. [19]). These are then translated into their central moment form, before each central moment is independently relaxed. The two-dimensional, nine velocity lattice is used, with velocities $v_{(i,j)}=(v_{(i)},v_{(j)})$, constructed as the tensor product of the velocities from the sets of two one-dimensional, three velocity lattices, with $v_{(i)}=i$, where $i=0,\pm1$. Moments of this product lattice can be written as [29]

$$\rho M_{pq} = \langle f_{(i,j)} v_{(i)}^{p} v_{(i)}^{q} \rangle, \quad p, q \in \{0, 1, 2\}, \tag{1}$$

where $\langle ... \rangle$ represents summation over all of the velocity indices. In this notation $M_{00}=1$ is the normalized density, and M_{10} and M_{01} the x and y velocities (u_x and u_y) respectively. We define the trace of the pressure tensor, T, and the normal stress difference, N, (both at unity density) as

$$T=M_{20}+M_{02},\ N=M_{20}-M_{02}. \tag{2}$$

$\Pi_{xy}=M_{11}$ is the off diagonal element of the pressure tensor (at unit density), and $Q_{yxx}=M_{21}$, $Q_{xyy}=M_{12}$ and $A=M_{22}$ are the third and fourth order moments. Populations can be expressed in terms of these moments as:

$$\begin{aligned} f_{(0,0)} &= \rho\left[1 - T + A\right], \\ f_{(\sigma,0)} &= \frac{1}{2}\rho\left[\frac{1}{2}(T+N) + \sigma u_x - \sigma Q_{xyy} - A\right], \\ f_{(0,\lambda)} &= \frac{1}{2}\rho\left[\frac{1}{2}(T-N) + \lambda u_y - \lambda Q_{yxx} - A\right], \\ f_{(\sigma,\lambda)} &= \frac{1}{4}\rho\left[A + \sigma\lambda \Pi_{xy} + \sigma Q_{xyy} + \lambda Q_{yxx}\right], \end{aligned} \tag{3}$$

where $\sigma,\lambda=\{-1,1\}$. Central moments are defined as in Geier et al. [28], as:

$$\rho \tilde{M}_{pq} = \left\langle (v_{(i)} - u_x)^p (v_{(j)} - u_y)^q f_{(i,j)} \right\rangle. \tag{4}$$

After some algebra, each of the raw moments can be expressed in terms of central moments,

$$
\begin{aligned}
\Pi_{xy} &= \tilde{\Pi}_{xy} + u_x u_y,\\
N &= \tilde{N} + (u_x^2 - u_y^2),\\
T &= \tilde{T} + u^2,\\
Q_{xyy} &= \tilde{Q}_{xyy} + 2u_y\tilde{\Pi}_{xy} - \frac{1}{2}u_x\tilde{N} + \frac{1}{2}u_x\tilde{T} + u_x u_y^2,\\
Q_{yxx} &= \tilde{Q}_{yxx} + 2u_x\tilde{\Pi}_{xy} + \frac{1}{2}u_y\tilde{N} + \frac{1}{2}u_y\tilde{T} + u_y u_x^2,\\
A &= \tilde{A} + 2u_x\tilde{Q}_{xyy} + 2u_y\tilde{Q}_{yxx} + 4u_x u_y\tilde{\Pi}_{xy} + \frac{1}{2}u^2\tilde{T} - \frac{1}{2}\left(u_x^2 - u_y^2\right)\tilde{N} + u_x^2 u_y^2.
\end{aligned}
\tag{5}
$$

and these can be substituted into Eq. (3), to give

$$
\begin{aligned}
f_{(0,0)} &= \rho\left[1 + u_x^2u_y^2 - u^2 + 4u_xu_y\tilde{\Pi}_{xy} - \left(\frac{u_x^2 - u_y^2}{2}\right)\tilde{N} + \left(\frac{u^2-2}{2}\right)\tilde{T} + 2u_x\tilde{Q}_{xyy} + 2u_y\tilde{Q}_{yxx} + \tilde{A}\right],\\
f_{(\sigma,0)} &= \frac{\rho}{2}\left[u_x^2 + \sigma u_x\left(1 - u_y^2\right) - u_x^2u_y^2 - \left(2\sigma u_y + 4u_xu_y\right)\tilde{\Pi}_{xy} + \left(\frac{1 + \sigma u_x + u_x^2 - u_y^2}{2}\right)\tilde{N}\right.\\
&\quad \left. + \left(\frac{1 - \sigma u_x - u^2}{2}\right)\tilde{T} - \left(\sigma + 2u_x\right)\tilde{Q}_{xyy} - 2u_y\tilde{Q}_{yxx} - \tilde{A}\right],\\
f_{(0,\lambda)} &= \frac{\rho}{2}\left[u_y^2 + \lambda u_y\left(1 - u_x^2\right) - u_x^2u_y^2 - \left(2\lambda u_y + 4u_xu_y\right)\tilde{\Pi}_{xy} + \left(\frac{-1 - \lambda u_y + u_x^2 - u_y^2}{2}\right)\tilde{N}\right.\\
&\quad \left. + \left(\frac{1 - \lambda u_y - u^2}{2}\right)\tilde{T} - \left(\lambda + 2u_y\right)\tilde{Q}_{yxx} - 2u_x\tilde{Q}_{xyy} - \tilde{A}\right],\\
f_{(\sigma,\lambda)} &= \frac{\rho}{4}\left[\sigma\lambda u_xu_y + \sigma u_xu_y^2 + \lambda u_yu_x^2 + u_x^2u_y^2 + \left(4u_xu_y + \sigma\lambda + 2\sigma u_y + 2\lambda u_x\right)\tilde{\Pi}_{xy}\right.\\
&\quad \left. + \left(\frac{-u_x^2 + u_y^2 - \sigma u_x + \lambda u_y}{2}\right)\tilde{N} + \left(\frac{u^2 + \sigma u_x + \lambda u_y}{2}\right)\tilde{T} + \left(\sigma + 2u_x\right)\tilde{Q}_{xyy} + \left(\lambda + 2u_y\right)\tilde{Q}_{yxx} + \tilde{A}\right].
\end{aligned}
\tag{6}
$$

With the populations written in this form, a collision operator with independent relaxation rates for each central moment can be derived. The LBM is written as

$$
f_{(i,j)}\left(\mathbf{x} + \mathbf{v}_{(i,j)}, t + 1\right) = f^*_{(i,j)}(\mathbf{x}, t),
\tag{7}
$$

where collisions are written in the familiar form

$$
f^*_{(i,j)} = (1 - \omega)f_{(i,j)} + \omega f^{eq}_{(i,j)}.
\tag{8}
$$

Using the form of $f_{(i,j)}$ in Eq. (6), for example for $f^*_{(0,0)}$ this becomes

$$\begin{aligned} f^*_{(0,0)} = \rho\Bigg[& 1 - u^2 + u_x^2 u_y^2 + 4u_x u_y \left((1-\omega)\,\tilde{\Pi}_{xy} + \omega \tilde{\Pi}^{eq}_{xy} \right) \\ & + \left(\frac{-u_x^2 + u_y^2}{2} \right) \left((1-\omega)\,\tilde{N} + \omega \tilde{N}^{eq} \right) + \left(\frac{u^2 - 2}{2} \right) \left((1-\omega)\,\tilde{T} + \omega \tilde{T}^{eq} \right) \\ & + 2u_x \left((1-\omega)\,\tilde{Q}_{xyy} + \omega \tilde{Q}^{eq}_{xyy} \right) + 2u_y \left((1-\omega)\,\tilde{Q}_{yxx} + \omega \tilde{Q}^{eq}_{yxx} \right) + \left((1-\omega)\,\tilde{A} + \omega \tilde{A}^{eq} \right) \Bigg]. \end{aligned} \tag{9}$$

where the equilibrium values for the moments are given by [29]

$$\tilde{\Pi}^{eq}_{xy} = \tilde{N}^{eq} = \tilde{Q}^{eq}_{xyy} = \tilde{Q}^{eq}_{yxx} = 0, \qquad \tilde{T}^{eq} = 2c_s^2, \qquad \tilde{A}^{eq} = c_s^4. \tag{10}$$

where $c_s^2 = 1/3$ is the speed of sound squared. The relaxation rate for the trace of the pressure tensor, T, can be replaced by ω_b, relating to the bulk viscosity, and the relaxation rates for the third and fourth order moments replaced by $\omega_3$and ω_4 respectively. This allows the bulk viscosity to be set independently of the kinematic viscosity, ν, and the higher order moments to be relaxed independently. Using the equilibrium values of the moments, this leads to:

$$\begin{aligned} f^*_{(0,0)} &= \rho\left[1 - u^2 + 4u_x u_y \tilde{\Pi}^*_{xy} - \left(\frac{u_x^2 - u_y^2}{2} \right) \tilde{N}^* + \left(\frac{u^2 - 2}{2} \right) \tilde{T}^* + 2u_x \tilde{Q}^*_{xyy} + 2u_y \tilde{Q}^*_{yxx} + \tilde{A}^* \right]. \\ f^*_{(\sigma,0)} &= \frac{\rho}{2}\Bigg[u_x^2 + \sigma u_x (1 - u_y^2) - (2\sigma u_y + 4u_x u_y)\,\tilde{\Pi}^*_{xy} + \left(\frac{1 + \sigma u_x + u_x^2 - u_y^2}{2} \right) \tilde{N}^* \\ &\quad + \left(\frac{1 - \sigma u_x - u^2}{2} \right) \tilde{T}^* - \left(\sigma + 2u_x \right) \tilde{Q}^*_{xyy} - 2u_y \tilde{Q}^*_{yxx} - \tilde{A}^* \Bigg]. \\ f^*_{(0,\lambda)} &= \frac{\rho}{2}\Bigg[u_y^2 + \lambda u_y (1 - u_x^2) - (2\lambda u_y + 4u_x u_y)\,\tilde{\Pi}^*_{xy} + \left(\frac{-1 - \lambda u_y + u_x^2 - u_y^2}{2} \right) \tilde{N}^* \\ &\quad + \left(\frac{1 - \lambda u_y - u^2}{2} \right) \tilde{T}^* - (\lambda + 2u_y)\,\tilde{Q}^*_{yxx} - 2u_x \tilde{Q}^*_{xyy} - \tilde{A}^* \Bigg]. \\ f^*_{(\sigma,\lambda)} &= \frac{\rho}{4}\Bigg[\sigma\lambda u_x u_y + \sigma u_x u_y^2 + \lambda u_y u_x^2 + (4u_x u_y + \sigma\lambda + 2\sigma u_y + 2\lambda u_x)\,\tilde{\Pi}^*_{xy} \\ &\quad + \left(\frac{-u_x^2 + u_y^2 - \sigma u_x + \lambda u_y}{2} \right) \tilde{N}^* + \left(\frac{u^2 + \sigma u_x + \lambda u_y}{2} \right) \tilde{T}^* + \left(\sigma + 2u_x \right) \tilde{Q}^*_{xyy} + (\lambda + 2u_y)\,\tilde{Q}^*_{yxx} + \tilde{A}^* \Bigg]. \end{aligned} \tag{11}$$

where fourth order velocity terms have been dropped, and

$$\tilde{\Pi}^*_{xy} = (1-\omega)\,\tilde{\Pi}_{xy},$$
$$\tilde{N}^* = (1-\omega)\,\tilde{N},$$
$$\tilde{T}^* = (1-\omega_b)\,\tilde{T} + \frac{2}{3}\omega_b,$$
$$\tilde{Q}^*_{xyy} = (1-\omega_3)\,\tilde{Q}_{xyy},$$
$$\tilde{Q}^*_{yxx} = (1-\omega_3)\,\tilde{Q}_{yxx},$$
$$\tilde{A}^* = (1-\omega_4)\,\tilde{A} + \frac{1}{9}\omega_4. \quad (12)$$

Under the constraint of $\omega_b=\omega_3=\omega_4=\omega$, this exactly recovers the BGK form of the collision operator. Using the Chapman–Enskog multi-scales expansion it can be shown that this scheme recovers the isothermal Navier–Stokes equations at reference temperature $T_0 = c_s^2$:

$$\frac{\partial \rho}{\partial t} + \nabla\cdot(\rho\boldsymbol{u}) = 0,$$
$$\frac{\partial}{\partial t}(\rho\boldsymbol{u}) + \nabla\cdot(\rho\boldsymbol{u}\boldsymbol{u}) + \nabla p = \nabla\cdot\boldsymbol{\tau}, \quad (13)$$

where

$$\tau_{\alpha\beta} = \rho\nu\left(\frac{\partial u_\beta}{\partial x_\alpha} + \frac{\partial u_\alpha}{\partial x_\beta} - \delta_{\alpha\beta}\nabla\cdot\boldsymbol{u}\right) + \rho\xi\delta_{\alpha\beta}\nabla\cdot\boldsymbol{u}, \quad (14)$$

and

$$\nu = \left(\frac{1}{\omega} - \frac{1}{2}\right)c_s^2, \qquad \xi = \left(\frac{1}{\omega_b} - \frac{1}{2}\right)c_s^2, \quad (15)$$

are the kinematic and bulk viscosities.

The form presented here is equivalent to the cascaded LBM given in Geier et al. [28], and results for increase in stability in the single phase case are therefore found to be the same as those given therein.

3. MRT METHOD

For comparison an MRT method is used [19–22]. This involves transformation from the population basis to a moment basis in which moments are relaxed, and in the original formulation the transformation between these bases was achieved via a transformation matrix. The MRT method can also be derived by revisiting the derivation of the cascaded LBM given above and simply removing the transformation step from the raw moment basis to the central moment basis, as is done in the following. The matrix form is also presented for completeness, although obviously the two different forms of the equations are equivalent. In the cascaded method post-collision states are written in terms of central moments relaxed towards their equilibria, in the MRT method they are written as raw moments relaxed towards their corresponding equilibria. In the equivalent to Eq. (9), the post-collision state $f^*_{0,0}$ in the LBGK case can be rewritten as

$$f^*_{(0,0)} = \rho\left[1 - \left((1-\omega)\tilde{T} + \omega\tilde{T}^{eq}\right) + \left((1-\omega)\tilde{A} + \omega\tilde{A}^{eq}\right)\right]. \tag{16}$$

In this form relaxation rates can again be replaced to allow bulk viscosity to be varied independently and the third and fourth order moments relaxed separately. The full set of post-collision populations is then

$$\begin{aligned}
f^*_{(0,0)} &= \rho\left[1 - T^* + A^*\right], \\
f^*_{(\sigma,0)} &= \frac{1}{2}\rho\left[\frac{1}{2}(T^* + N^*) + \sigma u_x - \sigma Q^*_{xyy} - A^*\right], \\
f^*_{(0,\lambda)} &= \frac{1}{2}\rho\left[\frac{1}{2}(T^* - N^*) + \lambda u_y - \lambda Q^*_{yxx} - A^*\right], \\
f^*_{(\sigma,\lambda)} &= \frac{1}{4}\rho\left[A^* + \sigma\lambda\Pi^*_{xy} + \sigma Q^*_{xyy} + \lambda Q^*_{yxx}\right],
\end{aligned} \tag{17}$$

where post-collision moments are

$$\begin{aligned}
\Pi^*_{xy} &= (1-\omega)\,\Pi_{xy} + \omega u_x u_y, \\
N^* &= (1-\omega)\,N + \omega\left(u_x^2 - u_y^2\right), \\
T^* &= (1-\omega_b)\,T + \omega_b\left(2c_s^2 + u^2\right), \\
Q^*_{xyy} &= \left(1-\omega_3'\right)Q_{xyy} + \omega_3' u_x\left(c_s^2 + u_y^2\right), \\
Q^*_{yxx} &= \left(1-\omega_3'\right)Q_{yxx} + \omega_3' u_y\left(c_s^2 + u_x^2\right), \\
A^* &= \left(1-\omega_4'\right)A + \omega_4'\left(c_s^2 + u_y^2\right)\left(c_s^2 + u_x^2\right).
\end{aligned} \tag{18}$$

Equilibrium values have been inserted and primes are used to distinguish raw moment relaxation rates from central moment relaxation rates.

To express this in terms of matrix transformations in general the LBM can be written as

$$f_i(\boldsymbol{x} + \mathbf{v}_i, t + 1) - f_i(\boldsymbol{x}, t) = -\sum_j \Lambda_{ij} \left(f_j(\boldsymbol{x}, t) - f_j^{eq}(\boldsymbol{x}, t) \right), \tag{19}$$

where for the specific case of the LBGK model the collision matrix Λij is given by

$$\Lambda_{ij} = \frac{1}{\tau}\delta_{ij}, \tag{20}$$

where τ=1/ω. In general, however, this is a full matrix, and solving Eq. (19)becomes complex. Through the use of a transformation matrix, ***K***, the collision matrix can be diagonalized. This transformation matrix is chosen such that

$$\boldsymbol{Kf}=\boldsymbol{M}, \tag{21}$$

where f is the vector of population distribution functions, and M is the vector of moments,

$$\boldsymbol{M} = \left(\rho, u_x, u_y, \Pi_{xy}, N, T, Q_{xyy}, Q_{yxx}, A\right)^T. \tag{22}$$

It transforms from the basis of populations to that of moments, and is given by

$$\boldsymbol{K} = \begin{pmatrix} 1 & 1 & 1 & 1 & 1 & 1 & 1 & 1 & 1 \\ 0 & 1 & 0 & -1 & 0 & 1 & -1 & -1 & 1 \\ 0 & 0 & 1 & 0 & -1 & 1 & 1 & -1 & -1 \\ 0 & 0 & 0 & 0 & 0 & 1 & -1 & 1 & -1 \\ 0 & 1 & -1 & 1 & -1 & 0 & 0 & 0 & 0 \\ 0 & 1 & 1 & 1 & 1 & 2 & 2 & 2 & 2 \\ 0 & 0 & 0 & 0 & 0 & 1 & 1 & -1 & -1 \\ 0 & 0 & 0 & 0 & 0 & 1 & -1 & -1 & 1 \\ 0 & 0 & 0 & 0 & 0 & 1 & 1 & 1 & 1 \end{pmatrix}. \tag{23}$$

Different transformation matrices have been used in different MRT methods, corresponding to different moment bases, and it is normal to orthogonalize this matrix, for example via the Gram–Schmidt procedure, however this is unnecessary for the present discussion. Using this transformation matrix the MRT method can now be written as

$$f_i(\boldsymbol{x}+\boldsymbol{v}_i, t+1) - f_i(\boldsymbol{x}, t) = -\rho \boldsymbol{K}^{-1}\left(\sum_{\beta} \hat{\Lambda}_{\alpha\beta}\left(M_{\beta}(\boldsymbol{x}, t) - M_{\beta}^{eq}(\boldsymbol{x}, t)\right)\right). \tag{24}$$

where $\boldsymbol{K}^{-1}$ transforms the relaxed moments back into velocity space for the propagation step, and $\hat{\Lambda} = \boldsymbol{K}\Lambda\boldsymbol{K}^{-1}$ is a diagonal matrix,

$$\hat{\Lambda} = \mathrm{diag}\left(1, \omega_b, \omega_4', 1, \omega_3', 1, \omega_3', \omega, \omega\right). \tag{25}$$

It is worth repeating that this is equivalent to the MRT as given by Eqs. (7), (17) and (18). Although different MRT schemes using different bases have been proposed it should be noted that the cascaded LBM cannot be recast in such a way by a linear transformation. However, as discussed by Asinari [30], the cascaded LBM can be cast in matrix form by linearizing the fourth order moment. The Chapman–Enskog procedure can be applied to this MRT scheme, and while this is not done here, the result is the same as for the cascaded LBM, with shear and bulk viscosities given by Eq. (15).

The MRT and cascaded methods are closely related, involving propagation of distribution functions in velocity space, followed by a transformation into moment space (using either raw moments in the MRT method, or central moments in the cascaded method), relaxation in this moment space, and transformation back to velocity space. As shown in Geier et al. [31], the third order terms in velocity are required to maintain Galilean invariance. For the decay of a sinusoidal shear wave, with amplitude in the y-direction, it was shown that a superimposed x-velocity reduced the measured viscosity by a factor proportional to u_x^2, unless the third order terms were included. For fair comparison, these terms are also included in the MRT method, and their effects on the multiphase results are discussed in Section 5.

4. EXACT DIFFERENCE METHOD

The original Shan–Chen method for multiphase flow calculated a force from a density dependent interaction potential, and introduced this force into the LBM through modifying the momentum in the equilibrium distribution function. It is well known that including the forcing term in this way leads to a scheme which is unstable for values of ω much higher than 1. A number of improvements to this method have been suggested, including the method of explicit derivatives, as used in the multiphase schemes derived from the kinetic theory of dense fluids [7–9], the method of Guo et al. [16] which takes into account discrete lattice effects, and the EDM. These schemes differ in the second order and higher moments of the forcing term, and as we are concerned here with relaxing higher order moments it is important to choose a method which introduces the lowest errors in the higher order terms. To compare each of the different schemes they can all be written in the general form

$$f_{(i,j)}(\mathbf{x} + \mathbf{v}_{(i,j)}, t + 1) - f_{(i,j)}(\mathbf{x}, t) = \Omega + F_{(i,j)}, \tag{26}$$

where Ω is a generic collision operator, and $F_{(i,j)}$ has moments

$$\sum F_{(i,j)} = 0, \tag{27}$$

$$\sum \mathbf{v}_{(i,j)} F_{(i,j)} = \boldsymbol{F}, \tag{28}$$

$$\sum \mathbf{v}_{(i,j)} \mathbf{v}_{(i,j)} F_{(i,j)} = \boldsymbol{\Psi}. \tag{29}$$

Here the general term Ψ has been introduced as the second order moment. While this should equal ($\boldsymbol{Fu}$+$\boldsymbol{uF}$) in the continuous case, in the discrete case it should include additional terms to cancel discretization errors, and differs in each of the different forcing methods. By series expansion of Eq. (26) the momentum equation is derived as

$$\frac{\partial}{\partial t}(\rho\hat{\mathbf{u}}) + \nabla \cdot (\rho\hat{\mathbf{u}}\hat{\mathbf{u}}) + \nabla p = \mathbf{F} + \nabla \cdot \hat{\boldsymbol{\tau}} + \nabla \cdot \mathbf{E}, \tag{30}$$

where $\rho\hat{\mathbf{u}} = \rho\mathbf{u} + \mathbf{F}/2$, $\hat{\boldsymbol{\tau}}$ is given by

$$\hat{\tau}_{\alpha\beta} = \rho\nu\left(\frac{\partial\hat{u}_\beta}{\partial x_\alpha} + \frac{\partial\hat{u}_\alpha}{\partial x_\beta} - \delta_{\alpha\beta}\nabla\cdot\hat{\mathbf{u}}\right) + \rho\xi\delta_{\alpha\beta}\nabla\cdot\hat{\mathbf{u}}, \tag{31}$$

and $\boldsymbol{E}$ is an error term given by

$$\mathbf{E} = \tau\left(\boldsymbol{Fu} + \boldsymbol{uF}\right) - \tau\boldsymbol{\Psi} + \left(\tau - \frac{1}{4}\right)\frac{\boldsymbol{FF}}{\rho}. \tag{32}$$

In the continuous case the second order moment of $F_{(i,j)}$ cancels the first term. Each of the different forcing schemes do this correctly, the leading order difference is in the third term. Ψ should also contain terms that cancel the third term, however in each scheme the coefficient in front of the $\boldsymbol{FF}$ term differs. The different resulting error terms are discussed below. Additionally, Wagner [32] concluded that as the pressure tensor contains second order derivatives that are large near to interfaces, the usual second order Chapman–Enskog expansion is insufficient to identify them. Using a fifth order Taylor expansion it was shown for a one-dimensional example that the error term should also contain terms proportional to the gradient of the forcing term.

For the Shan–Chen method the error term is given by

$$\boldsymbol{E}^{SC} = \left(\tau - \tau^2 - \frac{1}{4}\right)\frac{\boldsymbol{FF}}{\rho}. \tag{33}$$

The dependence on $\boldsymbol{\tau}$ of this error is responsible for the poor performance of the method as $\boldsymbol{\tau}$ is varied. Kupershtokh's derivation of the EDM was one attempt to solve this problem [15]. As in He et al. [7] the $\nabla_v f$ term in the Boltzmann equation can be written approximately as

$$\nabla_{\boldsymbol{v}} f \approx \nabla_{\boldsymbol{v}} f^{eq}. \tag{34}$$

As f cannot be expressed in terms of the microscopic velocity, v, then $\nabla_v f$ cannot be evaluated, however assuming that the main part of f is f^{eq} then the leading part of the gradient of f will be the gradient of f^{eq} and this approximation will be valid. He et al. [7] therefore wrote the forcing term as

$$\boldsymbol{F} \cdot \nabla_{\boldsymbol{v}} f \approx \frac{\boldsymbol{F} \cdot (\boldsymbol{v} - \boldsymbol{u})}{c_s^2} f^{eq}. \tag{35}$$

Kupershtokh noticed that for Galilean invariance the relationship

$$\nabla_{\boldsymbol{v}} f^{eq} = -\nabla_{\boldsymbol{u}} f^{eq} \tag{36}$$

must be true for the Maxwell–Boltzmann equilibrium distribution. Using the mathematical identity

$$\nabla_{\boldsymbol{u}} f^{eq} \frac{\mathrm{d}\boldsymbol{u}}{\mathrm{d}t} = \frac{\mathrm{d}f^{eq}}{\mathrm{d}t} \tag{37}$$

the discretized forcing term can then be expressed as

$$F_{(i,j)}^{\mathrm{EDM}} = f_{(i,j)}^{eq}(\rho, \boldsymbol{u} + \boldsymbol{F}/\rho) - f_{(i,j)}^{eq}(\rho, \boldsymbol{u}). \tag{38}$$

This can be written out explicitly using the expressions for the equilibrium distributions. It is important to note that when discussing results for second and third order terms in the collision operator that this expression is correspondingly truncated at second and third order. From the second order moment of $F_{(i,j)}^{\mathrm{EDM}}$ the error term can be calculated as

$$\boldsymbol{E}^{\mathrm{EDM}} = -\frac{1}{4}\frac{\boldsymbol{FF}}{\rho}. \tag{39}$$

Unlike in the Shan–Chen method the error term is no longer dependent on τ.

Guo et al. derive their scheme so as to eliminate the leading error, therefore the error term is

$$\boldsymbol{E}^{\mathrm{Guo}} = 0. \tag{40}$$

It should be noted that as the scheme of He et al. does not cancel any of the discretization errors, it has errors which are also dependent on τ. However the derivation given in He et al. also uses the trapezoid rule in discretising the force integral. The transformation of the resulting implicit scheme to an explicit scheme can be rewritten in the form of Eq. (26), for which the force term only differs to the scheme of Guo at third order.

Fig. 1 shows plots of the theoretically derived leading order error terms and the measured gas density for the different schemes, for varying $\boldsymbol{\tau}$. The experimental results are in good agreement with the theoretical predictions of the error, for the lack of dependence on $\boldsymbol{\tau}$ in both the EDM and Guo method, the equivalence of the Shan–Chen method and the EDM at $\boldsymbol{\tau}$ =1, and the approach of the Shan–Chen method to that of Guo as $\boldsymbol{\tau}$ tends to 0.5. Despite the scheme of Guo et al. having zero error from the second order Chapman–Enskog expansion, the results show greater errors in this scheme than in the EDM. This is likely due to the additional error term derived by Wagner [32], which was found to be proportional to the gradient of the forcing term. This will be high around interfaces and could therefore introduce significant error. Further study of this term is not the purpose of the present work, a possible solution is given by Wagner [32] and methods which appear to cancel this error with a tuneable parameter have been developed by Kupershtokh et al. [33] and Li et al. [34], although without specific reference to the error term.

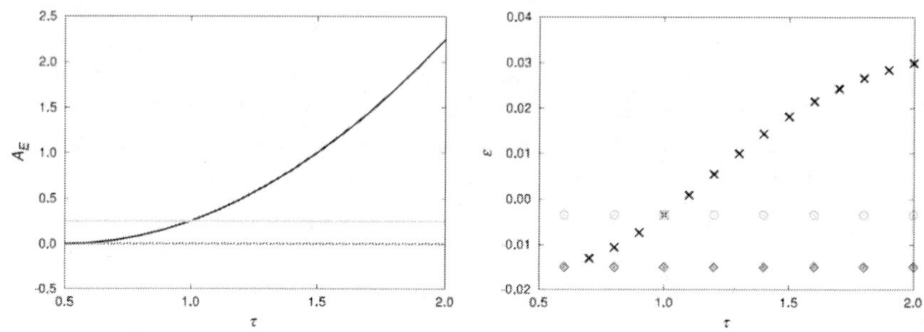

Figure. 1. Comparison between the coefficient of the leading error term, A_E, (left) and the error between the measured gas density and that predicted by the Maxwell rule, ε, (right). The solid black line and black crosses are for the Shan–Chen method [10], $A_E^{SC} = (1/4 - \tau + \tau^2)$, the dashed green line and green circles are for the EDM [15], $A_E^{EDM} = 1/4$, and the dotted red line and red diamonds are for the method of Guo [16], $A_E^{Guo} = 0$.

For the present purpose, the EDM is chosen as it gives only a small error which importantly is not dependent on the viscosity. Significantly for the present work, unlike the other methods, the EDM does not modify the collision operator, therefore the effect of the different collision operators on results can be studied. The result in Fig. 1 was repeated for the EDM with varying each of the relaxation parameters of the cascaded method and no effect on the result was observed, therefore the effect of the cascaded LBM on the higher order errors can be evaluated independently of any errors from the EDM. It should be noted that both MRT [35] and cascaded [36] models have been developed which reduce to the forcing scheme of Guo in the LBGK limit.

Following the Shan–Chen model the force term is calculated as

$$\boldsymbol{F} = -G\psi(\boldsymbol{x}) \sum w_{(i,j)} \psi(\boldsymbol{x} + \mathbf{v}_{(i,j)}) \mathbf{v}_{(i,j)}, \tag{41}$$

where $w_{(0,0)}=4/9$, $w_{(\sigma,0)}=w_{(0,\lambda)}=1/9$ and $w_{(\sigma,\lambda)}=1/36$. This force modifies the equation of state from that of an ideal gas to

$$P = \rho c_s^2 + \frac{Gc_s^2}{2} \psi(\boldsymbol{x})^2, \tag{42}$$

where G controls the interaction strength, and ψ is the effective mass, originally give as

$$\psi(\rho) = \rho_0 \left(1 - e^{-\frac{\rho}{\rho_0}}\right). \tag{43}$$

Yuan and Schaefer [14] showed that through rearranging the expression for ψ more realistic equations of state could be introduced, and that this significantly increased the density ratio attainable. The results given in the following section use the Carnahan–Starling equation of state, unless specified otherwise, given by

$$p^{CS} = \rho RT \frac{1 + \frac{b\rho}{4} + \left(\frac{b\rho}{4}\right)^2 - \left(\frac{b\rho}{4}\right)^3}{\left(1 - \frac{b\rho}{4}\right)^3} - a\rho^2, \tag{44}$$

where the constants are set to R=1, a=1 and b=4, in an effective mass given by

$$\psi(\rho) = \sqrt{\frac{2\left(p^{CS} - \rho c_s^2\right)}{Gc_s^2}}. \tag{45}$$

With ψ in this form the density ratio is no longer governed by G (now specified to keep the square root acting on a positive number), but by T.

5. RESULTS

5.1. Validation

Comparisons are now made between the results from the cascaded LBM and those of the MRT and LBGK methods. The effect of the third order velocity terms will also be considered. It is first necessary to ensure that adjusting the higher order relaxation rates does not affect the results. Therefore the properties of the system, including density ratio and surface tension, in equilibrium are studied, followed by those of an oscillating droplet. Finally the effects on the spurious velocities are presented.

Simulations on a 2D, periodic domain of size 5×199, using the Shan–Chen equation of state with G=−5.4, were used to evaluate equilibrium properties. The system was initialized with gas in one half of the domain and liquid in the other, and run to equilibrium. It is well known that the Shan–Chen model does not give a constant density ratio for varying viscosity, the EDM resolves this issue, giving a constant density across a range of viscosities. For the MRT method the three relaxation parameters, ω_b, ω'_3 and ω'_4, were each independently varied between 0.2 and 1.8, at ω=1, and at ν=0.5 and 0.0625. Comparing density ratios with those of the LBGK result at ω=1, results were found to be nearly identical across the range of viscosities and relaxation parameters (in the case of stable simulations), with the largest deviation found to be only 0.03% (for the case of ω_b=1.8). The same results was found for the cascaded LBM, varying ω_b, ω_3 and ω_4, with the largest variation again being only 0.03% (at ω_b=1.8). The only significant difference noted between the simulations was the time taken to reach equilibrium. Equilibrium is reached sooner for ω_b close to 0, and later for ω_b near to 2 (and unaffected by changes in the relaxation rates of the third and fourth order moments).

Fixing ω=1, and varying the density ratio (through varying G), the same setup was used to produce phase diagrams. Again the relaxation parameters were varied, and for both cascaded and MRT methods no visible variation in the phase diagrams were observed, with any differences in density ratio being of the same order as above.

Surface tension can be evaluated using the Laplace law for droplets in equilibrium,

$$\Delta P = \frac{\sigma}{R}, \tag{46}$$

where σ is the surface tension and R the droplet radius. One criticism of the original Shan–Chen model with equation of state in the exponential form was the dependence of surface tension on density ratio, this can however be overcome by tuning the parameters of the Carnahan–Starling equation of state, Eq. (44), or for example by using the grid-refinement method as introduced by Sbragaglia et al. [13]. Here we consider one value of the surface tension by fixing the parameters of the equation of state, as given previously. Droplets of different radii, up to a maximum of R=30, were initiated in the center of a 100×100 domain and simulations run to equilibrium. For this the Carnahan–Starling equation of state was used with T=0.063, giving a density ratio of approximately 100, at both ω=1 and ν=0.03125. This was repeated for different values of the relaxation parameters. For the case of ω=1, varying ω_b or ω_4 across their stable domain produced very little variation in the measured surface tension or offset from the origin, with the greatest deviations in surface tension being less than 0.9% and 0.5% for the case of ω_b=0.4 and ω_4=0.2respectively. Larger variations were observed when varying ω_3, with the largest being

11.3% at ω_3=0.2. Moving from the second order to the third order scheme reduces this maximum variation in surface tension to 6.3% (and has little effect on the ω_b and ω_4 results). The graph of Laplace law for the case of varying ω3 is given in Fig. 2. A very similar result is observed in the MRT case, with the greatest deviations being 0.9% and 0.1% for the case of ω_b=0.2 and ω'_4=0.4 respectively, and 11.9% in the case of $\omega'3$=0.2, reducing to 7.6% in the third order scheme. Reducing the viscosity to ν=0.03125 increases some of these errors slightly. For varying ω_b, ω_3 and ω_4 the maximum deviations in surface tension were found to be 4.0%, 3.7% and 2.6% at ω_b=1.0, ω_3=0.4and ω_4=0.8 for second order, and 4.1%, 3.7% and 2.5% respectively for third order, for the cascaded scheme. Again results are similar using the MRT scheme, for varying ω_b, ω'_3 and ω'_4 the maximum deviations in surface tension were found to be 2.4%, 5.8% and 1.5% at ω_b=0.8, ω'_3=0.2 and ω'_4=1.0 for second order, and 3.0%, 3.9% and 1.7% respectively for third order.

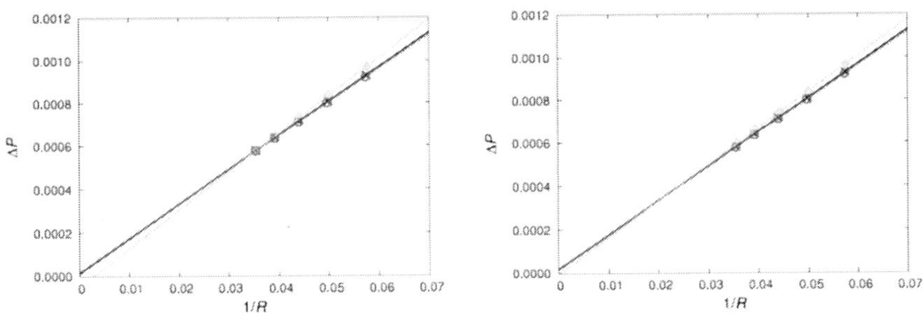

Figure. 2. Laplace law for varying ω_3, at ω=1, for the LBGK method (ω_3=1) (solid black lines), ω_3=0.2 (dashed green lines), and ω_3=1.8 (dotted red lines). Left and right figures show the results for the second and third order schemes respectively. The measured surface tensions are σ=0.0159 for the LBGK method, σ=0.0177 for ω_3=0.2 and σ=0.0157 for ω_3=1.8 at second order, and σ=0.0159 for the LBGK method, σ=0.0169 for ω_3=0.2 and σ=0.0157 for ω3=1.8 at third order.

The Laplace law results show that the relaxation rates can be varied across their whole stability range, without significantly affecting a droplet at equilibrium. Significantly the third and fourth order rates only have a small effect on the result at ω=1, although this increases for lower viscosity.

The case of an oscillating droplet is now considered. The same setup was used, with viscosity set to 0.03125. Once droplets reached equilibrium an initial velocity was applied, given by:

$$u_x = U_0 \frac{x - x_0}{R}$$
$$u_y = -2U_0 \frac{y - y_0}{R}, \qquad (47)$$

for droplets centered at (x_0, y_0). Again, this was repeated across the stable domain of each relaxation parameter. Results for the cascaded LBM are shown in Fig. 3. Varying ω_4 produced no visible deviation in result, with a maximum change in period of just 0.1%, and results are therefore not shown. The graphs show the deviation of the droplet interface from its position at equilibrium, along the x-axis. Each case shows the most extreme variation observed within the stable domain of each relaxation parameter, compared with the LBGK solution. For varying ω_b the largest variation in period, as shown in Fig. 3(left), was 2.1% at ω_b=1.0. This result does not change on moving to third order, as shown in Fig. 3(right). In the case of ω_3, the largest deviation in period from the LBGK result was 1.4% at ω_3=0.4 at second order, reducing to just 0.2% for third order. As with the Laplace law, results for the MRT case were very similar, and are therefore not shown. The maximum variations in period were found to be 4.7%, 1.9% and 0.1% at ω_b=0.8, ω'_3=0.4 and ω'_4=1.8, for second order, and 4.9%, 0.3% and 0.1% respectively for third order.

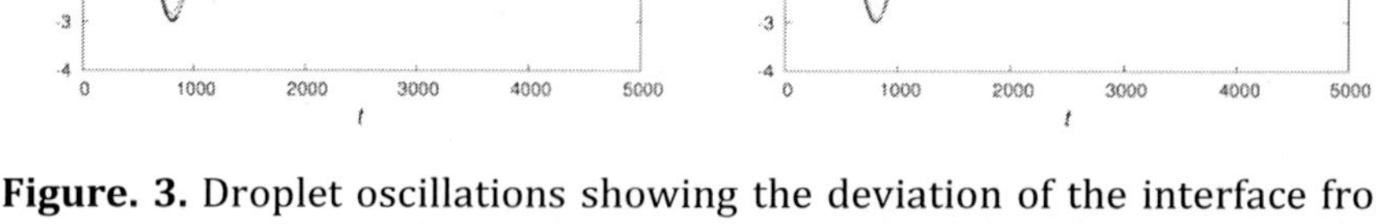

Figure. 3. Droplet oscillations showing the deviation of the interface from its position at equilibrium, ΔR (in lattice units), with time steps, t. Results shown are for ν=0.03125 for the LBGK method (solid black lines), ω_b=1.0 (dashed green lines), and ω_3=0.4 (dotted red lines). Left and right figures show the results for the second and third order schemes respectively. The measured oscillation periods are T_o=1074.2 for the LBGK method, T_o =1097.3 for ω_b=1.0, and T_o =1059.0 for ω_3=0.4 at second order, and T_o =1074.8 for the LBGK method, T_o =1101.3 for ω_b=1.0, and T_o =1072.8 for ω_3=0.4 at third order.

As with the cascaded method varying the fourth order moment relaxation rate has virtually no affect on results, with the same being true for the third order moment rate in the third order scheme. A similar result was observed at ω=1.

5.2. Spurious velocities

As it has been shown that the additional relaxation rates can be varied without having significant effect on the multiphase result, even at low viscosity, these parameters can be used to improve stability without a detrimental effect on accuracy. The following results describe the changes observed in the spurious velocities found around droplets, for varying these relaxation parameters. As well as spurious velocities, another cause of instability in the Shan–Chen LBM has been identified as the higher speed of sound in the liquid phase due to the modified equation of state [37]. Here the focus is on reducing spurious velocities, and both cascaded and MRT models are compared using the same equation of state.

Droplets of radius 20 were set up in the center of a 100×100 domain, with a density ratio of 20 (using T=0.073). At equilibrium the maximum spurious velocity magnitude and average spurious velocity magnitude in the gas phase were recorded. This was repeated for varying all three relaxation parameters simultaneously, with each varied from 0.2 to 1.8 in intervals of 0.2 (a total of 729 simulations). While the maximum spurious velocity, which usually occurs inside the interface, is normally reported, it was observed that this did not always give a good indication of the reduction in spurious velocity throughout the domain, as shown in Fig. 4. Therefore the following results report the reduction in the average spurious velocity in the gas.

Fig. 5 shows results for the minimum value found for the average spurious velocity in the gas around droplets, for a range of viscosities from 1 to 0.001. Results for the cascaded LBM and the MRT method are shown, along with the LBGK case for comparison. Both the cascaded LBM and the MRT method give similar significant reductions in spurious velocity over the LBGK method. This reduction is up to two orders of magnitude for certain viscosities, and taking for example 0.001 as the maximum average spurious velocity in the gas which can be tolerated for a simulation, increases the useable range of low viscosities by roughly two orders of magnitude.

Fixing ω=1, Fig. 6 shows results for varying density ratio. It can be seen that both the cascaded LBM and the MRT method provide significant reductions in spurious velocities over the LBGK case, with the cascaded LBM giving lower velocities than the MRT method at high density ratios. A two orders of magnitude reduction in spurious velocities over the LBGK method is seen at high density ratios with the cascaded LBM.

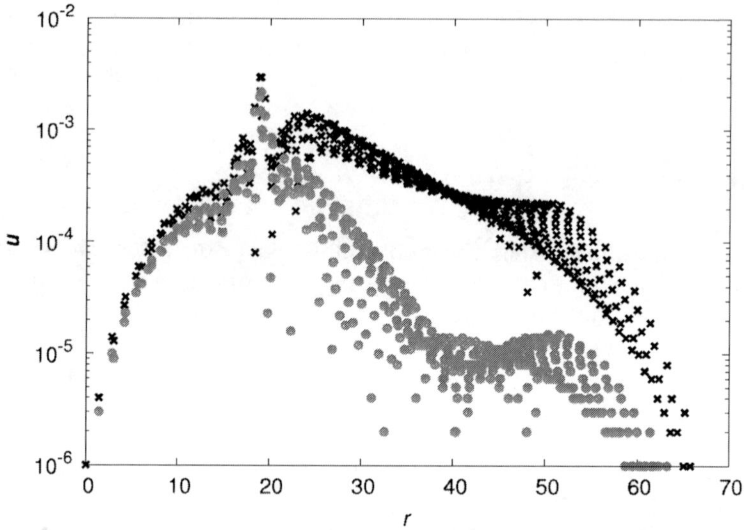

Figure. 4. Magnitude of the spurious velocities around a droplet against the distance from the droplet center, r, for a droplet of radius 20 at ω=1, for the LBGK method (black crosses) and the cascaded LBM with ω_4=0.2 (red circles). A small reduction in maximum spurious velocity (around r=20) is observed, while the reductions in the gas phase (r>20) can be greater than an order of magnitude.

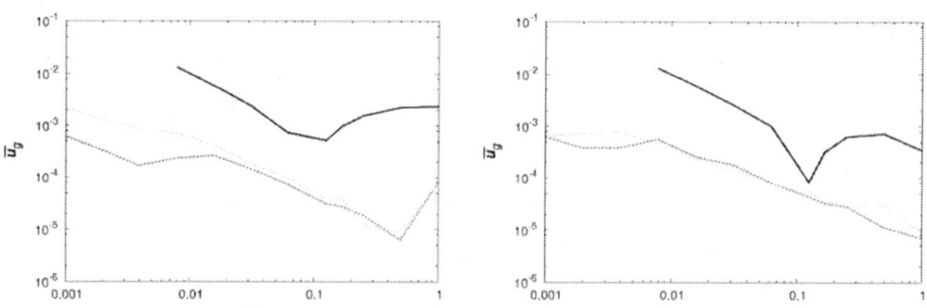

Figure. 5. Minimum average magnitude of the spurious velocities in the gas phase, for varying viscosity at a density ratio of 20. Results are for the LBGK method (solid black line), the MRT method (dotted green line) and the cascaded LBM (dashed red line), for the second order (left figure) and third order (right figure) schemes.

In the third order case, the improvement over the LBGK method is smaller, due to a large reduction in spurious velocities between the second and third order LBGK models. Results for the cascaded LBM are slightly worse than at second order, bringing them into line with those from the MRT method.

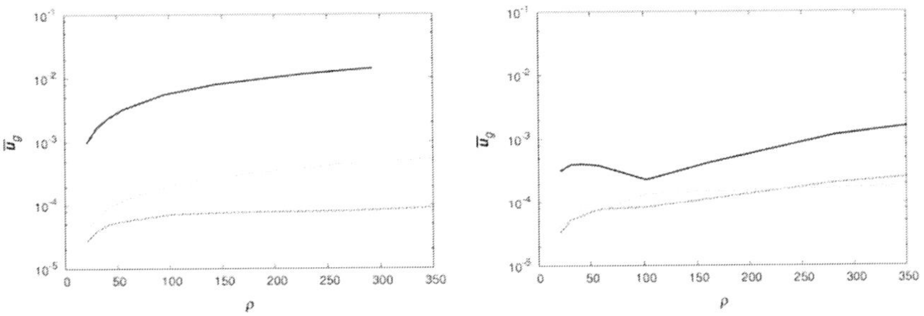

Figure. 6. Minimum average magnitude of the spurious velocities in the gas phase, for varying density ratio at ω=1. Results are for the LBGK method (solid black line), the MRT method (dotted green line) and the cascaded LBM (dashed red line), for the second order (left figure) and third order (right figure) schemes.

The cascaded LBM has given significant reductions in spurious velocities compared with the LBGK method, across a wide range of viscosities and density ratios, with results similar to or slightly better than those observed with the MRT method. At second order the cascaded method is seen to outperform the MRT method, especially at high density ratios. However in the third order case both the MRT method and the cascaded LBM give very similar improvement over the LBGK method. As the third order term is required to maintain Galilean invariance, and has been shown here in the case of oscillating droplets to be important when varying ω_3, it should be included in the model.

6. CONCLUSION

It has been shown that an implementation of the cascaded lattice Boltzmann method can significantly reduce the spurious velocities found around curved interfaces in a multiphase system, which uses the Shan–Chen interparticle model to calculate the forcing term. This is achieved through varying the relaxation rates of higher order moments defined in a co-moving reference frame. It has been shown that these relaxation rates can be varied without significant deterioration in the results, and that they can therefore be used to tune the system for lower spurious velocities and improved stability, without compromising the accuracy of the solution. This is in line with the finding of Geier et al. [28] for improved stability over the LBGK method in the single phase case. Additionally it has been shown that third order velocity terms play a significant role and should not be neglected.

Comparisons were made with an MRT implementation, in both cases the exact difference method was used, so differences between models due to the collision operator alone (and not the multiphase implementation) could be observed. The cascaded model was shown to perform as well as the more established MRT method across a large parameter range. This result, in combination with improvements over the MRT method in the single phase case [28,31], suggests that the cascaded LBM is a valuable addition to the family of lattice Boltzmann models. Finally, the reduction in spurious velocities over the LBGK model extends the useable region of the multiphase LBM in terms of both higher density ratios and lower viscosities, thus bringing the method closer to its goal of simulating the high density ratios and high Reynolds numbers observed in real world systems. A compromise exists between tuning the relaxation parameters for increased stability and reduced spurious velocity, therefore future work should focus on combining the cascaded LBM with other multiphase methods, for example the method of Lee and Fischer [17].

ACKNOWLEDGEMENTS

We gratefully acknowledge the funding from the Engineering and Physical Sciences Research Council for Grant No. EP/J016381/1 and a HEC Studentship, and insightful discussions with Prof. Ilya Karlin.

REFERENCES

1. Y.H. Qian, S. Succi, S.A. Orszag**Recent advances in lattice Boltzmann computing** Annu. Rev. Comput. Phys., 30 (1995), p. 195
2. S. Chen, G.D. Doolen, **Lattice Boltzmann method for fluid flows** Annu. Rev. Fluid Mech., 30 (1998), p. 329
3. S. Succi, **The Lattice Boltzmann Equation for Fluid Dynamics and Beyond** Oxford University Press, Oxford (2001)
4. M.R. Swift, W.R. Osborn, J.M. Yeomans, **Lattice Boltzmann simulation of nonideal fluids** Phys. Rev. Lett., 75 (1995), p. 830
5. E. Orlandini, M.R. Swift, J.M. Yeomans, **A lattice Boltzmann model of binary-fluid mixtures** Europhys. Lett., 32 (1995), p. 463
6. M.R. Swift, E. Orlandini, W.R. Osborn, J.M. Yeomans, **Lattice Boltzmann simulations of liquid–gas and binary fluid systems** Phys. Rev. E, 54 (1996), p. 5041

7. X. He, X. Shan, G.D. Doolen, **Discrete Boltzmann equation model for nonideal gases** Phys. Rev. E, 57 (1998), p. R13
8. X. He, G.D. Doolen, **Thermodynamic foundations of kinetic theory and lattice Boltzmann models for multiphase flows** J. Stat. Phys., 107 (2002), p. 309
9. L.-S. Luo, **Unified theory of lattice Boltzmann models for nonideal gases** Phys. Rev. Lett., 81 (1998), p. 1618
10. X. Shan, H. Chen, **Lattice Boltzmann model for simulating flows with multiple phases and components** Phys. Rev. E, 47 (1993), p. 1815
11. X. Shan, H. Chen, **Simulation of nonideal gases and liquid–gas phase transitions by the lattice Boltzmann equation** Phys. Rev. E, 49 (1994), p. 2941
12. X. Shan, G. Doolen, **Multicomponent lattice-Boltzmann model with interparticle interaction** J. Stat. Phys., 81 (1995), p. 379
13. M. Sbragaglia, R. Benzi, L. Biferale, S. Succi, K. Sugiyama, F. Toschi, **Generalized lattice Boltzmann method with multirange pseudopotential** Phys. Rev. E, 75 (2007), p. 026702
14. P. Yuan, L. Schaefer, **Equations of state in a lattice Boltzmann model** Phys. Fluids, 18 (2006), p. 042101
15. A.L. Kupershtokh, **New method of incorporating a body force term into the lattice Boltzmann equation** Proceedings of the 5th International EHD Workshop, University of Poitiers, Poitiers, France(2004), p. 241
16. Z. Guo, C. Zheng, B. Shi, **Discrete lattice effects on the forcing term in the lattice Boltzmann method** Phys. Rev. E, 65 (2002), p. 046308
17. T. Lee, P.F. Fischer, **Eliminating parasitic currents in the lattice Boltzmann equation method for nonideal gases** Phys. Rev. E, 74 (2006), p. 046709
18. D. Chiappini, G. Bella, S. Succi, F. Toschi, S. Ubertini, **Improved lattice Boltzmann without parasitic currents for Rayleigh–Taylor instability** Commun. Comput. Phys., 7 (2010), p. 423
19. D. d'Humières, **Generalized lattice Boltzmann equations, rarefied gas dynamics: theory and simulations** AIAA Prog. Astronaut. Aeronaut., 159 (1992), p. 450
20. P. Lallemand, L.-S. Luo, **Theory of the lattice Boltzmann method: dispersion, dissipation, isotropy, Galilean invariance, and stability** Phys. Rev. E, 61 (2000), p. 6546
21. D. d'Humières, I. Ginzburg, M. Krafczyk, P. Lallemand, L.-S. Luo, **Multiple-relaxation-time lattice Boltzmann models in three dimensions** Phil. Trans. R. Soc. A, 360 (2002), p. 437
22. P. Lallemand, L.-S. Luo, **Theory of the lattice Boltzmann method: acoustic and thermal properties in two and three dimensions** Phys. Rev. E, 68 (2003), p. 036706
23. M.E. McCracken, J. Abraham, **Multiple-relaxation-time lattice-Boltzmann model for multiphase flow** Phys. Rev. E, 71 (2005), p. 036701
24. J. Tölke, F. Sören, M. Krafczyk, **An adaptive scheme using hierarchical grids for lattice Boltzmann multi-phase flow simulations** Comput. & Fluids, 35 (2006), p. 820
25. S. Mukherjee, J. Abraham, **A pressure-evolution-based multi-relaxation-time high-density-ratio two-phase lattice-Boltzmann model** Comput. & Fluids, 36 (2007), p. 1149
26. Kuzmin, A.A. Mohamad, S. Succi, **Multi-relaxation time lattice Boltzmann model for multiphase flows** Int. J. Mod. Phys. C, 19 (2008), p. 875
27. Fakhari, M.H. Rahimian, **Phase-field modeling by the method of lattice Boltzmann equations** Phys. Rev. E, 81 (2010), p. 036707
28. M.C. Geier, A. Greiner, J.G. Korvink, **Cascaded digital lattice Boltzmann automata for high Reynolds number flow** Phys. Rev. E, 73 (2006), p. 066705
29. I.V. Karlin, P. Asinari, **Factorization symmetry in the lattice Boltzmann method** Physica A, 389 (2010), p. 1530
30. P. Asinari, **Generalized local equilibrium in the cascaded lattice Boltzmann method** Phys. Rev. E, 78 (2008), p. 016701
31. M.C. Geier, A. Greiner, J.G. Korvink, **Properties of the cascaded lattice Boltzmann automaton** Int. J. Mod. Phys. C, 18 (2007), p. 455

32. A.J. Wagner, **Thermodynamic consistency of liquid–gas lattice Boltzmann simulations** Phys. Rev. E, 74 (2006), p. 056703
33. A.L. Kupershtokh, D.A. Medvedev, D.I. Karpov, **On equations of state in a lattice Boltzmann method** Comput. Math. Appl., 58 (2009), p. 965
34. Q. Li, K.H. Luo, X.J. Li, **Forcing scheme in pseudopotential lattice Boltzmann model for multiphase flows** Phys. Rev. E, 86 (2012), p. 016709
35. Z. Yu, L.-S. Fan, **Multirelaxation-time interaction-potential-based lattice Boltzmann model for two-phase flow** Phys. Rev. E, 82 (2010), p. 046708
36. K.N. Premnath, S. Banerjee, **Incorporating forcing terms in cascaded lattice Boltzmann approach by method of central moments** Phys. Rev. E, 80 (2009), p. 036702
37. A.L. Kupershtokh, **Criterion of numerical instability of liquid state in LBE simulations** Comput. Math. Appl., 59 (2010), p. 2236

CHAPTER 18

A meshless method for an inverse two-phase one-dimensional nonlinear Stefan problem

B. Tomas Johansson[a,b], Daniel Lesnic[c], Thomas Reeve[d,*]

[a]*EAS, Aston University, Birmingham B4 7ET, UK*

[b]*ITN, Campus Norrköping, Linköping University, Sweden*

[c]*Department of Applied Mathematics, University of Leeds, Leeds LS2 9JT, UK*

[d]*School of Mathematics, University of Birmingham, Birmingham B15 2TT, UK*

ABSTRACT

We extend a meshless method of fundamental solutions recently proposed by the authors for the one-dimensional two-phase inverse linear Stefan problem, to the nonlinear case. In this latter situation the free surface is also considered unknown which is more realistic from the practical point of view. Building on the earlier work, the solution is approximated in each phase by a linear combination of fundamental solutions to the heat equation. The implementation and analysis are more complicated in the present situation since one needs to deal with a nonlinear minimization problem to identify the free surface. Furthermore, the inverse problem is ill-posed since small errors in the input measured data can cause large deviations in the desired solution. Therefore, regularization needs to be incorporated in the objective function which is minimized in order to obtain a stable solution. Numerical results are presented and discussed.

Keywords: Heat conduction; Inverse Stefan problem; Method of fundamental solutions; Two-phase change; Regularization

1. INTRODUCTION

The two-phase direct Stefan problem requires determining the temperature distribution and the moving free interface when the initial and boundary conditions, as well as the thermal properties of the bi-material involved, are known, see e.g. [19]. Under various boundary conditions it was shown to be well-posed, see [3,5,6]. In contrast to the direct problem, inverse Stefan problems require determining some initial temperature and/or boundary conditions, and/or thermal properties from additional information, which may involve the partial knowledge of the free surface, the temperature measured at some points inside the medium or on the boundary, the heat flux, etc., see [10].

In comparison to the studies on the one-phase flow, the literature on solving two-phase inverse Stefan problems is much more scarce, see [1,17,20]. However, these inverse design Stefan problems were linear because in their formulation the position of the moving interface is considered known. When the position of the moving interface is unknown and also no temperature or heat flux boundary conditions are specified on a part of the boundary then one deals with a nonlinear and ill-posed inverse Stefan problem, see [11]. Although the uniqueness of a solution in Hölder spaces for such a class of two-phase inverse nonlinear Stefan problems holds, see [10,12], these problems are still ill-posed because there is no continuous dependence of the solution on the input data.

The plan of the paper is as follows. In Section 2, we give the mathematical formulation of the one-dimensional two-phase inverse nonlinear Stefan problem and point out its ill-posedness. In Section 3, we describe the regularized numerical meshless method of fundamental solutions (MFS) for constructing a stable solution to the inverse problem. Section 4 presents and discusses numerical results obtained for some typical test examples with and without noise included in the input data. Finally, Section 5 presents conclusions and possible future work.

2. MATHEMATICAL FORMULATION

Assume that the interface

$s(t) \in (0,l]$, for $t \in (0,T]$, (2.1)

and $s(0)$ is given, and denote by

$$Q_T=\{(x,t)\in(0,l]\times(0,T]\}$$

the two-phase rectangular domain $(0, l) \times (0, T]$, which is subdivided by the interface into the two subdomains

$$D_T^1 = \{(x,t) \in Q_T | 0 < x < s(t), \quad t \in (0,T]\},$$

$$D_T^2 = \{(x,t) \in Q_T | s(t) < x < l, \quad t \in (0,T]\}.$$

We investigate the inverse nonlinear two-phase one-dimensional Stefan problem which requires finding the triplet solution $(u_1, u_2, s) \in C^{2,1}(D_T^1) \times C^{2,1}(D_T^2) \times (C([0,T]) \cap C^1(0,T]))$, satisfying (2.1), the heat equations

$$\frac{\partial u_1}{\partial t} = \alpha_1 \frac{\partial^2 u_1}{\partial x^2}, \quad (x,t) \in D_T^1 \qquad (2.2a)$$

$$\frac{\partial u_2}{\partial t} = \alpha_2 \frac{\partial^2 u_2}{\partial x^2}, \quad (x,t) \in D_T^2 \qquad (2.2b)$$

where $\alpha_n > 0$ is the thermal diffusivity of the heat conductor $D^n{}_T$ for $n = 1, 2$, the initial conditions at $t = 0$

$$u_1(x,0) = u_1^0(x), \quad x \in [0, s(0)], \qquad (2.3a)$$

$$u_2(x,0) = u_2^0(x), \quad x \in [s(0), l], \qquad (2.3b)$$

the interface Stefan conditions at $x = s(t)$

$$u_1(s(t), t) = u_2(s(t), t) = u^*(t), \quad t \in (0, T], \tag{2.4a}$$

$$s'(t) = -K_1 \frac{\partial u_1}{\partial x}(s(t), t) + K_2 \frac{\partial u_2}{\partial x}(s(t), t), \quad t \in (0, T], \tag{2.4b}$$

where $K_n = k_n/(\rho_2 L)$, and k_n, ρ_n, L are the thermal conductivities, densities and latent heat, respectively, of $D^1{}_T$ (water) and $D^2{}_T$ (ice), and the Cauchy boundary conditions at $x = l$

$$u_2(l, t) = f_l(t), \quad t \in (0, T], \tag{2.5a}$$

$$k_2 \frac{\partial u_2}{\partial x}(l, t) = g_l(t), \quad t \in (0, T], \tag{2.5b}$$

We also impose the compatibility conditions at the corners $(x, t) = (s(0), 0)$ and $(l, 0)$, namely

$$u_1^0(s(0)) = u_2^0(s(0)) = u^*(0), \tag{2.6a}$$

$$u_2^0(l) = f_l(0), \quad k_2 \frac{du_2^0}{dx}(0) = g_l(0). \tag{2.6b}$$

Remark that the fixed boundary $x = l$ is overspecified because both Dirichlet and Neumann (i.e. Cauchy) data are prescribed in (2.5a) and (2.5b), whilst the fixed boundary $x = 0$ is underspecified because no condition is prescribed on it. Physical quantities of interest related to this hostile or inaccessible boundary are the temperature

$$u_1(0, t) = f_0(t), \quad t \in (0, T], \tag{2.7a}$$

the heat flux

$$-k_1 \frac{\partial u_1}{\partial x}(0, t) = g_0(t), \quad t \in (0, T], \tag{2.7b}$$

and the mass

$$\int_0^{s(t)} u_1(x,t)\,dx = E(t), \quad t \in (0, T] \tag{2.7c}$$

This data can also be required to satisfy the compatibility conditions at the origin $(x, t) = (0, 0)$, namely,

$$f_0(0) = u_1^0(0), \quad g_0(0) = -k_1 \frac{du_1^0}{dx}(0), \quad E(0) = \int_0^{s(0)} u_1^0(x)\,dx \tag{2.8}$$

A sketch of the conditions in the two-phase inverse nonlinear Stefan problem is shown in Fig. 1.

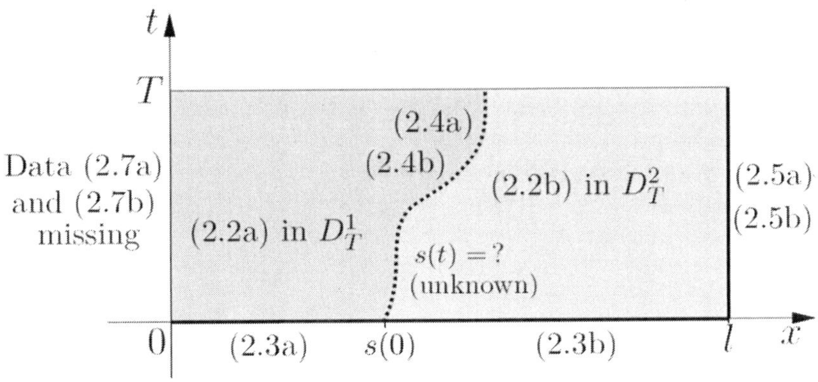

Figure. 1. Sketch of the two-phase inverse nonlinear Stefan problem (2.1)–(2.5).

Sometimes, in practice, the measurement of both the boundary temperature (2.5a)and the heat flux (2.5b) may not be easy and only one of this data may be available. In such a situation one could measure instead the upper base (i.e. final time) internal temperature at $t = T$, namely

$$u_1(x, T) = u_1^T(x), \quad x \in [0, s(T)], \tag{2.9a}$$

$$u_2(x, T) = u_2^T(x), \quad x \in [s(T), l], \tag{2.9b}$$

where $s(T) \in (0, l)$ is also given. However, it turns out, see [11], that this latter 'upper base data (2.9)' inverse problem is more ill-posed than the former 'Cauchy data (2.5a and 2.5b)' inverse problem because it can have more than one solution, i.e. the solution is not unique. However, as we shall see below, the former problem can have at most one solution, i.e. the solution is unique, though the problem is still ill-posed since small errors in the input data (2.5) can cause large errors in the output data (2.7). Therefore, in this study only the inverse problem given by Eqs. (2.1)–(2.6) will be investigated. This problem may be considered as a continuation problem of the solution of the parabolic linear heat equation from the boundary $x = l$, where the Cauchy data (2.5a and 2.5b) is given, into the domain Q_T. It can also be reinterpreted as a "backward in space" inverse heat conduction problem with an "initial" transient boundary, see [18]. However, in contrast to the non-characteristic Cauchy problem, there is the unknown phase transition moving boundary $x = s(t)$ in Q_T also to be determined and this essentially complicates the task of analytic continuation.

An initial attempt would be to split the two-phase inverse Stefan problem (2.1)–(2.6)into two problems. The first is the nonlinear inverse boundary determination problem for the pair (u_2, s) satisfying equations (2.1), (2.2b), (2.3b), (2.5a and 2.5b), (2.6) and

$$u_2(s(t), t) = u^*(t), \quad t \in (0, T] \tag{2.10}$$

with

$$u_2^0(s(0)) = u^*(0) \tag{2.11}$$

The solution of this problem is unique, see [9], even if the initial condition (2.3b) is not imposed, see [22]. Once the boundary $x = s(t)$ and the heat flux $\frac{\partial u_2}{\partial x}(s(t), t)$ have been determined, the second is the linear inverse problem for determining the temperature u_1 satisfying equations (2.2a), (2.3a),

$$u_1(s(t), t) = u^*(t), \quad t \in (0, T] \tag{2.12}$$

with

$$u_1^0(s(0)) = u^*(0) \tag{2.13}$$

and

$$-K_1\frac{\partial u_1}{\partial x}(s(t),t)=s'(t)-K_2\frac{\partial u_2}{\partial x}(s(t),t), \quad t\in(0,T] \tag{2.14}$$

The solution of this problem is unique, see [4] even if the initial condition (2.3a) is not imposed, see [14,21]. However, both the above problems are ill-posed since their solutions do not depend continuously on the input data. In order to obtain stable solutions regularization is necessary and this involves choosing at least two regularization parameters, one for each problem. Besides depending on the amount of noise in the input data they depend on each other since the first nonlinear ill-posed problem has to be solved first to provide the input for the second linear ill-posed problem. So, this two-parameter choice becomes complicated.

Therefore, it appears more useful to solve the composite problem (2.1)–(2.6) in one go for simultaneously determining the solution (u_1, u_2, s).

The problem is still ill-posed but it can now be regularized by choosing a single regularization parameter for the unknown temperature fields. This combined approach has been used previously by the authors for simultaneously determining a heat source and the initial temperature, see [15]. Finally, we will also investigate the case when the initial conditions (2.3a) and (2.3b), together with the compatibility conditions (2.6a) and (2.6b), are not prescribed.

3. THE METHOD OF FUNDAMENTAL SOLUTIONS

We approximate the solutions (u_1, u_2) of the heat equations (2.2a) and (2.2b) using the method of fundamental solutions (MFS) for the unsteady heat conduction in composite layered materials, recently developed by the authors in [7,16,17]. In the MFS, we approximate u_1 and u_2 by linear combinations of fundamental solutions of the heat equation

$$G_n(x,t;y,\tau)=\frac{H(t-\tau)}{\sqrt{4\alpha_n\pi(t-\tau)}}\exp\left(-\frac{(x-y)^2}{4\alpha_n(t-\tau)}\right), \quad n=1,2 \quad , \tag{3.1}$$

where H is the Heaviside function, of the form

$$u_n(x,t) = \sum_{j=1}^{M} c_j^{(n)} G_n(x,t;y_j^{(n)},\tau_j), \quad (x,t) \in \overline{D_T^n}, \; n = 1,2 \tag{3.2}$$

In expression (3.2), the source points $(y_j^{(n)},\tau_j)$ for $j=\overline{1,M}$ and n = 1, 2, are located outside the solution domains $\overline{D_T^n}$ in the following way:

$$y_j^{(1)} = \begin{cases} -h, & j=\overline{1,2M_1} \\ h + s_{3M_1-j+1}, & j=\overline{2M_1+1,3M_1} \\ h + s_{4M_1-j+1}, & j=\overline{3M_1+1,4M_1} \end{cases} \tag{3.3a}$$

$$y_j^{(2)} = \begin{cases} -h + s_{M_1-j+1}, & j=\overline{1,M_1} \\ -h + s_{2M_1-j+1}, & j=\overline{M_1+1,2M_1} \\ l+h, & j=\overline{2M_1+1,4M_1} \end{cases} \tag{3.3b}$$

where h is a preassigned MFS positive parameter giving the distance between the source points and the boundary, $M = 4M_1$,

$$\tau_j = \frac{(2j-1-2M_1)T}{2M_1} \quad \text{for} \quad j=\overline{1,2M_1},$$

$\tau_j=\tau_{j-2M_1}$ for $j=\overline{2M_1+1,4M_1}$, and $s_j = s(\tau_{j+M_1})$ for $j=\overline{1,M_1}$, see Fig. 2 for a representation of the domains, boundaries and placement of source points.

The $2M$ unknown coefficients $\mathbf{c} = (c_j^{(n)})_{j=\overline{1,M}}^{n=1,2}$ and the $M_1 = M/4$ discretization points $\mathbf{s} = (s_j)_{j=\overline{1,M_1}}$ of the unknown free boundary have to be determined by collocating the conditions (2.3)–(2.6), as described next. Let us select a uniform distribution of collocation points given by

$$t_0 = 0, \quad t_i = \frac{(2i-1)T}{2M_1} = |\tau_{2M_1-i+1}|, \quad i=\overline{1,M_1},$$

$$\tilde{t}_i = \frac{iT}{M_2} \quad \text{for } i=\overline{0,M_2},$$

$$x_1^{(k)} = \frac{ks(0)}{K+1}, \quad x_2^{(k)} = s(0) + \frac{k(l-s(0))}{K+1}, \quad k=\overline{1,K}, \tag{3.4}$$

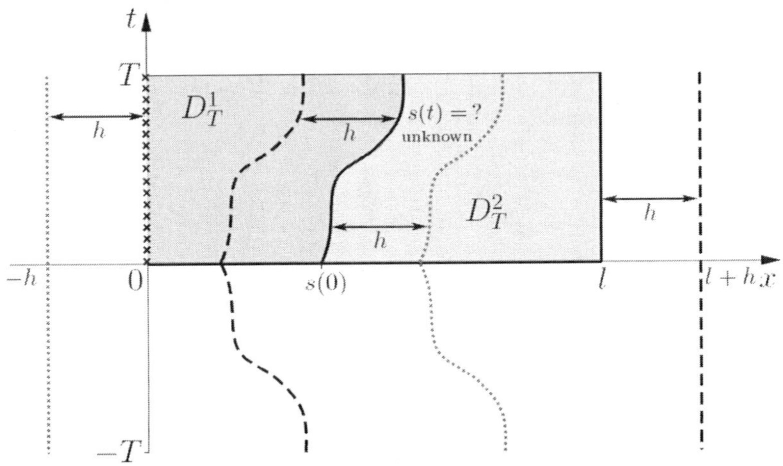

Figure. 2. Representation of the two-phase problem with domains D_T^1 and D_T^2, unknown boundary data (×), and source points (•••) and (- - -) placed externally to the domains D_T^1 and D_T^2, respectively.

and collocate equations (2.3)–(2.6) as follows:

$$u_n(x_n^{(k)}, 0) = u_n^0(x_n^{(k)}), \quad k = \overline{1, K}, \; n = 1, 2, \tag{3.5}$$

$$u_1(s_i, t_i) = u_2(s_i, t_i) = u^*(t_i), \quad i = \overline{0, M_1}, \tag{3.6}$$

$$-K_1 \frac{\partial u_1}{\partial x}(s_i, t_i) + K_2 \frac{\partial u_2}{\partial x}(s_i, t_i) = s'(t_i) = \begin{cases} \dfrac{s(t_1) - s(0)}{t_1}, & i = 1 \\ \dfrac{s(t_i) - s(t_{i-1})}{t_i - t_{i-1}}, & i = \overline{2, M_1} \end{cases}, \quad i = \overline{1, M_1}, \tag{3.7}$$

$$u_2(l, \tilde{t}_i) = f_l(\tilde{t}_i), \quad k_2 \frac{\partial u_2}{\partial x}(l, \tilde{t}_i) = g_l(\tilde{t}_i), \quad i = \overline{0, M_2} \tag{3.8}$$

In total, via (3.2), Eqs. (3.5)–(3.8) form a system of $(2K + 3M_1 + 2M_2 + 4)$ equations with $9M_1$ unknowns (**c**, **s**). In general, we require to have at least as many equations as unknowns and therefore we require

$$2M_2 + 2K + 4 \geq 6M_1, \quad \text{or} \quad M_2 + K + 2 \geq 3M_1$$

Note that this system is linear in **c**, but it is nonlinear in **s**. In addition, our inverse problem is ill-posed. Therefore, we apply the nonlinear Tikhonov regularization method based on minimizing the non-linear regularized least-squares functional

$$\begin{aligned}\mathcal{F}(\mathbf{c},\mathbf{s}) &= \sum_{n=1}^{2}\sum_{k=1}^{K}\left(\sum_{j=1}^{M} c_j^{(n)} G_n(x_n^{(k)},0;y_j^{(n)},\tau_j) - u_n^0(x_n^{(k)})\right)^2 + \sum_{i=0}^{M_1}\left(\sum_{j=1}^{M} c_j^{(1)} G_1(s_i,t_i;y_j^{(1)},\tau_j) - u^*(t_i)\right)^2 \\ &+ \sum_{i=0}^{M_1}\left(\sum_{j=1}^{M} c_j^{(2)} G_2(s_i,t_i;y_j^{(2)},\tau_j) - u^*(t_i)\right)^2 \\ &+ \sum_{i=1}^{M_1}\left(\sum_{j=1}^{M}\left[K_2 c_j^{(2)}\frac{\partial G_2}{\partial x}(s_i,t_i;y_j^{(2)},\tau_j) - K_1 c_j^{(1)}\frac{\partial G_1}{\partial x}(s_i,t_i;y_j^{(1)},\tau_j)\right] - s'(t_i)\right)^2 \\ &+ \sum_{i=0}^{M_2}\left(\sum_{j=1}^{M} c_j^{(2)} G_2(l,\tilde{t}_i;y_j^{(2)},\tau_j) - f_l(\tilde{t}_i)\right)^2 + \sum_{i=0}^{M_2}\left(\sum_{j=1}^{M} c_j^{(2)} k_2\frac{\partial G_2}{\partial x}(l,\tilde{t}_i;y_j^{(2)},\tau_j) - g_l(\tilde{t}_i)\right)^2 \\ &+ \lambda_1|\mathbf{c}|^2 + \lambda_2|\mathbf{s}|^2, \end{aligned} \tag{3.9}$$

where $\lambda_1, \lambda_2 \geq 0$ are regularization parameters which can be prescribed according to some criterion, e.g. the L-surface, or, more simply, by trial and error. Note that in the last term of (3.9), for simplicity and in a first attempt, we have imposed that $s \in C[0, T]$, but more regularity such as $s \in C^1[0, T]$ can also be imposed in order to get some stability estimates.

In imposing the flux boundary conditions (2.4b) and (2.5b) the x-partial derivative of (3.1) is needed, as given by

$$\frac{\partial G_n}{\partial x}(x,t;y,\tau) = -\frac{(x-y)H(t-\tau)}{2\sqrt{4\pi\alpha_n^3(t-\tau)^3}}\exp\left(-\frac{(x-y)^2}{4\alpha_n(t-\tau)}\right), \quad n = 1, 2.$$

The minimization of the functional (3.9) is performed using the MATLAB toolbox *lsqnonlin* which is designed to minimize a sum of squares of arbitrary differentiable functions. The gradient does not need to be supplied by the user and the simple bounds on the variables

$$0 < s_i < l \quad \text{for } i = \overline{1, M_1} \tag{3.10}$$

are also allowed.

The initial guess to start the iterative process is arbitrary and in this study we take $\mathbf{c}^0 = \mathbf{0}$ and $\mathbf{s}^0 = \mathbf{s}(0)$.

4. NUMERICAL RESULTS AND DISCUSSION

In this section, we apply the MFS outlined in the previous section to the inverse two-phase nonlinear Stefan problem (2.1)–(2.6). In the first two examples we have analytical solutions available and we also investigate for one of them the case when the initial conditions (2.3a) and (2.3b) are not given. In the third example, an analytical solution is not available. Previous experience with applying the MFS for the heat equation, [16,17], suggests that the MFS parameter h should be not too small (which will result in less accurate approximations) nor too large (which will increase the ill-conditioning of the system). In this section, the value of h, as well as the values of the regularization parameters λ_1 and λ_2, are chosen by trial and error. Nevertheless, more rigorous investigations on these choices should be undertaken in a future work.

4.1. Example 1

Let us take $T = 1$, $l = 2$, $\alpha_1 = 2$, $k_1 = 1$, $\alpha_2 = 1$, $k_2 = 2$, $K_1 = 1$, $K_2 = 2$. We also choose in Eqs. (2.3a) and (2.3b) the initial conditions

$$u_1(x,0) = u_1^0(x) = 2\left[\exp\left(\frac{0.5-x}{2}\right) - 1\right], \quad x \in [0, s(0) = 0.5] \tag{4.1a}$$

$$u_2(x,0) = u_2^0(x) = \exp(0.5-x) - 1, \quad x \in [0.5 = s(0), l = 2] \tag{4.1b}$$

We also take $u^*(t) = 0$ such that (2.4a) becomes

$$u_1(s(t),t) = u_2(s(t),t) = 0, \quad t \in (0, T = 1], \tag{4.2}$$

and take the Cauchy boundary conditions (2.5a) and (2.5b) specified by

$$u_2(2,t) = f_l(t) = \exp(t-1.5) - 1, \quad t \in [0, T = 1], \tag{4.3a}$$

$$k_2 \frac{\partial u_2}{\partial x}(2,t) = g_l(t) = -2\exp(t-1.5), \quad t \in [0, T = 1] \tag{4.3b}$$

Then the analytical solution of the inverse Stefan problem (2.1), (2.2), (2.4), (4.1)–(4.3) is given by

$$u_1(x,t) = 2\left(\exp\left(\frac{t+0.5-x}{2}\right) - 1\right), \quad (x,t) \in \overline{D_T^1}, \tag{4.4a}$$

$$u_2(x,t) = \exp(t+0.5-x) - 1, \quad (x,t) \in \overline{D_T^2}, \tag{4.4b}$$

$$s(t) = t + 0.5, \quad t \in [0, T = 1], \tag{4.4c}$$

which can be verified by direct substitution.

Of particular interest is to recover the missing data at the inaccessible hostile boundary $x = 0$, given by the boundary temperature

$$u_1(0,t) = f_0(t) = 2\left(\exp\left(\frac{t+0.5}{2}\right) - 1\right), \quad t \in [0, T = 1] \tag{4.5a}$$

the heat flux

$$-k_1 \frac{\partial u_1}{\partial x}(0,t) = g_0(t) = \exp\left(\frac{t+0.5}{2}\right), \quad t \in [0, T = 1] \tag{4.5b}$$

and the mass

$$\int_0^{s(t)} u_1(x,t)\,dx = E(t) = 2\left(2\exp\left(\frac{t+0.5}{2}\right) - t - 2.5\right), \quad t \in [0, T = 1] \tag{4.5c}$$

If we consider the boundary temperature (4.3a) at $x = l = 2$ as the quantity which is physically measured in practice, whilst the heat flux (4.3b) is prescribed, in order to take into account the uncertainties in the measurement we add to it random additive noise generated as

$$u_2^\delta(1,t) = f_l^\delta(t) = f_l(t) + N(0, \sigma^2), \tag{4.6}$$

where $N(0, \sigma^2)$ represents the normal distribution with mean zero and standard deviation σ which is taken to be

$$\sigma = \delta \times \max_{t \in [0,1]} |f_l(t)|, \tag{4.7}$$

where δ is the percentage of noise. In MATLAB, $N(0, \sigma^2)$ is generated by multiplying $\sigma$with randn (a matrix of normally distributed pseudorandom numbers).

Fig. 3(a)–(d) shows the numerical MFS solutions for $s(t)$, $u_1(0, t)$, $-k_1 \frac{\partial u_1}{\partial x}$ (0,t) and $E(t)$, as functions of $t \in [0, 1]$, obtained with $M_1 = 20$, $M_2 = 40$, $K = 40$, i.e. $2K + 3M_1 + 2M_2 + 4 = 224$ equations with $9M_1 = 180$ unknowns, for no noise, i.e. $\delta = 0$, and $\lambda_1 = \lambda_2 = 0$, in comparison with the exact solutions (4.4c), (4.5a)–(4.5c), respectively. In calculating the mass (2.7c) using the MFS the following integral is needed:

$$\int_0^{s(t)} G_1(x, t; y, \tau)\, dx = \frac{H(t-\tau)}{2}\left[\operatorname{erf}\left(\frac{s(t)-y}{\sqrt{4\alpha_1(t-\tau)}}\right) - \operatorname{erf}\left(\frac{-y}{\sqrt{4\alpha_1(t-\tau)}}\right)\right] \quad ,(4.8)$$

where erf is the error function.

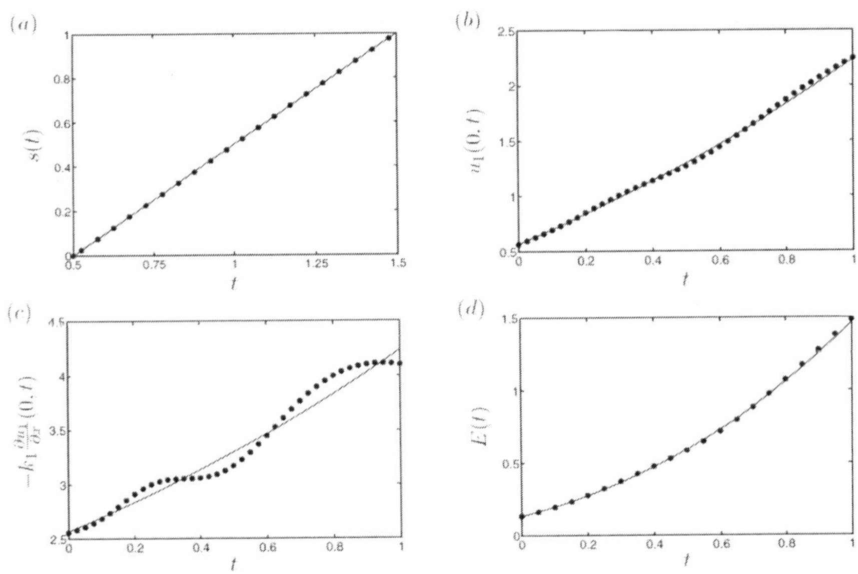

Figure. 3. The numerical (•••) MFS solutions for: (a) $s(t)$, (b) $u_1(0, t)$, (c) $-k_1 \frac{\partial u_1}{\partial x}$ (0,t), and (d) $E(t)$, as a function of $t \in [0, 1]$, obtained with $M_1 = 20$, $M_2 = 40$, $K = 40$, $h = 3$ for no noise $\delta = 0$ and $\lambda_1 = \lambda_2 = 0$ in comparison with the exact (—) solutions (4.4c), (4.5a)–(4.5c), respectively, for Example 1.

Fig. 4(a)–(d) shows the same as Fig. 3(a)–(d), but for δ = 1% and δ = 5% noise and $\lambda_1 = \lambda_2 = 10^{-6}$. In Figs. 3 and 4 it can be seen that stable and accurate numerical MFS solutions are obtained.

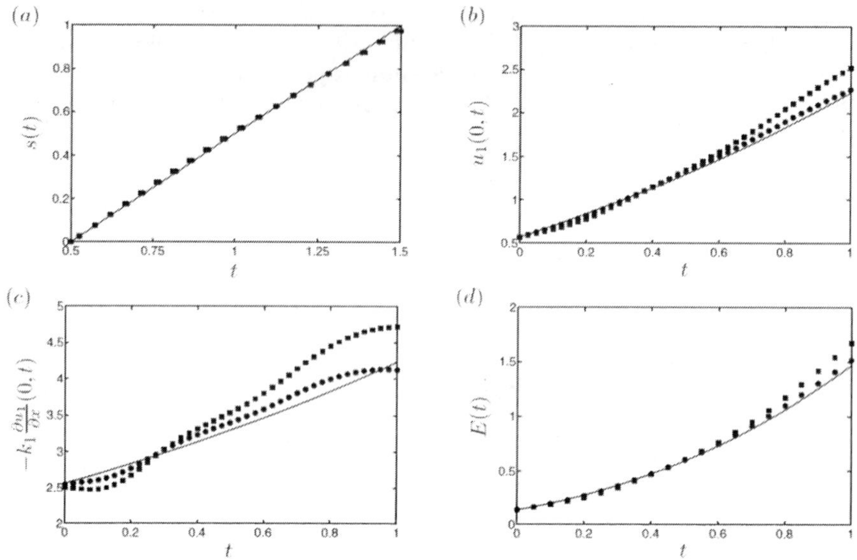

Figure. 4. The numerical MFS solutions for: (a) $s(t)$, (b) $u_1(0, t)$, (c) $-k_1 \frac{\partial u_1}{\partial x}$ (0,t), and (d) $E(t)$, as a function of $t \in [0, 1]$, obtained with $M_1 = 10$, $M_2 = 20$, $K = 20$, $h = 3$ for δ = 1% (•) and δ = 5% (▪) noise and $\lambda_1 = \lambda_2 = 10^{-6}$ in comparison with the exact (—) solutions (4.4c), (4.5a)–(4.5c), respectively, for Example 1.

Next, we look at the case when the initial conditions (4.1a) and (4.1b) are not imposed. In this case the first term in the right-hand side of (3.9) drops out, i.e. Eq. (3.5) is not imposed, such that, via (3.2), Eqs. (3.6)–(3.8) form now a smaller system of $(3M_1 + 2M_2 + 4)$ equations with $9M_1$ unknowns, and we require $M_2 + 2 \geq 3M_1$.

Figs. 5(a)–(d) and 6(a)–(d) represent the same quantities as Figs. 3(a)–(d) and 4(a)–(d), respectively, but obtained with $M_1 = 10$ and $M_2 = 40$, i.e. $3M_1 + 2M_2 + 4 = 114$ equations with $9M_1 = 90$ unknowns. In addition, Figs. 5e and 6e present the numerical results for the initial temperature

$$u(x,0) = \begin{cases} u_1(x,0), & x \in [0, s(0) = 0.5] \\ u_2(x,0), & x \in [0.5 = s(0), l = 2] \end{cases} \tag{4.9}$$

in comparison with the exact solution given by Eqs. (4.1a) and (4.1b). Again, even when we are missing the initial data (2.3a) and (2.3b), we obtain accurate and stable results in all figures, although some instabilities start to manifest in the retrieved heat flux in Fig. 6(c).

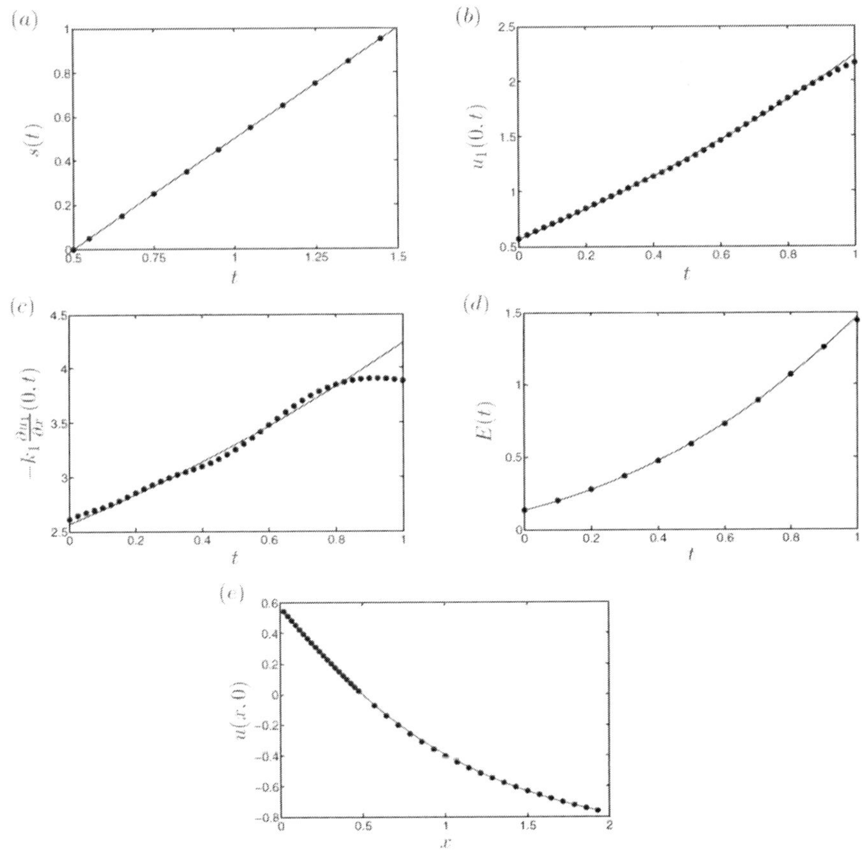

Figure. 5. The numerical (•••) MFS solutions for: (a) $s(t)$, (b) $u_1(0, t)$, (c) $-k_1 \frac{\partial u_1}{\partial x}$ (0,t), and (d) $E(t)$, as a function of $t \in [0, 1]$, and (e) $u(x, 0)$ as a function of $x \in [0, 2]$, obtained with $M_1 = 10$, $M_2 = 40$, $h = 3$ for no noise $\delta = 0$ and $\lambda_1 = \lambda_2 = 0$ in comparison with the exact (—) solutions (4.4c), (4.5a)–(4.5c), respectively, for Example 1.

So far, Example 1 has investigated retrieving a linear function of t for the free surface (4.4c). In the next example we consider a nonlinear variation.

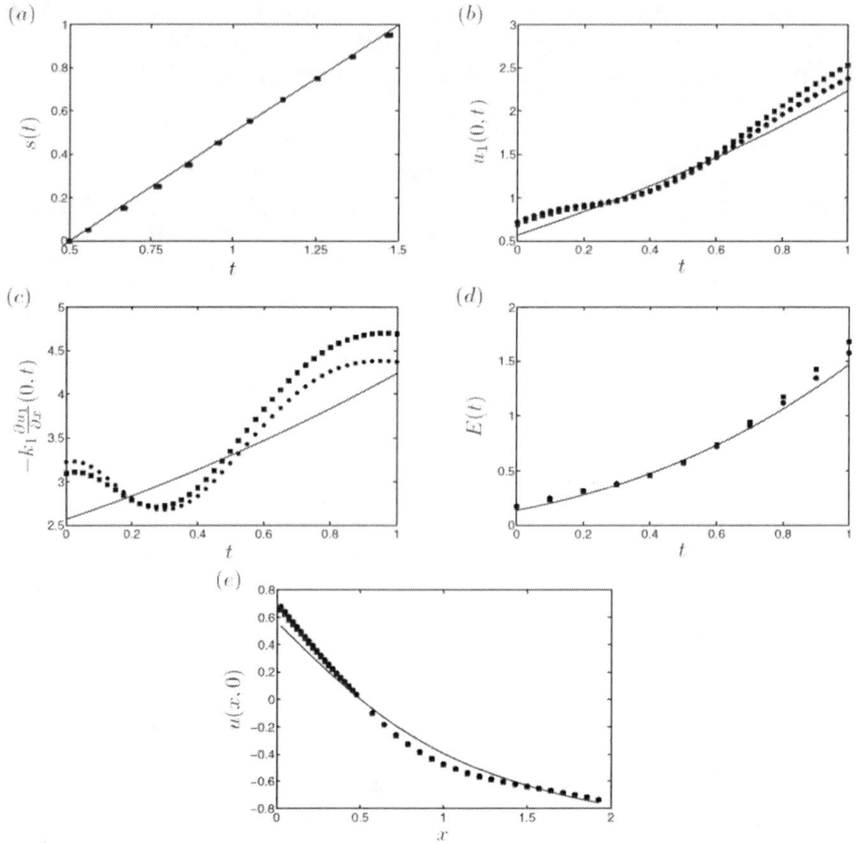

Figure. 6. The numerical MFS solutions for: (a) $s(t)$, (b) $u_1(0, t)$, (c) $-k_1 \frac{\partial u_1}{\partial x}$ (0,t), and (d) $E(t)$, as a function of $t \in [0, 1]$, and (e) $u(x, 0)$ as a function of $x \in [0, 2]$, obtained with $M_1 = 10$, $M_2 = 40$, $h = 3$ for $\delta = 1\%$ (•) and $\delta = 5\%$ (▪) noise with $\lambda_1 = \lambda_2 = 10^{-6}$ in comparison with the exact (—) solutions (4.4c), (4.5a)–(4.5c), respectively, for Example 1.

4.2. Example 2

Let us take $T = 1$, $l = 1$, $\alpha_1 = 0.5$, $\alpha_2 = 1$, $k_1 = 0.5$, $k_2 = 1$, $L = 1$, $\rho_2 = 1$, $K_1 = 0.5$, $K_2 = 1$, and $u^* = 0$. We also choose in Eqs. (2.3a) and (2.3b) the initial conditions

$$u_1(x,0) = u_1^0(x) = 1 - \frac{\operatorname{erf}\left(\frac{x}{2\sqrt{\alpha_1 t^0}}\right)}{\operatorname{erf}\left(\frac{\gamma}{2\sqrt{\alpha_1}}\right)}, \quad x \in [0, s(0) = 0.4]$$

(4.10a)

$$u_2(x,0) = u_2^0(x) = 1 + \frac{\operatorname{erfc}\left(\frac{x}{2\sqrt{\alpha_2 t^0}}\right)}{\operatorname{erfc}\left(\frac{\gamma}{2\sqrt{\alpha_2}}\right)}, \quad x \in [0.4 = s(0), l = 1]$$

(4.10b)

where $\gamma = 0.479611$, $t^0 = 0.695571$ and erf and erfc are the error and the complementary error function, respectively. We also take the interface condition (4.2)and the Cauchy boundary conditions (2.5a) and (2.5b) specified by

$$u_2(1,t) = f_l(t) = -1 + \frac{\operatorname{erfc}\left(\frac{1}{2\sqrt{\alpha_2(t+t^0)}}\right)}{\operatorname{erfc}\left(\frac{\gamma}{2\sqrt{\alpha_2}}\right)}, \quad t \in (0, T = 1],$$

(4.11a)

$$k_2 \frac{\partial u_2}{\partial x}(1,t) = g_l(t) = -\frac{k_2 \exp\left(-\frac{1}{4\alpha_2(t+t^0)}\right)}{\sqrt{\pi\alpha_2(t+t^0)}\,\operatorname{erfc}\left(\frac{\gamma}{2\sqrt{\alpha_2}}\right)}, \quad t \in (0, T = 1],$$

(4.11b)

Then the analytic solution of the inverse Stefan problem (2.1), (2.2), (2.4), (4.2), (4.10) and (4.11) is given by, see [7,8,17],

$$u_1(x,t) = 1 - \frac{\operatorname{erf}\left(\frac{x}{2\sqrt{\alpha_1(t+t^0)}}\right)}{\operatorname{erf}\left(\frac{\gamma}{2\sqrt{\alpha_1}}\right)}, \quad (x,t) \in \overline{D_T^1},$$

(4.12a)

$$u_2(x,t) = -1 + \frac{\operatorname{erfc}\left(\frac{x}{2\sqrt{\alpha_2(t+t^0)}}\right)}{\operatorname{erfc}\left(\frac{\gamma}{2\sqrt{\alpha_2}}\right)}, \quad (x,t) \in \overline{D_T^2},$$

(4.12b)

$$s(t) = \gamma\sqrt{t + t^0}, \quad t \in [0, T = 1], \tag{4.12c}$$

which can be verified by direct substitution. Of particular interest is to recover the missing data at the inaccessible hostile boundary $x = 0$, given by the boundary temperature

$$u_1(0, t) = f_0(t) = 1, \quad t \in [0, T = 1] \tag{4.13a}$$

the heat flux

$$-k_1 \frac{\partial u_1}{\partial x}(0, t) = g_0(t) = \frac{k_1}{\sqrt{\pi \alpha_1 (t + t^0)}\,\mathrm{erf}\frac{\gamma}{2\sqrt{\alpha_1}}}, \quad t \in [0, T = 1] \tag{4.13b}$$

and the mass

$$\int_0^{s(t)} u_1(x, t)\,dx = E(t) = \frac{2}{\mathrm{erf}\left(\frac{\gamma}{2\sqrt{\alpha_1}}\right)} \sqrt{\frac{\alpha_1 (t + t^0)}{\pi}} \left(1 - \exp\left(-\frac{\gamma^2}{4\alpha_1}\right)\right), \quad t \in [0, T = 1]. \tag{4.13c}$$

Noise is added in the boundary temperature (4.11a), as in (4.6).

Figs. 7 and 8 for Example 2 are the analogous of Figs. 3 and 4 for Example 1 and the same conclusions about the good performance of the method are obtained. To further improve the results obtained in Fig. 7, in Fig. 9 we increase the number of collocation and source points.

In both Examples 1 and 2 analytic solutions were available and this enabled assessing the accuracy of the numerically obtained results. The next example considers the case when an analytic solution is not available.

4.3. Example 3

In this example, partially taken from [1] where a linear inverse Stefan problem was addressed, an analytic solution is not available. We take $T = 1$, $l = \pi/2$, $\alpha_1 = 2$, $\alpha_2 = 1$, $s(0) = \pi/4$, $K_1 = 1$, $K_2 = 2$, $k_1 = 1$, $k_2 = 2$, $u^* = 0$, $g_l = 0$, and $u_2^0(x) = \cos(2x)$ for $x \in [\frac{\pi}{4}, \frac{\pi}{2}]$.

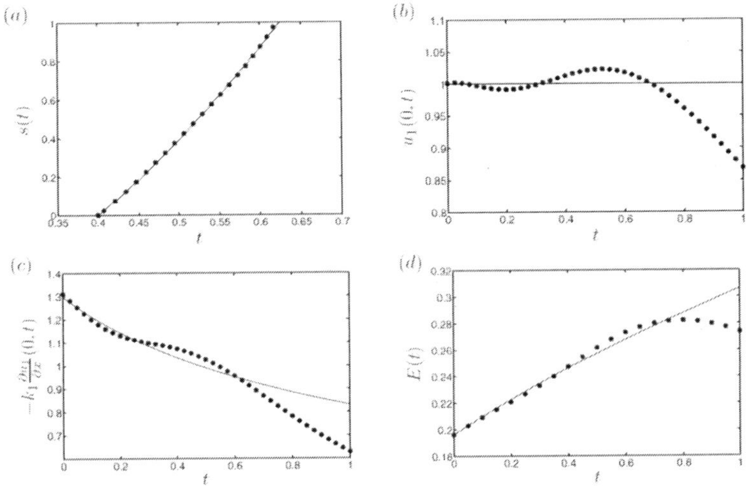

Figure. 7. The numerical (•••) MFS solutions for: (a) $s(t)$, (b) $u_1(0, t)$, (c) $-k_1 \frac{\partial u_1}{\partial x}$ (0,t), and (d) $E(t)$, as a function of $t \in [0, 1]$, obtained with $M_1 = 20$, $M_2 = 40$, $K = 40$, $h = 2$ for no noise $\delta = 0$ and $\lambda_1 = \lambda_2 = 0$ in comparison with the exact (—) solutions (4.12c), (4.13a)–(4.13c), respectively, for Example 2.

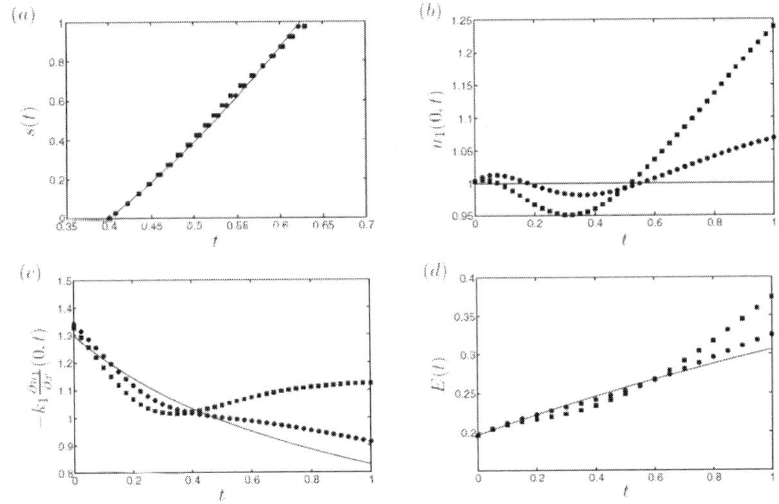

Figure. 8. The numerical MFS solutions for: (a) $s(t)$, (b) $u_1(0, t)$, (c) $-k_1 \frac{\partial u_1}{\partial x}$ (0,t), and (d) $E(t)$, as a function of $t \in [0, 1]$, obtained with $M_1 = 20$, $M_2 = 40$, $K = 40$, $h = 2$ for $\delta = 1\%$ (•) and $\delta = 5\%$ (▪) noise and $\lambda_1 = \lambda_2 = 10^{-6}$ in comparison with the exact (—) solutions (4.12c), (4.13a)–(4.13c), respectively, for Example 2.

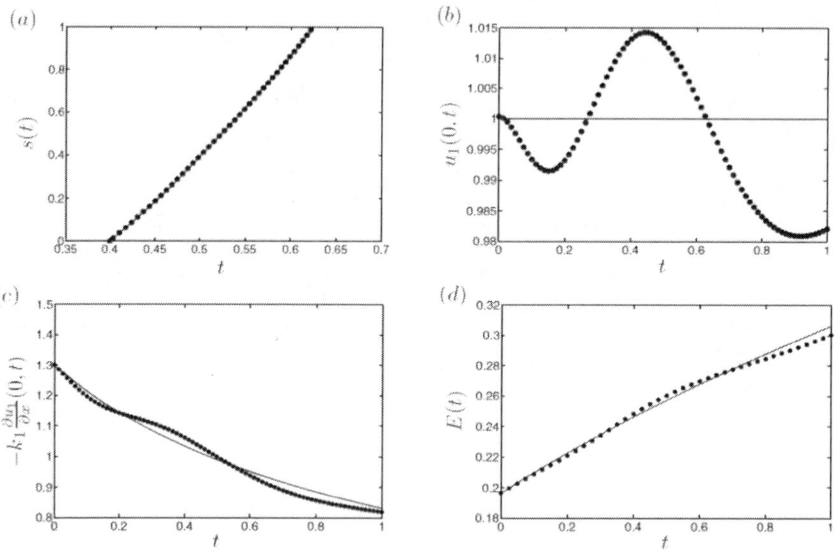

Figure. 9. The numerical (•••) MFS solutions for: (a) $s(t)$, (b) $u_1(0, t)$, (c) $-k_1 \frac{\partial u_1}{\partial x}$ (0,t), and (d) $E(t)$, as a function of $t \in [0, 1]$, obtained with $M_1 = 40$, $M_2 = 80$, $K = 80$, $h = 2$ for no noise $\delta = 0$ and $\lambda_1 = \lambda_2 = 10^{-12}$ in comparison with the exact (—) solutions (4.12c), (4.13a)–(4.13c), respectively, for Example 2.

Since an analytic solution is not available the data (2.5a) is numerically simulated by solving separately using the MFS the direct problem in the domain D_T^2 given by Eqs. (2.2b), namely

$$\frac{\partial u_2}{\partial t} = 2\frac{\partial^2 u_2}{\partial x^2}, \quad (x, t) \in D_T^2 = (s(t), l) \times (0, T], \tag{4.14}$$

Eq. (2.3b) given by

$$u_2(x, 0) = u_2^0(x) = \cos(2x), \quad x \in \left[\frac{\pi}{4}, \frac{\pi}{2}\right], \tag{4.15}$$

condition (2.4a) given by

$$u_2(s(t), t) = u^*(t) = 0, \quad t \in (0, 1] \tag{4.16}$$

the boundary condition (2.5b) given by

$$k_2 \frac{\partial u_2}{\partial x}\left(\frac{\pi}{2}, t\right) = g_l(t) = 0, \quad t \in (0, 1], \tag{4.17}$$

when the free surface is known and is given by

$$s(t) = \arctan(1 + t), \quad t \in (0, 1] \tag{4.18}$$

Observe that the compatibility conditions in (2.6a) and (2.6b) given by

$$u_2^0(s(0)) = u^*(0), \quad k_2 \frac{du_2^0}{dx} = g_l(0) \tag{4.19}$$

are automatically satisfied by the data (4.15)–(4.18). In the direct problem we collocate the Eqs. (4.15)–(4.17) and (4.19) as

$$u_2(x_2^{(k)}, 0) = u_2^0(x_2^{(k)}), \quad k = \overline{1, K} \tag{4.20}$$

$$u_2(s_i, t_i) = u^*(t_i), \quad i = \overline{0, M_1} \tag{4.21}$$

$$k_2 \frac{\partial u_2}{\partial x}(l, \tilde{t}_i) = g_l(\tilde{t}_i), \quad i = \overline{0, M_2} \tag{4.22}$$

resulting in, via (3.2), a system of (K + M_1 + M_2 + 2) linear equations with $4M_1$unknowns $\mathbf{c}^{(2)} = (c_j^{(2)})_{j=\overline{1,M}}$. A necessary condition for a unique solution is $K + M_2 + 2 \geq 3M_1$. This system of equations is ill-conditioned and therefore we employ linear Tikhonov regularization with regularization parameter λ. The numerical results obtained for the boundary temperature $u_2(\pi/2, t)$, as a function of $t \in [0, 1]$, are shown in Fig. 10. This data, to which noise is added as in (4.6), is then used as the input (2.5a) in the inverse problem.

The imposition of the initial condition (2.3a) cannot be arbitrary and in order to ensure that the solution exists we simply do not impose it. In this case the first term in the right-hand side of (3.9) for $n = 1$ drops out, i.e. Eq. (3.5) for $n = 1$ is not imposed, such that, via (3.2), equations (3.5) for $n = 2$, (3.6)–(3.8) form a system of ($3M_1$ + $2M_2$ + K + 4) equations with $9M_1$ unknowns, and we require $2M_2 + K + 4 \geq 6M_1$.

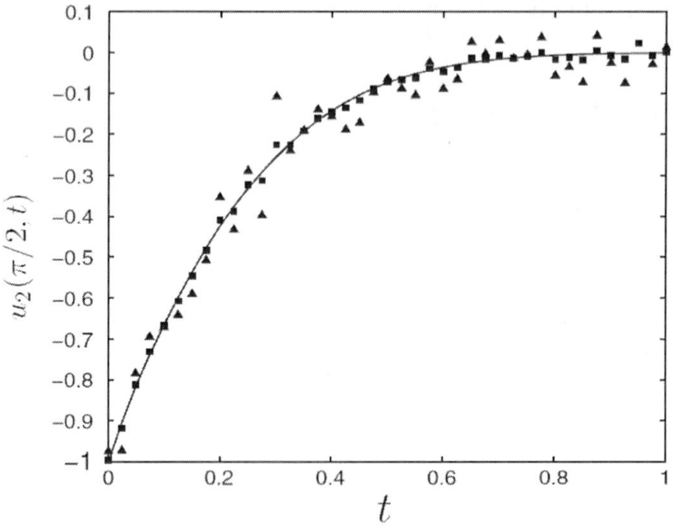

Figure. 10. The direct problem MFS for $u_2(\pi/2, t)$ (—), as a function of $t \in [0, 1]$, obtained with $h = 2$, $M_1 = 40$, $M_2 = 60$, $K = 58$ (i.e. $K + M_1 + M_2 + 2 = 160$ equations with $4M_1 = 160$ unknowns) and $\lambda = 10^{-14}$, and the perturbed data for $\delta = 1\%$ (▪) and $\delta = 5\%$ (▴), for Example 3.

Figs. 11(a)–(e) and 12(a)–(e) show the MFS solutions for s(t),u1(0,t), $-k_1 \frac{\partial u_1}{\partial x}$ (0,t),$E(t)$ and $u_1(x, 0)$ obtained for $M_1 = 20$, $M_2 = 40$, $K = 40$ (i.e. $3M_1 + 2M_2 + K + 4 = 184$ equations with $9M_1 = 180$ unknowns) for $\delta = 0$ and $\lambda_1 = \lambda_2 = 0$, $\delta = 1\%$ and $\lambda_1 = \lambda_2 = 10^{-6}$. We note that to generate the stable results in Fig. 11 the variable and function tolerances used in the MATLAB toolbox *lsqnonlin* were reduced from 10^{-6} to 10^{-9}.

For the free boundary, comparison between the MFS solution and the exact solution (4.18) made in Fig. 11(a) shows good agreement. We point out that the reconstructions become rather inaccurate when increasing the noise level, and for $\delta = 5\%$ it is not possible to obtain a reasonable approximation. Moreover, by inspecting Fig. 12(a)–(e) (see also Figs. 6(c) and 8(c)) we note that the numerical solutions seem to deviate from the 'exact' MFS approximations that were generated in [17], as the time t approaches the final time T.

This is to be somewhat expected since if we want to recover the heat flux at $x = 0$ over the whole time interval $[0, T]$ then we need to use the Cauchy data (2.5a) and (2.5b) over an extended interval $[0, T + r]$, where $r > 0$ is related to the concept of 'future times' in the inverse heat conduction literature, see [2,13].

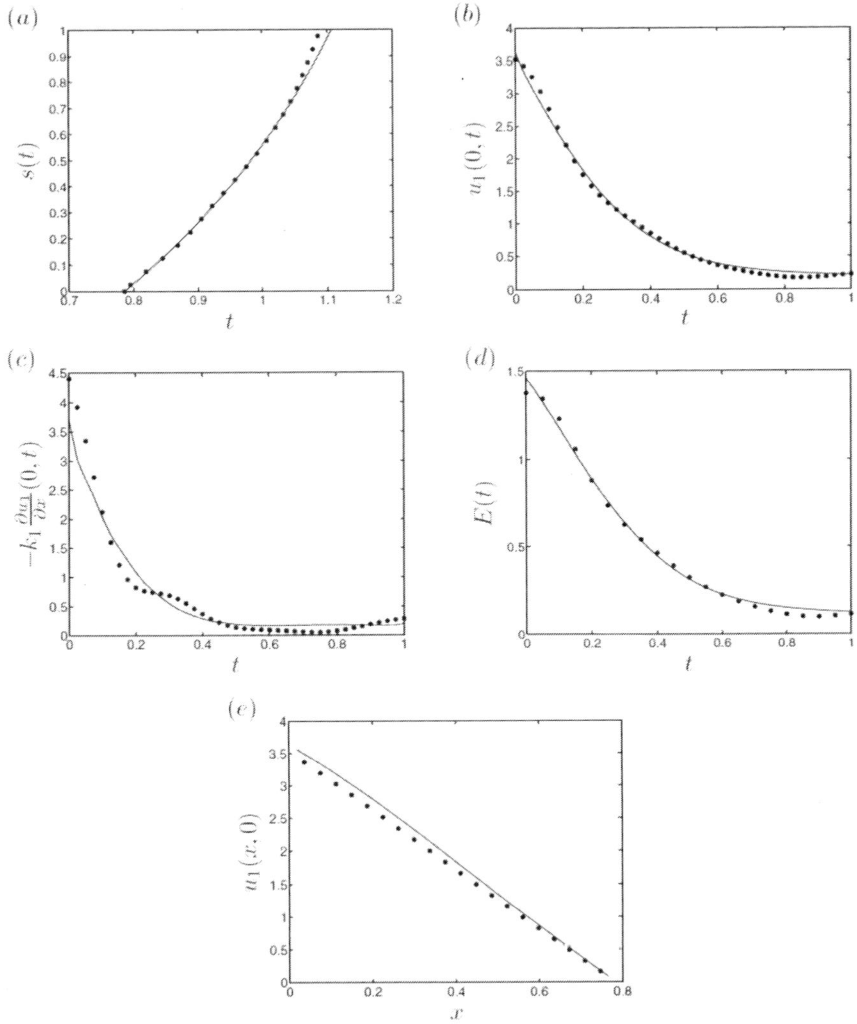

Figure. 11. The numerical MFS solutions (•••) for: (a) $s(t)$, (b) $u_1(0, t)$, (c) $-k_1 \frac{\partial u_1}{\partial x}$ (0,t), and (d) $E(t)$, as a function of $t \in [0, 1]$, and (e) $u_1(x, 0)$, as a function of $x \in [0, \pi/4]$ obtained with $M_1 = 20$, $M_2 = 40$, $K = 40$, for no noise $\delta = 0$ and $\lambda_1 = \lambda_2 = 0$, for Example 3. In case (a), the comparison with the exact solution (4.18) for $s(t)$ is also shown, and in cases (b)–(e) comparisons are made with the MFS approximation (—) that was generated in [17].

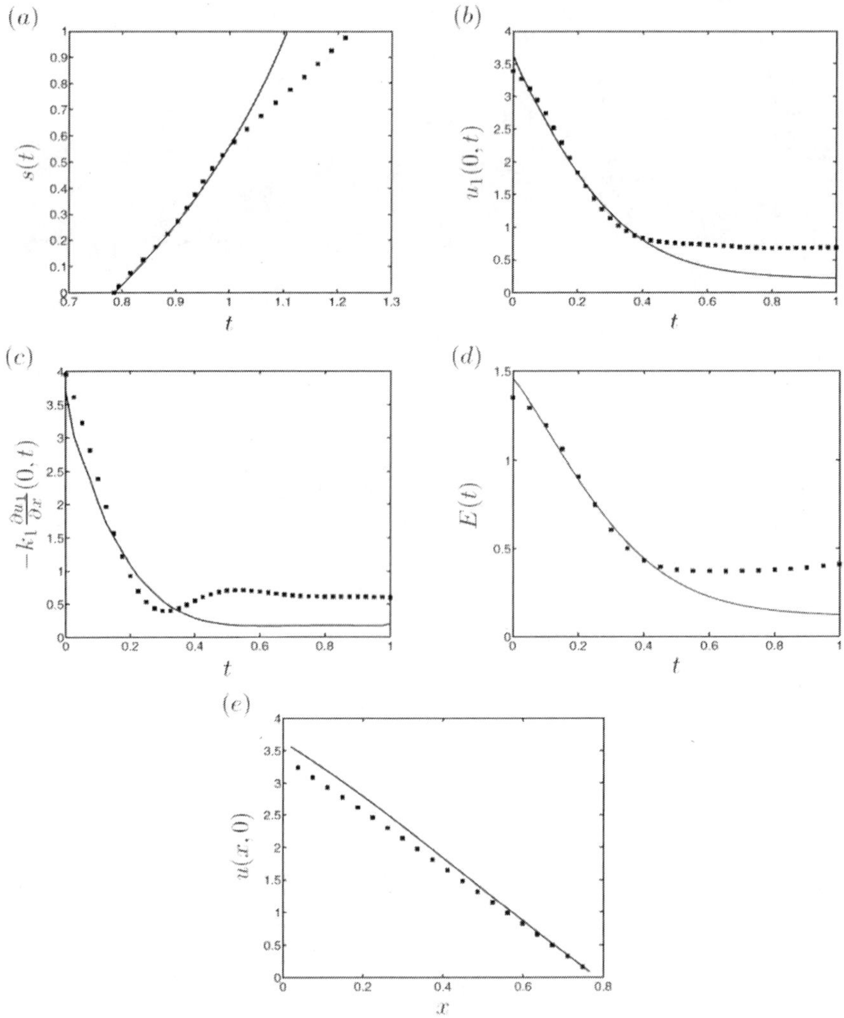

Figure. 12. The numerical MFS solutions for: (a) $s(t)$, (b) $u_1(0, t)$, (c) $-k_1 \frac{\partial u_1}{\partial x}$ (0,t), and (d) $E(t)$, as a function of $t \in [0, 1]$, and (e) $u_1(x, 0)$, as a function of $x \in [0, \pi/4]$ obtained with $M_1 = 20$, $M_2 = 40$, $K = 40$, for $\delta = 1\%$ (▪) noise and $\lambda_1 = \lambda_2 = 10^{-6}$, for Example 3. In case (a), the comparison with the exact solution (4.18) for $s(t)$ is also shown, and in cases (b)–(e) comparisons are made with the MFS approximation (—) that was generated in [17].

5. CONCLUSIONS

In this paper, the one-dimensional two-phase nonlinear inverse Stefan problem has been investigated using a regularized MFS. For both exact and noisy data the method has been shown to be accurate, stable and robust. At present there are no other results available to compare our MFS with since this paper undertakes the first numerical investigation to solve the inverse two-phase nonlinear Stefan problem. We mention that alternatively, one could employ the boundary element method, as a powerful and well-suited numerical boundary discretisation approach for solving the problem. Future work will concern extending the MFS developed in this study to multi-dimensional nonlinear Stefan problems.

ACKNOWLEDGEMENTS

T. Reeve would like to thank the financial support received from the EPSRC. B.T. Johansson and D. Lesnic would like to thank the Isaac Newton Institute for the Visiting Fellowships within the programme on "Inverse Problems" offered in November-December 2011 during which period some of this work has been performed. The comments and suggestions made by the referees are acknowledged.

REFERENCES

1. D.D. Ang, A. Pham Ngoc Dinh, D.N. TranhRegularization of an inverse two-phase Stefan problem Nonlinear Anal., 34 (1998), pp. 719-731
2. J.V. Beck, B. Blackwell, C.R. St-Clair Jr.Inverse Heat Conduction J. Wiley-Intersc. Publ., New York (1985)
3. J.R. Cannon, D.B. Henry, D.B. KotlowClassical solutions of the one-dimensional, two-phase Stefan problem Ann. Mat. Pura Appl., 107 (1975), pp. 311-341
4. J.R. Cannon, J. Douglas Jr.The Cauchy problem for the heat equation SIAM J. Numer. Anal., 4 (3) (1967), pp. 317-336
5. J.R. Cannon, M. PrimicerioA two phase Stefan problem with flux boundary conditions Ann. Mat. Pura Appl., 88 (1971), pp. 193-205
6. J.R. Cannon, M. PrimicerioA two phase Stefan problem with temperature boundary conditions Ann. Mat. Pura Appl., 88 (1971), pp. 177-191
7. S. Chantasiriwan, B.T. Johansson, D. LesnicThe method of fundamental solutions for free surface Stefan problems Eng. Anal. Bound. Elem., 33 (2009), pp. 529-538
8. J. CrankFree and Moving Boundary Problems Clarendon Press, Oxford (1984)
9. A.El Badia, F. MoutazaimA one-phase inverse Stefan problem Inverse Prob., 15 (1999), pp. 1507-1522
10. N.L. Gol'dmanInverse Stefan Problems Kluwer Academic Publ., Dordrecht (1997)

11. N.L. Gol'dmanInverse problems with phase transitions. O.M. Alifanov, N.V. Kerov, V.V. Michailov, A.N. Nenarokomov (Eds.), Proc. 3rd Int. Conf. Dynamic Systems Identification and Inverse Problems, Moscow-St. Petersburg, Russia (1998), pp. 128-139
12. N.L. Gol'dmanProperties of solutions of the inverse Stefan problem Differ. Equ., 39 (2003), pp. 66-72
13. D. Nho HàoMethods for Inverse Heat Conduction Problems Peter Lang, Frankfurt am Main (1998)
14. C.D. HillParabolic equations in one space variable and the non-characteristic Cauchy problem Comm. Pure Appl. Math., 20 (1967), pp. 619-633
15. B.T. Johansson, D. LesnicA procedure for determining a spacewise dependent heat source and the initial temperature Appl. Anal., 87 (2008), pp. 265-276
16. B.T. Johansson, D. LesnicA method of fundamental solutions for transient heat conduction in layered materials Eng. Anal. Bound. Elem., 33 (2009), pp. 1362-1367
17. B.T. Johansson, D. Lesnic, T. ReeveA meshless method for an inverse two-phase one-dimensional linear Stefan problem Inverse Prob. Sci. Eng., 21 (1) (2013), pp. 17-33
18. D.A. MurioSolution of inverse heat conduction problems with phase changes by the mollification method Comput. Math. Appl., 24 (1992), pp. 45-57
19. L. RubinsteınThe Stefan problem: Comments on its present state J. Inst. Maths Appl., 24 (1979), pp. 259-277
20. D. SlotaSolving the inverse Stefan design problem using genetic algorithms Inverse Prob. Sci. Eng., 16 (2008), pp. 829-846
21. Y.B. Wang, J. Cheng, J. Nakagawa, M. YamamotoA numerical method for solving the inverse heat conduction problem without the initial value Inverse Prob. Sci. Eng., 18 (2010), pp. 655-671
22. T. Wei, M. YamamotoReconstruction of a moving boundary from Cauchy data in one-dimensional heat equation Inverse Prob. Sci. Eng., 17 (2009), pp. 551-567

INDEX

Q

R

S

T

V

W